THE BODHISATTVA DOCTRINE IN BUDDHIST SANSKRIT LITERATURE

HAR DAYAL
M.A., Ph.D.

MOTILAL BANARSIDASS
DELHI :: PATNA :: VARANASI

Head Office : BUNGALOW ROAD, JAWAHAR NAGAR, DELHI-7
Branches : (1) CHOWK VARANASI-1 (U.P.)
(2) ASHOK RAJPATH, PATNA-4 (BIHAR)

By arrangement with
Routledge & Kegan Paul Ltd., London.
FIRST PUBLISHED 1932
REPRINT 1970

Price Rs. 25.00

PRINTED IN INDIA BY SHANTILAL JAIN AT SHRI JAINENDRA PRESS, BUNGALOW ROAD, JAWAHAR NAGAR, DELHI-7, AND PUBLISHED BY SUNDARLAL JAIN, MOTILAL BANARSIDASS, BUNGALOW ROAD, JAWAHAR NAGAR, DELHI-7.

To

SANKTA AGDA

In token of friendship and esteem

PREFACE

IN this essay an attempt has been made to discuss the Bodhisattva doctrine as it is expounded in the principal Buddhist Sanskrit treatises.

I beg to express my sincere gratitude to Professor R. L. Turner, M.A., D.Litt., Dr. C. A. F. Rhys Davids, M.A., D.Litt., Dr. W. Stede, Ph.D., Dr. Nalinākṣa Dutt, Ph.D., D.Litt., and Mr. Gokal Chand, M.A., LL.B. I am also greatly indebted to Dr. E. J. Thomas, M.A., D.Litt., for helpful criticism and many valuable suggestions.

HAR DAYAL.

LONDON,

October, 1931.

CONTENTS

CHAP.		PAGE
	List of Abbreviations	xi
I.	The Bodhisattva Doctrine	1
II.	Origin and Development of the Bodhisattva Doctrine	30
III.	The Thought of Enlightenment	50
IV.	The Thirty-seven "Dharmas"	80
V.	The Pāramitās	165
VI.	The Bhūmis	270
VII.	The Last Life and Enlightenment	292
	Notes and References	319
	Appendix	382
	Index	387

LIST OF ABBREVIATIONS

Ava.-ça.—*Avadāna-çataka*, edited by J. S. Speyer (St. Petersburg 1906, 1909). 2 vols. Bibliotheca Buddhica.

Aṅguttara.—*Aṅguttara-Nikāya*, edited by R. Morris and E. Hardy (London 1885–1910).

Aṅguttara trsln.—" Die Reden des Buddha," übers. von Nyāṇatiloka (München 1922–4).

Abhidharma-koça.—*L'Abhidharma-koça*, traduit par L. de la Vallée Poussin (Paris 1924–6).

Atharva-veda, edited by R. Roth and W. D. Whitney (2nd edition, Berlin 1924).

Attha-sālinī, edited by E. Müller (London 1897).

" Album Kern."—(Leyden 1903).

ARISTOTLE (" Ethics ").—" The Nicomachean Ethics," translated by R. W. Browne (London 1914).

ARISTOTLE (" Politics ").—" The Politics and Economics of Aristotle," translated by E. Walford (London 1881).

BEFEO.—" Bulletin de l'école française d'éxtrême Orient " (Hanoi).

Bo. Bhū.—*Bodhisattva-bhūmi* (Sanskrit Manuscript Add. 1702, Cambridge University Library).

B.C. Ava.—*Çāntideva's Bodhi-cary-āvatāra*, edited by I. P. Minayeff (Zapiski, vol. iv, 1889, pp. 155–225).

B.C. Ava. Pka.—*Bodhicaryāvatāra-pañjikā*, edited by L. de la Vallée Poussin (Calcutta 1901–14). Bibliotheca Indica.

B. Ct.—*Açvaghoṣa's Buddha-carita*, edited by E. B. Cowell (Oxford 1893).

Buddhavaṃsa, edited by R. Morris (London 1882).

R. G. BHANDARKAR (" Sects ").—" Vaiṣṇavism, Śaivism and Minor Religious Systems " (Strassburg 1913).

H. BECKH (" Buddhismus ").—" Der Buddhismus " (Berlin 1916, 1919). 2 Bde.

S. BEAL (" Abstract ").—" Abstract of Four Lectures on Buddhist Literature in China " (London 1882).

S. BEAL (" Catena ").—" A Catena of Buddhist Scriptures from the Chinese " (London 1871).

E. BURNOUF (" Int.").—" Introduction a l'histoire du Bouddhisme indien " (Paris 1876).

E. BURNOUF (" Lotus ").—" Le Lotus de la bonne loi " (Paris 1925).

L. D. Barnett ("Antiquities").—"Antiquities of India" (London 1913).

"Barlaam and Ioasaph," translated by G. R. Woodward (Loeb Classical Library, London 1914).

L. D. Barnett ("Path").—"The Path of Light" (London 1909).

A. Barth ("Religions").—"The Religions of India" (London 1906).

Çikṣā.—*Çāntideva's Çikṣā-samuccaya*, edited by C. Bendall (St. Petersburg 1897–1902).

Çiṣya-lekha.—*Candragomin's Çiṣya-lekha-dharma-kāvya*, edited by I. P. Minayeff (Zapiski, vol. iv, 1889, pp. 44–52).

Çikṣā tr.—*Çikṣā-samuccaya*, translated by C. Bendall and W. H. D. Rouse (London 1922).

Cariyā-piṭaka, edited by R. Morris (London 1882).

Csoma.—Alexander Csoma de Körös, *Mahā-vyutpatti*, edited by E. D. Ross and S. C. Vidyābhūṣaṇa (Calcutta 1910). Part I.

J. E. Carpenter ("Theism").—"Theism in Medieval India" (London 1921).

J. E. Carpenter ("Buddhism").—"Buddhism and Christianity" (London 1923).

Chalmers (*Majjh.* tr.).—"Further Dialogues of the Buddha," translated bv Lord Chalmers (London 1926–7). 2 vols.

H. T. Colebrooke ("Essays").—"Miscellaneous Essays" (London 1873). 2 vols.

R. S. Coplestone ("Buddhism").—"Buddhism, Primitive and Present" (London 1908).

"Compendium"—"Compendium of Philosophy," by S. Z. Aung and C. A. F. Rhys Davids (London 1910).

"Camb. Ind."—"Cambridge History of India," vol. i (Cambridge 1922).

Divy.—*Divy-āvadāna*, edited by E. B. Cowell and R. A. Neil (Cambridge 1886).

Dh. S.—*Dharma-saṅgraha*, edited by F. Max Müller, H. Wenzel, and K. Kassawara (Oxford, 1885).

Da. Bhū.—*Daça-bhūmika-sūtra*, publié par J. Rahder (Paris 1926).

Dīgha-Nikāya, edited by T. W. Rhys Davids and J. E. Carpenter (London 1890–1911). 3 vols.

Dhammapada.—Pāli Text Society's edition (London 1906–15).

Dhamma-saṅgaṇi, edited by E. Müller (London 1885). Translation by C. A. F. Rhys Davids (London 1923).

Dīpavaṃsa, edited by H. Oldenberg (London 1879).

"Dialogues."—"Dialogues of the Buddha," translated by T. W. Rhys Davids (London 1899–1921). 3 vols.

T. W. RHYS DAVIDS ("Buddhism").—"Buddhism: Its History and Literature" (New York 1896).

C. A. F. RHYS DAVIDS ("Psychology").—"Buddhist Psychology" (London 1924).

C. A. F. RHYS DAVIDS ("Gotama").—"Gotama the Man" (London 1928). "Sakya, or Buddhist Origins" (1931).

DIOGENES LAERTIUS.—"Lives of Eminent Philosophers," translated by R. D. Hicks (London 1925). 2 vols.

S. N. DASGUPTA ("Mysticism").—"Hindu Mysticism" (Chicago 1927).

P. DÖRFLER ("Anfänge").—"Die Anfänge der Heiligenverehrung" (München 1913).

S. N. DASGUPTA ("Yoga").—"Yoga as Philosophy and Religion" (New York 1924).

S. N. DASGUPTA ("History").—"A History of Indian Philosophy" (Cambridge 1922).

G. A. VAN DEN B. VAN EYSINGA.—"Indische Einflüsse auf evangelische Erzählungen (Göttingen 1904).

E. J. EITEL.—"Handbook of Chinese Buddhism" (Hongkong 1888).

A. J. EDMUNDS ("Gospels").—"Buddhist and Christian Gospels (Tokyo 1905).

C. ELIOT.—"Hinduism and Buddhism" (London 1921). 3 vols.

J. A. EKLUND ("Nirvāṇa").—"Nirvāṇa: en religionshistorisk undersökning" (Upsala 1899).

EUSEBIUS ("History").—"The Ecclesiastical History," translated by C. F. Cruse (London 1851).

ERE ("Encyclopædia of Religion and Ethics"), edited by J. Hastings (1908–26).

"The Expositor," by Maung Tin and C. A. F. Rhys Davids (London 1920–21). 2 vols.

P. E. FOUCAUX (*Lal. V.* tr.).—"Le *Lalita-vistara*, traduit du sanskrit en français," par. Ph. Ed. Foucaux (Paris 1884).

J. N. FARQUHAR ("Outline").—"An Outline of the Religious Literature of India" (Oxford 1920).

A. FOUCHER ("Art").—"L'art gréco-bouddhique du Gandhāra" (Paris 1905–8). 2 vols.

R. O. FRANKE ("Dīgha").—*Dīgha-Nikāya* in Auswahl übersetzt von R. O. Franke (Göttingen 1913).

A. GRÜNWEDEL ("Art").—"Buddhist Art in India" (London 1901).

A. GRÜNWEDEL ("Mythologie").—"Mythologie des Buddhismus" (Leipzig 1900).

M. and W. GEIGER (*Dhamma*).—*Pāli Dhamma* (München 1921).

H. S. Gour ("Spirit").—"The Spirit of Buddhism" (London 1929).
R. Garbe ("Sāṇkhya").—"Sāṇkhya und Yoga" (Strassburg 1896).
R. Garbe ("Christenthum").—"Indien und das Christenthum" (Tübingen 1914).
A. Gawronski ("Studies").—"Studies about the Sanskrit Buddhist Literature" (Crakowie 1919).

Lady Herringham ("Ajanta").—"Ajanta Frescoes" (Oxford 1915).
H. Hackmann ("Buddhism").—"Buddhism as a Religion" (London 1910).
M. Horten ("Islam").—"Die religiöse Gedankenwelt des Volkes im heutigen Islam" (Leipzig 1917–18).
S. Hardy ("Manual").—"Manual of Buddhism" (London 1881).
E. W. Hopkins ("India").—"India, Old and New" (New York, 1901).
F. Heiler ("Versenkung").—"Die buddhistische Versenkung" (München 1922).
B. Hodgson ("Lit.").—"Essay on the Literature of Nepal" (London 1874).

I-tsing.—"A Record of the Buddhist Religion," translated by J. Takakusu (Oxford 1896).
"Ind. Ant."—"Indian Antiquary" (Bombay).
"IHQ."—"Indian Historical Quarterly" (Calcutta).

Jā. Mā.—*Ārya-çūra's Jātaka-Mālā*, edited by H. Kern (Boston 1891)
Jātaka.—"The *Jātaka*, together with its commentary," edited by V. Fausböll (London 1877–97). 6 vols.
J. Jaini ("Outlines").—"Outlines of Jainism" (Cambridge 1916).
JRAS.—"Journal of the Royal Asiatic Society" (London).
JA.—"Journal Asiatique" (Paris).
JBTS.—"Journal of the Buddhist Text Society" (Calcutta).
JBAS.—"Journal of the Asiatic Society of Bengal" (Calcutta).
JPTS.—"Journal of the Pāli Text Society" (London).

Kar. Pu.—*Karuṇā-puṇḍarīka*, edited by S. C. Das and S. C. Çāstri (Calcutta 1898). (Buddhist Text Society.)
KSS.—*Kathā-sarit-sāgara*, edited by P. D. Prasād and K. P. Parab (Bombay 1915).
Kṣemendra.—*Bodhisattv-āvadāna-kalpalatā*, edited by S. C. Das and H. M. Vidyābhūṣaṇa (Calcutta 1888). 2 vols. Bibliotheca Indica.
Kā. Vy.—*Kāraṇḍa-vyūha*, edited by S. B. Samasrami (Calcutta 1873).
Kathā-vatthu, edited by A. C. Taylor (London 1894).

A. B. KEITH ("Philosophy").—"Buddhist Philosophy in India and Ceylon" (Oxford 1923).

C. F. KOEPPEN ("Buddha").—"Die Religion des Buddha und ihre Entstehung" (Berlin 1906).

J. H. C. KERN ("Histoire").—"Histoire du Bouddhisme dans l'Inde" (Paris 1901–3). 2 vols.

J. H. C. KERN ("Manual").—"Manual of Indian Buddhism" (Strassburg 1896).

W. KIRFEL ("Kosmographie").—"Die Kosmographie der Inder" (Bonn and Leipzig 1920).

R. KIMURA ("Study").—"A Historical Study of the terms Hīnayāna and Mahāyāna (Calcutta 1927).

A. B. KEITH ("Lit.").—"A History of Sanskrit Literature" (Oxford 1928).

Lal. V.—*Lalita-vistara*, edited by S. Lefmann (Halle a. S. 1902–8).

Lka.—*Laṅkāvatāra-sūtra*, edited by B. Nanjio (Kyoto 1923).

Lal. V. Tib.—*Rgya tch'er-rol-pa*, edited by P. Foucaux, vol. i (Paris 1847).

"Lesebuch."—"Religionsgeschichtliches Lesebuch," herausgegeben von A. Bertholet (Tübingen 1908).

"Lehrbuch."—"Lehrbuch der Religionsgeschichte," herausg. P. D. Chantepie de la Saussaye (Berlin 1925).

A. LILLIE ("Buddhism").—"Buddhism in Christendom" (London 1887).

F. LORINSER (*Gītā*).—*Bhagavad-gītā*, übers. von F. Lorinser (Breslau 1867).

Mtu.—*Le Mahā-vastu*, texte sanscrit publié par E. Senart (Paris 1882–97). 3 vols.

M. Vy.—*Mahā-vyutpatti*, edited by Sakaki (Kyoto 1928).

Milinda.—*Milinda-pañha*, edited by V. Trenckner (London 1928).

Mdh.—*Mūla-madhyamaka-kārikās* (*Mādhyamika-sūtras*) *de Nāgārjuna*, publié par L. de la Vallée Poussin (St. Petersburg 1903).

M. S. Al. and *M. S. Al.* tr.—*Mahāyāna-sūtrālaṅkāra*, édité et traduit par S. Lévi (Paris 1907, 1911).

Majjhima-Nikāya, edited by V. Trenckner and R. Chalmers (London 1888–99). 3 vols.

J. W. MCCRINDLE ("India").—"Ancient India" (London 1877).

J. H. MOULTON ("Zoroastrianism").—"Early Zoroastrianism" (London 1913).

I. P. MINAYEFF (Minaev) ("Recherches").—"Recherches sur le bouddhisme," traduit du rusee par R. H. Assier de Pompignan (Paris 1894).

J. Masuda ("Idealismus").—"Der individualistische Idealismus der Yogācāra-schule" (Heidelberg 1926).
P. Masson-Oursel ("Esquisse").—"Esquisse d'une histoire de la philosophie indienne (Paris 1923).
A. A. Macdonell ("Lit.").—"A History of Sanskrit Literature" (London 1900).
A. E. Medlycott ("Thomas").—"India and the Apostle Thomas" (London 1905).
W. M. McGovern ("Introduction").—"An Introduction to Mahāyāna Buddhism" (London 1922).
W. M. McGovern ("Manual").—"A Manual of Buddhist Philosophy," vol. i (London 1923).
Manu-smṛti, edited by J. Jolly (London 1887).
Montalembert ("Moines").—"Les Moines d'Occident," vol. i (Paris 1892).

Ngd.—*Harṣa's Nāgānanda*, edited by G. B. Brahme and D. M. Paranjape (Poona 1893).
Netti-pakaraṇa, edited by E. Hardy (London 1902).
K. E. Neumann (*Majjh.* tr.).—"Die Reden Gotamo Buddhos aus der mittleren Sammlung," 3 Bde. (München 1921).
R. A. Nicholson ("Studies").—"Studies in Islamic Mysticism" (Cambridge 1921).
B. Nanjio.—"A Catalogue of the Chinese Translation of the Buddhist Tripiṭaka" (Oxford 1883).
G. K. Nariman ("Lit.").—"Literary History of Sanskrit Buddhism" (Bombay 1920).

H. Oldenberg ("Buddha").—"Buddha: sein Leben, seine Lehre, seine Gemeinde" (Berlin 1897).
H. Oldenberg ("Indien").—"Aus dem alten Indien" (Berlin 1910).
P. Oltramare ("Bouddhique").—"La théosophie bouddhique" (Paris 1923).

Pr. Pā. Aṣṭa.—*Aṣṭa-sāhasrikā Prajñā-pāramitā*, edited by R. Mitra (Calcutta 1888). Bibliotheca Indica.
Pr. Pā. Çata.—*Çata-sāhasrikā Prajñā-pāramitā* (chapters i–xii), edited by P. Ghosa (Calcutta 1902–13). Bibliotheca Indica.
Puggala-paññatti, edited by R. Morris (London 1883).
J. Przyluski ("Açoka").—"La Légende de l'empereur Açoka" (Paris 1923).
Pāli Dicy.—T. W. Rhys Davids and W. Stede: Pāli Dictionary (Chipstead 1925).
R. Pischel ("Buddha").—"Leben und Lehre des Buddha" (Berlin 1917).

L. DE LA VALLÉE POUSSIN ("Etudes").—"Bouddhisme, Etudes et Materiaux" (London 1898).

L. DE LA VALLÉE POUSSIN ("Morale").—"La morale bouddhique" (Paris 1927).

L. DE LA VALLÉE POUSSIN ("Opinions").—"Bouddhisme : Opinions sur l'histoire de la Dogmatique" (Paris 1909).

L. DE LA VALLÉE POUSSIN (*Nirvāṇa*).—"The Way to *Nirvāṇa*" (Cambridge 1917).

RPP.—*Rāṣṭrapāla-paripṛcchā*, publié par L. Finot (Bibliotheca Buddhica). (St. Pétersbourg 1901).

Rāmāyaṇa.—*The Rāmāyaṇa*, edited by T. R. Krishnacarya (Bombay 1905).

Ṛgveda.—*Rigveda Sanhita*, edited by F. Max Müller (Oxford 1849–74). 6 vols.

RHR.—"Revue de l'Histoire des Religions" (Paris).

M. RATNACANDRAJI.—Ardha-māgadhī Dictionary (Ajmer 1923–7). 2 vols.

O. C. J. ROSENBERG ("Probleme").—"Die Probleme der buddhistischen Philosophie" (Heidelberg 1924). 2 Bde.

H. RAYCHAUDHURI ("Materials").—"Materials for the early History of the Vaishnava sect" (Calcutta 1920).

H. G. RAWLINSON ("Intercourse").—"Intercourse between India and the Western World" (Cambridge 1916).

J. RAHDER ("Glossary").—"Glossary of the Sanskrit, Tibetan, Mongol and Chinese versions of the *Daça-bhūmika-sūtra*" (Paris 1926).

Sāṅkhya-kārikā, edited by H. H. Wilson (Oxford 1837).

Sam. Rā.—*Samādhi-rāja-sūtra.* (Sanskrit Manuscript No. 4, Hodgson Collection, Royal Asiatic Society, London).

Su. Pr.—*Suvarṇa-prabhāsa.* (Manuscript No. 8, Hodgson Collection, Royal Asiatic Society, London).

Sad. Pu.—*Saddharma-puṇḍarīka*, edited by H. Kern and B. Nanjio (St. Petersburg, 1912).

Su. Vy.—*Sukhāvatī-vyūha*, edited by F. Max Müller and B. Nanjio (Oxford 1883).

Saund. Kā.—*Açvaghoṣa's Saundarānanda-kāvya*, edited by E. H. Johnston (London 1928).

Saṃyutta-Nikāya, edited by M. L. Feer (London 1884–1904). 6 vols.

Sutta-nipāta, edited by D. Andersen and H. Smith (London 1913).

SBE.—"Sacred Books of the East" (Oxford 1879–1910).

E. SENART ("Legende").—"Essai sur la Légende du Bouddha" (Paris 1882).

E. SENART ("Origines").—"Origines Bouddhiques" (Paris 1907).

Skt. Dicy. Pbg.—O. Böhtlingk and R. Roth, "Sanskrit-Wörterbuch" (St. Petersburg 1855–75).

Skt. Dicy. M.W.—Monier Williams, "A Sanskrit-English Dictionary" (Oxford 1872).

V. A. Smith ("Asoka").—"Asoka" (Oxford 1901).

D. T. Suzuki ("Outlines").—"Outlines of Mahāyāna Buddhism" (London 1907).

D. T. Suzuki ("Zen Essays").—"Essays in Zen Buddhism" (London 1927).

D. T. Suzuki ("Studies").—"Studies in the *Laṅkāvatāra-sūtra*" (London 1930).

K. J. Saunders ("Epochs").—"Epochs in Buddhist History" (Chicago 1924).

Th. Stcherbatsky ("Conception").—"The Central Conception of Buddhism" (London 1923).

Th. Stcherbatsky (*Nirvāṇa*).—"The Conception of Buddhist *Nirvāṇa*" (Leningrad 1927).

R. Seydel ("Legend").—"Die Buddha-Legende und das Leben Jesu" (Weimar 1897).

Sīlācāra (*Majjh.* tr.).—*The Majjhima-Nikāya* (München-Neubiberg 1924).

V. A. Smith ("Art").—"A History of Fine Art in India and Ceylon" (Oxford 1911).

T'oung-Pao (Leyden).

Thera-gāthā, edited by H. Oldenberg and R. Pischel (London 1883). Translation by C. A. F. Rhys Davids.

"Psalms of the Brethren" (London 1913).

Triglotte.—Buddhistische Triglotte, edited by A. Schiefner (St. Petersburg 1859).

S. Tachibana ("Ethics").—"The Ethics of Buddhism" (London 1926).

E. J. Thomas ("Buddha").—The Life of Buddha as Legend and History" (London 1927).

A Tibetan–English Dictionary.—By S. C. Das (Calcutta 1902).

A Tibetan–English Dictionary.—By H. A. Jäschke (London 1881).

Tāranātha—"Geschichte des Buddhismus in Indien," übers. von A. Schiefner (St. Petersburg 1869).

The Upaniṣads.—Ānandāçrama Series, Poona.

Uttarādhyayana-sūtra, edited by J. Charpentier (Upsala 1922).

Vajra.—*Vajra-cchedikā Prajñā-pāramitā*, edited by F. Max Müller (Oxford 1881).

Vinaya.—*The Vinaya-Piṭakaṃ*, edited by H. Oldenberg (London 1879–83). 5 vols.

The Vibhanga, edited by C. A. F. Rhys Davids (London 1904).
M. V. VASSILIEF.—"Le Bouddisme," traduit du russe (Paris 1865).

F. WELLER.—"Das Leben des Buddha," Tibetisch und Deutsch (Leipzig 1926–8).
U. WOGIHARA (*Bo. Bhū.*).—*Asaṅga's Bodhisattva-bhūmi* (Leipzig 1908).
L. A. WADDELL ("Buddhism").—"The Buddhism of Tibet" (London 1895).
M. WALLESER (*Pr. Pā.* tr.).—"*Prajñā-pāramitā:* die Vollkommenheit der Erkenntnis" (Göttingen 1914).
J. H. WOODS ("Yoga").—"The Yoga System of Patañjalī," translated by J. H. Woods (Cambridge, Mass., 1914).
M. WINTERNITZ ("Problems").—"Some Problems of Indian Literature" (Calcutta 1925).
M. WINTERNITZ ("Lit.").—"Geschichte der indischen Litteratur" (Leipzig 1909–20). 3 Bde.
E. WINDISCH ("Geburt.").—"Buddha's Geburt" (Leipsiz 1909).
E. WINDISCH ("Māra").—"Mara und Buddha" (Leipzig 1895).
H. C. WARREN ("Buddhism").—"Buddhism in Translations" (Cambridge, Mass., 1915).

Yo. Sū.—*Pātañjala-yoga-sūtrāṇi*, edited by K. Ç. Agāçe (Poona, 1904). Ānandāçrama Series.
S. YAMAKAMI ("Systems").—"Systems of Buddhistic Thought" (Calcutta 1912).

ZII.—"Zeitschrift für Indologie und Iranistik" (Leipzig).
Z.Bs.—"Zeitschrift für Buddhismus" (Leipzig).
E. ZELLER ("Stoics").—"The Stoics, Epicureans and Sceptics" (London 1870).
ZDMG.—"Zeitschrift der deutschen morgenländischen Gesellschaft."

N.B.—The abbreviations p. and pp. have generally been omitted after the titles of Sanskrit and Pāli works.

Chapter I

THE BODHISATTVA DOCTRINE

I. The Background

Early Buddhism inculcated the double ideal of *arhatva* (Pāli : *arahatta*) and *nirvāṇa* (Pāli: *nibbāna*). Gautama Buddha converted his first disciples by preaching the four Noble Truths and the eightfold Way and laying stress on the transitoriness and non-substantiality of all the constituents of human personality. The disciples were called *arhats* (Pāli: *arahā*, *arahant*), and Buddha himself was described as an *arhat*. The conception of *arhatship* was gradually widened and elaborated by the Teacher and his successors. Thus an *arhat* was also supposed to comprehend the formula of the twelve *nidānas* (Causes). He was defined as one, who had eradicated the three *āsravas* (Pāli : *āsava* = " Intoxicants ", sins and errors) of sense-desire, love of existence, and ignorance, and also the fourth supplementary *āsrava* of speculative opinion. He practised the seven Factors of Enlightenment (Pāli : *sambojjhaṅgā*) : mindfulness, investigation, energy, joy, serenity, concentration and equanimity. He got rid of the five *nīvaraṇas* (" Hindrances ", " coverings ") : sensuality, malice (ill-will), sloth-and-torpor, worry-and-excitement, and doubt. He freed himself from the three " Roots of Evil " : sense-desire, hatred and delusion. He practised self-restraint and Concentration, and acquired various wonder-working Powers. He fulfilled the triple discipline of virtuous conduct, Concentration and Wisdom. He followed the five ordinary ethical precepts and the ten strict rules for the monks. He had no craving or attachment to the five Aggregates that constitute human personality (form, feeling, perception, volitions and consciousness), or to the six elements of the universe (earth, water, fire, air, space and mentality). He obtained the six *abhijñās* (Super-knowledges). He put aside all evil dispositions, which remained far from him. He destroyed the ten Fetters (*saṃyojana*) of belief in substantial individuality, perverted notions about good works and ceremonies, doubt, sense-desire, hatred, love of life in the material worlds and the non-material worlds, pride, excitement and ignorance. He observed the tenfold righteous course of action by abstaining from killing, theft, unchastity, falsehood, slander, harsh speech, frivolous talk, covetousness, malice and wrong views. He was pure in his physical acts, his words and his thoughts. He was free from the threefold Craving for pleasure, life and annihilation. He practised the four Meditations, the four ecstatic Attainments and the supreme condition of Trance. He eschewed the extremes of severe austerities and sensual self-indulgence. He had faith in the Buddha, enjoyed good health, and cultivated sincerity, spiritual energy and insight. He was firmly established in the seven bases of *arhatship*, viz. keen desire for the discipline, for insight into the Doctrine, for the suppression of hankerings, for the need of solitude, for energy, Mindfulness, perspicacity and intuition of the Truth. He cultivated the eight Positions of Mastery and the eight Deliverances. He knew well the four sublime subjective states of love, compassion, sympathetic joy and equanimity. He practised all the thirty-seven principles that were conducive to Enlightenment, viz. the four Fields of Mindfulness, the four Right Efforts, the four Bases of wonder-working Power, the five controlling Principles, the five Powers, the seven Factors of Enlightenment and the eightfold Way. Above all, he was absolutely free from the three or four *āsravas*, and this freedom made him an *arhat*.

An *arhat*, who was thus liberated, knew that he would not be re-born. He had accomplished what was to be done. He had laid down his burden. He had lived the holy life. He attained undefiled and final emancipation of mind and heart. He was alone, secluded, zealous, earnest, master of himself.[1]

Such an *arhat* also went forth as a preacher and taught the doctrine of the Buddha to the people. The Master had exhorted his disciples to wander and preach the truth for the welfare and liberation of the multitude, as he loved his fellow-creatures and had pity on them.[2]

Such was the ideal of the *arhat*, as it was understood during the three centuries after Gautama Buddha's death. But it seems that the Buddhist monks began to neglect certain important aspects of it in the second century B.C., and emphasised a few duties to the exclusion of others. They became too self-centred and contemplative, and did not evince the old zeal for missionary activity among the people. They seem to have cared only for their own liberation from sin and sorrow. They were indifferent to the duty of teaching and helping all human beings. The *bodhisattva* doctrine was promulgated by some Buddhist leaders as a protest against this lack of true spiritual fervour and altruism among the monks of that period. The coldness and aloofness of the *arhats* led to a movement in favour of the old gospel of "saving all creatures". The *bodhisattva* ideal can be understood only against this background of a saintly and serene, but inactive and indolent monastic Order.

This tendency towards spiritual selfishness among the monks is exhibited in the later Pāli literature. The *Dhammapada* exalts self-control, meditation and absence of hatred, but it also exhibits an attitude of contempt for the common people and remoteness from their interests. Most poets of the *Thera-gāthā* only strike the note of personal salvation ; they seldom speak of the duty of helping others. The author of the *Milinda-pañha* declares that an *arhat* should aim at the destruction of his own pain and sorrow.[3] The singular ideal of a *pratyeka-buddha* was also evolved during this period (Pāli : *pacceka-buddha*). Such a Buddha is "one enlightened by himself, i.e. one who has attained to the supreme and perfect insight, but dies without proclaiming the truth to the world" (cf. *Puggala-paññatti*, p. 14).[4] It seems almost blasphemous to conceive of a "Buddha" without the attribute of love and altruistic activity. But the invention of this term and its recognition as an epithet of a certain type of "Buddhas" may be interpreted as a sign of the times. Some Buddhists thought that one could be very wise and holy through personal self-culture without fulfilling the equally important duty of teaching and helping suffering humanity. The *bodhisattva* ideal was taught in order to counteract this tendency to a cloistered, placid, inert monastic life. A *bodhisattva* is emphatically and primarily one who criticises and condemns the spiritual egoism of such *arhats* and *pratyeka-buddhas*. He declares at the outset that he is not an *arhat* or a *pratyeka-buddha*, with whom he should always be contrasted. He should also be clearly distinguished from them.

The exponents of the new ideal also protested against the *arhat's summum bonum* of *nirvāṇa*. They declared that mere cessation of *duḥkha* (pain, evil) or the conquest of the *āsravas* was not enough. They may have pointed out that the word *nibbāna* did not occur in the earliest records of Gautama Buddha's first sermons, but that *anuttarā sammā-sambodhi* (perfect supreme Enlightenment) was mentioned in them.[5] Gautama Buddha acquired such *bodhi* : hence every one could and should do the same. The *arhat's* ideal of *nirvāṇa* did not include intellectual Perfection and supreme Wisdom. The *arhats* also believed that a monk, who attained *nirvāṇa* in his life, could not remain in touch with this world of conditioned phenomena after his death, whatever his state of existence might be. He was not reborn on earth or in the heavens : that much was certain. He ceased to exist, or he existed in an undefinable, inconceivable sphere somewhere or nowhere (*asaṃskṛta*) ; or nothing could be predicated about him.[6] At any rate, he was lost to the world of men and *devas* as a friend and helper, as there was nothing that bridged the gulf between the *saṃskṛta* (conditioned) and the *asaṃskṛta* elements (unconditioned). *Nirvāṇa* was of course regarded as an *asaṃskṛta-dhātu.*[7] Thus the *arhat*, once deceased, was dead and gone, as far as his relations with the world of living beings were concerned, whatever his destiny, positive or negative, might be. The *bodhisattva* doctrine was promulgated also as a protest against this theory of *arhatship*, which was regarded as doubly defective. It disregarded the higher duty of acquiring the perfect Wisdom of a Buddha ; and it deprived the world of the services of the holy men and women who had attained *nirvāṇa* and passed away. A *bodhisattva* was defined as one who strove to gain *bodhi* and scorned such *nirvāṇa*, as he wished to help and succour his fellow-creatures in the world of sorrow, sin and impermanence.

II. "Bodhisattva"

The Sanskrit word *bodhisattva* has been explained in different ways. *Bodhi* means "Enlightenment". But several interpretations of the word *sattva* have been offered by ancient and modern scholars.

(1) *Sattva* may mean "Wesen, Charakter"; "essence, nature, true essence" (Skt. Dicy. Pbg. & Skt. Dicy. M.W.). The Pāli word *satta* may also mean "substance" (Pāli Dicy. s.v.). The great modern lexicographers seem to interpret *sattva* in this sense. Thus, according to Böhtlingk and Roth, *bodhisattva* means : "(adj.) dessen Wesen Erkenntniss ist ; (mas.) der im Besitz des Wesens der *Bodhi* Seiende." Monier

Williams translates: "one who has *bodhi* or perfect wisdom as his essence" (p. 688b). E. Burnouf seems to interpret the word in the same way as Böhtlingk and Roth: "celui qui possède l'essence de la *bodhi*."[8] P. Oltramare follows Monier Williams and translates: "un être dont l'essence consiste dans l'éveil". ("Bouddhique," p. 250). *C. F. Koeppen*: "Derjenige, dessen Wesenheit die höchste Weisheit (*bodhi*) geworden" ("Buddha", ii, 18).

C. Eliot: "One whose essence is knowledge" (Eliot, ii, 7).

H. Hackmann: "He whose essence is becoming Enlightenment" ("Buddhism," p. 52). It may be added that the modern Hindi word "*sat*," which is derived from Skt. "*sattva*", means "essence, extract".

(2) "*Sattva*" (masculine) may mean "any living or sentient being" (Skt. Dicy. M.W.), "ein lebendes Wesen" (Skt. Dicy. Pbg.). The Pāli word *satta* may mean "a living being, creature, a sentient and rational being, person" (Pāli Dicy. s.v.). Most modern scholars adopt this interpretation.

M. Winternitz: "Ein Erleuchtungswesen" ("Lit." ii, 183).

L. de la Vallée Poussin: "On peut le traduire 'creature' ou 'être vivant'" ("Opinions", p. 169, line 8).

M. Walleser: "Weisheitswesen" (*Pr. Pā.* tr., p. 5).

H. Kern: "A sentient or reasonable being, possessing *bodhi*" ("Manual," p. 65, line 11).

T. W. Rhys Davids and W. Stede: "a *bodhi*-being, i.e. a being destined to attain fullest Enlightenment" (Pāli Dicy. s.v.).

L. D. Barnett: "Creature of Enlightenment" ("Path", p. 20).

S. Lefmann: "Bodhisattva bedeutet einen, dessen Wesen Erweckung oder Erleuchtung ist" (*Lal. V.* tr., p. 50).

M. Aṇesaki: "A being seeking for *bodhi*" (ERE., v, 450).

E. J. Thomas: "a being of (or destined for) Enlightenment" ("Buddha", p. 2, note I).

P. Masson-Oursel: "un être d'illumination" ("Esquisse", p. 127).

R. Pischel: "Ein Wesen, das bestimmt ist, einst ein Buddha zu werden" ("Buddha", p. 50).

D. T. Suzuki: "Intelligence-Being" ("Outlines", p. 277).

Csoma de Körös: "Purified, mighty soul" (Csoma, p. 6).

The author of the *Samādhi-rāja-sūtra* interprets *sattva* as "being, creature", but thinks that the word *bodhisattva* means "one who admonishes or exhorts all beings" (*bodheti sattvān. . . Sam. Rā.* fol. 25*a*, 4). P. Ghosa seems to interpret *sattva* as "living being", but analyses the whole word in a peculiar way: "*bodhiḥ sa cāsau mahā-kṛp-āçayena sattv-ālambanāt sattvaç ceti bodhisattvaḥ.*" This would mean that the person *is* both *bodhi* and *sattva*! [9]

(3) "*Sattva*" may mean "spirit, mind, sense, consciousness"; "Geist" (Skt. Dicy. M.W. and Pbg.). The Pāli word *satta* may also mean "soul" (Pāli Dicy. s.v.). According to L. de la Vallée Poussin, the Indian lexicographers also explain *sattva* as a synonym for *citta* (thought) or *vyavasāya* (decision, determination).[10] Prajñākaramati, commenting on the *B.C. Ava*, says: "*tatra* (*bodhau*) *sattvam abhiprāyo'syeti bodhisattvaḥ.*" [11] P. Ghosa cites an old commentator, who also interprets *sattva* as meaning *abhiprāya* (intention, purpose): "*bodhau sattvam abhiprāyo yeṣām te bodhisattvāḥ*" (*Pr. Pā. Çata.*, p. 2, note 2). Thus the word would mean: "one whose mind, intentions, thoughts or wishes are fixed on *bodhi*". P. Oltramare rejects this interpretation as far-fetched and inaccurate; [12] but L. de la Vallée Poussin seems to be inclined to accept it, while he at the same time admits that the original meaning of the word may have been derived from the idea of "essence, own nature".[13]

(4) *Sattva* may mean "embryo" (Skt. Dicy. M.W.). H. S. Gour translates: "In whom knowledge is latent and undeveloped" ("Buddhism," p. XI).

(5) *Sattva* may have the same meaning as it has in the *Yoga-sūtras*, where it is opposed to *puruṣa* and means "mind, intelligence". This interpretation is offered by E. Senart, who believes that Buddhism was profoundly influenced by the *Yoga* system. He says: "*Sattva* ne désigne pas seulement le premier des trois *guṇas*, soit seul, soit complété par *buddhi* ou *citta*; il désigne l'esprit, mais en tant que l'esprit résume et exprime la *prakrti* et les *guṇas* qui la constituent . . . l'esprit actif, conscient, qui relèvent de la *prakṛti*. Expliqué par cette acception de *sattva* et comme *bahuvrīhi*, *bodhisattva* désignerait le futur Buddha, provisoirement retenu dans les liens de l'existence, comme 'possédant le *sattva* de la *bodhi*', c'est-à-dire une illumination encore liée aux conditions inférieures des *guṇas*, partant imparfaite." [14]

It is true that *sattva* occurs frequently in the *Yoga-sūtras*, and G. Jha translates it as "thinking principle or mind": (*Yo.*

Sū. II, 41, p. 109, "*Sattva-çuddhi-saumanasy-aikāgry-endriya-jay-ātma-darçana-yogyatvāni ca*").[15] E. Senart points out that *sattva* is declared to be distinct from *puruṣa* in the *Yoga-Sūtras* (III, 55, "*Sattva-puruṣayoḥ çuddhi-sāmye kaivalyam*," p. 174). He thus prefers the interpretation cited above, but I must confess that I do not really understand what he means by "le *sattva* de la *bodhi*".

H. Kern is of opinion that the first word *bodhi* may be related to the *buddhi* of the *Yoga* system, especially as the word *buddhisattva* is found in the literature of *Yoga*. A *bodhisattva* would thus be a personification of potential intelligence.[16]

(6) *Sattva* may be a wrongly Sanskritized form of the Pāli word *satta*, which may correspond to Skt. *sakta*. Thus Pāli *bodhisatta*, from which the Sanskrit word is derived, would mean *bodhi-sakta*, "one who is devoted or attached to *bodhi*".[17] *Sakta* (from the root *sañj*) means "clung, stuck or attached to, joined or connected with, addicted or devoted to, fond of, intent on" (Skt. Dicy. M.W.). According to the Pāli Dictionary, the Pāli word *satta* may correspond to several Sanskrit words: *sattva*, *sapta*, *sakta*, and *çapta*. It has been suggested that the Pāli word *sutta* is also related to Skt. *sūkta*, and not to Skt. *sūtra*, as the latter word is a very inappropriate designation for the lengthy and prolix Buddhist discourses. The Buddhists attached great importance to *subhāṣita* (good sayings), and the Pāli word *sutti* does correspond to Skt. *sūkti* (Pāli Dicy. s.v.). However that may be, it may be plausibly argued that Skt. *bodhi-sakta* is a possible equivalent of Pāli *bodhisatta*. The opinion of the Buddhist writers, who adopted the rendering *sattva*, need not be considered absolutely decisive in this question, as they have certainly given us other wrongly Sanskritized forms, e.g. *smṛty-upasthāna* (for Pāli *sati-paṭṭhāna*), *samyak-prahāna* (for Pāli *sammappadhāna*), etc. *Bodhisattva* may also belong to this class of wrongly Sanskritized terms. P. Oltramare rejects this interpretation, as the verb *sañj* is not used to denote attachment to moral and spiritual ideals, and the later writers could not make such "a strange mistake" in translating Pāli into Sanskrit.[18]

(7) "*Sattva*" may mean "strength, energy, vigour, power, courage" (Skt. Dicy. M.W. p. 1052). The word *bodhisattva* would then mean, "one whose energy and power is directed

towards *bodhi*." *Sattva* in this sense occurs frequently in Kṣemendra's *Avadāna-kalpa-latā*: "*sattv-ābdhiḥ*" (II, p. 713, verse 42); "*sattv-ojjvalaṃ bhagavataç caritaṃ niçamya*" (II, p. 85, verse 74); "*kumāraḥ sattva-sāgaraḥ*" (II, p. 723, verse 21); *sattva-nidhir* (II, p. 945, verse 21); "*bodhisattvaḥ sattva-vibhūṣitaḥ* (II, p. 113, verse 8). The word also seems to have the same signification in the *B. Ct.* (IX, 30—"*bodhisattvaḥ paripūrṇa-sattvaḥ*"). E. B. Cowell translates, "whose perfection was absolute"; but this rendering does not explain the precise meaning of *sattva*.

The Tibetan lexicographers translate *bodhisattva* as *byaṅ-chub sems-dpaḥ*".[19] In this compound, *byaṅ-chub* means *bodhi*, *sems* means "mind" or "heart", and *dpaḥ* signifies "hero, strong man" (= Skt. *çūra*, *vīra*). (Tib. Dicy. Jäschke, 374b and 325b; Tib. Dicy. Das, 883b, 787b and 1276b). This interpretation seems to combine two meanings of *sattva*, viz. "mind" and "courage" (Nos. 3 and 7 above). But it does not make the etymology of the compound word *bodhisattva* in any way clearer or more intelligible. It may be inferred that the Tibetan translators associated the ideas of "mind" and "courage" with the word *sattva*. According to E. J. Eitel, the Chinese interpret *bodhisattva* as "he whose essence has become *bodhi*" (p. 34*a*).

The principal Buddhist writers have not taken the trouble of discussing the exact meaning of *sattva*, though they mention many epithets in praise of a *bodhisattva*. Very little guidance is to be obtained from that quarter.

I may suggest that *sattva* cannot be accurately rendered by "essence", or "mind", or "intention", or "courage", or "embryo" or "the *sattva* of the *Yoga-sūtras*" (Nos. 1, 3, 4, 5, 7, above). If we interpret *sattva* as "essence", the word seems to be too lofty a title for a mere aspirant for wisdom. It would be a more suitable appellation for a perfect Buddha, who has realized the supreme *bodhi*. *Sattva*, interpreted as "intention", or "mind", or "embryo", does not yield a simple and natural sense: these renderings appear to be too scholastic and far-fetched. We need not wander into the distant fairyland of the *Yoga* system in order to explain an old Pāli word. H. Kern attempted to identify *bodhi* with the *buddhi* of the *Sāṅkhya-Yoga*; but *buddhi*, in Buddhist metaphysics, belongs to the lower phenomenal plane of existence, while *bodhi* is the supreme Wisdom. The *B.C. Ava.*

says: "*buddhiḥ saṃvṛtir ucyate*" (*IX*, 2—*buddhi* is called *saṃvṛti*, i.e. "obstruction, covering"). The word *buddhi-sattva* occurs in Vyāsa's commentary on *Yo. Sū.* I, 47 (p. 51): "*açuddhy-āvaraṇa-mal-āpetasya prakāç-ātmano buddhi-sattvasya.*" J. H. Woods translates the word as "the *sattva* of the thinking substance", but this does not seem to refer to a person like a *bodhisattva*. It is not found in the text of the *sūtras*. The *Yoga-sūtras* were composed between A.D. 300 and 500, and Vyāsa's commentary was written in the period A.D. 650–850.[20] The word *bodhisatta*, however, is as old as the Pāli *Nikāyas*, which date from the fifth and fourth centuries B.C.[21] (e.g. "*mayham-pi kho . . . . anabhisambuddhassa bodhisattass' eva*", *Majjh.* I, 17, 6; "*Vipassissa bhikkhave . . . . bodhisattassa sato.*" *Samyutta* II, 5, 8). It is not necessary to adopt the unsound method of appealing to comparatively modern treatises in order to explain a very ancient Pāli term.

One is tempted to believe that Pāli *satta* may really be rendered by Skt. *sakta*, as this interpretation seems to define the chief quality of an aspirant for *bodhi*. But the safest way is always to go back to the Pāli without attaching much importance to the later lexicographers and philosophers. Now *bodhisatta* in the Pāli texts seems to mean "a *bodhi*-being". But *satta* here does not denote a mere ordinary creature. It is almost certainly related to the Vedic word *satvan*, which means "Krieger", "a strong or valiant man, hero, warrior." In this way, we can also understand the final *dpaḥ* in the Tibetan equivalent. *Satta* in Pāli *bodhisatta* should be interpreted as "heroic being, spiritual warrior". The word suggests the two ideas of existence and struggle, and not merely the notion of simple existence.

The word *bodhisattva* is often coupled with *mahā-sattva* (great Being).

III. The Bodhisattva as Distinct from and Opposed to the Arhats (Çrāvakas) and the Pratyeka-Buddhas

The exponents and champions of the *bodhisattva* ideal carry on a vigorous controversy with the adherents of the two other ideals of the *çrāvaka* and the *pratyeka-buddha*. A *bodhisattva* is regarded as superior to a *çrāvaka* and a *pratyeka-buddha*, and the new ideal is set up as the *summum bonum* of the religious life. It appears that the reformers or innovators objected to the old gospel on two chief grounds :—

(1) A *bodhisattva* aims at the acquisition of *bodhi* and *buddha-jñāna* (Buddha-knowledge), while a *çrāvaka* and a *pratyeka-buddha* are content with the *nirvaṇā* that is attained by the destruction of the *āsravas*. The two latter stages are also marked by the development of certain kinds of *bodhi*, but they are inferior to the supreme Enlightenment of a Buddha. Thus three types of *bodhi* are recognised : *çrāvaka-bodhi*, *pratyeka-bodhi* and *anuttarā samyak-sambodhi* (the supreme and perfect *bodhi*). The last is declared to be the highest. This classification must have been devised at a comparatively early period, as it is found in the *Ava. Ça.* and the *Divy.* It is mentioned in almost all the later treatises. "*Çrāvaka-bodhiṃ pratyeka-bodhiṃ . . . mahā-bodhim* (*M.S. Al.* 169, 15). "He wishes to 'reveal or predict' the three kinds of *bodhi*" (*Av. Ça.* I, 5, 17 ff.). "Some produced in themselves the thought of, or the aspiration for, the *bodhi* of the *çrāvakas*, etc." (*Divy.* 209, 50). "They fulfil the Way of the *çrāvakas* . . . the Way of the *pratyeka-buddhas* . . . and then for the purification of the stage of *bodhisattvas*" (*Da. Bhū.* 25.23–26.3–26.7). "He acts as a father towards all *çrāvakas*, *pratyeka-buddhas*, and those who have started on the Way of the *bodhisattvas*" (*Sad. Pu.* 416, 14). "By giving such a gift, the position of an *arhat* is obtained ; by giving such a gift, *pratyeka-bodhi* is obtained ; by giving such a gift, the supreme and perfect *bodhi* is obtained" (*Pr. Pā. Çata.* 91, 19–21). *Arhatva*, *pratyeka-bodhi* and Omniscience are also mentioned as successive stages in the *Pr. Pā. Çata.* (p. 1373, lines 1–6). *Çrāvaka-bhūmi* and *pratyeka-bhūmi* are contrasted with Omniscience (*sarv-ākāra-jñāna. Pr. Pā. Çata.*, p. 964, 19–20).

In the earlier books like the *Sad. Pu.*, we find that the word "*arhat*" is more common than *çrāvaka*, but the latter gradually gained ground at the expense of the former. *Çrāvaka* is employed exclusively in connection with *bodhi*. We read of *çrāvaka-bodhi*, not of *arhad-bodhi*. The *Sad. Pu.* often describes Buddha's followers as *arhats*, while it also speaks of *çrāvakas* in the same sense. In the later literature, we read only of *çrāvaka-bodhi* and *çrāvaka-yāna*, and the term *arhat* seems to have disappeared altogether. Thus the eminent disciples of Buddha are called *çrāvakas* in the *M.Vy.* (xlvii, p. 79). Perhaps the word *çrāvaka* had a derogatory connotation, like *hīna-yāna*, as the author of the *Da. Bhū.* speaks disparagingly of the *çrāvakas* and explains that they are so called on account of their practice of simply hearing the preachers and following their word (*Da. Bhū.* 25, 23). But the author of the *Sad. Pu.* thinks that a *çrāvaka* is "a preacher" (one who makes others hear). *Çrāvaka-bodhi* is employed as a synonym of *nirvāṇa* as the ideal of the *arhats*.

Corresponding to these three kinds of *bodhi*, there are three *yānas* or "Ways", which lead an aspirant to the goal. The third *yāna* was at first called the *bodhisattva-yāna*, but it was subsequently re-named *mahā-yāna*. The other two *yānas* were spoken of as the *hīna-yāna*.[22] In the later treatises, the term *bodhisattva-yāna* is very rare, as *mahā-yāna* has taken its place. This is sometimes called the *Tathāgata-yāna*.

"*Trīṇi yānani çrāvaka-yānaṃ pratyeka-buddha-yānaṃ mahā-yānaṃ ca*" (*Dh. S.* II). "*Yāna-kramaḥ* .... *mahāyānaṃ pratyeka-buddha-yānaṃ çrāvaka-yānaṃ hīna-yānam*" (*M. Vy.* LIX, p. 95). "Lord, in this manner, this Mahāyāna belongs to the great Beings, the *bodhisattvas*" (*Pr. Pā. Çata.*, p. 1530, 6). "*Mahā-yān-ādhimuktānām arthe* .... *çrāvaka-pratyeka-buddha-yān-ādhimuktānām*" (*M.S. Al.*, p. 183, 24–25). "*Çrāvaka-yānam* . . . *pratyeka-buddha-yānam* . . . *mahā-yānam*" (*M.S. Al.*, p. 168, line 14). "*Arhad-dharmā* . . *pratyeka-buddha-dharmā* ... *bodhisattva-dharmā*" (*Pr. Pā. Çata.*, p. 552).

Now a *bodhisattva* strives to become a Buddha by attaining perfect *bodhi*, while an *arhat* is content with mere *nirvāṇa*, the cessation of the *āsravas*. The *pratyeka-buddhas* are not mentioned very frequently in the principal treatises, probably because they are so rare. The discussion centres on the comparative merits of the two chief Ways, the Way of the *çrāvakas* and the Way of the *bodhisattvas*. The Sanskrit writers frequently compare and contrast the two ideals of *nirvāṇa* and *anuttarā-samyak-sambodhi* (supreme and perfect Enlightenment). "To the *çrāvakas*, he preached the doctrine which is associated with the four Noble Truths and leads to the (formula) of Dependent Origination. It aims at transcending birth, old age, disease, death, sorrow, lamentation, pain, distress of mind and weariness; and it ends in *nirvāṇa*. But, to the great Beings, the *bodhisattvas*, he preached the doctrine, which is associated with the six Perfections and which ends in the *Knowledge of the Omniscient One* after the attainment of the supreme and perfect *bodhi*" (*Sad. Pu.* 17, 13 ff.–376, 5 ff.). "Each of these, the *Sūtra* (Discourses), the *Vinaya* (the Rules of Discipline), and the *Abhidharma* (Theory of the Doctrine; Philosophy and Psychology) have briefly a fourfold meaning. By knowing them, the *bodhisattva* acquires *Omniscience.* But the *çrāvaka* attains to the *destruction of the āsravas* by knowing the sense of even one verse" (*M.S. Al.* 54, 11 ff.). In the *Sad. Pu.*, the disciples say to Gautama Buddha :—

"Lord, we were afflicted by three painful states. By which three? The painful sensation caused by bodily pain; the pain, which has its origin in the *saṃskāras* (volitions), and the pain caused by change. Being in this transient world, we were intent upon the lesser things. Hence we have been taught by the Lord to reflect on the numerous lower *dharmas* (rules or doctrines), which are like a receptacle of filth.[23] Having applied ourselves to them, we have striven and struggled, O Lord, but we have begged and sought for only *nirvāṇa*, as if it were our wage.[24] We have been content, O Lord, with that *nirvāṇa*, which was obtained. We thought that we, having striven and struggled in diligently following those rules, have obtained much from the *Tathāgata.*[25] The Lord knows that we are intent on the lesser things, and therefore he neglects us and does not associate with us. He does not say to us: 'This treasure of Knowledge, which is the *Tathāgata's*, verily this, even this same, shall be yours.' The Lord, by his wisdom in the choice of means (for our salvation), appoints us heirs to that treasure of Knowledge, which is the *Tathāgata's.* But we ourselves have no desire for it. We know that even this is much for us, that we get *nirvāṇa* from the Lord as our wages (i.e. as a labourer gets his remuneration)" .... "If the Lord perceives the strength of our faith and utters the word *bodhisattva* with reference to us, then the Lord makes us do two things: we are said to be persons of little faith in the presence of the *bodhisattvas*, and these latter are roused to (the pursuit) of the noble Enlightenment of the Buddha. The Lord, now knowing the strength of our faith, declared this to us. In this manner, O Lord, we say: 'We have suddenly obtained this pearl of *Omniscience* as if we were the sons of the *Tathāgata*, though it was not desired or solicited by us, neither was it sought and striven after, nor was it thought of or asked for by us'" (*Sad. Pu.*, pp. 108–10). Even the highest form of *nirvāṇa* is clearly distinguished from *bodhi* in such a passage as the following :—

"The great Being, the *bodhisattva*, while girding on his armour, does not discriminate among the creatures, (saying): 'So many creatures shall I help to obtain complete *nirvāṇa*, in which no material substratum remains; [26] and so many creatures shall I not help in this way. So many creatures shall I establish in *bodhi*; and so many (others) shall I not so establish. But the *bodhisattva*, the great Being, verily dons his armour for the sake of all creatures" (*Pr. Pā. Çata.*, p. 1299, lines 13–17).

In an interesting passage, the author or authors of the *Pr. Pā. Çata.* enumerate several doctrines and practices, which lead to the *çrāvaka-bhūmi* (the Stage of a *çrāvaka*). They add that he, who tries to persuade a man to remain content with that lower state, is "a bad friend" (*pāpa-mitra*) and really does the work of the "Evil One" (*māra-karmāṇi*). The goal should be the attainment of the *anuttarā-samyak-sambodhi* (*Pr. Pā. Çata.*, pp. 1190–1). The *bodhisattva*, again, may lead other beings to *nirvāṇa*, but he himself must strive for the perfect *bodhi* (*Pr. Pā. Çata.*, p. 1264, lines 18–20). Gautama Buddha himself is represented in the *Sad. Pu.* as first teaching only the way to *nirvāṇa*, which enables a person to transcend birth, old age, disease, death and sorrow; but he further incites the *bodhisattvas* to the pursuit of the "supreme and perfect *bodhi*" (*Sad. Pu.* 71, 1–9). In fact, the entire sixth chapter of the *Sad. Pu.* elaborates the novel and startling idea that the most eminent of Gautama Buddha's disciples, who are described as liberated *arhats* in the old scriptures, should continue their spiritual development till they attain to the rank of Buddhahood. The condition of *nirvāṇa*, which they had acquired, belonged to a lower stage. None of the great *arhats* of the earliest period of Buddhist history are spared. Kāçyapa, Mahākātyāyana and Maudgalyāyana are mentioned, and their future Buddhahood is predicted (*Sad. Pu.*, pp. 144, 150, 153). In the 8th and 9th chapters, the same prediction is made with regard to Kauṇḍinya, Ānanda, Rāhula and 2,500 *arhats* (pp. 207.7–209–216.3–219.12–221.4 ff.). The inadequacy of the old ideal of *nirvāṇa* is vividly set forth in the words, which are put into the mouths of the 500 *arhats*. They say to Gautama Buddha:—

"We confess our transgressions, Lord. We have always and at all times thought thus (literally 'conceived the idea'): 'This is our final *nirvāṇa*; we are finally released.' We have been foolish and unwise; we have not known the right way. And why? Because we have been content (literally 'gone to contentment') with this sort of inferior (or insignificant) knowledge, whereas we should have acquired perfect Enlightenment through the Knowledge of the *Tathāgata*" (*Sad. Pu.* 210, 1–4).

At this point a parable is introduced. A man visits a friend's house and falls asleep or lies drunk there. That friend puts a priceless gem in his garment and ties a knot. The man does not know about it. He wanders to a far country and falls on evil days. He obtains food and raiment with the greatest difficulty. Then he happens to meet that old friend, who tells him of the precious gift that has always been with him, though unbeknown to him. The 500 *arhats* then proceed:—

"Even thus, O Lord, you produced in us the thoughts of Omniscience, while you formerly lived the life (or followed the spiritual career) of a *bodhisattva*. But we do not know or understand them. We imagined that we had been liberated through (reaching) the stage of the *arhat*. We can hardly be said to live, inasmuch as we are satisfied with such trifling (or insignificant, inferior) knowledge. But our aspiration for the Knowledge of the Omniscient One has never wholly perished. And the *Tathāgata*, O Lord, teaches us: 'O Monks, do not think that this is *nirvāṇa*. In your consciousness, there are roots of Merit,[27] which I have formerly ripened (or matured). This is now my wisdom in the choice of means (for conversion). I utter my words in preaching the religion and thereby you think that this now is *nirvāṇa*.' Having been taught thus, we have to-day received the prediction about our supreme and perfect Enlightenment" (*Sad. Pu.* 211, 8 ff.).

The author of the *Sad. Pu.* expresses the definite opinion that all *arhats*, who have destroyed the *āsravas*, must go further and seek the supreme *sambodhi* (*Sad Pu.* 43.11 ff.–137.5 ff.–142.3 ff.). The *Bo. Bhū.* explicitly declares that a *bodhisattva* should not take delight in the idea of *nirvāṇa*; he should be averse to *nirvāṇa* (*nirvāṇa-vimukhena vihartavyam. Bo. Bhū.* fol. 69a, 1, 2).

The ideal of *arhatship* is thus declared to be very inferior to that of Buddhahood, which is the goal of a *bodhisattva*. It may be added that the Sanskrit Buddhist writers have also described an *arhat* with reference to the formula of the ten Fetters (*saṃyojanāni*), which is elaborated in the Pāli writings. The four states of *çrota-āpanna* (one who has entered the stream), *sakṛd-āgāmin* (the once-returner), *anāgāmin* (one who does not return to earth) and the *arhat* are recognized by some Mahāyānist authors as the preliminary stages of a *bodhisattva's* career. They are mentioned in the *Laṅkāvatāra*, the *Avadāna-kalpalatā*, the *Daça-bhūmika-sūtra*, *the Prajñā-pāramitā* and the *Kāraṇḍa-vyūha.*[28] The *Pr. Pā. Çata.* indeed incorporates the entire scheme in its own metaphysics, but adds that all the Fetters can be destroyed only by *prajñā-pāramitā* (the Perfection of Wisdom). It thus seems to teach that even the old ideal of the *arhat* is unattainable without the practices enjoined by the new school. It mentions all the Fetters in this order: *sat-kāya-dṛṣṭi* (belief in substantial Individuality), *vicikitsā* (doubt), *çīla-vrata-parāmarça* (the perverted belief in good works and ceremonies), *kāma-rāga* (love of sense-pleasure), *vyāpāda* (malice, ill-will), *rūpa-rāga* (love of existence in the material worlds), *ārūpya-rāga* (love of existence in the non-material worlds), *avidyā* (ignorance), *māna* (pride) and *auddhatya*[29] (self-righteousness, exaltation, excitement). It defines an *arhat* as one who has destroyed all these Fetters. At the same time, it declares that the acquisition of the *prajñā-pāramitā* or *bodhi* is necessary for the eradication of these Fetters (page 478, line 12). Thus even *arhatship* is regarded as almost impossible of attainment without the *bodhi* of a *bodhisattva*.

In this connection, it is interesting to compare the stereotyped formulæ, which are found in the *Ava. Ça.*, the *Divy.* and other Sanskrit treatises. An *arhat* and a *bodhisattva* are described in two different sets of words, which indicate that the new ideal was radically divergent from the old. In the *Ava. Ça.*, the following passage recurs frequently:—

"He exerted himself and strove and struggled, and thus he realized that this circle (or wheel) of Life (or the Universe), with its five constituents, is in constant flux. He rejected all the conditions of existence which are caused by the *samskāras* (material compounds), as their nature is such that they decay and fall away, they change and are destroyed. He abandoned all the *kleças*[30] (sins, passions) and realized the state of an *arhat*. When he became an *arhat*, he lost all attachment to the three worlds;[31] gold and a clod of earth were the same to him; the sky and the palm of his hand were the same to his mind; he was like fragrant sandal-wood;[32] he had torn the egg-shell (of ignorance) by his Knowledge (i.e. as a bird is hatched); he obtained Knowledge, the *abhijñās* (Super-knowledges) and the *pratisaṃvids* (analytical Powers); he became averse to gain, avarice and honour in the world (or to existence, gain, etc.); he became worthy of being respected, honoured and saluted by the *devas*, including *Indra* and his younger brother,[33] *Viṣṇu* or *Kṛṣṇa*" (*Ava. Ça.* II, 348, 1–6 and passim).

In the *Divy-āvadāna*, we find the old Pāli formula of *arhatship*: "My rebirth is destroyed; the excellent (spiritual) life has been lived; what had to be done ('duty') has been done; I shall not know a birth (or existence) after this life" (*Divy.* 37, 14–16).

The epithets which are applied to the *arhats* in the *Sad. Pu.* and the *Pr. Pā. Çata.* are also very characteristic. The *arhats* are declared to be free from the *āsravas* and the *kleças* (passions); they are self-restrained; they are perfectly free in their hearts and minds (or in their thought and wisdom); they are of good birth and comparable to great elephants in nobility, strength and endurance; they have done their duty, accomplished all that was to be done, laid down their burden, and achieved their aim (or their highest Good); they have destroyed the fetters of existence; their minds are perfectly liberated through right knowledge; they have attained to the highest perfection in all forms of mind-control and are conversant with the *abhijñās* (Super-knowledges. *Sad. Pu.*, 6–9).

If we compare these epithets with those which are applied to the *bodhisattvas* in the same books, we shall understand the second point of difference between the ideals of the *bodhisattva* and the *arhat*.

The *arhats* are represented as very austere, saintly, self-restrained, meditative ascetics, but also as rather frigid and self-centred. The *bodhisattvas* are described as more compassionate and active. They will "roll the wheel of the Doctrine that will never turn back." They serve and worship hundreds of Buddhas. Their bodies and minds are suffused and penetrated with friendliness for all creatures (*maitrī*). They are fit for imparting the Buddha's Knowledge to others. They have attained the full perfection of Wisdom. They help many living beings to secure liberation and happiness (*santārakaiḥ. Sad. Pu.* 2, 11 ff.).

It is to be noted that the words "friendliness" (*maitrī*) and "saviour, liberator" (*santāraka*) do not occur in the passage that describes the *arhats*.

(2) The Mahāyānists accuse the *arhat* of selfishness and egotism, because he strives and struggles only for his own liberation from sorrow instead of working for the liberation and happiness of

all beings. A *bodhisattva*, who follows the ideal of the Mahāyāna, aims at the highest Good for himself and also for others. An *arhat* is rightly or wrongly represented by the Mahāyānist authors as a self-complacent, self-regarding and unsocial recluse, who is intent only on solving his own personal problem and does not think of others. A *bodhisattva*, on the contrary, thinks both of himself and others. The *Sad. Pu.* condemns the *arhats* and the *pratyeka-buddhas*, because they exert themselves only for their complete *nirvāṇa* (*ātma-parinirvāṇa-hetoḥ*), but the *bodhisattvas* aspire to the attainment of *bodhi* for the welfare and happiness of many beings, both men and *devas*.[34] They wish to help all creatures to obtain Liberation (*sarva-sattva-parinirvāṇa-hetoḥ*), because they love and pity the whole world. Their wisdom serves to liberate all beings;[35] but such is not the case with the wisdom of the *çrāvakas* and the *pratyeka-buddhas*, who never say to themselves: "Having acquired supreme and perfect Enlightenment, we shall help all beings to attain the complete and final *nirvāṇa*, devoid of any material substratum."[36] The thoughts of these two classes of saints are narrow and mean, as they promote only their own personal interests; but the thoughts of the *bodhisattvas* are noble and generous, as they deal with the interests of others.[37] Great Merit is obtained by the *bodhisattvas*, who devote themselves to the good of others (*par-ārtha*); but the *çrāvakas* think only of their own good (*sv-ārtha*).[38] A *bodhisattva* may be compared to a charitable man who gives food to other people; but a *çrāvaka* is like a person who consumes it himself.[39] The Mahāyānists thus attribute altruistic motives to the *bodhisattvas*, who are therefore declared to be infinitely superior to the *çrāvakas* in many passages of Buddhist Sanskrit literature.[40]

Here we find two remarkable ideas: (*a*) A *bodhisattva* helps all beings not only to attain the spiritual goal of *nirvāṇa*, but also to obtain the more material advantages of happiness and welfare in the world (*sukha*). The austere unworldiness of the old ideal is abandoned in favour of a more humane aim.

(*b*) A *bodhisattva* wishes to help all beings to attain *nirvāṇa*. He must therefore refuse to enter *nirvāṇa* himself, as he cannot apparently render any services to the living beings of the worlds after his own *nirvāṇa*. He thus finds himself in the rather illogical position of pointing the way to *nirvāṇa* for other beings, while he himself stays in this world of suffering in order to do good to all creatures. This is his great sacrifice for others. He has taken the great Vow: "I shall not enter into final *nirvāṇa* before all beings have been liberated."[41] He has girt on his spiritual armour and wishes to continue his work as a *bodhisattva* in all worlds and universes.[42] He does not realise the highest Liberation for himself, as he cannot abandon other beings to their fate.[43] He has said: "I must lead all beings to Liberation. I will stay here till the end, even for the sake of one living soul."[44]

The Mahāyāna thus preached the ideal of compassionate Buddhahood for all as opposed to cold *arhatship*. The *Sad. Pu.* clearly teaches this new gospel: "All shall become Buddhas."[45] Çāntideva declares that even worms and insects have finally risen to the supreme position of a Buddha.[46]

A *bodhisattva* will thus attain *bodhi* and become a Buddha. These two conceptions of *bodhi* and Buddhahood are integral elements of the *bodhisattva* doctrine.

IV. Bodhi

The word *bodhi* is derived from the root *budh*, which is thus explained by Monier Williams: "The original sense may have been 'to fathom a depth, penetrate to the bottom'; to observe, mark, heed, regard, attend to; to perceive, notice, become acquainted with, recognise; to know, understand, comprehend; to think, reflect; to deem, consider, regard as, esteem as; to recover consciousness (after a swoon or after sleep, etc.), come to one's senses; to wake up, awake; to admonish" (Skt. Dicy. 685b).

Bodhi, as understood by the Buddhists, is related to the meaning, "to know, understand," and not to the signification of "waking up",[47] as Sīlācāra and D. T. Suzuki incorrectly assume. The word occurs in the *Ṛg-veda* in the epithet *bodhin-manas*, which means "having an attentive mind" ("*bodhin-manasā rathy-esirā havana-çrutā*," *Ṛgveda V.* 75.5; vol. iii, page 530). In Buddhist philosophy, it signifies "supreme Knowledge", "Enlightenment", "perfect Wisdom" (Skt. Dicy. M.W. 688—Pāli Dicy. s.v.).

The conception of *bodhi* has been elucidated and explained by several Buddhist writers. Two qualifying adjectives are commonly associated with it: *samyak* (right, perfect) and *anuttarā* (nothing higher, without a superior, incomparable, unsurpassed, pre-eminent, supreme) The usual appellation in thus *anuttarā-samyak-sambodhi.*[48] (The prefix *sam* is also placed before the word *bodhi* in order to emphasise its excellence and completeness.) The form *bodha* is also found.[49]

Bodhi or *Sambodhi*, the *summum bonum* of a *bodhisattva*, is primarily and essentially equivalent to Omniscience. Of course, it has been analysed into its constituent elements, and its various aspects have been elucidated by the Buddhist philosophers. But the simple root-idea, shorn of all accretions and amplifications, is Omniscience. D. T. Suzuki defines *bodhi* in terms of the *dharma-kāya* [50] (cosmic spiritual Body). But the term *bodhi* was in use long before the doctrine of the *kāyas* was propounded. It is therefore inadmissible to introduce such later concepts into the simple definition of *bodhi.*

The final goal of a *bodhisattva's* career is always indicated by such words as *buddha-jñāna* [51] (Knowledge of a Buddha), *sarvajñatā* [52] (Omniscience), *sarv-ākārajñatā* [53] (the quality of knowing things as they are), *mārg-ākārajñatā* (the quality of knowing the forms of the Way), *anuttara-jñāna* [54] (supreme Knowledge), and *acintyaṃ jñānam* (inconceivable Knowledge).[55] *Bodhi* has been described as incomprehensible for the ratiocinative intellect.[56] It is infinite, because the qualities that produce it are infinite. It is pure and perfect Knowledge of all things, free from uncertainty and obscurity. It is the result of the complete destruction of the two *āvaraṇas* (veils, coverings), [57] which relate to the sins and passions (*kleç-āvaraṇa*) and to knowable things (*jñey-āvaraṇa*). It is pure, universal and immediate Knowledge, which extends over all time,[58] all universes, all beings and all elements, conditioned and unconditioned (*saṃskṛta, asaṃskṛta*). It is absolute, because it does not need repeated mental acts. It is identical with Reality and Suchness (*tathatā*),[59] and embraces all that exists. It is all-pervading, like space.[60] It is therefore the supreme and precious Wisdom that a *bodhisattva* seeks.

V. The Buddha

A Buddha is primarily a fully "enlightened" being. But the characteristic attributes and qualities of a Buddha have been described and enumerated in several definite formulæ. In the *Ava. Ça.*, a Buddha is said to possess ten Powers (*balāni*), four

Grounds of Self-confidence (*vaiçāradyāni*) and three Fields of Mindfulness [61] (*smṛty-upasthānāni*). But the last item is not mentioned in the standard Mahāyānist treatises, which replace it by eighteen "*āveṇika-dharmāḥ*" (special, exclusive, unique attributes). This formula gives us the accepted formal definition of a Buddha.[62] The Indian philosophers have the habit of devising precise numerical lists for all their ideas and ideals. A Buddha is one, who has acquired the ten *balas*, the four *vaiçāradyas* and the eighteen *āveṇika-dharmas*. No other being possesses these attributes.

(*a*) *The Ten Powers.*[63] A Buddha possesses the knowledge of correct and faulty conclusions.[64] He knows fully and truly the consequences of all actions in the past, the present and the future with regard to their causes and circumstances. He is cognisant of the various aspirations [65] or dispositions of the different types of persons. He knows the true nature of the various *dhātus* (elements) in the universe.[66] He understands the higher or lower powers of different creatures.[67] He knows the Way that leads everywhere.[68] He realises the defilement, purification and origination of all the forms of Musing, Deliverances, Concentration and Ecstatic Attainment.[69] He remembers all his previous existences. He discerns the process of the death and rebirth of all beings. He knows that his *āsravas* (Intoxicants: sins and errors) have been destroyed. Thus he acquires the Powers that are associated with such varied and accurate Knowledge.

The last three Powers are due to the threefold Knowledge (*tisro vidyāḥ*) that a Buddha gains immediately before Enlightenment.[70]

(*b*) *The Four Vaiçāradyas.* This word *vaiçāradya* (Pāli *vessārajja*) [71] means "perfect self-confidence, self-satisfaction", and the four *vaiçāradyas* are a Buddha's four "Grounds of Self-confidence". The term has also been translated as "conviction", "les assurances," "absence of hesitation," "la confiance," "les intrepidités," "les habiletés," "kinds of intrepidity," "die Selbstsicherheiten," "les certitudes," "vierfaches Selbstvertrauen," etc.[72] The root-idea seem to be "maturity, experience". The adjective *viçārada* (Pāli: *visārada*) means "experienced, wise, self-confident". It is the opposite of *sārada*, which is ultimately derived from the Sanskrit word *çarad* (autumn), and literally means "autumnal, this year's". Figuratively, it came to denote "unripe", "immature," "inexperienced." The Pāli substantive *sārajja* means "shyness", "timidity" (Pāli Dicy). A novice is sometimes said to suffer from *parṣac-chāradya* (diffidence or timidity in an assembly). The Tibetan equivalent is *mi-hjigs-pa*; [73] and *hjigs-pa* means "fear, apprehension, dread" (Tib. Dicy. Das, 457b). The Tibetans interpret *vaiçāradya* as "fearlessness". According to S. Lévi, the Chinese also translate it by a word which means "without fear". [74]

A Buddha has four Grounds or Subjects of Self-confidence, on account of which he boldly preaches the doctrine and "utters a lion's roar". He knows that he has attained perfect Enlightenment and understands all principles and phenomena (*dharmāḥ*).[75] He knows that he has destroyed all the *āsravas* (Intoxicants). He knows that the obstacles to the higher life, which he has described, really constitute serious hindrances.[76] He knows that the Way, which he teaches for the cessation of Pain and Evil (*duḥkha*), really leads to that goal. Thus no one in the entire universe, man or *deva*, or any other being, can accuse him of insincerity or falsehood in this respect. No one can say to him: "You claim to be perfectly enlightened; but here are things that you do not understand. You assert that you have destroyed the *āsravas;* but these are the *āsravas* that still remain in your personality. You declare that you have indicated the obstacles to the spiritual life; but some of these practices and ideas are no obstacles at all. You say that you teach the Way that leads to the destruction of Pain: but that Way does not help one to attain that end." A Buddha knows that no one can justly reproach him in this manner. For this reason, he is always serene, fearless and self-confident, and cultivates a noble and magnanimous spirit. (*Pr. Pā. Çata.*, pp. 1448–9.)

(*c*) *The Eighteen Āveṇika-dharmas.* A Buddha possesses eighteen special and extraordinary attributes, which are called his *āveṇika-dharmas*. This word *āveṇika* means "special, peculiar, extraordinary, exceptional" (Pāli Dicy. s.v.). Monier Williams derives it from *veṇi* (braiding, weaving, a tress, conflux of two or more streams), and translates: "Not connected with anything else; independent." Böhtlingk and Roth follow E. Burnouf, who gives the meaning: "qui ne se confondent pas." He says: "C'est par conjecture que je le traduis comme je fais, le prenant pour un dérivé du mot *aveṇi*, 'qui ne forme pas une tresse, ou qui ne se confond pas à la manière de plusieurs fleuves se réunissant en un seul.'" [77]

The term has also been translated as "independent conditions", "les vertus exclusives," "congenital qualities," "die Bedingungen der Unabhängigkeit," "les substances non-mêlées," "besondere Eigenschaften," "unique characteristics," "unmixed or pure virtues or qualities," "uncommon properties." [78]

V. Trenckner suggests that the word *āveṇika* is derived from *vinā* (without), with the prefix *ā*, and denotes "sine quâ non".[79] But it is difficult to understand how *āveṇika* can be related to *vinā*. A Buddha's three Fields of Mindfulness, mentioned above, are also described as *āveṇikāni*; and an educated woman is said to possess five *āveṇika-dharmas* (*Ava. Ça.*, i, 14, 7, translated as "cinq conditions distinctes" by E. Burnouf).[80] The adjectives *āveṇi* and *āveṇiya* are also found in Pāli literature; e.g. "*āveṇikammāni karonti - āveṇi - pātimokkhaṃ uddisanti*" (*Aṅguttara*, v, 74, line 10—where Nyāṇatiloka translates *āveṇi* as "*getrennt*").

"*Pañcimāni bhikkhave mātugāmassa āveṇikāni dukkhāni*" (*Saṃyutta*, iv, 239, line 10).

"*Āveṇi-uposathaṃ karonti āveṇi-pavāraṇaṃ karonti*" (*Vinaya* ii, 204, line 26), where T. W. Rhys Davids and H. Oldenberg translate, "perform *independently* Uposatha and Pavāraṇa" (S.B.E., xx, p. 267).

"*Devadatto .... āveṇi saṅgha-kammāni akāsi*" (*Jātaka*, i, 490, line 29), where R. Chalmers translates: "He performed the acts of a separate Brotherhood" (*Jātaka* Trsln., i, p. 305). The Tibetan equivalent is *ma-ḥdres-pa* (Csoma, p. 250—*M.Vy.*, p. 10). *Ḥdres-pa* means "mixed", and the term therefore signifies "pure, unadulterated, unmixed" (Tib. Dicy. Das, pp. 699, 948—Jäschke, p. 284). It is to be noted that the same root is employed in a phrase, which denotes "the influx of the Ganges into the sea" (Tib. Dicy. Jäschke, p. 284). This seems to confirm E. Burnouf's conjecture that the word *āveṇika* is related to *veṇi* in the sense of "confluence of rivers". According to E. J. Eitel, the Chinese translate *āveṇika-dharmāḥ* by a phrase which means "detached characteristics, the distinctive marks of a Buddha who is detached from the imperfections which mark ordinary mortals" (p. 26). The root-idea seems to be separation, as is evident from the Pāli passages, in which the word is almost always used with reference to schism in the Order. We may translate: "special, peculiar, exclusive."

These eighteen attributes[81] distinguish a Buddha from all other beings. "He is free from errors and faults. He is not noisy or loquacious.[82] He never loses Mindfulness. His mind is always composed and collected. He has no notion of multiplicity (i.e. he considers the universe under its aspect of unity and not with reference to the diversity of phenomena and objects). His equanimity is not due to want of judgment.[83] His Will and Resolution never falter. His Energy is never diminished. His Mindfulness is never relaxed. His Concentration always remains the same. His Wisdom never fails. His Deliverance knows no change. All his actions, performed with the body, are preceded by Knowledge and continue to be in accordance with Knowledge.[84] All his words and utterances are preceded by Knowledge and continue to be in accordance with Knowledge. All his thoughts are preceded by Knowledge and continue to be in accordance with Knowledge. He has absolute and infallible Knowledge and Insight with regard to the past time.[85] He has absolute and infallible Knowledge and Insight with regard to the future. He has absolute and infallible Knowledge and Insight with regard to the present (time)."

Such is the complete formula of the eighteen special attributes of a Buddha, with all its repetitions and redundancies and its partial unintelligibility. The *M.S. Al.* declares that six of these qualities refer to Method[86]; six deal with Acquisition (of Merit or Knowledge); three are descriptive of Actions, and three define a Buddha's Knowledge. As this list is not found in the Pāli canon and the early Sanskrit treatises, it must be assigned to a comparatively late period (third century A.D.).

This triple formula of the *balas*, *vaiçāradyas* and *āveṇika-dharmas* constitutes the stock definition of a Buddha. But there are several other essential factors in the conception of Buddhahood as it is developed by the Buddhist Sanskrit writers for the inspiration and edification of a *bodhisattva*. A *bodhisattva* should know and comprehend these qualities and characteristics of the Buddhas before he can appreciate the importance of striving for *bodhi*.

(*d*) A Buddha is distinguished from other beings by his deep and great pity, love, mercy and compassion for all beings (*karuṇā*).[87]

Here we come upon this great word, *karuṇā*, which recurs very frequently in Mahāyānist literature. A Buddha is endowed with *mahā-karuṇā*, the adjective *mahā* being prefixed in order to emphasise the importance of this attribute. He loves all creatures as his children. He says to them: "I am the Father of the world; you are my children."[88] A Buddha's *karuṇā* is discussed in the *M. Vy.* under thirty-two aspects; he pities all beings, because they are enmeshed in various sins, errors, dangers and calamities.[89] It was really necessary to lay stress on this attribute of a Buddha's personality. According to the *Kathā-vatthu*, some Buddhists taught that the Buddha could not feel compassion, as he was free from all passion (*rāga*).[90] This doctrine, which reminds us of the teaching of some Stoic philosophers of Greece, was vigorously combated by the Mahāyānists and others.[91]

(*e*) In addition to *karuṇā*, a Buddha is noted for his thorough and unblemished purity. His bodily actions, his speech, his thoughts and his very soul are pure; and there is not the slightest impurity in him. On account of this fourfold purity, he need not be on his guard against others. These are his four *Ārakṣyas* (Pāli: *arakkheyyā*).[92]

Many. other laudatory epithets have been applied to the Buddha by the pious Buddhists.[93] He is "self-existent", "a conqueror," "a physician," "self-luminous," "Lord of the Universe," "King of Kings," "peerless," "all-beholder," "sinless," "light-giver," "superior to all beings," "sweet-voiced," "the god of gods" (*devātideva*), etc.

(*f*) A *bodhisattva*, who becomes a Buddha, will not live in solitary grandeur, as the Buddhas are numerous. According to the oldest Pāli tradition, there were six Buddhas who lived before Gautama Çākyamuni. Their names are mentioned in the *Mahāpa-dāna-sutta* of the *Dīgha-Nikāya* (ii, 2 ff.). The number of these Buddhas is seven, because the ancient world believed in the existence of seven "planets" (Sun, Moon, Mercury, Venus, Mars, Jupiter and Saturn). These seven Buddhas correspond to the seven *ṛṣis* of the Indian tradition, who have also an astronomical origin. Their Sanskritized names are mentioned in the *Dh. S.* (Section 6), the *Lal. V.* and the *M. Vy.*[94] The number of the Buddhas, who preceded Gautama Çākyamuni and predicted his advent, was increased to twenty-four in the Pāli *Buddhavaṃsa*. But the Sanskrit writers continued the process of multiplying the Buddhas.

The *Lal. V.* speaks of *koṭis* (ten millions) of them, as does also the *Sad. Pu.* The *Suvarna-prabhāsa* tells us of "thousands", while the *Su. Vy.* estimates their exact number at 81 *koṭi-niyuta-çata-sahasrāṇi* (81 million million *niyutas*).[95] The *Kar. Pu.* and the *Pr. Pā. Çata.* speak of many Buddhas who have their *kṣetras* (fields).[96] The *Mahā-vastu* refers to 300 million Buddhas of the name of Çākyamuni, 60,000 Buddhas of the name of Pradyota, and so on.[97] Finally, the philosophers got tired of piling up high numbers in this fashion and declared that the Buddhas were really infinite in number. They hit upon the picturesque phrase: "The Buddhas are like the sands on the banks of the Ganges."[98] Having made the Buddhas innumerable, the Indian imagination could not go further.

It is likely that this idea was suggested by the star-lit tropical sky, and each star was regarded as an inhabited world ruled by a Buddha.

(*g*) A Buddha has his *buddha-kṣetra* (field), which he guides and "ripens" in spirituality. The *Sad. Pu.* contains predictions about the future Buddhahood of several saints, and their *kṣetras* are described.[99] A *kṣetra* consists of many worlds and universes, with their heavens, purgatories, earths, *devas*, *pretas*, human beings and animals.

(*h*) A Buddha, who appears on this earth or in any other world, can never cease to exist. This remarkable idea was developed very gradually by the Buddhist philosophers. In the old Pāli tradition, Gautama Çākyamuni after his demise was regarded as more dead than alive. He could not be seen by gods and men,[100] and honour paid to him after his death had only symbolic spiritual significance.[101] The six or twenty-four Buddhas of the past, who are mentioned in the Pāli canon, were not supposed to be living after their *parinirvāṇa*. But the *Mtu.* declares that a Buddha can live for many æons (*kalpas*).[102] In the *Sad. Pu.*, a Buddha is said to live for a very long time in his *kṣetra*, but he is not immortal. The length of life of each Buddha is specified, and he enters *parinirvāṇa* at the end of that period. Only in the case of Yaçodharā, the author shows that chivalry can be combined with theology, and he allots her an unlimited span of life as a future Buddha. Gautama Buddha also lives for ever (*sadā sthitaḥ*).[103] Here we find the first clear hint of immortality for the Buddhas. Further, the same writer contradicts himself by bringing on the scene a Buddha, who had really entered into *parinirvāṇa* long ago, but who suddenly re-appears as a living Buddha in order to sing the praises of the *Sad-dharma-puṇḍarīka* as a religious treatise.[104] Thus it is indicated that even *parinirvāṇa* does not imply extinction. The final doctrine on this question is elaborated by the author of the *Suvarṇa-prabhāsa*, who declares that a Buddha's duration of life is unlimited and immeasurable.[105] Gautama Buddha did not really perish after eighty years' sojourn on earth : he can never die.

(*i*) The Buddhas are not only numerous and immortal, but they are also superhuman (*lok-ottara*) in all their actions, even during their earthly lives. A Buddha is entirely free from sensual desires. He is above all human needs and weaknesses : his body has no limits and knows no fatigue.[106] He does not sleep or dream. He replies to all questions immediately and spontaneously without the necessity of thinking over the matter even for a moment. Every word uttered by a Buddha has deep spiritual significance and is intended for the edification of the people. His speech is always rational and perfect, and it is understood by the hearers. He is always in a state of profound concentration. His power of working miracles is unlimited.[107] He eats, drinks, and takes medicine in illness only in order to conform to the ways of the world (*lok-ānuvartanā*), as he is really not subject to hunger, thirst, disease, or any human needs and infirmities. His body is not formed by the physical union of his reputed parents, and he is born as a child merely in order to act like ordinary human beings.[108]

(*j*) Further, if a Buddha is immortal and superhuman, his physical body cannot represent his real nature. He must therefore be essentially a spiritual Being, who either assumes a human form as an *avatāra* (Incarnation) or shows an unreal physical body to the people for their edification. The doctrine of *avatāra* was rejected by the Buddhist thinkers, though it was accepted by the Hindus.[109] But the Buddha pretended to live and work in the world as a mortal in order to save all beings. His physical body (*rūpa-kāya*) was illusory and unreal like the shapes created by a magician (*nirmāṇa*). "The *rūpa-kāya* is not the Buddha," declares the author of the *Sam. Rā.* (fol. 95b, 4 ff.). The *Suvarṇa-prabhāsa* teaches that it is impossible to find any relic of a Buddha's body after his cremation.[110] It is a grave error to identify a Buddha with his *rūpa-kāya*, as a Buddha has no form or other material attributes.[111] A Buddha creates many phantom-bodies, which visit the worlds and preach the Doctrine. The people see them and believe that they are born and perish. All this illusion is due to a Buddha's wisdom in the choice of methods for converting the hearers (*upāya-kauçalya*).[112]

(*k*) If the fragile and limited *rūpa-kāya* is not the real Buddha, what and who is the Buddha? In contradistinction to the *rūpa-kāya*, the Mahāyānists speak of a Buddha's *dharma-kāya* (cosmic, spiritual Body).[113] A Buddha is the embodiment of *dharma*, which is his real Body.[114] He is also identified with all the constituents of the universe (form, thought, etc.).[115] This Body, which is also called *sad-dharma-kāya*, *bodhi-kāya*, *buddha-kāya*, *prajñā-kāya*, *svābhāvika-kāya* (essential Body), is invisible and universal.[116] It is imperishable and perfectly pure.[117] All beings "live and move and have their being in it".[118] It is the same as the Absolute Reality (*tathatā*), which is also one and indivisible for the entire Universe.[119] It is immutable and undifferentiated.[120]

(*l*) If a Buddha's real body is the cosmic Absolute, then it follows that all Buddhas are spiritually united in the *dharma-kāya*. This final step was taken by the Mahāyānists. "All Buddhas are one," declares the *M.S. Al.*[121] There cannot be many Buddhas in reality.[122] Buddhahood, which belongs to the realm of Freedom and Perfection (*anāsrave dhātau*), unites them all, as they have one Wisdom and one Aim.[123] Gautama Buddha could therefore rightly say: "I was that Buddha of the past, named Vipaçyin."[124]

A Buddha also possesses a Body of Bliss or Enjoyment, which is radiant and glorious, and bears thirty-two special marks and eighty minor signs[125] (*sambhoga-kāya*, *sāmbhogika-kāya*, *sāmbhogya-kāya*). It is the result of the Merit, which a Buddha has acquired by his good deeds during many æons.[126] It is visible only to the faithful *bodhisattvas*, who assemble to hear a Buddha preach.[127] It must, however, be emphasised that the fundamental distinction is between the physical body and the *dharma-kāya*, which are often mentioned together and contrasted. The *saṃbhoga-kāya* was added subsequently in order to give the Buddhas something like the celestial bodies of the Hindu *devas*. It belongs to the stage of deification, not to that of spiritualisation and unification.

Thus the conception of Buddhahood was developed to its ultimate conclusion in universal pan-Buddhism (as distinct from

Pantheism). The Buddhas were subjected to a sixfold process of evolution: they were multiplied, immortalised, deified, spiritualised, universalised and unified.

(*m*) There were many causes, which led to this radical transformation of the ideal of a Buddha's personality. The idea of a Buddha's enduring *dharma*-body is found in the Pāli canon.[128] Gautama Buddha was at first regarded as only an *arhat* like the other monks,[129] and he disclaimed omniscience.[130] But several Pāli passages indicate that he was in some way also superhuman. He could make Yasa invisible,[131] and work miracles at Uruvelā and other places.[132] He declared that he was neither a man nor a *deva*, but a Buddha, as if the Buddhas formed a distinct species or class of beings by themselves.[133] He is said to be unlike the other monks, as he first found the Way of Enlightenment and showed it to others.[134] He promised rebirth in *svarga* (heaven) to those who should have faith in him and love him.[135] His body was transfigured,[136] and his birth was accompanied by miracles.[137] He could have lived much longer, if he had wished to do so.[138] He could enable a visitor to see the hidden parts of his body under his garments.[139] Such details show that the process of deification began soon after Gautama Buddha's death. It was continued and intensified by the *Mahāsaṅghikas*, the *Vetulyakas*, the *Andhakas* and other Buddhist sects.[140] The uneducated masses and their enthusiastic leaders always love to exalt and glorify their prophet. Hero-worship is ingrained in human nature and takes strange forms among the uncultured sections of society. The Arians of Europe were finally defeated by the more superstitious followers of Athanasius.[141] The competition of the rival Indian sects and movements also led the Buddhists to advance new claims on behalf of their leader. The Jainas taught that Mahāvīra survived death and existed as a Spirit in beatitude. The Hindus deified *Kṛṣṇa* and prayed to their *devas*, *Viṣṇu*, *Çiva* and others. The *Sāṅkhya* philosophers promised an eternal future of unalloyed felicity as *puruṣa*. The *Vedāntins* looked forward to identification with the eternal *Brahman*. It would have been impossible for the Buddhists to succeed in their ethical propaganda, if they had adhered to the old doctrine that the survival of a Buddha after death was an "unexplained question" (*avyākṛta*), or if they had taught that a monk perished altogether at death after attaining *nirvāṇa*, like Godhika and Vakkali of unhappy memory.[142]

Such a dismal message of agnosticism or annihilation could not win many converts in that unscientific age. The Buddhists had to follow the line of least resistance. They perhaps also thought and felt that so wise and virtuous a man as Gautama Buddha could not end in blank nothingness. They transformed him into a living, immortal, powerful and gracious *deva*. They also bestowed on him all the mystical attributes of the impersonal *Brahman* of the *Upaniṣads*. His humanity, his physical body and his death were therefore denied or thrown into the background, and he was endowed with the *sambhoga-kāya* and the *dharma-kāya*. The Mahāyānists borrowed and assimilated the entire theology and metaphysics of Hinduism and Jainism, and then evolved their impressive and comprehensive conception of the Buddha. The life of Gautama was the foundation of the edifice: the rival sects supplied the material for the superstructure.

Such a Buddha every man and woman, nay every living creature, can and must become. This is a *bodhisattva's* goal and ideal.

The *bodhisattva* ideal reminds us of the active altruism of the Franciscan friars in the thirteenth century A.D. as contrasted with the secluded and contemplative religious life of the Christian monks of that period.[143] The monk prayed in solitude: the friar " went about doing good ". The great Franciscan movement in the history of Christianity offers an interesting parallel to the Mahāyāna " revival " in Buddhism. Both the *arhat* and the *bodhisattva* were unworldly idealists; but the *arhat* exhibited his idealism by devoting himself to meditation and self-culture, while the *bodhisattva* actively rendered service to other living beings. In the phraseology of modern psychology, an *arhat* was an " introvert ", while a *bodhisattva* was an " extrovert ".[144]

Chapter II

ORIGIN AND DEVELOPMENT OF THE BODHISATTVA DOCTRINE

I

The *bodhisattva* doctrine may be regarded as the final outcome of the tendencies that were at work in India during several centuries after Gautama Buddha's death. These may be grouped and classified as follows :—

(1) The natural tendencies of development within the Buddhist Church.

(2) The influence of other Indian religious sects like the *Bhāgavatas* and the *Çaivas*.

(3) The influence of Persian religion and culture.

(4) The influence of Greek art.

(5) The necessities of propaganda among new semi-barbarous tribes.

(6) The influence of Christianity.

These different factors, that contributed to the rise and growth of the new doctrine, may be considered in detail.

(1) Natural Development of Buddhism

The most important factor was the natural and inevitable tendency of Buddhism to grow and develop in the changing circumstances of the age. A great religion is not a dead static formula of salvation and ethics : it is always a living, dynamic, self-evolving and self-adjusting spiritual movement. The founder's disciples try to render explicit all that was implicit in the original teaching, and they also contribute new ideas and ideals. Only an ultra-orthodox Mahāyānist would support S. Kimura's contention that the philosophers of the Māhāyana really expounded Gautama Buddha's own "ontological and introspectional principles", which were not communicated to the ordinary disciples.[1] This is an unwarranted assumption. Gautama Buddha took pride in being free from the fault, that was described as *ācārya-muṣṭi* (Pāli : *ācariya-muṭṭhi*, "the teacher's fist, close-fistedness, keeping things back, esotericism"). His teaching was open to all, like the light of the sun and the moon.[2] The fiction of an "esoteric" Buddhism need not be invoked in order to explain the natural development of Buddhism after the death of the founder.

The *bodhisattva* doctrine was the necessary outcome of two movements of thought in early Buddhism, viz. the growth of *bhakti* (devotion, faith, love) and the idealisation and spiritualisation of the Buddha. *Bhakti* was at first directed towards Gautama Buddha. But he was soon idealised, spiritualised and universalised, as has already been indicated. He then became an unsuitable and unattractive object for the pious Buddhist's *bhakti*. That deep-rooted feeling found an outlet in the invention and adoration of the *bodhisattvas*.

The ideal of *bhakti* arose and flourished among the Buddhists. Some scholars are of opinion that it originated in the Hindu sects and was subsequently adopted by the Buddhists. They think that the *bhakti* literature of the Buddhists is an imitation of Hindu scriptures like the *Bhagavad-gītā*. M. Winternitz says : "It was under the influence of the *bhakti* doctrine of the *Bhagavad-gītā*, ... that the Mahāyāna Buddhism was developed."[3] H. Kern finds that "the *Sad. Pu.* is full of un-Buddhistic notions, allied with, if not directly taken from, the *Gītā*".[4] É. Senart writes : "La tradition bouddhique se meut certainement dans une atmosphère Krishnaite."[5] He also thinks that the Buddhists borrowed the idea of *bhakti* from the *Bhāgavata* sect.[6] K. J. Saunders has tried to show that the author of the *Sad. Pu.* borrowed much from the *Bhagavad-gītā*.[7] L. de la Vallée Poussin thinks that Buddhism in its entirety is only a form or aspect of Hinduism : "une modalité de l'Hindouisme," "une cristallisation particulière de l'Hindouisme."[8] This view is based on an inaccurate interpretation of the history of religion.

It is almost certain that the Buddhists were the originators and innovators in several new developments, and the Hindus followed suit. If Buddhism were only a "modality" of Hinduism, the Buddhists would have adopted the whole Hindu pantheon of gods and goddesses instead of exercising their ingenuity and imagination to invent the class of beings known as the *bodhisattvas*. Buddhism had its own independent genius, which kept it distinct from Hinduism during many centuries, as is evident from the oft-recurring significant phrase, "*çramaṇas* and *brāhmaṇas*." The Hindus priests of India resolutely refused to preserve Buddhist literature or to acknowledge Buddhist metaphysics as an "orthodox" system. Hinduism absorbed the *Bhāgavatas* and other new sects, but Buddhism and Jainism could resist its assimilating power. Buddhism has spread among other Asiatic nations, because it is universal in spirit, like Christianity and Islam; but Hinduism is a national religious and social system, like Confucianism and Judaism. Buddhism borrowed some ideas and institutions from Hinduism, and the latter was indebted to Buddhism for fundamental changes in its ethics and ritual. But both maintained their individuality as systems of doctrine and discipline. The idea of *bhakti* was not a borrowed feather, with which Buddhism adorned itself. It was an integral part of the Buddhist ideal from the earliest times. In fact, the very word *bhakti*, as a technical religious term, occurs for the first time in Indian literature in a Buddhist treatise and not in a Hindu scripture. The *Theragāthā* speaks of *bhatti*: "*so bhattimā nāma ca hoti paṇḍitō ñatvā ca dhammesu visesi assa*" (p. 41, lines 1–2). This anthology contains verses that go back to the earliest period of the history of Buddhism, and its final redaction took place in the middle of the third century B.C.[9] But the idea of *bhakti* is found in the ancient Pāli *Nikāyas*: it was called *saddhā* in the fifth century B.C. *Saddhā* was a very important concept in early Buddhism. Faith in the Buddha is repeatedly declared to be essential for the spiritual development of the monks and the laymen.[10] It can even lead to rebirth in a heaven. A novice must "take refuge" first in the Buddha and then in the Doctrine and the Confraternity. It is a great mistake to under-estimate the importance of *saddhā* in early Buddhism, which has been wrongly represented as a dry "rationalistic" system of precepts and theories.[11] Even in the Pāli canon, the impression left on the reader's mind is that Gautama Buddha is the centre of the whole movement, and that the Doctrine derives its vitality and importance from his personality. This is true of all great religions and churches. When the Christians love and exalt Jesus Christ and the Moslems praise and glorify their Prophet, they evince personal *bhakti*, which can be thoroughly justified by an appeal to history and psychology. Even if the Buddha had advanced no extraordinary claims on his own behalf, his greatness as a man would have given rise to the cult of *bhakti* for him. The disciples of a wise and virtuous teacher must love and revere him personally, even though he should modestly declare that his personality is of no importance. It is Personality that secures the triumph of a religious movement; the dogmas and precepts shine in the light reflected from Personality. *Bhakti* cannot arise without the historical fact of the life and work of a great man. For this reason, it could not have originated among the metaphysicians of the *Upaniṣads*, as A. B. Keith has assumed.[12] There was no great man like Buddha or Mahāvīra among them. Apart from the irresistible influence of Personality, the absence of any other objects of adoration led the Buddhists to concentrate their love and devotion on the Buddha. They did not hold the ancient *devas* in high esteem. They could not have any devotional feeling for them or pray to them. The *devas* were regarded by the Buddhists as glorified super-men, who enjoyed bliss and power, but who were subject to the law of death and rebirth and needed wisdom and liberation as much as the human beings on earth. They were far inferior to the Buddha in character and knowledge. They visited him as disciples and suppliants, and even rendered menial service to him.[13] Having reduced the great *devas* of Hinduism to such a subordinate position, the Buddhists had no object of love and devotion except the Buddha himself. They, like all men and women, had hearts as well as brains; and the heart will not be denied its rights, whatever the logicians may say. Man is not merely "a reasoning self-sufficing thing, an intellectual all-in-all". As the Buddhists despised the *devas*, they put the Buddha in their place. It was therefore quite natural that the ideal of *bhakti* should first grow and flourish among the Buddhists, and not among the Hindus. As a matter of fact, *Viṣṇu* and *Çiva* are mentioned only as secondary deities in the list of *devas* in the *Dīgha-Nikāya* (*Veṇhu* and *Isāna*).[14] They are not regarded as the equals of the old *devas*, *Brahmā* and *Çakra*. Their cults could not have been very important at that period (fifth century B.C.). *Bhakti* was chiefly associated in Hinduism with the sects devoted to these two *devas*. The *Bhagavad-gītā* also belongs to a much later period (200 B.C. to A.D. 200). It may therefore be inferred on *a priori* grounds, and also on the basis of historical data, that Buddhism originated the idea of *bhakti* and did not borrow it from Hinduism. If we find similar epithets applied to Gautama Buddha and Kṛṣṇa in the *Sad. Pu.* and the *Bhagavad-gītā*,[15] we must conclude that they were first invented by the Buddhists and subsequently adopted and adapted by the Hindu sectarian leaders. The latter tried to find some heroes in their own tradition and discovered Kṛṣṇa and Rāma for their cult of *bhakti*.

This stage in the evolution of Buddhism is represented by the two treatises, the *Sad. Pu.* and the *Su. Vy.* In the *Sad Pu.*, Gautama Buddha is described as the loving Father of all creatures, and all pious Buddhists are exhorted to worship and adore him.[16] The *Su. Vy.* promises rebirth in the Buddha *Amitābha's* paradise (*buddha-kṣetra*) to all who should think of him and utter his name with love and devotion.[17] The larger *Su. Vy.* excludes from this privilege all sinners, who have committed any of the five heinous, mortal sins (*ānantaryāṇi*). But the *Amitāyur-dhyāna-sūtra* abolishes this restriction and offers a happy rebirth (not *nirvāṇa*) to all creatures as the reward of *bhakti*.[18] *Bhakti* is directed towards a Buddha at this period.

The conception of Buddhahood was widened and elaborated under the influence of Jainism and Hindu theology and metaphysics, as has been indicated above. As a consequence, a Buddha ceased to appeal to the popular imagination as an object of devotion. He had been de-humanised and universalised. He was also theoretically far removed from this world of change and sin. He lost Personality and became cosmic Law. As the Hindus could not love or adore the metaphysical *Brahman* of the *Upaniṣads*, but needed deities of flesh and blood for their cult, so the Buddhists too could not approach the idealised and transcendental Buddha of the Mahāyāna with prayer and worship. He had become too great, vast, nebulous, impersonal and incomprehensible for such relations. The Mahāyānists turned in their need to the earlier history of Gautama Buddha, when he was not the remote metaphysical Buddha, but only a charitable, patient and wise *bodhisattva*, a married citizen and a denizen of this workaday world. As a *bodhisattva*, he had helped many men and women with gifts of wealth and knowledge. He was a more humane and lovable figure at that stage of his career. The pious worshippers could pray to a *bodhisattva* for health, wealth and mundane blessings, and that was all that they really wanted. The cult of *bhakti* is partly an expression of egoism, as it involves supplication for selfish interests. Ordinary men and women are more anxious to secure welfare and happiness in this world than to strive for the distant and doubtful goal of

Buddhahood. The *bodhisattvas* were thus chosen for worship and adoration in order to satisfy the needs of the devout and pious Buddhists. The *bodhisattva* doctrine may be said to have been the inevitable outcome of the tendency towards *bhakti* and the new conception of Buddhahood. This view seems to be confirmed by the fact that the Hīnayānists, who did not de-humanise and universalise the Buddha, did not feel the necessity of inventing and adoring the *bodhisattvas*. The analogy of other religious movements also proves that uneducated men and women require some attributes of human personality in the superhuman beings, whom they are willing to worship. They feel more at home with such helpers. They shrink from the measureless immensity and unapproachable sublimity of the universal Spirit, whether it is called *Brahman*, *Dharma-kāya*, *Allah* or *God*. The development of saint-worship in Islam and Christianity was due to the same causes as led to the cult of the *bodhisattvas* in Buddhism. Both Islam and Christianity teach that God has personality and love and answers prayers ; but millions of Moslems and Christians have found solace in the worship of the saints. They have felt the need of these human intercessors as intermediate objects of worship. They have placed them between God and Man. Saint-worship was firmly established in the Christian Church as early as the fourth century A.D., as P. Dörfler and H. Thurston have pointed out.[19] The Moslems, too, are fervent worshippers of their saints. R. A. Nicholson says : " In Mohammedan religious life, the *walī* occupies the same middle position : he bridges the chasm which the Koran and scholasticism have set between man and an absolutely transcendent God. He brings relief to the distressed, health to the sick, children to the childless, food to the famished. . . . His favour confers blessing." [20] W. M. Patton writes : " Every neighbourhood in the Muslim world has its patron saint. . . . . Since the days of al-Ghazāli (twelfth century A.D.), the Sunnite branch of Islam (excepting the Hanbalite school) has given its approval to the cult of the saints. . . . . In reality, the saint is a far more real God to them than Allah is . . . . The Shiahs are enthusiastic worshippers of the saints." [21] M. Horten expresses the same opinion : " Der Heiligen-kultus hat im islamischen Volke eine ungeheure Ausdehnung gewonnen, von der die zahllosen heiligen Stätten (die Gräber von Heiligen), Feste und sonstige Gebraüche ein beredtes Zeugnis ablegen." [22] The universal practice of saint-worship shows that it has satisfied certain fundamental needs of human nature at a certain stage of intellectual development.

The Buddhists invented their class of saints (*bodhisattvas*) chiefly by personifying the different virtues and attributes of Gautama Buddha's personality. They also took up certain epithets that were applied to Gautama Buddha, and converted them into the names of some *bodhisattvas*. The *bodhisattvas* thus derive their existence and attributes from the central historical fact of Gautama Buddha's life and work. The two chief *bodhisattvas*, Mañjuçrī and Avalokiteçvara, are personifications of Wisdom (*prajñā*) and Mercy (*karuṇā*) respectively. Maitreya typifies *maitrī* (friendliness). Some other *bodhisattvas* owe their names to the adjectives that were first employed to describe the great Teacher. Buddha is spoken of as "*samantato bhadraka*" and "*samanta-bhadra-kāya*" (auspicious or excellent in all ways) in the *Ava. Ça.* and the *Lal. V.*; and we find that Samantabhadra is the name of a *bodhisattva*.[23] Even "Mañjuçrī" may perhaps be derived from *mañju-ghoṣa* and *mañju-svara*, as these two epithets are used to describe Buddha's voice.[24] Çāntideva in fact refers to this *bodhisattva* as "*ajita-mañju-ghoṣa*" (*B.C. Ava.* ii, 13). In other cases, the descriptive titles of the Hindu *devas* have been transferred to the *bodhisattvas*. Thus *Brahmā* is described as "*mahā-bala-sthāma-prāpta*" in the *Da. Bhū.* (81.31), and an important *bodhisattva* is called Mahāsthāma-prāpta (having great strength).[25] Such names as Vajra-pāṇi and Kṣiti-garbha also suggest the influence of Hindu mythology.

(2) The Influence of Hinduism

Although the idea of *bhakti* originated among the Buddhists and was adopted in self-defence by the Hindus, yet the new sects, which arose after the fifth century B.C., exercised a profound influence on the further development of Buddhism. They established the cults of certain *devas* and deified heroes, and the Buddhists were compelled to endow their Buddhas and *bodhisattvas* with similar attributes and powers.

The *Bhāgavata* sect, which was probably founded in the fifth century B.C. in the west of India, inculcated the worship of *Bhagavat* (the Adorable) as the supreme Deity and was almost monotheistic. In course of time, the *Bhāgavatas* came to identify *Vāsudeva* with *Bhagavat* and the ancient sun-god *Viṣṇu*. This name *Vāsudeva* has been explained as referring to Kṛṣṇa, who is mentioned as a hero and also as a divine Incarnation in the *Mahābhārata*. He is also supposed to have been the disciple of Ghora Āṅgirasa, the sage mentioned in the *Chāndogya Upaniṣad*. It is not relevant to our purpose to discuss whether Kṛṣṇa was a warrior, a religious leader, a tribal god, a solar deity or the spirit of vegetation.[26] But the existence of a sect of *Vāsudeva*-worshippers at this period explains certain features of the *bodhisattva* doctrine. This sect is mentioned in the *Mahāniddesa* (vol. i, p. 89, lines 19–20 : "*Vāsudeva-vattikā vāhonti*"). *Vāsudeva* as a deity is also spoken of by Pāṇini in his grammar ("*Vāsudevārjunābhyāṃ vun*," iv, 3, 98, page 198 ; *bhaktiḥ*, iv, 3, 95, page 197). Several inscriptions of the second century B.C. also refer to the cult of *Vāsudeva*, e.g.

> "*Devadevāsa Vā(sude)vasa garuḍadhvaj(ō)ayam.*"
> (Besnagar inscription, J.R.A.S., 1909, p. 1055, line 16.)
> (Epigraphia Indica X, H. Lüder's list, No. 669.)
> "*janā bhagavabhyā sakaṣaṇa-vāsudevābhyām.*"
> (Ghasundī inscription, J.R.A.S., 1887, vol. lvi, Part I, page 78, line 10.) (Epigraphia Indica X, H. Lüder's list, No. 6.)

These inscriptions date from the second century B.C. Megasthenes, who lived as an ambassador at the court of Candragupta about 300 B.C.,[27] declared that the Indians worshipped Herakles : "This Herakles is held in especial honour by the Sourasenoi, an Indian tribe who possess two large cities, Methora and Cleisobora."[28] As Mathurā was a centre of Kṛṣṇa-worship, it is supposed that Megasthenes refers to Kṛṣṇa as "Herakles". Historical evidence thus establishes the existence of the powerful *bhakti*-cult of the worshippers of *Vāsudeva* in the centuries that followed the rise of Buddhism. The *Çaiva* sect was making progress during the same period. *Çiva* is spoken of in the *Çvetāçvatara Upaniṣad* as *bhagavān*, and devotion to him is inculcated.

> "*sarva-vyāpī sa bhagavāṃs tasmāt sarva-gataḥ çivaḥ*" (iii, 11, page 50).
> "*devam ātma-buddhi-prakāçaṃ . . . çaraṇam ahaṃ prapadye*" (vi, 18, page 73).

This *Upaniṣad* is assigned to a date posterior to Buddhism. *Çiva* is also praised in the *Mahābhārata*, but the chronology of that immense poetical encyclopædia is uncertain.[29] Patañjali mentions a *Çaiva* sect in his commentary on Pāṇini's grammar (about 150 B.C.—" *Kiṃ yo ayaḥ-çūlen-ānvicchati sa āyaḥ-çūlikaḥ kiṃ cātaḥ Çiva bhāgavate prāpnoti*," v, 2, 76; vol. ii, page 387—" *apaṇya ity-ucyate tatr-edaṃ na sidhyati çivaḥ skandaḥ viçākha iti*," v. 3, 99; vol. ii, page 429). The *Çaivas* are also mentioned along with the *Vāsudeva*-worshippers in the *Milinda-pañha* (p. 191, lines 6 ff., "*sivā vāsudevā ghanikā*"). The sect of the *Pāçupatas*, who worshipped *Çiva*, existed in the second century B.C., if not earlier.[30] Megasthenes wrote that the Indians also worshipped " Dionysos ": " The Indians worship the other gods, and Dionysos himself in particular, with cymbals and drums . . . he instructed the Indians to let their hair grow long in honour of the god." [31] This " Dionysos " has been identified with *Çiva*. The cumulative evidence of all these historical data points to the existence of a vigorous sect of *Çiva*-worshippers, who had chosen the ancient *Rudra* and *Īçāna* of the *Veda* as their deity.

These sects were soon controlled and assimilated by the Hindu priests, who were exerting themselves to stem the tide of Buddhism. The great revival of Hinduism under the *Çuṅga* dynasty in the second century B.C. obliged the Buddhists to develop new methods of popular propaganda. As E. W. Hopkins has pointed out, the second century B.C. was a critical period in the history of Buddhism.[32] The palmy days of royal patronage had ended with the fall of the Maurya dynasty in 184 B.C.,[33] and Buddhism had to fight for its life against the *Brahmins*, who had converted the *Bhāgavatas* and the *Çaivas* into their allies. The *arhats* were becoming too meditative and inert. The Buddhist leaders, who inaugurated the Mahāyāna movement, saved Buddhism from shipwreck by popularising it and inventing compassionate *bodhisattvas* as Buddhist counterparts of the Hindu deities and their Incarnations. Their methods bear a strong resemblance to the devices employed by the Christian Church in its struggle against the other religions of the Roman Empire.

(3) Persian Religion and Culture

Persia was a great empire from the time of Cyrus to the invasion of Alexander, and Darius I annexed the valley of the Indus about 518 B.C.[34] Persian culture continued to exercise considerable influence on the nations of Asia during many centuries. Persia and India were close neighbours, and the Persians were in many respects more advanced in civilisation than the Indians. D. B. Spooner's fantastic theory of the Persian origin of the Çākyas and the Mauryas is now dead and buried; [35] but India certainly borrowed much from Persia during this period. The lion-capital of Açoka's pillar at Sārnāth, the architecture of the palaces at Pāṭaliputra and certain usages of the Maurya court point to the influence of Persian culture.[36] Zoroastrianism, the religion of ancient Persia, may also have contributed to the rise of the *bodhisattva* doctrine in India. We know that it supplied a great deal of mythology to Judaism. Its *fravashis* and *amesa-spentas* bear a certain resemblance to the *bodhisattvas*.[37] The six *amesa-spentas* (immortal holy or beneficent ones, archangels), who are associated with Ahura-Mazdah, are personified abstractions, and the chief *bodhisattvas* are also really personifications of Wisdom and Love. The *amesa-spentas* are *asa* (Truth, Order, Right), *vohu manah* (Good Thought), *aramaiti* (Piety), *hauravatāt* (Welfare, Salvation, Wholeness), *Kshathra* or *Kshathra-vairya* (Dominion) and *amèrètat* (Immortality). The *fravashis* may be compared to the *bodhisattvas* in the *Tuṣita* heaven. Zoroastrianism influenced the development of Buddhism more directly through the cult of sun-worship, which was introduced into India in the third century B.C.[38] Sun-worship is referred to in the *Dīgha-Nikāya* (i, 11, line 21), and it is ridiculed in the *Ādiccupatthāna-jātaka* (*Jātaka* ii, pp. 72–3). Many familiar names of the Mahāyāna are suggestive of sun-worship, e.g. *Amitābha* (Measureless Light), *Vairocana* (the Brilliant One), *Dīpaṅkara* (Light-maker). Gautama Buddha himself is called *āditya-bandhu* (Kinsman of the Sun).[39] The Magas (*Magi*) are mentioned in Indian literature as the priests of the temples of the Sun in north-western India.[40] It is probable that they established an organised sect of sun-worshippers on the basis of Zoroastrianism and the ancient Indian domestic rites of sun-worship. The solar myth penetrated deep into every phase of Buddhism, and many *bodhisattvas* were endowed with solar attributes.

(4) Greek Art

The art of Gandhāra in north-western India was based on the ideals and methods of Hellenic sculpture as applied to the representation of Buddhist subjects. The figure of Buddha appears first in Gandhāra art; he was represented only by symbols at Bharhut and Sānchī. The Greek invaders, immigrants and sculptors thus taught the Buddhists the value of clear-cut definite personality, and the Buddhists invented their pantheon of *bodhisattvas* in order to worship half-divine half-human beings, such as the Hellenic gods were.[41]

(5) Propaganda Among New Tribes

During the centuries that followed Alexander's invasion of India, the north-western part of India was repeatedly overrun by foreign invaders like the Pahlavas, the Çakas and the Kuṣāṇas. It was a real meeting-place of nations. The Kuṣāṇas established a vast empire. H. G. Rawlinson says: "These great rulers, about whom we know only too little, built up a vast empire, comprising a variety of nationalities. In the Panjāb were semi-Asiatic Greeks, Parthians, Scythians, Hindus. In Afghanistan and Baktria, besides the remnants of the older Scythian and Iranian settlers, were Greeks, Parthians, and their own countrymen from Central Asia." [42] This international atmosphere favoured the introduction of new ideas in Buddhism. The Buddhists grappled with the task of converting these sturdy and semi-barbarous tribes to their faith. Polytheism had to be tolerated and even rendered attractive. The *bodhisattva* doctrine exalted Love and Activity and peopled the heavens with gracious Beings, who could be worshipped. It is likely that some deities of the new tribes were adopted as *bodhisattvas*. This period in the history of Buddhism corresponds to the mediæval period of Christianity, when the Teutons of Central Europe were converted.

(6) Christianity

As the *bodhisattva* doctrine was formulated before the advent of Christianity, there can be no question of Christian influence with regard to the origin of the new ideal. Christianity certainly influenced the development of Mahāyāna Buddhism at a later period and was also influenced by Buddhism to some extent. There were several channels of communication between the Buddhists and the Christian countries of Western Asia, Africa and Europe. The Buddhists could establish intercourse with the Christians in Alexandria, Southern India and Central Asia. Clement of Alexandria (c. A.D. 150–c. 215) mentions the presence of Indians at Alexandria and also refers to Buddha and the "Samanas".[43] Porphyry, the Neo-Platonist (233–c. 304), gives interesting details from the lost work of Bardesanes, the Gnostic teacher, who wrote about the Indian monasteries.[44] St. Jerome (c. A.D. 340–420) speaks of Buddha in connection with the dogma of the virgin-birth.[45] The Gnostics, who were numerous in the Roman Empire in the early centuries of the Christian era, borrowed some ideas from Buddhism, though one need not regard the word "gnosis" as the equivalent of *bodhi* or compare their three "qualities" to the *guṇas* of the *Sāṅkhya* system.[46] Analogy does not always imply a common source. But it is certain that the Indian religion was not unknown to the leaders of the Christian Church during the second and succeeding centuries. Further, there is the tradition that St. Thomas visited India and preached to King Gondophares. It is not possible to determine if this legend is true or false. R. Garbe rejects it, but A. E. Medlycott is of opinion that "the Apostle Thomas had entered King Gondophares' dominions in the course of his apostolic career". E. W. Hopkins also regards the tradition as worthy of credit.[47] But the story of the Apostle's martyrdom is intrinsically improbable, as the Indians did not approve of religious persecution. They have always been very tolerant and broad-minded, and there is no reason why a solitary innocent preacher should have been put to death. The Indians were free from the fanaticism of the Jews and the calculating cruelty of the Roman imperialists. Another missionary, St. Pantaenus (second century A.D.), is mentioned by Eusebius, the ecclesiastical historian.[48] Apart from these doubtful traditions, the existence of a Christian community in Southern India during the sixth century is attested by the Egyptian writer, Kosmas Indikopleustes.[49] G. A. Grierson indeed thinks that India learned the *bhakti* doctrine from this Christian Church;[50] but *bhakti* was inseparably associated with early Buddhism, as has been indicated above. It was not, however, in Alexandria or the Deccan that Christianity and Buddhism exercised that mutual influence, which cannot be doubted or denied. They met and mingled in Central Asia and Syria. Açoka sent Buddhist missionaries to Bactria and Syria in the third century B.C.,[51] and Buddhism was known in those regions during the centuries that witnessed the rise and growth of the Mahāyāna. Buddhism and Christianity borrowed much from each other. Diligent investigators have discovered many striking parallels between Christian and Buddhist legends, rites, miracles and precepts, which need not be discussed in detail.[52] Many of these alleged analogies are very superficial and unconvincing. But two great religious systems, which were in close contact with each other, must have exercised some mutual influence, as is evident from the fact that the very word *bodhisattva* has been taken over by the Greek and Roman Churches in the name of "St. Josaphat"[53]. It is not the right method to collect isolated passages from the *Bhagavad-gītā* and then proceed to trace them to Christian influence, as E. W. Hopkins and F. Lorinser have done.[54] Even if we could find precisely similar phrases in the Gospels and the *Gītā*, the fact would remain that the *spirit* of the Gospels is not the spirit of the *Gītā*. The ideals of life taught by the two scriptures are fundamentally different. The *Gītā* teaches pantheism, caste-duty, asceticism, war and intellectual insight; the Gospels inculcate monotheism, loving service, social equality, peace and faith. In the same way, it is idle to compare the two parables of the lost son in the *Sad. Pu.* and the New Testament, as the moral of the stories is not the same. They are intended to illustrate quite different ideas. If we apply this test, we should not attach much importance to the Madonna-worship, the fish-symbol, the story of the temptation, the episodes of Simeon and Asita, the miracles of walking on the water or multiplying food, Nathanael's fig-tree, the scenes of transfiguration, and other such external and secondary matters as have been discussed by van der B. van Eysinga and R. Seydel.[55] We should try to discover where and how the Mahāyāna was really influenced by Christian *ideas* and *ideals*. A religion is distinguished and defined only by its *spirit*. We may safely assert that the spirit of the later Mahāyāna is not the same as that of the earlier Mahāyāna. Nāgārjuna and Vasubandhu follow the real Indian tradition in attaching equal importance to Wisdom and Love, and even stressing the former more than the latter. But Çāntideva seems to ignore *prajñā* (Wisdom) altogether, though he offers lip-homage to it. He moves in an entirely different atmosphere: he talks with genuine feeling of sin and service, confession and forgiveness. His ideal of perfection is different from that of the earlier Mahāyānists. He seems to have drunk deep at some other fountain. *If* Christianity has at all influenced Indian thought, we shall look in vain for that influence in the *Bhagavad-gītā* or the *Sad-dharma-puṇḍarīka*. We shall perhaps find it in that remarkable poem, the *Bodhi-cary-āvatāra*. It has been compared to Thomas à Kempis's "Imitation of Christ", but it is more Christian in spirit than that manual of a mere monk. Here, if anywhere, we may discern some traces of external influence, as a new spirit is in evidence. The Mahāyāna was true to its genius in thus assimilating foreign ideals, which were very similar to its own. There is indeed much in common between Christianity and the later Mahāyāna, though it is not quite correct to speak of "theistic Buddhism",[56] a misleading phrase coined by J. E. Carpenter.

II

Phases of Development of the Doctrine

The *bodhisattva* doctrine probably originated in the second century B.C. The word *bodhisatta* is very old and occurs in the Pāli *Nikāyas*. Gautama Buddha speaks of himself as a *bodhisatta*, when he refers to the time before the attainment of Enlightenment. This seems to be the earliest signification of the word. It was applied to Gautama Buddha as he was in his last earthly life before the night of Enlightenment. The following clause recurs frequently in the *Majjhima-Nikāya*: "In the days before my Enlightenment, when as yet I was only a *bodhisatta*, etc."[57] The word also seems to be used only in connection with a Buddha's last life in the *Mahāpadāna-sutta* (*Dīgha-Nikāya* ii, 13) and the *Acchariy-abbhuta-dhamma-sutta* (*Majjhima-Nikāya* iii, 119). In the *Kathā-vatthu*, certain questions are raised with regard to the *bodhisatta's* actions; the signs on his body, his rebirth in a state of woe, and the possibility of his harbouring heretical opinions or practising asceticism are discussed.[58] It is clear that the previous lives of Gautama Buddha and other saints have now begun to excite interest and speculation. But there was no new systematic doctrine in the middle of the third century B.C., when the *Kathā-vatthu* was composed. The idea of a *bodhisattva's* renunciation of personal *nirvāṇa* is stated clearly and unequivocally in the *Pr. Pā Aṣṭa.*; and *bodhi* is set up as the new ideal in the *Sad. Pu.* These treatises belong mainly to the first century B.C. We may infer that the Mahāyāna doctrine in its earliest form was definitely formulated in the second century B.C. This was also the period of the Hindu revival under the *Çuṅga* dynasty. Most scholars are of opinion that the Mahāyāna doctrine originated in the centuries immediately preceding the Christian era. M. Walleser says: "Welchen Umfang die Herstellung von Mahāyāna-sūtras zur zeit des dritten Konzils des Kaniṣka..... erreicht hat, erhellt aus der Notiz des Tāranātha, dass damals die 1,000 Abschnitte umfassende *Ratnakūta*gruppe und das ebenso umfangreiche *Avataṃsaka* entstanden sein....... so ist andererseits doch nicht unwahrscheinlich, dass die grosse Masse der Mahāyānasūtras noch in die vorchristliche Zeit zurückreicht." [59] W. McGovern writes: "The religious aspect of the Mahāyāna developed sometime immediately prior to the Christian era." K. Saunders assigns the date 50 B.C.–A.D. 50 to what he calls "the half-way Mahāyāna". S. Dutt suggests 100 B.C. for the first beginnings of the Mahāyāna. We may regard the second century B.C. as the chronological starting-point for the development of the *bodhisattva* doctrine.

In the course of several centuries (second century B.C. to seventh century A.D.), the *bodhisattva* doctrine was modified in its essential features. The chief lines of development may be indicated as follows:—

(1) In the early Mahāyāna, the *bodhisattvas* are inferior and subordinate to the Buddhas; but they acquire greater importance in course of time till they are at last regarded as equal to the Buddhas in many respects. They are also endowed with ten *balas*, four *vaiçāradyas* and eighteen *āveṇika-dharmas*.[60] They are to be worshipped like the Buddhas, or even in preference to them. This gradual exaltation of the *bodhisattvas* at the expense of the Buddhas culminates in the apotheosis of Avalokiteçvara, who is declared to be a kind of "Buddha-maker". He helps others to acquire Buddhahood, while he himself remains the eternal *bodhisattva*.

(2) In the early Mahāyāna, Wisdom and Mercy are regarded as equally important, and a *bodhisattva* must possess the double Equipment of Knowledge and Merit (*jñāna-sambhāra*, *puṇya-sambhāra*).[61] In fact, Wisdom is considered to be somewhat more important than Mercy. Mañjuçrī, who represents Wisdom, is invoked in the opening verses of several treatises, and he is

praised in the *Sad. Pu.* The glorification of Wisdom reaches its climax in the writings of the *Mādhyamika* school of philosophy, which was founded by Nāgārjuna in the second century A.D. *Prajñā* is extolled *ad nauseam*, while Mercy (*karuṇā*) is not discussed in detail. But the later Mahāyāna emphasises Mercy more than Wisdom. It is emotional rather than argumentative. It sometimes seems to ignore and discard Wisdom altogether, as when it declares that *karuṇā* is the one thing needful for a *bodhisattva*.[62] As this ideal gains ground, the *bodhisattva* Avalokiteçvara increases in importance till he becomes the supreme and unique *bodhisattva*. The Mahāyāna slowly passes from the ascendancy of Mañjuçrī to the reign of Avalokiteçvara.

(3) The early Mahāyāna attaches equal importance to social life and to ascetic retirement from the world. It is, in fact, inclined to exalt the layman-householder and the women in comparison with the solitary recluses. But the later Mahāyāna reverts to the old ideal of celibacy and forest-life.[63] The monk triumphs in the end even in the Mahāyāna, and an inferior position is assigned to family life and to women.

(4) Many practices of *Yoga* are borrowed from external sources by the *Vijñāna-vādin* (or *Yogācāra*, *Yogācārya*) school of philosophers (fourth century A.D.). A *bodhisattva* is described as the *yogin* par excellence. The number of *samādhis* (modes of Concentration) is increased, and wonderful properties are ascribed to them.[64] *Yoga*, which is endemic in India, is accepted as an integral part of the *bodhisattva* doctrine.

(5) The quest of *bodhi* (Enlightenment) is relegated to the background, while active Altruism in this world of sin and suffering is regarded as almost sufficient in itself. The early Mahāyāna teaches that altruistic activity is one of the means of attaining Enlightenment, which is the goal. But the later Mahāyāna seems to forget even that far-off destination and prefers to loiter on the way. A *bodhisattva* need not be in a hurry to win *bodhi* and become a Buddha, as he can help and succour all living beings more effectively during his mundane career as a *bodhisattva*.[65] This idea also resulted in the subordination of the Buddhas to the *bodhisattvas*. There is a marked tendency to regard Altruism as an end in itself. Avalokiteçvara does not seem to think seriously of becoming a Buddha.

(6) The early Mahāyāna recognises an oligarchy of *bodhisattvas*, and eight are mentioned as a group of equal rank.[66]

Perhaps Mañjuçrī is regarded as *primus inter pares.* In the later Mahāyāna, the oligarchy is changed into an absolute monarchy. Avalokiteçvara is first and the rest nowhere. He absorbs all the virtues, powers, functions and prerogatives of the other *bodhisattvas*, because he is the Lord of Mercy. He occupies the supreme position in the Universe and reigns without a rival.

Karuṇā (mercy, pity, love, compassion) and its personified symbol, Avalokiteçvara, are all-in-all. This is the last word and the consummation of the Mahāyāna.

III.

Mañjuçrī and Avalokiteçvara

Many eminent *bodhisattvas* are named in the Sanskrit treatises, e.g. Mañjuçrī, Avalokiteçvara, Samanta-bhadra, Gagaṇa-ganja, Vajra-pāṇi, Vajra-garbha, Sarva-nivaraṇa-viṣkambhī, Kṣiti-garbha, Kha-garbha, Vyūha-rāja, Indra-jālī, Ratna-garbha, etc. But only a few are really important. Mahāsthāma-prāpta is one of the two active ministers in the Buddha *Amitābha's* paradise *Sukhāvatī*, and Vajra-garbha figures in the *Da. Bhū.* Samanta-bhadra promises to protect all preachers (*Sad. Pu.*, chapter 26); Vajra-pāṇi is described as the chief of Buddha's servants (*Çikṣā* 316, 7). But all these are rather shadowy figures. The two most important *bodhisattvas* are Mañjuçrī and Avalokiteçvara.

Mañjuçrī ("Gentle Glory," "Sweet Splendour"). He is named in the *Sad. Pu.* (chapter 11), and is regarded as a master of wisdom and knowledge. He has trained and disciplined many *bodhisattvas* (*Sad. Pu.*, p. 261). He has been aptly called "a male Athene, all intellect and chastity".[67] The epithet "*kumāra*" or "*kumāra-bhūta*" is often applied to him. It has been interpreted as "ever young" or "prince royal, a consecrated heir of the Buddha". S. C. Das explains that he is so called, because he observes celibacy (J.B.T.S., vol. i, p. 39, 1893). But this title does not present any problem, as it is also conferred on other very ordinary *bodhisattvas* (*Pr. Pā. Çata.* 30—*Kar. Pu.* 106—*Sam. Rā*, fol. 95*a*, 4). The passage in the *Kar. Pu.* shows that it means "young", as a *bodhisattva* is said to become a *kumāra*, "twenty years old". E. W. Hopkins thinks that Mañjuçrī was a missionary in northern India [68]; but we do not possess any historical data about him, and he is associated with the ocean in the *Sad. Pu.* The title "*kumāra*" is probably nothing more than a complimentary epithet for the *bodhisattvas*, who are regarded as "ever youthful", and perhaps also as "princes of Buddha's realm".

Avalokiteçvara. This name has been translated in different ways :—

"The Lord, who sees, or looks down."
"The Lord, who is seen or manifested, or is everywhere visible."
"The Lord of what is seen, of the visible world."
"The Lord, who is seen from on high" (i.e. by *Amitābha* Buddha, as a small Buddha-figure is often placed in the head of the statues of Avalokiteçvara).
"The Lord, who looks from on high" (i.e. from the mountains, where he lives, like *Çiva*).
"The Lord of View." "Lord of compassionate glances."
"The Lord of the dead and the dying."

The Pāli verb *oloketi* means "to look at, to look down or over, to examine, inspect, consider". The word *avalokita* may have an active signification, and the name would mean, "the lord who sees (the world with pity)". The Tibetan equivalent is *spyan-ras-gzigs* (the lord, who looks with eyes). The *Kāraṇḍa-vyūha* explains that he is so called, because he regards with compassion all beings suffering from the evils of existence. According to N. D. Mironov, the original form of the name was *avalokita-svara*, which has been found in the fragments of the manuscript of the *Sad. Pu.* brought by Count K. Otani's expedition from E. Turkestan.[69] It is a remarkable fact that Sanghavarman (third century), Dharmarakṣa and other early translators translated the name into Chinese as *kuang-shih-yin* (illuminating the sounds of the world). J. Edkins says: "*Kuan* (looks on), *shih* (the 'region' of sufferers), *yin* (whose voices of many tones, all acknowledging misery and asking salvation, touch the heart of the pitiful *Bodhisattva*)." [70] The Chinese equivalent of the form *avalokiteçvara* (*kuan-tzŭ-tsai*) appeared first in Yuan Chwang's writings in the seventh century. It has been objected that *avalokita-svara* is a queer sort of compound, which would convey no clear meaning to an Indian.[71] But the present form is also a puzzling compound which cannot be interpreted with any degree of certainty. It may be inferred that the Chinese knew the form *avalokita-svara*, but it was subsequently changed to *avalokiteçvara* on account of the confusion between *lok-eçvara* and *avalokita-svara*. There was probably some Çivaite influence. A tentative suggestion may be offered: the word *avalokita* may mean "wisdom", as it is employed in the *Mtu.* to denote the essence of Buddha's Enlightenment (*Mtu.*, ii, 294, 2). There is also a *samādhi*, called *avalokita-mudrā* (*Pr. Pā. Çata*, p. 483). In that case, the name would mean "Lord of Wisdom". This interpretation is neither better nor worse than those mentioned above, all of which are unsatisfactory. There is also no valid reason for associating this *bodhisattva* with the dead and the dying: such an idea is not found in the texts that describe his activities.

Avalokitecvara is the chief minister in the Buddha *Amitābha's* paradise (*Sad. Pu.*, chapter xxiv). He is also regarded as an emanation of that Buddha. He is not mentioned by name in the early treatises like the *Mtu.* and the *Lal. V.* But he is prominent in the supplementary portion of the *Sad. Pu.* and in the *Su. Vy.* and the *Kā. Vy.* In the *M. Vy.* (Section 23), he stands at the head of a list of ninety-one *bodhisattvas*. His origin is obscure. K. J. Saunders thinks that he is a sun-god of Central Asia.[72] M. Winternitz refers to the story of King Vipaçcit in the *Mārkaṇḍeya-purāṇa* and says: "This king is a counterpart, perhaps a forerunner, of the *bodhisattva* Avalokiteçvara in Mahāyāna Buddhism".[73] He can hardly be a "forerunner", as the Buddhist texts mentioning Avalokiteçvara are certainly older than this *purāṇa*. Avalokiteçvara's name, his association with *Amitābha*, his lordly and leisurely movements throughout the Universe, the stress laid on his "eyes" (*Sad. Pu.*, 452, 2), his capacity of illuminating the world (*Su. Vy.*, 56, 5), and his epithet of *samanta-mukha* point to a solar deity. The cult of Avalokiteçvara seems to be a Buddhist adaptation of the sun-worship of the *Sauras* and the *Magi*.

As a *bodhisattva*, Avalokiteçvara is the personification of Mercy. He abrogates and nullifies the old law of *karma*, as he visits the purgatory of *avīci* and makes it a cool and pleasant place (*Kā. Vy.*, p. 6). He goes to the realm of the *pretas* and gives them plenty of food and drink; they thus regain a normal figure. The beings, who are liberated from these realms, are reborn in the paradise of *Sukhāvatī*. In the purgatories, he creates a lake of honey and wonderful lotuses, which are as large as chariot-wheels. He visits the demonesses (*rākṣasīs*) in Ceylon and they fall in love with him; but he converts them to the true religion (*Kā. Vy.*, p. 43). In the country of Magadha, he finds that the people have become cannibals on account of a famine: he helps them by raining down water, rice, cereals, clothes and other things (*Kā. Vy.*, p. 47). In Benares, he assumes the shape of a bee and preaches to the worms and insects in their foul and humble abode. They seem to hear this buzzing sound (*ghuṇa-ghuṇāyamānam çabdam*): "Salutation to Buddha." They are reborn as *bodhisattvas* in *Sukhāvatī*. Such are Avalokiteçvara's deeds of mercy.

It is distinctly stated in the *Kā. Vy.* that Avalokiteçvara is much greater than the Buddhas in Merit, intelligence and sphere of influence (*Kā. Vy.*, pp. 14, 19, 23). His Merit is incalculable, like drops of rain falling continually for a year (p. 19). He is the father and mother of all (pp. 48, 66). The devotee, who recites his name, is freed from pain; and the man or woman, who worships him with one flower, is reborn as a *deva* (pp. 48, 49).

The apotheosis of Avalokiteçvara culminates in identifying him with the Spirit of the Universe and bestowing on him all the attributes of *Brahman* and *Īçvara*. He has a hundred thousand arms and several millions of eyes. The sun and moon have sprung from his eyes, *Brahmā* and other gods from his shoulders, *Nārāyaṇa* from his heart, and *Sarasvatī* from his teeth. He has innumerable pores (*roma-vivara*), which are intangible, like space (p. 62). In each pore there are many Buddhas, gods, mountains of gold and silver, etc. Pious worshippers can be reborn in these pores and attain felicity (p. 67). Above all, they should learn and recite the mysterious formula, "*Oṃ maṇipadme hūṃ*," which is called "the lore of six letters or syllables". It is Avalokiteçvara's special gift to the world and leads to *mokṣa* (Liberation). This seems to be an invocation of a female deity, "the deity of the jewel-lotus." F. W. Thomas and A. H. Francke have shown that the popular interpretation is incorrect (*Om*, "the Jewel in the Lotus").[74] With this formula, we enter the dark realm of Çakti-worship and Mantra-yāna, which should be clearly distinguished from the historical Mahāyāna.

Chapter III

THE THOUGHT OF ENLIGHTENMENT

A *bodhisattva's* career is said to commence with the "production of the Thought of *bodhi*" (*bodhi-citt-otpāda*). He thinks of becoming a Buddha for the welfare and liberation of all creatures, makes certain great vows, and his future greatness is predicted by a living Buddha. These three events mark the conversion of an ordinary person into a *bodhisattva*. But the later Buddhist philosophers have also introduced a kind of novitiate, which must be gone through before an ordinary person can arrive at the stage of the *citt-otpāda*. We find that the several factors of this period of preliminary preparation were gradually devised and elaborated. The *Da. Bhū.* does not speak of any such conditions; it mentions the *citt-otpāda* as the first step in a *bodhisattva's* career.[1] It represents the earliest tradition with regard to this question. But the authors of the *M.S. Al.* and the *Bo. Bhū.*, who belong to the fourth century A.D., add the conception of *gotra* ("family", "predisposition"), which must precede the *citt-otpāda*.[2] In the chapters on the *vihāras* and the *bhūmis* in the *Bo. Bhū*, *adhimukti* (Aspiration) is also put forward for the first time as an element in the novitiate.[3] These chapters are certainly later in date than the other parts of the treatise, as the first chapter discusses only *gotra* and the second chapter deals with the *citt-otpāda* without mentioning *adhimukti* at all. The *M. Vy.* shows the theories of *gotra* and *adhimukti* in their completely developed form.[4] The works of Çāntideva (seventh century) exhibit the latest phase of this tendency towards the increased elaboration of the factors and conditions appertaining to the preliminary period. He does not attach great importance to *gotra* or *adhimukti*, but lays much stress on faith, worship, prayer, confession of sins and other practices of piety and devotion as the necessary antecedents that should lead up to the *citt-otpāda*.[5] The *Dh. S.* mentions only such practices, and it ignores *gotra* and *adhimukti* altogether.[6] Thus three subsidiary problems must be discussed before we can take up the crucial question of the *citt-otpāda*, with the Vow and the Prediction that follow it.

I

Gotra.—It is probable that the Mahāyānists borrowed the conception of *gotra* from the Hīnayānists, as the latter inserted the stage of a *gotrabhū* between the ordinary unconverted person (*puthujjano*) and the *sotāpanno* (Stream-attainer), who represented the lowest order of Buddhist laymen in the earliest texts. In two passages of the *Aṅguttara-Nikāya*, nine or ten worthy types of persons, who are "fields of Merit", are mentioned, and the *gotrabhū* is of the lowest rank.[7] He has not entered the Stream or acquired Faith. In a passage of the *Majjhima-Nikāya*, the *gotrabhū* is spoken of contemptuously as a nominal "member of the spiritual clan".[8] The *Puggala-paññatti* defines an "ordinary person" as one who is not even inclined to abandon the three "fetters"; and it proceeds to describe a *gotrabhū* as one who is endowed with the conditions that immediately precede the advent or appearance of the noble nature (*ariya-dhammassa avakkanti*; i.e. he is ripe for conversion as a *sotāpanno*, but has not yet been converted).[9] T. W. Rhys Davids and W. Stede derive this word *gotra* from Sanskrit *goptṛ gup*, and explain thus: "a technical term used from the end of the *Nikāya* period to designate one, whether layman or *bhikkhu*, who, as converted, was no longer of the Worldlings, but of the *ariyas*, having *nibbāna* as his aim." The *M. Vy.* mentions *gotra-bhūmi* as one of the seven *bhūmis* (Stages) of the Hīnayānists (Section 50). It may be inferred that the idea of placing an intermediate Stage between the unconverted worldling and the fully converted adept of the first Stage was borrowed from the Hīnayānists and applied to the development of the *bodhisattva* doctrine. The Hīnayānists seem to have adopted the term *gotrabhū* in order to endow the numerous new converts of the lower castes and classes with a *gotra.* This word originally meant "family", and was then used to denote the group of persons descended in the male line from a common ancestor, who was often assumed to have been a holy sage of ancient times like Kāçyapa, Gautama, Bharadvāja, etc. Thus the three higher castes are divided into several *gotras*, but the *çūdras* do not belong to any *gotra.*[10] This has been the theory of Hinduism. But early Buddhism used an old term in a new sense, and declared that all Buddhists belonged to the family or clan of Gautama Buddha, as they were his spiritual sons and heirs.[11] Such a notion of democratic equality and spiritual kinship probably led to the adoption of the Brahmanic word *gotra* by the Buddhists, who preserved the original Sanskrit form in *gotrabhū* instead of employing the Pāli equivalent, *gotta*. The Sanskrit form also betrays its origin.

Gotra, as applied to a *bodhisattva's* preliminary preparation, has been translated as "Family" and "Breeding".[12] The Tibetan equivalent *rigs* shows that the qualities of a class or clan are meant, as that word also denotes "caste" S. C. Das translates: "breed, culture, also spiritual descent" (Tib. Dicy., 1180). The *Da. Bhū.*, which does not speak of *gotra* as preceding the *citt-otpāda*, contains references to *buddha-gotra*;[13] and a *bodhisattva* is said to "follow the *gotra* of the Buddha". The idea was subsequently developed and elaborated till *gotra* became merely a technical term, meaning "tendency, pre-disposition, diathesis"

Thus different persons are qualified by their *gotra* to become *çrāvakas*, or *pratyeka-buddhas*, or perfect Buddhas, while the *gotra* of some individuals cannot be determined and others have no *gotra* at all. There are thus five species of *gotra*, as enumerated in the *M. Vy.* (Section 61). The person, who is first to become a *bodhisattva* and then to develop into a Buddha, must have the proper and requisite *gotra* for his mission, otherwise he cannot enter on the first stage of his career by "producing the Thought of Enlightenment" and taking the Vows. *Gotra* is either innate or acquired. Innate *gotra* depends on some superiority in the faculties and is due to a person's deeds in the previous existences; while acquired *gotra* is obtained in this present life by developing the "Roots of Merit".[14] A *bodhisattva's gotra* is distinguished by certain signs or marks, which indicate his fitness for the practice of the six *pāramitās* (Perfections). He attaches the greatest importance to the cultivation of Virtue and thinks of the future life.[15] He is a severe critic of his own actions, and he fears and avoids the slightest sin.[16] He helps others and eschews strife and discord.[17] He exhorts others to abstain from improper actions.[18] He is always merciful and virtuous and loves the truth.[19] He speaks pleasantly even to dumb servants and appreciates the merits of others.[20] He is forbearing and patient even towards those who injure him.[21] He is by nature energetic and courageous, and does his duty without succumbing to indolence and inactivity.[22] He is strong-willed in all preparations for success, and aids other people even in their worldly pursuits.[23] He is not over-diffident, but believes that he can achieve his aims, even if the task be difficult.[24] He finds happiness in the thought of renunciation; he loves the solitude and silence of the woods.[25] He is by nature not very prone to passion or vice.[26] His mind is not disturbed by evil thoughts.[27] He is pure and bears within himself the seed of all the principles and attributes of perfect Enlightenment.[28] He cannot commit a heinous mortal sin.[29] He possesses great powers of endurance.[30] In fact, his condition is called *gotra*, because good qualities arise from it.[31] It may be compared to gold and precious gems.

A *bodhisattva* must be on his guard against certain dangers and obstacles in this preparatory stage. He should beware of passions and vices of all kinds.[32] He must shun bad friends and companions.[33] He must acquire an independent position in life. He must not be dependent on masters and kings, and he must not be exposed to the attacks of thieves and enemies.[34] He must not be altogether indigent, as he must be free from anxiety for the necessaries of life.[35] He must properly understand the teaching or advice of his good friends, and evince zeal and energy in following it.[36]

A *bodhisattva's* excellent *gotra* protects him against the worst consequences of his evil deeds, even if he should lapse into sin. He may be reborn in a state of woe, but he is soon released from it[37]; and he does not endure terrible anguish like an ordinary worldly man.[38] He also learns to feel pity for other suffering creatures.[39]

Such are the characteristics, dangers and privileges of the *gotra* stage of a *bodhisattva*. As it is by nature associated with bright virtue and is thus auspicious and sublime, it must be regarded as a necessary and indispensable condition for the attainment of the supreme position of a Buddha.[40]

The Buddhist philosophers developed the theory of *gotra* in order to explain why all persons do not try or desire to become *bodhisattvas*.

II

Adhimukti.—The second idea, which is associated with this preliminary stage, is that of *adhimukti* (Aspiration). The *M.S. Al.* mentions *adhimukti* as a quality possessed by a *bodhisattva* in the *gotra* Stage,[41] but it does not devote a special chapter to *adhimukti-caryā*. In this stage, a *bodhisattva* is afraid of pain and is not prepared to suffer pain for the sake of others.[42] But he has now commenced his progress towards the goal.[43] When he has purified himself in this condition, he will be fit to enter on the first of the ten real *bhūmis* (Stages) of his career.[44] But he is as yet deficient in virtuous action ; he is not free from faults and imperfections; and he is not regular and consistent in his life.[45] He possesses the idea of perfection only in the state of germ or cause, as a latent possibility ; and his Aspiration may be feeble, moderately strong, or very intense.[46] Noble Aspiration must always precede " the Thought of *bodhi* ".

III

Anuttara-pūjā (Supreme Worship).—As the ideal of Faith and Worship gradually became predominant in the Mahāyāna during the fifth and sixth centuries, the Buddhist teachers were not content with prescribing only *gotra* and *adhimukti* as the necessary preliminaries to the *citt-otpāda*. They introduced more devotion and ritual, and also propounded the new and startling ideas of Sin and Confession.

This development is reflected in the *Dh. S.*, the *Çikṣā* and the *B.C. Ava.*[47] A *bodhisattva* must perform the following religious exercises before he can attain to the "Thought of Enlightenment" :—

(*a*) *Vandanā* and *Pūjā* (Worship and adoration of the Buddhas, the *bodhisattvas* and the Doctrine).

Çāntideva is the chief representative of this devotional type of Buddhism. In the second canto of the *B.C. Ava.*, he sings a hymn of love and adoration for the Buddhas and the great *bodhisattvas*. He wishes to worship them in a fitting manner in order to attain to the *citt-otpāda*. He lavishly offers them everything that is beautiful and gorgeous,—all flowers, fruits, jewels, limpid waters, gem-producing mountains, woods and forests, flowering creepers and fruit-laden trees, celestial perfumes and incense, the wish-fulfilling tree of heaven, lakes adorned with lotuses and swans, wild and cultivated plants, and all other valuable things in the entire universe that may be offered in worship.

At this point in the rhapsody, the poet seems to feel that he is giving away what does not belong to him and that this sort of *pūjā* really costs him nothing. He suddenly pulls himself up and adds these touching lines, which breathe the true spirit of devotion :—

"I give myself to the *Jinas* (the conquerors). I give myself entirely and utterly to their sons (i.e. the *bodhisattvas*). O noble Beings, take possession of me. I have become your slave through Love." (*B.C. Ava.*, ii, 8.)

Çāntideva then declares that he would render humble service to the Buddhas and the *bodhisattvas*. He would gladly prepare their bath, massage their bodies, spread perfumes over them, etc. He yields again for a moment to the temptation of bestowing on them costly lamps, spacious palaces, lustrous gems and lovely flowers. But he ends in a happier vein, and praises and worships the Buddhas and the *bodhisattvas* in these words :—

"I bow to the Buddhas of the past, present and future, to the Doctrine, and to the noble band (of *bodhisattvas*) with as many obeisances (as many times) as there are atoms in all the buddha-fields."[48]

(*b*) *Çaraṇa-gamana.*—Çāntideva then repeats the formula of "taking refuge" in the Buddha, the Doctrine and the *bodhisattvas*. The threefold formula dates from a very ancient period.[49] The Mahāyānists subsequently substituted "the group of the *bodhisattvas*" for the old third term, *Saṅgha*. The triad is also known as the "three jewels" (*tri-ratna*). Novices are always described as taking this first step of confessing their faith in these three "jewels" before they proceed to the higher duties of practising the ethical precepts.[50]

(*c*) Confession of Sins (*pāpa-deçanā*).—The poet confesses his sins, declares that he is a miserable sinner, promises not to sin again, and takes refuge in the *bodhisattvas* for protection and succour. These verses introduce a new note in Buddhist literature, which was not heard before in the Hīnayāna or the Mahāyāna. Çāntideva exclaims :—

"I am a brute :[51] whatever sins I have committed, or caused others to commit, either in this life or in the endless series of previous existences, and whatsoever sins I have approved, all those sins I confess. I am consumed with remorse, and I have earned death through my folly (have slain myself).

"O Leaders! Whatever grievous sins I have committed with my body, speech and mind against the 'three jewels', or my parents, or my teachers, or others, I confess them all now. I am a sinner soiled with many transgressions (vices, faults).

"How shall I escape from is? I am always beset by fear and anxiety lest I should die soon before the burden (accumulation) of my sins is diminished." (*B.C. Ava.*, ii, 28–32.)

Çāntideva calls on the *bodhisattvas* to save him. He reflects that death suddenly smites living beings like a thunderbolt. He has sinned through lust, hatred and delusion. He has sinned through the love of kinsmen and friends, who cannot protect him in the hour of death, as every man must reap as he has sown. He has sinned through the pursuit of pleasure, forgetting that all external objects must be left behind by Man, who is only a stranger and a pilgrim on earth. He thinks of the terrible punishment that awaits him after death, and asks: "Who can save me?" He repents of his folly in neglecting the cultivation of virtue. He has failed to amass spiritual Merit. He promises to follow the Buddha's precepts, as a sick man must obey the physician. He is mortally afraid of the pain of rebirth in purgatory, and again confesses all his transgressions against natural law and against the rules and precepts of the Buddhist Community.[52] He ends by declaring that he will sin no more. (*B.C. Ava.*, ii, 33 ff.)

This remarkable Confession, the "De Profundis" of the pious Buddhist poet, bears witness to the influence of the completely developed Hindu doctrine of *bhakti* (devotion) on Buddhist thought. The ideas of self-reliance and personal retribution are discarded, and the *bodhisattvas* are invoked to save a sinner from the evil consequences of his deeds. It is assumed that frank confession is meritorious and can induce the *bodhisattvas* to help him. This trend of thought reminds us of the ancient Vedic hymns to *Varuṇa* and the later devotional literature of the Hindu sects like the *Vaiṣṇavas* and the *Çaivas*.[53] The ideas of sin as an offence against higher deities, and of confession, repentance and extraneous protection were alien to the spirit of Buddhism during several centuries. It is true that King Ajātasattu confessed his sin before Gautama Buddha, who declared that he "accepted the confession", whatever that may mean.[54] But the iron law of *karma* was not effectively relaxed in favour of erring humanity before *bhakti* came to be regarded as an easy and alternative device to escape pain and attain felicity. In later Buddhist literature, repentance and confession are held to absolve the sinner from the sin and its punishment. They can at least mitigate the disastrous consequences of sin. As many as thirty-five Buddhas are supposed to hear Confession.[55]

(*d*) *Puṇy-ānumodanā* (Rejoicing in the Good). Çāntideva declares that he rejoices in thinking of the good deeds of all beings, of the Liberation obtained by the *arhats*, and of the spiritual heights attained by the *bodhisattvas* and the Buddhas.[56]

(*e*) *Adhyeṣaṇā* and *Yācanā* (Prayer and Supplication). Çāntideva prays and implores all the Buddhas to preach the true Doctrine and not to disappear in final *nirvāṇa*. The people will remain blind, if they do not receive instruction from the Buddhas.[57]

(*f*) *Declaration of Altruism and Self-Denial.*

The last stage, which immediately precedes the *citt-otpāda*, has been described as *pariṇāmanā* (the application of one's Merit to the welfare of others) and *ātma-bhāvādi-parityāgaḥ* (renunciation of one's body, or of oneself, etc.). These descriptive terms have been invented by the later commentators, and the *Dh. S.* even puts *pariṇāmanā* after the production of the Thought of Enlightenment.[58] Çāntideva really gives us a magnificent Canticle of love and charity. It deserves to be quoted in full, as it reveals the spirit that should animate and inspire the novice, who would become a *bodhisattva*. As Çāntideva speaks in the first person, he brings us into touch with the living soul of the *bodhisattva* ideal as distinguished from the dry bones of the tiresome numerical lists of a *bodhisattva's* qualities and powers.

He says: "Whatever Good I have acquired by doing all this, may I (by that Merit) appease and assuage all the pains and sorrows of all living beings.[59]

May I be like unto a healing drug for the sick! May I be the physician for them, and also tend them till they are whole again! (literally, 'till the disease does not arise again').[60]

May I allay (literally, kill) the pain of hunger and thirst by showers of food and drink (by raining down food and drink). And may I myself be food and drink (for the hungry and the thirsty) during the intermediate æon of famine![61]

May I be an inexhaustible treasure for poor creatures! May I be foremost in rendering service to them with manifold and various articles and requisites!

I renounce my bodies, my pleasures and all my Merit in the past, present and future, so that all beings may attain the Good (accomplish their welfare): I have no desire (for all those things).

To give up everything, that is *nirvāṇa*: and my mind seeks *nirvāṇa*. If I must give up everything, then it is best to bestow it upon the living beings.

I have devoted this body to the welfare of all creatures. They may revile me all the time or bespatter me with mud; they may play with my body and mock me and make sport of me; yea, they may even slay me. I have given my body to them: why should I think of all that?

They may make me do such things (actions) as bring happiness to them. May no one ever suffer any evil through me! (literally, 'having had relations with me').

If they have thoughts of anger or of friendliness towards me, may those very thoughts be the means of accomplishing all that they desire!

Those persons who revile me, or do me harm, or scoff at me, may they all attain Enlightenment! [62]

May I be the protector of the helpless! May I be the guide of wayfarers! May I be like upon a boat, a bridge and a causeway for all who wish to cross (a stream)! May I be a lamp for all who need a lamp! May I be a bed for all who lack a bed! May I be a slave to all who want a slave! May I be for all creatures a *cintāmaṇi* (the philosopher's stone) and a *bhadraghata* (a vessel from which a lottery is drawn, a pot of fortune), even like unto an efficacious rite of worship and a potent medicinal herb! May I be for them a *kalpa-vṛkṣa* (the wish-fulfilling tree) and a *kāma-dhenu* (the cow yielding all that one desires)!" [63] (*B.C. Ava.*, iii, 6–19.)

IV

Bodhi-citt-otpāda.—When a person has fulfilled the requirements of *gotra*, *adhimukti* and *anuttara-pūjā*, he is ready for the decisive step, "the production of the Thought of Enlightenment." D. T. Suzuki defines *bodhi-citta* as "intelligence—heart", and says: "Theoretically speaking ... the *Bodhi* or *Bodhicitta* is in every sentient being .... In profane hearts, it may be found enveloped in ignorance and egoism." [64] He thus identifies *bodhi-citta* with *bodhi* itself! M. Anesaki also takes a metaphysical view of *bodhi-citta*, and defines it as "the primordial essence of our mind, which in itself consists in the supreme *bodhi*".[65] But it is not necessary to indulge in such subtleties in order to explain this simple term. *Bodhi-citta* simply means: "the Thought of *bodhi*". The word *citta* has also been translated as "heart", "soul," "mind." But it should be interpreted as "Thought, idea", in the compound *bodhi-citta*. It is derived from the root *cit*, meaning "to perceive, to form an idea in the mind, etc." (Skt. Dicy., M.W., 323b). The fanciful etymology suggested by the author of the *Laṅkāvatāra-sūtra* need not be taken seriously. He explains *citta* as "that by which *karma* (action or its result) is gained or accumulated" (*cittena cīyate karma*).[66] The compound word *citt-otpāda* is employed in its ordinary non-technical sense in a passage of the *Divy.* (394,19—*sādhu sādhu mahārāja çobhanas te citt-otpādaḥ*). Here it means "thought, idea". When the Buddhists developed the *bodhisattva* doctrine, they attached a special meaning to it, and it became a technical term. *Bodhi* is the prize that a thoughtful person should strive to secure. But it is perhaps "too bright and good for human nature's daily food". The Buddhist writers have therefore adduced several reasons, motives and considerations, which should induce the average man to produce the Thought of *bodhi* in himself. He should reflect that birth as a human being is a very rare privilege.[67] He may be born as an animal, a *preta* or a denizen of purgatory many times, and there is no chance of becoming a *bodhisattva* in those existences. Even if he has escaped these three calamities, it is extremely difficult to find the five or six other favourable conditions that are indispensable for his initiation as a *bodhisattva*.[68] He may be born as one of the long-lived *devas*, who cannot aspire to *bodhi*, though they are very happy. He may be born among foreigners or in a barbarous country. He may be defective in his faculties and organs. He may be misled by false doctrines. And lastly, he may find himself on earth during a period when no Buddha has lived and taught, for the perfect Buddhas are very rare.[69] He should consider himself fortunate in being free from these eight or nine difficulties and disqualifications, and, above all, in being born as a human being at all, for human life is a blessing that perhaps falls to one's lot only once in billions of years. He should never forget the famous simile of the blind turtle, which explains that the chance of being born as a human being is infinitesimally small. Buddha himself has spoken thus: "Suppose a man should throw into the ocean a yoke with a single aperture in it. It is blown west by an easterly wind or east by a westerly wind; again it is carried north by a southern wind or south by a northerly wind. Now suppose there were a blind turtle in that ocean, and he came to the surface once in a hundred years. What think you, Monks? Would that blind turtle get his neck into that single aperture of the yoke? . . . Verily, that turtle would more quickly and easily perform that feat than a fool in his misery can be born as a human being once again ".[70] So difficult it is to enjoy the blessing of life as a man or woman under fortunate and favourable circumstances (*kṣaṇa-sampad*)! Further, an ordinary worldly person should realise that his life and the external world are painful, impermanent and unsubstantial.[71] He should think of death and the inevitable retribution after death. Death and dissolution are everywhere around us.[72] Nothing endures. The clouds, that strike terror into men's hearts with thunder, lightning and rain, melt away.[73] The mighty rivers, that uproot the trees on their banks in the rainy season, shrink again to the size of small and shallow streams.[74] The cloud-compelling winds, that smite the mountains and the oceans, abate their fury and die away.[75] The beauty of the woodland too is evanescent.[76] All happiness ends in sorrow, and life ends in death.[77] All creatures begin their journey towards death from the very moment of their conception in the womb.[78] Powerful monarchs, skilled archers, clever magicians, haughty *devas*, furious elephants, ferocious lions and tigers, venomous serpents and malignant demons—all these can quell, subdue and slay their enemies, but even they are powerless against Death, the fierce and irresistible foe of all living beings.[79] Realising the peril of death and suffering after death, a wise man should feel fear and trepidation (*saṃvega*) and resolve to become a *bodhisattva*.[80]

Besides thinking of his own lasting weal, a thoughtful person should be incited to the pursuit of the ideal of *bodhi* by the spectacle of the misery and folly of the people around him. They are foolish worldlings, deluded by ignorance.[81] They are attached to sense-pleasures and enslaved by egotism, pride, false opinions, lust, hate, folly, doubt, craving and evil imaginations.[82] They are without refuge and protection and have no haven of rest.[83] They are blind, and there is no one to guide them.[84] They are travelling through this jungle of mundane existence and towards the precipice of the three states of woe.[85] They do not love virtue and duty, and are ungrateful to their parents and spiritual teachers.[86] They are addicted to violence, strife, falsehood and cunning.[87] Their sins are many, and they suffer from dire diseases and famines.[88] The true religion is rejected, and false creeds arise and flourish.[89] The world is groaning under the five dreaded calamities of degeneracy (*kaṣāya*).[90] The duration of life is decreasing. The living beings are degenerate, their sins and passions increase, and they hold wrong views. The great Æon itself is nearing its end. Such is the terrible situation, in which the world finds itself. Reflecting on this sad state of things, one should resolve to become a *bodhisattva* in order to help and save all creatures. Such pity, mercy, love and compassion (*karuṇā kṛpā*) are at the very root of the Thought of Enlightenment.[91] A *bodhisattva* produces this Thought in himself for his own good and for the welfare and liberation of all living beings. He says: "As the Buddhas of yore accepted the Thought of *bodhi* and regularly followed the discipline of the *bodhisattvas*, even so I too produce (in my mind) this Thought of *bodhi* for the good of the world, and I will follow that discipline in due order." [92] With this resolve, the man or woman becomes a *bodhisattva*. The *Bo. Bhū.* gives the decisive declaration in these words: "He thinks thus: 'O may I obtain supreme and perfect Enlightenment, promote the good of all beings, and establish them in the final and complete *nirvāṇa* and in the Buddha-knowledge!' Such is his prayer (*prārthanā*)." [93] The two objects (*ālambana*) of the Thought are thus *bodhi* and the good of the living beings (*sattv-ārtha*).[94]

Great are the merits and advantages of this heroic step. It cancels and annuls all the sins and transgressions of a *bodhisattva*'s past lives, thus transcending even the law of *karma*.[95] It is one of the three "Roots of Merit" (*kuçala-mūlāni*), the other two being purity of thought and freedom from egotism in all its forms.[96] It increases spiritual Merit,[97] and even those, who encourage it, share in that *puṇya*.[98] It leads to happy rebirths, even if one does nothing to realise it in practice, as even a broken diamond is more precious than gold! [99] It saves a *bodhisattva* from punishment in purgatory, even if he should be guilty of murder.[100] It is superior to all good resolutions, mundane or supra-mundane.[101] One may count the stars in the sky, but it is impossible to estimate the virtues and merits that are associated with the *bodhi-citta*.[102] It is the occasion of rejoicing in the heavens and hells.[103] Nature exhibits miraculous phenomena at such an auspicious moment.[104] A person at once becomes worthy of respect, like a teacher or a father; and others can acquire Merit by helping him, as he is a "field of Merit".[105] He is now born in the "Buddha's family".[106] His Merit cannot be impaired, and he cannot be injured by beasts, *yakṣas* or other non-human beings. His body does not feel any fatigue, and he acquires a retentive memory (or abiding Mindfulness).[107] He is freed from anger, falsehood, envy, hypocrisy and all such faults of character.[108] He acquires four powers[109]:—(1) *adhyātma-bala*, i.e. joy (*ruci*) in *bodhi*, produced by one's own strength; (2) *para-bala*, i.e. the joy conferred by others; (3) *hetu-bala*, i.e. joy experienced on account of exercise in past existences; and (4) *prayoga-bala*, i.e. power obtained by practice in the present life, the company of virtuous persons, etc. The Thought of *bodhi* is supremely blessed and auspicious,[110] and may rightly be compared to a pearl, to the ocean, to sweet music, to a shade-giving tree, to a convenient bridge, to the soothing moonbeams, to the rays of the sun, to a universal panacea and an infallible elixir.[111]

Having sung the praises of the *bodhi-citta* in the usual florid style, the hair-splitting Buddhist philosophers proceed to describe its different species, the causes that produce it, and the practices that fortify it. It may be regarded as of two sorts. One kind is conducive to Liberation and cannot be turned back, as it persists perpetually.[112] The other variety of *bodhi-citta* does not lead to Liberation, as it can be turned back, either temporarily or irrevocably.[113] Further, the *bodhi-citta* may be divided into two categories from another point of view: (1) the mere resolution, and (2) the actual progress (or starting) towards *bodhi* (*bodhi-praṇidhi-citta* and *bodhi-prasthāna-citta*).[114]

As regards the occasions and causes that may lead to the the *bodhi-citta*, special importance is attached to the effect produced by seeing some miracle wrought by a Buddha or a *bodhisattva*, or hearing of it.[115] A person may study the true Doctrine and the Scriptures, and thus find the chief motive for conversion.[116] He may be instructed and encouraged by a Buddha or his disciple; he may hear the praise of *bodhi* or *bodhi-citta*; or he may realise how perfect a Buddha's personality is. Some benign Buddhas may even rouse the Thought of *bodhi* in others by a deceptive stratagem. Even an ordinary worldly person, who has the proper predisposition, can acquire the *bodhi-citta*, as a new-born tiny sparrow, which has not completely broken its shell, utters a sparrow's cry. So none need despair.[117]

It is a pleasing feature of Buddhist literature on this subject that it lays stress on the advantages of having a good friend (*kalyāṇa-mitra*). The spirit of haughty self-sufficiency is not inculcated. On the contrary, a good friend is regarded as an indispensable factor in the attainment of the *bodhi-citta*, just like *gotra* and *karuṇā*. The possession of such a helper is indeed a blessing (*kalyāṇa-mitra-parigraha-sampad*).[118] He should be intelligent, and he should not hold wrong views. He should not lead the would-be *bodhisattva* to negligence or evil actions. He should aspire to the highest ideals and be a man of deep faith.[119] Not only is a *kalyāṇa-mitra* necessary for this first step in a *bodhisattva's* career, but he is useful and valuable at all times. Only a lucky person, who has been very charitable to the poor in a previous existence, can find such a friend.[120] A *kalyāṇa-mitra* helps a *bodhisattva* to remain fearless and courageous at all times, and always exhorts him to follow the precepts and ideals of the Mahāyāna (as distinct from the other systems).[121] A bad friend (*pāpa-mitra*), on the contrary, dissuades a *bodhisattva* from practising the *pāramitās* (Perfections), drags him down and does not warn him against errors and inferior ideals.[122] When a *bodhisattva* has found a good friend, he should never desert him, but try to keep him by all means in his power.[123] He should hold that friend as dear as his own life.[124]

Last, but not least, fearlessness is necessary for the production of the *bodhi-citta*. The would-be *bodhisattva* must not be timid.[125] He can develop such a courageous spirit, if he is noble by nature and also acquires the strength that comes from knowledge (*paṇḍito bhavati*)[126] and the habit of meditation and reflexion.[127] Sincere faith in Enlightenment and intense enthusiasm for it, combined with deep compassion for others, will also dispel all fear.[128]

When the *bodhi-citta* has been attained, it can be rendered firm and strong like adamant (*vajr-opamaḥ*),[129] if the *bodhisattva* loves all creatures like a wife (*kadatra-bhāvena*) without being contaminated by such affection.[130] He should also entertain the good purpose of promoting their spiritual and physical welfare. He should adopt the practice (*prayoga*) of daily augmenting and strengthening that double purpose and endeavouring to mature the principles (or qualities) of Buddhahood in himself and others.[131]

A *bodhisattva*, who has once accepted the *bodhi-citta*, must not swerve from the right path or abandon the career. He must reflect that he has given a sacred promise to all creatures, whose welfare and liberation depend on him.[132] He belongs to the family of the Buddhas and must be worthy of his distinguished position.[133] He must be alert and vigilant from the very first day.[134] He should not give up his *bodhi-citta*, even if *Māra* (the god of Desire and Death) tries to weaken his resolve with the most dreadful menaces and threats.[135] He should also know that he will certainly suffer torment in the purgatories, if he voluntarily abandons the *bodhi-citta* through weakness and vacillation. Such a betrayal is a cardinal sin (*mūl-āpatti*).[136]

V

Praṇidhāna or Praṇidhi.—Having accepted the *citt-otpāda*, the *bodhisattva* makes a great *praṇidhāna* in order to strengthen his resolve and avert the danger of giving up his glorious task.[137] This term, *praṇidhāna*, is explained by Monier Williams as meaning "prayer, entreaty, supplication" (Skt. Dicy. 609*c*). D. T. Suzuki interprets it somewhat differently and says: "*Praṇidhāna* is a strong wish, aspiration, prayer, or an inflexible determination to carry out one's will."[138] L. Feer explains thus: "*Praṇidhāna* signifie 'disposition particulière d'esprit, application de l'esprit à un objet determiné'."[139] The word has been translated as "vow", "resolve," "solemn aspiration," "prayer," etc. The Tibetan equivalent is *smon-lam* (*Lal. V. Tib.*, p. 4, line 6). S. C. Das translates: "meditation, prayer, supplication; as a prayer, it seems to be rather for the enjoyment of the fruits of one's merits and seldom for a favour of a necessity undeserved." According to H. A. Jäschke, it means: "Prayer, whether it be in the general way of expressing a good wish or offering a petition to the Deity, or in the specific Brahmanic-Buddhistic form, which is always united with some condition or asseveration, as: if such and such a thing be true, then may . . . ; wishing-prayer" (Tib. Dicy., 428*a*). The Tibetan verb *smon-pa* means "to wish, to desire". According to E. J. Eitel, the Chinese translate *praṇidhāna* by a phrase, which means "prayers and vows" (p. 121). It may be inferred that the idea underlying *praṇidhāna* is that of an earnest wish, and not strictly that of a vow or resolve. It may be rendered as "Earnest Wish" or "Aspiration".

Praṇidhāna is both the cause and the result of the Thought of Enlightenment.[140] It is of three kinds: that which relates to happy rebirths; that which aims at the good of all beings; and that which is intended to purify the buddha-fields.[141]

The earliest formula of a *bodhisattva's praṇidhāna* was quite simple. The *Pr. Pā. Aṣṭa.*, for instance, gives it in these words: "We having crossed (the stream of transmigratory existence), may we help the living beings to cross! We being liberated, may we liberate others! We being comforted, may we comfort others! We being finally released, may we release others!"[142] In the *Ava. Ça.*, Pūrṇabhadra and others add a very short declaration to these four sentiments: "By this Thought of Enlightenment, the Root of Good, and by my renunciation of everything that can be given away, may I become a Buddha in this blind world, which is without a guide and leader."[143] The four clauses of the *Pr. Pā. Aṣṭa.*, which form the kernel of the formula, are repeated in the *Mtu.* (iii, 138.16). In the *Lal. V.*, the *bodhisattva* Siddhārtha is reminded of the *praṇidhāna* that he had made in his previous existences: "I will attain the immortal, undecaying, pain-free *bodhi*, and free the world from all pain."[144] The *bodhisattva* Dharmākara's *praṇidhāna* in the *Su. Vy.* is more elaborate.[145] He aspires to free all creatures from the fear of being reborn in a state of woe as animals, *pretas*, *asuras* or denizens of purgatory. He expresses such earnest wishes as the following: "May all beings be of a golden complexion! May human beings be equal to the *devas* in every respect! May all beings possess the wonder-working Powers in such perfection as to be able to traverse many buddha-fields in a moment! May they have the power of remembering their former existences! May they possess the supernal organ of sight and see many worlds and universes! May they obtain the supernal organ of hearing and listen to the words of the preachers in many buddha-fields! May they acquire the power of discerning the thoughts of others! May they be free from the notion of possession and property, even with regard to their own bodies! May they be firmly established in Righteousness (*samyaktva*) till they attain the great final Liberation![146] May they not know even the name of Evil (*akuçala*)! May they be blessed with great bodily strength! May they enjoy supreme felicity! May they not be born as females! May they be free from pain and keep all their faculties unimpaired! May they never turn back from the quest of Enlightenment![147]

These are a few "wishes", selected from the long list of miscellaneous aspirations, which the *bodhisattva* Dharmākara cherishes for himself and for the beings, who should be born in his buddha-field in the remote future. It is clear that the concept of *praṇidhāna* has been considerably extended and amplified by the author of the *Su. Vy.* and the sect to which he belonged. But the most detailed formula of a *bodhisattva's praṇidhāna* is found in the *Da. Bhū.*, which mentions ten Wishes or Aspirations.[148] Each *praṇidhāna* is characterised as "great" (*mahā-praṇidhāna*), and certain epithets are also applied to it, viz.: "Wide and comprehensive as the element of the phenomena, co-terminous with the element of Space (ether), dwelling on infinite futurity, uninterrupted for the entire number of æons and the Buddhas to be born." These ten *praṇidhānas* may be summarized as follows:—

(1) To provide for the worship of all the Buddhas without exception.

(2) To maintain the religious Discipline that has been taught by all the Buddhas and to preserve the teaching of the Buddhas.

(3) To see all the incidents in the earthly career of a Buddha.

(4) To realise the Thought of Enlightenment, to practise all the duties of a *bodhisattva*, to acquire all the *pāramitās* and purify all the stages of his career.[149]

(5) To mature all beings[150] and establish them in the knowledge of the Buddha, viz. all the four classes of beings who are in the six states of existence.

(6) To perceive the whole Universe.

(7) To purify and cleanse all the buddha-fields.

(8) To enter on the Great Way and to produce a common thought and purpose in all *bodhisattvas*.

(9) To make all actions of the body, speech and mind fruitful and successful.

(10) To attain the supreme and perfect Enlightenment and to preach the Doctrine.

The later writers seem to have preferred a simple form of *praṇidhāna* to the prolix and grandiose declarations of the *Su. Vy.* and the *Da. Bhū.* Kṣemendra describes several persons as making a *praṇidhāna* "for the acquisition of *bodhi* and the liberation of the world", when they give away wealth, certain limbs of their bodies, or their lives, for the benefit of others.[151] But the importance of the idea of *praṇidhāna* was realised in an increasing degree in course of time, as *praṇidhāna* was finally incorporated in the lists of the *bodhisattva's balas* (Powers), *vaçitās* (Mights, Sovereignties), and *pāramitās* (Perfections).[152] Thus did the Buddhist philosophers evince their appreciation of the Will as a factor in spiritual progress.

VI

Vyākaraṇa or Vyākṛti.—According to the accepted doctrine, a *bodhisattva* must declare his *praṇidhāna* in the presence of a living Buddha, who then predicts his future success in attaining Enlightenment. This "Prediction" is called *vyākaraṇa* or *vyākṛti.* The Tibetan equivalent is *luṅ-bstan-pa*, which means "precept, inspired command, prophecy" (Tib. Dicy. Das, 1216*a*). The idea of *vyākaraṇa* seems to have fallen into abeyance in course of time, as Çāntideva does not attach any importance to it.

The typical formula for such a prediction is given in the *Sad. Pu.*[153] Gautama Buddha's prophecy with regard to Çāriputra's future Buddhahood is uttered in these words: "O Çāriputra, at a future period, after the lapse of immeasurable, inconceivable, innumerable æons, when you have learned the true Doctrine from hundred thousand *nayutas* of *koṭis* of Buddhas, worshipped them in various ways, and completed this discipline (or career) of a *bodhisattva*, you will be a *Tathāgata* who will bear the name of Padmaprabha. You will become a perfectly enlightened Buddha, venerable, perfect in knowledge and conduct, knower of all the worlds, peerless trainer of men who need discipline, teacher of *devas* and men, a Buddha worthy of adoration ....[154] The field of that Buddha will be called *Viraja* (pure). The duration of his life will be twelve intermediate *kalpas*. After his final Liberation, his religion will endure for thirty-two intermediate *kalpas*, and the counterfeit of that religion will also last for as many intermediate *kalpas*." Another shorter formula, which describes the perfect Buddha in different terms, is found in the *Ava. Ça.* It seems to be later in date than that given in the *Sad. Pu.* It runs thus: "By this thought of Enlightenment, the Root of Good, and by this renunciation of everything that can be given away, Pūrṇa will realise *bodhi* after three *asaṅkhyeyas* of *kalpas* and fulfil the six *pāramitās*, cultivated with great Love. He will be a perfectly enlightened Buddha, Pūrṇabhadra by name, endowed with the ten Powers, the four Grounds of Self-confidence, and the three special and characteristic Fields of Mindfulness, together with great Love."[155] These details are communicated by the Buddha in each "Prediction", which varies according to the time and the individual.[156] It is a Buddha's duty to give such a *vyākaraṇa* before he dies.[157] A *bodhisattva*, who has received such a Prediction, can attain Wisdom more easily than others.[158] The prophecy may also be made in the *bodhisattva's* absence.[159] Curiously enough, the *deva Indra* is also described as uttering such a prediction[160]; but, as a general rule, *vyākaraṇa* is the prerogative of a perfect Buddha. Kṣemendra records many *vyākaraṇas*, couched in very short and simple terms, which were made by Gautama Buddha with regard to the future of Puṇyabhadra, Madhurasvara and Sumati, and also of a hare.[161]

It must be noted that the *vyākaraṇa* assumes the theory or doctrine of a *bodhisattva's* rebirth in future existences. He will cultivate many virtues and acquire knowledge and wisdom during many lives to come. Most Buddhist writers divide living beings into five classes (*gatis*, goings, modes or states of existence): the *devas*, the human beings, the *pretas*, the animals and the denizens of the purgatories.[162] Some authors also mention a sixth class, the *asuras* ("demons, titans, furious spirits"). Birth as an *asura* is regarded as a state of misery in the *Su. Vy.*, but the *asuras* are associated with the *devas* by Çāntideva.[163] Now a *bodhisattva* cannot (as a rule) be reborn in a purgatory, or as an animal or a *preta*. These are the three states of woe. He will therefore be born in the cycle of transmigration or re-incarnation as a *deva* or a human being till he attains *bodhi*. This doctrine of rebirth, which is not found in the *Vedas*, suddenly makes its appearance in the *Çatapatha-Brāhmaṇa*, in which the stress is laid on the idea of repeated deaths (*punar-mṛtyu*).[164] The theory is nowhere discussed as a debatable question, and no arguments are adduced for or against it. The dogma was regarded as self-evident and axiomatic. It has been suggested that it was borrowed by the Aryan immigrants from the aboriginal inhabitants of India, or that it may have been the popular belief of the lower strata of Aryan society.[165] The Indian philosophers adopted and elaborated it in the seventh and eighth centuries B.C. Whatever the origin of the idea may be, it forms the starting-point and the basis of Buddhist philosophy and religion. The series of lives in the past is declared to be without a beginning,[166] and that is all that is vouchsafed to us in the way of argument.

A *bodhisattva* will thus die and be reborn many times in the different worlds and universes, which are supposed to exist. But an initial problem must be discussed before we proceed further. The Buddhist philosophers teach that a human being has no *ātman* (Pāli : *attan*), but consists of five *skandhas* [167] (Aggregates), which are all impermanent and non-substantial. The word *ātman* has usually been translated as "soul", and the question has been asked : "If a *bodhisattva* has no soul, who and what survives death ? How can he be reborn ? What is the principle of identity in his numerous existences ?"

The five *skandhas* (Pāli : *khandha*), which Gautama Buddha himself is said to have mentioned in his second sermon, are as follows :—[168]

(*a*) *Rūpa* : ("form," "matter," "material qualities," "das Sinnliche," "the body," etc).

(*b*) *Vedanā* : ("feeling" or "sensation", or both).

(*c*) *Saṃjñā*: ("perception" or "ideas"). Th. Stcherbatsky, citing the *Abhidharma-koça*, defines *saṃjñā* as "operations of abstract thought", "that which abstracts a common characteristic sign from the individual objects".

(*d*) *Saṃskārāḥ*.—This untranslatable term has been variously rendered [169] as "plastic forces", "syntheses," "pre-natal forces," "potentialities," "conformations," "mental confections," "conditions," "precedent conditions," "complexes of consciousness," "activities," "activities and capabilities," "mental activities," "actions," "synergies," "dispositions," "predispositions," "die Taten," "die psychische Gestaltungen," "die Hervorbringungen," "les concepts," "die Gestaltungen," "die gestaltenden Kräfte," "die Kräfte oder Prozesse," "impressions," "volitions," "volitional complexes," "constituents," "mentations," "aggregates," "les formations," "die Unterscheidungen," "Unterbewusstsein (latente Bildekräfte)," "conceptions," "a complex including will, attention, faith and other conative groups," "die Betätigungen," "die Willensakte," "constituents of being," "potencies," "the fashion or forms of the perceiving mind," "die verborgenen Prädispositionen," "les dispositions morales," "the grosser conditions precedent to thought, speech and action," "Geistige Gebilde (Willenstätigkeiten)," "merit and demerit," "mental co-efficients," "mental qualities," "actions or deeds," "l'idée," "volitions and other faculties," "energies," "co-ordinated energies," "productions," etc. etc.

The Pāli word *saṅkhāra*, derived from the root "*kṛ*", literally denotes either (1) that which is put together, compounded, conditioned, produced by a combination of causes (= *saṅkhata*), or (2) that which puts together or creates. In the passive sense, it means "phenomena, physical or material life, all conditioned things, which have been made up by pre-existing causes" (Pāli Dicy. s.v.). In its active signification, the word is employed to denote the fourth of the five *skandhas* and the second of the twelve *nidānas* (Causes) in the formula of *pratītya-samutpāda* (Dependent Origination). As a *skandha*, it has been explained thus: "The mental concomitants, or adjuncts, which come, or tend to come, into consciousness at the uprising of a *citta* or unit of cognition ... The concrete mental syntheses, called *saṅkhārā*, tend to take on the implication of synergies, of purposive intellection" (Pāli Dicy.) R. C. Childers and D. T. Suzuki identify this *skandha* with the fifty odd "mental properties or elements", which are mentioned in a late metaphysical treatise (*phasso vedanā* etc., etc.).[170] This irrelevant catalogue does not throw any light on the precise meaning of the term, and it need not be taken seriously. A. B. Keith thinks that "the root conception is the impressions resulting in dispositions, pre-dispositions, or latent tendencies, which will bear fruition in action in due course."[171] R. O. Franke states his conclusion thus: "*Saṅkhāra*: das psychische Hervorbringen der Anschauungs-Auffassungsformen, d.h. Vorstellungen, durch den Geist des 'Nichtwissenden' (d.h. des über das Wesen der Dinge Unaufgeklärten), resp. auch die Vorgestellten (und nur in der Vorstellung existierenden) Dinge selbst bedeutet."[172] P. Oltramare says: "Les *saṃskāra* sont les predispositions et les tendances qui expliquent le *dharma* actual par un des *dharma* anterieurs, et qui, dans le *dharma* actuel, préparent les *dharma* à venir."[173]

In the Pāli canon, the term is explained in these words: "And why, O Monks, do you say '*saṅkhāras*'? Because they compose a compound (*saṅkhataṃ abhisaṅkharonti*). They compose the body (*rūpa*) into the body-compound, feelings (*vedanā*) into the feeling-compound, perception (*saññā*) into the perception-compound, and consciousness or soul (*viññaṇa*) into the consciousness-compound ".[174] In another passage, three *saṅkhāras* are mentioned: "*puññ-ābhisaṅkhāra*," "*apuññ-ābhisankhāra*" and "*āneñj-ābhisaṅkhāra*", which have been interpreted as "act of merit", "act of demerit" and "stationary act".[175] The *Dhammasaṅgaṇi* includes a long list of about forty-seven qualities and powers in this *skandha*, and gives this general and comprehensive definition: "These and all other incorporeal, causally induced states, exclusive of the *khandhas* of feeling, perception and consciousness, are called the *khandha* of the *saṅkhāras*."[176] This is very elaborate, but not helpful at all. The *Abhidharma-koça* follows the same line of thought and explains thus: "Le *saṃskāra-skandha*, c'est les *saṃskāras* différents des quatre autres *skandhas*. Les *saṃskāras*, c'est tout ce qui est conditionné; mais on réserve le nom de *saṃskāra-skandha* aux conditionnés, qui ne rentrent ni dans les *skandhas* de *rūpa*, de *vedanā*, de *saṃjñā* . . . ni dans le *skandha* de *vijñāna*."[177] Vasubandhu also mentions a *sūtra*, which identifies the *saṃskāras* with the six kinds of *cetanā* (active thought, intention, purpose, will); but he rejects that explanation and prefers his own omnibus definition, which is really no definition at all. The *M. Vy.* outdoes both the *Dhammasaṅgaṇi* and the *Abhidhammattha-sangaha* by enumerating ninety-four mental elements (*caitàsikā dharmāḥ*), which are included in the *saṃskāra-skandha*.[178] The Tibetan equivalent is *ḥdu-byed*, which is explained by S. C. Das as "that which is or seems to be compounded, as opposed to the simple and elementary, anything pertaining to either body, speech or mind that can be analysed. It is thus particularized: mental association, thoughts, ideas, etc.; material or physical compounds; phrases, epigrams, sententious expressions, etc." (Tib. Dicy., 682). H. A. Jäschke leaves the word untranslated (Tib. Dicy., 276). According to E. J. Eitel, the Chinese translate *saṃskāra* by a term which means "action, *karma*" (p. 144).

So many unsatisfactory and bewildering explanations and translations, ancient and modern, seem to make confusion worse confounded. But the passage of the Pāli canon, cited above (*Saṃyutta-Nikāya*, iii, 87), and the dictum of the author quoted by Vasubandhu in the *Abhidharma-koça* give a clue to the fundamental idea that the early Buddhists tried to convey by this term. The *saṃskāra-skandha* is the fashioner, the "together-maker", the architect of the other four *skandhas*, not excepting even *vijñāna*. The author, whom Vasubandhu quotes, identifies it with *cetanā*. In the *Milinda-pañha*, *cetanā* is even substituted for the *saṃskāra-skandha*, and it is described as *abhisaṅkharaṇa-lakkhaṇā* ("characterized by purposive 'putting together'").[179] *Cetanā* is defined in the *Abhidharma-koça* in exactly the same words as the *saṃskāras* : *saṃskṛtam abhisaṃskaroti* (that which puts together the compounds).[180] It may therefore be inferred that the *saṃskāra-skandha* stands for *cetanā* (Volition) and can best be interpreted as "The Will". An eminent scholar has complained that Buddhist literature has no word for "Will".[181] Perhaps this is the word for it. It is necessary to clear away the cobwebs spun round the term by the mediaeval commentators.

(*e*) *Vijñāna* (Pāli *viññāṇa* : "consciousness," "soul"). It has also been rendered as "mind", "intellection," etc. The *Dhamma-saṅgaṇi* defines it as "thought, ideation, the heart, that which is clear, ideation as the sphere of mind, as the faculty of mind, the appropriate element of representative intellection".[182] The *Abhidharma-koça* explains thus : "*Vijñāna*, c'est l'impression relative à chaque objet. Le *vijñāna-skandha*, c'est l'impression (*vijñapti*) relative à chaque objet, c'est la préhension nue (*upalabdhi*) de chaque objet. Le *vijñāna-skandha*, c'est six classes de connaissances, connaissance visuelle, auditive, olfactive, gustuelle, tactile, mentale."[183]

Now these five *skandhas* are said to constitute a human being. They are severally and collectively impermanent and non-substantial, as there is no *ātman* in them. This doctrine of *pudgala-nairātmya* (non-substantiality or phenomenality of the individual) is taught by almost all the Buddhist philosophers.[184] It is enunciated in Gautama Buddha's second sermon, in which he declares that the five *skandhas* are devoid of *ātman*, and that a wise man should say with regard to *rūpa*, *vedanā*, *saṃjñā*, *the saṃskāras* and *vijñāna* : "This is not mine. I am not this. This is not *ātman*."[185] These three simple sentences have been expanded and elaborated into the oft-repeated *nairātmya* theory. The Mahāyānist philosophers attach such great importance to this doctrine that they have elaborated a formula of no fewer than fourteen terms, which are regarded as synonyms of *ātman*, and which are declared to be non-existent and illusory. In this way, they have tried to "rub it in", so that there may be no possibility of error or misunderstanding on this point. These fourteen terms are : *ātman*, *sattva*, *jīva*, *jantu*, *puruṣa*, *poṣa*, *manuja*, *kārāpaka*, *mānava*, *vedaka*, *kāraka*, *vedayitṛka*, *jānaka* and *paçyaka*.[186] These redundant words may be translated collectively: "being, individual, person, agent, doer, knower, beholder, one-who-makes-another-do, one-who-makes-another-know." It is held that a *bodhisattva*, who does not believe in the *ātman*, will find it easy to get rid of sensual desire, pride and egotism in all its forms (the idea of "I" and "Mine").[187] The theory is thus considered to be conducive to spiritual progress. The Buddhist philosophers regard it as an essential and fundamental principle of their systems. The heresy of *sat-kāya-dṛṣṭi* must be destroyed before the first step towards perfection can be taken. This term *sat-kāya-dṛṣṭi* means "belief in permanent substantial individuality". It is the *bête noire* of all Buddhist writers of the Hīnayāna and the Mahāyāna.[188] Both schools agree in condemning this wrong view as the root of all evil. The *Pra. Pā. Aṣṭa.* goes so far as to declare that all the sixty-two wrong speculative opinions, which Gautama Buddha rejected, are included in this one monstrous error of *sat-kāya-dṛṣṭi*.[189] It is compared to a mountain with twenty peaks, as a person may harbour the following four false notions with regard to each of the five *skandhas*: [190]

(1) This *skandha* (*rūpa*, etc.) is *I*.
(2) *I* have this *skandha*.
(3) This *skandha* is the essence of *Me*.
(4) The essence of *Me* is in this *skandha*.

It may be asked how a *bodhisattva* is reborn and makes spiritual progress during many lives, if there is no "soul". This difficulty has arisen from the regrettable mistake of translating *ātman* by the English word "soul". The idea has gained ground that the Buddhist philosophers do not believe in "the soul", and at the same time teach that a *bodhisattva* goes through a long series of rebirths during many æons. This illogical and absurd position has been made the butt of ridicule and criticism. But it is certain that the Mahāyānist writers believed in the continuity of personal identity between one life and the next. They assert the principal of personal identity in the most unmistakable terms. They identify Gautama Buddha and others with the persons that figure in the stories of his past lives. Thus Buddha says at the end of a story: "I was that Viçvantara, and that priest was

Devadatta."[191] The Super-knowledge (*abhijñā*) of *pūrva-nivās-ānusmṛti-jñāna* (knowledge of previous existences)[192] would also be an impossible and meaningless acquisition, if the person were not the same in each life, and if he did not know and feel that he was the same, just as a normal person is conscious of personal identity in the course of his or her life on earth. But it may be asked: "How is this possible, if there is no 'soul' that survives death?" This relevant question may be answered by declaring once for all that the Buddhist Sanskrit writers teach the existence of the "*soul*" in the ordinary sense of that word, but that they deny the existence of "*spirit*" as an immutable, non-composite, unconditioned, noumenal, absolute Substance, exempt from the law of change and causality. *Ātman* should be translated as "Spirit", and not as "soul". When the Buddhists condemned and combated the *ātman* doctrine, they meant that they did not believe in the *ātman* as it was described in the *Upaniṣads* and the treatises of the *Vedānta* system. The *Chāndogya Upaniṣad* declares that the *ātman* is immortal (8, 14, page 510—*tad brahma tad amṛtaṃ sa ātmā*). The *Bṛhadāraṇyaka Upaniṣad* also speaks of "that *ātman*, that *Immortal*, that *Brahman*, that *All*". The *Kaṭha Upaniṣad* teaches that the *Ātman* (which is also *Brahman*) is undecaying and unchangeable. Similar ideas are expressed in several other passages of the *Upaniṣads*.[193] But the Buddhists made no exception to the universal law of change and relativity, and they carried on a vigorous polemic against this *ātman-brahman* doctrine. Now it is clear that *ātman* in this sense should be translated in philosophical language as "Reality, the Absolute", and in religious phraseology as "Spirit", as in the Biblical saying, "God is Spirit."[194] The human "soul", which thinks, feels and wills, does not belong to this category of pure "Spirit", as it is subject to change and experiences pain and pleasure in this life and after death. This "soul" survives death and represents the principle of personal identity in non-Buddhist systems. The Buddhists recognise its existence and call it *vijñāna*. This term has been translated by the cumbrous and unwieldly word "consciousness". But it is advisable to interpret it as "soul". It is distinctly stated in the Pāli canon that *vijñāna* is that *skandha*, which continues to exist after death and enters the mother's womb for the next re-birth (*mātu kucchiṃ na okkamissatha*, etc.).[195] *Māra*, the *deva* of Desire and Death, could not find the *vijñāna* of Godhika and Vakkali after the death of those nonks, though he looked for it everywhere. They had attained final and complete *nirvāṇa*, and their *vijñāna* was not reinstated in a new embryo.[196] *Vijñāna* thus corresponds to the "soul", as this latter word is understood by most non-Buddhist religious teachers. "Soul" is defined as "the spiritual part of man regarded as surviving after death and as susceptible of happiness or misery in a future state" (New English Dictionary, 1919, IX, i, p. 461*c*). *Vijñāna* is explained as meaning "a mental quality as a constituent of individuality, the bearer of individual life, life-force (as extending also over rebirths), principle of conscious life, general consciousness (as function of mind and matter), regenerative force, animation, mind as transmigrant, as transforming (according to individual *kamma*) one individual life (after death) into the next" (Pāli Dicy. s.v.). It may therefore be suggested that Buddhist *vijñāna* should be regarded as the nearest equivalent of the Christian "soul".

Having established the personal identity of a *bodhisattva* during all his rebirths, we may now proceed to discuss his duty and discipline.

VII

Caryā.—A *bodhisattva*, who has fulfilled the conditions of the *citt-otpāda*, *praṇidhāna* and *vyākaraṇa*, is fit to commence his *caryā*. This word *caryā*, derived from the root *car*, means "course, proceeding, behaviour, conduct" (Skt. Dicy. M.W.). It denotes the whole duty of a *bodhisattva*, all that he has to do. This comprehensive term covers his complete discipline and career. The forms *cari* and *carikā* are also found.[197] *Caryā* is divided into four parts in the *Mtu.*[198] (1) *Prakṛti-caryā* (the *caryā* of Nature). This seems to correspond to *gotra*, which has been discussed above. (2) *Praṇidhāna-caryā* (the *caryā* of Aspiration). (3) *Anuloma-caryā* (the *caryā* of regular practice). This refers to a *bodhisattva's* early training. (4) *Anivartana-caryā* (or *avivarta-caryā*). This denotes a *bodhisattva's* higher career, when he is sure that he cannot be a backslider.

This rudimentary scheme of sub-division was subsequently amplified in the list of the *bhūmis* (Stages), which a *bodhisattva* progressively occupies.

Another group of four *caryās* is mentioned in the *Bo. Bhū.* and the *M.S. Al.*[199]

(1) *Bodhi-pakṣya-caryā* (Practice of the "*bodhi-pakṣyā dharmāḥ*", i.e. principles conducive to Enlightenment).

(2) *Abhijñā-caryā* (Practice of the Super-knowledges).

(3) *Pāramitā-caryā* (Practice of the Perfections).

(4) *Sattva-paripāka-caryā* (Practice of maturing the living beings, i.e. preaching and teaching).

This latter scheme of classification is preferable to that given in the *Mtu.*, as it really indicates the various duties and qualities of a *bodhisattva*. It is therefore advisable to adopt this plan of treating the somewhat complicated theme of a *bodhisattva's* career and discipline. The *bodhi-pakṣya-dharmas* and the *abhijñās* will be discussed before the *pāramitās*, the *bhūmis* and the details of the last earthly life of a successful *bodhisattva*, who attains Enlightenment and thus finishes the long and laborious " Pilgrim's Progress "

VIII

THE QUESTION OF TIME.—A *bodhisattva*, who has taken the Vow, has an incredibly long pilgrimage before him. He will reach his goal and become a Buddha after the lapse of a very long period of time, in comparison with which even geological and astronomical figures pale into insignificance. According to the Pāli canon, many persons could attain *arhatship* very quickly,[200] but the idea seems to have gained ground that spiritual growth could not be so rapid and easy. Even the Hīnayānists began to think that " thousands of years " were required for that consummation.[201] They also spoke of *kalpas* in connection with the more difficult task of attaining to the stage of a *pratyeka-buddha*. Thirteen or fifteen *kalpas*, or twenty *antara-kalpas*, were considered to be necessary for this result.[202] The unit of a *kalpa* was adopted for such calculations. The Mahāyānists and the semi-Mahāyānists either speak in general terms of a " long time " or reckon the time in *kalpas*. Thus we read of " many " kalpas, or of hundreds, thousands or *koṭis* of kalpas. Sometimes *nayutas* are added to the word *koṭi*.[203] But the grandiose Indian imagination soon devised the phrase, " immeasurable innumerable *kalpas*." According to the *Mahā-vastu*, the *devas* tell Maudgalyāyana that Enlightenment is attained after a hundred thousand *kalpas*, but Gautama Buddha thinks that the *devas* are wrong, and he utters these staggering words, *aprameyehi asaṅkhyeyehi kalpehi.*[204] Çāntideva tries to give a more moderate estimate and reckons sixty *kalpas* for each *pāramitā* (i.e. 360 or 600 *kalpas* in all); but he also declares that a *bodhisattva* will struggle for "*acintya*" *kalpas*. This word *acintya* may simply mean "inconceivable", "unthinkable"; or it may denote a very high number, which is mentioned in the *M. Vy.*[205] But the Buddhist philosophers perhaps found that precise definition was necessary, and they commenced a regressive movement. They discontinued the practice of speaking vaguely of an "immeasurable" number of *kalpas*, and fixed the limit at three or seven *asaṅkhyeyas* of *kalpas*. The lower figure was then adopted, and three *asaṅkhyeyas* of *kalpas* was generally accepted as the duration of a *bodhisattva's* career.[206]

Now the terms *koṭi*, *nayuta*, *kalpa*, *antara-kalpa* and *asaṅkhyeya* must be explained. *Koṭi* means "10 millions". *Nayuta* is probably equivalent to a hundred thousand millions. The *Abhidhāna-ppadīpikā* mentions *nahuta*, which is interpreted by S. Hardy and W. Kirfel to mean "a hundred thousand millions"; but T. W. Rhys Davids and W. Stede explain it as signifying only "a vast number, a myriad".[207] The *M. Vy.* informs us that a hundred *koṭis* make an *ayuta* and a hundred *ayutas* make a *nayuta* (Section 248). Thus a *nayuta* is equal to a hundred thousand millions. The same result is confirmed by the system of enumeration given in Section 249 of the *M. Vy.*, where the numbers increase in a geometrical progression, with 10 as the common ratio. An *asaṅkhyeya* (Pāli: *asaṅkheyya*) is explained by T. W. Rhys Davids and W. Stede as "an immense period", and they do not specify any definite number. M. Williams translates, "an exceedingly large number," and Böhtlingk & Roth also explain the word as "eine best. ungeheure Zahl". M. A. Rémusat gives it the value, "10,^{17} or 1 followed by 17 cyphers."[208] The *Abhidhāna-ppadīpikā* mentions the word, and W. Kirfel interprets it to mean 10,^{140} or 1 followed by 140 cyphers. S. Hardy thinks that it is equivalent to 10^{133}, or 1 followed by 133 cyphers.[209] It occurs in the Pāli Jātaka (i, 27, 15), and T. W. Rhys Davids leaves it untranslated.[210] In the *Milinda-pañha* (p. 232, line 8), T. W. Rhys Davids also translates in general terms: "millions of years, æon after æon" (S.B.E., vol. xxxvi, p. 38). L. de la Vallée Poussin has calculated, according to the data furnished by the *Avataṃsaka-sūtra*, that an *asaṅkhyeya* is equivalent to the 104th term of the series $(10^2)^0$, $(10^2)^1$, $(10^2)^2$, ... ; an *asaṅkhyeya* would thus be $(10^2)^{103}$, or 1 followed by 206 cyphers. But he also offers another suggestion and explains that an *asaṅkhyeya* is the 66th term of the series 0, 10, 10^2, 10^4, 10^{16}, ...[211] J. E. Carpenter adopts the value, "1 followed by 140 cyphers."[212]

If it is at all necessary to calculate the exact value of an *asaṅkhyeya*, we should rely on the *Mahā-vyutpatti*, which gives two lists of numerals, one of which is based on the *Lal. V.* and the other on the *Abhidharma-koça*. The former list does not mention *asaṅkhyeya* and is therefore of no value for our purpose (Section 248, *M. Vy.*). The latter, however, contains the term *asaṅkhyeya*, and it has also the merit of agreeing with the tables of numerals given in the *Abhidharma-koça*[213] and the Tibetan literature (Tib. Dicy. Das, p. 241). According to these lists, there is a number, called *mahā-balākṣam* (Tibetan, *stobs migchenpo*), which is equal to 10^{50}, or 1 followed by 50 cyphers. The *M. Vy.* proceeds with the enumeration, and an *asaṅkhyeya* (*asaṅkhyam* in the text) is ten times a *mahā-balākṣa*, or "1 followed by 51 cyphers." The Tibetan lexicon inexplicably omits to mention *asaṅkhyeya* and leaves a gap in its place. We may conclude from the concurrent testimony of these three authoritative sources that the Buddhist system of enumeration finally reckoned an *asaṅkhyeya* as the equivalent of 10^{51}, or 1 followed by 51 cyphers. A *bodhisattva's* career lasts for 3×10^{51} *kalpas*, or three thousand billion billion billion billion *kalpas* (reckoning a billion as equivalent to a million million).

According to Buddhist cosmogony, a *mahā-kalpa* denotes a complete period of the Evolution and Involution (or Re-integration and Disintegration) of a universe. Each universe is periodically evolved and dissolved, and such a cyclic period is called a *mahā-kalpa*. It is divided into four *kalpas*, which are as follows :—

(1) *Vivarta-kalpa* (the period of incipient Evolution, Renovation, Re-integration or Re-appearance).

(2) *Vivṛtt-āvasthā-kalpa* (the period of continued Evolution, Renovation or Re-integration).

(3) *Saṃvarta-kalpa* (the period of incipient Involution, Disintegration, Dissolution or Disappearance).

(4) *Saṃvṛtta-āvasthā-kalpa* (the period of continued Involution, Disintegration or Dissolution).[214]

Each *kalpa* is divided into twenty *antara-kalpas* (small or intermediate *kalpa*). An *antara-kalpa* denotes a period of time, during which the length of human life increases from ten years to about 80,000 years, and then decreases to ten years, the rate of change being one year in a century. Thus an *antara-kalpa* lasts for 16 million years and the duration of a *mahā-kalpa* is four times 320 million years. A *bodhisattva's* career thus covers about four times $3 \times 10^{51} \times 320 \times 10^{6}$ years, or four times nine hundred sixty thousand million billion billion billion billions of years.

If we interpret *kalpa* as an ordinary *kalpa* and not as a *mahā-kalpa*, the above figure must be divided by four. But if a *kalpa*, as defined above, is interpreted as meaning an *asaṅkhyeya* of the Pāli literature, the *bodhisattva's* career lasts for only 960 million years. According to E. J. Eitel, the Chinese reckon 1,344,000 or 1,344,000,000 years for a *mahā-kalpa* (p. 68).

Some Buddhist authors, however, have warned us against wasting our time on such fantastic arithmetical computations. In the *Mtu.*, Kātyāyana tells Ānanda that a *kalpa* is "unmeasured" (*aparimitaḥ*) according to Buddha's teaching, but there would be somehow many of them.[215] This logical riddle is left unsolved by the saintly Kātyāyana. And we shall leave it at that. With regard to a *bodhisattva's* career, the word *asaṅkhyeya* is really intended to create an awe-inspiring impression of vast and sublime grandeur. We convert the poetry of religion into bald prose, if we speak of exactly three *asaṅkhyeyas* and try to confine an *asaṅkhyeya* of the *bodhisattvas* within the bounds of our mathematics.

CHAPTER IV

THE THIRTY-SEVEN "*DHARMAS*"

The Buddhist philosophers devised a formula of thirty-seven "*bodhipakṣyā dharmāḥ*", which enumerates and comprises thirty-seven practices and principles. They are held to be conducive to the attainment of Enlightenment. The word is met with in several forms :—

Bodhipakṣāḥ (*M.S. Al.* 159.9–177 ; *Kar. Pu.*, 127.8 ; *Pr. Pā. Aṣṭa.*, 194.18 ; *Divy.*, 350.14, etc.).

Bodhipakṣyāḥ (*Sam. Rā.*, fol. 193*b*.2 ; *Bo. Bhū.*, fol. 36*b*.4.1, fol. 100*b*.3.3, and passim).

Bodhipakṣikāḥ (*Bo. Bhū.*, fol. 90*a*.2.2 ; *Mtu.* ii, 290.6).

Bodhipākṣikāḥ (*Da. Bhū.*, 53.22 ; *Kar. Pu.*, 10.13 ; *Lal. V.*, 424.12 ; *Dh.* S., section 43.)

The first two forms (*pakṣāḥ* and *pakṣyāḥ*) occur more frequently than the others. The *dharmas* are also called *bodhipakṣyāni mārg-āṅgāni* in the *Da. Bhū.* (42.9), and the *Ava. Ça.* speaks of *bodhi-karakā dharmāḥ* and *bodhisattva-karakā dharmāḥ*, which are presumably the same as the "*bodhipakṣyā dharmāḥ*" (*Ava. Ça.* i, 69.12 ; i, 86.15 ; i, 75.4).

The term "*bodhipakṣyā dharmāḥ*" has been variously translated as follows :—

T. W. Rhys Davids and W. Stede (s.v. *bodhipakkhika* and *pakkhiya*) : "belonging to Enlightenment, qualities or items constituting or contributing to *bodhi*" (Pāli Dictionary).

E. Burnouf : "les conditions qui sont du côté de la *bodhi*" (Lotus : p. 430).

S. Lévi : "Les Ailes d'illumination" (*M.S. Al.* tr. p. 291).

T. W. Rhys Davids : "The principles, which are the wings of wisdom" (Dialogues, ii, 348).

L. de la Vallée Poussin : "Principles conducive to Enlightenment" (*Le Muséon*, 1905, p. 7).

L. Feer : (1) "Les lois qui forment les 37 ailes de la *bodhi*" (*Ava. Ça.* tr., p. 101).

(2) "Les 37 lois relative à la *bodhi*" (*Ava. Ça.* tr., p. 229).

C. F. Koeppen: "Die begleitenden Bedingungen der *bodhi*" (Buddha, i, 436).

E. J. Thomas: "Principles tending to Enlightenment" (Buddha, p. 183, note).

P. Oltramare, "Conditions favorables à l'Illumination" (Bouddhique, p. 348).

A. B. Keith: "Wings of Enlightenment" (Philosophy, p. 292).

It seems probable that the form *pakṣya* is not related to the word *pakṣa*, which means "wing". That simile would not be very appropriate, as no bird has thirty-seven wings. We find other similes referring to the two wings of a bird. The Pāli word *bodhipakkhiya* is probably derived from the Sanskrit form, which was the earlier of the two, as this word does not occur often in the *Nikāyas* or the *Milinda-pañha*, though all the factors are mentioned in the *Mahāparinibbāna-sutta* (*Dīgha*, ii, 120; *Mil.*, pp. 37ff.; *Vibhaṅga*, p. 372). As E. Hardy has pointed out, the collective term *bodhipakṣā dharmāḥ* is found in the *Lalita-vistara* (8.6; 182.11).[1] It also occurs in the *Mtu.* (ii, 290.6). The number "thirty-seven" is first mentioned in the *Sad. Pu.* (458.1). The term emphatically refers to *bodhi* and not to the *nirvāṇa* of the Pāli scriptures. Both the term and the complete formula seem to have originated among the Sanskritists or quasi-Sanskritists, who were the forerunners of the Mahāyāna. The Pāli rendering points to *pakṣya* as the correct Sanskrit form, which is also used in the *Bo. Bhū.* in connection with other words, e.g. *sukha-pakṣya*, etc. (fol. 5*a*.2, fol. 83*b*.4). It is derived from the substantive *pakṣa*, which means "a side, party, faction" (Skt. Dicy. M.W. 520*b*), as in such words as *pakṣapāta*, *pratipakṣa*, etc. Literally it means "belonging to a side" (Skt. Dicy. M.W. 521*a*). *Pakṣyāḥ* makes both good sense and good grammar. We are therefore justified in accepting this latter form and translating: "Principles which are conducive to Enlightenment." The Tibetan equivalent renders *pakṣa* or *pakṣya* by *phyogs*, which means "side, party, direction", and not "wing" (Tib. Dicy. Das, 840*a*; J. Rahder, Glossary, 134).

I

It is a curious circumstance that the thirty-seven items of the formula are enumerated in several passages of Buddhist Sanskrit literature without being called by the collective appellation, *bodhipakṣyā dharmāḥ*, e.g. *Divy.* 208.7ff. : *Pr. Pā. Çata.* 56–7, 133, 162, 1473 ; *M. Vy.* sections 38ff. The term *bodhi-pakṣāḥ* occurs in the *Pr. Pā. Çata.* (p. 1636, line 10), but the list includes more than thirty-seven *dharmas*. The numeral " thirty-seven ", however, is also found in the same book (p. 1410.19 ; 274.22). It may be inferred that the exact number and the name of these *dharmas* were determined at a comparatively late period. The Pāli *Nettipakaraṇa*, which dates from the beginning of the Christian era, mentions forty-three *bodhipakkhiyā dhammā*.[2] Açvaghoṣa mentions only twenty-eight items in the *Saund.-kāvya* (xvii, 24, ff.), and he does not use the term *bodhipakṣya*.

The formula, in its final form, includes the following thirty-seven *dharmas*, which are usually given in this order :[3]

Four *Smṛty-upasthānāni*	4
Four *Samyak-prahāṇāni*	4
Four *Ṛddhi-pādāḥ*	4
Five *Indriyāṇi*	5
Five *Balāni*	5
Seven *Bodhy-aṅgāni*	7
The Noble Eightfold Way (*Āry-āṣṭ-āṅga-mārgaḥ* or *Āry-āṣṭ-āṅgika-mārgaḥ*) . . .	8
Total	37

These principles and practices are regarded as highly beneficial in this life and also for the purposes of a happy rebirth. They are supposed to embody the last precepts and injunctions of Gautama Buddha himself.[4] They also lead to the attainment of the spiritual stage of a *pratyeka-buddha*. They are common to the Hīnayāṇa and the Mahāyāna. The latter starts with these *dharmas*, but adds the *pāramitās* and the *bhūmis*, which constitute its special contribution to the development of Buddhism.

II

The Smṛty-upasthānas

A *bodhisattva* must cultivate the four *smṛty-upasthānāni*. This term *smṛty-upasthānāni* has been interpreted by modern scholars in different ways :—

T. W. and C. A. F. Rhys Davids: (1) "Applications of Mindfulness" (Dialogues, iii, 214). (2) "Earnest meditations" (Dialogues, ii, 128).

S. Lévi: "Les Aides-Mémoires" (*M.S. Al.*, tr., p. 203).

R. O. Franke: "Die vierfache Geistessammlung" (*Dīgha*, p. 218).

A. Schiefner: "Die vier Handlungen des Gedächtnisses" (Triglotte, iii).

H. Oldenberg: "Die vierfache Wachsamkeit" (Buddha, p. 227).

W. H. D. Rouse: "Subjects of intent contemplation" (*Çikṣā*, tr., p. 216).

M. Winternitz: "Die Richtungen des Gedenkens" (Lesebuch, p. 251).

E. Burnouf: "Les soutiens de la mémoire" (Introduction, p. 85, edition 1844).

L. de la Vallée Poussin: "Subjects of mindful reflexion" (ERE, ii, 752*b*).

C. F. Koeppen: "Die Handlungen oder Zustände des Gedächtnisses" (Buddha, i, 436).

E. J. Thomas: "Meditations" (Buddha, p. 183, note 2).

Lord Chalmers: (1) "Applications of Mindfulness" (Majjh., tr., ii, 246). (2) "The four starting-points for mustering up Mindfulness" (Majjh., tr., ii, 6).

Csoma de Körös: "The four kinds of recollection or self-presence" (Csoma, p. 13).

D. T. Suzuki: "Subjects of Recollection" (Zen Essays, p. 72, note).

M. Anesaki: "The fourfold fixation of mind" (ERE, v, 455).

H. C. Warren: "Intent Contemplations" (Buddhism, p. 353).

Böhtlingk and Roth (s.v. *upasthāna*): "Das Dabeistehen, Dasein, Gegenwart. Hierher gehören vielleicht auch die *catuḥ-smṛtyupasthānāni* der Buddhisten."

T. W. Rhys Davids and W. Stede: "Intent contemplation and mindfulness, earnest thought, application of mindfulness" (Pāli Dicy., s.v. *sati*).

S. C. Das: "The four essential recollections" (Tibetan Dicy., 650*b*, s.v. *dran-pa-ñe-bar-bahig-pa*. *Lal. V. Tib.*, p. 10, line 12).

F. Heiler: "Die Meditationsobjekte" (Versenkung, p. 17).

K. E. Neumann: "Die Pfeiler der Einsicht" (*Majjh.*, tr., ii, 327).

M. Walleser: "Die vier Stützen des Gedenkens" (*Pr. Pā.*, tr., p. 56).

P. Oltramare: "Les assistances de l'attention" (Bouddhique, p. 348).

P. E. Foucaux: "La présence de la mémoire" (*Lal. V.*, tr., p. 9).

The term *smṛty-upasthāna* is composed of two words, *smṛti* and *upasthāna*. *Smṛti* (Pāli : *sati*) is derived from the root *smṛ*, and it has therefore been interpreted as "memory" by some scholars, (S. Lévi, E. Burnouf, A. Schiefner, C. F. Koeppen, cited above). Other translations have also been suggested, e.g.

T. W. Rhys Davids and W. Stede: (1) Memory, recognition, consciousness. (2) Intentness of mind, wakefulness of mind, mindfulness, alertness, lucidity of mind, self-possession, conscience, self-consciousness (Pāli Dicy, s.v. *sati*).

H. Oldenberg: "Gedenken, Wachsamkeit" (Buddha, pp. 350, 351).

K. E. Neumann: "Einsicht" (*Majjh.*, tr., ii, 327).

R. O. Franke: (1) "Sittlicher Ernst, Sammlung" (*Dīgha*, p. 27, note 6). (2) Ernstes sichbesinnen" (*Dīgha*, p. 157).

H. Beckh: "Die Besonnenheit" (Buddhismus, ii, 37).

F. Max Müller: "Intense thought" (SBE, vol x, part i, p. 99).

C. A. F. Rhys Davids: (1) "Mindfulness" (Psychology, p. 90, line 19). (2) "Mental clearness" (IHQ, vol. iii, No. 4, p. 701).

F. Heiler: "Gedenken" (Versenkung, p. 96).

E. Senart: "Raison, conscience" (*Mtu.*, i, 554).

M. Winternitz: "Das Gedenken, die Bedachtsamkeit" (Lesebuch, p. 319).

P. E. Foucaux: "Le souvenir"; "la mémoire" (*Lal. V.*, tr., pp. 34, 35).

L. de la Vallée Poussin: "La mémoire de la loi de Bouddha" (*B. C. Ava.*, tr., p. 30).

R. S. Hardy: (1) "The ascertainment of truth by mental application" (Manual, p. 517). (2) "Attention" (*ibid.*, p. 516).

The word *smṛti* has the ordinary meaning of "memory" in many passages, but it cannot be so rendered in the term *smṛty-upasthāna*. As F. Max Müller has pointed out,[5] the root *smṛ* originally denoted "intense thought". *Smṛti* in that sense would signify "Mindfulness". Almost all modern scholars are now agreed in translating *smṛti* (and *sati*) by this expressive English word, "Mindfulness." *Upasthāna* means "das Dabeistehen, Dasein, Gegenwart, das Hinzutreten, Erscheinen; standing near, presence . . . approaching, appearing, obtaining, getting" (Skt. Dicy. Pbg. and M.W.). The term may thus be interpreted as the four *upasthānas* (risings, appearances, or starting-points) of *smṛti*. But it is probably a wrongly Sanskritized form. The Pāli word is *sati-paṭṭhāna*.[6] *Paṭṭhāna* may be derived from *pra-sthā*, or it may be a contracted form of *upaṭṭhāna*. As a Pāli substantive, *paṭṭhāna* means the resort or feeding-ground of an animal, and figuratively the area, field or sphere of Mindfulness (Skt. *gocara*). But *paṭṭhāna*, as a derivative of the root *sthā*, cannot be a contracted form of *upaṭṭhāna*, and the Pāli term *sati-paṭṭhāna* is always masculine. Hence the term cannot be a compound of *sati* and the derivative *upaṭṭhāna*, and we must interpret it as "the *prasthāna* of *sati*". The word *paṭṭhāna* also occurs in the title of the seventh book of the *Abhidamma-piṭaka*, and it has been held to mean "starting-point, origin, cause".[7] L. Sadaw explains *paṭṭhāna* as meaning "principal cause",[8] but that meaning does not yield a proper sense in the compound *sati-paṭṭhāna*. There is no Sanskrit term that corresponds to the Pāli masculine substantive *paṭṭhāna*. The Mahāyānists have interpreted it, not as *prasthāna*, but as *upasthāna*, and they have recklessly changed the sense in order to get an intelligible Sanskrit word. It is an unfortunate blunder, as the four meditations are not merely the "appearances" or "risings" of *smṛti*; they include the whole of it. They are in fact the fields or spheres, in which *smṛti* is to operate. Most scholars have failed to convey the exact sense of *paṭṭhāna* in their translations. Perhaps it is best to translate, "The Four Fields of Mindfulness", thus preserving the original metaphor to a certain extent.

Smṛti is a very important adjunct of a *bodhisattva's* personality. It is often associated with another quality, *samprajanya* (Pāli, *sampajañña*), which means "sustained cognizing, deliberateness, self-awareness, self-possession".[9] The latter word denotes mental alertness and self-control, and emphasizes the intellectual factors implied in such self-mastery.

Smṛti is the *sine quâ non* of moral progress for a *bodhisattva.* All Buddhist writers emphasize the necessity of cultivating, safeguarding and developing it. It is the theme of many homilies in prose and verse. Its importance in Buddhist philosophy may be gauged by the circumstance that it is included in several of those overlapping numerical formulæ, which the Buddhist philosophers devised with an ingenuity that was worthy of a better cause. *Smṛti* is reckoned as the seventh of the eight items in the time-honoured, ancient Eightfold Way (*vide infra*). It is also the first of the seven *bodhy-aṅgas* ("Factors of Enlightenment", *vide infra*) and the third of the five *balas* (Powers) and the five *indriyas* (Ruling Principles). It thus appears four times on the list of the thirty-seven "*bodhipakṣyā dharmāḥ*" (Principles conducive to Enlightenment). It is also mentioned in the well-known sentence, which describes the fourth *dhyāna* (*Mtu.*, i, 228.10). It is even mentioned as a factor of the third *dhyāna* (*Da. Bhū.*, 34.4). Such frequency of occurrence in these formulae shows that the Buddhist teachers attached the greatest importance to it.

Smṛti is one of the words that recur very frequently in Buddhist Sanskrit literature. Right *smṛti* is the entrance to the light of the Faith, and a *bodhisattva* does not pay attention to anything that is adverse or prejudicial to it.[10] When the *bodhisattva* Siddhārtha visits the sage Ārāḍa Kālāma as a wandering seeker after truth, he boasts that he possesses *smṛti* along with other virtues, and that he is therefore vigilant and ardent.[11] One of the titles of a perfect Buddha is *amuṣita-smṛtiḥ* (one whose *smṛti* never falters or disappears),[12] and this quality is also reckoned among his eighteen special characteristic attributes.[13] A Buddhist writer goes so far as to say that Gautama's very gait was suggestive of *smṛti*, as he wended his way to the *bodhi*-tree at Gayā immediately before the attainment of perfect Enlightenment.[14] He possessed *smṛti* even during his residence in the *Tuṣita* heaven before his birth.[15] *Smṛti* is the axe that is laid to the root of the tree of mundane existence in order to cut it down.[16] A *bodhisattva* never loses *smṛti* and is therefore never confused or distracted in mind.[17] Indeed, he regards *smṛti* as his principal asset.[18] He teaches others the duty of safeguarding it.[19] It purifies his *buddhi* (intellect), gives constancy and consistency to his thoughts, and helps him always to keep the doctrine in his mind.[20] A *bodhisattva* always cultivates self-possession,[21] and Mindfulness is indeed an essential element in his Equipment, like virtue and knowledge,[22] (*smṛti-sambhāra*). It is like a door for the control of the senses [23] (i.e. to detach the sense-organs from the external objects). It is the chief instrument with which the senses, which are naturally in a state of unrest, can be diverted from the objects by which they are attracted.[24] It leads to the attainment of Truth.[25] Without *smṛti* and *samprajanya*, one cannot expect to succeed in the struggle against sin.[26] *Smṛti* confers great power on a *bodhisattva* (*smṛti-balam*).[27]

Almost all Buddhist writers have something to say about *smṛti* and *samprajanya*, but Açvaghoṣa and Çāntideva have especially distinguished themselves by their earnest and eloquent exhortations. Açvaghoṣa thus sings the praises of *smṛti* in the *Saundarānanda-kāvya* (xiv, 35 ff.) :—

"So you should preserve Mindfulness and self-possession in all actions, such as sitting, looking round and speaking.

"He who has established Mindfulness as a doorkeeper at the gate cannot be menaced (overpowered) by sins, even as enemies cannot (conquer) a well-guarded (or concealed) town.

. . . . .

"He who lacks the defensive armour of Mindfulness is indeed a target for sins (i.e., regarded as arrows), even as a warrior in battle, who has no armour, is (exposed to the arrows of) his foes.

"That mind, which is not protected by Mindfulness, is indeed to be regarded as helpless, like a blind man (literally, "one deprived of sight") walking about on uneven ground without a guide.[28]

"(People) are addicted to evils; they are averse to their own highest good; they feel no trepidation when fearsome things are nigh; all this is due to the loss of Mindfulness.

"Virtuous conduct and all the other good qualities remain in their own spheres, and are as it were separated from one another (scattered), but Mindfulness follows them as a cowherd (goes after) the cows.

"Whoever loses Mindfulness loses the Deathless; but he who applies Mindfulness to the body, the Deathless is his (literally, "rests in his hands").

"Who hath not Mindfulness, how can noble Justice (or

Right) be his? And whoever lacks noble Justice goes astray from the true path (literally, "the true path is lost for him").

"Who has lost the true path loses also the seat of the Deathless. Who loses the Deathless cannot win release from Evil (literally, "is not freed from Evil").

"Therefore, you should keep Mindfulness at all times and in all actions. When you are walking, you should reflect, 'I am walking.' When you are sitting, you should reflect, 'I am sitting,' and so on."

In the verses cited above, Açvaghoṣa has given us a beautiful lyric on *smṛti*, but its simple and terse style cannot be reproduced in a literal prose translation. Çāntideva, on the other hand, has described, analysed and classified *smṛti* in the spirit of a theologian and philosopher. He says :—

"The teaching of a *bodhisattva* is nothing but the preparation of the mind" (i.e., of the mind when it is not in a state of unrest).

"The mind will not be diverted from calmness, if external activity is inhibited.

"The mind of one, who has lost Mindfulness and self-possession through being dependent on others, is in a state of unrest, as it is being led towards something else than the desired object. When external activities are kept off (inhibited) by means of Mindfulness and self-awareness, then the mind, for that reason, remains fixed on a single object as long as he desires". (*Çikṣā.*, p. 123.)

In the fifth canto of Çāntideva's immortal poem, the *Bodhicary-āvatāra*, a *bodhisattva* is exhorted to keep his great Vow under all circumstances, and he has need of *smṛti* and *samprajanya* for this purpose. The following verses breathe a spirit of profound earnestness :—

"He, who wishes to keep the Rule, should make a great effort to guard his mind.

"He, who does not guard the restive (inconstant, unstable) mind, cannot keep the Rule.

"Mad and uncontrolled elephants do not cause so much pain in this world as will be occasioned by an unrestrained mind in *avīci* and the other purgatories. If the elephant of the mind is bound with the rope of Mindfulness on all sides, then all danger vanishes and all Good makes its appearance.

"Tigers, lions, elephants, bears, serpents, all the guardians of purgatory, the ogres and demonesses, yea, all one's enemies can be bound (in fetters), if one's mind is bound. All of them can be controlled, if only the mind is controlled. . . .

. . . . .

"I do obeisance to those who desire to guard their minds, and (say to them): 'Safeguard carefully Mindfulness and Self-awareness in all their aspects.'

"If the mind has lost these two, it is unable to perform any actions (auspicious deeds), as a man, who is afflicted with illness, is unable to do anything.

"The man, who is not self-possessed in his mind, cannot retain in his memory (the truths) that he has heard, pondered or cultivated, as water cannot remain in a pot that has a hole in it. Many there be who have learning, faith and energy, but they soil themselves with sin through the fault of lacking Self-awareness.

"Lack of Self-awareness is like a thief; it follows in the wake of the loss of Mindfulness. Those who are thus robbed go to painful rebirths, even though they may have accumulated spiritual Merit.

"The sins are like a band of thieves, who are looking for a chance to enter. If they enter (literally, "obtain entry"), they steal (one's Merit) and destroy happy rebirths.

"Therefore, Mindfulness should never be removed from the gate of the mind. Even if it has been lost, it should be re-established by thinking of the pain of evil rebirths (i.e., in purgatory, or as a *preta* or an animal). . . .

"When Mindfulness is seated at the gate of the Mind for its protection, then Self-awareness appears; and it does not disappear, when once it has arisen."

(*B.C. Ava.*, v, 1–5, 23–29, 33.)

So much for *smṛti* in general. The Buddhist philosophers have devised the special formula of the four Fields of Mindfulness. *Smṛti* should be applied to

Kāya (the body),
Vedanā (feelings),
Citta (thoughts), and
the Dharmas (phenomena).

These four *smṛty-upasthānas* are often mentioned in Buddhist Sanskrit literature (*M. Vy.*, xxxviii, p. 73; *Dh. S.*, xliv, p. 9; *Pra. Pā. Çata.*, pp. 1,427 ff.; *Da. Bhū.*, p. 38; *M.S. Al.*, p. 140; *Cikṣā.*, pp. 228 ff.). It should be noted that the *Lalita-vistara* calls them only *anusmṛtis* without adding the word *upasthāna* (p. 33.11).

It seems probable that the *kāya-smṛty-upasthāna* was the only one at the beginning, as we find *kāya-gatā-smṛti* frequently mentioned by itself without any reference to the others. The Pāli canon has also a whole *sutta* devoted to this one form of *smṛti* ("*kāya-gatā-sati-sutta*", *Majjh.*, iii, 88 ff.). The *Karuṇā-puṇḍarīka* and the *Lalita-vistara* sometimes mention only this kind of *smṛti* (*Lal. V.*, 209.1—*Kar. Pu.* 13.9). Açvaghoṣa also speaks only of *kāya-gatā-smṛti* in a verse of the *Saund. Kā.* (xiv, 42). Only *kāya* (the body) figures among the ten *anusmṛtis*, which a *bodhisattva* should cultivate (*Pra. Pā. Çata.*, p. 1443). The next step in the evolution of the formula was presumably taken by adding *citta* as an object of *smṛti*. *Kāya* and *citta* (body and mind) are a natural pair, and they are often mentioned together. Thus Açvaghoṣa speaks of them in the *Saund. Kā.* (xiv, 37):—

> "Sin does not arise for him who applies Mindfulness to the body: he guards his mind under all circumstances, as a nurse protects a child."

Kāya and *citta* are also spoken of together in the *B. C. Ava.*, the *Avadāna-çataka* and the *Sam. Rā.*[29] The *Bodhisattva-bhūmi* speaks of a virtuous man as *prasrabdha-kāyaḥ prasrabdha-cittaḥ* (fol. 87*b*, 6). The other two items, *vedanā* and *dharma*, were added in order to make up the number four. As a matter of fact, the Buddhist authors have written a great deal only about *kāya-smṛty-upasthāna*; they dismiss the other three with a few words. This shows that this *kāya-smṛty-upasthāna* is the chief theme. The other *smṛty-upasthānas* are merely ancillary in character.

Before discussing each *smṛty-upasthāna* in detail, it may not be out of place to refer to certain comments that have been made about them collectively as a group.

Açvaghoṣa and Vasubandhu agree in regarding these four meditations as antidotes to the four *viparyāsas*[30] (*Saund. Kā.*, xvii, 25; *M. S. Al.*, 140.24). Açvaghoṣa declares that the four *viparyāsas* (perversions), which cause evil, should be destroyed by the four *smṛty-upasthānas* respectively. These *viparyāsas* are mentioned in several passages of Buddhist literature (e.g. *Da. Bhū*, 29.12, 63.6; *Çikṣā*, 198.11; *Pr. Pā. Çata.*, 478; *Lal. V.*, 372.2). Çāntideva explains that a man is afflicted with the four *viparyāsas*, when he harbours these wrong opinions :—

(1) What is really impermanent (*anitya*) is permanent.
(2) The things, which have really no substantial permanent individuality (*anātman*), possess it.
(3) What is really impure (*açuci*) is pure.
(4) What is really painful (*duḥkha*) is pleasant.

The *viparyāsa* of impurity was probably introduced through the influence of the *Yoga* system, which defines *avidyā* in exactly the same terms (*Yo. Sū*, ii, 5, p. 61). The old Pāḷi texts speak of *açubha* and not of *açuci* (*Aṅguttara*, ii, 52, line 6). Now the four *smṛty-upasthānas* are regarded as the opposites (*pratipakṣatvāt*) of these four errors, as a man learns that the body, the feelings, the thoughts and the phenomena are really impermanent and have no substantial existence (*M. S. Al.*, 140.25).

Vasubandhu goes further and ascribes other merits to these four meditations taken collectively. They help a *bodhisattva* to understand the four Noble Truths about the existence of Evil, the origin of Evil, the cessation of Evil and the Eightfold Way. They are based on the threefold Wisdom and promote the cultivation of the *pāramitās*. They are adapted by a *bodhisattva* to the instruction of the ordinary people and of the leaders of the Hīnayāna. They confer superior capacity on a *bodhisattva*, even if they are practised only to a small extent. The beneficial results accruing from them do not disappear even in complete *nirvāṇa*, and they lead to the Perfections of the ten *bhūmis* (stages) and the Wisdom of the Buddha. (*M. S. Al.*, p. 141.)

The four *smṛty-upasthānas* may now be considered in detail.

(A) *Kāya-smṛty-upasthāna*

A *bodhisattva's* attitude towards the body should be determined by this simple rule: "He should see the body in the body, i.e. regard it as the body should be regarded" (*kāye kāy-ānudarçī*). The complete formula runs thus :—

"A *bodhisattva* envisages the body internally, externally, and both internally and externally as it should be envisaged. He is ardent, self-possessed and mindful, and he has got rid of covetousness and despondency in the world. He does not harbour any perverse thoughts associated with the body."[31]

The same words are used to describe the other *smṛty-upasthānas*, substituting *vedanā*, *citta* and *dharmāḥ* respectively for *kāya*.

Kāye kāy-ānudarçī: This simple rule seems innocuous enough. But it has let loose a flood of cynical diatribes against the body in Buddhist Sanskrit literature. We find two currents of thought on this subject in these treatises. *First*, the body is condemned, reviled, despised and anathematized as the source of evil, filth and sin. St. Francis called the body "Brother Ass", but the Buddhist philosophers indulge in more virulent invective. They touch the lowest depths of morbid cynicism. *Secondly*, the body is valued and cherished as the instrument of altruistic service and final perfection.

According to the *Lalita-vistara*, Mindfulness with regard to the body is "an entrance to the light of the Faith", which helps a *bodhisattva* to isolate himself from the body.[32] Almost all Buddhist writers approve of the threefold dictum that the body is foul and filthy, that it is transient and unsubstantial, and that it is the seat and source of sinful passions and desires. These are the three main charges in their scathing indictment of the body.

Physiologically considered, the body is a mass of filth and putridity. It exudes such malodorous and impure substances as sweat, pus, bile, phlegm, urine, saliva and excrements through its nine apertures.[33] It is indeed a rotten carcass,[34] and it is infested by eighty thousand worms.[35] Its natural foulness is not realised by ordinary men and women, as it is usually covered with clothes and ornaments.[36]

The body is thus revolting and repulsive from the æsthetic point of view. But the chief burden of complaint against it is that it is transient and unsubstantial. A *bodhisattva* analyses the body with his keen insight, and scrutinises it "from the soles of the feet to the crown of the head". He sees that it is merely an artificial collection of "feet, toes, legs, chest, loins, belly, navel, backbone, heart, ribs, flanks, hands, forearms, upper-arms, shoulders, neck, jaw, forehead, head, skull", to which are added other things like the hair, the bones, the sinews, etc.[37] It is composed of the four elements—earth, water, fire and wind.[38] A *bodhisattva* clearly recognises its composite nature, just as a butcher or his apprentice may cut up a cow's carcass into four pieces and examine them.[39] A *bodhisattva* never forgets that the body is made up of many separate ingredients and members, just as a farmer knows exactly that his granaries contain wheat, rice, barley, sesasum seeds, beans, mustard seeds, kidney beans, lentils, and other pulses and cereals.[40] As the body is thus a merely composite structure, it cannot be really said to exist, as the name corresponds to no reality. A *bodhisattva* may therefore reasonably ask, "Then what is this body ?"[41] And he understands that it is only like *ākāça*. Further, the body is thus nothing more than an instrument or tool, as it has no essential and independent existence. It cannot feel, or perform actions, or maintain its identity in the past, present and future.[42] It is also transient and fragile.[43] It is subject to hunger, thirst, disease, old age and death.[44] It is like unto a foam-bubble[45] or a lamp of straw.[46] Man, the Wayfarer, cannot stay long in this abode of the body.[47] It is indeed more fragile than a pot of clay : the latter may be kept intact for a long time with proper care, but the body is destroyed very soon like a tree growing on the bank of a river.[48] By its very nature, it is exposed to the five calamities of "decaying, falling, breaking, scattering and crumbling".[49] Indeed, it cannot be otherwise, for the body is the outcome of one's deeds in a previous life, one's *karma* ; it grows in the soil of *karma* and is watered by sensual passion. *Karma*[50] is its artificer. It can know no happiness or peace ; it must continually be in a state of pain.[51]

The body is also the seat and source of sin. It suffers from sensual desires, the emotions of hate, fear and despondency, and the fatal malady of delusion and folly. All these are like thieves and robbers, that attack it.[52] It is the abode of sinful deeds.[53] The elements, of which it is composed, are unruly and dangerous, like wild horses and serpents. They always cause physical and spiritual evil.[54]

This threefold arraignment of the body culminates in the famous (or infamous) formula of the nine meditations on the Impure (i.e. the impurity of the body—*açubha-bhāvanā* or *açubha-pratyavekṣā*; *M. Vy.*, lii, p. 87 ; *Pr. Pā. Çata.*, 59, 1258, 1431 ff. ; *Lal. V.*, 32.21). This method of realising the transitoriness of the body consists in visiting a cemetery (or thinking of it) and seeing or visualising the different aspects of a corpse in process of disintegration and decomposition. It is called the realisation (*bhāvanā*) or the examination (*pratyavekṣā*) of that which is inauspicious, foul or loathsome. The Pāli texts mention ten offensive conditions of a corpse (*Dhammasaṅgaṇi*, Sections 263 and 264, page 55), but the Sanskrit writers discuss only nine. The *Mahā-vyutpatti* gives the following list :—

(1) *vinīlaka* (a discoloured, bluish, livid corpse).
(2) *vidhūtika* (*vipūyaka*, a festering corpse).
(3) *vipaḍumaka* (a worm-eaten corpse).[55]
(4) *vyādhmātaka* (a bloated, swollen corpse).
(5) *vilohitaka* (a bloody corpse).
(6) *vikhāditaka* (a devoured and mangled corpse).
(7) *vikṣiptaka* (a scattered corpse).
(8) *vidagdhaka* (a burned corpse).
(9) *asthi* (bones).

The *bodhisattva* is exhorted to frequent cemeteries and reflect on the fate of the body. The idea of a visit to the cremation-ground was probably suggested by the old legend, which related that the *bodhisattva* Siddhārtha saw a funeral procession. A dead man's body was being carried to the cremation-ground.[56] This was regarded as one of the four incidents that preceded his flight from his home. Kṣemendra, indeed, improves upon the ancient biographies and tells us that the young Siddhārtha actually visited a cemetery and gave expression to edifying sentiments.[57] The vivid Indian imagination played with the idea and did not recoil from suggesting these lugubrious meditations. The author or authors of the *Pr. Pā. Çata.* follow an old tradition in recommending these meditative exercises, which are also mentioned in the Pāli canon.[58] A *bodhisattva* should go to a cemetery and see the corpses of the persons who died one, two, three, four, or five days before. As he observes them in different stages of decomposition, he should apply the moral to his own body and say to himself: "This body has also the same constitution : it is of such a nature, and it cannot escape this condition." Then he may observe corpses, which have lain in the cemetery for six or seven days, or which have been devoured and mangled by crows, eagles, vultures, dogs, jackals and worms. Again, he may see heaps of bones hanging together by the tendons, with the flesh and blood on them ; or such bones as have altogether lost the flesh, blood and tendons, and look like sea-shells ; or such bones as are scattered on all sides, the bones of the feet in one direction, and the bones of the thighs and other limbs in other directions. Finally, he may see such bones as have lain in the cemetery for several years and have been reduced to rotten powder-dust of a bluish colour. Seeing such corpses and bones, he should constantly think of his own body, and say to himself: "Such is the nature of this body". (*Pr. Pā. Çata.*, pp. 1431–3; *Çikṣā*, pp. 210 ff.)

In justice to the Mahāyānist writers, it must be stated that most of them do not mention these meditations at all. They are not discussed in such standard treatises as the *Dh. S.*, the *M. S. Al.* and the *Da. Bhū.* This circumstance shows that they were not practised or recommended by all the sects. The idea was probably borrowed from the Jainas, who attached great importance to the *açuci-bhāvanā* (*anuprekṣā*).[59]

These diatribes against the body and such funereal meditations are intended to help the *bodhisattva* in his spiritual development. They lead to the abandonment of the sins of sensual passion.[60] A *bodhisattva* is soon delivered from the darkness of delusion, as he constantly practises these meditations.[61] He also uses them as the means of converting others.[62] When he regards the transient body as the abode of calamities and the victim of evil destiny, he is filled with disgust for it (*nirveda*).[63] The meditation on the Impurities is the real antidote to sensual desire.[64] Even an arrant deluded fool would not love the body and its lusts, if he practised these exercises. Self-sacrifice is not difficult for a *bodhisattva*, if he regards the body as impermanent. He can render service as a servant and a disciple to all living beings.[65] He avoids all wickedness, crookedness and hypocrisy, and does not commit any sins for the sake of the body. He does not hanker after pleasures, and gives his all for others. As he grows in spiritual stature, he understands the fundamental unity of all beings and identifies their bodies with his own. He then thinks of establishing all of them in the eternal unity of the Buddha's spiritual Body, which is free from sin and ignorance. He knows that his own body, the bodies of other beings and the Buddha's universal spiritual Body are essentially of the same nature.[66] Thus the application of Mindfulness to the body gradually leads him to the highest Wisdom.

In the course of development of Buddhist thought, the body ceased to be despised and condemned, as it came to be regarded as the blessed instrument of altruistic service and final perfection. This constructive idea finds frequent expression in the works of Çūra, Çāntideva and Kṣemendra. The *Lalita-vistara* warns a *bodhisattva* that a weak body is unfit for the attainment of Wisdom.[67] The body is transient and unsubstantial, but it should be used to achieve substantial results by earning spiritual merit (*asāra*, *sāra*).[68] In that case, it becomes an instrument (*sādhana*) for the service of others.[69] The body, which is troubled with hundreds of diseases and various afflictions, should be employed as a ship to carry other creatures across the sea of troubles.[70] It is indeed frail, unsubstantial, unreal, miserable, impure and ungrateful; but when it is used for the good of others, a *bodhisattva* rejoices exceedingly, as a wise man should do.[71] He, who does not use this mortal body to secure enduring benefit for himself and others, is indeed unable to discern the difference between the ephemeral things that are worthless and the things that are "a possession for ever".[72] In the end, the body will be devoured by vultures and jackals, but it should be preserved as an instrument of Action.[73] It is indeed subject to old age, disease, sorrow and death; it must suffer the pangs of union and separation; but if it is inspired by the wisdom and resolution of a *bodhisattva*, it can pursue the long career of a *bodhisattva*, ripen all beings, and fulfil the law of the Buddha.[74] A *bodhisattva* should regard every action and movement of his body as an occasion for the cultivation of friendly thoughts for the good of all creatures.[75] When he sits down, he thinks thus: "May I help all beings to sit on the throne of *bodhi!*" When he lies on his right side, he thinks thus: "May I lead all beings to *nirvāṇa!*" When he washes his hands, he thinks thus: "May I remove the sinful propensities of all creatures!" When he washes his feet, he thinks thus: "May I take away the dirt of sins and passions from all creatures!" In this way the body can be converted into a holy vessel of benediction. And who can deny that the great Buddha's body was auspicious (*kalyāṇa-niketana*)?[76] Blessed indeed is he who loses this frail body in doing good to others.[77] Such a sacrifice can be made only by those who have already cultivated virtue and acquired much spiritual Merit.[78] A *bodhisattva* can never love the body for its own sake, as it is foul, dirty and illusory; if he cherishes it, he does so only because he will gird himself up to save someone sometime somewhere on some occasion in the moment of tribulation.[79] This journey of life is fruitful only if one does good to others, for who knows what the end of the body will be? [80] A *bodhisattva* should therefore be indifferent to the body and even to his life. His actions can lead to Enlightenment only if he maintains such a heroic spirit.[81]

(b) *Vedanā-smṛty-upasthāna*

Vedanā is a "term of very general import, meaning sentience or reaction, bodily or mental, on contact or impression". It is derived from the root *vid* in the sense of experiencing a feeling or sensation. It may be interpreted as "sensation", as it is regarded as the immediate outcome of the contact (*sparça*) between the sense-organs and the external objects in the well-known formula of the twelve *nidānas*. It is also described as sixfold according to the sense-organ, whose contact originates it (*cakṣuḥ-sparçajā vedanā*, *çrotra-sparçajā vedanā*, etc.).[82] T. W. Rhys Davids, L. de la Vallée Poussin, L. Feer, P. Oltramare and P. E. Foucaux agree in translating *vedanā* here as "sensations".[83] M. Anesaki's rendering, "senses," is perhaps inadmissible.[84] But *vedanā* also seems to mean "feeling", as it is said to be of three kinds: pleasant (*sukhā*), painful (*duḥkhā*), and neither-painful-nor-pleasant, i.e. neutral, indifferent (*aduḥkh-āsukhā*).[85] In the famous Tibetan pictorial representation of the twelve *nidānas*, the symbol of *vedanā* is a couple of lovers.[86] Surely this is suggestive of "feeling", and not of mere "sensation!"

It appears that *vedāna* is something which is both feeling and sensation. We cannot perhaps find a proper word for it in the terminology of European psychology, which has adopted a different principal of analysis and classification. The Buddhist did not regard feeling and sensation as mutually exclusive terms. In any case, *vedanā* as a *smṛty-upasthāna* should be interpreted as "feeling", as there is no sense in speaking of Mindfulness with regard to the sensations, which reach the mind from the external world. The feelings, which arise in the mind, can be the objects of mindful reflexion. It seems proper to follow the lead of R. O. Franké and W. H. D. Rouse, and translate "feeling".[87]

A *bodhisattva*, who practises Mindfulness with regard to Feeling, learns to restrain and control all feelings. He girds himself up in order to teach all beings that they should suppress Feeling, as happiness is possible only when Feeling does not exist. Feeling is a perversion and a delusion. He exhorts all beings to adopt this negative attitude towards Feeling ; but he himself, as a *bodhisattva*, tries to sublimate the three kinds of Feeling into universal compassion. He reflects upon his feelings in such a manner that he achieves two results: he feels deep compassion for all creatures, and he improves his own personality by destroying or diminishing *rāga* (sense-desire), *dveṣa* (hate, ill-will) and *moha* (delusion, folly). Mindfulness with regard to Feeling can thus subserve the highest ends of a *bodhisattva's* discipline. When he experiences a pleasant feeling, he is on his guard against *rāga*. At the same time, he thinks with infinite pity of all those beings who are the slaves of pleasurable feelings. When he experiences a painful feeling, he is free from hatred and ill-will, and he pities those whose hearts are darkened by those emotions. When he experiences a feeling which is neither painful nor pleasant, he hastens to get rid of *moha*, and thinks compassionately of those creatures who are the victims of *moha*. Further, he also realises other truths. He understands that pleasant feeling is impermanent, that painful feeling is just like a thorn, and that neutral feeling should leave him calm and serene. Finally, he comprehends that there is no enduring Self behind Feeling, no Ego that feels. He regards Feeling as altogether illusory, like a dream. (*Lal. V.*, 33.12 ; *M. S. Al.*, 141 ; *Çikṣā*, 232.)

(c) *Citta-smṛty-upasthāna*

A *bodhisattva* applies Mindfulness internally, externally, and both internally and externally to *citta*. This word may be interpreted as "Thought", "thoughts," or "the mind." The rendering "heart" has also been suggested. As the word is always used in the singular in all the texts dealing with this *upasthāna*, it is best to render it as "Thought".

A *bodhisattva*, who practises Mindfulness with regard to *citta*, understands that it is by nature luminous, like *ākāça*. This is Vasubandhu's teaching on the subject. But all the other writers take up a different line of argument, which culminates in unalloyed subjective nihilism. They hold that *citta* is produced and conditioned by the external objects, which are perceived by the senses ; it moves among them and is unstable and restless, like a monkey or the wind. It may be compared to a flowing stream, a flash of lightning, or the flame of a lamp. It is also sensuous and sensual in its nature, as it takes delight in the five kinds of sensations derived from the external world. It finds pleasure in form, sound, smell, taste and touch, and is therefore nothing better than a moth's eye, a battle-drum, a hog, a servant that eats of the leavings of food, and a fly in a vessel filled with oil. Further, Thought is altogether illusory and non-existent, as it is related to Time, and a *bodhisattva* knows that Time is a figment of the imagination. The past is gone, the future is still unborn, and the present cannot stand still. Thus the dependence of Thought on Time shows that it is altogether unreal and impossible. The relation between Thought and the external world leads a *bodhisattva* to the same conclusion. Çāntideva propounds a dilemma in connection with the vexed question of Subject and Object in philosophy and psychology. He says: "If Thought exists before the Object, on what does its origination depend? And if it arises with the Object...", the same query can be repeated. As this conundrum is insoluble, we must conclude that Thought does not exist. An examination of one's own consciousness also confirms this opinion. Thought cannot be the object of mental cognition, as a sword-blade cannot cut itself or a finger-tip cannot touch itself. How, then, can one be sure of its reality? It cannot be found inside us, nor outside us, nor anywhere between the two. It is without form and habitation, and no Buddha has ever perceived it, does perceive it, or shall perceive it at any time. It is a false notion and an illusion.

Having argued thus, a *bodhisattva* should remember a few striking similes with regard to Thought. It is like a bad friend, as it is the cause of all evil. It is like a fish-hook, as it looks pleasant to the fishes, but is really a calamity for them. It is like a blue fly, which regards filthy things as pure. It is like an enemy, as it torments a person in various ways. It is like a strength-destroying ogre, which always seeks for a loophole to enter. It is like a thief, as it steals all the "Roots of Merit" that have been accumulated. Thus does a *bodhisattva* look upon *citta*! (*Lal. V.*, 33.13; *Mdh.*, 62–3; *B.C. Ava.*, ix, 103 ff.; *Çikṣā*, 233 ff.; *M. S. Al.*, 141.)

(d) *Dharma-smṛty-upasthāna*

A *bodhisattva* also practises Mindfulness with regard to "the *dharmas*". This word, in this context, has been variously translated as follows:

T. W. Rhys Davids and W. T. Stede: "Phenomena" (Pāli Dicy. s.v. *sati*).

M. Anesaki: "The ultimate nature of things" (ERE, v, 455).

R. O. Franke: "Die seelischen und äusseren Daseinserscheinungen" (*Dīgha*, p. 187, note).

W. and M. Geiger: "Die Dinge" (Pāli *Dhamma*, p. 89, l. 7).

M. Winternitz: "Die Erscheinungen" (Lesebuch, p. 251).

H. Beckh: "Die Natur der Dinge" (Buddhismus, i, 20, note).

T. W. Rhys Davids: (1) "Reason and Character" (Dialogues, ii, 129). (2) "Ideas" (Dialogues, ii, 334).

S. Lévi: "L'idéal" (*M. S. Al.* tr., p. 105, note).

J. Masuda: "Die Gegenstände ausser den drei vorhergehenden" (Idealismus, p. 8, note).

W. H. D. Rouse: "The Elements of Existence" (*Çikṣā* tr., p. 221).

K. E. Neumann: "Die Erscheinungen" (Majjh. tr., ii, 327).

P. E. Foucaux: "La loi" (*Lal. V. Tib.*, ii, 42).

S. C. Das translates the Tibetan equivalent (*chos*) as "conditions of existence".

It is to be noted that the word *dharma* is almost always used in the plural number in this *smṛty-upasthāna*: *Dharmeṣu dharmānudarçī*. The detailed comments of the Buddhist writers also show that it cannot mean "the ideal, virtue, character". We must also dismiss the long disquisition on the different principles and precepts (*nīvaraṇas*, *skandhas*, etc.) at *Dīgha-Nikāyā*, ii, 300 ff. as irrelevant and misleading. *Dharmāḥ* cannot refer to all those doctrinal categories as the objects of this *smṛty-upasthāna*. If we interpret *dharmāḥ* here as "Phenomena", "Things," we find that the sense suits the context. Having reflected on the elements of his own personality, like the body, the feelings and the mind, a *bodhisattva* now turns his thoughts towards the outer world, the universe in general. Thus both the Ego and the non-Ego are included in the operations of Mindfulness. This natural climax gives symmetry and completeness to the formula.

A *bodhisattva*, who applies Mindfulness to the Phenomena, understands that they are adventitious and extraneous, just as dust, smoke, clouds and frost are merely accidental adjuncts of Space. He acquires perfect knowledge, which is free from all delusion and darkness. He realises that the Phenomena arise from causes and are thus relative and inter-dependent. They are impermanent and fragile, like a pot of unbaked clay or a town built of sand. They may be compared to the sand on the bank of a river, the flame of a lamp, a clot of foam, a gust of wind, the plaster washed away in the rainy season, the stem of a plantain tree and an empty fist. Such similes can be appropriately applied to the Phenomena. They are caused by Ignorance and they do not really exist. Grass can be twisted and made into a rope, and the buckets of water are turned by a wheel at the well; but there is no "turning" in them one by one. Similarly, the movements of the things in the universe are dependent on one another. The Phenomena are in fact unintelligible. The sprout springs from the seed, but it is neither the same as the seed nor different from it. A seal can give an impression, which is neither the same as the seal nor different from it. We see things on account of the contact between the eye and external forms, but the latter are not in the eye. Fire is produced by the friction of two pieces of wood, but no man can see or tell whence it came and whither it has gone. In the same way, sound is produced by the combined action of the bodily organs and the mind, but all sound is but an echo. It may be produced by means of a stringed musical instrument, which is played with the hand; but no one can perceive whence it comes or whither it goes. Thus the Phenomena are due to primary and secondary causes, and they are void within and without. There is no essence and reality in them. (*Lal. V.*, 33; *M. S. Al.*, 141; *Çikṣā*, 236 ff.)

III. The Samyak-Prahāṇas

A *bodhisattva* should cultivate the four "*samyak-prahāṇāni*" (Pāli *sammappadhānā*).[88] The term has been variously translated as follows:—

T. W. Rhys Davids and W. Stede: "Right exertions" (Pāli Dicy., s.v. *padhāna*).

S. Lévi: "Les abandons réguliers" (*M. S. Al.* tr., p. 238).

A. Schiefner: "Die vier vollkommenen Entsagungen" (Triglotte, iii).

P. E. Foucaux: "Les quatre abandons complets" (*Lal. V.* tr., p. 34).

W. H. D. Rouse: "The four kinds of quietism" (*Çikṣā* tr., p. 107).

H. Oldenberg: "Das vierfache rechte Streben" (Buddha, p. 227).

R. O. Franke: "Das vierlei rechte Ringen" (*Dīgha*, p. 218).

M. Winternitz: "Die tüchtigen Anstrengungen" (Lesebuch, p. 251).

M. Anesaki: "Right control or exertion" (ERE, v, 455).

E. Burnouf: "Les quatre abandons complets" (Introduction, p. 85, ed. 1844).

E. Eklund: "Den fyrfaldiga stora kampen mot synd" (the fourfold great struggle or fight against sin). (*Nirvāṇa*, p. 133.)

T. W. and C. A. F. Rhys Davids: "Four Supreme Efforts" (Dialogues, iii, 215).

Lord Chalmers: (1) "The four Right Struggles" (*Majjh.* tr., ii, 6). (2) "The four Efforts" (*Majjh.* tr., ii, 320).

C. F. Koeppen: "Die vollkommenen Entsagungen" (Buddha, i, 436).

K. E. Neumann: "Die vier gewaltigen Kämpfe" (*Majjh.* tr., ii, 327).

S. C. Das (s.v. Tibetan *spoṅ-ba* and *chos*): "The Renunciations" (Tib. Dicy., 429*a* and 802*a*).

The four *samyak-prahāṇas* are mentioned in several passages of Buddhist literature (*M. Vy.*, Section 39, p. 73; *Dh. S.*, xlv; *M. S. Al.*, 141; *Da. Bhū.*, 39; *Çikṣā*, 356; *Pr. Pā. Çata.*, 1436).

It is clear that *prahāṇa* is a wrongly Sanskritized form. The usual Pāli word is *padhāna* (*Dhamma-saṅgaṇi*, 1366), and the correct Sanskrit rendering would be *pradhāna*, derived from the root *dhā* (and not from the root *hā*, *jahāti*, as in *prahāṇa*). In fact, we find the correct form in a few passages of Buddhist literature, e.g. *samyak-pradhānā caturo me açvā* (*Mtu.*, iii, 120.14); *samyak-pradhān-ottama-vāhanasthaḥ* (*Saund. Kā.*, xvii, 24). The derivative *prahita* also occurs in the *Mtu.*: *prahit-ātmā vyapakṛṣṭo* (*Mtu.*, ii, 118.11, 120.3). In describing the four struggles, some writers have employed the correct verb, *samyak pradadhāti* (*Pr. Pā. Çata.*, 1436; *M. S. Al.*, 142.6). The *Da. Bhū.* has *praṇidadhāti* (38.26). But when the incorrect form *prahāṇa* was once accepted, the original meaning was forgotten. Thus the *Kar. Pu.* explains that the Equipment (*sambhāra*) of the *samyak-prahāṇas* consists in the abandonment of all evil conditions (104.23). The *M. Vy.* omits the word *samyak* and speaks only of *prahāṇāni*.

The first Effort is intended to prevent the inception of such evil and sinful conditions as have not yet arisen, so that new evil and sinful conditions or mental states may not arise. A *bodhisattva*, who practises this *samyak-prahāṇa*, rouses (produces) in himself a keen desire (intention, resolution, will—*chanda*) to attain this end. He strives, puts forth Energy, controls his mind, and exerts himself well.[89] Thus he obtains protection from evil.

The second Effort is directed towards the abandonment (or destruction) of such evil and sinful conditions or mental states as have already arisen. The *bodhisattva* rouses in himself a keen desire or resolution to attain this end He strives, puts forth Energy, controls his mind and exerts himself well. Thus he obtains purification.

The third Effort is directed towards the production of such right and meritorious conditions or mental states as have not yet arisen. The *bodhisattva* rouses in himself a keen desire or resolution to attain this end. He strives, puts forth Energy, controls his mind, and exerts himself well. Thus he secures growth.

The fourth Effort is directed towards securing the permanence and promotion of such right and meritorious conditions or mental states as have already arisen, so that they may not be lost, but should increase, multiply and receive full cultivation with a view to their perfection. A *bodhisattva* strives, puts forth Energy, controls his mind and exerts himself well. This also leads to growth.

In the scheme of the ten *bhūmis*, a *bodhisattva* cultivates these "Efforts" in the fourth *bhūmi*. They are compared to the chariot of a spiritual warrior by Açvaghoṣa: the *bodhisattva* fights his enemies (the sins and passions), while he is seated in such an impregnable vehicle. They are particularly useful in combating the five hindrances and besetting sins, which are called *nīvaraṇāni* (coverings, veils, obstacles).[90] They enable a *bodhisattva* to rise above the stage of a Hīnayānist adept and enter on the career of advanced spirituality in the seventh and higher *bhūmis*, until he reaches final perfection as a Buddha. (*M. S. Al.*, 141; *Da. Bhū.*, 38; *Çikṣā*, 356; *Saund. Kā.*, xvii, 24.)

IV. The Ṛddhi-pādas (with the Prātihāryas and the Abhijñās)

A *bodhisattva* should cultivate the four "*Ṛddhi-pādāḥ*" (Pāli : *iddhipādā*). This term, which consists of two words, *ṛddhi* and *pādāḥ*, has been translated in the following ways :—

T. W. and C. A. F. Rhys Davids : (1) "Stages to Efficiency" (Dialogues, iii, 215). (2) "Roads to Saintship" (Dialogues, ii, 129).

H. Beckh : "Die Elemente oder Voraussetzungen der übersinnlichen Vollkommenheit" (Buddhismus, ii, 75).

E. J. Thomas : "Kinds of magic power" (Buddha, p. 183, note 2).

A. Schiefner : "Die vier Grundlagen der Wunderkraft" (Triglotte, iii).

H. Kern : "The subdivisions of the power of working miracles" (Manual, p. 60).

R. O. Franke : "Die Grundlagen übernaturlicher Kräfte" (*Dīgha*, p. 218).

E. Eklund : "Vägarne till *arhatship*" ("Ways to *arhatship*"). (*Nirvāṇa*, p. 133).

C. A. F. Rhys Davids : "Bases or preliminaries to potency" (*Thera-gāthā* tr., p. 265).

H. Oldenberg : "Die vier Teile Heiliger Macht" (Buddha, p. 227).

T. W. Rhys Davids and W. Stede : "Bases of, or steps to, psychic power" (Pāli Dicy).

E. Burnouf : "Les principes de la puissance surnaturelle" (Introduction, p. 75, ed. 1844).

C. F. Koeppen : "Die Principien der Wunderkraft" (Buddha, i, 436).

S. Lévi : "les pieds-de-Magie" (*M. S. Al.* tr., p. 239).

L. Feer : "Les bases de la puissance surnaturelle" (*Ava. Ça.* tr., p. 9).

Lord Chalmers : "Bases of psychic power" (*Majjh.* tr., ii, 7.)

S. C. Das (for Tibetan *rdsu-ḥphrul-gyi-rkaṅ-pa*) : "The bases for magical transformations" (Tib. Dicy. 429*a*).

K. E. Neumann : "Die vier Machtgebiete" (*Majjh.* tr., ii, 328).

Böhtlingk and Roth (s.v. *ṛddhi*) : "übernaturliche Kraft" (Skt. Dicy. Pbg.).

The Tibetan term for *ṛddhi* is *rdsu-ḥphrul* (*M. Vy.*, p. 74; J. Rahder, Glossary, p. 44; *Lal. V. Tib.*, p. 10). S. C. Das translates and explains: "A miracle, a magical illusion, an apparent marvel, the power to cause which is considered the highest manifestation of moral acquirements" (Tib. Dicy., 1058*b*). *Ṛddhi* (Pāli: *iddhi*) cannot be adequately translated by such a word as "magic". "Magic" has now a specialized sense in anthropology, and it is quite different from the *ṛddhi* of the Buddhists. We are also not justified in introducing the peculiar theological notion of the "supernatural" into a Buddhist term. The adjective "*psychic*" is also unsuitable, as it has now acquired certain modern associations; and *ṛddhi*, as described in the Buddhist treatises, far transcends what is commonly called "psychic power". "Saintship" is too wide of the mark as a rendering of *ṛddhi*. "Efficiency" and "potency" are too general, and do not convey a clear idea of what *ṛddhi* really is. "Super-will," "more-will," "wondrous gift" are also unsatisfactory renderings.[91]

The word *ṛddhi* is derived from the root *ṛdh*, meaning "to grow, increase, prosper, succeed; to cause to increase and prosper" (Skt. Dicy., M.W.). This verb and its derivatives have this original meaning in several passages of Buddhist literature, e.g.: *Tvaṃ ṛddhi-prāpto vicaresi loke* (*Mtu.*, ii, 321.21); *rāja-dhānī . . . ṛddhā ca sphītā ca kṣemā ca* (*Divy.*, 291.13). (Cf. *Mtu.*, ii, 67.21. *Ava. Ça.*, i, 117.14.)

The Pāli word *iddhi* came to mean "potency", "virtue", (almost like Greek ἀρετή), as when birds are said to fly by *iddhi* (*Dhamma-pada*, 175). We do not find many passages in Buddhist Sanskrit literature, in which *ṛddhi* bears this generalised sense. But *ṛddhi* (like Pāli *iddhi*) is very frequently employed to denote "wonder-working Power". This is perhaps the best translation of the term, which implies the possession of such Power, but which excludes the irrelevant and extraneous notions of "magic", "miracle", "supernaturalism" or "mysticism".

The word *ṛddhi* is sometimes coupled with *prātihārya*, which means "jugglery, working miracles, a miracle; Gaukelei, Erzeugung von Wundern, Wundertätigkeit" (Skt. Dicy. Pbg. and M.W.). The latter term is of wider import than *ṛddhi*, as there are three kinds of *prātihārya*, of which *ṛddhi-prātihārya* is one. The other two may be described as "wonders" only in a metaphorical sense: they are given as *ādeçanā-prātihārya* and *anuçāsanī-prātihārya*.[92] These terms may be translated as "manifestation-wonder" and "education-wonder". They are not of great importance as far as a *bodhisattva* is concerned. But the first *prātihārya*, which is associated with *ṛddhi*, is frequently mentioned in connection with a *bodhisattva's* activity. We may regard the two terms, *ṛddhi* and *ṛddhi-prātihārya*, as synonymous for all practical purposes. *Ṛddhi* is also reckoned as one of the six *abhijñās* and will be discussed in detail as such.

The word *pāda* in the term *ṛddhi-pādāḥ* has been variously translated as "basis", "mode", "part", "step", "kind", "foot", "way", "stage", "subdivision", etc. H. A. Jäschke translates the Tibetan equivalent *rkaṅ-pa* as "base, foundation" (Tib. Dicy. 15*b*). We may translate: "Bases."

The four *ṛddhi-pādas* are frequently described in Buddhist Sanskrit literature (*M. Vy.*, xl, p. 74; *Dh. S.*, xlvi; *Pra. Pā. Çata.*, 1436; *M. S. Al.*, 142; *Da. Bhū.*, 38.30 ff.; *Lalita-vistara*, 33).[93]

A *bodhisattva* develops (or cultivates) the first *ṛddhi-pāda* by uniting a strong Desire or Will (*chanda*) to the moulding forces of concentration and effort.

He develops the second *ṛddhi-pāda* by uniting Thought (*citta*) to the moulding forces of concentration and effort.

He develops the third *ṛddhi-pāda* by uniting Energy (*vīrya*) to the moulding forces of concentration and effort.

He develops the fourth *ṛddhi-pāda* by uniting Investigation (*mīmāmsā*) to the moulding forces of concentration and effort.

All the *ṛddhi-pādas* help a *bodhisattva* in the attainment of all his aims for his own good and for the good of others. They produce lightness and elasticity of body and mind. They may be compared to a chariot, which is driven by Wisdom and Mindfulness.[94]

V. The Abhijñās

A *bodhisattva* acquires the five or six *abhijñās* (Pāli: *abhiññā*) in the course of his career. This word *abhijñā* has been translated by modern scholars in the following ways:—

T. W. Rhys Davids and W. Stede: "Psychic powers" (Pāli Dicy., s.v. *abhiññā*).

Böhtlingk and Roth: "Eine höhere übernaturliche Kenntniss und Macht" (Skt. Dicy. Pbg.).

Monier Williams: "Supernatural science or faculty of a Buddha" (Skt. Dicy., 62*b*).

C. A. F. Rhys Davids: "Super-knowledge" (Psychology, p. 161).

H. Kern: "Transcendent knowledge" (Manual, p. 60).

E. Burnouf: "Connaissances surnaturelles" (Lotus, p. 818).

S. Lévi: "Les super-savoirs" (*M. S. Al.* tr., p. 5).

L. de la Vallée Poussin: (1) "Pouvoirs mystiques" (Morale, p. 88). (2) "Facultés transcendantes" (*Le Muséon*, 1911, p. 156).

L. Feer: "Connaissances supérieures" (*Ava. Ça.* tr., p. 141).

C. F. Koeppen: "Die übernaturalichen Einsichten" (Buddha, i, 440).

H. Beckh: "Die höheren Seelenfähigkeiten" (Buddhismus, ii, 77).

F. Heiler: "Höhere Erkenntniss" (Versenkung, p. 92).

Lord Chalmers: "Transcendent knowledge" (*Majjh.* tr., i, 320).

M. Anesaki and J. Takakusu: "Supernatural powers" (ERE, iv, 704*a*).

F. Max Müller: "Supernatural faculties" (*Dh. S.*, p. 39).

The Tibetan equivalent is *mñon par çes pa* (*M. Vy.*, p. 18). S. C. Das translates: "Gifts of supernatural perception" (Tib. Dicy. 365*b*). Perhaps it is best to translate, "Super-knowledges"—a literal and satisfactory rendering.

These *abhijñās* present a difficult problem in Buddhist Sanskrit literature. The formula in its final form comprises six *abhijñās*, but five *abhijñās* are most frequently mentioned. The same author sometimes speaks of five *abhijñās* in one passage and of six in another.[95]

The six *abhijñās* are given in the Sanskrit treatises in the following order[96]:—

M. Vy. (xiv, p. 18) (1) *Divyaṃ cakṣuḥ.*
(2) *Divyaṃ çrotram.*
(3) *Parasya cetaḥ-paryāya-jñānam; para-citta-jñānam.*
(4) *Pūrva-nivās-ānusmṛti-jñānam.*
(5) *Ṛddhi-vidhi-jñānam.*
(6) *Āsrava-kṣaya-jñānam.*

Dh. S. (xx, p. 4) : 1, 2, 3, 4, 5 (No. 6 omitted).
Pr. Pā. Çata. (pp. 97–8) : 1, 2, 3, 4, 5.
Ibid. (p. 252) : 1, 2, 3, 4, 5, 6.
Ibid. (p. 1453) : 1, 2, 3, 4, 5, 6.
Da. Bhū. (pp. 34–5) : 5, 2, 3, 4, 1 (No. 6 omitted).
M. S. Al. (p. 25) : 1, 2, 3, 4, 5, 6.
Su. Vy. (p. 12) : 4, 1, 2, 3,
Ibid. (p. 52) : 5, 1, 2, 4.

The *M. Vy.* has the heading, *Six Abhijñās*, but it enumerates seven of them ! The third and the fourth in its list are really the same, viz. *para-citta-jñānam* and *cetaḥ-paryāya-jñānam.* The copyist has probably made a mistake. The Tibetan version omits *cetaḥ-paryāya-jñānam.*

The order, in which the *abhijñās* are placed, may throw some light on the process of growth, which culminated in the final formula. According to the latest Buddhist authors, *āsrava-kṣaya-jñāna* always occupies the last place and is regarded as the sixth *abhijñā*. The *Dh. S.* omits it altogether. It is also understood that the term *pañc-ābhijñāḥ* refers to the other five *abhijñās*. In that case, we should be justified in holding the view that *āsrava-kṣaya-jñāna* was added to the original group of the five *abhijñās*. But as a matter of fact, *āsrava-kṣaya-jñāna* was included in the fivefold group even in its oldest form ; and *ṛddhi-vidhi-jñāna* was the intruder that ousted the former from its position and relegated it to the sixth place.

The starting-point for the evolution of the formula must be sought in the three *vidyās* of the early Buddhists. Buddha is said to have attained *divya-cakṣus*, *pūrva-nivās-ānusmṛti* and *āsrava-kṣaya-jñāna* during the night, in which he acquired perfect Enlightenment. Both the *Lalita-vistara* and the *Mtu.* record this tradition (*cf. Lal. V.*, pp. 344–5 ; *Mtu.*, iii, 67.7 ; ii, 283.15 ff., 284.6, 285.5).

Two other thaumaturgic powers were added to these three in order to make up the group of five, viz. *divya-çrotra* and *ṛddhi*. These two are mentioned along with *divya-cakṣus* and *jātismaratā* in the *Su. Vy.* (52.16 ff.). It is to be noted that *āsrava-kṣaya-jñāna* has already dropped out, so that only four such powers are recognised. This may have been a stage in the development of the formula, as the *Laṅkāvatāra* also speaks of four *abhijñās* (*caturvidhāḥ* ; *Lka.*, p. 292, verse 211). Finally, *para-citta-jñāna* was tacked on to the formula. The order, in which the *abhijñās* are placed in the *Kassapa Saṃyutta*, is significant (*Saṃyutta-Nikāya*, ii, 212–13). It shows that three new items were added to the three old *vidyās*, which are put together as the 4th, 5th and 6th *abhijñās*. But this order was changed by the Sanskritists, and *āsrava-kṣaya-jñāna* also disappeared from the group of five. As *ṛddhi* was a new item, it would naturally be put at the beginning or at the end of the old lists; and the later writers perhaps attached more importance to wonder-mongering than to the purely spiritual quality of freedom from the *āsravas*. Further, many texts show that the old term *āsrava* was not in favour with the Sanskritists. In the Pāli canon, it occupies the place of honour, as *arhatship*, the *summum bonum* of the religious life, was gained only after the destruction of the "*āsavas*".[97] But a remarkable change of phraseology can be noticed even in such early books as the *Divy-āvadāna* and the *Ava. Ça*. *Arhatship* is described as the result of *kleça-prahāṇa* (the abandonment of the *kleças*) and not of *āsrava-kṣaya* (cf. *Divy*., 50.9; 166.17. *Ava. Ça*., ii, 38.2). Now the *kleças* are by no means the same as the *āsravas* either in the Hīnayāna or the Mahāyāna, despite the author of the *Bo. Bhū*.[98] The *kleças* are ordinary faults of character. In Pāli literature, ten *kilesas* are mentioned: *lobho* (greed), *doso* (hatred), *moho* (delusion), *māno* (pride), *diṭṭhi* (speculative opinion), *vicikicchā* (doubt), *thīnam* (stolidity), *uddhaccam* (excitement, exaltation), *ahirikam* (unconscientiousness), and *anotappam* (shamelessness, or disregard of social censure).[99] The Mahāyāna reckons six *kleças*: *rāga* (sense-desire), *pratigha* (anger), *māna* (pride), *avidyā* (ignorance), *kudṛṣṭi* (wrong views), and *vicikitsā* (doubt: *Dh. S*., lxvii.) The *āsravas*, on the other hand, are more metaphysical and fundamental sins and errors: they were originally three in number, *kām-āsrava*, *bhav-āsrava*, and *avidy-āsrava*; and a fourth, *dṛṣṭy-āsrava*, was added at a later period.[100] It appears that some leaders of the Hīnayāna and the Mahāyāna quietly ignored the more difficult ideal of *āsrava-kṣaya*, which was considered too strenuous for ordinary monks. Only a perfect Buddha and some eminent saints were supposed to possess all the six *abhijñās*. Most monks and teachers are usually spoken of as only *pañc-ābhijñaḥ* (having five *abhijñās*). This latter epithet occurs far more frequently than the other, *ṣaḍ-ab hijñaḥ*, which is indeed a name of the perfect Buddha in the *Mahā-vyutpatti* (Section 1, p. 4). *Āsrava-kṣaya-jñāna* is thus not much in evidence as an *abhijñā* in the Sanskrit treatises. Its old associations with the *nirvāṇa* ideal of the Hīnayānists must have deterred the Māhāyanists from attaching much importance to it.

It is probable that the Buddhists borrowed the three additional *abhijñās*, *divy-çrotra*, *para-citta-jñāna* and *ṛddhi* from the schools of wonder-working ascetics or impostors, that have always flourished in India. The *Yoga-sūtras* belong to a comparatively late period in the history of Indian literature, but they represent a very old tradition. These three Super-knowledges are mentioned in that treatise, which also refers to the knowledge of previous lives (*Yo. Sū*., iii, 18, 19, 21, 41, 42). (Cf. Vyāsa's Commentary on the *Yoga-Sūtras*, iii, 45, p. 164.)[101]

We shall discuss the six *abhijñās* in the order in which they are given in the *Mahā-vyutpatti*.

(1) *Divya-cakṣus* (supernal organ of sight). This *abhijñā* is also called *cyuty-upapāda-jñāna* (the knowledge of death and rebirth) or *cyuty-upapatti-jñāna*.[102]

The powers of the saint, who possesses this *abhijñā*, are described in a sterotyped passage, which is found in several treatises. "A *bodhisattva* observes all beings with his pure and superhuman eye, as they die and are reborn according to their actions. Some of them are handsome, while others are ugly. Some are in a happy state and others are in a wretched condition. Some are excellent and others are mean. Some are reborn after death in painful states and the purgatories, because they had done evil with their body, speech and mind, held wrong views, and reviled the noble saints. Others are reborn in heaven and the worlds of the *devas*, because they had done virtuous deeds with their body, mind and speech, held right views and honoured the noble saints. A *bodhisattva* thus sees all creatures as they die and are reborn, in all their forms, details and characteristics". (*Da. Bhū*., 36 ; *Pr. Pā. Çata*., 1447 ; *Lal. V*., 344.9 ; 375.13.)

A *bodhisattva* surpasses all the *devas* of all the heavens in this respect. He knows the powers which they possess in virtue of their divine Eyes, but they do not know of the wonders of the *bodhisattva's divya-cakṣus*. He sees the death and rebirth of all beings in the ten directions throughout the worlds and universes, which are innumerable like the sands of the Ganges.[103]

C. A. F. Rhys Davids interprets *divya-cakṣus* as "clairvoyance", as it belongs to the *devas*, i.e. "men happily reborn" (I.H.Q., vol. iii, No. 4, p. 709). But it is doubtful if the word *deva* can have this simplified signification and if "clairvoyance" covers all the powers of the *divya-cakṣus* as described above.

(2) *Divya-çrotra* (supernal organ of hearing).

A *bodhisattva* can hear all kinds of human and divine sounds in the whole universe right up to the highest heaven, whether they are voluminous or slight, distinct or indistinct, artificial or natural, distant or near. He enjoys the privilege of hearing the voices of all the Buddhas, who teach and preach in their *kṣetras* (fields). He can hear even the sounds uttered by gadflies, mosquitoes, worms and flies.[104] Kṣemendra relates that Gautama Buddha heard the cries of some merchants at a great distance. He could also hear the prayers of Bimbisāra and Subhadra in the same way, as the author of the *Avadāna-çataka* would have us believe.[105]

The *divya-çrotra* is not included in the threefold knowledge (*tevijjā* ; *tisro vidyāḥ*), as is wrongly supposed by M. Anesaki (ERE, xii, 430*a*).

(3) *Para-citta-jñāna* (the discernment or knowledge of the mind or the thoughts of others).

If a *bodhisattva* has acquired this *abhijñā*, his mind can truly discern the thoughts of other creatures and individuals. He discerns the mind that is subject to sensual desire, and the mind that is free from it. He discerns the mind that is full of hate, and the mind that is free from it. He knows the deluded mind as such and the enlightened mind as such, the sinful mind as such and the sinless mind as such, the small mind as such and the great mind as such. In the same way, he knows exactly if the mind of another person is or is not lofty, boundless, attentive, diffused, concentrated or un-concentrated, liberated or un-liberated, pure or impure, noble or ignoble (*Da. Bhū.*, 35.14 ff.).[106]

(4) *Pūrva-nivās-ānusmṛti-jñāna*. This power is also called *cyuty-upapāda-darçana* (seeing death and birth).

A *bodhisattva* can remember his own previous existences and those of others. He can know the actions, great and small, that were done in those lives.[107] He can thus relate the stories of the previous lives of the great *bodhisattvas*, who have observed wonderful practices and displayed extraordinary energy.[108] He can lead his hearers to faith in Buddha, teach the law of *karma*, and refute the erroneous views of the Eternalists (*çaçvata-dṛṣṭikānām*).[109]

This power has been described in a graphic manner in the *Mtu.*, the *Lal. V.* and the *Da. Bhū.* "A *bodhisattva* remembers one, two, three, four, five, ten, twenty, thirty, forty, fifty, hundred, many hundreds, many thousands of his previous lives. He remembers the æon (*kalpa*) of Involution, the æon of Evolution, and many æons of Involution and Evolution. He remembers a hundred *kalpas*, a thousand *kalpas*, a *koṭi* (ten millions) of *kalpas*, a hundred *koṭis* of *kalpas*, a thousand *koṭis* of *kalpas*, a hundred thousand *koṭis* of *kalpas*, in short, many hundred thousand *niyutas* of *koṭis* of *kalpas*. He remembers thus: 'There I was, had such and such a name, was born in such and such a family. Such was may caste or clan, such was my food, such was the length of my life, such was the duration of my sojourn, such were my experiences of happiness and sorrow. Then I died there and was reborn at that other place; again died there and was reborn here.' Thus he remembers his various previous existences, in all their forms, details and characteristics." This is the Super-knowledge of *pūrva-nivās-ānusmṛti*. Gautama Buddha declares: "I remember immeasurable *niyutas* of *kalpas*, as if I were awakened from a dream."[110]

(5) *Ṛddhi.*—*Ṛddhi* as an *abhijñā* is spoken of as *ṛddhi-vidhi-jñāna*, *ṛddhi-viṣay-ābhijñā* and *ṛddhi-vikurvaṇa*.[111] It also figures among a *bodhisattva's* ten *vaçitās* (powers).

The earliest stereotyped description of *ṛddhi*-wonders was probably borrowed from the Pāli canon.[112] The *M. Vy.*, the *Da. Bhū.* and the *M. S. Al.* added a few other items, and the *Bo. Bhū.* completed the process by describing eighteen different ways, in which *ṛddhi* could be manifested.[113] This was the high-water mark of wonder-mongering in Buddhism. This development is easily explained by the natural tendencies of the uneducated masses and the Indian thinkers' ingrained love of exaggeration. The biographies of Christian and Moslem saints also abound in incredible miracles, which are supposed to indicate superior sanctity. It is possible that some genuine psychic phenomena were observed, and superstition erected the vast superstructure of marvels on this slender basis. The authentic testimony of reliable scientific investigators seems to show that thought-reading, levitation and other strange phenomena can be witnessed on rare occasions in India and other countries.[114] However that may be, the accounts of *ṛddhi*-wonders as given in the Buddhist treatises add a ton of sensationalism to an ounce of truth. The final outcome is the systematic catalogue of miracles in the *Bodhisattva-bhūmi*, which is reproduced below.

The *Dh. S.* does not give even the simple original formula of *ṛddhi*-wonders, which is as follows :—

" He realizes *ṛddhi* in its various aspects. Being one, he becomes many ; having become multiple, he becomes one ; he enjoys the experience of becoming visible or invisible ; he goes unimpeded through a wall, a rampart or a mountain ; he travels cross-legged in the sky, like a winged bird ; he dives up and down the earth as if it were water ; he touches and feels with his hands the sun and the moon, which are so potent and powerful ; he can reach as far as the *brahma*-world with his body." [115] (*Da. Bhū.*, 34.23 ff. ; *M. Vy.*, xv ; *Mtu.*, iii, 409.20 ff.)

The author of the *Bodhisattva-bhūmi* teaches that *ṛddhi* is of two kinds : *pāriṇāmikī* (i.e. of the nature of transformation) and *nairmāṇikī* (i.e. of the nature of creation).

The first kind of *ṛddhi* can be exhibited in sixteen different ways :—

(*a*) A *bodhisattva*, who possesses the requisite qualifications, can shake (*kampana*) a monastery, a house, a village, a town, the realms of purgatory, of the *pretas*, of animals, of men and of *devas*, and even an infinite number of worlds and universes (fol. 26*a*, 7, 2, to fol. 26*b*, 2, 1).

(*b*) *A bodhisattva* can emit flames (*jvalana*) of fire from the upper or lower part of his body, while streams of cold water issue from the other limbs. This wonder is also called the *yamaka-prātihārya* (the miracle of pairs) ; it is described in the *Divy-āvadāna*, the *Māha-vastu*, the *Da. Bhū.*, and the *M. Vy.* Further, a *bodhisattva* can glow with fire and light all over his body and emit rays of different colours, blue, yellow,[116] red, white, scarlet and crystalline (fol. 26*b*, 2, 1, to 3, 2

(*c*) A *bodhisattva* can illumine with light a monastery, a house, etc., as in (*a*) above : *spharaṇa* (3.2 to 4.1).

(*d*) He can show all the worlds and buddha-fields with their inhabitants to the monks and other creatures : *vidarçana* (fol. 26*b*, 4.1 to 6.2).

(*e*) He can transmute the four elements into one another (earth, water, fire and wind) ; and he can change forms into sounds, sounds into smells, and so on. He can even transmute cow-dung and clay into food and clothing (*anyathī-bhāva-karaṇa*), and turn stones and sugar into pearls and precious stones (fol. 26*b*, 6.3 to fol. 27*a*, 4.2).

(*f*) He can pass through walls and other such obstacles, and rise to the highest heaven of the *akaniṣṭha devas* (*gamanāgamana*; fol. 27*a*, 4.2 to 5.3).

(*g*) He can reduce and increase the size and volume of all things. He can make a mountain as small as an atom, and he can make an atom as large as a mountain (*saṃkṣepa-prathana*; fol. 27*a*, 5.3 to 6.1).

(*h*) He can make all things and forms enter into his body, and the spectators, who witness this wonder, also find themselves in the *bodhisattva's* body (*sarva-rūpa-kāya-praveçana*; fol. 27*a*, 6.2 to 7.1.).

(*i*) He can assume the external appearance and ways of speech of different kinds of congregations (*kṣatriyas*, *brahmins*, etc.; *sabhā-gat-opasaṃkrānti*).

(*j*) He can make himself visible or invisible to other persons, and appear or disappear a hundred times, a thousand times (*āvirbhāva-tirobhāva*).

(*k*) He can control and dominate all the creatures in such a way that they come, go, stop, and speak as he wills (*vaçitva-karaṇa*).

(*l*) He can control and surpass the *ṛddhi* of others, except the Buddhas or other *bodhisattvas*, who are superior or equal to him (*pararddhy-abhibhava*).

(*m*) He can confer intelligence and understanding on those who lack it (*pratibhā-dāna*).

(*n*) He can confer Mindfulness on those who need it (*smṛti-dāna*).

(*o*) He bestows material comforts on all creatures (*pratiprasrabdhi-sukham*; fol. 28*a*, 1, 1.2). They can then hear the preaching without being troubled by disease and other calamities (*sukha-dāna*; fol. 28*a*, 1).

(*p*) He can emit rays, which allay and assuage the torments of the creatures suffering in the purgatories. He does good to all beings in this way (*raçmi-pramokṣa*).

The second species of *ṛddhi* (*nairmāṇikī*) is manifested in two ways:—

(*a*) A *bodhisattva* can create a phantom body, which may be similar to or different from himself (*kāya-nirmāṇam*; fol. 28*a*, 6.2). Such an illusory body is created in different aspects for the welfare of the beings. It may be intended only to be seen by others, or it may fulfil all its natural functions. Çūra relates how a saint created a phantom monkey (*Jā. Mā*, p 147).

(*b*) A *bodhisattva* can create a voice, which preaches the doctrine. Such a magical voice is harmonious and clear. When it is associated with the *bodhisattva* himself (*sva-sambaddha*), he uses it to rebuke those who are spiritually slack and negligent. It may also be associated with other persons, or it may not be associated with anything or any person (*par-asambaddha*, *asambaddha*; fol. 28*b*, 3.1–2–3).

By means of these two powers, a *bodhisattva* converts the people to the doctrine of the Buddha, and also renders service to all afflicted creatures in many different ways.

The chief object of *ṛddhi*-wonders is said to be the conversion of the people. Such miracles facilitate the preacher's task of converting the living beings to the faith of the Buddha.[117] "Conversion by the *ṛddhi*-wonder," declares Vasubandhu in his usual laconic style.[118] Ordinary persons are thus quickly induced to listen to the teaching.[119] A *bodhisattva* displays these powers for the good of the creatures.[120] Such deeds may produce the thought of *bodhi* in an eye-witness and induce him to take the vow of becoming a *bodhisattva*.[121] An unconverted person may even attain this stage by hearing of the inconceivably wonderful miraculous power of a Buddha or a *bodhisattva*.[122] A *bodhisattva* always associates such wonders with his propaganda, as was done by the famous *bodhisattva* Sadāparibhūta.[123] The exhibition of miracles is indeed one of the twenty-seven means of ripening the creatures that should be employed by a *bodhisattva*.[124] Gautama Buddha himself set the example, when he converted Mahākāçyapa and his two brothers by means of five hundred miracles.[125] Another Buddha emitted glorious rays from his body or wrought other miracles, so that the people may be filled with joy on seeing his power.[126] Every Buddha obtains stupendous *ṛddhi*-power as a necessary adjunct of his duties as a preacher, and it is one of his ten imperative duties to perform great miracles.[127] A *bodhisattva* exerts himself more assiduously for his spiritual improvement, when he can plainly see all the terrors and miseries of the purgatories by his *ṛddhi*-power.[128] He can also refute and confound rival teachers by working miracles, as Gautama Buddha did on a memorable occasion.[129]

Besides this general purpose of *ṛddhi*, the power may also be employed in other ways. Perhaps the most frequent exhibition of *ṛddhi*, that is mentioned in the Buddhist treatises, is the feat of flying through the air in order to reach a certain destination.

The author of the *M. S. Al.* indeed restricts the use of *ṛddhi* to the purpose of going to the place, where the people, who should be converted or taught, are to be found.[130] Many saints are said to fly through the air on different occasions.[131] The monks, who came to Rājagṛha to attend the Council, flew through the air.[132] A *bodhisattva* can also use his *ṛddhi*-power for other purposes. He can create phantom forms of animals or human beings.[133] He can come and go anywhere in the entire universe.[134] He can hypnotise other persons and make them see things according to his desire.[135] He can visit different buddha-fields and heavens without any difficulty.[136] He can rise in the air in order to prove his sanctity.[137] He can prolong his life to an æon of time.[138] He can do good to others by healing the sick, giving sight to the blind and the power of hearing to the deaf, clothing the naked, feeding the hungry, releasing those who are in bonds, and bestowing Mindfulness on the heedless sinners.[139]

(6) *Āsrava-kṣaya-jñāna* (the knowledge of the destruction of the *āsravas*). This word, *āsrava*, is found in two forms, *āsrava* and *āçrava*, e.g. *āsrava* at *Pr. Pā. Aṣṭa.*, 330; *M. S. Al.*, 105.3; *Ava. Ça.*, ii, 143.7; *Da. Bhū*, 78.9; *Mdh.*, 118.10., etc.; *āçrava* at *Lal. V.*, 348.20, 376.11, 405.21; *Mtu.*, i, 147.1, iii, 337; *Su. Vy.*, 76.3, etc. This word has been variously translated as follows :—

T. W. Rhys Davids and W. Stede : "that which flows (out or onto), outflow and influx, the intoxicating extract or secretion of a tree or flower, technical term for certain specified ideas, which intoxicate the mind (bemuddle it)" (Pāli Dicy. s.v. *āsava*).

Böhtlingk and Roth : "Leiden, Fehler, Laster, Gebrechen, Fluss, Strom" (Skt. Dicy. Pbg.).

Monier Williams : "Distress, affliction, pain" (Skt. Dicy., 162*a*).

M. Walleser : "Ausfluss" (*Pr. Pā.* tr., p. 9).

O. C. J. Rosenberg : "Die Unruhen" (Probleme, ii, 240).

E. Burnouf : "Les souillures" (Introdn., p. 379, line 18, edition 1844).

L. de la Vallée Poussin : (1) "Les depravations" (Le Muséon, 1911, p. 159). (2) "Les Passions" (ERE., viii, 256*a*).

T. W. and C. A. F. Rhys Davids : "Deadly Floods or Taints" (Dialogues, i, 93).

H Kern : "Defiling passions" (Manual, p. 60).

L. Feer: "Les mauvais désirs, la souillure morale, proprement les courants qui viennent du dehors au dedans ou vont du dedans au dehors" (*Ava. Ça.* tr., p. 477).

J. Masuda: "Die Leidenschaften" (Idealismus, p. 45).

Csoma de Körös: "Imperfections" (Csoma, p. 49).

R. S. Copleston: "Corruptions" (Buddhism, p. 93).

S. Lévi: "Les Écoulements" (*M. S. Al.* tr., p. 75 note).

Lord Chalmers: "Cankers: Running sores or neoplasms of character, with their metastases of evil (*Majjh.*, tr., i, 2).

R. O. Franke: "Die falsche, weltliche Daseinsauffassung" (*Dīgha*, p. 82.30).

E. Max Müller: (1) "The vices, affections, appetites, passions" (S.B.E., X, part 1, pp. 13, 14). (2) "Appetites" (*Dh. S.*, p. 52).

Sīlācāra: "Banes" (*Majjh.* tr., p. 11).

H. Neumann: "Der Wahn" (*Majjh.*, tr., ii, 366).

P. Oltramare: "Les infections" (Bouddhique, p. 116).

P. E. Foucaux: "Les corruptions" (*Lal. V.* tr., p. 292).

C. A. F. Rhys Davids: "Intoxicating Drugs" (Psycholo p. 127).

H. Beckh: "Ein die Fesselung der Seele bewirkender Wahn" (Buddhismus, ii, 134).

D. T. Suzuki: (1) "Evil leakages" (Zen Essays, p. 50 (2) "Impure outflows of the mind" (Studies, p. 391).

H. Jacobi: "Sinful inclinations" (S.B.E., xlv, p. 81).

A. B. Keith: "Infection, defilement, intoxicants" (Philosophy, pp. 128, 333).

It appears that the earlier Sanskrit treatises employed the form *āçrava*, while the later writers preferred *āsrava*.

The root *sru* means "to flow, stream, trickle, ooze, drip, drop, distil, exude" (Skt. Dicy. M.W. 1155*c*). Böhtlingk and Roth are of opinion that the form *āçrava* is incorrect ("schlechte schreibart"). As F. Max Müller has pointed out, the word *āsrāva* occurs in the *Atharva-veda*, 1, 2, 4 (page 1)[140]:

Eva rogaṃ c-āsrāvaṃ c-āntas tiṣṭhatu muñja it.

It is translated as "a running, a sore" by F. Max Müller. In the *Suçruta*, it means "flow, issue, running discharge" (Skt. Dicy. M.W. 162*a*). According to M. Williams, *āsrava* also means "the foam on boiling rice, and a door opening into water, allowing the stream to descend through it" (Skt. Dicy. 162*a*). The term *āsrava* is used by the Jainas to denote "the influx of *karma*-matter into the soul". It is one of the seven *tattvas* in Jaina metaphysics (*jīva*, *ajīva*, *āsrava*, *bandha*, *etc.*).[141] The *Dravya-saṅgraha* speaks of *bhāv-āsrava* and *dravy-āsrava*, and defines them thus: "That activity of the soul, whereby *karma* flows into it, is said by the Jina to be *bhāv-āsrava* (subjective influx). . . Matter of various colours, etc., which flows (*āsavadi*) into the active soul is to be known as *dravyāsrava* (objective influx)."[142] The *Tattvārtha-sūtra* (vi, 1.2) declares that *āsrava* means "action by body, mind, and speech".[143] Muni Ratnacandraji explains *āsrava* as "a door, a sluice for the inflow of *karma*" (*Ardha-Māgadhī* Dictionary). H. T. Colebrooke says: "*Āsrava* is the impulse, called *Yoga* or 'attention', by which the soul participates in the movement of its various bodies (*audarika*, etc.). As a door opening into the water makes the stream descend through it, so actions flow in upon the soul by the pipe of *yoga*; or again, as a wet garment exposed to the wind collects the dust from every part, so the soul, wet with previous sins, on all sides collects actions which are brought to it by *yoga*. *Āsrava* is good or evil, as it is directed to right or wrong objects. *Āsrava* has also been defined as 'the action of the senses which impels the soul towards external objects'."[144] The *Uttarādhyayana-sūtra* mentions *āsrava* as one of the nine *tattvas* (principles or categories) and also speaks of five *āsravas*.[145] A saint is said to have annihilated the *āsravas*, and the prince Balaçrī or Mṛgaputra is described as one, who prevented the arising of the *āsravas* through all bad channels. H. Jacobi thus translates and explains the word in these passages: "the influx of *karman*", "sinful inclinations", "that which causes the soul to be affected by sins" (S.B.E., vol. xlv, pp. 81, 99, 154). H. Jacobi is of opinion that the Buddhists borrowed the term *āsrava* from the Jainas, as the latter employed the word in its literal sense.[146] But the meaning attached to the word by the Buddhists is very different from the Jaina category of *āsrava*. The figurative sense of "extract, juice, beverage" originated in the natural development of the language, and the Buddhists probably adopted it without having recourse to the Jaina scriptures.

Āsava, meaning "intoxicating beverage", occurs in several Pāli passages: e.g. "*merayo nāma pupphāsavo phalāsavo madhvāsavo guḷāsavo* (*Vinaya*, iv. 110, line 15). (Cf. also *Jātaka*, vi, 9, line 12; iv, 222, line 19.) But it means "discharge from a sore" in some passages, e.g. *duṭṭharuko āsavaṃ deti*" (*Aṅguttara*, i, 127, lines 3–4). Buddhaghoṣa does not define the exact meaning of the word. The *Attha-sālinī* suggests several different explanations (page 48, lines 9 ff.). "*Āsavas* are things which flow (*āsavanti*), i.e. flow or arise from the senses and the mind. Or *āsavas* may be defined as things, which, as states, 'flow' up to the stage of adoption, and which, as in space, flow as far as the topmost plane of existence. The meaning is that they occur keeping these states within that extent of space. The prefix 'ā' in *āsava* is indeed used in the sense of 'keeping within'. Or, as the juices of the *madira* fruits (*Bassia latifolia*), etc., become intoxicants by fermentation for a length of time, so certain states, which are like these intoxicants, are termed *āsavas*. . . . Or, *āsavas* are those states, which fructify or beget the pains of the ocean of births of long duration" (The Expositor, i, 63–4). A fanciful etymology is given by a commentator of the *Pr. Pā. Çata.*: *āsaṃsāraṃ çravanti* (*Pr. Pā. Çata.*, p. 3, note 2: they flow as far as, or as long as, transmigratory existence). It has also been suggested that *āsrava* is connected with *āçraya*.[147] But this is not sound etymology. E. J. Thomas has suggested that Buddhaghoṣa derives the word from the root "*su*" (to press) or "*pa-su*" (to beget).[148]

The Tibetan equivalent is *zag-pa* (*M. Vy.*, p. 10). S. C. Das translates *zag-pa med-pa* (=*anāsrava*) as "that which does not flow out", and he renders *zag-pa* as "depravity, sin" (Tib. Dicy., 1089*b*). According to J. Eitel, the Chinese translate *āsrava* by a word meaning "stream", "the stream of transmigration" (p. 21*a*).

Several other derivatives from the root *sru* are met with in Buddhist Sanskrit literature: e.g. *prasrāva* (= urine, *Ava. Ça.* i, 245.2—*Kṣem. Latā.*, ii, 513.15); *srāvaṇa* (of a wound, *M. S. Al.* 30.15).

It seems to have escaped the attention of most lexicographers and translators that the Sanskrit form *āsava* (identical with the Pāli word) occurs in the writings of Çūra and Kṣemendra. It means "intoxicating beverage", when it is employed in its ordinary signification. As a philosophical term, it occurs after such words as *rāga* and *viṣaya-bhoga*, and thus seems to have the same connotation as *āsrava*: e.g. *sur-āsava-çīdhu-maireya-madhu* (*Jā. Mā.*, 101.9); *vadan-āsava*, *rāg-āsava* (*Kṣem. Latā.*, i, 935.9: ii, 1021.18).

Thus it may be inferred that *āsrava*, derived from the root *sru*, means "intoxicating beverage", and not "canker" or "stream".

Āsrava-kṣaya-jñāna is an important term in Buddhist philosophy. It is not only the sixth *abhijñā*, but also one of the ten *balas* (Powers) and the four *vaiçāradyas* (Grounds of Self-confidence) that appertain to a perfect Buddha (*M. Vy.*, Sections 7, 8; *Dh. S.*, Sections 76, 77). Gautama Buddha is said to have cried on attaining Enlightenment: "Dried-up *āsravas* do not flow again" (*āsravāḥ* here = "streams or running sores"). In the *Lal. V.* (348.20), *āsrava* is regarded as almost synonymous with *duḥkha*, and the conception of *āsrava* thus becomes a fundamental idea in the philosophical system of Buddhism. Gautama Buddha is said to have discovered the origin and cessation of the *āsravas*, just as he discovered the origin and cessation of *duḥkha* (pain, evil). The eightfold Way is also said to lead to the cessation of the *āsravas*. The indentification of the *āsravas* with *duḥkha* naturally led to the notion that only a perfect Buddha knows that he has destroyed all the *āsravas*. Ordinary monks and nuns could not be expected to possess the sixth *abhijñā*, "*Āsrava-kṣaya-jñāna*". It was therefore excluded from the formula of the five *abhijñās*, as has already been indicated above.

In the oldest Pāli texts, three *āsavas* are mentioned (*Majjh.* ii, p. 39, lines 3 ff.—*Dīgha* iii, 216.9, etc.). These were *kāma*, *bhava* and *avijjā*. This old formula is found in the Sanskrit *Da. Bhū.* (18.5), which speaks only of these three. But the later Pāli texts added a fourth *āsava*, "*diṭṭhi*," and placed it third on the list (*Vinaya*, iii, 5, lines 31 ff.—*Dhammasaṅgaṇi*, Section 1448 and Sections 1096–1100). This development is also reflected in Buddhist Sanskrit literature. The *Lal. V.* mentions these four *āsravas*, but puts *dṛṣṭi* last (p. 348.21). The *Da. Bhū.* speaks of four *bandhanāni* (bonds), from which a *bodhisattva* almost frees himself in the third *bhūmi* (p. 36). These bonds are the same as the three old *āsravas*, *kāma*, *bhava* and *avidyā*, and a fourth, *rūpa* (form). But the author has not altogether forgotten the Pāli tradition, as he immediately adds that a *bodhisattva* has previously destroyed the bonds arising from *dṛṣṭi*. He thus attempts to substitute *rūpa* for *dṛṣṭi* as the new *āsrava*. The aversion of the Mahāyānists to the ideal of *nirvāṇa* may have led to the invention of the term *bandhana* instead of *āsrava*, which was closely and indissolubly associated with the old conception of *nirvāṇa* and *arhatship*. It is presumably for the same reason that the *āsravas* are not enumerated at all in the *Dh. S.* and the *M. Vy.*

A *bodhisattva* knows if and when he himself or some other person has succeeded in destroying the *āsravas*. He understands the means for attaining this result. He also knows that other persons are puffed up with conceit, when they arrive at this stage. He himself knows all this, but he does not finally realise the *abhijñā* known as *āsrava-kṣaya*,[149] as he does not wish to enter *nirvāṇa*. He lives in this world of the *āsravas*, but he is not soiled and polluted by it. He is thus in the world but not of it. He works in and for the world of sin and sorrow, but transcends it in spirit.[150] This is his greatest glory and his duty.[151] The author of the *Bo. Bhū.* here expounds the true and developed doctrine with regard to a *bodhisattva*'s ideal of life. But an earlier writer has not thought of making such reservations in respect of *āsrava-kṣaya* and its results. The *Pr. Pā. Çata.* simply reproduces the old Pāli formula of *arhatship* in describing the sixth *abhijñā*. "Through the destruction of the *āsravas*, he knows and realises the undefiled deliverance of the mind and heart, and abides in it. Rebirth is destroyed; the higher spiritual life has been lived. What had to be done has been accomplished. After this life, there will be no Beyond" (*Pra. Pā. Çata.*, p. 1448.2 ff.). It may be inferred that the Sanskritists only gradually came to realise the full import of *āsrava-kṣaya* and its implications with reference to a *bodhisattva*'s career.

The four *āsravas* may now be considered in detail. (*a*) *Kāma*. This word has been variously translated as "love of sensual pleasure", "desire," "lust," "passion," "sensuality." It may be rendered as (1) "love of sense-pleasures", and (2) "love of sensual pleasures, sensuality, lust." It refers to the gratification of the five senses in general, and also to sensuality (carnal lust) in particular.

As a general term, *kāma* is spoken of as five-fold. There are five *kāma-guṇas*,[152] corresponding to the five *indriyas* (sense-organs): the eye (*chakṣus*), the ear (*çrotra*), the olfactory organ (*ghrāṇa*), the tongue (*jihvā*), and the body or skin (*kāya*). These five "factors or elements of *kāma*" are referred to in several passages of Buddhist Sanskrit literature.[153] The terms *kāma-rāga* (love of Pleasure) and *kāma-cchanda* are also met with.[154] *Kāma-cchanda* is the technical name for the first of the five *nīvaraṇas* (Hindrances), which is indeed identified with *kām-āsava* in the *Dhammasaṅgaṇi* (Section 1153, p. 204). The external objects, which are perceived or enjoyed by the five sense-organs, are called *rūpa* (form), *çabda* (sound), *gandha* (odour), *rasa* (savour) and *spraṣṭavya* or *sparça* (tangible things) respectively.[155] The sense-organs and the external objects, taken together in pairs, are called *āyatanas* (spheres of sense). But *manas* (the mind) is spoken of in connection with the *kāma-guṇas* only in a few passages.[156] It may be stated here, for the sake of completeness, that *manas* is regarded as the sixth "sense-organ" (*indriya*), and the mental objects, ideas or phenomena perceived by it are called *dharmas*. Thus there are altogether twelve *āyatanas*.

It is almost impossible to give an adequate idea of the vehemence and pertinacity, with which the Buddhist writers have preached the duty of curbing, controlling, suppressing, crushing and conquering the senses. They are never tired of repeating themselves on this theme, and they have hit upon many apt similes and metaphors to embellish their homilies.

In view of the crucial importance of the subject, no apology is perhaps needed for two lengthy quotations from Buddhist Sanskrit treatises.

The Buddhist writers have found several opportunities to inveigh against the *kāmas* (in the plural), when they record the events of Gautama Buddha's life. The *bodhisattva* Siddhārtha, who is known as Gautama Buddha after attaining Enlightenment, declaims against the *kāmas* on five important occasions. He is disgusted with the worldly life of selfish pleasure and decides to leave his home at night. He witnesses the beautiful women of the palace, as they lie asleep in different postures. This sight moves him to the following outburst against the *kāmas* :

"Oh how foolish are those, who are enmeshed in the dense darkness of delusion. They think that there is some good in the pleasures of sense, which are really worthless, even as the birds placed in a cage can never escape from it (literally, "never obtain egress").

These pleasures, in them fools are slain, as those, who are condemned to death, (are killed) in a slaughter-house.

These pleasures,—ignorant fools take delight in them, as they may like beautifully painted vases, which are filled with filth.

These pleasures,—in them fools are drowned, like elephants in the water (of rivers, pools, etc.).

These pleasures,—in them fools find joy, as swine (wallow) in filth.

These pleasures—fools cleave to them, like dogs to a heap of bones.[157]

These pleasures—fools fall into them, like moths into the flame of a lamp.

These pleasures—fools are caught with them, like monkeys with smearing ointment.[158]

These pleasures—in them fools are destroyed, like the fish brought up in a net.

These pleasures—in them fools are cut to pieces, like rams on the wooden floor of a slaughter-house.

These pleasures—on them fools are impaled, like malefactors on the point of a pike (or stake).

These pleasures—in them fools perish, like old elephants in a bog.

These pleasures—in them fools are wrecked, like shipwrecked persons on the wide seas.

These pleasures—into them fools fall, as the blind (literally, "born blind") fall over a high precipice.

These pleasures—in them fools come to their end, like water that has gone into the chasm leading to the nether world.

These pleasures—in them fools are choked with smoke, like the great Earth during the dissolution of the Universe at the close of the æon.

These pleasures—by these fools are kept in a whirl, like the potter's pierced wheel.

These pleasures—in them fools go astray and wander about, like blind persons (literally, "born blind") in the interior of a mountain.

These pleasures—by them fools are made to turn round and round, like dogs tied in a leash.[159]

These pleasures—through them fools wilt and wither, like grass and the trees in the hot season.

These pleasures—in them fools wane (in strength), like the moon in the dark fortnight.

These pleasures—by them fools are devoured, as the serpents (are devoured) by Garuḍa.

These pleasures—by them fools are swallowed up, as a ship (is swallowed up) by a huge leviathan (sea-monster).[160]

These pleasures—by these fools are despoiled, as a trading-caravan (is despoiled) by a band of robbers.

These pleasures—by these fools are broken, as trees (are broken) by the wind.

These pleasures—by them fools are slain, as the living creatures (are slain) by snakes.

These pleasures—the fools, who regard them as agreeable and delicious, are wounded by them, as by the edge of a razor-blade, besmeared with honey.

These pleasures—by them fools are carried away, like logs of wood by a flood of water.

These pleasures—with them fools play, like children with their own urine and excrements.

These pleasures—by them fools are made to turn round,[161] like elephants with the driver's goad (or hook).

These pleasures—by them fools are cheated,[162] as simple-minded folk (are cheated) by rogues.

These pleasures—in them fools throw away their roots of merit, as gamblers (throw away) their wealth.

These pleasures—by them fools are devoured, as travelling merchants (are devoured) by the female ogres". (*Lal. V.*, pp. 206 ff.)

Here we see that the author is terribly in earnest and piles up many telling similes in order to warn a *bodhisattva* of the dire dangers that lurk in the pleasures of the senses. Certainly no one, who has once read this passage, can ever forget it.

The *bodhisattva* Siddhārtha's interview with King Bimbisāra of Rājagṛha furnishes another occasion for an eloquent sermon on the evils of Pleasure. The King tries to dissuade the young *bodhisattva* from his purpose, offers him half the kingdom and promises to aid him in conquering a new kingdom, if he prefers that course. The *bodhisattva* thanks the well-meaning friend, and replies in these burning words (*Buddha-carita*, xi, 7 ff., pp. 86 ff.):—

"I know the danger of old age and death. I wish to obtain final Release, and have adopted this mode of life. I have left my beloved kinsfolk in tears (literally, "with tears on their faces"). Of course, with even greater determination have I abandoned Pleasures, which cause Evil.

I fear Pleasures (literally, "external objects of sense") much more than I fear serpents, or thunderbolts fallen from the sky, or even a fire fanned by the wind (literally, "flames associated with the wind"). Pleasures (the *kāmas*) are evanescent ; they rob a person of his possessions of spiritual Merit[163]; they are hollow and illusory in this world. They delude the minds of men, even if they are only hoped for; they can do so in a much greater degree, if they abide in the mind.

The slaves of Pleasures (literally "those conquered by Pleasures") do not obtain happiness, even in the heaven of the *devas*, still less in this world of mortals. He, who thirsts for Pleasures, cannot be satisfied, as Fire, the friend of Aeolus, has never enough of fuel.

There is no evil in the world like Pleasures; but people are addicted to them through folly. A wise man, who is afraid of evil, knows this truth; how then should he himself long for what is evil?

Having obtained possession of the sea-robed Earth,[164] they (i.e. kings) wish to conquer the other shore of the great ocean. People are never satisfied with Pleasures, as the ocean has never enough of the river-water that falls into it.

For *Māndhāt̤r*, it rained gold from heaven; he conquered the four continents and oceans; he won even half of *Çakra's* throne; still he was not satisfied with the things that give Pleasure.[165]

Nahuṣa enjoyed the pleasure of ruling over the *devas* in heaven, when *Çata-kratu* (*Indra*) had gone into hiding for fear of *Vṛtra*; in his pride, he employed the great sages (*ṛṣis*) as his litter-bearers; but he was not satisfied with Pleasures and so fell (from his high estate).[166]

King *Purūravas*, the son of *Iḍā*, entered the third heaven, and got the famous goddess *Urvaçī* into his power; but he was still not satisfied with Pleasures. In his greed, he wished to rob the sages of their gold and so fell into perdition.[167]

Who would put his trust in these things that give Pleasure? They were transferred from *Bali* to *Mahendra*, from *Mahendra* to *Nahuṣa*, and back again from *Nahuṣa* to *Indra*. In heaven and on earth, they are indeed exposed to many vicissitudes.[168]

These are Enemies, which we call "Pleasures". Who would seek them? They have ruined even the ascetics, who had really other things to do, and who were clad in the bark of trees, lived on roots, fruits and water, and wore matted hair as long as snakes.[169]

Even the thought of these Pleasures is inauspicious and brings about Death. What (should one say) then of the lawless persons, who are habitually addicted to them?[170] For the sake of these Pleasures, *Ugrāyudha* met his death at the hands of *Bhīṣma*, though he was formidable, when armed with his weapons.[171]

One should reflect that Pleasures give very little delight and yield no satisfaction, even if one possesses them up to the culminating point. Righteous men despise them and they are certainly sinful. Who would take this poison, which is named "Pleasure"?[172]

Those, who are masters of their minds, should give up Pleasures. They learn of the misery of those people, whose hearts are set on Pleasure, and who are engaged in agriculture and other similar pursuits. And they (see) the happiness of those who are indifferent to Pleasures.

If the slave of Pleasure succeeds in his desires, it should be regarded as a calamity for him. When the desires are gratified, he falls into Pride. Through Pride, he does what should not be done, and he does not do what should be done. Then he is stricken and goes to a miserable destiny (in rebirth).

What man, who is master of his mind, can find delight in Pleasures, which are obtained and kept with much trouble, and then cheat us and again disappear? They are indeed like borrowed things.

What man, who is master of his mind, would love Pleasures, which resemble a firebrand made of a wisp of straw. Those, who feel a hankering for them, seek them and take them. But if they do not let them go, they come to grief.[173]

What man, who is master of his mind, would love Pleasures? They are like angry and fierce snakes. Those weak-willed men, who are bitten by them in their inmost souls, are destroyed and do not find happiness.[174]

What man, who is master of his mind, would love Pleasures? They are like a skeleton of old bones. Dogs feel the pangs of hunger for bones.[175] Even so, those, who enjoy Pleasures, are never satisfied. What man, who is master of his mind, would love Pleasures? They cause misery, as they have to be shared with kings and thieves, and also with fire and water[176] (i.e. may be destroyed by them). They are like meat, that has been thrown away.

What man, who is master of his mind, would love Pleasures? Those, who are addicted to them, are exposed to dangers on all sides, from their relatives and their enemies.

Pleasures are indeed death-dealing things, like the Spheres of Sense.[177]

What man, who is master of his mind, would love Pleasures?

Those, who strive to get them, come to a miserable end in the mountains and the forests, or on the waters of the ocean.

Pleasures resemble the fruits that hang on the topmost branch of a tree. . . ."

The poet continues his scathing invective and compares Pleasures to glowing cinders, to the joyful sensations of a dream, to a stake for impaling criminals, to a sword, and to ferocious beasts.[178] He then proceeds and explains the philosophy of the simple life of asceticism :—

"Antelopes are lured to their death by songs ; moths fall into the flame (fire) for the sake of the beauty of form ; the fish, avid of flesh, swallows the iron-hook. Thus Pleasures bear evil fruit.

As to the idea that 'Pleasures are enjoyments', they cannot be reckoned as enjoyable objects, when they are well scrutinised. Clothes and other things should be regarded only as remedies for pain (antidotes to pain).

Water is desired to quench thirst, and food is sought in the same way for appeasing hunger. A house (is needed) to keep off the wind, heat and rain ; and clothes serve to cover the nakedness of the body and keep off the cold.

Sleep serves to counteract drowsiness. A carriage allays the fatigue of a journey. A seat obviates the necessity of standing. Bathing gives cleanliness and the strength that comes of good health.[179]

The things that give pleasure are therefore only the means of alleviating pain for human beings ; they are not objects of enjoyment.[180]

What wise man would admit that he enjoys them, when they are used only as remedies?

A man, who is burning with bilious fever, may think that the application of cold is an enjoyment ; but he is only intent on finding the method for assuaging pain. Such a man may indeed have the idea that Pleasures are enjoyments.[181]

Pleasures have no absolute quality[182] of their own ; for this reason also, I cannot think that they are enjoyments. The same conditions (or things), as point the way to happiness, bring misery again.

Heavy garments and aloe-wood give pleasure in the cold, but cause pain in the heat. The moonbeams and sandal-wood are pleasant in the heat, but painful in the cold".[183] (*B. Ct.* xi, 7–42.)

Açvaghoṣa thus puts some positive arguments into the *bodhisattva's* mouth, and does not merely indulge in glowing rhetoric on this theme.

When the *bodhisattva* arrives at *Gayā-çīrṣa*, he thinks of three new similes on the subject of the *kāmas*. He says to himself: "There are monks (*çramaṇas*) and priests (*brāhmaṇas*), who have not freed their bodies and minds from Pleasures.[184] They delight in Pleasures; they are attached to Pleasures; they are intent on Pleasures; they lust after Pleasures; they thirst for Pleasures; they are deluded and infatuated by Pleasures; they are consumed by Pleasures; their attachment to Pleasures never ceases. Further, they experience acute, sharp, bitter, harsh and disagreeable sensations of pain, which consume their bodies and torment their souls. Thus they are incapable of fully realising the special insight into transcendental, noble knowledge. This is just as if a man, who wishes to have fire and light, and seeks for them, were to take two moist pieces of wood and rub them against each other after throwing them into the water. It is impossible for him to produce fire and light. Even such are these monks and priests". In the second simile, the *bodhisattva* compares the slaves of Pleasure to a man, who should try to produce fire by the attrition of two moist pieces of wood on dry land. In the third simile, he speaks of a saint who has renounced Pleasure, and compares him to a wise man, who tries to get fire by the friction of two dry pieces of wood in a dry place. His efforts are crowned with success. (*Lal. V.*, pp. 246 ff.–*Mtu.* ii, 121 ff.)

When the *bodhisattva* Siddhārtha enters on a conflict with *Māra*, the *deva* of Desire and Death, he carries on a lively debate with him and his daughters, and expatiates on the evils and dangers of the *kāmas*. He points out that Pleasures are rooted in evil and pain.[185] They only intensify craving and lust, as salt water makes a man more thirsty than before.[186] The beautiful bodies of fair women are really infernal machines of Evil, full of filth and impurity.[187] Even the pure and ethereal bodies of the celestial nymphs are transient and must perish.[188] Pleasures are fleeting like autumn clouds.[189] They destroy a man's spiritual Merit, as lightning can burn up a field of ripe rice.[190] A *bodhisattva* despises them, as if they were a heap of burning, ill-smelling dried excrements.[191]

Finally, when the *bodhisattva* Siddhārtha has attained Enlightenment and begins to preach his doctrine, he condemns sensual

Pleasures as vulgar, ignoble and degrading in his very first sermon.[192] Thus we find that he rejects and repudiates Pleasure at each step in his career from the eventful night of Renunciation to the still more eventful night of Enlightenment. On five occasions he utters the warning, like an ever-recurring refrain : " Beware of the *kāmas*."

In the *Divy-āvadāna*, aversion to the six-fold pleasures of sense (including those associated with *manas*, the mind) is regarded as the sum and substance of Gautama Buddha's teaching.[193] When Buddha preaches a very short sermon for the benefit of Pūrṇa, he exhorts him not to take delight in attractive forms, sounds, odours, savours, tangible things and mental objects. That ideal is declared to be essential to liberation (*nirvāṇa*). Even *manas* is here regarded as a source of evil, and the number of the dangerous *kāma-guṇas* is thus raised to six.

The Buddhist writers had thus ample authority in Buddha's alleged deeds and words for their vehement denunciation of all kinds of sense-pleasures. The tradition was maintained by a long line of teachers from Açvaghoṣa to Çāntideva, who repeated the stock similes and the familiar arguments. They sometimes added a few touches of foul cynicism, and imagined that they had improved upon their predecessors. Açvaghoṣa has inserted several homilies against the *kāmas* in his poem, the *Saundarānanda-kāvya*, which relates the conversion of Nanda to the monastic ideal of Buddhism. Nanda was madly in love with his consort Sundarī, and could not think of becoming a monk. As the Buddhist teachers did not contemplate the possibility of sublimating, ennobling and idealising the sentiment of love, they could only condemn and combat it as a vile and dangerous passion. They saw only bestial lust in human love.

According to the legend, Gautama Buddha took Nanda up to *svarga*, and showed him the celestial nymphs, who were immeasurably more beautiful than Sundarī. Nanda forgot his wife and was now infatuated with the nymphs ; but these could be won only through severe austerities. Nanda began to practise penance with the ultimate object of winning a nymph and enjoying sensual pleasure. There is a touch of cynical irony in this situation. He thus tasted the higher joys of the ascetic life, though his motive was ignoble. He was taunted and rebuked by the other monks for practising penance with a worldly aim. The upshot was that Nanda really appreciated the merits of the monks'

Rule and was weaned from his love for his wife. He joined the Order of Monks.

This story gives Açvaghoṣa several opportunities of putting edifying words into Gautama Buddha's mouth. His views and exhortations may be summarised as follows :—

The senses (*indriyas*) are by nature fickle and restive. They must cause pain always and everywhere. They smite both the body and the mind. The five *indriyas* may be compared to arrows besmeared with the poison of wrong thoughts. Carking care is their feathered part, and their fruit is Pleasure. They fly in the firmament of material objects. They slay human beings like deer, when Eros, the hunter, shoots them at the heart. They can be parried by means of the armour of Mindfulness. When one sees a living form, one should not think if it is a man or a woman. Desire ruins the pleasure-loving world ; it is a false and treacherous friend. If the mind feels no inclination for the objects that give pleasure, it cannot be enslaved by them. As both fuel and the wind are necessary for the burning fire, so both external objects and the inclination of the mind [194] must be present before sinful attachment can arise. The same object can produce different feelings in the minds of different persons : love, repulsion, indifference or disgust. The mind is therefore the prime cause of slavery to sensual pleasure. One should always be vigilant and watchful in controlling and restraining the five sense-organs. Even if a person should be reborn in *svarga* as the reward of good deeds, he must descend again to Earth after the lapse of a certain period of time, as a traveller comes home from strange climes. He may be reborn as an animal, a *preta*, or a denizen of a purgatory. He must then be tormented by the memory of the pleasures that he had enjoyed in *svarga*. Even the great *devas* must leave *svarga* sooner or later through the power of *karma*, and thus suffer terrible agonies. The pleasures of *svarga* abide not for ever : one should therefore aim at obtaining final Liberation. A soul, which is enmeshed in Ignorance, must sooner or later return to Earth, as a bird, which is tied to a string, must come back even after a long flight from home. As a leper obtains no relief by the application of warmth, even so a sensual man finds no happiness by indulging in pleasures. If some remnants of Desire should remain in the mind, as fire sometimes lies concealed under the ashes, then they should be eradicated by spiritual cultivation (*bhāvanā*)."

(*Saund. Kā.*, ix, 43 ff.—xi, 32 ff.—xiii, 30 ff.—xv, 5 ff.)

Other Buddhist writers have also warned a *bodhisattva* against the snares of Pleasure. A *bodhisattva* should know the misery and danger and disadvantages of the *kāmas*.[195] They are like the water seen in a mirage in the hot weather.[196] They expose a person to legal punishments and penalties like mutilation, imprisonment and death.[197] They cause rebirth in painful states of woe. Sensual pleasure is associated with the lovely bodies of men and women, but these must be reduced to dust and ashes in the cemetery. All men and women are really walking skeletons covered with flesh.[198] A *bodhisattva* should think with disgust of kisses, which make two persons imbibe each other's saliva; and the saliva is just like the faeces, as both derive their origin from food.[199] And why should a wise man seek another person's impure and malodorous body and thus eat filth? [200] Pleasures cannot be enjoyed without money.[201] Money cannot be earned without enduring much trouble and tribulation and committing heinous sins, for which one must be punished in the dreadful purgatories. Foolish people waste the days of their youth in hard work and in self-imposed exile in order to earn money: and how can they really enjoy Pleasure in old age? [202] They serve cruel masters and sell themselves for money. Even their wives and children are exposed to severe hardships in travelling at home and abroad.[203] These fools risk their lives in battle for the sake of false glory.[204] Wealth must first be acquired and then guarded, and it may be lost: it is thus a source of misery at all times. It absorbs all the energy and interest of worldly persons, and leaves them no time to think of their eternal Liberation.[205] The slaves of Pleasure thus incur many dangers and misfortunes and reap only a meagre reward, like the beasts harnessed to a chariot, which get only a handful of grass for their labour.[206] Even the brutes can gratify the sensual appetites: a wise man should rise above them and make a better use of his precious life as a human being.[206] He can attain Enlightenment with a thousand millionth part of the toil and trouble undergone by foolish people in the vain pursuit of Pleasure.[206] The love of Pleasure sows strife and discord among friends, and incites men to falsehood and cunning.[207] It is at the root of all quarrels, conflicts, struggles and rivalries in society.[208] It makes men forget virtue, law and duty.[209] Verily, it is a diabolical thing, and begets untold evil.[210] The pleasure-loving man should always remember the parable of the crow. A dead elephant's carcass was floating down the river Ganges. A crow sat on it and began to eat of the flesh. It was sweet and good to eat, and the crow was glad at heart. So he did not cease eating of it. But he did not know, poor fool, that he was being carried down to the briny ocean, wherein no bird can live. And when he reaches the ocean, still sitting on the elephant's carcass and eating of the sweet flesh, he will be slain and devoured by the monsters of the deep. A pleasure-loving man is like unto that foolish crow. He will find himself in an evil state of woe, when he is reborn as a *preta* or an animal, or in a purgatory. This is the famous Parable of the Crow.[211]

The Buddhist philosophers have devoted all their powers of rhetoric, exposition and argumentation to this important theme of the *kāmas*. It is not difficult to understand and explain their attitude. Buddhism depended for its success and progress on the Order of celibate monks. It had rejected the old Indian ideal of the married sage (*ṛṣi*) and had approved of the new mode of life, which was adopted by the unmarried *muni*, the lonely hermit and thinker. Celibacy cannot be maintained without a deep-rooted and unnatural aversion to sense-pleasures. It was the duty of the Buddhist philosophers to decry and denounce Pleasure in unmeasured and even repulsive terms, if their disciples were to live unspotted from the world. Similar cynical diatribes against Pleasure and Love are found in the writings of the medieval Christian monks.[212] The institution of celibacy rendered it necessary to forget the sweet and sane moderation of the ideals taught in the *Rāmāyaṇa* and the *Mahābhārata*, and even in the *Upaniṣads*. The spirit of Buddhism is in this respect quite different from that of ancient Hinduism and Hellenism. It is marked by exaggeration, abnormality, cynicism and sophistry. Self-restraint, self-control and self-discipline, which must be inculcated and practised by all philosophers, were thus interpreted as implying the complete suppression and repression of some vital and essential elements in human nature.

(*b*) *Bhava-*(*āsrava*). "*Bhava*" means "existence", "form of rebirth," "life." It usually denotes continuing existence in one of the three states or spheres, which are mentioned in Buddhist cosmology, viz. *kāma-dhātu*, *rūpa-dhātu* and *arūpa-dhātu* or *ārūpya-dhātu* (sensual-material existence, *deva*-corporeal existence, and formless, non-material existence).[213]

An advanced *bodhisattva* is free from the craving for existence in any form.

(*c*) *Avidyā-(āsrava)*. The Intoxicant of Ignorance or Nescience. *Avidyā* is discussed in the section on the twelve *nidānas* (*vide infra*).

(*d*) *Dṛṣṭi-(āsrava)*. The Intoxicant of metaphysical speculation.[214] It refers especially to the fourteen questions, that are regarded as unsolved and insoluble (*avyākṛta-vastūni*, "unexplained subjects"). Speculation on such problems is condemned as fruitless and dangerous. These questions are as follows [215] :—

(1) The Universe is eternal.
(2) The Universe is non-eternal.
(3) The Universe is both eternal and non-eternal.
(4) The Universe is neither eternal nor non-eternal.
(5) The Universe is finite (literally, "has an end").
(6) The Universe is infinite.
(7) The Universe is both finite and infinite.
(8) The Universe is neither finite nor infinite.
(9) The *Tathāgata* exists after death.
(10) The *Tathāgata* does not exist after death.
(11) The *Tathāgata* both exists and does not exist after death.
(12) The *Tathāgata* neither exists nor becomes non-existent after death.
(13) The *jīva* is the same as the body.[216]
(14) The *jīva* is one thing and the body another (i.e. they are different).

The order of the questions is not the same as in the Pāli texts, and the number has been increased from ten to fourteen by discussing the eternity and infinity of the Universe in four statements.

Nāgārjuna and Candrakīrti have attempted to prove that such theories must be regarded as antinomies, because they end in logical absurdities, and both the positive and negative solutions can be justified.[217] They have also applied the doctrines of *çūnyatā* (emptiness, relativity, interdependence) and *pratītya-samutpāda* (interdependent origination) in order to show that it is foolish and unprofitable to discuss these problems. As the *Tathāgata* is really "void by nature" (*svabhāva-çūnya*), he cannot be said to exist or become non-existent after death. As the Universe has only a contingent and phenomenal existence, it cannot be said to be eternal or non-eternal, finite or infinite. A *bodhisattva*, who accepts any such opinions, is hindered in his development. The foolish non-Buddhist heretics wrangle about such conundrums;[218] but the wise Buddhists maintain the great Silence. They "condemn all theories of the Thing-in-Itself, the Ding-an-sich", as L. de la Vallée Poussin has rightly pointed out.[219]

For the sake of completeness, it must be stated that the same four items (*kāma*, *bhava*, *avidyā*, *dṛṣṭi*) are also known as the group of four *oghas* (floods) or *mah-aughas* (great floods).[220] They are also spoken of as the four *yogas* (yokes, bonds, attachments).[221]

Such exuberant redundancy of names and terms testifies to the fertility of the Buddhist philosophers' imagination. It also proves the earnestness of their endeavours to warn the world against these four deadly Intoxicants.

The six *abhijñās*, that have been discussed, are of two kinds; mundane and supra-mundane.[222] They are acquired through meditation, inward peace, moral conduct and insight.[223] He, who wishes to obtain them, must live in the forest or a mountain-cave, ponder on the Truth and the Doctrine, and abandon his sins, evil passions and worldly desires.[224] He must also practise severe austerities, which are known as *dhūta-guṇāḥ*. Thus stern asceticism and self-mortification must be practised by a *bodhisattva* in order to gain the *abhijñās*. When he has obtained them, he realises that he had been a blind fool before, and that all his actions in that unenlightened state had been fruitless. A saint may lose the *abhijñās* that he has acquired; but he can recover them.[225] Faith and resolution lead to the rapid acquisition of the *abhijñās*.[226] By their means, a *bodhisattva* can see and hear all the Buddhas of the entire universe.[227] He can help other men by interpreting their dreams.[228] He acquires these Super-knowledges in the third or eighth *bhūmi*.[229] They are so important that they are reckoned as one of the four *caryās* (practices, duties, branches of discipline) that a *bodhisattva* must accomplish.[230]

VI. The Dhūta-guṇas

The *abhijñās* are to be acquired by living as a hermit and practising the *dhūta-guṇas* (ascetic practices). The word *dhūta-guṇa* or *dhuta-guṇa* is generally understood to mean the "qualities or attributes of a *dhuta* or *dhūta* (i.e. a person who has shaken off sins)," from the root *dhu* (to shake). Or the word may be a synonym of *dhauta*, derived from the root *dhāv*, and thus signify "a purified, cleansed, holy person". T. W. Rhys Davids and W. Stede derive it from *dhu* and interpret it as meaning "a scrupulous or punctilious person" (Pāli Dicy. s.v.). The Tibetan equivalent of *dhūta-guṇa* is *sbyaṅs-pahi-yon-tan*, and *sbyaṅs-pa* means "washed or used", from the verb *sbyoṅ-ba* (= to clean or cultivate). It seems likely that *dhūta* here is derived from the root *dhāv* and not from *dhu*. S. C. Das explains that *dhūta* in this term does not refer to the person, who has "shaken off" his sins or who has been "cleansed", but that the adjectival participle qualifies the substantive *guṇa*. He translates: "talents or qualifications kept up, used or practised,—ascetic practices" (Tib. Dicy., Das., 939*a*). The verb *sbyoṅ-ba* is often used to denote the purification and cultivation of the mind by training and exercise (Tib. Dicy., Jäschke, 405*b*). This interpretation seems to be more acceptable than that given in the Pāli Dictionary.

The Pāli texts mention thirteen *dhūtaṅgas*,[231] but the Sanskrit treatises speak of twelve *dhūta-guṇas*.[232] They are earnestly recommended by the author of the *Sam. Rā.*[233] The great saint, Kāçyapa, was an expert in such practices.[234] Çāntideva and the author of the *Da. Bhū.* also teach that a *bodhisattva* should persistently practise them.[235]

The twelve items are not placed in the same order in the *Dh. S.* and the *M. Vy.* They are as follows (*M. Vy.* Section 49—*Pr. Pā. Aṣṭa.*, p. 387) :—

(1) *Pāṃçu-kūlikaḥ.* The *bodhisattva* wears clothes made of rags taken from a dust-heap (Skt. Dicy. M.W., 560*b*).

(2) *Traicīvarikaḥ.* The *bodhisattva* does not possess more than three robes at a time. *Cīvara* means "the dress of a Buddhist mendicant or any mendicant" (Skt. Dicy. M.W., 327*b*).

(3) *Nāmatikaḥ* (*Nāmantikaḥ* in the *M. Vy.*). The meaning of this word is not clear. The word *namataḥ* occurs in the *M. Vy.* (Section 233, page 381) among *vastra-nāmāni* (names of articles of clothing), where it is rendered as *phyiṅ-pa* in the Tibetan. It also occurs in Section 272 (page 575) of the *M. Vy.* *Namataka* is also found in the *Cullavagga*:—"*anujānāmi bhikkhave satthakaṃ namatakanti* (v, 11.1; *Vinaya*, ii, page 115); "*tenkho pana samayena chabbaggiyā bhikkhuniyo . . . . namatakam dhārenti*" (x. 10.4—*Vinaya* ii, page 267). T. W. Rhys Davids

and H. Oldenberg translate it as "felt" in these passages.[236] E. Burnouf is of the opinion that *nāmatikaḥ* is a meaningless word [237] and may perhaps be changed to "*kāmbalikaḥ*"; but F. Max Müller rejects this suggestion and points out that the Chinese equivalent of *namata* is "hair-cloth" or "cloth made of hair".[238] The Tibetan term, *phyiṅ-pa*, is thus explained by S. C. Das, who also mentions *namata* and *kambalya* as the Sanskrit equivalents:—"the quantity of wool necessary for making a blanket; felt much used by Dokpa nomads of Tibet for tents and carpets" (Tib. Dicy, 836*a*). Csoma de Körös also gives the form *nāmacika* (p. 19), and translates: "clothed or clad in felt."

A *bodhisattva*, who practises this *dhūta-guṇa*, wears a garment made of felt or wool.

(4) *Paiṇḍapātikaḥ.* The *bodhisattva* lives only on food obtained by begging from door to door (and does not accept invitations to the houses of the laymen, etc.).

(5) *Aikāsanikaḥ* (*Ekāsanikaḥ* in the *Dh. S.* and the *Pr. Pā. Aṣṭa.*). The *bodhisattva* eats his meal at one sitting, or he has only one seat. The Tibetans translate, *stan-gcig-pa* (*M. Vy.*, p. 86). *Stan* means "a seat, mat, anything to sit upon". E. Burnouf thinks that the Tibetan equivalent means, "having only one seat." [239] But the practice of eating at one sitting is mentioned in Buddhist literature and is probably referred to here.[240] The Tibetan version is quite literal, and does not explain the meaning of the word. Csoma de Körös translates: "having only one mat" (p. 19).

(6) *Khalu-paçcād-bhaktikaḥ.* This term is also puzzling. The Pāli form is *khalu-pacchā-bhattika* and is interpreted by T. W. Rhys Davids and W. Stede as meaning "a person, who refuses food offered to him after the normal time (i.e. midday)". But the prefix *khalu* in the Sanskrit word seems to be inexplicable. E. Burnouf boldly conjectured that the whole word should be read as *svādv-apaçcād-bhaktika*, and translated as "celui qui ne mange pas de douceur après son repas." [241] The Tibetan equivalent, "*Zas phyis mi len-pa*" is interpreted by E. Burnouf as meaning "celui qui ne prend rien après son repas": (*Zas* = food, *len-pa* = to receive, to accept. Tib. Dicy., Das, 1093*a*, 1220*a*). The Sanskrit word appears to be meaningless in its usual form. E. Burnouf's emendation seems plausible. Csoma de Körös translates: "taking no food a second time on the same day" (p. 19).

(7) *Āraṇyakaḥ*. The *bodhisattva* lives in the woods.

(8) *Vṛkṣa-mūlikaḥ*. The *bodhisattva* dwells at the foot of a tree, or under a tree.

(9) *Ābhyavakāçikaḥ*. The *bodhisattva* lives in an open unsheltered place (not under a roof in a house). It is derived from *avakāça* (open or wide space, Skt. Dicy. M.W., 87*c*). The Pāli word *abbhokāsika* is translated by T. W. Rhys Davids and W. Stede as "one who lives in the open, the practice of certain ascetics" (Pāli Dicy., s.v.). H. Oldenberg suggests the reading *abhrāvakāçika*,[242] which means, "exposed to the rain, and so doing penance; not seeking shelter from the rain; having the clouds for shelter; open to the sky" (Skt. Dicy. M.W., 74*b*). This word occurs in the *Manu-smṛti* (vi, 23, page 117), "*grīṣme pañca-tapās tu syād varṣāsv-abhrāvakāçikaḥ.*" But this suggestion seems to be rather far-fetched and unnecessary.

(10) *Çmāçānikaḥ*. The *bodhisattva* lives in or near a cemetery, or visits a cemetery or cremation-ground frequently.

(11) *Naiçadikaḥ* (*naiçadyikaḥ* in the *Dh. S.* and the *Pr. Pā. Aṣṭa.*). The *bodhisattva* remains in a sitting posture while sleeping. The Tibetan equivalent *cog-bu-pa* also means, "one who lives in a lonely mountain-cavern, or in a small tent that accommodates but one man" (Tib. Dicy. Das, 384*b*). Csoma de Körös prefers this interpretation (p. 20).

(12) *Yāthā-saṃstarikaḥ* (*Yathā-saṃstarikaḥ* in the *Dh. S.*). T. W. Rhys Davids and W. Stede interpret the Pāli word *yathā-santhatika* as "accepting whatever seat is offered" (Pāli Dicy.). But H. Kern translates: "Spreading a night-couch where one happens to be."[243] The Tibetan version is vague and may be interpreted in two ways, according to E. Burnouf: (1) "Celui qui reste à la place où il est", (2) "Celui qui garde son tapis tel qu'il l'a une fois placé."[244] As this ascetic practice is forbidden to nuns, H. Kern's interpretation is likely to be correct. S. C. Das translates the Tibetan term as "a recluse, who stays where he is" (Tib. Dicy., 1080*a*). Csoma de Körös translates: "who accommodates himself as he can" (p. 20).

Thus we see that the old Indian practice of *tapas* (austerities) has become an integral part of the discipline of a *bodhisattva*. The beginnings of this innovation may be noted in the *Lal. V.*, which adds *tapas* to the virtues of charity and moral conduct in several passages. Gautama Buddha is said to have practised rites and penances for many æons, and to have lived the higher life by cultivating liberality, virtuous conduct and *tapas*.[245] He has fulfilled his resolve with *tapas*.[246] *Tapas* is indeed declared to be indispensable for Enlightenment, which cannot be attained without performing severe penances for many *kalpas*.[247] The *Mtu.* also describes Gautama Buddha as "endowed with virtue, forbearance and *tapas*".[248] This tendency to exalt *tapas* is a curious feature of Buddhist Sanskrit literature, though the *Lal. V.* and the *Mtu.* also faithfully insert Gautama Buddha's first sermon, in which he condemned such austerities and mortifications (*ātma-kāya-klamatha*).[249] Çūra praises the *bodhisattva* Viçvantara for practising *tapas* during half a year.[250] But the glorification of *tapas* and the *dhūta-guṇas* reaches its climax in that authoritative treatise, the *Sam. Rā.* Its author enumerates ten advantages that result from the practice of the *dhūta-guṇas*. He says :—"There are ten advantages that accrue to a *bodhisattva*, who is firmly established in the noble family of recluses that are content with the four requisites. He is free from deceit and loquacity (or from deceitful talk). He does not exalt himself; and he does not revile (or decry) others. He moves about in the houses (of the laity) without undue friendliness or repugnance. He preaches the Doctrine (literally, "bestows the gift of the *dharma*") in a disinterested spirit. His religious teaching is effective". (*Sam. Rā.*, fol. 119*a*, 6 ff.)

It is not difficult to understand the causes of this intrusion of the idea of *tapas* into Buddhist philosophy. Although Gautama Buddha clearly and emphatically condemned austerities and also rejected Devadatta's suggestions, yet we find that the *dhūta-guṇas* are mentioned in several passages of Pāli literature.[251] The *Milinda-pañha* devotes a whole chapter to them (chapter vi); it enumerates twenty-eight virtues (*guṇā*) that are inherent in them and eighteen good qualities that are acquired by the monks through these practices.[252] The Mahāyānist writers also approve of *tapas*, though Kṣemendra reverts to the original teaching and proclaims its futility.[253] But he was only a voice crying in the wilderness. It may be surmised that the acceptance of *tapas* as a condition of the *bodhisattva's* discipline was due to several irresistible tendencies that were at work in India. The Jainas valued *tapas* very highly as a means of Liberation.[254] It destroys *karma* and purifies the soul, as the *Uttarādhyayana-sūtra* teaches. The views of the Jainas are referred to in the Pāli canon.[255] The *Majjhima-Nikāya* speaks of other preachers, who taught the ordinary social virtues and *tapas*.[256] The competition of these rival sects led the Buddhists to practise similar austerities, as the people admired and followed such self-torturing ascetics. Vanity may have been the motive of many monks, who adopted the *dhūta-guṇas*. The common people always revere the spiritual athletes, who can curb and control the body and its appetites with such self-restraint and resolution. It is also probable that some earnest souls are born with a deep-seated longing for such a life of excessive self-denial. They wish to enjoy the spiritual luxury of completely dominating and crushing the sensual elements of human nature. Perhaps a few are called to this task in each generation, and they fulfil their peculiar mission. The history of all great spiritual movements exhibits this phase of stern asceticism. The Greeks as a people loved life, beauty and joy ; but they too produced Diogenes, "the mad Socrates," and the School of the Cynics.[257] Jesus Christ "came eating and drinking", and St. Paul advised Timothy to drink a little wine for the sake of his health.[258] But the Christian Church honoured the ascetics of Egypt and Syria, and the names of St. Anthony and St. Simeon Stylites are famous in world-history.[259] Thus it seems to be the universal law of historical development that Religion should have a few fanatical heroes, who assert the supremacy of Mind over Matter in the most striking and uncompromising fashion.

It is probable that the recorded account of the austerities practised by Gautama Buddha himself suggested the idea of *tapas* to the later Buddhists. It is true that Buddha repudiated those experiences as fruitless and dangerous, but the fact remained that he had gone through them at a certain stage in his career.[260] The champions of *tapas* may have appealed to those texts, as the Christian ascetics referred to Christ's long fast of forty days. Further, it was held that all the events and experiences of Gautama Buddha's life would be repeated in the last earthly life of every advanced *bodhisattva* before he attained Enlightenment. He must be born in a wealthy family, marry, renounce his home, and so forth.[261] But the episode of the penances was a stumbling-block for these devout Buddhists, who idealised Buddha in this way. The *Lal. V.* explains the laudable motives of the wise *bodhisattva* in practising *duṣkara-caryā* (austerities). He wished to exhibit a wonderful deed to the world. He intended to humiliate, confound and instruct the deluded heretics by excelling them even in those austerities, which they prized, but which he really knew to be vain and foolish.[262] He desired to show the fruits of perfect Wisdom and to analyse the different factors of meditation. He aimed at utilising the merits of his virtuous deeds. He hoped to convert the *devas* by a special form of meditation. He could thus display his physical strength and endurance and also acquire fortitude.[262] He thought that he could thus more easily convert the people. He aspired to cultivate the *āsphānaka* meditation, which is difficult even for the *pratyeka-buddhas*.[262] He expected to obtain *yoga-kṣema* (peace from bondage, uttermost safety, Liberation). The *Mtu.* also declares that the salvation of all creatures was the *bodhisattva's* only motive in practising penance.[263] The specious pleas adduced in the *Lal. V.* show that the Buddhists found it difficult to reconcile this episode with the perfect wisdom of a spiritually advanced *bodhisattva*. But even the *Lal. V.* admits that the *bodhisattva* derived some positive benefit from his *tapas*. Thus the old tradition relative to Gautama Buddha's own *tapas* could be interpreted in such a way as to induce the Buddhist monks to engage in similar practices. But Kṣemendra resolutely adheres to the ancient doctrine and consistently condemns *tapas*. He goes so far as to say that the *bodhisattva* Siddhārtha had to perform penance, because he had committed a sin in his previous existence.[264] It may be inferred that there were at all times two schools of thought among the Buddhists. Some approved of *tapas* and the *dhūta-guṇas*, while others condemned them. It is worthy of note that they are not discussed in such standard treatises as the *Bo. Bhū.* and the *M. S. Al.*

VII. The Vaçitās

Vasubandhu teaches that a *bodhisattva*, who is spiritually advanced, can exhibit all the wonders of *ṛddhi*, as he has acquired ten *vaçitās* (Powers, Sovereignties).[265] These ten powers are enumerated in the *Da. Bhū.*, the *M. Vy.*, and the *Dh. S.* But the order, in which they are placed, is not the same in the different treatises. They are also referred to in several other passages of Buddhist literature.[266]

According to the author of the *Da. Bhū.*, a *bodhisattva* acquires them in the eight *bhūmi*. They are as follows :—

(1) *Āyur-vaçitā* (power of longevity). A *bodhisattva* has sovereignty over the length of life. He can prolong it to an immeasurable number of *kalpas* (æons).

(2) *Ceto-(Citta)-vaçitā.* He has sovereignty over the mind, as he has acquired the knowledge of an infinite number of *samādhis* (modes of Concentration).

(3) *Pariṣkāra-vaçitā.* He has the mastery of Equipment, as he knows all the arrangements and adornments of all the worlds and universes.

(4) *Karma-vaçitā.* He has sovereignty over Action, as he comprehends the consequences of deeds at the proper time.

(5) *Upapatti-vaçitā.* He has mastery over Birth, as he understands the origin of all the worlds and universes.

(6) *Adhimukti-vaçitā.* He has sovereignty over Faith (or Aspiration), as he sees well all the Buddhas of all the worlds and universes.

(7) *Praṇidhāna-vaçitā.* He has mastery over all the Vows, as he sees well the time for Enlightenment in any buddha-field according to his desire.

(8) *Ṛddhi-vaçitā.* He is lord of the wonder-working Power, as he sees well the marvels of all the buddha-fields.

(9) *Dharma-vaçitā.* He has mastery over the Doctrine, as he beholds the light of the source of the Doctrine in the beginning, the middle and the end.

(10) *Jñāna-vaçitā.* He comprehends thoroughly the attributes of a Buddha, viz. his Powers, his Grounds of Self-confidence, his special exclusive attributes, and the principal marks and the minor signs on his body. Therefore he is the Lord of Knowledge.

VIII. The Indriyas and the Balas

The five *indriyas* and the five *balas*, which have the same names, are included among the thirty-seven *bodhipakṣya-dharmas*.

In the final formula, these are :—(1) *çraddhā* (Faith), (2) *vīrya* (Energy), (3) *smṛti* (Mindfulness), (4) *samādhi* (Concentration), (5) *prajñā* (Wisdom). But it is almost certain that this group of five was accepted after a process of change and selection. The Pāli texts speak of four, five or seven *balas*, and the names vary.[267] Only three items (*vīrya*, *samādhi*, and *prajñā*) are mentioned at *Mtu.* ii, 290.9, and *samādhi* is omitted at *Lal. V.*, 434.22. *Chanda* takes the place of *çraddhā* in several passages of the *Lal. V.* (239.1—262.8—434.19). This substitution of *chanda* for *çraddhā* gives us a glimpse into the early history of the pentad. *Chanda* was associated with the idea of personal effort, as in the formulæ of the *ṛddhi-pādas* and the *samyak-prahāṇas*. But *çraddhā* suggested pious devotion to the Buddha. *Chanda* gave place to *çraddhā*, as the Buddhists tended more and more to exalt the Buddha and depend on his help and grace instead of working out their own salvation with diligence and being their own "islands of refuge".[268] It is also to be noted that the same group of five (with *chanda* in the place of *çraddhā*) is incorporated in the formula of the eighteen *āveṇika-dharmas* (special exclusive attributes) of a perfect Buddha (Nos. 7, 8, 9, 10, 11).[269] It is almost certain that *chanda* originally occupied the place now accorded to *çraddhā*.

Another group of five *balas* is also mentioned in the *Lal. V.*: *puṇya*, *prajñā*, *jñāna*, *kṣānti*, *vīrya*—(*Lal. V.* 316.15).

We may also surmise that an attempt was made by some thinkers to add the two terms *vimukti* and *vimukti-jñāna-darçana* to the group of the five *balas*. The innovators failed in this case, though they succeeded in tacking these notions on to the three old *skandhas* of *çīla*, *samādhi* and *prajñā*.[270] The five *balas* and *indriyas* represent important and fundamental Buddhist concepts. They are related more to the needs of the heroic monk than to those of the ordinary layman. They begin with Faith, take up three *aṅgas* (parts, limbs) of the eightfold Way (*vīrya* = *vyāyāma*, *smṛti* and *samādhi*), and end with the highest Wisdom. The formula was found so helpful that the *Yoga* school borrowed it from the Buddhists. It is found in identically the same form in the *Yoga-sūtras* (i, 20, page 23).

It is probable that the five *balas* were introduced into the formula of the thirty-seven *dharmas* after the five *indriyas*, as the latter are always mentioned before the *balas* in the list. Açvaghosa indeed omits all mention of the *indriyas* at xvii, 26 of the *Saund. Kā.*, where he speaks of the *balas*. This circumstance may lead us to suppose that the *indriyas* were not recognised as a group in his time. But he knew of them, as he refers to *çraddh-endriya* in the same poem (xii, 37). In fact, the five *indriyas*, which are included among the "*bodhipakṣya-dharmas*", have been taken over from another old list of twenty-two *indriyas*, which also occurs in the Pāli canon.[271] These twenty-two *indriyas* are enumerated in the *M. Vy.* (Section 108, page 156), but not in the *Dh. S.* It has been suggested that this list of *indriyas* is a revised and more elaborate form of the twenty-three or twenty-five categories (*tattvas*) of the *Sāṅkhya* system.[272] But the

Buddhist list seems to include only the categories referring to the individual living being, and it does not analyse the external world. Thus the six external *āyatanas* (form, sound, odour, etc.) are excluded. It seems more likely that the philosophers of the *Sāṅkhya* school developed the idea suggested by the Buddhist categories and extended its scope (cf. *Sāṅkhya-kārikā*, verse 22, page 20). The twenty-two *indriyas* are placed in a peculiar order in the Pāli and Sanskrit texts, and the *M. Vy.* makes matters worse by putting *jīvita* at the end (instead of the ninth place, which it occupies in the Pāli list: *Vibhaṅga*, p. 123, lines 3 ff.).

The *M. Vy.* also places *duḥkha* before *sukha*. It will perhaps make the list more intelligible, if we mention the items in the following order :—

(1) *Jīvita* (life, vitality, vital spirits, vital principle).
(2) *Puruṣa* (male).
(3) *Strī* (female).
(4) *Cakṣus* (the eye, or vision).
(5) *Çrotra* (the ear, or hearing).
(6) *Ghrāṇa* (the olfactory organ, or smelling).
(7) *Jihvā* (the tongue, or taste).
(8) *Kāya* (body-sensibility).
(9) *Manas* (mind).
(10) *Duḥkha* (pain).
(11) *Sukha* (pleasure).
(12) *Saumanasya* (joy).
(13) *Daurmanasya* (grief).
(14) *Upekṣā* (hedonic indifference, or equanimity).
(15) *Çraddhā* (faith).
(16) *Vīrya* (energy).
(17) *Smṛti* (mindfulness).
(18) *Samādhi* (concentration).
(19) *Prajñā* (wisdom).
(20) *An-ājñātam ājñāsyāmi* (*indriya*), (the thought, "I shall come to know the unknown").
(21) *Ājñā* (gnosis, knowledge).
(22) *Ājñātāvī* (one who possesses knowledge).

This list may be easily divided into its component parts. The first three categories are biological; the next six are the sense-organs and sense-functions. The five from No. 10 to No. 14 are feelings;

the next five (Nos. 15–19) are the important factors of Enlightenment, and the last three relate to the thought of Enlightenment, Enlightenment and the perfectly enlightened man.

Five *indriyas* (Nos. 15–19) have been taken out of this list and included among the thirty-seven *bodhipakṣya-dharmas*. This word *indriya* means, "belonging to the ruler," "governing, ruling, controlling principle," "directive force." "These five *indriyas* are related to moral and spiritual qualities and values" (Pāli Dicy.). The Sanskrit authors also interpret the term in the same sense. Açvaghoṣa says that the categories are called *indriyas* as they are "chief or principal" factors: (*Saund. Kā.*, xii, 37). Vasubandhu explains that they are of "sovereign importance" (*ādhipaty-ārthen-endriyāṇy-ucyante*: *M. S. Al.*, 143, 21.) The Tibetan equivalent, *dbaṅ-po*, also indicates the etymology of the term, as it means "Indra, powerful, mighty, a ruler, lord or sovereign" (Tib. Dicy., 908*a*). The word has been variously translated as "faculties", "mental energies," "organs of spiritual sense," "de fem organen for andlig förnimmelse," "organs of moral practice," "moral qualities," "die Vermogen," "les sens," etc. But it is advisable to avoid confusion by eschewing the words "organ" and "faculty" in translating this term, when it refers to these five *indriyas*. It should be rendered as "chief categories" or "chief controlling principles."

These five *indriyas* and *balas* are mentioned as a group in several passages of Buddhist Sanskrit literature (*M. Vy.* Sections 41, 42; *Dh. S.* Sections 47, 48; *M. S. Al.*, 143, 19 ff.; *Da. Bhū.*, 39; *Pr. Pā. Çata.*, 1437). They are sometimes not called *indriyas* or *balas* (*Lal. V.*, 245.5). A *bodhisattva* must cultivate them (*bhāvayati*: *Da. Bhū.*, 39.) H. Kern thinks that the only difference between the *indriyas* and the *balas* is that the latter are more intense than the former.[273] But there seems to be a radical distinction between the two categories. The *indriyas* are regarded as static in character, while the *balas* are dynamic. The word *bala* has been variously translated as "moral powers", "strengths," "forces," "virtues," etc. It is perhaps best to render it as "powers". The *M. S. Al.* explains that they are so called, because their contraries or opposites (*vipakṣāḥ*) are feeble (p. 143). Açvaghoṣa teaches that the *balas*, which he describes as "noble" (*āryāḥ*), serve to destroy the five "mental obstructions" (*cetaḥ-khilāni*, literally, "waste or fallow land"; hence, "barrenness of mind"; *Saund. Kā.*, xvii, 26). These five *khilas* are the following:—(1) Doubt or misgivings about the Teacher (Buddha). (2) Doubt about the Doctrine. (3) Doubt about the Confraternity, or Order of Monks. (4) Doubt about the course of training. (5) Anger towards the other monks.[274]

The items, *vīrya* and *prajñā*, will be discussed as *pāramitās*; *smṛti* has been dealt with in the section on the *smṛty-upasthānas*; and *samādhi* will be treated in detail in connection with the *dhyāna-pāramitā*. We shall therefore now discuss only *çraddhā* and its relation to a *bodhisattva's* career.

Çraddhā (as *indriya* and *bala*)

Çraddhā (Pāli: *saddhā*) is an important factor in a *bodhisattva's* development. Faith is frequently mentioned in the Pāli canon.[275] It acquires even greater importance in the hands of the Sanskritists. In the Buddhist Sanskrit treatises, it is regarded as the Alpha of a *bodhisattva's* career, whose Omega is *prajñā* or *bodhi* (Wisdom, Enlightenment). It occupies the first place in the list of the five *balas* and *indriyas*. But it has the same position of predominance and distinction in the list of the seven *dhanas* (*dhanāni*—treasures), which embodies some of the most important categories of Buddhist ethics and metaphysics. *Çraddhā* heads the list, and the other six follow: (*çīla*, *hrī*, *apatrāpya*, *çruta*, *tyāga*, *prajñā*).[276] *Çraddhā* is also mentioned as the first of the four *sampads* (blessings, accomplishments), viz. *çraddhā*, *çīla*, *tyāga*, *prajñā*, which are often spoken of in connection with the conversion and moral improvement of unbelieving, wicked, selfish or deluded persons.[277] A *bodhisattva* is said to "establish unbelievers in the *sampad* of Faith". *Çraddhā* is placed first in the list of the 108 *dharm-āloka-mukhas* (entrances to the light of the Religion) in the *Lal. V.*, and it figures twice again in that list as an *indriya* and a *bala*.[278] According to the scheme of the ten *bhūmis*, a *bodhisattva* acquires ten "purifying principles" (*pariçodhakā dharmaḥ*) in the very first *bhūmi*; and here too *çraddhā* occupies the first place, the other *dharmas* being love, friendliness, etc.[279] It is also mentioned in the *Çikṣā* as the first of the four principles or qualities, which prevent a *bodhisattva* from falling away from the right path, the other three being Reverence (*gaurava*), Humility (*nirmānatā*) and Energy (*vīrya*).[280] Thus there is remarkable unanimity among the Buddhist writers in giving *çraddhā* the first place in several numerical lists and formulae.

Çraddhā is said to be recommended by Gautama Buddha

himself as the starting-point of a pious Buddhist's life in the new faith. The *Lal. V.* relates that Buddha did not wish to preach the Doctrine to the world after his Enlightenment, as he was not sure that the people were ripe for it. If they did not accept his teaching, it would mean only fruitless work and fatigue for him.[281] But the *deva Mahābrahmā* persuaded him to teach the people. Gautama Buddha then spoke of *çraddhā* as the first necessary condition for receiving religious instruction.[282] Similarly, when Buddha exhorts Nanda in the *Saund. Kā.*, he puts *çraddhā* first: "Henceforward you should again guard your conduct. Cultivate first the *indriya* of *çraddhā* (or 'let *çraddhā* be your guide'). Thus, friend, you will attain to the Deathless" (*Saund. Kā.*, xiii, 10).

Çraddhā has been accorded a prominent position by the Mahāyānist authors in another remarkable context. They have put *çraddhā* right into the old formula, which describes the renunciation of a monk and his initiation into the Order. This formula reads thus: "He left his home for the homeless life with right Faith, having removed his hair and his beard and donned reddish-yellow orange-coloured garments."[283] *Çraddhā* is often mentioned in connection with the renunciation of the home and the world (*çraddhayā pravrajita*).[284]

Almost all Buddhist writers have sung the praises of *çraddhā* in eloquent words. "It leads to inviolable aspiration.[285] It renders a person independent of the guidance of others.[286] It enables a *bodhisattva* to escape the power of Evil (*Māra*) and to put forth great Energy[287]; but it must be rooted in *Dharma* (righteousness and religion).[288] It is indeed the most excellent of all possessions.[289] He, who has faith, will be rich in virtues. Faith gives constancy and strength.[290] It is a rare gift, which is not easy to come by.[291] *Çraddhā* is so blessed that she should be accorded divine honours and worshipped as a goddess.[292] If a deed is purified by Faith, it will bear great fruit in increasing spiritual Merit.[293] Faith is indeed like unto ambrosia,[294] and its power fulfils all desires, when it is combined with the Thought of Enlightenment and Renunciation.[295] Faith is like a ship, in which a *bodhisattva* can safely enter the great ocean of Virtue and Merit; but if he makes shipwreck, he cannot acquire supreme Wisdom.[296] Faith is the seed of bright virtue (*çuklo dharmaḥ*): if the seed be burned by fire, how can it put forth green sprouts?[297] A *bodhisattva*, who is lacking in Faith, will easily fall into the grievous sin of Pride.[298] Without Faith, no one can even start on the long career of a *bodhisattva*, which begins with the "Thought of Enlightenment". Faith is the root of that idea.[299] It leads the way ; it is the parent of all virtues ; it fosters and promotes them.[300] It dispels all doubt and shows us the City of Bliss.[301] It destroys Pride and gives joy to the pure mind. Through Faith, a *bodhisattva* rejoices in renunciation and charity, and becomes invincible on account of the increased keenness and radiance (clearness) of all his faculties and powers. He never swerves from the path of righteousness and discipline, especially as he is always devoted to the Church (*saṅgha*) and cannot be misled by bad friends. He is protected by the Buddhas ; he acquires purity of will and purpose, and practises the *pāramitās*. He constantly thinks of the Buddhas and attains the ideal. Faith thus leads to the highest Enlightenment."

In this way, the Buddhist authors extol and magnify Faith. Açvaghoṣa also adds the human touch in a few simple verses :—

"When a man needs water, he believes by Faith that it exists in the bowels of the earth. Then he digs the ground."

"The husbandman believes by Faith that grain will grow in the soil, otherwise he would not expect a crop or sow the seed". (*Saund. Kā.*, xii, 33, 35.)

The persons, towards whom *çraddhā* should be directed, are the Buddhas, especially Gautama Buddha, and the higher *bodhisattvas*.

Three Additional Indriyas. It has been indicated above that the five *indriyas* have been taken from the comprehensive list of twenty-two, and then included among the thirty-seven *bodhi-pakṣya-dharmas*. But some philosophers have also attempted to associate three other important categories of that list with a *bodhisattva's* discipline. These are Nos. 20, 21 and 22, which represent the supreme goal of Wisdom. The *Pr. Pā. Çata.* interprets these three last *indriyas* as referring to the initiation, development and consummation of the process of cultivating the five *indriyas* of *çraddhā*, *vīrya*, *smṛti*, *samādhi* and *prajñā*.[302] The novice is in the condition indicated by the *indriya* No. 20, "I shall know the unknown." When he has made some progress, he is in the stage of Gnosis (*ājñā*). When he has thoroughly acquired the five *indriyas*, he is a perfect adept (*ājñātāvī*). It should be stated, however, that most Buddhist writers do not deal with these three *indriyas* at all.

Ten Additional Balas. The Mahāyānist authors were inclined to exalt and glorify the *bodhisattvas* and accord them a position of equal dignity and importance with the Buddhas. According to an old tradition, a Buddha possesses ten *balas*; (these have been enumerated in the section on "The Buddha"). An advanced *bodhisattva* was therefore also supposed to have ten *balas* (*M. Vy.*, Section 26; *Dh. S.*, Section 75). But the epithet *Daça-bala* generally denotes a perfect Buddha, as the older tradition maintained itself in literature. These ten *balas* of a *bodhisattva* are of merely theoretical interest, and they are not described in detail in the principal treatises.

Here we have another of those numerical lists, with which Buddhist literature is over-burdened. To make matters worse, the items are not the same in the *M. Vy.* and the *Dh. S.*, which give two different lists. The *Dh. S.* attributes the following *balas* to a *bodhisattva*:—

(1) *Adhimukti:* "Faith," "Devotion"; Tibetan: *mospa* = "faith, devotion, adoration, satisfaction." (Tib. Dicy., 977).

(2) *Pratisaṅkhyāna:* "Power of computation" (Pali Dicy.) [303] Tibetan: *So-Sor brtags-pa* = "detailed examination" (Tib. Dicy., 557).

(3) *Bhāva:* "Cultivation or production by thought" (Pāli Dicy.). Tibetan: *bsam-pa* = "thought, inclination" (Tib. Dicy., 1316).

(4) *Kṣānti:* Forbearance, patience.

(5) *Jñāna:* "Knowledge."

(6) *Prahāṇa:* "Renunciation" (or perhaps, "Exertion").

(7) *Samādhi:* "Concentration."

(8) *Pratibhāna:* "Intelligence," or "Readiness of Speech."

(9) *Puṇya:* "Spiritual Merit."

(10) *Pratipatti:* "Accomplishment," "Attainment," "Way, method, conduct, practice, performance, behaviour, example" (Pāli Dicy.). Tibetan: *sgrub-pa*, "to complete, to accomplish." Tib. *nan-tan du bya-ba*, "accomplished, practised with earnestness" (Tib. Dicy. 736).

The *M. Vy.* gives the following list:—

(1) *Āçaya-balam*: "The Power of Thought." The Tibetan equivalent is *bsam-pahı-stobs*. *Bsam-pa* means "thought, reflection," and also "will, inclination" (Tib. Dicy., Das, 1316). S. Lévi translates: "la force de Tendance" (*M. S. Al.*, tr. p. 27). "Inclination, intention, will, hope" (Pāli Dicy., s.v. *āsaya*).

(2) *Adhyāçaya-balam:* "The Power of Will." S. Lévi translates: "la force de l'archi-tendance." "Intention, desire, wish, disposition, bent" (Pāli Dicy., s.v. *ajjhāsaya*).

(3) *Prayoga-balam:* "The Power of Practice." *Tibetan: Sbyor-ba*, "to prepare, to establish" (Tib. Dicy., 941). S. Lévi translates: "la force d'emploi." "Preparation, undertaking, occupation, exercise, business, action, practice" (Pāli Dicy., s.v. *payoga*).

(4) *Prajñā-balam:* "The Power of Wisdom."

(5) *Praṇidhāna-balam:* "The Power of Resolution or Aspiration."

(6) *Yāna-balam:* "The Power of the Way or Career."

(7) *Caryā-balam:* "The Power of the Discipline or Practice." S. Lévi translates: "la force de conduite." *Tibetan: spyod-pa*, "deed, action, practice, behaviour" (Tib. Dicy., 808).

(8) *Vikurvaṇa-balam:* "The wonder-working Power." S. Lévi translates: "la force de transformation." The Tibetan equivalent is the same as for *ṛddhi* (*ḥphrul-ba*).

(9) *Bodhi-balam:* "The Power of Enlightenment."

(10) *Dharma-cakra-pravartana-balam:* "The Power of preaching the Doctrine" (literally, "of turning the wheel of the Doctrine").[304]

IX. The Seven Bodhy-aṅgas or Sambodhy-aṅgas.

A *bodhisattva* must cultivate and practise the seven *bodhy-aṅgas* or *sambodhy-aṅgas* (Factors or Constituents of Enlightenment. Pāli: *bojjhangā sambojjhangā*).[305] This term *bodhyaṅga* has been variously translated as follows:—

E. Burnouf: "Les parties constituantes de la *bodhi*" (Lotus: p. 796).

T. W. Rhys Davids and W. Stede: "Factors or Constituents of Knowledge or Wisdom" (Pāli Dicy.).

M. Anesaki: "Divisions of *bodhi*" (ERE. V. 455).

S. Lévi: "Les membres de l'Illumination" (*M. S. Al.*, tr., p. 241).

E. Hardy: "Forms of Wisdom" (*Nettipakaraṇa*, xxxi).

P. E. Foucaux: "Les parties de l'intelligence parfaite" (*Lal. V.* tr., p. 35).

K. E. Neumann: "Die sieben Erweckungen" (*Majjh.* tr., ii, 329).

These Factors of Enlightenment are mentioned in several passages of Buddhist Sanskrit literature (*Dh. S.*, Section 49; *M. Vy.*, Section 43; *Lal. V.*, 34.3 ff.; *Divy.*, 208.9; *M. S. Al.*, 144; *Da. Bhū.*, 39; *Çikṣā*, 144.10; *Pr. Pā. Çata.*, 1437, etc.). They are called *bodhy-aṅgikā dharmāḥ* in the *Da. Bhū.* (57.22). According to the scheme of ten *bhūmis*, outlined in that treatise, the *bodhy-aṅgas* are associated with all the *bhūmis*. This teaching shows that the Mahāyānists also attached considerable importance to them. The Equipment (*sambhāra*) of the *bodhy-aṅgas* serves to enlighten a *bodhisattva* with regard to the true nature of all phenomena.[306] He accumulates and acquires this Equipment with unflagging zeal, and is never satisfied with his achievement.[307]

These seven Factors of Enlightenment are as follows :—

(1) *Smṛti* (Mindfulness). *Smṛti* has been discussed in the section on the four *smṛty-upasthānas*.

(2) *Dharma-pravicaya* (Pāli : *Dhamma-vicaya*).

The word *pravicaya* has been variously translated as "examination", "research," "investigation," "study," "discernment," "discrimination," "le tri," "das Nachdenken," etc. The form *vicaya* is also found (*M. S. Al.*, 144.10). The form *pravicinoti* occurs in the *Da. Bhū.* (22.18), and *pravicita* in the *Mtu.* (ii, 346.3), which also speaks of Buddha's *loka-pravicaya* (ii, 290.3). T. W. Rhys Davids and W. Stede translate *vicaya* as "investigation", which seems to be a suitable rendering (Pāli Dictionary).

The other word, *dharma*, presents some difficulties. Does it mean "the Law, the Doctrine, Buddhist Scriptures", or does it signify "things, phenomena"? L. de la Vallée Poussin and M. Anesaki approve of the latter interpretation.[308] T. W. Rhys Davids and W. Stede translate : "Investigation of Doctrine" (Pāli Dicy., s.v.); and Lord Chalmers and R. O. Franke agree with them.[309] The *Lal. V.* states that this *bodhy-aṅga* helps a *bodhisattva* to fulfil the whole *dharma*.[310] Vasubandhu teaches that this *bodhy-aṅga* dispels all causes of doubt and uncertainty,[311] and enables a *bodhisattva* to preach the *dharma* effectively.[312] Such passages seem to prove that *dharma* in the name of this *bodhy-aṅga* means "Doctrine, Scripture", and not "phenomena or things". E. R. J. Gooneratne thinks that it refers only to the four Truths.[313] But this interpretation is perhaps too narrow. "*Dharma*" includes all that has been uttered and taught by the Buddha. The teaching of the Buddha has been divided into twelve sections and sub-divisions:[314] *sūtra* (discourses), *geya* (mixed verse and prose), *vyākaraṇa* (expository answers), *gāthā* (poems), *udāna* (solemn or triumphant utterances), *ityukta* (quotations), *avadāna* (edifying stories), *jātaka* (birth-stories), *vaipulya* (extended treatises or longer texts), *adbhuta-dharma* (tales of wonder, miracles) and *upadeça* (treatises on esoteric ritual). These twelve categories of Scripture are collectively described as *dharma-pravacana* (exposition of the Doctrine). An earlier list mentions only nine items and omits *nidāna*, *avadāna* and *itivṛttaka* (*ityukta*).[315] A *bodhisattva* gains several advantages from the study and investigation of the Doctrine. He develops all the elements of his personality and experiences sublime happiness at the hour of death. He is reborn according to his desire and always remembers his past existences. He associates with the Buddhas and hears the Doctrine preached by them. He is protected by magic spells, acquires Wisdom, Faith and Concentration, and finally attains Enlightenment.[316]

A *bodhisattva* may also learn much about the *dharma* by receiving instruction orally from a competent teacher. In that case, he should listen with reverence, love and faith, and earnestly desire to acquire virtue and the knowledge of the Doctrine.[317] He must get rid of pride and mental distraction.

(3) *Vīrya* (Pāli : *viriya*). *Vīrya* will be discussed in the section on the *pāramitās*.

(4) *Prīti* (Pāli : *pīti*). This word, derived from the root *prī*, means "emotion of joy, delight, zest, exuberance" (Pāli Dicy.). It has been variously translated as "bliss", "rapture," "le plaisir," "die Heiterkeit," "l'amabilité," "pleasurable interest," "le contentement," "joy in what one has attained," "die Fröhlichkeit," etc. It is often associated with *prasāda* (joy, satisfaction) and *prāmodya* (delight).[318] The *sukha* (happiness, pleasure) of *prīti* (joy) is sometimes mentioned, especially in connection with the first *dhyāna*.[319] *Prīti* is one of the indispensable qualifications of a *bodhisattva*. The *Dhammasaṅgaṇi* explains it thus: "Gladness, rejoicing at, rejoicing over, mirth and merriment, felicity, exultation, transport of mind."[320] As C. A. F. Rhys Davids has pointed out, *prīti* connotes emotion as distinct from bare feeling. It is referred to the *skandha* of *saṃskāras*, and not to *vedanā* (feeling), as it is a complex psychological phenomenon. The five species of *prīti*, mentioned by Buddhaghoṣa, are not discussed by the principal Sanskrit writers.[321] *Prīti*

is regarded as something ethereal, as some *devas* are said to have *prīti* for their food.[322] A *bodhisattva* attains to rapt Concentration by means of *prīti*. Açvaghoṣa teaches that *prīti* arises from the cultivation of virtue, and it can save a *bodhisattva* from sloth and languor.[323]

(5) *Praçrabdhi* (Pāli: *passaddhi*). This word also occurs in two other forms: (1) *prasrabdhi* (*Ava. Ça.*, i, 32.4). (2) *Prasraddhi* (*Pr. Pā. Çata.*, 1438.4).

The adjective, *prasrabdha*, is often applied to the body and the mind.[324] Literally, the word means "cessation, stopping", as in the passages of the *Divy.* and the *Ava. Ça.*, where the stopping or cessation of miraculous power and of pain is spoken of.[325] In the compound *apratipraçrabdha-margaḥ* (*M. Vy.*, Section 30, page 63), it means "interrupted". As a philosophical term, *praçrabdhi* came to signify "cessation of pain", "serenity," "tranquillity."

It has been variously translated as follows:—

D. T. Suzuki: "Modesty" ("Outlines," p. 317).

M. Anesaki: "Satisfaction" (ERE, v. 455).

P. E. Foucaux: "L'assurance" (*Lal. V.* tr., p. 35).

E. Burnouf: "La confiance" ("Lotus," p. 798).

E. R. J. Gooneratne: "Pacification of the mental and bodily defilements" (*Aṅguttara* trsln., p. 55).

W. M. McGovern: "Serenity or cheerfulness" ("Manual," p. 143).

E. H. Johnston: "*Praçradbhi* is properly the feeling of intense, almost buoyant calm, that ensues on the sudden cessation of great pain, and has a similar meaning, as applied to the mind" (*Saund. Kā.*, p. 156).

T. W. Rhys Davids and W. Stede: "Calm, tranquillity, repose, serenity" (Pāli Dicy.).

R. O. Franke: "Die Beruhigung (der Körper-Ideen") (*Dīgha*, p. 184).

Monier Williams: "Trust, confidence" (Skt. Dicy. 646).

Böhtlingk and Roth: "Vertrauen."

K. E. Neumann: "Die Lindheit" (*Majjh.* tr., ii, 329).

S. Lévi: "La Rémission" (*M. S. Al.* tr, p. 242).

Lord Chalmers: "Serenity" (*Majjh.* tr., ii, 7).

In the terminology of Buddhist philosophy, *praçrabdhi* signifies "tranquillity, serenity," whatever the original meaning of the root *çrambh*, *çrabh* may have been. It is often associated with *prīti.*[326] As a *bodhy-aṅga*, it helps a *bodhisattva* to do his duty.[327] Açvaghoṣa teaches that tranquillity springs from joy and leads to felicity.[328]

(6) *Samādhi.* *Samādhi* will be discussed in the section on *dhyāna-pāramitā.*

(7) *Upekṣā* (Pāli: *upekkhā*, *upekhā*). This word is derived from the root *īkṣ*, and literally means "looking on". It has been variously translated as follows :—

T. W. Rhys Davids and W. Stede : "hedonic neutrality or indifference, zero point between joy and sorrow ; disinterestedness, neutral feeling, equanimity" ; "sometimes equivalent to feeling, which is neither pain nor pleasure" (Pāli Dicy.).

S. Lévi : "L'Apathie" (*M. S. Al.* tr., 242).

W. M. McGovern : "Self-sacrifice" ("Introduction," p. 165).

R. O. Franke and R. Pischel : "die Gleichmut" ("Buddha," p. 77 ; *Dīgha*, p. 184).

Lord Chalmers : "The Poise of Indifference" (*Majjh.* tr., ii, 7).

Csoma de Körös : "Unbiassedness" ("Csoma," p. 108).

P. E. Foucaux : "La patience" (*Lal. V.* tr., p. 35).

H. Oldenberg : (1) "die Gleichmut," ("Buddha," p. 343). (2) "Alle Wesen als nicht Freund und nicht Feind empfinden" ("Indien," p. 5).

D. T. Suzuki : "Large-heartedness" ("Outlines," p. 317).

Upekṣā (Equanimity) is an important term in Buddhist philosophy. It is one of the twenty-two *indriyas*, which have been mentioned above. It is also one of the four *brahma-vihāras* (Excellent or Sublime States), which a *bodhisattva* cultivates. Thus it occurs in three numerical lists. It is also mentioned in the sentences that describe the four *dhyānas.*[329]

The exact connotation of this term has been indicated in several Pāli passages. *Upekkhā* is one of the ten *pāramīs* (Perfections), which are mentioned in the later Pāli treatises.[330] According to the *Cariyā-piṭaka*, it consists in preserving the same mental attitude in all circumstances, in joy and sorrow, in fame and obloquy, and in gain and loss.[331] The *Dhamma-saṅgaṇi* explains it thus : "It is the mental condition, which is neither pleasant nor unpleasant, the sensation or the feeling, which is neither easeful nor painful."[332] In the *Jātaka*, the Perfection of *upekkhā* is described in these words : "I lay down in the cemetery (cremation-ground) and my pillow consisted of the bones of the corpses." . . . .

"His equanimity was not disturbed, even when the villagers tried to vex or please him by spitting or by offering garlands and perfumes, and thus he acquired the Perfection of *upekkhā*."[333] The Tibetan equivalent is *btaṅ-sñoms* (*Lal. V. Tib.*, p. 36, line 18). According to S. Lévi, it means, "l'équilibre par rejet."[334] S. C. Das explains thus: "*Btaṅ-sñoms* is a word signifying impartial and equal treatment of friend or foe, i.e., to abstain from anger or affection for friends and relations, equal treatment to all living beings without either attachment or hatred" (Tib. Dicy. 529*a*). *Upekṣā* thus seems to denote the mental state of equanimity under all favourable and unfavourable circumstances, and also the practice of impartiality in one's conduct towards others. Kṣemendra and a commentator of the *Pr. Pā. Aṣṭa.* emphasize the latter aspect of *upekṣā*.[335] The other Mahāyānist authors also regard it as a principle of action, and not merely as a subjective psychological phenomenon. When *upekṣā* is regarded as "equanimity", it is the neutral middle term between *sukha* and *duḥkha*. When it is interpreted as "impartiality", it is the neutral middle term between *anunaya* (friendliness) and *pratigha* (repugnance); it then corresponds to *udāsīna* (neutral), which is the mean between *mitra* and *amitra*. *Upekṣā* has something in common with the "Apathy" of the Stoics of Greece and Rome.[336]

A *bodhisattva*, who cultivates *upekṣā*, does not hurt or injure any living being.[337] He does not love or hate anything or anyone. Gold and a stone are the same to him.[338] He develops a feeling of aversion to mundane existence (or to the idea of personal existence).[339] He acquires the certitude of knowledge.[340] He is free from sorrow, as he has transcended the feelings of love and hate.[341]

These seven *bodhy-aṅgas* as a group are highly valued and appreciated by all the Sanskrit authors, Hīnayānists and Mahāyānists alike. A Buddha is said to be richly endowed with "the flowers of the *bodhy-aṅgas*";[342] but they are usually spoken of as "jewels and gems" (*ratnāni*).[343] The commentator of the *M. S. Al.* works out the simile in detail and compares the seven *bodhy-aṅgas* to the seven *ratnas* of a universal monarch. According to the Indian tradition, a monarch (*cakra-vartin*) possessed seven "jewels": a wheel (*cakra*), an elephant (*hastī*), a horse (*açva*), a gem (*maṇi*), a woman (*strī*), a treasurer or manager (*gṛha-pati*), and an adviser or Marshal (*pariṇāyaka*). Vasubandhu applies this idea to a *bodhisattva*, who cultivates the seven *bodhy-aṅgas*.

Smṛti (Mindfulness) gains the knowledge that has not been acquired, as a monarch's *wheel* conquers new territory. *Dharma-pravicaya* (Investigation of the Doctrine) dispels all doubt, as the monarch's *elephant* destroys his enemies. *Vīrya* (Energy) enables a *bodhisattva* to understand everything quickly and acquire the Super-knowledges (*abhijñā*) rapidly, as the monarch's *horse* traverses the whole earth as far as the ocean. A strenuous *bodhisattva* gains more and more of the Light of Truth and is therefore filled with Joy (*prīti*), as the monarch is pleased with the lustre of the *gem*. A *bodhisattva*, who has cultivated *praçrabdhi* (Tranquillity), is freed from all mental obstructions and evil qualities [344] and attains felicity, as the monarch enjoys happiness with the *woman* (*queen*). By *samādhi*, a *bodhisattva* succeeds in the aim that he has contemplated, as the monarch achieves success with the help of his *gṛha-pati* (*steward*). By *upekṣā*, a *bodhisattva* lives and goes wherever he likes, without let or hindrance, as the monarch's *adviser or Marshal* manages the army with its four divisions, and leads it to the place where it can have its encampment without any trouble.[344]

Thus does Vasubandhu, the commentator of the *M. S. Al.*, show his appreciation of the seven *bodhy-aṅgas*. Açvaghoṣa does not indulge in such play of fancy, but he exhorts a *bodhisattva* to destroy the seven *anuçayas* (evil proclivities and tendencies) of the heart by means of these seven Factors of Enlightenment.[345] These *anuçayas* are pride, doubt, ignorance, lust, hatred, delusion, and the craving for rebirth.

X. The Eightfold Way and the Four Noble Truths

It is a curious circumstance that the eightfold Way is included among the thirty-seven *bodhi-pakṣya-dharmas*, but the four Noble Truths (*ārya-satyāni*) are not found in that formula. The eightfold Way itself is the fourth of the "Truths" that Gautama Buddha is said to have discovered on the night, during which he attained Enlightenment.[346] The eightfold Way is thus torn from its original context in the formula of the *bodhi-pakṣya-dharmas*. It cannot be explained or understood without reference to the three other Truths that lead up to it. The Mahāyānists or semi-Mahāyānists, who devised that numerical list of the *bodhi-pakṣya-dharmas*, attached more importance to the eightfold Way than to the three other Truths, as the latter are merely theoretical in character and also suggest pessimism. The "eightfold Way", on the contrary, consists of positive and practical precepts, and it breathes a spirit of optimism. The author of the *Da. Bhū.* even puts the cart before the horse in his scheme of the ten *bhūmis*. A *bodhisattva* is supposed to practise the virtues and comprehend the principles that are embodied in the eightfold Way, while he is in the fourth *bhūmi*; but he understands the four Noble Truths subsequently in the fifth *bhūmi*.[347] It is not explained how a *bodhisattva* can start on the eightfold Way without first realising the other three Truths, of which it is only a sequel. As a matter of fact, the Mahāyānists did not attach much importance even to the eightfold Way. They taught that the six or ten *pāramitās* (Perfections) were the most important factors in a *bodhisattva's* career. The *Sad. Pu.* explicitly declares that the *arhats* (i.e. the Hīnayānists) preach the four Noble Truths and the twelve *nidānas*, while the *bodhisattvas* (i.e. the Mahāyānists) teach the *pāramitās*.[348] The *Da. Bhū.* and the *M. S. Al.* devote only a few lines to the eightfold Way. This difference of opinion between the Hīnayānists and the Mahāyānists is reflected in Buddhist Sanskrit literature. The *Ava. Ça.* and the *Divy.*, which belong mainly to the Hīnayāna, speak of the four Truths as the fundamental doctrines of Buddhism, while the later treatises only mention them briefly without attaching great importance to them. The *Lal. V.* and the *Mtu.* transmit the older tradition, as they record the earliest sermons of Gautama Buddha; but they also value the *pāramitās* as the essential elements of a *bodhisattva's* discipline.

(*a*) *The Four Noble Truths.*

The four Truths are called *ārya-satyāni* (Pāli: *ariyasaccāni*).[349] The word *ārya* (Pāli: *ariya*) literally means, "that which is in accord with the customs and ideals of the Aryan clans, held in esteem by Aryans, generally approved. Hence: right, good, ideal" (Pāli Dicy., s.v.). The four Truths may thus be described as "sublime or noble" Truths. They are mentioned in several passages of Buddhist Sanskrit literature (*Lal. V.*, 350.5, 416.2 ff.; *Mtu.*, ii, 285.3; iii, 331.17 ff.; iii, 408.17 ff.; *M. Vy.*, Sections 54, 56, 112; *Dh. S.*, Section 21; *Da. Bhū.*, 42.17 ff.; *Mdh.*, 475 ff., etc.).

The *Lal. V.* relates that Gautama Buddha explained the four Truths to the five disciples in his first sermon after the attainment of Enlightenment. He said: "O monks (*bhikṣus*), these are the four sublime Truths. What are the four? Pain (*Duḥkha*),[350] the origination (*samudaya*) of Pain, the cessation (*nirodha*) of Pain, and the Way (*mārga*) leading to the cessation of Pain. Then what is Pain? Birth is Pain (or Evil); old age is Pain; disease is Pain; death is Pain; union with that which is disagreeable is Pain; separation from that which is agreeable is Pain; when one does not obtain what one desires and seeks, that is Pain. In short, the five elements or substrata of sensory existence, which depend on attachment to existence, are Pain. All this is called Pain. Then what is the origin of Pain? This Craving (*tṛṣṇā*), which leads to renewed existence, which is accompanied by the lust of sense-desire, and which takes delight in various objects (literally, "there and there"), even this is called the origin of Pain. Then what is the cessation (or destruction—*nirodhaḥ*) of Pain? The complete renunciation and destruction of this same craving,[351] accompanied by the lust of sense-desire, which takes delight in various objects, and which, as the cause of Birth and Rebirth, leads to renewed existence. Then what is the Way leading to the cessation of Pain? It is this same eightfold Way (literally, "with eight members or limbs"): Right Views, Right Intention, Right Speech, Right Action, Right Livelihood, Right Endeavour, Right Mindfulness and Right Concentration. These are the four sublime Truths." (*Lal. V.*, 417.2 ff.)

The *M. Vy.* analyses the clauses in this sermon that refer to the different forms of Pain, and it enumerates the eight items (birth, old age, etc.). These are called "the eight *duḥkhatās*" (forms of *duḥkha*).[352] Çāntideva adds a few others, e.g., the pain of poverty, the pain of rebirth in a state of woe, and the pain of a sojourn in the world of *Yama*.[353] Another scheme of classifying the *duḥkhatās* (forms or states of pain) was also introduced. Three *duḥkhatās* are spoken of, viz. (1) *duḥkha-duḥkhatā* (painful sensation caused by bodily pain); (2) *saṃskāra-duḥkhatā* (pain having its origin in the *saṃskāras*, volitions or compounds, which are impermanent); and (3) *vipariṇāma-duḥkhata* (pain caused by change).[354] The author of the *Da. Bhū.* places them in this order: *saṃskāra-duḥkhatā*, *duḥkha-duḥkhata* and *pariṇāma-duḥkhatā*. He changes *vipariṇāma* to *pariṇāma* in describing the third *duḥkhatā*, and also attempts to relate these *duḥkhatās* to the twelve *nidānas* ("causes"; *vide infra*). Thus *saṃskāra-duḥkhatā* is due to the first five *nidānas* (*avidyā*, *saṃskārāḥ*, *vijñāna*, *nāma-rūpa* and *ṣad-āyatana*); *duḥkha-duḥkhatā* arises from the next two *nidānas* (*sparça* and *vedanā*); and the third *duḥkhatā* originates in the remaining five *nidānas* (*tṛṣṇā*, *upādāna*, *bhava*, *jāti* and *jarā-maraṇa*, etc.).

The Buddhist philosophers have also mentioned three aspects of each of the Truths, thus making a twelvefold scheme of "insight into Knowledge" (*jñāna-darçanam*) or of "the wheel of the Doctrine" (*cakram*). Each Truth receives three *parivartas* (turnings, revolutions), and is regarded in three ways, viz. (1) As the knowledge of the Truth obtained by thorough reflexion; (2) as something which is to be realised, practised and cultivated; (3) as something which has already been known, realised, practised and cultivated.[355] This scheme of classification seems to have been generally accepted, as it is explained at length in the *Lal. V.* and also frequently mentioned in other treatises. An attempt was also made to introduce another formula with sixteen sub-divisions, but it failed to win general recognition. This formula is as follows:—

Duḥkha. (*a*) *Duḥkhe dharma-jñāna-kṣāntiḥ* (Acceptance of the knowledge of the Law with regard to Pain).

(*b*) *Duḥkhe dharma-jñānam* (Knowledge of the Law with regard to Pain).

(*c*) *Duḥkhe-'nvaya-jñāna-kṣāntiḥ* [356] (Acceptance of the traditional or retrospective knowledge with regard to Pain).

(*d*) *Duḥkhe-'nvaya-jñānam* (Retrospective or traditional knowledge with regard to Pain).

Similarly, each of the three other Truths (*samudaya*, *nirodha* and *mārga*) are amplified in these four ways, thus making sixteen items in all (*M. Vy.*, Section 56; *Dh. S.*, Section 96; *Mdh.*, p. 482).

Apart from these elaborate and systematic statements, the Buddhist writers have also given us a few concise aphorisms, which assert the universal nature of *duḥkha*. "All this is Pain, not Happiness." "All the five *skandhas* are Pain." "Pain is like disease." "Pain grows surely and certainly, like weeds in a field." "Pain is assuredly everywhere, and Happiness is nowhere to be found." "Life is the epitome of all Pain." [357] This fundamental pessimism became the cardinal feature of almost all Indian systems of philosophy. The *Yoga* school borrowed the idea and the fourfold formula from the Buddhists. Patañjali declares that life is only Pain to a wise man; and Vyāsa, the commentator, speaks of *saṃsāra* (transmigratory existence), its cause (*hetu*), liberation (*mokṣa*) and the means or expedients for its attainment (*mokṣ-opāya*). (*Yo. Sū.*, ii, 15, p. 74.) Vyāsa also refers to the usual formula of medical science: "disease, its cause, health, and the medicine or drugs prescribed" (p. 78). It has been suggested that the Buddhists borrowed the formula from the medical treatises.[358] But medical science was not highly developed in India in the sixth and fifth centuries B.C. It is more likely that the writers on medicine were indebted to Buddhist literature for the four terms. There is nothing very original or striking in the idea of putting these four propositions together, and the formula belongs to the earliest Buddhist texts in a historical sense. From that source, it found its way into the literature of *Yoga* philosophy and medical science.

The few Sanskrit treatises that belong mainly to the Hīnayāna represent the four Truths as the central and fundamental dogmas of Buddhism. The *Ava. Ça.* and the *Divy.* teach that a person, who understands these Truths, has attained the first stage on the way to *arhatship*. Gautama Buddha converts the people by first expounding these Truths, which are always mentioned as constituting the theme of the sermons.[359] The Mahāyānist authors, on the contrary, do not attach much importance to the four Truths. The *M. S. Al.*, for instance, does not mention them at all. The Mahāyānists really took up a new attitude towards the problem of *Duḥkha*. The older tradition of Buddhism emphasised the fact of Pain so persistently that it tended to generate a kind of morbid cowardice in the *arhat*, who learned to avoid Pain at all costs and under all circumstances. But the Mahāyāna introduced the new and revolutionary idea that Pain (*duḥkha*) should be welcomed with joy, if it is endured in the service of other creatures. This alchemy of altruism transmuted evil into good, and led to a thorough re-valuation of all values. *Duḥkha* and *sukha* were recognised to be relative terms, and a *bodhisattva* was exhorted to suffer *duḥkha* for the good of others. The whole basis of Buddhist philosophy, theoretical and practical, was thus radically altered. The centre of gravity was shifted from *duḥkha* (Pain) to *karuṇā* (Love), and the formula of the four Truths was not regarded as the central doctrine of the religion. The new ideal is expounded by almost all the Mahāyānist authors. Candragomin defines it in a concise phrase: "Pain (endured) for the sake of others is Happiness" (*par-ārthe duḥkhaṃ sukham*).[360]

Kṣemendra says: "Pain is regarded as happiness by those, who sacrifice themselves for doing good to others." [361] The author of the *M. S. Al.* declares that a *bodhisattva* feels profound joy even in Pain on account of his great compassion.[362] He is prepared to suffer in a purgatory or other states of woe in order to save all creatures.[363] He thinks only of the interests of others, and not of the pain endured.[364] He is not afraid of *duḥkha*, and he may indeed be said to be closely associated with *duḥkha*, though he is free from it in another sense.[365] It is clear that these Mahāyānist philosophers exhibit a new attitude towards *duḥkha*, and they have travelled far from the negative and pessimistic standpoint of the early Buddhists. For this reason, they do not think that the comprehension of the four Truths is the beginning of Wisdom. They also rise to a higher point of view, when they declare that an advanced *bodhisattva* is really beyond and above both Pain and Pleasure. He does not associate the notion of Pain or Pleasure with anything in the universe.[366] Such is a *bodhisattva's* perfection of insight with regard to Pain.

(*b*) *The Eightfold Way*

The fourth of the Noble Truths is "the eightfold Way" (Pāli: *aṭṭhaṅgiko maggo*). In Sanskrit, the first word is found in two forms: (1) *aṣṭāṅga* (*Mtu.* iii, 332.10; *Lal. V.*, 417.13; *M. Vy.*, section 44; *Pr. Pā. Çata.*, 1010.14; *Kar. Pu.*, 106.31; *Sam. Rā*, fol. 193*b*, 3; *Ava. Ça.*, i, 232.3, etc.).

(2) *Aṣṭāṅgika* (*Divy.* 164.14; *Kā. Vy.*, 46.1; *Dh. S.*, section 50; *Mtu.*, iii, 331.12; *Lka.*, 204, verse 117, etc.).

The latter form corresponds to the Pāli, but the former occurs more frequently in the Sanskrit treatises. The phrase means; "The Way, which has eight constituents or parts, or embraces eight items." It is also called a *vīthi* (street or road).[367]

This Way was taught by Gautama Buddha to his first disciples as a middle path between excessive unbridled sensuality on the one hand and severe self-mortification on the other. He said to them in his first sermon: [368] "O monks (*bhikṣus*), there are two extremes that a monk should avoid. Attachment to sensual pleasures is low and vulgar; it is fit only for the ordinary persons and not at all for the noble disciples; it is associated with evil; it is not conducive in the sequel to the spiritual life, to disgust with the world, to dispassionateness, to destruc on (of Pain), to insight, to perfect Wisdom and to final Liberation. And this (other) extreme course, which consists in the practice of mortifying (tormenting) one's body, this is also painful and associated with evil; it causes Pain in this present existence and also results in Pain in the future. The *Tathāgata*, avoiding these two extremes, teaches the Doctrine of the Middle Way."

It may be inferred that the eightfold Way occupies an independent position by itself, although it is also included in the formula of the Four Truths. It is placed before those Truths in the *Lal. V.* and the *Mtu.* Those Buddhist Sanskrit writers, who maintain the tradition of the Hīnayāna, hold it in high esteem; but the Mahāyānists dismiss it with a few words. The author of the *Ava. Ça.* relates the story of Subhadra, who is told by Gautama Buddha that the eightfold Way constitutes the essential and central principle of the new religion. "In whatever religious Discipline, the noble eightfold Way is not found, there the *çramaṇas* (holy, saintly men) of the first, second, third or fourth degree are not found ... In this religious Discipline, the eightfold Way is found, and the *çramaṇas* of the four degrees are also found in it."[369] A perfect Buddha is praised in the same treatise as "the teacher of the eightfold Way".[370] The ideal of moderation is also emphasised by Kṣemendra, who employs the simile of the lute-string for this purpose. "If the string is stretched too much or too little, no music can be produced; even so a wise man should cultivate moderation." The Middle Way is indeed the ambrosia of piety; it is the one blessed Way for all Buddhists.[371]

The eightfold Way is mentioned in several passages of Buddhist Sanskrit literature;[372] but it is not thoroughly discussed in detail, as it is in the Pāli canon.[373] The eight items are as follows:—

(1) *Samyag-dṛṣṭi* (Pāli: *sammā-diṭṭhi*). "Right Views." The word *dṛṣṭi* has been variously translated as "doctrine", "la vue", "belief", "faith", "outlook", "opinion", etc. The English word "View" corresponds literally and etymologically to Sanskrit *dṛṣṭi*. The *Dhamma-saṅgaṇi* seems to identify *samyag-dṛṣṭi* with Wisdom in general, and its verbose explanation does not exactly define the meaning of this word.[374] In other Pāli passages, *samyag-dṛṣṭi* is said to denote belief in the utility of alms, sacrifices, oblations and good deeds, and in the existence of other worlds, of spontaneously generated beings and of holy saints and monks.[375] But such interpretations seem to be unsuitable and far-fetched. The author of the *Pr. Pā. Çata.* explains *samyag-dṛṣṭi* as faith

in the Buddha, the Doctrine and the Confraternity or Church (*dharma*, *saṅgha*).[376] The *M. S. Al.* defines it as "conformity to the knowledge of things as they are (or to the insight into Truth)."[377] But it is perhaps admissible to suppose that *samyag-dṛṣṭi* originally referred to the comprehension of the four Noble Truths, which were mentioned with the eight-fold Way in Buddha's first sermon and which were regarded as the cardinal dogmas of Buddhism. This view is also confirmed by several important Pāli passages.[378] The *Lal. V.* teaches that *samyag-dṛṣṭi* helps a *bodhisattva* to observe the Rule.[379]

(2) *Samyak-saṅkalpa* (Pāli: *sammā-saṅkappo*): The word *saṅkalpa* has been variously translated as "aspiration", "resolve", "thoughts", "aim", "intention", "decision", "la combinaison", "la volonté", "le jugement", "die Gesinnung", "das Entschliessen", etc. The *Dhammasaṅgaṇi* regards it as synonymous with *vitakka* (Sections 7, 283 and 298). It explains thus: "The discrimination, the application, which is the disposing, the fixing, the focussing, the super-posing of the mind, right intention, which is a component of the Way, and is contained in the Way." The *Saṅgīti-suttanta* of the *Dīgha-Nikāya* mentions three *kusalā saṅkappā* and three *akusalā saṅkappā*, the latter being "sense-desires, enmity, and cruelty".[380] The same triad is mentioned in several passages of the *Majjhima-Nikāya*, and *sammā-saṅkappo* is said to consist in renunciation, goodwill (amity) and kindness (harmlessness).[381] T. W. Rhys Davids and W. Stede render *sammā-saṅkappo* as "Right thoughts or intentions" (Pāli Dicy.). It is perhaps best to translate, "Right Intention," thus preserving the singular number as in the original. The Tibetan equivalent *rtog-pa* (*Lal. V. Tib.*, 362.21) means "ideas, thought, full comprehension" (Tib. Dicy., Das, 539). According to Vasubandhu, *samyak-saṅkalpa* consists in the analysis and arrangement of the knowledge that constitutes *samyag-dṛṣṭi*.[382] He thus establishes a close relation between *samyag-dṛṣṭi* and *samyak-saṅkalpa*. The *Lal. V.* teaches that right Intention enables a *bodhisattva* to get rid of all doubt, uncertainty and indecision.[383]

(3) *Samyag-vāk* (Pāli: *sammā-vācā*): Right Speech. A *bodhisattva's* duties with regard to Speech will be discussed in the sections on *çīla* and the *saṅgraha-vastūni* (*vide infra*).

(4) *Samyak-karmānta* (Pāli: *sammā-kammanto*). The word *karmānta* has been translated as "conduct", "action", "la

fin de l'œuvre", etc. Its general meaning is "doing, acting, working, work, business, occupation, profession". The *Dhammasaṅgaṇi* (Section 300) defines it as "*tīhi kāya-duccaritehi ārati virati*" (aversion to and abstention from the three errors of conduct), and it is understood as referring to the avoidance of the bodily sins of killing, theft and unchastity in some other Pāli passages.[384] But this interpretation is surely too narrow. It is best to interpret it in a general sense : "Right Action."

(5) *Samyag-ājīva* (Pāli : *sammā-ājīvo*) : Right livelihood or mode of earning one's livelihood. A *bodhisattva* must have a pure and honest mode of gaining his livelihood.[385] Various dishonest or unsuitable pursuits and professions are described in some Pāli passages.[386] But we do not find a similar list in the principal Sanskrit treatises.

(6) *Samyag-vyāyāma* (Pali : *sammā-vāyāmo*) : "Right Endeavour." The word *vyāyāma* is derived from the root *yam*, "to stretch out," "to extend." It originally signified "struggle, fight", and also "physical exertion and athletic exercise". But the Buddhists employed it in a spiritual sense to denote "moral striving, effort, exertion, endeavour". The *Dhammasaṅgaṇi* (Sections 13, 22, 289, 302) regards it as a synonym of *vīrya* (Energy), and it is interpreted in the same way thus : "the striving and the onward effort, the exertion and endeavour, the zeal and ardour, the vigour and fortitude, the state of unfaltering effort, the state of sustained desire, the state of unflinching endurance, etc."[387] A *bodhisattva*, who practises *vyāyāma* indefatigably, eliminates all obstacles to knowledge and reaches the further shore of transmigratory existence.[388]

The word *vyāyāma* has been translated as "effort", "energy", "exertion", "l'application", "la tension", "perseverance in well-doing", "das Mühn", etc. The Tibetan equivalent *rtsol-ba* (*Lal. V. Tib.*, p. 363, line 1) means "zeal, endeavour, exertion, diligence, perseverance" (Tib. Dicy., Das, 1015).

(7) *Samyak-smṛti* (Pāli : *sammā-sati*) : Right Mindfulness. The term has been discussed in the section on the four *smṛty-upasthānas*.

(8) *Samyak-samādhi* (*Pāli : sammā-samādhi*) : Right Concentration. The term *samādhi* will be discussed in the section on *Dhyāna-pāramitā*.

It is probable that the Buddhists borrowed the word *samyak* from the Jainas, who employed it in their well-known formula: *Samyag-darçana-jñāna-caritrāṇi.*[389] The Jainas also reckon eight *aṅgas* of the *samyag-darçana*. E. Senart has suggested that the eightfold Way may be compared to the eight *aṅgas* of the *Yoga* philosophy.[390] But there is really very little in common between these two formulae, for the eight *aṅgas* of *Yoga* are: *yama* (moral abstentions), *niyama* (observances), *āsana* (postures), *prāṇāyāma* (regulation of the breath), *pratyāhāra* (withdrawal of the senses), *dhāraṇā* (fixed a tention), *dhyāna* (contemplation) and *samādhi* (concentration: *Yo. Sū*, ii 29, page 101). The number of the items in such formulae is due to the old custom of counting by tetrads, which was also applied to the Olympiads of Greece.

The principle of moderation, which is embodied in the eightfold Way, constitutes a link between Indian and Hellenic thought. Aristotle defined Virtue as the mean between two extremes: "Virtue is a mean state between two vices, one in excess, the other in defect."[391] This noble ideal was discovered and formulated independently in India and Greece.

Chapter V

THE PĀRAMITĀS

A *bodhisattva* must practise the six or ten *pāramitās* (Perfections). This important word *pāramitā* has also been translated as "transcendental virtue", "perfect virtue", "highest perfection", "complete attainment", "die Vollkommenheit", etc. The form *pārami* is also found (*Divy.*, 637, 5, *mantrāṇāṃ pāramiṃ gatāḥ*). In Pāli, the forms *pāramī* and *pāramitā* occur in the *Sutta-nipāta*, the *Jātaka*, the *Nettipakaraṇa* and other treatises [1]; and T. W. Rhys Davids and W. Stede translate: "completeness, perfection, highest state" (Pāli Dicy.). The term *pāramitā* has been wrongly explained by Böhtlingk and Roth, Monier Williams, E. Burnouf, B. Hodgson and M. Vassilief as consisting of two words, *pāram* (the opposite bank, the further shore), and *ita* (gone, from the root *i*, Skt. Dicy., M.W. 566*c*).[2] Böhtlingk and Roth regard it as a contracted form of the abstract substantive *pāramitatā* (the quality of having gone to the further shore). But E. Burnouf thinks that it is an adjectival participle, which really qualifies a suppressed substantive like *buddhi*, but which is employed as a substantive on account of its similarity to other abstract nouns ending in *-tā*. He says: "Ce mot, en effet, est le féminin de l'adjectif *pāramita* signifiant, 'celui qui est allé à l'autre rive, transcendant,' mais ce n'est ni ce ne peut être un substantif. Or c'est comme substantif que l'emploient les Bouddhistes . . . Peut-être le mot de *pāramitā* se rapporte-il à quelque terme sous-entendu, comme celui de *buddhi*, l'Intelligence, par exemple, de sorte qu'on devrait traduire les noms des diverses Perfections de cette manière: (l'Intelligence) parvenue à l'autre rive de la sagesse, de l'aumône, de la charité, et ainsi des autres . . . Je dirai seulement que l'expression de *pāramitā*, une fois introduite dans la langue avec l'ellipse que je suppose, a pu y rester et y prendre par extension la valeur d'un substantif, à cause de sa ressemblance extérieure avec un nom abstrait tel que ceux qu'on forme au moyen de la syllabe *-tā*".[3] E. Burnouf also refers to T. Goldstücker's view that the word is derived from Sanskrit *parama* (= "most distant, last; highest, first, most excellent or distinguished, best, greatest, chief, primary, principal, superior". Skt. Dicy., M.W. 535*a*). T. Goldstücker was on the right track, but he unfortunately thought that *pārami* meant "daughter of *parama*, i.e. of Buddha". *Pāramitā* is really derived from *parama* (and not from *pāra* with the root *i*), as the *Bo. Bhū.* clearly explains. The *pāramitās* are so called, because they are acquired during a long period of time (*parameṇa kālena samudāgatāḥ*), and are supremely pure in their nature (*paramayā svabhāva-viçuddhyā viçuddhāḥ*). They also transcend the virtues or qualities of the *çrāvakas* and the *pratyeka-buddhas*, and lead to the highest result (*paramaṃ ca phalam anuprayacchanti*).[4] It is not necessary to accept all the details that are given in the *Bodhisattva-bhūmi*. But the derivation of the term from *parama* is thus placed beyond the possibility of doubt. It simply means, "highest condition, highest point, best state, perfection." F. W. Thomas, T. W. Rhys Davids and W. Stede explain it as a substantive derived from *parama*, while L. de la Vallée Poussin expresses himself enigmatically: "les vertus d'au-dela, parceque leur mérite est appliqué à l'acquisition de la qualité de Bouddha." [5] The Tibetan equivalent is *pha-rol-tu-phyin-pa*. S. C. Das explains thus: "to get to the other side; in Buddhism, crossing to the other side of this life, i.e. to *Nirvāṇa*; absolute transcendental virtue" (Tib. Dicy., 817*b*). This seems to confirm E. Burnouf's view that *pāramitā* is derived from *pāra*. But it only proves that the Tibetan translators did not know the correct etymology of the term. The *Bodhisattva-bhūmi*, cited above, connects it with *parama*. Unfortunately, the Chinese also seem to have made the same mistake as the Tibetans. According to E. J. Eitel, they translate *pāramitā* as "means of passing, arrival at the other shore" (p. 115*a*).[6]

The earlier and alternative form *pārami* also points to the derivation from *parama*. The suffix *-tā* was probably added to it on the analogy of the abstract substantives ending in *-tā*. It has been suggested that a compound like *dāna-pāramitā* may be explained as "the quality or condition of a person, who is a *dāna-pārami*, i.e. who possesses the *pārami* or highest point of *dāna* or charity." In this case, the suffix *-tā* would be added to a *bahu-vrīhi* compound (*dānasya pāramir yasya*). But the two words in such a compound as *dāna-pāramitā* seem to stand in direct apposition, and it is better to construe thus: *dānam eva* *pāramitā dāna-pāramitā*. The virtue of charity is itself the Perfection.

The six *pāramitās* are really the chief factors in a *bodhisattva's* discipline, and the four additional *pāramitās* are merely supplementary in character. The six *pāramitās* are mentioned and discussed in many passages of Buddhist Sanskrit literature,[7] while the seventh, eighth, ninth and tenth *pāramitās* are mentioned only in a few passages and are not explained at great length.[8] Thus the *Bo. Bhū.* classifies each of the six chief *pāramitās* under nine separate headings, but it dismisses the other four *pāramitās* in a few sentences in another chapter. The *M. S. Al.* adopts the same method of treatment. The *Dh. S.* gives six *pāramitās* in one section and ten in another; but the *M. Vy.* speaks only of ten *pāramitās*. The *Da. Bhū.* definitely increases the number of the *pāramitās* to ten, as it teaches that a *bodhisattva* practises one of the *pāramitās* in each of the ten *bhūmis* (stages) of his career. This alteration may have been due to the rivalry with the Hīnayānists, who had devised the Pāli formula of the ten *pāramīs* (*dāna*, liberality; *sīla*, virtuous conduct; *nekkhamma*, renunciation; *paññā*, wisdom; *viriya*, energy; *khanti*, forbearance; *sacca*, truthfulness; *adhiṭṭhāna*, resolution; *mettā*, love or friendliness; *upekkhā*, equanimity).[9] But it is more probable that the number of the *pāramitās* (and the *bhūmis*) was raised to ten as a consequence of the invention of the decimal system of computation in the science of arithmetic in the third or fourth century A.D. A. F. R. Hoernle assigns the subject-matter of the Bakhshālī manuscript to that period.[10] The oldest epigraphical evidence for this remarkable discovery dates from the sixth century, and the literary evidence belongs to the same period, as the system is employed by Varāhamihira.[11] Many old formulae of Indian philosophy and religion were recast according to the decimal system on account of the enthusiasm evoked by this epoch-making invention. Even the time-hallowed *yamas* and *niyamas* of the *Yoga* system are increased to ten in the later treatises.[12] The *Samādhi-rāja-sūtra* mentions ten advantages of each *pāramitā* (chapter xxviii). The *Bo. Bhū.* assigns ten causes for the phenomena.[13] In the *Da. Bhū.*, a *bodhisattva* acquires ten qualities in each stage, must beware of ten faults, and so on. The *M. S. Al.* speaks of ten marks, and the *M. Vy.* raises the number of *caryās* from four to ten.[14] There is a sudden transition to the decimal system in many categories and formulae of Indian religion and philosophy. Previous teachers had preferred the numbers Seven and Eight (e.g. seven *bhūmis*, fourteen *guṇa-sthānas* of the Jainas, the eightfold Way, the eight *aṅgas* of *Yoga*, etc.). But the number Ten is associated with many lists and items after this period. The six *pāramitās* were also increased to ten, when the *bhūmis* were reckoned as ten instead of seven.

The six chief *pāramitās* are given as follows [15] :—

(1) *Dāna* (giving, generosity, liberality).
(2) *Çīla* (virtuous conduct, morality, righteousness).
(3) *Kṣānti* (forbearance, patience).
(4) *Vīrya* (energy).
(5) *Dhyāna* (rapt musing).
(6) *Prajñā* (wisdom).

The four supplementary *pāramitās* are the following [16] :—

(7) *Upāya* or *Upāya-kauçalya* (skilfulness in the choice or adaptation of means for conversion or succour).
(8) *Praṇidhāna* (aspiration or resolution).
(9) *Bala* (strength, power).
(10) *Jñāna* (knowledge).

The formula of the six chief *pāramitās* was evolved after a process of selection and experimentation. Thus only two of these virtues are mentioned together (*çīla* and *kṣānti*) in several passages of the *Mtu.* (ii, 327, 9 ; ii, 353, 20 ; ii, 408, 18 ; iii, 441, 1). In another passage, *vīrya* is not mentioned (ii, 296, 6) ; and *dhyāna* and *kṣānti* are left out at *Mtu.*, iii, 249, 13 ff. In the *Su. Vy.*, another item (*çamatha*, "calm") is added after *dāna* (p. 8, lines 6–7), and *prajñā* is omitted. Another puzzling problem is presented by the fact that the *Sad. Pu.* mentions only five *pāramitās* in an important passage (p. 334, line 2), and the Tibetan literature has a treatise on "the five *pāramitās*" (Tib. Dicy., Das, p. 817*b*). It seems likely that the formula included only five "Perfections" at a certain period.

The origin of the sixfold formula of the *pāramitās* must be sought in the early Buddhist triad, *çīla* (virtuous conduct), *samādhi* (concentration) and *prajñā* (wisdom), which are known as the three *skandhas* [17] (groups constituting the factors of spiritual progress) and also as the three *çikṣās* (branches of instruction, the threefold training and discipline).[18] It is probable that *prajñā* was added to the original group of two, viz. *çīla* and *samādhi*, which are mentioned together in several passages (*Mtu.*, ii, 361.8 ; *Çikṣā.*, 121.1). *Çīla* is often said to lead to *samādhi*, and *prajñā* is not spoken of in that context. The eightfold Way also ends with *samādhi*. The threefold *çikṣā* is defined as *adhi-çīla*, *adhi-citta* and *adhi-prajñā* in the *M. Vy.* (Section 36); the prefix *adhi* denotes pre-eminence and importance. *Citta* is here synonymous with *samādhi*. The last two items are identical with the fifth and sixth *pāramitās* (*dhyāna* and *prajñā*). *Çīla* is the second *pāramitā*, to which *kṣānti* was gradually attached as an important virtue. These two were mentioned together even before the final formulation of the six Perfections. The fourth *pāramitā* (*vīrya*) was placed between the *çīla* section (which appertained especially to the laymen) and the *dhyāna-prajñā* section (which was really cultivated by the monks). The first *pāramitā* occupied an independent position from a very early period, when it was coupled with *çīla*. *Dāna* and *çīla* were regarded as the laymen's special duties, which paved the way to a happy re-birth. The well-known sentence, which describes Buddha's preaching, begins thus: "*dāna-kathaṃ sīla-katham sagga-kathaṃ*."[19] This was the complete gospel for the layman-householder. The higher virtues of renunciation and celibacy are then mentioned in the latter part of the same sentence: "*kāmānaṃ ādīnavaṃ okāraṃ saṃkilesam*," etc. (*Dīgha*, i, 110.2, 148.7). *Dāna* was thus the first step that an ordinary person was taught to take; and it was placed before *çīla* as a distinct duty, though it is logically included in moral conduct (*çīla*). It may be inferred that *dāna* and *prajñā* were added to the central dyad of *çīla* and *samādhi*, and they were emphasised on account of the influence of Hinduism. Vasubandhu clearly explains in the *M. S. Al.* commentary that the six *pāramitās* are fundamentally related to the three *çikṣās*. The first three *pāramitās* correspond to *adhi-çīla*, and the fifth and sixth to *adhi-citta* and *adhi-prajñā* respectively; while the fourth (*vīrya*) is regarded as belonging to all the three branches of discipline. The third *pāramitā* is sometimes coupled with the fourth, thus making three pairs of *pāramitās*.[20]

In this connection, it may be pointed out that the division of the *pāramitās* into two sections (with *vīrya* as the common or neutral middle term) is based on the doctrine of the twofold Equipment (*sambhāra*) of a *bodhisattva*, which has already been referred to above. *Sambhāra* means "what is carried together", hence "materials and requisite ingredients", "necessary conditions", "equipment". It consists of *puṇya*

(Merit acquired by good deeds in social life) and *jñāna* (Knowledge acquired by concentration and wisdom).[21] "Merit" leads to happiness, sense-pleasure, and welfare on earth and in the heavens; but "Knowledge" confers final Liberation. The accumulation of "Merit" is therefore the aim of the layman, while the acquisition of "Knowledge" is the goal of the monk. According to Vasubandhu, the first two *pāramitās* (*dāna* and *çīla*) lead to Merit, the last *pāramitā* (*prajñā*) constitutes Knowledge, while the other three partake of the characteristics of both kinds of *sambhāra*. Thus one may even speak of three divisions of *sambhāra*. But the application of the results of all the *pāramitās* for the attainment of Enlightenment really abolishes the distinction between mundane Merit and supra-mundane Knowledge, and all the *pāramitās* may be regarded as conducive to the equipment of Knowledge.[22] In this way, Vasubandhu attempts to unify and sublimate social Action and ascetic Meditation in the single ideal of the quest for *bodhi*.

The six *pāramitās* are thus related to several basic concepts of early Buddhism. The Buddhist Sanskrit writers attach the greatest importance to the *pāramitās*, which distinguish the *bodhisattvas* from the inferior *arhats* and *pratyeka-buddhas*. These latter are regarded as representatives of merely *negative* ethical ideals, while the *pāramitās* are put forward as a scheme of *positive* moral development. It is not easy to understand the claims advanced by the Mahāyānists in this respect. There is nothing new in the formula of the six *pāramitās*: all the items are found in the old Buddhist scriptures. But the Mahāyānists really contrast their *pāramitās* with the thirty-seven *bodhi-pakṣya-dharmas*, which are supposed to constitute the highest ideal of the so-called Hīnayāna. It is certainly surprising that the terms *dāna*, *çīla* and *kṣānti* are absent from that curious and comprehensive catalogue of a monk's duties, which does not seem to include social sympathy and altruistic service. The early Mahāyānists were perhaps proud of having combined the social virtues of a righteous layman-householder with the ascetic ideals of a meditative monk in this formula of the *pāramitās*. They thus bridged the gap that yawned between popular and monastic Buddhism. They taught that a *bodhisattva* should not cease to practise charity and forbearance in social life, when he ascended to the higher stages of Concentration and Wisdom. The six *pāramitās* were not new, but the new method of juxtaposition was devised by the Mahāyānists. They preferred their new formula to the thirty-seven *bodhi-pakṣya-dharmas*, which were regarded as too monastic and anti-social in their scope and tendency. Charity and moral conduct, which could lead a Buddhist only to the gates of a heaven of temporary pleasure in the old Dispensation, were now considered to be as important as Concentration and the higher Wisdom. All are classed together as indispensable factors in the attainment of Enlightenment.

The *pāramitās* are extolled to the skies in many passages of Buddhist literature. They are "the great oceans of all the bright virtues and auspicious principles", and confer prosperity and happiness on all creatures.[23] They are a *bodhisattva's* best friends. They are "the Teacher, the Way and the Light". They are "the Refuge and the Shelter, the Support and the Sanctuary". They are indeed "Father and Mother to all".[24] Even the Buddhas are their "children".[25]

Certain general characteristics are ascribed to all the *pāramitās* as a group. They are sublime, disinterested, supremely important and imperishable.[26] They lead to welfare, happy re-births, serenity, unremitting spiritual cultivation, successful Concentration and the highest Knowledge.[27] They are free from contamination by sensual pleasure, partiality, love of reward and culpable self-complacency.[28] They are placed in this order, as they imply one another and form a progressive scheme of action. The practice of each *pāramitā* is impossible without the cultivation of the preceding one.[29] Each Perfection has three degrees: it may be ordinary, extraordinary, or superlatively extraordinary (i.e. good, better, and the best).[30] It is ordinary, when it is practised by the ordinary worldly persons for the sake of happiness in this life or the next; it is extraordinary, when it is cultivated by the Hīnayānists for the sake of personal *nirvāṇa*; but it is of the highest degree, when it is acquired by the Mahāyānist *bodhisattvas* for the welfare and liberation of all beings. All the Perfections can be cultivated only by means of attentive thought, resolute purpose, self-mastery, and wisdom in the choice of means.[31] But foolish and boastful persons may abuse all the *pāramitās* to their own destruction, as they may be puffed up with pride and arrogance on account of their moral superiority.[32] In that case, the Perfections really become obstacles and hindrances. Such disastrous consequences may be avoided by applying and devoting them only to the attainment of Enlightenment.

The different Perfections may now be considered in detail.

1. Dāna-pāramitā. The word *dāna* literally means "giving", and this seems to be the best rendering in this context. The other equivalents, "generosity," "liberality," "charity," "munificence," do not suggest the vast variety of the things that a *bodhisattva* gives away, when he practises the Perfection of Giving.

The practice of *tyāga* (renunciation, Pāli: *cāga*) is almost synonymous with *dāna*, though the former term is not employed in the formula of the *pāramitās*. The Mahāyānists attach great importance to this Perfection, and *dāna* or *tyāga* is included in several numerical lists. It figures among the six or ten *anusmṛtis* (subjects of recollection), the seven *dhanas* (treasures), the four *sampads* (blessings, accomplishments), the three, four or five items of meritorious action (*puṇya-kriyā-vastūni*), the four means of conversion or sympathy (*saṅgraha-vastūni*) and the four resolutions (*adhiṣṭhānāni*).[33] Such frequency of occurrence in these different formulae indicates its crucial importance for a *bodhisattva's* discipline. The Mahāyānists speak much and speak often of what they love. They simply maintain and develop a very ancient Indian tradition in thus exalting and inculcating the practice of charity and self-sacrifice. The duty of *dāna* is emphasised in the *Upaniṣads*, the *Gṛhya-sūtras* and other Hindu scriptures.[34] The motives, methods and merits of Giving are also discussed in detail in several striking passages of the Pāli canon.[35] The Mahāyānists developed the idea of *dāna* in five ways. They coloured it with the avarice and selfishness of a mendicant monastic Order. They extended its scope and included life and limb among the objects, which should be sacrificed for others. They introduced a spirit of exaggerated sentimentality by praising imaginary men and women, who sacrificed themselves for the protection of animals. They gradually eliminated the noble self-regarding motive of attaining *nirvāṇa* or *bodhi*, and taught that *dāna* should be based solely on the feeling of mercy and compassion (*karuṇā*). They evolved the new and revolutionary idea of the "gift of Merit", by which a *bodhisattva* could save all sinners from punishment or bestow undeserved happiness on all creatures. The spirit of the Mahāyāna may be described in Wordsworth's words:—

> "Give all thou hast. High Heaven rejects the lore
> Of nicely calculated less or more."

Dāna is classified and analysed in the first place according to the things given away. The *Dh. S.*, which divides each Perfection into three parts, speaks of three kinds of *dāna*: the gift of wealth and material objects, of religious instruction and of friendliness (or security and protection).[36] Çāntideva teaches that a *bodhisattva* gives away his body, his pleasures and his Merit.[37] The author of the *Bo. Bhū.* divides *dāna* into three categories: personal *dāna* (i.e. the gift of life and limb), external *dāna* (i.e. the gift of material objects), and such *dāna* as is partly personal and partly external.[38] The love of logic, however, leads him into a difficult situation, as he is at a loss to find an example of the third species of *dāna*. He mars his valuable dissertation on *dāna* by the repellent remark that the gift of food, which has been eaten and then vomited by a *bodhisattva*, is partly personal and partly external! The same writer has also devised a scheme of classification under nine headings, which he applies to all the Perfections. *Dāna*, for instance, is described as being of nine kinds [39] :—

(1) *Svabhāva-dānam* (i.e. *dāna* in its essential aspects).
(2) *Sarva-dānam* (i.e. *dāna* in general).
(3) *Duṣkaraṃ dānam* (i.e. difficult *dāna*).
(4) *Sarvato-mukhaṃ dānam* (i.e. all-round *dāna*).
(5) *Satpuruṣa-dānam* (i.e. the *dāna* of a virtuous man).
(6) *Sarvākāraṃ dānam* (i.e. omniform *dāna*).
(7) *Vighātārthikaṃ dānam* (i.e. the *dāna*, which prevents other persons from being hostile and converts them into suppliants; or, which makes poor persons rich).
(8) *Ih-āmutra-sukhaṃ dānam* (i.e. the *dāna*, which is pleasant in this life and the next).
(9) *Viçuddhaṃ dānam* (i.e. purified *dāna*).

This elaborate scheme of classification is used only as a framework for a lengthy disquisition on the *pāramitāṣ*.

(1) The recipients of a *bodhisattva's* gifts are frequently mentioned. In a general way, all suppliants (*arthī*, *yācaka*) [40] should be helped. But certain classes of people are especially indicated. They may be divided into three categories. First, a *bodhisattva* should bestow gifts on his friends and relatives (*bandhuṣu*; *mitra-sva-janebhyaḥ*; *kalyāṇa-mitra-mātā-pitṛbhyaḥ*).[41] Secondly, he should help the needy, the poor, the sick, the afflicted and the helpless (*daridra-sattva-parigrahaḥ*; *dīn-ātura-modakaḥ*; *kṛpaṇa-vanī paka-yācakebhyaḥ*; *dīne jane*; *duḥkhito niḥpratisaraṇo*).[42] Thirdly,

he should offer gifts to the Buddhist monks and the Hindu priests (*çramaṇa-brāhmaṇebhyaḥ*). These two classes are often mentioned together with the poor and the needy as deserving recipients of charity. The phrase *çramaṇa-brāhmaṇa-kṛpaṇa-vanīpakebhyaḥ* recurs frequently in Buddhist literature.[43] The claims of the poor are not overlooked; but monasticism slowly casts its sombre shadow on Buddhist ethics, and the poor are sometimes forgotten. But we find that only the poor are spoken of in certain passages. The miseries and difficulties of the indigent sections of society are described with real sympathy and insight by Kṣemendra and other writers. We seem to hear the cry of the poor of India in such verses as the following: "His heart melted with pity, when he saw the afflicted and helpless farmers. Their hair looked yellow, as it was covered with dust; their hands and feet were torn and rent; they suffered from hunger, thirst and fatigue; they were troubled with the wounds and hard scratches inflicted by the plough and the spade."[44] Çāntideva teaches that a monk should even share his scanty alms with the poor.[45] But it must be admitted that the Buddhist authors often forget the poor and speak only of charity to the monks and the priests. In such passages, mendicant monasticism stands out naked and unashamed.[46] In the story of Açoka's gifts to the monks, the poor are not mentioned at all.[47] The economic interests of the monastic Order also led to the formulation of the curious doctrine that the merit of a charitable deed depended on the spiritual status of the recipient, and not on the greatness of his need or the nature of the social service rendered by the donor. It is more meritorious to give to a monk than to a pious layman or an ordinary person.[48] A Buddha is the worthiest recipient of gifts (a *kṣetra* or field).[49] This teaching throws a lurid light on the sub-conscious psychology of the monks, who depended for their subsistence on the alms of the laity.

(2) As regards the objects that should be given in charity, a *bodhisattva* should give all that he has,[50] his wealth, his limbs, his life, his "Merit" (*puṇya*), and also his wife and children, who are evidently regarded as a man's property. The heroes of many edifying legends are kings and princes, and they are described as giving away "food, beverages, medicine, couches, seats, gardens, houses, villages, towns, perfumes, garlands, ointments, silver, gold, elephants, horses, chariots, clothes, corn, gems, ornaments, musical instruments, men-servants and maid-servants", etc.[51] But

there is also a moving story of "the widow's mite" in the *Avadāna-çataka*.[52] A poor woman gives a piece of cotton cloth (*paṭaka*), which is all that she can afford. A monk does not need superfluous luxuries, and accepts only his simple "requisites", viz. clothing, food, lodging and medicine.[53]

A *bodhisattva* should exercise his discretion in the choice of gifts. He should not give anything which may be used to inflict injury on other living beings.[54] He should also refrain from supplying others with the means of gratifying their sensual appetites and passions[55] (*rati-krīḍā-vastu*). He should not give away poisons, weapons, intoxicating liquor, and nets for the capture of animals.[56] He should not bestow on others a piece of land, on which the animals may be hunted or killed.[57] He should not give anybody the instruments for suicide or self-torture. He should not offer unsuitable gifts: thus, for example, he should not give alcoholic beverages to teetotalers or unwholesome food to the sick. The wealth, that he gives in charity, must be acquired righteously and peacefully.[58] If he has little, he gives what he has. If he possesses something, which is very rare and precious, or which has been obtained with great difficulty, he does not refuse to part with it.[59]

Besides wealth and material objects, a *bodhisattva* should be ready to sacrifice his limbs for the good of others, "his hand, foot, eye, flesh, blood, marrow, limbs great and small, and even his head."[60] This teaching is, however, modified by the sensible author of the *Bodhisattva-bhūmi*, who expresses the opinion that a *bodhisattva* need not give away his body and limbs, if his mind is pure. But he can sacrifice his body by becoming a servant or a slave for the sake of others.[61] The idea of giving away one's limbs has given rise to some curious stories, which are intended to be highly instructive and inspiring, but which are simply silly and puerile.

A *bodhisattva* should also give away his wife and children to such suppliants as need their services.[62] But he may not sacrifice his parents in the same way, as they should be honoured and protected.[63] The gift of one's wife and children is regarded as the acme of liberality. It is indeed necessary for an advanced *bodhisattva* to be married in order that he may be able to exhibit this virtue in its perfection!

(3) A *bodhisattva* should also know *how* to give. He should always be very courteous to the suppliants, and receive them

with every mark of respect and deference (*satkṛtya*).[64] He should also be happy and joyful, when he gives away anything.[65] This condition is important and essential. The donor should be even happier than the recipient of the gift. A *bodhisattva* should not repent of his generosity after bestowing gifts on others.[66] He should not talk of his charitable deeds.[67] He should give quickly (*tvaritam*) and with a humble heart.[68] He should make no distinction between friends and enemies, but should give to all alike.[69] He should give to the deserving and the undeserving, the wicked and the righteous, everywhere and at all times.[70] But he should not lose the sense of measure and proportion in his charity. He owes a duty to many living beings and must not sacrifice himself in vain for an unimportant purpose. He must combine wisdom with mercy.[71]

(4) A *bodhisattva*, who knows *what* to give and *how* to give, should also understand *why* he should give. The Buddhist writers have mentioned almost all the motives, high and low, that may actuate a donor. Charity confers fame on the generous man (*dātṛ-kīrti*).[72] The love of fame, that "last infirmity of noble minds", is regarded as a motive, that should not be severely condemned. Charity leads to the accumulation of *puṇya* (Merit) and to happy rebirths on earth or in a heaven of the *devas*.[73] It should be practised even by selfish persons, as it confers inward happiness and peace of mind. It also affords protection against premature death and all other evils.[74] It is indeed the source of power, longevity, welfare and prosperity during many æons.[75] A gift cannot fail to bring a corresponding reward in the next life: they who give food, money or a lamp will get strength, beauty or lovely eyes respectively as their recompense.[76] Gautama Buddha himself enjoyed good health on account of his charitable deeds in a former life,[77] and a *bodhisattva's* great physical strength is acquired in the same way.[78] A very generous donor (*dāna-pati*) is praised by the poets as a sandal-tree, a cloud, a drug-tree, a *kalpa-vṛkṣa* (wish-fulfilling tree), a *cintāmaṇi* (philosopher's stone) and a baited hook; and other similes are employed in order to exalt and glorify him.[79] The Buddhists put their well-known *dāna-sūtra* (text or aphorism on *dāna*) into the mouth of Gautama Buddha, who is represented as speaking these words: "If the living beings knew the fruit and final reward of charity and the distribution of gifts, as I know them, then they would not eat their food without giving to others and

sharing with others, even if it were their last morsel and mouthful. If they should meet a person, who is worthy of receiving a gift, selfishness (niggardliness), that has once arisen, would not abide in their hearts. But they do not know the fruit and final reward of charity and the distribution of gifts, as I know them. For this reason, they eat without giving and sharing with others; and selfishness, that has once arisen, abides in their hearts." [80] This passage describes the merits of charity in a general way, but the author of the *Samādhirāja-sūtra* mentions ten advantages resulting from the practice of *dāna*. He says: "A *bodhisattva*, who is devoted to charity, conquers the sin of selfish niggardliness; his heart is ennobled by the spirit of renunciation; he really enjoys pleasures in sharing them with many persons; he is born in wealthy families, which command many enjoyments; he is of a charitable disposition from the moment of his birth; he becomes popular among the four kinds of assemblies (i.e. monks, nuns, laymen and laywomen); he enters all assemblies with self-confidence; his noble fame as a donor spreads in all directions; his hands and feet are soft and small; . . . [81] he is always blessed with good friends until he acquires Enlightenment." (*Sam. Rā.*, fol. 112*a*, lines 4 ff.) The author of the *Bodhisattva-bhūmi* also speaks of the four glorious powers (*prabhāva*) of charity. A *bodhisattva* gives up the vice of selfish niggardliness, which is the opposite of generosity. He matures himself and others for Enlightenment, and his gifts are the means of converting the people. He experiences heartfelt joy before giving, during the act of giving, and after it. He thus serves his own best interests. He allays the pain suffered by others through hunger, thirst, heat and cold. He acquires wealth and power, and also learns to love charity for its own sake (*Bo. Bhū.*, fol. 31*a*, 5.2–7.2.). Charity thus brings great rewards, but niggardliness (*mātsarya*) is a sin that is punished in the next life, especially if a gift is refused to a monk.[82] The selfish miser is reborn as a *preta*, who is perpetually tormented with hunger and thirst. The ordinary worldly motives for charity are thus fully and adequately set forth by these Buddhist writers. But the highest teaching of the Mahāyāna seems to be that a *bodhisattva* should practise charity without any selfish motives whatsoever. His generosity should be absolutely disinterested. He should not think of the reward of *dāna*, and he should not desire or expect any recompense.[83] He should not wish to secure rebirth as a king or a *deva* as the result of his sacrifice.[84] He should not give in order to obtain honour and fame.[85] He does not desire to be respected as a *dāna-pati* by the king, ministers, priests and citizens.[86] He knows that all such advantages and enjoyments are impermanent and valueless, and this wisdom helps him to act without the thought of reward (*phala-darçanam*).[87] He gives unselfishly and also teaches others to do likewise.[88]

(5) *Karuṇā.* If a *bodhisattva* has no selfish motives for his charitable deeds, he can be actuated and inspired only by love, pity, mercy and compassion (*karuṇā, anukampā, kṛpā, dayā*). This great virtue, *karuṇā*, which has already been mentioned as an attribute of a perfect Buddha and of a budding *bodhisattva*, is exhibited, practised and developed chiefly by *dāna*. It is intimately associated with the *dāna-pāramitā*, though it is also the guiding-star of a *bodhisattva's* entire career. It should be rendered in English by such words as "love", "pity", "mercy", "compassion", and all their synonyms or approximate synonyms put together. No one word can convey an adequate idea of what *karuṇā* means. It is mentioned in an enormous number of passages in all the principal treatises.[89] It is perhaps the word that occurs most frequently in Mahāyānist literature. According to the *Pr. Pā. Çata.*, a *bodhisattva* shows his *karuṇā* chiefly by resolving to suffer the torments and agonies of the dreadful purgatories during innumerable æons, if need be, so that he may lead all beings to perfect Enlightenment.[90] He desires Enlightenment first for all beings and not for himself.[91] He is consumed with grief on account of the sufferings of others, and does not care for his own happiness.[92] He desires the good and welfare of the world.[93] All his faults and sins are destroyed, when his heart is full of *karuṇā*.[94] He loves all beings, as a mother loves her only child.[95] This famous simile sums up a *bodhisattva's* ideal of *karuṇā*. He loves all creatures more than he loves himself or his wife and children.[96] He does not love his own children more than other children, as his love is the same for all.[97] He is like a mother, a father, a relative, a friend, a slave and a teacher for all beings.[98] Aryaçūra and Çāntideva exalt *karuṇā* above all other virtues and attributes. Āryaçūra says: "The earth, with its forests, great mountains and oceans, has been destroyed a hundred times by water, fire and wind at the close of the æons: but the great compassion of a *bodhisattva* abides for ever."[99] The same author goes so far as to declare that even Liberation and

the highest Knowledge are superfluous, if *karuṇā* is mistress of the soul. Another great poet says: "Of what use are Knowledge (Gnosis), salvation or ascetic practices (matted hair and besmearing the body with ashes) to the man, whose heart melts with pity for all living creatures?" Çūra teaches that Mercy (*dayā*) is really the sum and substance of ethics and religion, as wickedness and corruption will be impossible, when all men learn to love others as their kinsmen.[100] He also anticipates Shakespeare's well-known simile by comparing Mercy to "the gentle rain from heaven".[101] As the rain makes all the crops grow, so Mercy produces all the virtues that should adorn a *bodhisattva's* personality. Çāntideva also regards *karuṇā* as the one thing needful. He teaches that a *bodhisattva* need not learn many things, but only *karuṇā*, which leads to the acquisition of all the principles and attributes of Buddhahood. As the soldiers follow their king, and as all the activities of mankind depend on the sun, even so all the principles, which are conducive to Enlightenment, arise and grow under the aegis of *karuṇā*. It is indeed the life and soul of Religion (*jīvit-endriya*).[102]

The Buddhist writers have not only sung the praises of *karuṇā*, but have also attempted to analyse and explain it in a philosophical spirit. They teach that it may be considered from two points of view. It consists in realising the equality of oneself and others (*par-ātma-samatā*) and also practising the substitution of others for oneself (*par-ātma-parivartana*).[103] When a *bodhisattva* cultivates the habit of regarding others as equal to himself, he gets rid of the ideas of "I and Thou" and "Mine and Thine".[104] He learns to feel the joys and sorrows of others like his own, and does not prefer his own happiness to that of others.[105] He loves and guards others, as he loves and guards himself.[106] He is also willing to exchange his happiness for the miseries of others.[106] He gives himself for the sake of others. He returns good for evil, and helps even those who have injured him. He identifies himself with the poor and the lowly, and looks upon himself as if he were another person.[106] He follows the two Golden Rules of the Mahāyāna: (1) "Do unto others as you would do unto yourself"; (2) "Do unto others as they wish that you should do unto them."

What is the relation of *karuṇā* to Egoism and Altruism? This question has been answered in different ways by the principal philosophers. Some of them teach that a *bodhisattva* acts for his own good and also for the good of others. His motives are both egoistic and altruistic. He achieves his own purpose(*svārtha*) and also promotes the best interests of others (*par-ārtha*). *Svārtha* and *par-ārtha* are mentioned together in many passages of Mahāyānist literature.[107] The author of the *Bodhisattva-bhūmi* declares that only the perfect Buddhas and very advanced *bodhisattvas* can act from purely altruistic motives, as when they condescend to be born in a lower world for the good of the living beings.[108] All ordinary *bodhisattvas* must work both for themselves and others, as they wish to attain Enlightenment, even though they do not care for any temporal advantages or sensual pleasures. Every charitable action is a step forward on the path to *bodhi*. Many donors declare that the Merit of their good deed may be the means of attaining *bodhi*.[109] This is their higher spiritual egoism. They think of their own final liberation from mundane existence and their goal of Enlightenment, when they help others out of love and compassion. They combine and reconcile self-interest with the service of others.

In course of time, the term *svārtha* was dropped, and only *par-ārtha* is spoken of in many passages.[110] This development indicates the triumph of the ideal of pure Altruism. The *bodhisattva* should not think of self at all, when he exerts himself for the good of others. He should be filled with love, and love alone, without any admixture of self-interest, however sublime and spiritual it may be. His mind must be so overwhelmed and saturated with the feeling of pity for others, that it is not possible for him to think of his own Enlightenment at the same time. The *bodhisattvas*, who follow this ideal, do not declare that they wish to obtain *bodhi* in exchange for their sacrifices. They utter such sentiments as the following :—

" By the Merit of my sacrifice, may I also use my body in my future lives for the good of all creatures."

" I do not make this sacrifice in order to secure a happy rebirth as a king or a *deva* ; and I do not think even of the felicity of Liberation. By the Merit of my charitable deed, may I become the guide and saviour of the world, which is lost in the wilderness of mundane existence. I wish to accomplish the good of others." [111] The hero of the ninety-second story in Kṣemendra's *Avadāna-kalpa-latā* cries : " For the sake of others, I shall bear this torturing wheel (discus) on my head." [112] The *Pr. Pā. Çata.* also teaches that a preacher should not desire even Enlightenment as the reward of his disinterested work.[113] Thus only Altruism is finally recognised and recommended as the motive of a *bodhisattva's* self-sacrifice. Çāntideva teaches this ideal as a paradox: "If thou lovest thyself, thou shouldst not love thyself. If thou wishest to protect thyself, thou shouldst not protect thyself." [114] The last word on this difficult problem is said by the author of the *M. S. Al.*, who declares that Egoism and Altruism are one and the same in the case of an advanced *bodhisattva*. When the *bodhisattva* thinks of others in the same way as he thinks of himself, the words *svārtha* and *par-ārtha* become synonyms, and there is no distinction between them.[115] In the highest synthesis, Egoism and Altruism are merged in perfect Love.

Kṣemendra also discusses the origin and nature of *karuṇā*. Is it natural and innate? Or is it the result of Merit acquired in a former existence? Or does it depend on practice? The poet teaches that compassion is natural and innate in all creatures, even in such ferocious beasts as lions.[116] It can be developed by practice. Thus does the Mahāyāna discover mercy and pity even in the nature and essence of cruel and rapacious brutes. Altruism is here united to the highest optimism. Kṣemendra, like Tennyson, voices the faith that

"Love is creation's final law." [117]

(6) *Stories of Dāna*. Buddhist literature abounds in stories and legends of charitable and self-sacrificing men, women and animals. They should be regarded as "parables", as most of them are the products of the luxuriant Indian imagination. Some animals are represented as models of virtue, partly because Buddhism does not draw a sharp line of demarcation between the human and sub-human species, and partly because the writers wish to indulge in a little caustic irony against mankind.[118] The birth of a *bodhisattva* in such a state of woe is explained as being the result of some remnants of Demerit.[119] This explanation must be taken for what it is worth. The Buddhists could not resist the temptation of employing the fable as a medium of religious instruction. India is noted as the original home of this interesting and popular literary genre. The Mahāyānists often teach wisdom out of the mouths of the beasts of the field. The heroes and heroines of these stories give away wealth, limbs, life, wives and children in a spirit of exaggerated and fantastic philanthropy. The lack of a sense of proportion and harmony is the fatal flaw of the Indian temperament as exhibited in literature and religion. The Indian thinkers

and writers often push a good idea to such extremes that it becomes grotesque and ridiculous. But we can read these quaint parables with pleasure and interest, if we appreciate their spirit without thinking too critically of the details. Only a few typical stories can be related very briefly in this essay.

Story of the Tigress. A *bodhisattva* threw himself before a hungry tigress, which had several little cubs. She would have devoured the cubs, if the *bodhisattva* had not sacrificed his body for her sake. This curious story is related in the *Jātaka-mālā*, the *Suvarṇa-prabhāsa* and the *Avadāna-kalpa-latā*.[120] Kṣemendra narrates it twice and gives Satyavrata and Karuṇarekha as the names of the *bodhisattvas*. He adds the interesting detail that the cubs were reborn as thieves in their next lives! In the *Jātaka-mālā*, the scene of the story is quite different from the milieu described in the *Suvarṇa-prabhāsa*. Āryaçūra's *bodhisattva* is a learned teacher, who goes out for a walk with his disciple and sees the tigress in a deep ravine. The *bodhisattva's* name is not given, but the disciple is called Ajita. The number of the cubs is not indicated. The *bodhisattva* asks the disciple to leave him and go in search of food for the tigress. In the meantime, he throws himself down into the ravine near the tigress, which devours his dead body. The legend, according to the *Suvarṇa-prabhāsa*, is as follows:—

Gautama Buddha, wandering about in the region of the *Pañcala* with his disciples, arrived at a beautiful spot in the woods. He asked Ānanda to prepare a seat for him, and said that he would show them the relics of the great *bodhisattvas* who had performed difficult feats. He struck the ground with his hands. The earth shook, and a *stūpa* made of gems, gold and silver rose up. Buddha directed Ānanda to open the *stūpa*. It contained a golden sarcophagus covered with pearls. Ānanda saw some bones, which were as white as snow and the *kumuda* flower (white water-lily). All present paid obeisance to the relics. Buddha then told the story of the hero. A long time age, there lived a king named Mahāratha. He had three sons, Mahāpraṇāda, Mahādeva and Mahāsattvavān. These princes were one day wandering about in a great park and came to a lonely place called "The Twelve Shrubs". Mahāsattvavān was not disturbed by any fears or misgivings, but his brothers were not so brave. Suddenly they saw a tigress in that hollow of "The Twelve Shrubs". She had whelped seven days before, had five cubs, and was emaciated through hunger and thirst. The three brothers talked of her sad plight and said: "What can this poor creature eat?" Mahāsattvavān asked his brothers to walk on and said, "I shall go into this hollow to do something." He then uttered these words: "I, moved by compassion, give my body for the good of the world and for the attainment of *bodhi*". When he threw himself before the tigress, she did not do anything to him. The *bodhisattva* understood that she was very weak. He looked round for a weapon, but could find none. He took a strong hundred-year-old bamboo creeper, cut his throat, and fell dead near the tigress. (*Su. Pr.*, fol. 73*b*, 3ff.)

King Çivi (*Çibi*). The story of King Çivi is found in four different versions in Buddhist Sanskrit literature. It is related in the *Avadāna-çataka*, the *Jātaka-mālā* and the *Avadāna-kalpa-latā*. According to the *Avadāna-çataka*,[121] King Çivi, having distributed all his wealth among the people, thinks of the small insects. He inflicts several wounds on his body with a weapon, and feeds the fleas and mosquitoes with his blood, as if they were his children. In the meantime, *Çakra*, the chief of the *devas*, assumes the shape of a vulture in order to put King Çivi to the test. The king offers the vulture a feast of his own flesh, and tells him to eat as much as he needs. *Çakra* then appears in the guise of a Hindu priest (*brahmin*), and asks for the king's eyes, which are willingly given. *Çakra* praises and blesses the king for his generosity. In Kṣemendra's first story of Çivi, the king feeds an ogre (*rākṣasa*) with his flesh and blood as a recompense for a few beautiful verses, which *Indra*, disguised as an ogre, recites in his presence. *Indra* asks him if he felt any pain or grief at the sacrifice of his limbs. Çivi replies in the negative, and says: "If it is true that my mind was not touched by that pain, then may I, by the power of this truthful asseveration, regain my body as it was." His body immediately becomes whole and sound again. It may be stated that this device of *saty-ādhiṣṭhāna* (resolution by Truth) is employed by the later Mahāyānist writers in order to restore their heroes and heroines to their normal physical condition after the mutilation suffered by them in the exercise of charity. In some stories, *Indra*, who often appears as the tempter, compensates them at the end by his divine power; but Kṣemendra prefers this curious method of *saty-ādhiṣṭhāna* for avoiding a tragic conclusion of the moving tales. The hero cannot be left torn and bleeding after his superhuman sacrifice. This tendency to finish the stories in a happy vein is most marked in Kṣemendra's writings, while Çūra does not always care to restore his mauled and mangled heroes to their pristine strength and beauty. The same King Çivi (or Çibi) is also the hero of the second story in Çūra's *Jātaka-mālā*. *Çakra*, in the guise of a blind priest, asks for the gift of one eye, but the king gives him both eyes. Çibi remains blind for some time, but *Çakra* restores his eyes to him in the end and bestows on him the power of seeing things at a distance.

Kṣemendra also narrates a second story of King Çivi. His capital was called *Çikhi-ghoṣā*. When a violent epidemic raged in the country, the physicians declared that the sick could be cured only by drinking the blood of a man, who had always practised forbearance since the day of his birth. The king knew that he had never yielded to anger, and that his mother had also completely eschewed it during the pre-natal period. He gave his blood to the sick during six months.

Rukmavatī or *Rūpāvatī*. The story of Rukmavatī is told in the *Divy-āvadāna* and the *Avadāna-kalpa-latā*.[122] In the *Divy-āvadāna*, the name is given as Rūpāvatī. Rukmavatī was a charitable lady of the town of Utpalāvatī. She once saw a famished woman, who had been delivered of a child and who was on the point of eating her own offspring. Rukmavatī was in a dilemma. If she ran home to fetch food for the poor creature, the starving wretch would devour the child in the interval. If she took the child home with her, the mother would perish of starvation. She helped the woman by cutting off her own breasts and giving them to her for food! *Indra*, the chief of the *devas*, appeared on the scene, and she was transformed into a man as a reward for her sacrifice! According to the *Divy-āvadāna*, she first recovered her limbs by the device of the *saty-ādhiṣṭhāna*. Kṣemendra continues the story into Rukmavatī's next life. She was born as Sattvavara, the son of the chief of a guild. He took pity on the birds of the air, and cut off bits of his flesh to feed the vultures and other carnivorous birds in the cremation-ground. His eyes were also torn out by the birds, and nothing at last remained of him but a heap of bones.[123]

Jīmūtavāhana. The famous story of Jīmūtavāhana is related in the *Kathā-sarit-sāgara* and the *Avadāna-kalpa-latā*, and it is dramatised in Harṣa's play, "*Nāgānanda*."[124] Jīmūtavāhana was a prince, who lived in the forest with his aged father. He was married to a princess, named Malayavatī. As he was walking about, he saw on a certain occasion that a boy, named Çaṅkhacūḍa, was followed by an attendant, who carried two red garments. The boy belonged to the *Nāga* tribe and was chosen as the victim for *Garuḍa*, who claimed such a bloody sacrifice every day. His mother was weeping and wailing in the neighbourhood. Jīmūtavāhana offered to give his own life and save the unfortunate creature. In spite of the boy's protests, he donned the red garments and sat on the stone of sacrifice. *Garuḍa* came, seized him, and began to devour him. Jīmūtavāhana looked happy and contented. *Garuḍa* was astonished at this spectacle, and soon learned his mistake. He expiated his error by repenting of his cruelty, promising to kill no living beings in future, and restoring all the dead *Nāgas* to life. In Harṣa's play, the goddess *Gaurī* also appears on the scene and Jīmūtavāhana is restored to life.

Other heroes and heroines of this type are also mentioned in Buddhist literature. Jñānavatī, daughter of King Jñānabala, gave her flesh and blood in order to provide medicine for a sick monk.[125] King Puṇyabala sacrificed his eyes and limbs during many lives.[126] King Surūpa gave his body, his queen and his son to be eaten up by a *Yakṣa*, whose form *Indra* had assumed in order to test the king.[127] King Sarvandada gave refuge to a bird, which was pursued by a fowler. He offered to compensate the poor man by giving him an equivalent weight of his own flesh. But the bird became so heavy in the balance that the king had to sacrifice his whole body in order to keep his promise. He regained it by the usual method of *saty-adhiṣṭhāna*.[128] Padmaka killed himself in order that he might be reborn as a *rohita* fish, whose flesh was needed as medicine for curing the sick.[129] King Çrīsena gave away his wife and half of his own body.[130] Maṇichūḍa fed a demon with his flesh and blood.[131] King Maitrībala converted some ogres to the true faith by giving them his flesh to eat.[132]

The *Samādhirāja-sūtra* explains why a *bodhisattva* does not feel any pain, when he mutilates himself for the good of others. Ānanda asks Buddha how a *bodhisattva* can cheerfully suffer the loss of his hands, feet, ears, nose, eyes and head; Buddha explains that pity for mankind and the love of *bodhi* sustain and inspire a *bodhisattva* in his heroism, just as worldly men are ready to enjoy the five kinds of sensual pleasure, even when their bodies are burning with fever. (*Sam. Rā.*, fol. 160*a*, 5 ff.)

The Hare. Another story, which is found in several versions, is that of the self-immolating hare. This hare is perhaps the most famous animal in history, not excepting Balaam's ass, Alexander's horse, Robert Bruce's spider, St. Jerome's lion, or the wolf of Gubbio. The hare figures in this parable, probably because he is India's "man in the moon".[133] The story is related in the *Jātaka-mālā*, the *Avadāna-kalpa-latā* and the *Avadāna-çataka.*[134]

According to the *Avadāna-çataka*, Gautama Buddha had a young disciple, who had such a vacillating disposition that he left the monastery for his home three times, and was at last persuaded by Buddha to return to the spiritual vocation and persevere in it. This disciple had been a sage in a previous existence, and Buddha had been the hare that had then dissuaded him from abandoning the hermit's life. The sage, who lived in a forest far from the haunts of men, duly performed the daily religious rites, including the worship of fire. This last point is important, as a fire must somehow be kindled in this story. The hare possessed human speech and felt almost filial affection for the sage. Unfortunately, a drought dried up the brooks and destroyed the roots and fruits, on which the sage subsisted. He resolved to return to the town, where he could live on alms. The hare persuaded him to put off his departure for a day. Next morning, he threw himself into the fire and asked the sage to eat the flesh and continue to live and meditate in the forest. The sage was much moved at this deed, and promised that he would not return to the town. But he refused to save his life by eating the flesh. The hare then resorted to the device of *saty-ādhiṣṭhāna* and cried: "Since I came to the forest, my heart has taken delight in solitude. By the power of this true speech, may *Indra* now send down rain." No sooner had he uttered these words than rain began to fall, and the sage could soon obtain the roots, fruits, herbs and flowers that he needed.

This is the earliest version of this story in Sanskrit. But Āryaçūra tells quite a different tale and assigns another motive for the hare's self-sacrifice. In the *Ava. Ça.*, the hare is ready to die for the sake of friendship and anti-social asceticism, but Āryaçūra evinces the new Mahāyāna spirit by making the hare give his life for the fulfilment of the social duties of hospitality. The fire is miraculously provided by *Indra*, who comes in the guise of a priest (*brahmin*). The *Jātaka-mālā* gives the story as follows :—

Once upon a time, four animals, an otter, a jackal, a monkey and a hare, lived as friends in a forest. On the eve of the *poṣadha*, the hare reminded his friends that it was their duty to show hospitality to some guests the next day.[135] But he was sad at heart, because he himself was not in a position to offer suitable food to any guest. He could procure only a few blades of bitter grass. He silently resolved to offer his own body. On the *poṣadha* day, *Indra* came to the forest in the guise of a priest (*brahmin*) and asked for help as a weak and weary wayfarer. The animals pressed him to stay several days in their midst as a welcome guest. The otter offered him seven fishes; the jackal regaled him with sour milk and a lizard, and the monkey treated him to ripe mangoes. But the hare asked the *brahmin* to eat his flesh, as he had nothing else to give. The *brahmin* refused this offer and said, "How can I kill a living being, especially a friend?" But the hare leaped into the fire, which *Indra* had created near by in order to test him. *Indra* then assumed his own shape; a shower of flowers fell from the sky; and the hare was honoured by having his image placed in the halls of the *devas* in heaven and on the disc of the moon.

Such is Āryaçūra's version of the legend, which is really more instructive and interesting than that given in the *Avadāna-çataka*. Kṣemendra adopts the latter, and only adds the detail that the sage's name was Suvrata. The *Ava. Ça.* describes him only as a *ṛṣi*, and gives no name. The Buddhists had evidently learned to appreciate the meaning and value of personality in the interval that elapsed between the *Ava. Ça.* and the *Avadāna-kalpa-latā*. Kṣemendra also points out that the story illustrates the advantages of having virtuous friends. His choice of this version of the story proves the vitality and persistence of the old Hīnayānist tradition.

Other animals are also represented as sacrificing their lives for the benefit of human beings. An elephant throws himself down from a rock in order that a caravan of famished travellers in the desert may be kept alive by eating his flesh. A tortoise also sacrifices his life under similar circumstances. A lion and an elephant lose their lives in saving a group of men from the jaws of a fiery dragon.[136] In such stories, the noble character of the animals is often contrasted with the meanness and selfishness of ordinary men.

Viçvantara. The famous story of Viçvantara is related in

the *Jātaka-mālā* and the *Avadāna-kalpa-latā*.[137] It is regarded as the most pathetic and edifying of all the stories of *dāna*.

Viçvantara was the son of King Sañjaya. He was a very charitable and merciful prince. He gave abundant alms to all, and at last presented even the white elephant of the royal stables to the priests. His inordinate generosity led to such an outcry against him that his father was compelled to banish him to Mount Vaṅka. His wife Madrī and his two children accompanied him in his exile. The family rode in a chariot driven by four horses. When a priest asked for the horses, he gave them to him. Another priest obtained the gift of the chariot. Viçvantara took the boy Jālin in his arms, and his wife carried the girl Kṛṣṇājinā. They walked on foot till they reached their destination, and lived in a hut of leaves. An old *brahmin* came one day, when Madrī was away. He asked Viçvantara to give the two children to be his servants and attendants. The prince could not refuse this demand. Then *Çakra*, the chief of the *devas*, appeared in the guise of a poor priest and begged Viçvantara to let him have Madrī, who was of course given away. *Çakra* assumed his own shape and blessed Viçvantara. In the meantime, the priest, who had taken the two children, brought them to their grandfather King Sañjaya, who redeemed them for a heavy price. The King and the people were so moved by Viçvantara's self-denial that they recalled him from exile and reinstated him in his rank.

This story, which at least does not reek of the shambles, is especially important. According to the Buddhist tradition, Viçvantara practised the virtue of charity in its full perfection, and was reborn in his next life as the historic teacher, Gautama Buddha.

(7) *Transfer of Merit.* There is something even more precious than a *bodhisattva*'s wealth, limbs, wives and children, and that is his Merit (*puṇya*). He should give it for the good of all beings. The technical term for this gift is *pariṇāmanā* ("bending round or towards," transfer, dedication). The idea of *puṇya* is one of the central concepts of Buddhism. Every act, which is inspired by charity, or by charity and morality (*çīla*), produces some *puṇya*, which leads to welfare in this life and also secures happy re-births.[138] *Puṇya* is generally regarded as the power of good deeds that were done in previous existences. It is also called *kuçala*, and it is collectively termed *puṇya-skandha* (mass of Merit) and *kuçala-mūlāni*

(roots of weal).[139] A virtuous person "accumulates" Merit (*kuçala-sañcaya*), as a thrifty man deposits money in the bank. No simile appears to be more suitable than that of a bank-account. *Puṇya* is supposed to result automatically and inevitably from a righteous action. It is an invisible cosmic force that confers happiness on the individual, to whom it belongs. The Buddhists have developed a precise quantitative view of *puṇya*, which seems to convert their much-vaunted ethics into a sordid system of commercial arithmetic. Every good deed produces a certain fixed amount of *puṇya* and no more. A unit of *puṇya* confers a certain kind of happiness on earth or in a heaven only for a certain period of time, after which it is exhausted. This quantitative notion of *puṇya* has culminated in the doctrine of *pariṇāmanā* (transfer of Merit). *Puṇya* acts surely and silently. It cannot be destroyed except by evil actions, which produce Demerit and therefore reduce the sum-total of Merit. It is a mighty Agent in the universe. All that is noble, beautiful, auspicious, glorious and desirable in the world is the result of *puṇya*.[140] The *Lalita-vistara* frequently refers to Gautama Buddha's *puṇya*, by which he acquired mystical attainments without difficulty, defeated *Māra*, and recovered his strength after eating a meal at the end of the period of austerities.[141] The *devas* derive their power and felicity from their *puṇya*.[142] Kings and wealthy men owe their good fortune to their *puṇya*.[143] Merit protects a person and can even work miracles in his favour: it can make trees bloom out of season and convert a fiery furnace into a lovely lotus-pond.[144] It can save mariners from shipwreck, and ward off the attacks of demons and hobgoblins.[145] Even the cyclic evolution and dissolution of the Universe are due to Merit. The sun and the moon owe all their splendour to it.[146] *Puṇya* is thus a wonderful Power, and it is exalted and glorified in Mahāyānist literature to such an extent that it is finally regarded almost as the equivalent of Wisdom (*prajñā*) and *bodhi*. In the early period of the Mahāyāna, *puṇya* was considered to be only the means of securing happy re-births, while Enlightenment was reserved for those who acquired *jñāna* (Knowledge) through Musing and Concentration. But the increasing appreciation of active altruism in social life gave rise to the new idea that *puṇya* by itself could lead to Enlightenment. This startling view is clearly expressed by the later Mahāyānist teachers. Çāntideva even substitutes the "transfer of *puṇya*" for the Perfection of Wisdom (*prajñā-pāramitā*) as the final goal of a *bodhisattva's* career.[147] *Puṇya* usurps the position, which is theoretically accorded to supreme Wisdom (*prajñā*).

Merit is thus a beneficent power, but Demerit is also a terrible power that causes misery and pain. Sins and transgressions of different kinds lead to rebirth in a purgatory, or as an animal or a *preta*. They also produce disease, poverty, dishonour and unhappiness in human life on earth.[148] Demerit can even affect Nature by drying up wells and creating waterless forests.[149] It is the source and root of all evil.

According to the old and approved doctrine of Buddhism, Merit or Demerit, produced by a person's actions (*karma*), is strictly personal. It is also imperishable. The *Bo. Bhu.* and the *Mdh.* teach that the result of actions cannot be destroyed even after many æons.[150] It is impossible to escape the consequences of one's deeds. This teaching is illustrated by many stories in the *Avadāna-çataka*,[151] and Kṣemendra also reverts to this doctrine of personal retribution. Even the great Buddha suffered pain ten times in his life on account of the remnants of his Demerit, which had not been expiated.[152] Every man or woman must reap as he or she has sown.[153] Every creature is born alone and dies alone.[154] His deeds always follow him everywhere.[155] He may dive into the ocean or climb lofty mountains; he may take refuge in the heavens or the nether world: but his *karma* cannot be baulked of its fruition.[156] As all beings are under the power of their own actions, no one has a personal relation to another, and it is folly to be attached to any person.[157] No one can help another in the next life.[158] This rigidly individualistic doctrine of *karma* is also taught in the Pāli canon. The *Sutta-nipāta* says: "No one's *karma* is lost; it comes back and its owner meets it. The fool, who does evil, himself experiences the pain in the other world."[159] All the Buddhas teach the doctrine of *kamma* and *kiriya* (*kamma-vādā*, *kiriya-vādā*).[160] It is a heresy to believe that actions do not bear fruit.[161] The inequalities among men are due to their deeds, which are their possession and heritage. *Karma* is indeed the begetter, the kinsman and the refuge of all beings.[162] In the later Pāli writings, however, the idea of the transfer of Merit is adumbrated. Some *pretas* are said to derive benefit from the charitable deeds of their living relatives, but an evil deed cannot be shared with others.[163] The transfer of Merit does not exhaust it, but leads to growth in virtue.[164] This idea was developed to its logical conclusion by the Mahāyānists.

Several circumstances must have contributed to soften the harsh and uncompromising individualism of the old *karma* doctrine. As E. W. Hopkins and A. B. Keith have pointed out, Hinduism itself exhibited a tendency to modify the doctrine by recognising the transfer of Merit in certain cases.[165] According to the *Rāmāyaṇa*, a woman shares the Merit of her husband's deeds, but other relatives enjoy their own *puṇya* (ii, 27, 3–4; vol. i, p. 123). A faithful wife participates in the husband's destiny after death (*Manu*, ix, 29, p. 196). A king gets the sixth part of the *dharma* and *adharma* (virtue and sin) of his subjects (*Manu*, viii, 304, p. 180). The householder, who fails to entertain a guest, loses all his Merit (*Manu*, iii, 100, p. 50). Hinduism, which was broad-based on social solidarity, was thus led to deny the validity of the individualistic doctrine of *karma*. The Mahāyāna also owed its teaching of *pariṇāmanā* partly to the influence of Hinduism. As it laid stress on altruistic service, it could not fail to recognise the universal inter-dependence of mankind. The doctrine of *karma* in its unmitigated form repudiated the bond of social solidarity and dissolved society into a vast number of isolated spiritual atoms. Such a theory evidently did violence to the facts of life. The early Buddhists forgot that man was essentially what Aristotle called "a social being".[166] The Mahāyānists insisted on social sympathy and sacrifice, and they realised that no one was born unto himself alone and no one died unto himself alone. The people of India were also growing more sensitive to suffering on account of the climate, the practice of vegetarianism, and the teaching of love and mercy as inculcated by the Buddhists and the Jainas. They developed a genuine repugnance to the idea of pain and torture of any kind. They lived in an atmosphere of peace, toleration, gentleness and refined culture. They became more and more averse to the contemplation of the sufferings and torments of the creatures, who were condemned to the hot and cold purgatories or imprisoned in the vile bodies of *pretas* and animals. In the *Mtu.*, Maudgalyāyana returns from a visit to the purgatories and only delivers a sermon on the well-deserved punishment of the sinners.[167] But a few centuries later, the people of India could not bear to think of such cruel pains and penalties as the doctrine of *karma* inflicted on the unfortunate transgressors of the moral law. They had developed that almost feminine tenderness and sentimentality, which would not allow the representation of tragic scenes on the stage and banned real tragedy from Indian literature. The same gentle temper rose in revolt against the old doctrine of *karma* with its horrid array of purgatories and miserable rebirths during long æons. The Mahāyānists evolved the humane teaching that even a sinner was not destined to suffer in the three states of woe, as the *bodhisattvas* could cancel his Demerit by giving him some of their Merit. Avalokiteçvara was described as releasing the sufferers from the purgatories without paying any regard to the law of *karma*. Here again the Mahāyānists nearly abrogated the old law of *karma* and replaced it by the new gospel of *karuṇā*. The old teachers proclaimed that the cosmic law demanded " an eye for an eye and a tooth for a tooth ". But the Mahāyānists taught that love was the supreme law. It was the conflict between the Old and New Testaments of Buddhism. D. T. Suzuki and J. E. Carpenter explain this change in terms of the metaphysical theory of the *dharma-kāya*.[168] But the doctrine of *pariṇāmanā* (or *parivarta*) did not grow in the arid soil of logic and metaphysics. It sprang from the heart of the Indian people, who could not tolerate the idea of protracted suffering of any description. The philosophers subsequently provided it with a rationale.

According to the developed Mahāyāna doctrine, *pariṇāmanā* is of two kinds. A *bodhisattva* may "apply" the Merit of a good deed for his own Enlightenment (*bodhi*). This practice is mentioned very frequently.[169] But a *bodhisattva* may also "apply" his Merit for the welfare and spiritual progress of all creatures. Such *pariṇāmanā* is regarded as more commendable in the later Mahāyāna, which prefers altruistic activity even to the ideal of Enlightenment. In this case, a *bodhisattva* shares his "roots of Merit" with all beings.[170] He declares that he wishes to allay and appease their pain and misery, to save them from all fear, and to lead them to virtue, serene meditation and true knowledge.[171] He desires that all beings should enjoy the blessings of health, strength, friendship, purity and unity, and also gain the knowledge of the Buddhas.[172] As a concrete instance of *pariṇāmanā*, we may refer to the concluding verses of Çāntideva's *Bodhi-cary-āvatāra* and Candragomin's *Çiṣya-lekha*. Many Buddhist authors "transferred" the Merit that might accrue to them from the good deed of writing a book.[173] Çāntideva devotes a whole canto to this *pariṇāmāna*. He utters such philanthropic sentiments as the following: "May all, who suffer pain in body or mind, obtain abundant joy and happiness! May all the denizens of the purgatories rejoice! May all the purgatories be divested of their terrors and become pleasant habitations for those beings! May they soon be released from their misery by the great and powerful *bodhisattvas*! May the wild brutes cease to attack and devour one another! May the famished *pretas* get plenty of food! May the blind see and the deaf hear! May the women bear children without travail! May all creatures obtain food, drink, clothes and ornaments according to their desires! May none be troubled with fear or grief! May the sick recover health, and may the feeble gain strength! May all wayfarers travel safely and succeed in their enterprise! May the ugly become beautiful! May all women become men! May all creatures shun sin and vice, and love virtue and righteousness! May they have eternal life, and may the very name of Death perish for ever!" These verses exhibit the spirit, in which a *bodhisattva* should dedicate his Merit to the service of all beings.

This idea of *pariṇāmanā* may be compared to the Christian doctrine of participation in the merits of the saints.[174]

II. Çīla-pāramitā. *Çīla*, the second *pāramitā*, includes all the ordinary virtues of an honest, respectable layman-householder. The word is explained as a derivative of the root *çīl*, meaning "to exercise, to practise".[175] Açvaghoṣa connects it with *çīlana* (repeated practice, frequent exercise[176]). The *M. S. Al.* gives a fanciful etymology for it: *çaityasya lambhanāt* (from the acquisition of coldness, i.e. the suppression of the passions[177]).

Çīla as a *pāramitā* has been defined in three ways. It has been identified with Virtue in general, and many admirable qualities have been enumerated as its characteristics. It has also been interpreted in relation to the ideals of purification and restraint, as they are realised with the body, the speech and the mind (deed, word and thought). It is usually understood as referring to the five moral precepts and the ten good and meritorious "Ways of Action", which constitute the Buddhist layman's definite code of practical ethics.

Çīla is a very important category in Buddhist philosophy. It occurs in several numerical formulae. It figures among the six *anusmṛtis* (recollections), the four *sampads* (blessings, accomplishments), the seven *dhanas* (treasures), and the three, four or five items of meritorious action (*puṇya-kriyā-vastūni*).[178]

It is also one of the three original *skandhas* (group of factors in spiritual progress), the other two being Concentration and Wisdom, as has already been indicated above.

The Buddhist writers have pointed out the fundamental importance of *çīla* in eloquent words. *Çīla* is compared to a flawless gem, crystal or lapis lazuli, and the expressive adjective *acchidra* is often applied to it.[179] It is more precious than silver and gold.[180] A Buddhist without *çīla* is an impostor, and he can be neither a layman nor a monk.[181] All auspicious actions depend on *çīla*.[182] A virtuous man is infinitely superior to a great conqueror.[183] *Çīla* adorns a person like a beautiful silk garment. Its " fragrance " spreads far and wide.[184]

(*a*) *Çīla*, as a general term for many virtues, embodies the Buddhist's ideal of moral perfection. It is attained by completely extinguishing the fire of the passions.[185] It is especially related to the qualities, which are the opposites of the three basic faults, the "Roots of Evil or Demerit" (*akuçala-mūlāni*). These three sources of " all our woe " are *rāga* (passion, lust, sense-desire), *dveṣa* (hatred, ill-will) and *moha* (delusion, folly).[186] The last term has also been rendered as " bewilderment ", " infatuation ", " stupidity ", " dullness ", " confusion of mind ", etc. *Rāga*, which is derived from the root *rañj*, is regarded as almost synonymous with *lobha* (greed, appetite). The *Dhamma-saṅgaṇi* defines it thus : " lust, passion, seducing, compliance, . . . cupidity, voracity, attachment, covetousness, longing, fondness, affection ; appetite for visual forms, sounds, odours, savours and tangible things ; appetite for wealth, children and life ; craving for sensual pleasures, for existence, and for non-existence." [187] The conquest of *rāga* is the essence of righteousness.[188] It can be achieved by the meditations on Impurity and by the realisation of the impermanence of all phenomena.[189] *Dveṣa* (Pāli: *doso*) is derived from the root *dviṣ*, and not from *duṣ*, as Candrakīrti wrongly assumes.[190] The *Dhamma-saṅgaṇi* defines it thus : " When annoyance springs up at the thought, ' he has done me harm, is doing, will do me harm,' ' he has done harm, is doing harm, will do harm to some one dear and precious to me,' ' he has conferred a benefit, is conferring, will confer a benefit on someone I dislike and object to ' ; or when annoyance springs up without any ground ; all such vexation of spirit, resentment, repugnance, hostility, ill-temper, irritation, anger, hate, antipathy, abhorrence, mental disorder, detestation, wrath, hatred, hate, hating, derangement, opposition, churlishness, . . . disgust of heart—this is what is called *doso*."[191] After such a deluge of synonyms, one should understand what *dveṣa* in Buddhist philosophy really means! It can be eradicated by the cultivation of the feeling of friendliness.[192] *Moha*, which is derived from the root *muh*, is thus defined in the *Dhamma-saṅgaṇi*: "Lack of knowledge about the four Noble Truths; lack of knowledge about the former things, about the latter things and about both taken together; lack of knowledge about the assignable causation of causally determined states; lack of insight, of understanding, of comprehension, of enlightenment, of penetration, . . . of reflection, of perspicacity; dullness, obtuseness, ignorance: this is called *moho*."[193] *Moha* can be destroyed by the comprehension of the fundamental tenets of Buddhism, especially the four Noble Truths and the formula of Dependent Origination (*pratītya-samutpāda*).[194]

These three dire causes of all evil are like a devastating fire.[195] A *bodhisattva* frees himself from them in the third or fifth *bhūmi* (stage).[196]

The Buddhists seem to teach that all sins and vices are due to *rāga* and *dveṣa*, which are mentioned together in several passages.[197] All errors and heretical views spring from *moha*. *Rāga* and *dveṣa* are the enemies of Virtue, while *moha* cuts at the root of Wisdom. The suppression or control of *rāga* and *dveṣa* may thus be regarded as the general principle for the cultivation of *çīla* as a *pāramitā*.

Çīla is thus rooted in the absence of sensuality and hatred, but its ramifications are many. The Buddhist philosophers' catalogue of virtues is long and varied. Āryaçūra ascribes eleven virtues to the *bodhisattva* Sutasoma: "generosity, mercy, self-control, ardour, forbearance, fortitude, humility, modesty, conscientiousness, politeness and purity."[198] The virtues of the beings, who inhabit *Sukhāvatī* (the Region of Bliss), are enumerated in the *Su. Vy.* They are distinguished for unselfishness, purity, love of equality and peace, fortitude, equanimity, friendliness, tenderness of disposition, honesty, love, joyfulness, activity, forbearance, patience, composure, serenity, self-control, calmness, and complete freedom from avarice, arrogance and envy."[199] The *M. S. Al.* declares that the *bodhisattvas* are temperate, pure, firm, benevolent, earnest, conscientious, merciful, resolute, unselfish, calm and intrepid.[200] A similar list of virtues is found in the *Lal. V.* and the *M. Vy.*[201] Such general descriptions convey an adequate idea of the traits of character that the Buddhist teachers admired.

(*b*) These rambling and over-lapping lists of virtues were reduced to some kind of order in the threefold classification, which was based on the ideal of restraint and self-control (*saṃvara*) as applied to body, speech and mind. This triad of deed, word and thought may have been borrowed from Zoroastrianism, but it is probably of indigenous origin, as it is also found in Jaina literature.[202] The Jainas employ the term *gupti* (restraint, guarding) instead of *saṃvara*. *Çīla* is often defined as the control and restraint of *kāya* (body), *vāc* (speech) and *manas* (mind). The author of the *Samādhirāja-sūtra* attaches particular importance to this aspect of *çīla*.[203] The *Bo. Bhū.* and the *Dh. S.* divide *çīla* into three categories, the first of which is *saṃvara-çīla*.[204] The other two categories are really equivalent to benevolence, as they are defined as *kuçala-dharma-saṅgrāhaka-çīla* (i.e. *çīla*, which is conducive to the accumulation of Merit) and *sattv-ānugrāhaka-çīla* or *sattva-kriyā-çīla* (i.e. *çīla*, which consists in rendering service to the living beings). The former of these two categories may refer to the particular moral precepts of Buddhism; but the latter variety of *çīla* is identical with *dāna*, which has already been discussed. *Saṃvara* is thus regarded as the keynote of *çīla* by several Buddhist philosophers. A *bodhisattva*, who practices *saṃvara*, examines himself and discovers his own faults and short-comings.[205] He does not care for worldly honour or gain of any kind.[205] He scorns even the power and privileges of universal sovereignty.[205] He acquires perfect spiritual vigilance (*apramādaḥ*) and exhibits it in five ways. He combats and counteracts the sins and vices (*āpatti*) of the past, the present and the future; and he is inspired by the ardent zeal to act in such a way that no new sins may arise. Finally, all his actions are free from sin.[205] Such is his watchfulness or vigilance against himself. He is also firm and serene in deportment, self-confident and pure.[205]

The body, speech and mind must be controlled and disciplined; they must also be purified. This idea of purification is applied to the *bodhisattva's* personality; it is probably of Persian origin.[206]

According to the accepted Buddhist doctrine, the body can be controlled and purified by practising abstention from the three sins of killing a living being, theft and unchastity; speech can be controlled and purified by abstaining from falsehood (untruthfulness), slander, harsh or impolite speech and frivolous, senseless talk; and the mind can be purified by the avoidance of covetousness, malevolence and wrong views. Thus we come to the ten "Ways of good or meritorious Action", which constitute the Decalogue of Buddhism (*kuçala-karma-pathāḥ*).[207]

(*c*) These ten precepts owe their origin to the fusion of four old Indian ethical rules with the three "Roots of Evil" (*rāga*, *dveṣa*, *moha*). The ancient Hindu sages inculcated four virtues and discouraged four vices by teaching the people to abstain from killing, falsehood, theft and unchastity. These four basic articles of social ethics are found in several ancient Hindu scriptures and also in the *Yoga-sūtras*.[208] They represent the minimum of morality, without which organised society cannot exist. They are therefore common to all civilised nations, and are also included in the Hebrew Decalogue.[209] The Buddhists and the Jainas borrowed them from Hinduism. These four precepts are mentioned in several passages of the Pāli canon.[210] The rules with regard to speech were increased and amplified by the Buddhists, and three other faults were added to "falsehood". It is a peculiar characteristic of the Indian ethical systems that the duty of pleasant speech is especially emphasised. The number of the precepts was thus raised to seven, and this group of seven is also found in the Pāli canon.[211] Only these seven rules are discussed in the opening sections of the *Brahma-jāla-sutta* and some other passages. It may be inferred that the formula included only these seven precepts at a certain stage of its development. Finally, the three "Roots of Evil" were added in order to reach the round number Ten. The eighth sin to be avoided is called *abhidhyā*, which is almost a synonym of *rāga*. The ninth item is *vyāpāda*, which is the same thing as *dveṣa*; and the tenth is *mithyā-dṛṣṭi*, which is equivalent to *moha*. It was not a happy idea to combine these general terms with the seven definite rules for practical action. The two groups of precepts do not mix well, like oil and water. The spirit of the first set of seven is different from that of the second set of three. The former is concrete and relates to action; the latter is abstract and deals with general motives and ideas. The Buddhist teachers have foisted upon their Church this singular conglomeration of dissimilar items as the standard code of practical ethics, as *çīla par excellence*.

Before discussing these ten constituents of *çīla*, it must be stated that there was also another line of development, in which the four ancient Hindu rules were increased to five by adding the injunction against the use of alcoholic beverages (" abstaining from any state of indolence arising from the use of intoxicants "). This set of five precepts is known as the five *çikṣā-padāni* in Sanskrit literature, though the Pāli term *sikkhāpada* seems to refer to the ten special regulations for the monks, which are given in the *Vinaya*.[212] They are also spoken of as the *çikṣā-padas* of an *upāsaka* (layman).[213] A Buddhist convert promises to observe these five precepts immediately after declaring his faith in the Buddha, the Doctrine and the Confraternity.[214] In Pāli, they are also mentioned as the *pañca-sīla*,[215] but this term is not generally employed in Sanskrit. It is probable that the prohibition of alcoholic beverages was at first intended only for the monks. It was subsequently extended to the laity. Some writers attempted to incorporate this important fifth rule in the formula of the ten " Ways of meritorious Action " by omitting the item " Harsh speech " (*pāruṣya*) and substituting teetotalism for it.[216] Others inserted it as the third item without omitting any other rule, and thus raised the number of the precepts to eleven ! [217] But these attempts to secure a place in the Decalogue for the new rule did not succeed. It retained its position only in the smaller group of the five *çikṣā-padas*. The Mahāyānists carried on vigorous propaganda against the use of alcohol, but they did not attach much importance to this separate list of five items. It is not given in the *Mahā-vyutpatti*, which, however, speaks of liquor-drinking as a sin. Āryaçūra describes the evil consequences of alcoholism in the *Kumbha-jātaka*.[218] The ancient special rules for the monks are also found in the Mahāyānist treatises, though they are not considered very important. They include the five *çikṣā-padas* mentioned above and the following five additional rules [219]:—

Not to use perfumes, garlands and unguents.

Not to use a high big bed.

Not to eat at the wrong hour.

Not to take part in worldly amusements, like music, dancing, etc.

Not to accept silver and gold.

The ten " Ways of Action " are given in both positive and negative forms. The sins and errors are mentioned as the ten "evil or demeritorious Ways of Action" (*daç-ākuçalāḥ karma-pathāḥ*).[220] When the word *virati* or *viramaṇa* (abstention) is added to them, the different items are called "good or meritorious Ways of Action".[221] (The word *prativirati* is also found in this connection).[222] The word *pathāḥ* is sometimes dropped, and they are described only as "actions" (*kuçala-karmāṇi*).[223] Both words are sometimes omitted, and only the ten *kuçalāni* or *akuçalāni* are spoken of.[224] The author of the *Da. Bhū.* adds some comments of a positive and constructive character to each precept, so that a *bodhisattva* may understand the complementary ideas of "Thou shalt not" and "Thou shalt" at the same time.

The ten "Ways of Action" may now be considered in detail.

1. Abstention from killing living beings (*prāṇ-ātipātād viratiḥ*). The form *prāṇ-ātighātād* is also found. But the Pāli words are : *pāṇātipātā veramaṇī*.[225] It is therefore proper to accept the form *prāṇ-ātipāta*.

This precept corresponds to the *ahiṃsā* of the Hindu scriptures. A *bodhisattva* does not use weapons of any kind. He does not hate any being, and cannot kill a living creature even in thought.[226] He understands that all things originate in causes, and cultivates pity and compassion.[227] He knows that he has Free Will in action, and he believes in the doctrine of re-birth. Life is dear to all creatures, and a *bodhisattva* does not do unto others what he wishes that others should not do unto him.[228] *Ahiṃsā* (not killing) is indeed the highest virtue.[229] From all these motives and considerations, a *bodhisattva* abstains from taking the life of any living being. He also condemns and shuns the barbarous custom of war among the states and kings of the world.[230] War has its origin in hatred, avarice, cruelty and selfishness, and the glory of victorious kings is stained with blood. It is better for a king to abdicate than to wage war. A virtuous king tries his best to avoid war, as he knows that the so-called duty (*dharma*) of the warrior-caste (*kṣatriyas*) is based on cruelty and unrighteousness. Such "pacifist" sentiments are expressed by Kṣemendra.

The Mahāyānists also extended the scope of this precept to the relations between human beings and animals, as an animal is also a *prāṇin* (living being). The idea of humaneness to animals is found in the Pāli canon.[231] *Maitrī* (friendliness) to the brute creation is inculcated in the *Avadāna-çataka* ; and Kṣemendra cries, "I cannot endure the pain even of an ant." [232] This tendency towards the humane treatment of animals is also fostered by the doctrine that sinful men and women may be reborn as animals. Some animals are said to possess a few human attributes. They can speak as a result of "Merit", and some snakes and parrots can even hear and understand sermons.[233] Certain animals are reborn in a heaven, because they have eaten of a *bodhisattva's* flesh.[234] Gautama Buddha was born as a hare, a swan, a fish, a quail, an ape, a woodpecker and an elephant in his previous existences.[235] Avalokiteçvara preaches to the worms and insects,[236] which can rise to the position of a Buddha after many æons.[237] A doe bears a son to a sage in the forest.[238] Prince Kuṇāla is punished with blindness, because he had inflicted the same calamity on some animals in a former life.[239] These details, which have been culled from different treatises, prove that the Buddhists did not regard the animal world only with disdainful contempt. They acknowledged the rights and virtues of the dumb beasts. This feeling of sympathy also led to the condemnation of hunting and flesh-eating. Āryaçūra declares that it is wicked to discharge arrows at the frightened fleeing antelopes.[240] The chief Mahāyānist writers also teach that it is a sin to eat meat. They abrogate the old rule that a monk may eat meat, if it is not especially cooked for him.[241] The *Laṅkāvatāra-sūtra* devotes a long chapter to this subject, and several arguments are adduced in favour of vegetarianism.[242] It is possible that an animal may really be one's relative, who is reborn in this state of woe; one's father, mother, brother, sister, son or daughter may reappear on earth in the form of a brute. There is no reason why the meat of some species should be eaten, while other species are spared: hence meat of all kinds should be regarded as uneatable. Meat is impure and repulsive, as it is always blended with blood and the secretions of the body. It is not right to spread terror and agony among the animals, which flee from man as from a ruthless demon. Meat is really nothing but foul ill-smelling carrion, and one should not eat the carcasses of animals. The practice of flesh-eating makes men cruel and sensual. Men are not carnivorous by nature, like tigers or wolves. Hence such diet paves the way for rebirth in the dreadful purgatories. For these reasons, the author of the *Laṅkāvatāra-sūtra* teaches that vegetarianism is the only proper course for a *bodhisattva*. Çāntideva shares this view, but he allows the use of meat as medicine, if human life is in danger.[243] The Mahāyānist interpretation of *ahiṃsā*, as applied to the animal world, has been accepted by the vast majority of the Indian people.

Apart from strict vegetarianism, extreme moderation in eating and drinking is also enjoined on a *bodhisattva*, who practises the *saṃvara* of the body. He should eat neither too much nor too little. He should eat only to keep the body healthy and active, as ointment is applied to a wound and as a ship is rigged and repaired. Intemperance in eating and drinking causes disease, torpor and weakness.[244]

2. Abstention from theft (literally, "from taking what is not given": *adatt-ādānād viratiḥ*). The form *adatta-haraṇam* is also found (instead of *adatt-ādānam*).[245] Both the Hindus and the Jainas employ the term *asteya* (not stealing), but the Buddhists have resorted to this curious periphrasis. A *bodhisattva* is contented with his possessions and does not covet those of other people. He respects the rights of property in things that belong to others. He does not steal even a leaf or a blade of grass.[246]

3. Abstention from unchastity (literally, "false conduct with regard to sensual pleasures," *kāma-mithy-ācāraḥ*). The form *kāma-mithyā-vādaḥ* is also found.[247] The author of the *Samādhirāja-sūtra* retains the old Hindu term *abrahmacarya* (fol. 193*b*, 6).

A *bodhisattva* is contented with his own wife and does not cast longing eyes on the wives of other men. He does not harbour even a lustful thought with regard to other married women. Adultery is like poison, that mars and destroys human life, even if it is committed in secret.[248]

4. Abstention from telling lies (*mṛṣā-vādād viratiḥ*, or, *anṛta-vacanād viratiḥ*). The Hindus employ the simple term *satyam* (truthfulness).

A *bodhisattva* speaks the truth and nothing but the truth, and he does so at the proper time. His actions are in harmony with his words.[249] He does not tell a lie even in a dream. Truthfulness is the highest spiritual austerity.[250] The power of Veracity is like a force of Nature and can work miracles. When it is employed by truthful persons according to the procedure of *saty-ādhiṣṭhāna*, it can give sight to the blind and heal the torn and bleeding limbs of self-sacrificing *bodhisattvas*. It can cure disease and produce rainfall. It can allay the fury of the elements and save mariners from shipwreck. It can even restore the dead to life.[251] Truth is great and prevails against all the powers of evil.

5. Abstention from slander (*paiçunyād viratiḥ*, or *piçuna-vacanād viratiḥ*).

A *bodhisattva* does not sow strife and discord in society by uttering slanderous libels. He does not act as a tale-bearer. He does not repeat what he has heard. He does not separate good friends or take delight in causing disunion among people by his words.[252]

6. Abstention from harsh speech (*pāruṣyād viratiḥ*, or *paruṣa-vacanād viratiḥ*).

A *bodhisattva* does not indulge in harsh, bitter, offensive, vulgar and angry speech, which cuts others to the quick and wounds and lacerates their feelings. His speech is always sweet, polite, gentle, pleasant, agreeable, beneficial and dignified. It gives joy both to him and to others, as it is sweet both to the ear and the heart. But he may speak harshly in order to restrain foolish persons from evil actions.[253]

7. Abstention from frivolous and senseless talk (*sambhinna-pralāpād viratiḥ*. In Pāli : *samphappalāpā veramaṇī*).

A *bodhisattva* speaks at the proper time, and his utterances are always cogent, relevant and instructive. He speaks of righteousness and religion. He avoids all conversation about common stories and legends.[254] He is not interested in aimless gossip about "kings, robbers, soldiers, villages, towns, countries, kingdoms, capital cities, ministers, officials, eunuchs, carriages, gardens, palaces, monasteries, tanks, ponds, lakes, mountains, demons, ogres, hobgoblins, food, drink, clothes, ornaments, music, dance, love," etc., etc.[255] The Mahāyānists are very severe on what is called "light talk". Pleasant and useful speech is also regarded as one of a *bodhisattva's* four *saṅgraha-vastus* (items of sympathy or conversion). A *bodhisattva* is not talkative or loquacious : he is inclined to be reticent and speaks little.[256] "Sweet speech" is the means of teaching the doctrine (*deçanā*). It removes the doubts of the inquirer and sets forth the proper arguments. It may therefore be characterised as *grāhaka* ("that which makes people take").[257] A *bodhisattva's* speech should be pleasant, true, and conducive to the Good.[258] It is the mark of a *bodhisattva*, who cannot fall from his high estate (*avinivarttanīya*). Dharmākara, the saint who rose to be the great Buddha *Amitābha*, was a man of sweet speech.[259] Prince Sutejas was also gentle in speech.[260]

As a general rule, a *bodhisattva's* speech is intended to encourage, delight or instruct others. He encourages others by being the first to speak to them with a smiling and joyous countenance. He inquires about their welfare and their health, and addresses words of hearty welcome to them.[261] He also delights other people by conforming to the ways of the world like a fellow-citizen, and wishes them abundant increase of sons, wives and relatives, or of wealth and worldly goods.[262] He expresses the hope that they will grow in faith, virtue, knowledge, charity and wisdom.[263] He instructs them in religion for their good and weal (*hita*, *sukha*), and is always ready to benefit them by his speech, which is devoted to spiritual teaching.[264] It is a very difficult task indeed to speak sweetly to one's enemies and adversaries, or to preach to very stupid and dull persons with great patience, or to hold encouraging and uplifting converse with false, dishonest and cunning people.[265] But a *bodhisattva* cultivates sweet speech even in his intercourse with such individuals. Further, he exhorts the people to abandon the five *nīvaraṇas* (Hindrances), to aim at happy rebirths, and to ponder on the four Noble Truths. He rebukes and admonishes lax monks and easy-going householders, removes their doubts and helps them to enter the path of earnestness.[266] He preaches the ten ethical precepts, which free a person from sin and show him the way leading out of all sorrow. As a general rule, a *bodhisattva* permits others to do what is permissible according to the Scriptures, and prohibits them to do such things as are forbidden.[267] He comforts and solaces those creatures, who are afflicted with diverse fears.[268] He purifies his speech in four ways: he abstains from lying, slander, harsh words and frivolous talk. He speaks exactly as he has seen, heard, thought or known; and if he has not seen, heard, thought or known anything, he speaks accordingly. These are his eight noble ways of speech (*āryā vyavahārāḥ*).[269] He soothes and allays the grief of all persons, who are suffering from bereavement or loss of wealth. He speaks to those who are ill, vicious or heterodox, and he teaches them how to acquire health, virtue or right views (*Bo. Bhū.*, fol. 86*a*, *b*).

8. Abstention from covetousness (*abhidhyāyā viratiḥ*). The Pāli word *abhijjhā* is explained as a synonym of *rāga* in the *Dhamma-saṅgaṇi* (Section 1136). Açvaghoṣa teaches that it destroys the man, who is the slave of sensuality. A *bodhisattva* is free from this fault. He does not covet the wealth and

possessions of other persons. He does not think thus: "May I get what belongs to other people." His heart is not corrupted by avarice.[270]

This precept may be compared to the tenth Commandment of the Hebrew Decalogue.

9. Abstention from malevolence (malice, ill-will: *vyāpādād viratiḥ*). The Pāli word *byāpāda* is given as a synonym of *dosa* (hatred) in the *Dhamma-saṅgaṇi* (Sections 419, 1137). A *bodhisattva's* heart is free from malice. He is friendly, merciful, benevolent, compassionate and kind-hearted towards all living beings. He abandons all anger, hatred, ill-will and enmity. He cultivates thoughts of love and pity towards all creatures, and desires their welfare and happiness.[271]

10. Abstention from wrong views (heretical opinions: *mithyā-dṛṣṭer viratiḥ*). The form *mithyā-darçanam* is also found.[272]

A *bodhisattva* walks in the path of righteousness. He has firm faith in the Buddha, the Doctrine and the Confraternity. He is straightforward, honest and sincere. He does not think of evil and improper pursuits and actions.[273]

The *Da. Bhū.* explains *mithyā-dṛṣṭi* in this general way. But the *Dhamma-saṅgaṇi* repeats the formula, which has already been referred to in the section on *samyag-dṛṣṭi* (unbelief in the existence of the next life and the fruit of actions, etc.).[274] The term probably refers to the whole system of Buddhist doctrine, and may be interpreted as "heterodoxy". A *bodhisattva* must be "orthodox" in his views and should not accept the doctrines of the Jainas, the Hindus, and other sects.

(*d*) As regards the motives and sanctions for rignt action, the Buddhist philosophers speak of the ordinary worldly inducements and allurements, as in the case of Charity (*dāna*). *Çīla* leads to fame, popularity, beauty, happiness, and rebirth in a wealthy family on earth or as a *deva* in a heaven.[275] It enables a person to meet death calmly and peacefully.[276] The *Samādhirāja-sūtra* mentions ten advantages of *çīla*. A *bodhisattva*, whose conduct is pure, attains complete knowledge, follows the example of the Buddhas, is never blamed by the learned, does not break his promises, remains firm in the right ways of behaviour, flees the world, lives free from any hindrance caused by prepossessions or adverse conditions, acquires

Concentration, and is not afflicted with poverty. (*Sam. Rā.*, fol. 113*a*, lines 1–2.)

Pure hedonism thus seems to be the ruling theory of Buddhist ethics. But it sometimes degenerates into spiritual terrorism of the worst sort. The ten precepts are more or less negative in character, and the fear of punishment in the purgatories is held to be the chief sanction for virtuous conduct. The hope of reward is supposed to be the mainspring of *dāna* (Giving) ; but threats of terrible penalties are considered to be necessary for the observance of *çīla*. The Buddhist teachers speak of eight hot and eight cold purgatories in connection with the ten precepts of *çīla*.[277] The eight hot *narakas* (purgatories) are called *sañjīva*, *kāla-sūtra*, *saṅghāta*, *raurava*, *mahā-raurava*, *tapana*, *pratāpana* and *avīci*. Some of these names have perhaps a meaning. *Raurava* may signify "the place of cries" ; *tapana* means "heating". The two purgatories, *raurava* and *avīci*, are mentioned more frequently than the others. The eight cold purgatories are named *arbuda*, *nirarbuda*, *aṭaṭa*, *hahava* (or *apapo*), *huhuva* (or *hāhādhara*), *utpala*, *padma*, *mahāpadma*. Some of these names are evidently onomatopœic ; *aṭaṭa* and *hahava* suggest the effects of extreme cold. *Padma* and *utpala* (lotus) are probably euphemistic terms. This scheme of sixteen purgatories was the final product of the vivid imagination of the Mahāyānists, who elaborated the idea of retribution after death. The *Mahā-vastu* devotes a long chapter to the subject (vol. i, pp. 5–26) ; but it mentions only the eight hot purgatories and speaks vaguely of sixteen smaller purgatories (*utsada*) attached to each great *naraka*. It offers a fanciful etymological explanation for each name, and describes the tortures and the sins associated with each purgatory. Açvaghoṣa and Çāntideva have also described the terrors of the purgatories.[278] As the Indians are past masters in the art of exaggeration, there is no lack of burning, boiling, baking, rending, tearing, wounding, bleeding, freezing, shivering, piercing, sawing, splitting, mauling, mutilating and other pains and torments in these purgatories. Çāntideva has in fact drawn up a systematic penal code for the sinners, who violate any of the ten ethical precepts.[279] As in Dante's Inferno, the punishment is often suited to the transgression. Thus a thief sees unreal gold and jewels, which he tries to appropriate in vain ; an adulterer pursues phantoms of women, who mock his lust ; a liar's tongue is cut out of his mouth, and so on. The only redeeming feature of this hideous nightmare of the Mahāyānists is that the sojourn in these purgatories does not last for ever. Each sin is completely expiated after a certain period of time, though that period may be very long.

A sinner may also be punished by being reborn as an animal or a *preta*. The troubles and calamities of the animals are described in the *Mahā-vastu* and the *Buddha-carita*.[280] An irascible teacher, who told his dull pupils that they were buffaloes, was reborn as a buffalo. Some careless persons, who spat on the walls of sacred buildings, were even reborn as walls! The Mahāyānists certainly do not lack a sense of humour.[281] The *pretas*, whose mouths are as small as the eye of a needle and whose bellies are as large as a mountain, are always tormented with hunger and thirst. This class of imaginary creatures is a peculiar product of Indian wit and folklore. Finally, a sinner may be reborn as a poor, ugly, diseased and deformed man or woman, and may be unfortunate and unsuccessful in his or her life on earth.[282]

Such are the terrible sanctions behind the Mahāyānist Decalogue.

(*e*) Some Mahāyānist philosophers have risen to the noble conception that a person should do the right, because his conscience prompts and compels him to act in that manner. *Çīla* is regarded as the means of leading others to Enlightenment, and not as the price paid in advance for the pleasures of heaven.[283] The ruling and controlling principle of a *bodhisattva's çīla* should be *hrī* (conscientiousness) and *ātma-lajjā* (shame in or before oneself). This important term *hrī* denotes a remarkable concept in Mahāyānist ethics. It is often coupled with *apatrāpya* (*vyapatrāpya*, *apatrapā*. Pali : *ottappa*), which means "shame with regard to others, fear of social censure". These two are included in the formula of the seven *dhanas* (treasures).[284] *Apatrapā* belongs after all to the sphere of enlightened hedonism, as it is associated with social approval and popularity. But *hrī* (Pāli : *hiri*) introduces us to a new order of ideas.[285] It has been explained as "purity of intention, and modesty with regard to oneself".[286] The idea of "shame" can easily develop into that of "self-respect", as the Greek word αἰδώς clearly shows.[287] *Hrī* represents an inner self-determining disinterested principle, which inspires a *bodhisattva* to the practice of *çīla*.[288] It is synonymous with *lajjā*, which is extolled in the *Bo. Bhū.* and the *M. S. Al.* A *bodhisattva* feels shame, if he is not energetic in the cultivation of the *pāramitās*. *Çīla* is destroyed in the absence of this quality, which is also indispensable for the Equipment that leads to Enlightenment.[289] It raises a *bodhisattva* above the eight ordinary motives and deterrents: viz. gain and loss, fame and obloquy, praise and blame, pleasure and pain.[290] Āryaçūra teaches that a *bodhisattva* does not commit any sin, because he has *ātma-lajjā* (self-shame) and witnesses his own actions, even if they are concealed from others.[291] *Hrī* thus points to the existence of that inner Mentor, which is also recognised by Marcus Aurelius and Kant as the necessary postulate of true ethics.[292]

(*f*) The Mahāyānists have thus gone through the entire gamut of the motives that govern human conduct. But they have rather stultified themselves by teaching the strange doctrine that a *bodhisattva* may violate any or all of the precepts of *çīla*, if he is moved by compassion for others.[293] This view has led to much subtle casuistry. The *Bo. Bhū.* and other treatises explain that the ethical rules are not absolute. They may be infringed, if a *bodhisattva* can thereby render service to an unfortunate creature. This doctrine must have originated on account of three circumstances. These keen thinkers must have realised that no ethical laws can be universally and eternally valid, and that the ordinary social code must break down under certain circumstances. They attached such exaggerated importance to mercy and compassion that they began to take a short-sighted view of ethical obligation. They thought that the immediate relief of pain and suffering outweighed the permanent loss inflicted on the individual and on society by the deliberate violation of the great moral principles. It is also probable that they wished to excuse and condone the moral laxity of the Buddhist monks, to which the well-known passage in the *Rāṣṭrapāla-paripṛcchā* bears witness.[294] Çāntideva also speaks with suspicious frequency of the sins of *rāga* (passion, lust) as venial and even commendable offences, when a *bodhisattva* commits them in order to please and gratify others.[295] The medieval monks of Europe also passed through a period of widespread corruption; but they did not formulate a regular philosophy of degeneracy. The later Mahāyānists sought to justify the sensual escapades of the monks (alias *bodhisattvas*) by referring to the assumed motive of *karuṇā*. Tantrism cast its shadow before.

The author of the *Bodhisattva-bhūmi* indicates the circumstances, in which a *bodhisattva* may infringe the seven chief precepts. He may kill a person, who intends to murder a monk or his own parents. He should say: "It does not matter if I suffer in the purgatories for this sin: but I must save this misguided creature from such a fate."[296] He can "take what is not given", if it is necessary to deprive unjust kings and wicked robbers of their ill-gotten gains, which must lead to their ruin and destruction.[297] He may have carnal knowledge of an unmarried woman, if he can thus prevent her from harbouring thoughts of hatred and ill-will.[298] He may tell lies for the sake of others. He may slander someone in order to separate another *bodhisattva* from a bad friend. He may speak harshly to a sinner in order to warn and reproach him.[299] He may indulge in frivolous talk in order to win over such persons as are addicted to music, dancing and gossip. He may adopt an objectionable mode of livelihood in order to approach and convert the people, who follow such sinful practices.[300] He may take part in amusements, if he wishes to soothe the grief, worry and anxiety of those who are depressed in mind; but he should not be boisterous or undignified in his behaviour. As a general principle, he is not forbidden to conform to the ways of the world, as he must help others and maintain amicable relations with them.[301] He should not be afraid of sinning now and then for the sake of others, as he has a long period of time at his disposal before Enlightenment can be attained.[302] In this way, the Mahāyānists teach that the end justifies the means and that a *bodhisattva* may sometimes adopt St. Paul's device of "becoming all things to all men".

(g) *Stories of Çīla*. The stories of *çīla* are not so numerous or sensational as those relating to *dāna*.

Çakra, the chief of the *devas*, observed the first precept by turning back his aerial car in order to spare some tiny nests, even though he was hotly pursued by his enemies, the Demons, after the defeat of his army.[303] But his humane action gave him the victory, as the Demons were bewildered and thrown into confusion by this sudden and unexpected movement. A quail and a whale lived on vegetarian food, as they did not wish to kill small animals.[304] A prince was troubled with keen qualms of conscience, because he drank the water out of a pot that belonged to a sage, and he was thus guilty of theft.[305] A *bodhisattva* disobeyed the command of his *brahmin* teacher, who asked his pupils to steal for his benefit.[306] A king, who was deeply infatuated with the beautiful wife of one of his officials, refused to gratify his passion, even though the husband was willing and eager to give up his wife as a loyal subject.[307] Upagupta and Padmaka rejected and repelled the advances of certain prostitutes.[308] Prince Kuṇāla and Prince Kalyāṇakārī also refused to be seduced by passionate women, who fell in love with them.[309] Kṣemendra relates a foolish story of incest and its terrible consequences.[310] A fish saved his comrades from death by calling down rain from the heavens through the power of veracity.[311] A young quail saved his parents and himself by extinguishing a forest-conflagration in the same manner.[312] Pūrṇa was reborn as a slave-girl's son, as he had committed the sin of using harsh language in his previous existence.[313] Sthaviraka and Hastaka were also visited with condign punishment for the same fault.[314] Raivata was condemned to twelve years' imprisonment for a crime, which he had not committed, because he had falsely accused another man of such a crime in his former life.[315]

The stories relating to chastity and the punishment of harsh speech are more interesting than the others.

III. KṢĀNTI-PĀRAMITĀ (Forbearance and Endurance). A *bodhisattva* should practise the Perfection of *kṣānti.* This word has been rendered as "forbearance", "patience", "meekness", "die Milde", etc. A. B. Keith, following D. T. Suzuki, interprets it as "not feeling dejected in the face of evils".[316] But this explanation is not adequate. *Kṣānti* is always described as the opposite of *krodha* (anger), *dveṣa* (hatred), *pratigha* (repugnance) and *vyāpāda* (malice).[317] It is defined as freedom from anger and excitement (*akopanā, akṣobhanatā*) and as the habit of enduring and pardoning injuries and insults (*par-āpakārasya marṣaṇam*).[318] This is the primary and fundamental connotation of *kṣānti.* But it is also used in two other subsidiary senses: (1) patient endurance of pain and hardship (*duḥkh-ādhivāsana*), and (2) acquiescence in or acceptance of the ideals and doctrines of the religion with faith (*dharma-nidhyān-ādhimukti*).[319]

These three aspects of *kṣānti* may be discussed in detail.

1. *Forbearance.* A *bodhisattva* knows that the Buddhas are "the ocean of forbearance"[320]; gentle forbearance (*kṣānti-sauratyam*) is their spiritual garment.[321] He cultivates this virtue in its full perfection. He forgives others for

all kinds of injury, insult, contumely, abuse and censure.[322] He forgives them everywhere, in secret and in public. He forgives them at all times, in the forenoon, at noon and in the afternoon, by day and by night. He forgives them for what has been done in the past, for what is being done at present and for what will be done in the future. He forgives them in sickness and in health. He forgives them with his body, as he never thinks of striking them with his hands or a stick or a stone; he forgives them with his speech, as he never utters harsh words; and he forgives them with his mind, as he harbours no anger or evil thoughts against them. Even if his body is destroyed and cut up into a hundred pieces with swords and spears, he does not conceive an angry thought against his cruel persecutors.[323] He forgives all without exception, his friends, his enemies, and those who are neither. He forgives even weak and socially inferior persons, who may insult or injure him. He forgives wicked and cruel persons, who may have inflicted terrible and unendurable pain and loss on him for a very long time. Being reviled, he reviles not again; being beaten, he beats not again; being annoyed, he annoys not again. He does not show anger towards one who is angry. He is like a dumb sheep in quarrels and squabbles. In a word, his forgiveness is unfailing, universal and absolute, even as Mother Earth suffers in silence all that may be done to her.[324]

A *bodhisattva* should cultivate certain modes of thought and ponder on some great principles, so that he may understand why he should forgive others. He should remember Buddha's words: "The strength of a religious teacher is his patience." [325] He should love all beings and therefore bear with them.[326] His enemy of to-day may have been a friend, a relative or a teacher in a previous existence and should therefore be regarded as an old comrade.[327] A *bodhisattva* also knows that there is no permanent substantial individuality in any man or woman. Hence it follows that there is really no one who reviles, beats and injures, or who is reviled, beaten and injured.[328] All beings are ephemeral and mortal; it is improper to be angry with such miserable creatures. They are also afflicted with pain. Even those, who live in great affluence, cannot escape the three kinds of pain that are inseparable from the very nature of things.[329] A *bodhisattva* should try to alleviate their pain, not to increase it by lack of forbearance. He should also be more or less of a determinist in judging others, who harm him. Those enemies are not free agents: their wicked deeds are produced by causes, over which they have no control, as disease originates in physiological conditions.[330] All men are driven and dominated by the forces set in motion by their actions in past lives, even though they may not know this law. "Tout comprendre, c'est tout pardonner." Further, a *bodhisattva* cannot really blame others for the injuries that they may inflict upon him, because he suffers on account of his own sins and misdeeds in his previous existence.[331] His enemies are only the instruments of the cosmic law of *karma*.[332] In fact, they are his best friends, and he should thank them for their services. They deprive him of the dangerous impedimenta of wealth, fame and worldly happiness. They enable him to exhibit the virtue of forbearance, which leads to heaven and also to Enlightenment.[333] They do him much good, while they ruin their own chances of a happy rebirth. A *bodhisattva* should also reflect that anger is a grievous sin, which must certainly be expiated in the dreadful purgatories. It destroys all the Merit that has been acquired in many lives.[334] It is therefore better to suffer a little in this life at the hands of one's enemies than to yield to anger and endure the terrible consequences of that heinous sin after death. Anger and Envy should be shunned, as a fish would swim clear of the fisherman's net.[335] The envious man forgets that his neighbours only enjoy the fruits of their good deeds. He should learn to rejoice in the prosperity of others and to praise their virtues. Lack of forbearance is often due to Pride (*māna*). Pride is a very dangerous, destructive and demoralising sin, which a *bodhisattva* must combat and subdue with all his might. It is the work of *Māra*, the deity of Desire and Death. A *bodhisattva* must never praise and exalt himself, or belittle and depreciate others. He should be humble in spirit, like a servant or an outcaste. Humility is indispensable for the attainment of *bodhi*. It also facilitates the practice of Forbearance. A wise *bodhisattva* should forgive others even from fear, as vindictiveness always ends in evil.[336] The Buddhas will not forgive him, if he does not forgive those who trespass against him.[337] His own best interests can also be promoted in this way, as he, who is at peace with all, must be happy in life and at the moment of death.[338] Such a man is also invulnerable: he cannot be burned by fire, drowned in water, or wounded by weapons. He is sure of rebirth in a heaven. He finally attains Enlightenment, if he practises large-hearted, all-embracing, measureless Forbearance towards all.[339]

Thus do Çāntideva and the author of the *Bodhisattva-bhūmi* argue and preach on this theme. But it is really difficult to reconcile the law of *karma* with the spirit of forbearance. Such frigid metaphysics may teach passive resignation, but not loving forbearance. But the same writers also mention mercy and love as the motive forces behind *kṣānti*; and here they seem to get at the root of the matter. We forgive with the heart, and not with the head.

2. *Endurance.* A *bodhisattva* also exhibits the virtue of *kṣānti* by enduring hunger and thirst, cold and heat, and also all the severity and inclemency of wind and weather.[340] He lives happily even in places infested with fleas, gnats, serpents and other such obnoxious and dangerous insects and reptiles. He is also capable of enduring any amount of labour, drudgery, hardship and privation, because he loves all who suffer in this world of woe, and wishes to help them.[340] In spite of all this, he is happy and cheerful. He experiences pleasure even when he is subjected to the most excruciating pain, torture and mutilation, because he sends out loving thoughts and wishes to all creatures.[340] He also knows that only the body suffers in this way, and he does not identify his personality with the body. He reflects that he has undergone many troubles and tribulations during many lives only for the sake of transient pleasure and a wretched livelihood; but now he must endure comparatively slight pain in order to acquire Merit and attain *bodhi*.[340] Thinking thus, he resolves to meet all kinds of pain calmly and joyfully. He is prepared to starve and suffer, if he does not get even the necessaries of life. He can bear the loss of all perishable worldly possessions, taken separately or collectively.[340] He works hard day and night to purify his heart from all evil, and he does not yield to indolence and lassitude. He does not rest or recline on a couch or a seat, or even on a bed of grass and leaves, at the wrong hour.[340] He is not afraid of the toil and exertion that are necessary for the service of the Buddha, the Doctrine, the Confraternity and his teachers, for the study of the principles of the religion and their dissemination among others, for the task of careful self-examination in the privacy of solitude, and for the cultivation of calm and insight.[340] He observes the hard rules of the monastic Order—lifelong celibacy, poverty, mendicancy, ugliness of face and features

after the tonsure, the robe of peculiar hue, and the permanent loss of all amusements and social amenities.[340] If he is a householder, he has to work and labour as a farmer, a merchant or an official. But a *bodhisattva*, monk or layman, is not discouraged or depressed on account of all this pain and misery. He does not turn back from his quest.[340]

3. *Acceptance of the Truth.* A *bodhisattva* exercises *kṣānti* of the highest and most difficult kind by the realisation of insight into the real Law and Truth of the universe. He investigates the Doctrine thoughtfully and intelligently, and thus acquires firm faith in the merits of the Buddha, the Doctrine and the Confraternity, in the Truth, in the power and glory of the Buddhas and the *bodhisattvas*, in the Cause, in the Fruit, in the *summum bonum* and in his own methods and efforts for its attainment.[341] Such *kṣānti* can be developed only through pure knowledge and persistent practice. It is of three kinds.[342] A *bodhisattva* may only hear some preacher and accept his teaching (*ghoṣānugā kṣāntiḥ*); or he may observe and follow the regular religious discipline and practise reflexion (*ānulomikī kṣāntiḥ*); or he may reach the highest stage by accepting and realising the truth that nothing is produced or originated. The *Samādhirāja-sūtra* describes the great powers and privileges of a *bodhisattva*, who acquires these three forms of *kṣānti*, which it does not, however, define or explain (fol. 26*a*, 6 ff.). The *Da. Bhū.* and the *M. S. Al.* explain the third kind of *kṣānti* (*anutpattika-dharma-kṣāntiḥ*) as the comprehension and acceptance of the doctrine that all phenomena and things are illusory, non-existent, un-produced and un-differentiated.[342] It is obtained by an advanced *bodhisattva* in the eighth *bhūmi* (stage). In modern parlance, he "sees life steadily and sees it whole".

4. *Stories of Kṣānti* There are some beautiful stories relating to this *pāramitā*, one or two of which have perhaps also the merit of being true.

Story of Pūrṇa. Pūrṇa was a Buddhist apostle in the early period of the history of Buddhism. His story is related in the Pāli canon.[343] In Sanskrit, it is found in the *Divy-āvadāna* and the *Avadāna-kalpa-latā*.[344] It is one of the gems of Buddhist literature. Some irrelevant details need not be considered here (e.g. his birth as a slave-girl's son, his attachment to one of his half-brothers, his success in business, etc.). The story of his *kṣānti* begins with his ordination as a monk. He resolved to go as a missionary to a country, which was inhabited by wild barbarous tribes. He asked permission of Gautama Buddha, who tried to dissuade him from his risky enterprise. Buddha said : "The people of Çroṇāparānta are fierce, violent and cruel. They are given to abusing, reviling and annoying others. If they abuse, revile and annoy you with evil, harsh and false words, what would you think?" Pūrṇa replied : "In that case, I would think that the people of Çroṇāparānta are really good and gentle folk, as they do not strike me with their hands or with stones (clods of earth)."

Buddha : "But if they strike you with their hands or with clods, what would you think?"

Pūrṇa : "In that case, I would think that they are good and gentle folk, as they do not strike me with a cudgel or a weapon."

Buddha : "But if they strike you with a cudgel or a weapon, what would you think?"

Pūrṇa : "In that case, I would think that they are good and gentle folk, as they do not take my life."

Buddha : "But if they kill you, Pūrṇa, what would you think?"

Pūrṇa : "In that case, I would still think that they are good and gentle folk, as they release me from this rotten carcass of the body without much difficulty. I know that there are monks, who are ashamed of the body and distressed and disgusted with it, and who slay themselves with weapons, take poison, hang themselves with ropes or throw themselves down from precipices. (So I shall thank those people for rendering me a service)."

Buddha : "Pūrṇa, you are endowed with the greatest gentleness and forbearance. You can live and stay in that country of the Çroṇāparāntas. Go and teach them how to be free, as you yourself are free". (*Divy-āvadāna*, pp. 38, 39)

This story is probably based on historical facts, and therefore deserves to be related in detail.

Story of Kuṇāla. King Açoka had a son, named Dharma-vivardhana, whose eyes were as beautiful as those of the Himalayan bird, called *kuṇāla*. He was therefore also called Kuṇāla. When he grew to manhood, his step-mother Tiṣyarakṣitā fell in love with him, but he tried to preach virtue to her. He thus incurred her enmity, and she resolved to destroy him. Kuṇāla was sent by the king to the town of Takṣaçilā in the north in order to quell a revolt of the citizens. Kuṇāla ruled Takṣaçilā as a successful and popular governor. In the meantime, Açoka fell ill, and

Tiṣyarakṣitā his wife restored him to health by her efforts. She asked to be allowed to exercise royal power for a week, and Açoka complied with her request in order to show his gratitude to her. She despatched an order in Açoka's name to the citizens of Takṣaçilā, commanding them to put out Kuṇāla's eyes. The citizens did not know what to do; but Kuṇāla gladly submitted to the ordeal, as he had thoroughly understood the Buddhist doctrine that all external things are transient and worthless. He even took the eyes in his hands and began to philosophise in verse. He left the town and wandered back to Pāṭaliputra as a beggar, accompanied by his wife Kāñcanamālā. He begged his bread on the way by singing and playing the *vīṇā* (lute). The unfortunate couple found refuge in the royal garage (*yāna-çālā*), where they were discovered by the palace-servants. When they were taken into the king's presence, the lascivious and vindictive queen's intrigue was exposed. Açoka was furious with rage and grief, and threatened to put her to death with cruel tortures. But Kuṇāla had learned the duty and virtue of forbearance so well that he interceded for her. He said to King Açoka: "O King! I am not troubled with pain at all. In spite of the terrible wrong (inflicted on me), there is no burning anger in me (*manyu-tāpaḥ*). My heart is full of love for my mother, who put out my eyes."[345]

This is the moral of the story. The author of the *Divy-āvadāna* ruins the tragedy by adding that Kuṇāla then cried: "If these words are true, may both my eyes immediately become as they formerly were." He thus got back his eyes by the process of *saty-ādhiṣṭhāna*.

We seem to hear distant echoes of a palace-intrigue in this story. Or is it only a piece of fiction, like the other *avadānas*?

Story of Kṣāntivādin. This famous story is told in the *Jātaka-mālā* and the *Avadāna-kalpa-latā.* Kṣemendra relates it twice, first as the *Kāçīsundar-āvadāna* and then as the *Kṣānti-avadāna.*[346]

A holy monk lived in a wood. He was called Kṣāntivādin, because he often preached the virtue of forbearance. Now it happened that the king of that country came to the wood on a pleasure-trip with his wives and attendants. When he had strolled about for a time, he drank some wine and fell asleep. His wives came to the monk's hermitage in the course of their ramble. They listened to an excellent sermon on forbearance. When the king awoke from his sleep, he set out in search of the ladies. When he saw them at the hermitage, he was beside himself with rage and jealousy. He reviled and abused the monk, called him a charlatan and hypocrite, and cut off his hands, arms, ears, nose and feet. But the monk's forbearance and serenity remained unshaken. He was sorry for the king and pitied him. He even uttered sincere wishes for his future welfare. That king had in the meantime met the guerdon of his *karma*: the earth opened and swallowed him up. The monk died peacefully and went to a heaven.

Kṣemendra avoids this tragic conclusion. He restores the monk to his normal condition by the device of *saty-ādhiṣṭhāna*.

Is this story based on a real tragedy? It is a simple story, but it has become very popular and important. Perhaps it had its origin in the capricious cruelty of a drunken despot.

These three names, Pūrṇa, Kuṇāla and Kṣāntivādin are famous in Buddhist literature. The halo of *kṣānti* surrounds them. There are other minor tales relating to the same Perfection. Gautama Buddha forgave his assailants, and offered hospitality to the men who were sent to kill him.[347] Queen Padmā asked her husband not to punish her wicked rivals.[348] A boy did not curse the king who shot him.[349] Dharmapāla forgave his executioners.[350] And so on. *Kṣānti* is one of the favourite themes of the Buddhist story-tellers.

IV. Vīrya-pāramitā. *Vīrya* as a *pāramitā* is a many-sided and comprehensive term. The word *vīrya*, derived from *vīra* and *vīr*, literally means " the state of a strong man, vigour, strength, power, heroism, prowess, valour, fortitude, courage, firmness, virility " (Pāli Dicy. and Skt. Dicy. M. W.). As a *pāramitā*, it has been translated as " strength ", " energy ", " strenuousness ", " manliness ", " zeal ", " courage ", " power ", " die Tapferkeit ", " diligence ", " vigour ", etc. It is advisable to leave it untranslated, or to adopt "Energy" as a conventional rendering.

Vīrya is an important category in Buddhist philosophy and religion. It is also reckoned among the five *balas* and *indriyas* and the seven *bodhy-aṅgas*, as has already been indicated above. The *Dhamma-saṅgaṇi* defines it thus: " The striving and onward effort, the exertion and endeavour, the zeal and ardour, the vigour and fortitude, the state of unfaltering effort, the state of sustained desire, the state of not putting down the yoke and the burden, the solid grip of the yoke and the burden, energy, right endeavour, this is *viriya*" (Section 13). The *M. S. Al.* gives a fanciful etymology: *vareṇa yojayati* (it unites one to that which is excellent).[351] *Vīrya* is generally defined as "energy in the pursuit of the Good", "vigour in well-doing", "effort for the Good" (*kuçal-otsāhaḥ*).[352] The *Bodhisattva-bhūmi* describes it as "the great energy or vigour of the mind in the accumulation of meritorious principles" (*cittasy-āty-utsāhaḥ kuçala-dharma-saṅgrahe*).[353] The words *apramāda* (vigilance, alertness, watchfulness) and *dhṛti* (fortitude, steadfastness) also denote certain aspects of *vīrya* and are frequently employed.[354] The opposite of *vīrya* is *kausīdya* (*kauçīdya*), "indolence, sloth." Other words, which are synonyms of *kausīdya*, are also contrasted with *vīrya*, e.g. *middha*, *nidrā*, *ālasya*, etc. But Çāntideva also mentions three other faults in this connection, viz. attachment to ignoble and evil things, despondency (*viṣāda*: "despair, discouragement"), and self-contempt (diffidence, *ātm-āvamanyanā*).[355]

Vīrya is often praised by the Mahāyānist writers, and its fundamental importance is indicated in unequivocal terms. Enlightenment depends entirely on *vīrya*; where there is *vīrya*, there is *bodhi*.[356] *Vīrya* is the chief and paramount cause of all the auspicious principles that are conducive to Enlightenment (*bodhi-karakāṇāṃ kuçala-dharmāṇāṃ pradhānaṃ kāraṇam*).[357] It promotes a *bodhisattva's* material and spiritual well-being.[358] It is far better to live only for a day with full *vīrya* than to vegetate without energy during a hundred years.[359] *Vīrya* destroys all pain and darkness, and it has therefore been praised by all the Buddhas.[360] It ensures success and protection, and counteracts all fears and evil proclivities.[361] Gautama Buddha himself was a great *vīra* (hero) and owed his victory over *Māra* chiefly to his *vīrya*.[362]

Vīrya is of two kinds: the *vīrya* of preparation and initiative (*sannāha-vīryam*, i.e. putting on the armour) and the *vīrya* of practice and activity (*prayoga-vīryam*).[363] The *Dh. S.* adds a third variety, which is not clearly intelligible (*para-niṣṭhā-vīryam*, or *pari-niṣṭhā-vīryam*).[364] It may signify "the *vīrya* that leads to the supreme End"; but it is not important, as it is not discussed in detail. If we attempt to arrange and analyse the prolix and redundant statements of the Buddhist authors on this subject, we find that *vīrya* may be considered under the following aspects:—

1. *Moral Development.* A *bodhisattva* resolutely combats all the great and small sins and vices (*kleça, upakleça*) that may drag him down.[365] He employs a suitable antidote to every dangerous fault and weakness. He dispels hatred by the cultivation of love, counteracts sensuality by the meditations on Impurity, and so on.[366] He exerts himself continually and seriously (*sātatya-satkṛtya*).[367] He keeps vigils and restrains his senses.[368] He is not contented with a little progress and achievement, but hopes to equal and surpass the great *bodhisattvas* of old.[369] He is inspired, and not discouraged, by their example. He does not yield to despair, as he knows that all shall and can become Buddhas. He knows that self-sacrifice will become easier with practice. He, who can give only herbs and vegetables at first, will end by sacrificing even his life.[370]

2. *Study of the Scriptures and General Education (Çikṣā-vīrya).* In the early days of the Mahāyāna, learning was perhaps not considered very important. The *Sad. Pu.* contrasts Gautama Buddha, who possessed *vīrya*, with Ānanda, who had much knowledge, but who lagged behind in the race for Wisdom.[371] In course of time, the importance of religious instruction and liberal education was fully recognised. A *bodhisattva* is diligent in studying the Scriptures. He knows the Doctrine well. Çāntideva mentions eighty different ways of commencing the acquisition of religious learning.[372] But a *bodhisattva* also studies the arts and sciences, and thus gets a good liberal education. He devotes his energy to the acquisition of a thorough knowledge of the five principal subjects of study or branches of learning (*vidyā-sthānāni*). These five *vidyā-sthānas* are: Buddhist philosophy, logic or dialectics, grammar, medicine, and the technical arts and crafts.[373] These accomplishments help a *bodhisattva* in his work of converting the people, healing the sick, and conferring material benefits on all.[374] He studies with attention and mental concentration.[375] His learning is then profound and accurate. He is well-versed in all the arts and sciences (*kalās* and *çāstras*[376]; *çāstrajñatā; sarva-vidyāḥ; bāhu-çrutya*). In order to acquire such encyclopaedic knowledge, he must be very diligent and industrious. This is his *çikṣā-vīrya* (Energy in Education).

It is probable that the ideal of a liberal education was borrowed by the Buddhists from Hinduism. Early Buddhism did not attach much importance to Learning, perhaps because the latter was almost identical in that age with the hated threefold *vidyā* of the *brahmins*. Gautama Buddha laid stress chiefly on morality, monasticism and meditation. But the conversion of many Hindu priests to Buddhism must have led to a movement in favour of higher education among the Buddhist monks. The heroes of the *Mahābhārata* and the *Rāmāyaṇa* are described as well-educated and cultured men. Rāma is spoken of as "*vidvān sarva-çāstr-ārtha-tattvajña*" in the opening verses of the *Rāmāyaṇa*.[377] This ancient Indian ideal was also accepted by the Mahāyānists, who taught that a *bodhisattva* must be a prodigy of erudition and even learn the mechanical arts. The Buddhists improved on what they borrowed and very nearly approached the modern ideal of education.

3. *Altruistic Activity* (*sattv-ārtha-kriyā-vīryam*). A *bodhisattva* reflects carefully before he embarks on an enterprise; but he carries all his work to a successful issue.[378] He does not leave it half-done, and he is not daunted and discouraged by difficulties and dangers.[379] He maintains the same energy and resolution under all circumstances (*samaṃ vīryam*).[380] He devises the proper expedients for attaining his end. He is indefatigable and optimistic (*açlatha-vīrya*).[381] He does not lose hope on account of the stupidity and wickedness of the people; he does his daily task like the sun.[382] Like a king, he has his devoted soldiers, whose names are Zeal, Strength, Joy, Exclusive Application, Self-mastery and Courage. He also acts on the two great principles: "Equality of self and others," and "Regard of others in place of self". He develops a healthy pride in himself and his own capacity, and is therefore eager to undertake the most difficult tasks. The same pride gives him the strength to overcome all passions and endure all trials. He says: "I will conquer everything: nothing shall conquer me." This pride, which stimulates noble ambition, self-confidence and self-respect, must be clearly distinguished from vanity, conceit and arrogance, which ruin the soul.[383] Such noble pride leads a *bodhisattva* to regard himself as the very embodiment of virtue and wisdom. He can even say with truth: "The six Perfections do not help me; it is I, who help the Perfections."[384] He is determined to observe the five "continuities" (*ānantaryāṇi*) by persistence in his devotion to the Mahāyāna, to the ideal of self-sacrifice, to the duty of saving all beings, and to the pursuit of true knowledge and perfect wisdom.[385] For such a *bodhisattva*, nothing is impossible.[386]

As regards the reasons and motives for the cultivation of *vīrya*, the Buddhist writers adduce the usual arguments based on the certainty of death, the fear of punishment after death, the promotion of one's welfare on earth, the assurance of a happy rebirth, the rarity of the Buddhas and the difficulty of moral development in this life. We have heard all this before. Çāntideva only adds a few picturesque similes in order to inspire a *bodhisattva* with unflagging zeal and intense ardour. A *bodhisattva* is like a man carrying a vessel full of oil, who is surrounded by soldiers armed with swords; he will be killed, if he stumbles. When a drowsy man sees that a snake has come upon his breast, he suddenly rises up; even so a *bodhisattva* should always remain alert and active. He should rout the passions, as a lion slays the deer.[387] There is one new idea, however, which must be appreciated. It comes as an agreeable surprise. It is like an oasis of positive affirmation in the vast desert of Indian pessimism and negativism. In the midst of the gently soporific metaphysics of Buddhism, Çāntideva suddenly propounds the idea that happiness consists in activity. He thus reminds us of Aristotle's definition of happiness as the energy or activity of the soul in accordance with virtue.[388] A *bodhisattva* finds his happiness in his work. He does not work in order to obtain something, which will make him happy. For him, work is happiness and happiness is work.[389] Hence he is always active. When he has finished one task, he straightway commences another. This ideal of unremitting activity is a distinct and valuable contribution to the developed *bodhisattva* doctrine.

Stories of Vīrya. There are a few stories of *vīrya*, but they are not very interesting. In the *Lal. V.*, a few of Gautama Buddha's extravagant exploits in his previous lives are mentioned. He dried up the ocean by emptying out the water in order to recover a precious gem that had fallen into it.[390] This feat is also referred to in the *Mahā-vastu* as the most remarkable exhibition of the Perfection of *vīrya*.[391] Gautama Buddha also counted the leaves on a tree in a previous life.[392] The hero Kanakavarmā fought single-handed against a host of *Yakṣas*.[393] Prince Sudhanu undertook a perilous journey, braved many dangers and went through numerous adventures in order to meet his wife, a Himalayan woman, who had returned to her father's house on account of a palace-intrigue. This story is related in the *Mtu.*[394] and the *Avadāna-kalpa-latā*, but Kṣemendra gives Sudhana as the prince's name.[395] Sudhanu was thus united to his sweetheart "with great labour and great *vīrya*". Some earnest men also showed uncommon *vīrya* in their efforts to join the monastic Order. Tripita's father refused to give his permission for this step, but the young man fasted six times and his father then relented.[396] Gaṅgika tried to put an end to his life in order to be reborn as a monk.[397] Lack of *vīrya* in study can sometimes have tragic consequences. Some students, who were slack and lazy, were reborn as parrots and swans as a punishment for their indifference to duty.[398] Another novice, who was negligent in keeping a fast, was reborn as a snake.[399]

V. Dhyāna-pāramitā. With this Perfection, we enter the realm of asceticism and abnormal psychological phenomena, and the Mahāyāna now begins to be anti-social and unintelligible. *Dhyāna*, derived from *dhyā*, is one of the terms that cannot be translated. It has been rendered as "meditation", "trance", "ecstasy", "contemplation", "rapture", "die Versenkung", "die Vertiefung", etc. But C. A. F. Rhys Davids has pointed out that *jhāna* in Pāli "does not mean meditation", as this English word implies intellectual effort.[400] E. J. Thomas has shown that "ecstasy" is also an inadequate rendering.[401] It is really inadvisable to apply European terms to Indian concepts, as the lines of intellectual development in Europe and India have been different. It is easier and more profitable to understand the Indian terms than to search for an exact equivalent, which does not exist. C. A. F. Rhys Davids explains *dhyāna* as "the practice of rapt musing or abstraction".[402] This may be accepted as a conventional rendering for the present.

Dhyāna is defined in the *Bodhisattva-bhūmi* as "concentration and stability or fixity of the mind" (*citt-aikāgryaṃ citta-sthitiḥ*).[403] The *M. S. Al.* gives a fanciful etymological explanation: "*dhārayaty-adhyātmaṃ mana iti dhyānam*" (that which supports the mind).[404] The opposite of *dhyāna* is *vikṣepa* (distraction of mind) or *manaḥ-kṣobha* (agitation or disturbance of the mind).[405] *Dhyāna* is thus primarily and principally the means of experiencing and attaining serenity and calm (*çamatha*), which is indeed coupled with mental Concentration in the *Pr. Pā. Çata*.[406]

1. *Preliminaries of Dhyāna*. A *bodhisattva*, who begins to practise *dhyāna*, must go through a preliminary stage of

preparation, which may be said to include Renunciation and Solitude, the cultivation of the four Sublime or Perfect States (*brahma-vihārāḥ*), and the use of the *kṛtsnāyatanas*.

(*a*) *Renunciation and Solitude.* A *bodhisattva* must now give up family life and ordinary social intercourse, and retire to a secluded spot in the forest. He must live as a celibate hermit and recluse. M. Anesaki expresses the opinion that "the Mahāyānists find the life of nobles or householders in no way incompatible with the practice of the *pāramitās* and the attainment of *bodhi*" (ERE, v, 453). But the principal Sanskrit writers do not support this view. The well-known Pāli aphorism, which condemns the householder's life, is found in the Sanskrit version in several passages. "Life in the home is narrow and full of hindrances ('cabin'd, cribbed, confined'), while a monk's life is like the open air. It is difficult to lead the pure, austere and holy spiritual life as a householder."[407] According to the *Pr. Pā. Çata.*, celibacy is necessary for Enlightenment. Even if a *bodhisattva* is married, his marriage is really a "pious fraud" for the conversion of others. He does not really enjoy sensual pleasure: he remains a celibate.[408] The *Da. Bhū.* teaches that a *bodhisattva* becomes a monk in the first stage of his career.[409] The *Jātaka-mālā* distinctly favours the monastic life, and the married state is regarded with contempt and aversion by some of Çūra's noblest heroes. *Kṣāntivādin* thinks that life in the home is prejudicial to the growth of virtue, as it is associated with money-making pursuits, love of pleasure, jealousy, anger and pride.[410] *Ayogṛha* also expresses similar sentiments.[411] *Agastya* condemns the householder's life as troublesome, irksome and undesirable.[412] In the *Bisa-jātaka*, a whole party of seven brothers, their sister and several servants and friends renounce home-life and retire to the forest.[413] In the *Aputra-jātaka*, Çūra admits that a householder may be able to observe the precepts of religion; but he adds that it is well-nigh impossible, as the layman must tell lies, use violence, and injure others in order to earn wealth and keep it. A home is always infested with the serpents named Sensuality, Pride and Infatuation.[414] This is Çūra's idea of a home! Çāntideva declares that a married man cannot attain Enlightenment, and he also indulges in that amazing tirade against Passion, which has already been referred to. He teaches that a *bodhisattva* must renounce the world in all his lives after taking the great Vow.[415] Kṣemendra also regards celibacy and renunciation as indispensable for a *bodhisattva*. He even relates the story of a couple, who maintained a purely spiritual relation in married life, though they could not avoid marriage on account of the pressure of external circumstances.[416] A similar story is told in the *Avadāna-çataka*, which also praises several women for their aversion to marriage.[417] Kṣemendra goes so far as to say that ordination as a monk confers absolution even for the sin of matricide.[418] It is true that the *Sad. Pu.* speaks of the duties of a *bodhisattva* who is a king; and Çāntideva also seems to admit that a *bodhisattva* may be a householder.[419] The *Bodhisattva-bhūmi* definitely mentions both "laymen and monks" in connection with the first four *pāramitās*, but it does not refer to the laymen in the chapter on *dhyāna*. On the whole, it may be inferred that the Mahāyānist philosophers exalt and glorify monastic celibacy and seclusion, while they only condone and tolerate domestic life as an inferior state.

In this connection, it is interesting to note that these writers also adopt the misogynist's attitude towards women. In the early treatises of the Mahāyāna, women are not always regarded with contempt and suspicion. The *Lal. V.* treats Siddhārtha's marriage as a romantic episode.[420] The *Sad. Pu.* prophesies the future Buddhahood of Gautama Buddha's wife Yaçodharā, and of King Sāgara's daughter. It speaks of the "sons and daughters of good families" as potential *bodhisattvas*, and mentions five hundred women, who will certainly become Buddhas.[421] The eighth *varga* (section) of the *Ava. Ça.* is devoted to the stories of spiritual heroines.[422] The idealism and devotion of women are celebrated in the legends relating to such married couples as Viçvantara and Madrī, Kuṇāla and Kāñcanamālā, and others.[423] Kṣemendra even admits that a virtuous daughter like Sumāgadhā is better than a son![424] These details show that the better instincts of the Buddhist philosophers sometimes prevailed in spite of their one-sided theories. But the general trend of thought in their treatises points to the conclusion that women are spiritually and intellectually inferior to men. Even in the *Sad. Pu.*, which acknowledges a woman's right to be a *bodhisattva*, final Enlightenment is reserved only for men, and a woman's sex is changed before that consummation.[425] The *Mtu.* declares that a *bodhisattva* is not born as a woman[426]; but it is probable that this dictum refers to an advanced *bodhisattva's* last life.

The *Bodhisattva-bhūmi* is more definite on this point. It explains that a *bodhisattva* may be born as a woman during the first *asaṅkhyeya* of his career, but not during the second and third *asaṅkhyeyas* (fol. 39*b*.4). A woman can never be a Buddha (fol. 39*b*.3.3). The greatest boon that a woman can crave is speedy rebirth as a man.[427] In numerous passages, women are described as wicked and dangerous. They are foolish and fatuous creatures.[428] They are very prone to vice and sin (fol. 39*b*.4 . 3). They are the slaves of lust and passion. They are fond of intrigue, gossip and crooked ways. Birth as a woman is a calamity.[429] A *bodhisattva* should avoid women, even if they are nuns.[430] If he is married, he should fear and despise his wife ; and he should understand that the married state is merely a concession to the prejudices of society.[431] A *bodhisattva*, who preaches the Doctrine, should not pay too much attention to women.[432] It may be inferred that a woman is eligible for the first step of the "Thought of Enlightenment",[433] but must be reborn as a man in order to ascend to the higher stages of a *bodhisattva's* career. A male *bodhisattva*, married or unmarried, should beware of the wiles and charms of the fair sex. And a model male *bodhisattva* should be an unmarried monk.

It is probable that the influence of Hinduism at first led to the conception that a woman should be a man's friend and comrade in spiritual progress. The householder's life was praised and appreciated to the fullest extent in the ancient Hindu Scriptures.[434] The *Rāmāyaṇa* and the *Mahābhārata* usually mention couples of famous persons, e.g. Rāma and Sītā, Vasiṣṭha and Arundhatī, Nala and Damayantī, etc. This tradition was maintained in some Buddhist stories, like the legends of Viçvantara and Kuṇāla. The *Mtu.* also recounts several tales of Gautama Buddha's previous lives, in which his wife had been very helpful to him.[435] But monastic celibacy triumphed in the end. It must also be remembered that Gautama Buddha's wife did not play an important part in his movement, and she was not present at his death-bed. These celibate monks were bound to drift into an attitude of contempt and aversion with regard to women. The Christian monks of Europe have also written virulent diatribes against women.[436] Monasticism not only lowered the status of women, but also created an anti-social bias in the minds of the Mahāyānist teachers. They rail not only again the family, but also against society and social life in general. It is always a short step from violent misogyny to unalloyed cynicism. Most Buddhist philosophers belittle and revile common humanity, and prefer the solitude of the forest to the delights of social intercourse. Ordinary men are spoken of as "children" (*bālāḥ*), which is really a euphemistic term for "fools". They are avaricious, envious, quarrelsome, vain, stupid, conceited, demoralised and incorrigible.[437] A *bodhisattva* should wander alone like a rhinoceros.[438] The trees and flowers in the forest are pleasant friends that give no trouble, and their company is preferable to that of these silly and selfish men of the world.[439] A *bodhisattva*, who has retired to the forest, should "find tongues in trees, books in the running brooks".[440] He should be free from the ideas of Self and Property, like the trees around him. He should not be afraid of the wild beasts, but should be prepared to sacrifice his life for them in a compassionate spirit, if they attack him.[441] He should devote himself to meditation and self-examination, and also preach occasionally to the laymen, who may visit him in his hermitage.[442] The Mahāyānist effusions on this theme contain some excellent Nature-poetry and a great deal of bad philosophy.

(*b*) *The Brahma-vihāras.* A *bodhisattva* should practise the four meditations called the *brahma-vihāras.* The forms *brāhma-vihāra* and *brāhmya-vihāra* are also found (*Kar. Pu.* 114.30; *Bo. Bhū.*, fol. 38*a*, 4.2; *M. S. Al.*, 122.7).

The word has been variously translated as follows:—

T. W. Rhys Davids and W. Stede: "Sublime or divine state of mind" (Pāli Dicy.).

Monier Williams: "Pious conduct, perfect state" (Skt. Dicy., 740*a*).

C. A. F. Rhys Davids: (1) "God-moods" ("Gotama," p. 183). (2) "Sublime occupations" ("Psychology", p. 103).

S. Lévi: "Les stations brahmiques" (*M. S. Al.*, tr., p. 318).

M. Walleser: "Die brahman-wohnungen" (*Pr. Pā.* tr., p. 124).

H. C. Warren: "Sublime states" ("Buddhism," p. 291).

Lord Chalmers: "Excellent states" (*Majjh.* tr., ii. 40).

F. Heiler: "Brahma-zustände" ("Versenkung", p. 24).

T. W. and C. A. F. Rhys Davids: "Divine states" ("Dialogues," iii, 216 note).

P. Oltramare: "Les conditions saintes" ("Bouddhique," p. 361).

T. W. Rhys Davids: "The highest condition" ("Buddhism," p. 148).

It is very doubtful if the term implies any reference to the neuter *Brahman* of the *Upaniṣads* or the masculine *Brahmā*, the *deva* of Hinduism. It is true that the practice of these meditations is said to ensure rebirth in the world of *Brahmā* (*brahma-loka*),[443] but that idea may itself have originated in mistaken notions about the etymology of this term. The word *brahma*, derived from *bṛh* (to increase), here means "excellent, perfect", as in other words like *brahma-jāla-sutta* (the perfect net), *brahma-cariyā*, *brahma-vāda*, etc. (Pāli Dicy., s.v.). Perhaps it is best to translate: "Perfect or Excellent States."

These four meditations are also known as *apramāṇāni* (the "infinitudes", "infinite feelings", "measureless meditations"). The *Pr. Pā. Çata.* speaks of them throughout as *apramāṇāni*, and not as *brahma-vihārāḥ.*[444] Perhaps the latter term was discarded, when the word *vihāra* was employed to denote the different stages of a *bodhisattva's* spiritual career, as in the *Bo. Bhū.*[445]

These *brahma-vihāras* seem to have been borrowed by the Buddhists from another school of philosophers. In the *Makhādeva-sutta* of the *Majjhima-Nikāya* (*Majjhima*, ii, 82), it is hinted that they did not constitute Buddha's original contribution to Indian religious thought. C. A. F. Rhys Davids is of the opinion that they were taught by an important preacher, whom she calls "the unknown co-founder of Buddhism".[446] They are also found in the same order in the *Yoga-sūtras* (1.33, p. 38). The first three are also mentioned in Vyāsa's commentary on *Yo. Sū.*, iii, 23 (p. 148). This shows that they belonged to the common tradition of the Indian religious world. In Buddhist Sanskrit literature, they are mentioned and described in many passages (*M. Vy.*, Sections 69, 82; *Dh. S.*, xvi; *M. S. Al.*, 121; *Da. Bhū.*, 34.18 ff.; *Pr. Pā Çata.*, 1314, 1444; *Mtu.*, iii, 421; *Lal. V.*, 297.10, etc.).

The four *brahma-vihāras* consist in the cultivation of four feelings, according to a certain method, viz. *maitrī* (love or friendliness), *karuṇā* (compassion), *muditā* (sympathetic joy) and *upekṣā* (equanimity).

It is possible to indicate the growth of this fourfold formula in Buddhist Sanskrit literature. In many passages, only *maitrī* is mentioned: (e.g. *Pr. Pā. Çata.*, 261.4; *Saund. Kā.*, xviii, 11, 34; *Lka.*, 259.2; *Mtu.*, iii, 373.11; *Kṣemendra*, ii, 501.57; *Ava. Ça.*, ii, 34.15; *Lka.*, 259, verse 23, etc.). At other places, only *maitrī* and *karuṇā* are mentioned together. These form a natural pair, and are spoken of as such at *Da. Bhū.*, 19.21, 39.13; *Pr. Pā. Çata.*, 19.8, 134.4, 136.4; *M. S. Al.*, 180.29, 47.71; *Mtu.*, ii, 340.20, etc. But it is more puzzling to find only *maitrī*, *karuṇā* and *muditā* mentioned in several passages, e.g. *Mtu.*, ii, 362.5; *Sam. Rā.*, fol. 193*b*, 4. Vyāsa, in his commentary on *Yo. Sū.*, iii, 23, refuses to recognise *upekṣā* as a *bhāvanā* (practice for realisation). It differs also in its aim and spirit from the other three meditations.

In course of time, these social virtues were appreciated in an increasing degree. The Mahāyānist writers even reckon *mahā-karuṇā* among a perfect Buddha's attributes. It is considered as important as the *balas*, the *vaiçāradyas*, and the *āveṇika-dharmas*. The *Mtu.* exalts the *brahma-vihāras* to such an extent that it promises *nirvāṇa* and the *summum bonum* to the person who practises them.[447] This was a daring innovation, as the old Pāli writers regarded them only as the means of securing rebirth in the heaven of *Brahmā*. All the *brahma-vihāras* were thus emphasised and inculcated with greater zeal, and *karuṇā* was chosen as the most important among them. The honorific title *mahā* was also prefixed to all, especially to *maitrī* and *karuṇā*.[448]

As *karuṇā* and *upekṣā* have been discussed in the sections on *dāna* and the *bodhy-aṅgas* respectively, the two other *brahma-vihāras* will now be considered in detail.

Maitrī ("friendliness or love". Pāli: *mettā*). Some scholars have translated this word as "love", but others prefer "friendliness, benevolence, la bonté, goodwill" as the proper rendering, as they believe that "love" has certain Christian associations.[449] *Maitrī* is a feeling that is directed towards those who are happy in life. Its opposite is *vyāpāda* (malice). It is thus distinguished from *karuṇā*, which is shown to unhappy and afflicted living beings. "Love," as defined and described by Jesus Christ and St. Paul, approximates more to *karuṇā* than to *maitrī*: (cf. St. Matthew v, 43; St. Luke vi, 27 ff.; St. John xv, 13; 1 Corinthians xiii). "Friendliness" seems to indicate the the content of the term *maitrī* with a sufficient degree of accuracy. It is characterised by the desire to do good to others and to provide them with what is useful.[450] *Maitrī* is mentioned and extolled more frequently in the Pāli canon than *karuṇā*.[451] The Hīnayāna emphasises *maitrī*, while the Mahāyāna lays stress on *karuṇā*. This seems to be their distinctive note. As a *brahma-vihāra*, *maitrī* is exercised through a certain meditative practice, and the same formula is applied to all the other *brahma-vihāras*. This practice belongs to the *dhyāna-pāramitā* in the Mahāyāna, and the *Pr. Pā. Çata.* actually places these *brahma-vihāras* between the four *dhyānas* and the four *samāpattis* in its oft-repeated lists of a *bodhisattva's* duties.[452] The process of meditation is thus described in the case of all the *brahma-vihāras*, substituting *karuṇā*, *muditā* and *upekṣā* respectively for *maitrī*: "He (the *bodhisattva*) abides pervading the whole Universe (with its chief element, the Truth, and its remotest element, Space) with his mind, accompanied by *maitrī*, with vast, great, undivided, unlimited and universal freedom from hatred, rivalry, narrow-mindedness and harmfulness". (*Da. Bhū.*, p. 34.)

This formula differs in some respects from its Pāli original [453] (cf. *Dīgha* i, 250, section 76 ff.). The *Da. Bhū.* gives it in a form, which is not exactly the same as that found in the *Pr. Pā. Çata.*[454] It has been suggested that these meditations are directed towards particular individuals and not towards the world in general.[455] But the wording of the sentence does not warrant such a conclusion. It is as vague and abstract as it can possibly be. *Maitrī* is regarded as a great Power in the universe (*maitrī-bala*).[456] It prompts a *bodhisattva* to hope, pray and wish for the welfare of others, without passion or expectation of reward.[457] It can tame wild beasts and venomous serpents. It prevents and allays physical and mental pain and evil.[458] It establishes peace and concord among mankind.[459] It is of three kinds according as it is directed towards the living beings, towards all things and phenomena, or towards no particular objects.[460] The perfect Buddhas can emit *rays of maitrī* from their bodies, which are diffused over the world and promote peace and joy everywhere.[461]

Muditā (Sympathetic joy). This word has been variously translated as "appreciation", "die Mitfreude", "satisfaction", "joy", "delightfulness", "happiness in the happiness of all", "das Freundschaftsgefühl", etc. E. Senart suggests that it may be a *Prākṛt* form of *mṛdutā* (gentleness, softness).[462] But this feeling is said to be directed towards virtuous and righteous persons (*puṇy-ātmakeṣu*). Its chief characteristics are joy, faith, and freedom from despondency, craving, jealousy, insincerity and hostility. It is associated with the alertness of all the faculties.[463]

(*c*) *The Ten Kṛtsnāyatanas* (Pāli: *kasiṇāyatana*). A *bodhisattva* should practise certain exercises in concentration and self-hypnotism, in which his attention is fixed on one of the ten *kṛtsnāyatanas* (bases or objects of such exercises). These ten objects are the four colours and the six elements: blue, yellow, red, white, earth, water, fire, air, space and mentality (intellection).[464] By gazing at them, visualizing them, or concentrating his mind on them in other ways, a *bodhisattva* can produce that mental state of calm and quiet somnolence, which is favourable to *dhyāna*.

2. *Dhyāna and the Nine States.* The conception of *dhyāna* has been amplified and modified in course of time; but the central doctrine revolves round the nine psychological states, real or imaginary, which are called the *anupūrva-vihāras* (i.e. states that follow one another in regular succession). The first four of these states are known as the four *dhyānas*,[465] and the last five are usually spoken of as *samāpattis* (Attainments).[466] These latter are really the fourth, fifth, sixth, seventh and eighth items of a list of eight *vimokṣas* (Deliverances, or Stages of Deliverance).[467] The first three Deliverances are not relevant to our subject in this section. The early history of these categories is obscure. They probably existed before the rise of Buddhism, as the *Brahma-jāla-sutta* connects them with non-Buddhist sects.[468] According to the *Lal. V.*, Rudraka Rāmaputra, who was Gautama Buddha's teacher for some time, practised them.[469]

The first four *dhyānas* were borrowed by the Buddhists at an early period, and special importance was attached to them. Gautama Buddha attains them on the night of Enlightenment. He is also described as passing away to *nirvāṇa* from the fourth *dhyāna* and not from the eighth, though he had also reached the latter stage.[470] Perhaps the four *dhyānas* and the eight "Deliverances" belonged to different systems until five "Deliverances" were added to the original four *dhyānas*. These five highest stages are generally called *samāpattis*, and not *dhyānas*, in the Sanskrit treatises. The *Pr. Pā. Çata.* always speaks of them as *ārūpya-samāpattayaḥ*.[471] Four of these are frequently mentioned, but the last of the nine *anupūrva-vihāras* is rarely discussed. Perhaps it inspired a kind of fear, as it seemed to be too much like extinction and death. All the nine are also called *anupūrva-vihāra-samāpattayaḥ*.

It is not possible to find any regular system of "mystical" meditation in these nine states. They are most probably nothing but mere verbiage, which corresponds to no real experience. This subject cannot be properly discussed in the absence of ascertained and verifiable facts. The nine states are described as follows [472] :—

(*a*) *First Dhyāna*. He (i.e. the *bodhisattva*), free from sensual pleasures and evil demeritorious states of mind, attains and abides in the first *dhyāna*, which arises from seclusion, and which is associated with the pleasure of joy and accompanied by reflection and investigation.

(*b*) *Second Dhyāna*. With the cessation of reflection and investigation, he, serene at heart, concentrates his mind on one point, and attains and abides in the second *dhyāna*, which is associated with the pleasure of joy, and arises from rapt concentration in the absence of reflection and investigation.

(*c*) *Third Dhyāna*. Having renounced the attachment to joy, he remains equable, mindful and self-possessed; experiences in his body the pleasure that the Noble ones describe as "living in equanimity, mindfulness and happiness"; and attains and abides in the third *dhyāna* which is devoid of joy.[473]

(*d*) *Fourth Dhyāna*. On account of the abandonment of pain and pleasure and the previous disappearance of elation and dejection, he attains and abides in the fourth *dhyāna*, which is neither painful nor pleasant, and which is absolutely pure through equanimity and mindfulness.[474]

(*e*) *The Non-material Samāpattis*. He transcends entirely the perceptions of material form, eliminates the perceptions of resistance (repulsion), does not pay attention to the perceptions of diversity, realises that "Space is infinite", and attains and abides in the sphere of the Infinity of Space.[475]

(*f*) He transcends entirely the sphere of the Infinity of Space, realises that "Consciousness is infinite", and attains and abides in the sphere of the Infinity of Consciousness.

(*g*) He transcends entirely the sphere of the Infinity of Consciousness, realises that "there is nothing", and attains and abides in the sphere of Nothingness.

(*h*) He transcends entirely the sphere of Nothingness, and attains and abides in the sphere of "neither-Consciousness-nor-non-Consciousness" (or, "neither-Perception-nor-non-Perception").

(*i*) He transcends entirely the sphere of "neither-Consciousness-nor-non-Consciousness" and attains and abides in the Cessation of Consciousness and Feeling.

(*Da. Bhū.*, 34; *Pr. Pā. Çata.*, 1443-5).

This Sanskrit formula differs in some respects from its Pāli original. These psychological states are also supposed to bring a *bodhisattva* into direct touch with the different worlds and spheres, whose existence is assumed in the cosmology of the Buddhists. C. A. F. Rhys Davids says: "This was so to sink the whole world of sense, and the work of mind on the world of sense, that the other worlds might arise in the man's awareness". She believes that the Buddhists could even establish communication with the dead by means of the *dhyānas*.[476] However that may be, the cosmology of the Mahāyānists divides the universe into three divisions: the sphere or realm of sensuous Desire (*kāma-dhātu*), the sphere of Form or Matter (*rūpa-dhātu*), and the sphere of Formlessness or non-Materiality (*arūpa-dhātu*, *arūpya-* or *ārūpya-*).[477] As W. Kirfel has pointed out, these three categories were first applied to the conception of *bhava* (Existence), and then extended to the entire universe.[478] The macrocosm and the microcosm were thus brought into harmony.

The sphere of Desire includes the earth, the firmament, the four Guardians of the cardinal points, the group of thirty-three *devas*, the denizens of the realms of *Yama* and of the *Tuṣita* heaven (Delight), and the *devas* called *nirmāṇa-ratayaḥ* (who rejoice in their creations) and *para-nirmita-vaça-vartinaḥ*.[479] Excluding the inhabitants of the earth and the firmament, there are thus six classes of celestial *devas* in this sphere. But a *bodhisattva* rises above this low region by means of the four *dhyānas* and the four *samāpattis*. The four *dhyānas* can transport him to the heavens of the *devas* that inhabit the second sphere of Form or Matter (*rūpa-dhātu*). These *devas* are called *rūp-āvacarā devāḥ* (the *devas* of the realm of Form). They have bodies, but are free from sense-desire. The number of these heavens is not quite fixed. The *Pr. Pā. Çata.* mentions twenty-one in one passage and seventeen in another. The *Mtu.* mentions fifteen names and also gives another list of sixteen. The *Divy-āvadāna* speaks of seventeen classes of *devas* in this sphere. The *Abhidharma-koça* and the *Lal. V.* give the same number. The *Dh. S.* and the *M. Vy.* agree in enumerating eighteen *deva*-groups, and this seems to be the accepted tradition.[480] These eighteen heavens are mentally accessible to a *bodhisattva* in a regular order by means of the four *dhyānas*. They are as follows (*M. Vy.*, sections 157–63) :—

First Dhyāna.

(1) *Brahma-kāyikāḥ* (the *devas*, who belong to the company of *Brahmā*).

(2) *Brahma-pāriṣadyāḥ* (*brahma-pārṣadyāḥ* in the *Dh. S.* Pāli : *brahma-pārisajjā*. The *devas*, who are in the retinue of *Brahmā*).

(3) *Brahma-purohitāḥ* (the ministers or priests of *Brahmā*).

(4) *Mahā-brahmāṇaḥ* (the *devas* attached to the great *Brahmā*).

Second Dhyāna.

(5) *Parīttābhāḥ* (the *devas* of limited splendour).

(6) *Apramāṇ-ābhāḥ* (the *devas* of immeasurable splendour).

(7) *Ābhāsvarāḥ* (Pāli : *ābhassarā*. The radiant *devas*, " shining in splendour ").

Third Dhyāna.

(8) *Parītta-çubhāḥ* (the *devas* of limited lustre or aura).

(9) *Apramāṇa-çubhāḥ* (the *devas* of immeasurable lustre or aura).

(10) *Çubha-kṛtsṇāḥ* (Pāli : *subha-kiṇṇā*. The *devas* of steady aura).

Fourth Dhyāna.

(11) *Anabhrakāḥ* (The *devas* of the cloudless heaven).

(12) *Puṇya-prasavāḥ* (the *devas* of auspicious birth).

(13) *Vṛhat-phalāḥ* (Pāli : *vehapphalā*. The *devas* of the heaven of great results or abundant reward).

(14) *Avṛhāḥ* (Pāli : *avihā*. The immobile *devas*).

(15) *Atapāḥ* (the serene *devas*).

(16) *Sudṛçāḥ* (the beautiful *devas*, " well-looking ").

(17) *Sudarçanāḥ* (the clear-sighted *devas*, well-seeing).

(18) *Akaniṣṭhāḥ* (the highest *devas* ; literally, " not the smallest ").[481]

The *Dh. S.* omits the *apramāṇa-çubhas* and inserts the *asaṃjñi-sattvas*, who correspond to the *asañña-sattas* of the Pāli list of sixteen *deva*-classes. This name means " unconscious beings " (cf. *Divy.*, 505.23). The *M. Vy.* adds three items to the Pāli list : the *anabhrakas*, *puṇya-prasavas* and *brahma-kāyikas*. It leaves out the *asañña-sattas*.

These names betray the influence of Hinduism and

Zoroastrianism, as they seem to be derived from *Brahmā* and from words meaning "Light". The number eighteen was probably regarded as mystical, because it is equal to 2 × 9. The *M. Vy.* adds two other names, *aghaniṣṭhas* (the "rare" *devas*, "not too dense"?) and *mahā-maheçvar-āyatanam* (the realm of the great *Çiva*). The fourth *dhyāna* is sometimes divided into two parts, and the different heavens are then allotted to five *dhyānas*: Nos. 1–4 to the first *dhyāna*, Nos. 5–7 to the second, Nos. 8–10 to the third, Nos. 11–13 to the fourth, and Nos. 14–18 to the fifth. This scheme of division is apparently adopted in the *M. Vy.*

The four heavens of the Formless Sphere are reached by the *dhyānas* of the four *samāpattis*, which have been mentioned above. They have the same names as these *samāpattis*.

3. *Dhyāna and the Samādhis*. Emerging from this perplexing labyrinth of *dhyānas* and *devas*, we may remark that these standard *dhyānas* are not regarded as very important by the Mahāyānist authors, who are more interested in different *samādhis* (modes of Concentration). These *samādhis* bear definite names and can produce certain results. *Samādhi* originally also denoted self-restraint and contentment,[482] but it is synonymous with *dhyāna* in the Sanskrit treatises. Many new forms of Musing and Concentration are spoken of. One may remain absorbed in them for several years or even during many millions of æons.[483] The *Laṅkāvatāra-sūtra* mentions another set of four *dhyānas*, which seem to belong to a different tradition. They are as follows [484]:—

(*a*) *Bāl-opacārikaṃ dhyānam*. This *dhyāna* is practised by the Hīnayānists and the Yogins, who believe in the non-substantiality of the Ego. It is meant only for beginners (*bālas*).

(*b*) *Artha-pravicayaṃ dhyānam*. This *dhyāna* is practised by the *bodhisattvas*, who understand the principle of the non-substantiality of all phenomena. It consists in the investigation and examination of propositions.

(*c*) *Tathat-ālambanaṃ dhyānam*. This *dhyāna* consists in comprehending the principle of Suchness or Reality and meditating on the Truth.

(*d*) *Tāthāgataṃ dhyānam*. This *dhyāna* belongs to the perfect Buddhas, who have personally realised the highest Knowledge and rendered service to all beings.

Other treatises also mention different kinds of *samādhi*. The

M. Vy. gives as many as 118 *samādhis* in Section 21 and nine more in Section 24. Some *samādhis* have significant names, e.g. *vajr-opama* (like adamant), *ratna-mudrā* (seal of gems), *vidyut-pradīpa* (having the splendour of lightning), *tejovatī* (fiery, ardent), *avaivarta* (irrevocable, not turning back), etc. The *Sam. Rā.* extols a particular *samādhi* and prescribes certain moral qualifications for its successful attainment.[485] The *Dh. S.* mentions eight names of *samādhis*, some of which are also found in the *M. Vy.*[486] The *Laṅkāvatāra-sūtra* speaks of "thousands of *samādhis*".[487] The *Pr. Pā. Aṣṭa.* enumerates the *samādhis* acquired by a *bodhisattva*. The *Pr. Pā. Çata.* names and describes an enormous number of *samādhis*.[488] It opens the list with the famous *samādhis* known as *çūraṅgama* ("going to the brave", "accessible to the brave") and *siṃha-vikrīḍita* (lion-play). Out of this plethora of *samādhis*, three should be selected for special mention, as they are considered to be very important. They are also called *vimokṣa-mukhāni* (mouths or entrances of Liberation). They destroy the three "Roots of Evil" (*rāga*, *dveṣa* and *moha*). They are as follows[489] :—

(i) *Çūnyatā* (Emptiness). The doctrine of *çūnyatā* will be discussed in the section on *prajñā-pāramitā*.

(ii) *Ānimitta*. The Tibetan equivalent for this term is *mtshan ma med pa*, and S. C. Das translates it as "unconditioned". He gives the Sanskrit equivalent as *animitta*, but *ānimitta* is the more correct form. T. W. Rhys Davids and W. Stede render it as "signless", as also do S. Lévi ("sans-signe") and M. Walleser ("das Zeichenlose"). H. Kern translates, "groundless, reasonless." The idea seems to be that the *bodhisattva* attains a state, in which he enters the realm of the Unconditioned and the Causeless.

(iii) *Apraṇihita*. The Tibetan equivalent of this term is *smon pa med pa*. S. C. Das translates it as "passionless". T. W. Rhys Davids and W. Stede render it as "aimless", and C. A. F. Rhys Davids suggests "not hankered-after". M. Walleser interprets it as "das Neigunglose", and S. Lévi gives a very literal translation, "sans-vœu." W. H. D. Rouse explains it as "untrammelled". Perhaps it means "free from Desire". The root-meaning of *praṇidhāna* seems to be "wish", as the Tibetan equivalent indicates.[490]

The *samādhis* are very useful to a *bodhisattva* for all possible purposes. *Samādhi* is said to be the means of attaining final Liberation.[491] But the different *samādhis* can be used to perform many miracles in this life. Pūrṇa flew in the air and saved certain travellers from shipwreck by means of a *samādhi*.[492] Another *samādhi* can call the *devas* to one's aid.[493] Another confers perpetual youth, while others enable a *bodhisattva* to travel everywhere in the universe.[494] A *bodhisattva* can employ the *samādhis* in order to heal the sick, protect the people from all dangers, produce rainfall in a period of drought and famine, bestow wealth on the poor, and warn and admonish the heedless sinners.[495]

4. Some scholars have attempted to compare these *dhyānas* and *samādhis* to the ecstatic states of the *Yoga* system and of Christian mysticism. E. Senart says: "Les *yogin* ont fait l'éducation et préparé les voies du bouddhisme." He thinks that the "ultra-cognitive" *samādhi* (*asamprajñāta*) of *Yoga* is equivalent to the fourth *dhyāna* of the Buddhists.[496] H. Beckh writes: "Der ganze Buddhismus ist durch und durch nichts als *Yoga*."[497] R. Garbe says: "Die Lehren des *Yoga* zu den Grundlagen des Buddhismus gehören."[498] But it is probable that the *Yoga* system in its developed form did not exist, when the Pāli canon was composed. The word *yoga* has sometimes a pejorative sense in the Pāli scriptures, and even in the *Mahā-vastu*[499]; it means "bond", "fetter". It is not till we come to the *Laṅkāvatāra-sūtra* that we find the term *yogin* applied to a *bodhisattva*.[500] Further, the four *dhyānas* do not correspond to anything in the *Yoga* system. There are four stages in *Yoga*, but they are entirely different in their spirit and scope.[501] The Buddhists do not believe in the existence of *Īçvara*, but that doctrine is an integral part of the *Yoga* system. *Dhyāna* in the *Yoga-sūtras* is only a means of attaining *samādhi* (*Yo. Sū.*, iii, 1–3, pp. 118, 119). But the Buddhists regard the four or eight *dhyānas* as ladders reaching to the highest regions of the universe. All that can be maintained is that certain practices of Concentration were borrowed by the early Buddhists from other schools, and that the later Mahāyāna was deeply influenced by the *Yoga* system as it is known to us. At the same time, it must be emphasised that the spirit of the Mahāyāna is quite different from that of the *Yoga* philosophy. C. A. F. Rhys Davids and F. Heiler have tried to compare the *dhyānas* to the experiences of the Greek and Christian "mystics".[502] But the *dhyānas* and *samādhis* of Buddhism have very little in common with the practices and aspirations of Plotinus, St. Theresa, Eckhart and other European "mystics". Christian mysticism is based on fervent

emotion and pious theism: the *dhyāna* of Buddhism is rooted in thought and spiritual autonomy, as it ends in mindfulness and equanimity, or in total coma and unconsciousness. The Christian mystic loses himself in God and has a vision of Christ: the Buddhist monk is intensely conscious of his own personality, and does not aspire to meet another higher Personality, immanent or transcendental. The formulae of the Buddhists do not help us to understand the psychological states that are produced (if they are produced at all). "Mysticism" is a vague term, and it is difficult to compare and contrast two such nebulous growths as Buddhist *dhyāna* and Christian "mysticism". It is perhaps impossible to find a common denominator for these radically different historical phenomena.

VI. Prajñā-pāramitā (The Perfection of Wisdom).

This Perfection represents the *summum bonum* of Buddhist philosophy. *Prajñā* has been translated as "gnosis", "wisdom", "insight", "intuition", "la science transcendante", "transcendental idealism", "knowledge", "spiritual enlightenment", "la science de la nature des choses", etc. The English word "wisdom", derived from Gothic "witan, weis", is related in meaning to *prajñā*, which is derived from *jñā*. The opposite of *prajñā* is often given as *avidyā* (ignorance), *moha* (delusion, folly), or simply *dauṣprajñā* (non-wisdom).[503] H. Kern suggests the untenable theory that *prajñā* is the female consort of *Çiva*, or *Durgā*, who is also identical with Nature.[504]

Prajñā is of three kinds: that which depends on hearing the teaching from another person and on the study of Scripture; that which arises from reflexion; and that which is developed by cultivation and realisation (*çrutamayī*, *cintāmayī*, *bhāvanāmayī*).[505]

The concept of *prajñā* is so important that it is mentioned in several numerical lists, e.g. among the *balas*, the *indriyas*, the *dhanas*, the *cakṣus* and the *adhiṣṭhānas*.[506] It is explained in three different ways by the Buddhist authors.

1. *Prajñā* as ordinary knowledge and learning. The *Bodhisattva-bhūmi* and the *Lal. V.* sometimes interpret *prajñā* as the knowledge of the arts and sciences.[507] But this original sense of *prajñā* was not adopted in systematic Buddhist philosophy.

2. *Prajñā and the Vijñāna-vādins.* The two great Mahāyānist schools of Buddhist philosophy do not agree in their interpretation

of *prajñā*. The *Vijñāna-vādins* (*Yogācāras*) explain *prajñā* in a positive manner as "the Knowledge of the supreme Good or the supreme Truth" (*param-ārtha-jñāna*), or simply as "Knowledge" (*jñāna*).[508] It depends on right investigation and concentration, which lead to the knowledge of that which exists and as it exists.[509] It consists in an unobscured and lucid knowledge of all that is knowable (*sarva-jñey-ānāvaraṇa-jñānam: Bo. Bhū.*, fol. 84*b*.6). It implies the knowledge of the four Noble Truths, of what should be done or not done (*karaṇīya, akaraṇīya*), of the philosophical categories and arguments, and of moral corruption and purification (*saṅkleçasya, vyavadānasya*).[510] The *Vijñāna-vādins* thus identify *prajñā* with perfect Knowledge in all its aspects, and regard it as insight into Reality (*tathatā*).[511]

3. *Prajñā and the Mādhyamikas.* The *Mādhyamika* philosophers have interpreted *prajñā* in a negative sense, but they have expounded their ideas with remarkable prolixity and pertinacity. They have even composed voluminous treatises, which deal only with this *pāramitā*. They also extol and glorify it in eloquent terms. They invoke it in the exordium of the *Pr. Pā. Aṣṭa.*, as if it were a substitute for the "triple jewel" of the Buddha, the *Dharma* and the *Saṅgha*. They apply the epithets *āryā* (noble) and *bhagavatī* (adorable) to it, and we know that Buddha was always described as *bhagavān*. The *Mādhyamikas* do not shrink from declaring that the *prajñā-pāramitā* is the mother of all the Buddhas and *bodhisattvas*.[512] It is the good friend of the *bodhisattvas*. It is a pearl of great price. It is immeasurable, pure, lovely, profound, wonderful, infinite, indivisible, unshakable and inconceivable. It is greater than all the other *pāramitās*, as the moon is greater than the stars. All the other *pāramitās* should be transmuted and sublimated into the *prajñā-pāramitā*, which really includes all of them. The other *pāramitās*, without *prajñā*, lead to the lower stage of the Hīnayāna, while this *prajñā-pāramitā* is the essence of the Mahāyāna and is even sufficient by itself without the other Perfections. It produces, maintains and promotes them all.[512]

This *prajñā-pāramitā* is understood to mean *çūnyatā* (literally, "emptiness, void"). This elusive term may be translated as "conditioned, contingent, phenomenal Existence" or as "Non-existence". It is explained in these two different ways by the *Mādhyamika* philosophers.

(*a*) *Çūnyatā as conditioned Existence.* The original doctrine of the *Mādhyamikas* was regarded as a middle way between the dogmas of absolute Existence and absolute Non-existence. The *Samādhirāja-sūtra* says: "'Is' and 'Is not' are both extreme opinions; 'Purity' and 'Impurity' are also the same." [513] The *Mdh.* declares that the foolish people, who believe in Existence or Non-existence, do not understand the real nature of things.[514] The *Laṅkāvatāra-sūtra* shows that absolute Existence and Non-existence are relative terms, as each proves the necessity of the other.[515] Nāgārjuna has expressed this view in his famous aphorism :—

"No destruction, no production; no discontinuity, no permanence; no unity, no diversity; no appearance (coming), no disappearance (going)." [516]

These eight negatives sum up the early teaching on *çūnyatā*, which really amounts to a systematic exposition of the old Buddhist formula of the *pratītya-samutpāda* (Pāli: *paṭicca-samuppāda*, "Dependent Origination") or the twelve *nidānas* (bases, grounds, causes). It is distinctly stated in the *Mdh.* that *çūnyatā* does not mean "Non-existence" (*abhāva*) and that it is identical with the principle of the *pratītya-samutpāda* (*Mdh.*, 503.10 ff.; 491.15 ff.). The root-idea of the obscure and unintelligible formula of the twelve *nidānas* is found in the Pāli canon: "This being, that becomes; from the arising of this, that arises; this not becoming, that does not become; from the ceasing of this, that ceases." [517] The term *suññatā* also occurs in several passages of the Pāli canon,[518] and the *Andhakas* had a definite theory of *çūnyatā* (*Kathā-vatthu*, xix, 2, p. 578). The Mahāyānists only re-iterated the old doctrines and developed them to their logical conclusion. The fundamental notion is thus explained in the *Mdh.*: "There is nothing that arises without a determining cause; hence there is nothing that is not empty or void (*çūnya*)." (*Mdh.*, 505.2–3.) "Things and phenomena do not arise by themselves." (*Mdh.*, 76, 1.) This doctrine of universal causation and inter-dependence is embodied and formulated in the numerical list of the twelve *nidānas*, which has been devised to explain how the law of causality operates.

Pratītya-samutpāda and the Nidānas. The word *pratītya* (Pāli: *paṭicca*) is derived from the root *i* (with *prati*) and literally means "resting on, falling back on". The term *pratītya-samutpāda* signifies "arising on the grounds of a preceding cause, happening by way of cause, causal-genesis, dependent origination" ("*hetu-pratyay-āpekṣo bhāvānām utpādaḥ.*" *Mdh.*, p. 5). The *Mdh.* also gives an incorrect grammatical interpretation: "the production or origination of successively perishable things or phenomena." E. Burnouf has also mentioned this explanation: "la production connexe des conditions faites pour disparaître successivement." [519] The twelve items of this formula are also called *nidānas.* This word, derived from *dā* (*dyati*, to bind) and *ni* (along), suggests a series or connected chain. It means "Grundursache, Wesen, Grundform; a first or original cause, basis, a primary or remote cause; source, origin, cause" (Skt. Dicy. Pbg. and M.W.; Pāli Dicy.). These twelve *nidānas* are given as follows in the Sanskrit treatises:—

"From Ignorance (*avidyā*) as cause arise the *saṃskāras*; from the *saṃskāras* as cause arises Consciousness (*vijñāna*); from Consciousness as cause arises Name-and-form (*nāma-rūpa*); from Name-and-form as cause arises the sixfold Sphere of the Senses (*ṣaḍ-āyatana*); from the sixfold Sphere as cause arises Contact (*sparça*); from Contact as cause arises Sensation (*vedanā*); from Sensation as cause arises Craving (*tṛṣṇā*); from Craving as cause arises Grasping (clinging, *upādāna*); from Grasping as cause arises Becoming (*bhava*); from Becoming as cause arises Birth (*jāti*); from Birth as cause arise old age, death, grief, lamentation, pain, dejection and despair". (*Lal. V.*, 346, 419; *Mtu.*, iii, 448.) [520]

In the *Da. Bhū.*, "the five *indriyas*" are mentioned in place of the "sixfold Sphere of the Senses", and *abhinandanā* (delight, pleasure) is inserted as a synonym of *tṛṣṇā.* Instead of *jāti*, the *Da. Bhu.* speaks of "the emergence of the five *skandhas* (aggregates)." [521] The *Lal. V.* also mentions all the *nidānas* in the reverse order, but most treatises always begin with *avidyā.*

1. *Avidyā* (Pāli: *avijjā*). *Avijjā* is defined in the *Dhamma-saṅgaṇi* as "lack of knowledge about the four Noble Truths" etc., exactly in the same way as *moha*, with which it is thus identified (Sections 1100, 1162). The *Da. Bhū.* explains *avidyā* as "delusion or folly (*moha*) with regard to the things, which are material compounds". [522] It infatuates the beings. Kṣemendra equates *avidyā* and *vāsanā* (subliminal impressions), and declares that it is the root of the tree of phenomenal existence and of all pain. [523] *Avidyā* is mentioned in the *Yoga-sūtras*, where it is defined as the error of imagining that

transient, impure, painful and non-substantial things have just the opposite characteristics (*Yo. Sū.*, ii, 5, p. 61). J. Woods translates it as "undifferentiated consciousness" (p. 110). A Tibetan symbolic picture of the *nidānas* represents it as a blind man feeling his way with a stick. The idea of blindness seems to be essential.[524] T. W. Rhys Davids interprets *avidyā* as "a productive, unconscious Ignorance", while S. Lévi stresses the point that it is an objective entity.[525] As *avidyā* is absent from the list of the *nidānas* in the *Mahāpadāna-sutta* and the *Mahānidāna-sutta* of the *Dīgha-Nikāya*, it was probably borrowed from a Hindu school which had affiliations with the *Upaniṣads*. It is difficult to understand its exact nature as the first link of the chain of causation. Perhaps it is something like the "Unconscious" of C. R. E. von Hartmann's metaphysics.[526]

2. *Saṃskāras*. Kṣemendra refers to the threefold division of the *saṃskāras* that belong to the body, speech and the mind.[527] In an Ajanta fresco, they are represented by a potter working at his wheel, surrounded by pots; but the Tibetan picture has only the wheel and the pots, without the potter. The latter symbol is more appropriate, as the Buddhists do not recognise the existence of Omar Khayyām's "potter".[528] The *Da. Bhū.* teaches that the *saṃskāras* bring about the realisation of the results (of actions) [529] in the future.

3. *Vijñāna*. Kṣemendra identifies *vijñāna* with the six "organs of sense" (including *manas*).[530] According to the *Da. Bhū.*, it causes the reunion of Becoming.[531] In the Ajanta fresco and the Tibetan picture, it is represented as an ape, or an ape climbing a tree. It is also considered under six aspects according to its connection with the six *indriyas* (the eye, the mind, etc.).

4. *Nāma-rūpa*. This term denotes "mind-and-body" *Nāma* includes the four non-material "aggregates" of sensation, perception, volitions and consciousness, while *rūpa* means "form, the body composed of the four elements". Contact and attention are also comprised in *nāma*, which is a comprehensive term for the individual's mental life. In the Tibetan picture, it is represented by a boat crossing a stream (i.e. a living being on the ocean of *saṃsāra* or transmigratory existence). *Nāma-rūpa* was borrowed by the Buddhists from the *Upaniṣads*: (cf. *Chāndogya Upd.*, vi, 3.2., p. 337, "*tad etad amṛtaṃ satyena-cchannaṃ prāṇo vā amṛtaṃ nāma-rūpe satyaṃ tābhyām ayaṃ prāṇaç channaḥ*"; *Bṛhadāraṇyaka Upd.*, i, 6.3., p. 249).

5. *Ṣaḍāyatanam* (Pāli : *saḷ-āyatana*). *Āyatana* literally means " place or sphere for meeting or of origin ; ground of happening ". It denotes both the six " organs of sense " (including *manas*) and the corresponding objects. The former are called the internal *āyatanas*, and the latter are the external *āyatanas*.[532] In the Ajanta and Tibetan pictures, they are represented by a mask of a human face, or a house with six windows.

6. *Sparça* (Pāli : *phasso*). Contact is of six kinds according as it is produced by each of the six organs of sense (the eye, the ear, etc.). It is represented in the Tibetan picture by a man seated with an arrow entering the eye.

7. *Vedanā*. Sensation or Feeling has been discussed in the section on the *smṛty-upasthānas*. In the pictures, it is represented by a couple of lovers embracing each other (cf. T. W Rhys Davids, " Buddhism," p. 158).

8. *Tṛṣṇā* (Pāli : *taṇhā*). After *avidyā*, *tṛṣṇā* (Craving, Thirst) is the root-cause of evil. It is of three kinds according as it produces the desire for sensuous pleasures, for existence, and for non-existence (*vibhava*). It is often compared to a fever and a stream.[533] It leads to the wrong idea of the reality of the phenomena.[534] The *Laṅkāvatāra-sūtra* declares that *avidyā* is the father and *tṛṣṇā* is the mother of the phenomenal world.[535] *Tṛṣṇā* is also the name of a daughter of *Māra*, the *deva* of Desire and Death.[536] According to the *Da. Bhū.*, it produces attachment to the objects of enjoyment.[537] In the Tibetan picture, it is represented by a man drinking wine.

9. *Upādāna*. This word, derived from *dā* with *upa* and *ā*, literally means " that material substratum by means of which an active process is kept alive or going ", hence " fuel " (for a fire). In Buddhist philosophy, it denotes " grasping, clinging to existence or to external objects ", as this tendency feeds the fire of Becoming and leads to rebirth.[538] According to the *Da. Bhū.*, it creates the bond of moral corruption. There are four kinds of *upādāna*, arising from sensuous Desire, heresy, belief in rites and ceremonies, and the wrong idea of a substantial Ego (*ātman*).[539] In the Tibetan picture, *upādāna* is represented as a man picking flowers and storing them up in large baskets. E. Burnouf translates the term as " la conception ".[540]

10. *Bhava* (Becoming, " das Werden "). Kṣemendra mentions the three divisions of *bhava*, viz. the spheres of *kāma* (sense-desire), *rūpa* (form) and *arūpa* (*ārūpya*, formlessness).

H. Oldenberg interprets *bhava* as rebirth and the continuance of existence.[541] But the Tibetan picture represents it as a married woman. L. A. Waddell says: " She is the wife of the individual, whose life-history is being traced . . . It is literally fuller Becoming, —Life as enriched by satisfying the worldly desire of home and as a means of obtaining an heir to the wealth amassed by Greed." [542]

11. *Jāti* (Birth). The *Da. Bhū.* explains *jāti* as the emergence or appearance of the five *skandhas*. Kṣemendra refers to the round of different lives.[543] The Tibetan picture shows the birth of a child. L. A. Waddell says: " It is the maturing of the man's life by the birth of an heir and as a result of the married existence of the tenth stage." [544]

12. *Jarā-maraṇa*, etc. Only *jarā-maraṇa* is sometimes mentioned.[545] *Vyādhi* (disease, sickness) is added to the seven items in several passages.[546] The Tibetan picture shows a corpse, which is being carried off to cremation or burial.

This famous formula of the twelve *nidānas* has given rise to much controversy. E. J. Thomas has refuted R. Pischel's theory that the terms are borrowed from the phraseology of the *Sāṅkhya-Yoga* system, which did not exist in its developed form in the fifth and fourth centuries B.C.[547] The tentative attempts of the early Buddhists have left clear traces in the Pāli canon. The *Mahāpadāna-sutta* and the *Mahānidāna-sutta* do not mention all the twelve items (*Dīgha*, ii, 31 ff., 55 ff.). The *Sutta-nipāta* gives a somewhat different series (*Dvayatānupassanā-sutta*, pp. 139 ff.), adding other terms, *ārambha*, *āhāra*, *iñjita*, etc. The series is prolonged in the *Saṃyutta-Nikāya* by adding *saddhā* and other positive concepts after " old age and death ".[548] But the Sanskrit writers took up the ready-made formula with its twelve factors. It is probable that there were only six items in the earliest form of the series, viz. *vijñāna*, *nāma-rūpa*, *ṣaḍ-āyatana*, *sparça*, *vedanā* and *tṛṣṇā*. These form a coherent group, and the discussion in the *Mahānidāna-sutta* is abruptly broken off at *taṇhā*. It is a sort of anti-climax to continue the series after *tṛṣṇā*, which is the central theme. In this shorter form, the formula was perhaps originally intended as an expansion of the second and third of the four Noble Truths (the origin and the cessation of Pain, which is due to Craving). The traditional explanation is that the first two terms refer to a past life, the next eight describe the present life, and the last two are related to a future existence.[549] This interpretation is unconvincing and unsatisfactory, as "Birth" is unnecessarily repeated, and the sense of the entire formula is obscured and distorted. In the third section, according to this analysis, there is a gap between Birth and Death, and the transition is too abrupt. H. Beckh thinks that the individual is really born at the stage of *bhava* (Empfängnis), and that the nine preceding terms refer only to the activities of a "super-sensible spiritual being", which is called a *gandharva*.[550] This *gandharva* carries with it all the *skandhas* of the person, who is not yet born: ("Dieses Seelenwesen, das die vor der irdischen Empfängnis vorhandenen übersinnlichen Wesensteile *skandha's* des Menschen in sich hat"). All this is very ingenious; but the *gandharva* cannot possess *rūpa* or the sense-organs, and it cannot feel *tṛṣṇā* (Craving). H. Beckh's interpretation cannot solve this curious problem. His irrelevant references to *Sāṅkhya* terminology do not call for serious comment. H. Oldenberg accepts the traditional *Theravāda* explanation, and says: "So wird die Region des Geborwerdens zweimal berührt, und das Irreführende, die tatsächlich vorhandene Unklarheit liegt darin, dass dies beidemal mit verschiedenen Ausdrücken geschieht." But why should this item occur twice? L. de la Vallée Poussin thinks that the twelve items have been arranged by taking pairs of terms from the *Dvayatānupassanā-sutta* and the *Kalaha-vivāda-sutta* of the *Sutta-nipāta*. He mentions the theory of the *gandharva*, and says: "La pensée (*citta* = *vijñāna*) revêt une forme corporelle (pas où il faut entendre le *nāma-rūpa*), qui se munit des organes (*ṣaḍ-āyatana*). Ainsi constitué, l'être intermédiaire contemple les créatures, et . . . il voit certain couple embrassé : il entre en contact (*sparça*) avec ce couple,"[551] etc. This explanation is repugnant to good taste, unconvincing and far-fetched. P. Oltramare points out that the formula has also been applied to the universe in general, and not merely to the individual life: "Expression d'une loi universelle absolue, le *pratītya-samutpāda* est mis en dehors du temps et de la relativité." He is of opinion that it was intended only to explain the origin of suffering for the practical aim of edification and that it is very unsatisfactory in its present form: "Que dans l'application de ce principe, il y ait des bizarreries et des enfantillages, personne n'en disconviendra."[552] J. Kirste begins with old-age-and-death and tries to trace the causal connection backward. He defines *avidyā* as "Unbewusstsein", "da darin Nichtwissen und Nichtsein verschmolzen sind"

(Album Kern, pp. 75–7). P. Oltramare also thinks that the *nidānas* do not really succeed one another in time, but act simultaneously to produce Pain. He says: "En réalité, tous les douze se trouvent coopérer à la fois, directement ou indirectement, à la souffrance que l'individu éprouve d'instant en instant." [553] But the simultaneous existence of such factors as Contact and Craving would be impossible. Some items must precede the others. There is an essential time-plan in this formula. We may do worse than follow the Indian tradition as it has been preserved and interpreted by the Tibetan priests, who explained to L. A. Waddell that *bhava* and *jāti* introduced the romantic elements of marriage and parenthood into this all-too-dull formula. The same person is not born again, but his child appears on the scene. This explanation may not be absolutely correct; but it at least makes sense out of the series, while almost all other interpretations make nonsense out of it.

A *bodhisattva* understands the truth of the *pratītya-samutpāda* in the sixth *bhūmi* (stage). He is then freed from all delusion and error (*moha*).[554]

When *çūnyatā* is understood to mean "conditioned Existence", it denotes the absence of an absolute self-existent Substance or Substratum in all things and phenomena (*dharma-nairātmya*).[555] It also implies the non-existence of any uncaused or self-caused entities and phenomena. It is thus equivalent tc Causality and Phenomenalism, and may perhaps be compared tc the basic ideas of the systems of Auguste Comte and Herbert Spencer.

(*b*) *Çūnyatā as Non-existence.* Some Buddhist philosophers go further and explain *çūnyatā* as absolute Non-existence (*abhāva*). The authors of the *Pr. Pā. Çata.* and the *Vajra. Pr. Pā.* seem to revel in a veritable orgy of negation. The *Pr. Pā. Çata.* says [556]: "Ignorance is non-existent; the *saṃskāras* are non-existent; Consciousness, Name-and-form, the Sixfold Sphere of the Senses, Contact, Sensation, Craving, Grasping, Becoming, Birth, Eld-and-Death are all non-existent (*avidyamāna*) . . . A *bodhisattva* does not find and discern the origination or cessation, corruption or purification, this side or the other side of any thing or phenomenon. If a clever magician or his apprentice were to create a great crowd of people in a square and preach the Perfection of Wisdom to them in order to establish them therein, then he would not thereby establish any being in the Perfection of

Wisdom, because all things and beings are of such a nature that they are illusory (*māyā-dharmatā*) . . . All *dharmas* exist in that they do not exist. They are not merely empty; they are identical with Emptiness. They are transient, painful, non-substantial, quiescent, void, signless, aimless, unproduced and unrelated. There are no form, sensation, perception, volitions and consciousness; no eye, ear, nose, tongue, body and mind; no forms, sounds, odours, savours, tangible things and mental objects; no Pain, or its origin or cessation; no eightfold Way; no past, present or future; no uncompounded elements; no *bodhisattva*, no Buddha and no Enlightenment . . . A *bodhisattva* is himself like a phantom of illusion (*māyā-puruṣa*)." Thus does the *Pr. Pā. Çata.* expound its doctrine of negation, which is surely carried to the utmost limit. The *Vajracchedikā Pr. Pā.* exhibits the same tendency. It declares that there are no individuals, no qualities, no ideas, no Doctrine, no beings to be delivered, no production or destruction, no *bodhisattva*, no Buddha and no *bodhi.*[557] Such absolute nihilism seems to border on absurdity. But these writers, like Tertullian, are perhaps not deterred by the difficulties inherent in absurdity. Çāntideva also adds his mellifluous note to this shrill chorus of "non-existent" philosophers, and perpetrates such verses as the following:—

"Nothing exists in the causes, taken separately or collectively. It cannot come from another place, and it cannot stay or go. How does it differ from illusion? . . . If something exists, why should it need a cause? And if it does not exist, why should it need a cause? If Existence is not present at the time of Non-existence, when will it come to be? So long as Existence does not appear, Non-existence will not disappear; but there is no possibility of the appearance of Existence, so long as Non-existence has not disappeared. Hence there is no Becoming and no Cessation at any time; this whole world is not produced or destroyed. All things are empty."[558]

To such puerile logomachy can these champions of *çūnyatā* descend! They have also devised a set of stock similes. All phenomena and beings are like a dream, an echo, a mirage, the stem of the plantain-tree, the image of the moon seen in water, etc.[559]

(*c*) *Cūnyatā* has also been classified, and very much so. There are eighteen or twenty kinds of *çūnyatā*. They are described as follows:—

(1) Inward or internal Emptiness (*adhyātma-çūnyatā*).
(2) External Emptiness (*bahirdhā*).
(3) Emptiness, which is both internal and external.
(4) The Emptiness of Emptiness (i.e. extreme Emptiness).
(5) Great Emptiness.
(6) The supreme or transcendental Emptiness (*paramārtha*).
(7) The Emptiness of the compounded phenomenal elements (*saṃskṛta*).
(8) The Emptiness of the uncompounded noumenal elements (*asaṃskṛta*).
(9) Absolute Emptiness (*atyanta*).
(10) Emptiness without beginning and end (*anavarāgra*: cf. *Divy.*, 197.15).
(11) Emptiness without a residuum, or ceaseless Emptiness (*anavakāra*).
(12) Emptiness by nature (*prakṛti*).
(13) Emptiness of all phenomena (*sarva-dharma*).
(14) Emptiness of Characteristics (*lakṣana*).
(15) Non-acquisitional Emptiness (i.e. it is difficult to acquire results: *anupalambha*).
(16) Emptiness of Non-existence (*abhāva*).
(17) Emptiness of Existence (*svabhāva*).
(18) Emptiness of both Existence and Non-existence.
(19) Emptiness of that which is not a characteristic (*alakṣana*).
(20) Emptiness of Other-existence (*para-bhāva-çūnyatā*).

The last two items are found only in the *Dh. S.*[560] The *Pr. Pā. Çata.* applies these different aspects of *çūnyatā* to all the concepts and categories of Buddhist philosophy (*rūpa*, *vedanā*, etc.), and even to the attributes of a Buddha. The *Laṅkāvatāra-sūtra* mentions seven kinds of *çūnyatā*, some of which are included in the list given above.[561]

(*d*) Some Buddhist thinkers have also arrived at the conclusion that nothing can be predicated about Reality. The nature of all things and phenomena is undefinable and indescribable.[562] There is neither transiency nor permanence, neither Emptiness (*çūnyatā*) nor its opposite, neither pain nor pleasure. An advanced *bodhisattva* rises above all such pairs of opposites and says nothing. He is also above Good and Evil, which really belong to the phenomenal world.[563] He does not recognise the existence of either virtue or sin (*puṇya*, *pāpa*). He is beyond Merit and Demerit. This view betrays the influence of the *Upaniṣads*.[564]

(*e*) The idea of Emptiness is also applied to all the Perfections (*pāramitās*). They are then "purified" and exercised in their highest potency. Thus a *bodhisattva* should "purify" the *pāramitā* of Giving by thinking that the donor, the recipient and the gift do not really exist.[565] In the same manner, all the persons and things that he meets in practising the other Perfections should be regarded as illusory and unreal. This is the best way of exhibiting the *pāramitās* in all their glory!

(*f*) The Buddhist philosophers, having so vociferously asserted the non-existence of all things, at last manage to "deviate into sense" by the subtle theory of the "two kinds of Truth".[566] Truth may be regarded under two aspects: *saṃvṛti-satya* (or *vyavahāra-satya*, "veiled, relative, conventional, contingent, experimental Truth") and *paramārtha-satya* (supreme, absolute, metaphysical Truth). The *Laṅkāvatāra-sūtra* says: "Everything exists relatively and contingently; but nothing exists absolutely."[567] The *M. S. Al.* declares that the relative world is like a magically constructed wooden elephant, which is fundamentally unreal and illusory, but which may be said to exist.[568] Çāntideva teaches that the phenomenal world, which can be grasped by the discursive intellect (*buddhi*), exists in a relative sense, as far as ordinary men and women are concerned; but the absolute Truth of Reality is beyond the sphere of Intelligence.[569] This monastic device of dividing Truth into two mutually incompatible parts is intended to reconcile the philosophy of *çūnyatā* with the common sense of mankind. The laymen live and love and work in the relative world of Phenomena; the monks live and think and dream in the absolute realm of Emptiness. Monasticism meddles even with metaphysics!

(*g*) *Prajñā* and *çūnyatā* are the sources of a *bodhisattva*'s moral strength. He is not attached to anything, and he is freed from all desires and fears.[570] *Prajñā* routs the army of *Māra*, as water destroys a vessel of unbaked clay.[571] According to the *Samādhirāja-sūtra*, a *bodhisattva*, who has acquired *prajñā*, gives away everything and is perfect and flawless in character. He loves rapt Musing, and cannot be shaken or conquered by the hosts of *Māra*. He remains detached in mind and body. He is animated by deep and great Love and Mercy (*adhimātra-karuṇā*). He acquires all the *dhyānas*, *samādhis* (modes of Concentration) and *samāpattis* (Attainments) of a Buddha (*Sam. Rā.*, fol. 115*a* and *b*).

This is the acme of Wisdom, and its positive aspects are thus emphasised.

VII. Upāya-kauçalya-pāramitā (also *Upāya-kauçala*).

This is the most important of the four supplementary *pāramitās*. It is also given as *upāya-pāramitā*.[572] It may be explained as " skilfulness or wisdom in the choice and adoption of the means or expedients for converting others or helping them ". It is especially related to a *bodhisattva's* work as a preacher and teacher. The Mahāyāna was a " revival " movement and attached great importance to successful propaganda. The *Bodhisattva-bhūmi* declares that it is a *bodhisattva's* duty to be an effective preacher (*avandhya-dharma-deçako bhavati*, fol. 152*a*, 6.2). According to the *Pr. Pā. Çata.*, all the *pāramitās* are fulfilled by preaching.[573] The *Sad. Pu.* also emphasises the importance of such missionary zeal.[574] The *Da. Bhū.* teaches that a *bodhisattva* becomes a preacher in the fifth *bhūmi* (stage).[575] Preaching and teaching are known as a *bodhisattva's* " gift of the Doctrine or Truth " (*dharma-dāna*).[576] It is more valuable and meritorious than the gifts of material objects (*āmiṣa-dāna*). A *bodhisattva* knows all kinds of devices and expedients for the instruction and discipline of the living beings (*Bo. Bhū.*, fol. 152*b*, 5.2). The Merit acquired by such service is a treasure that belongs to him.[577]

Upāya-kauçalya is frequently mentioned along with the six *pāramitās* in the *Pr. Pā. Aṣṭa.*,[578] but it was subsequently raised to the rank of a *pārāmitā*. Its object is stated in the *Bodhisattva-bhūmi* to be the conversion of those who are hostile or indifferent to the faith, and the development and liberation of those who already profess Buddhism (*Bo. Bhū.*, fol. 116*b*.5). This Perfection is generally exercised in order to gain access to the people, to win their sympathy, to explain the principles of the religion in a popular manner and to facilitate propaganda in other ways. A *bodhisattva* should always adapt his teaching to the capacity of the audience. He is like a physician, who prescribes different remedies for different diseases and different persons.[579] He speaks only of heaven to those who desire a happy rebirth.[580] He does not lay heavy burdens on his congregation. He does not ask them to keep long fasts, but shows an easier way to the simple, pious folk, who try to increase their "Merit".[581] He does not frighten them with the profound teaching of Emptiness, which he reserves for more advanced aspirants.[582]

A *bodhisattva* can adopt other methods suggested by his *upāya-kauçalya.* The *Sad. Pu.* relates some interesting parables, which illustrate this Perfection. It seems that trickery and falsehood are permitted, if the end of converting or helping others is achieved. The *pāramitā*, as described in the *Sad. Pu.*, comes perilously near the vice of duplicity and insincerity. Some Christian divines have also recommended "economy of truth" and "pious frauds" in the interests of religion.[583] But *upāya-kauçalya* can also take many unobjectionable forms. Two parables of the *Sad. Pu.* may be briefly related as follows :—

Parable of the Burning House. There was an old man, who was wealthy and owned a ramshackle dilapidated house with but one door. When he was outside the house one day, he saw that it was on fire. He had five, ten or twenty children, who were playing in the house. He did not know what to do. If he had entered the house and tried to take hold of the boys in order to save them, the foolish children would have run away from him in all directions. He called to the boys and cried: "Come, my children. The house is on fire." But the boys did not heed his words, and they did not even understand what he meant by "fire", so ignorant were they. He then showed his *upāya-kauçalya* by calling out: "Boys, I have put bullock-carts, goat-carts, deer-carts and other beautiful toys for you outside the door. Come out and take them." When the children heard this, they straightway ran out of the house and were saved from the jaws of death. The father gave them splendid and costly carriages.

In this parable, the father is Buddha ; the children are ordinary men and women ; the burning house is life in the world ; the three carts are the three Ways of the Buddhist Church, which lead to different degrees and kinds of sanctity ; the costly carriage is the highest Way, the Mahāyāna.[584]

Parable of the Lost Son. A certain poor man had a beloved son, and it so happened that the son left his home and wandered to a far country. He lived in the strange land for fifty long years, but still remained poor. During all those years, his father throve and prospered in the world and rose to be a rich man with much substance and many servants and attendants. Now that poor young man, wandering about in search of food and raiment, came to the town and the street in which his father lived. He saw that rich man sitting at the door of a fine mansion, and knew not that he saw his father. But the father saw his face and recognised him at once. The poor young man was filled with fear at the thought that he had perhaps come into the wrong street and might be punished for his rashness. So he ran away in great haste. But the old father said to his servants: "Go, my men, and quickly bring that fellow to me." When the servants came upon the young man, he cried, "I have done nothing against you . . . O, I am undone." He fainted and fell to the ground. His father looked after him, but did not tell him who he really was. The old man now exhibited his *upāya-kauçalya* in this way. He let the poor fellow go away. He then called two poor men of humble origin and said to them: "Go, and hire that young man for double wages, and tell him to work here in my house and clean the receptacle of filth." So the son worked as a labourer in that house and his father saw him from the window. Then the old man put on dirty clothes, took a basket in his hand, and, going near unto his son, said: "Work here, my man; do not go anywhere else . . . Look upon me as your own father . . . Henceforward you are unto me like my son." In this way, the father found the chance of speaking to his son, who thereupon felt happier in the house. But he continued to live in his hovel of straw and did the same menial work for twenty years. At last, the rich man fell sick and felt that his days were numbered. So he first gave much wealth to the young man, and then he gathered together his kinsfolk and fellow-citizens and said to them: "He is my son: I am his father. To him I leave all my possessions." The son was greatly astonished at this, and rejoiced exceedingly in his heart.

In this parable, the father is Buddha: the son is every pious Buddhist: the labour of cleaning the refuse-barrel is the lower teaching about *nirvāṇa* (Liberation); and the declaration of the filial relation is the higher doctrine of the Mahāyāna.[585]

There are other stories of the same type. A man causes a false message to be sent to his children in order to induce them to use a certain beneficial medicine.[586] That was his *upāya-kauçalya*. The *Sad. Pu.* teaches that Gautama Buddha really attained Enlightenment many æons ago and lives for ever; he pretends to be born as a man and attain *bodhi* under the tree. He does so in order to help mankind, and this is his *upāya-kauçalya*.[587] An advanced *bodhisattva* can assume different forms in order to preach to different congregations. And so on. It is clear that a certain amount of trickery and falsehood is regarded as permissible.

The *bodhisattva*, who acts as a preacher, must have certain moral qualifications. He should be patient and unworldly. He should not be afraid of sacrificing his life, if need be.[588] He should not ask the people for gifts. He should avoid the company of nuns and women. He should not mix with butchers, actors, and other low people. If he preaches to women, he should not be alone, and he should beware of frivolity. He should not think of food and raiment, but devote himself entirely to his work.[589] He should not keep back anything, as he should not have the "closed fist" of the teacher (*ācārya-muṣṭi*, *Bo. Bhū.*, fol. 44*b* 2.2). He should not discourage the people or preach the lower ideal of the Hīnayāna; but he should not condemn the Hīnayāna in a bitter or intolerant spirit.[590] He should not quarrel with the teachers of other sects or enter into unseemly controversy with them. He should not praise himself. He should not judge and censure others harshly, and he should be very tactful in dealing with sinners and heretics.[591]

Such a preacher needs three other things for complete success in his mission. These are: (1) the *saṅgraha-vastus* (means or items of sympathy or conversion); (2) the *pratisaṃvids*; and (3) the *dhāraṇīs*. These requisites of effective propaganda may be discussed very briefly.

1. *The Saṅgraha-vastus.* The Buddhist leaders showed great sagacity in exhorting the preacher to cultivate four virtues or practices in order to facilitate the task of converting the people to the new faith. These four requisites of propaganda are called *saṅgraha-vastūni* (Pāli: *saṅgaha-vatthūni*). The second word is sometimes omitted, as at *Lka.*, 346, verse 656, and *Sad. Pu.*, 142. This term has been translated in several ways:—

L. de la Vallée Poussin: (i) "Topics leading to the sympathy of creatures" (ERE, ii, 740*a*). (ii) "Moyens de séduction" (Le Muséon, xii, 1911, p. 160).

H. Kern: "Articles of sociability" (SBE., vol. xxi, p. 140, note 4).

L. Feer: "Les bases de la réunion" (*Ava. Ça.* tr., p. 9).

S. Lévi: (i) "Les matières de rapprochement" (*M. S. Al.*, tr., p. 319). (ii) "Les choses de cohésion" (*M. S. Al.*, tr., p. 201 note). This is S. Lévi's rendering of the Tibetan equivalent.

E. Burnouf: "Les éléments de la bienveillance" ("Lotus", p. 405).

P. E. Foucaux: "Les bases de la réunion" (*Lal. V.* tr., p. 36).

T. W. Rhys Davids and C. A. F. Rhys Davids: "Grounds or Bases of popularity" ("Dialogues", iii, 145, 223).

E. B. Cowell and R. Neil: "Elements of popularity" (*Divy.*, p. 692).

S. Tachibana: "Elements of friendliness" ("Ethics", p. 70).

T. W. Rhys Davids and W. Stede: "Objects (characteristics) of sympathy" (Pāli Dicy.).

F. Max Müller: "Elements of popularity" (*Dh. S.*, p. 39).

The Pāli word *saṅgaha* means: (1) collecting, gathering; (2) kind disposition, kindliness, sympathy, friendliness, help, assistance, protection, favour (Pāli Dicy.). M. Anesaki interprets it as "sympathy or altruism" (ERE, v. 451). A comparison of several Sanskrit texts would perhaps lead us to prefer a very literal interpretation (viz. "gathering together", "converting"). We read of *sattvānāṃ saṅgrahaḥ* in *Kar. Pu.* (p. 65). The *bodhisattvas* are said to "bring together" the creatures (*sattvān saṅgṛhṇanti*, *Pr. Pā. Çata.*, p. 280, line 12); *sattva-gaṇasya saṅgṛhītā* (*M. S. Al.*, 117.19); *saṅgraha-vastu-jñānena saṅgṛhya janatām-aham* (*Lal. V.*, 437.15). It is clear that *saṅgraha* refers more to the creatures than to the *bodhisattva*. But such renderings as "popularity" or "sympathy" make us think of it as something possessed by a *bodhisattva*. The Tibetan word *bsdu bahi dnôspo* means: "essentials of partnership or cooperation" (J. Rahder, "Glossary," p. 180; *M. Vy.*, p. 71; Tib. Dicy., Das, 724*b*). It is perhaps preferable to translate, "Means of conversion" There is also a suggestion of "sympathy" in the term, but not of "popularity".

The four *saṅgaha-vatthūni* are enumerated in several passages of the Pāli canon.[592] These are: *dānaṃ*, *peyyavajjaṃ*, *attha-cariyā* and *samānattatā*. This is a fixed and invariable formula in the Pāli scriptures. But it is a remarkable fact that we can trace its growth in the Sanskrit treatises. Thus we find that only *artha-caryā* is mentioned at *Mtu.*, iii, 383.11 and iii, 407.13. Açvaghoṣa mentions only the last two (*artha-caryā* and *sāmānyaṃ sukha-duḥkhayoḥ*) as the qualities of a good friend (*Saund. Kā.*, xi. 17). Only the first two are spoken of at *Pr. Pā. Çata.*, p. 280, line 12. The *Bo. Bhū.* devotes a whole chapter to the four *vastus*, but it particularly emphasises *dāna* and *samān-ārthatā* at fol. 31*a* and 31*b*. The last is again omitted by Çūra at *Jā. Mā.*, p. 95, line 12, while only three are mentioned in the same treatise at p. 2, line 1; the fourth *vastu* is indicated only by *ādi* and *prabhṛtibhiḥ* (= et cetera). It is probable that the complete formula grew up slowly and gradually in the Sanskrit tradition, and that the fourth *vastu* gained recognition at a late period. Hence perhaps the constant reiteration of *samān-ārthatā* in the *Bodhisattva-bhūmi.* This treatise does not discuss this *vastu* in detail with reference to the ninefold classification, which is applied to the *pāramitās* and the other three *vastus*. This circumstance may also point to the comparatively late origin of the fourth *vastu*. Another puzzling problem is raised by the entire absence of the *vastus* from the long list of a *bodhisattva's* duties and practices, which is found at several places in the *Pr. Pā. Çata.* (pp. 1182 ff., 1373 ff., 375 ff.). The familiar *vastus* are conspicuous by their absence in these passages, though they are mentioned in the *Lal. V.*, the *Da. Bhū.*, the *Mtu.*, the *Ava. Ça.* and other treatises (*Mtu.*, i, 3, 11–12; *Da. Bhū.*, 22.3, 57.16, 45.13; *Ava. Ça.*, 1.16, 12; *M. S. Al.*, 116; *Lal. V.*, 160.6; *M. Vy.*, xxxv, p. 71; *Dh. S.*, xix, p. 4).

The four *vastus* are as follows:—

(*a*) *Dāna* (Giving, liberality, generosity).

(*b*) The second *vastu* is given in several forms, though the meaning is the same: "pleasant, agreeable speech." The usual form is *priya-vāditā* (*M. Vy.*, xxv, p. 71; *M. S. Al.*, p. 116; *Bo. Bhū.*, fol. 32*a*, line 3, section 1; etc.). But other variants are also met with, e.g.

priya-vadya (*Lal. V.*, 38.17).
priya-vacanam (*Jā. Mā.*, 95.12; *Dh. S.*, xix, p. 4).
priya-vadyatā (*Da. Bhū.*, 45.13; *Pr. Pā. Çata.*, p. 280, line 12).
priya-vākya (*Lal. V.*, 160.6).
priy-ākhyānam (*M. S. Al.*, 116.4).
priya-vādyam (*Mtu.*, i, 3.12).

The following renderings have been suggested:—

T. W. and C. A. F. Rhys Davids: "Kind words, kindly speech" ("Dialogues", iii, 145, 183); "Affability" ("Dialogues", iii, 183, note 2).

S. Yamakami: "Loving words" ("Systems", p. 306).

S. Tachibana: "Kind-wordedness" ("Ethics", p. 70).

These two subjects, Charity and Speech, have been discussed above.

(*c*) The third *vastu* is given in two forms :—

(i) *artha-caryā* (*M. Vy.*, xxv, p. 71 ; *Bo. Bhū.*, fol. 87*b*. etc.).

(ii) *artha-kriyā* (*Lal. V.*, 182.6).

Artha-caryā is the word that occurs most frequently. It has been translated in several ways :—

T. W. and C. A. F. Rhys Davids: "Justice" ("Dialogues", iii, 223).

T. W. and C. A. F. Rhys Davids: "Sagacious conduct" ("Dialogues", iii, 145).

T. W. and C. A. F. Rhys Davids: "Beneficence" ("Dialogues", iii, 183, note 2).

L. de la Vallée Poussin: "Service" (Le Muséon, 1911, xii, 161).

L. de la Vallée Poussin: "Putting into practice rules of altruism" (ERE, ii, 740*a*).

J. S. Speyer: "Succour" (*Jā. Mā.* tr., p. 2, line 15).

J. Alwis: "Fruitful conduct, well-being in law" (JBTS., 1894, vol. ii, part 2, p. 22, note 2).

S. Lévi: "La conduite dans le Sens" (*M. S. Al.*, tr., p. 201).

H. Kern: (i) "Officiousness" (?) ("Manual", p. 67). (ii) "Promoting another's interest" (SBE., vol xxi, p. 140).

Perhaps it is best to translate : "Promoting the interest of others." The hallowed Biblical phrase "Doing good" seems to be a suitable and literal rendering.

The *Bodhisattva-bhūmi* explains *artha-caryā* in detail as follows :—

A *bodhisattva* does good to others by exhorting them to the practice of virtue, and his *artha-caryā* has the effect of inducing the people to pursue the Good (*pravartakaḥ kuçale pravartanāt*). It leads to action in accordance with the dictates of religion. It removes the people from evil conditions and establishes them in the Good, and it may be described as *avatāraka* (that which makes one enter). A *bodhisattva* thus renders service to those, to whom he has already preached the faith. He is merciful, pious and disinterested in spirit. The most general form of his service to others consists in ripening the beings who are spiritually immature, and in liberating those who are already mature. He also helps others to further their worldly interests by earning, keeping and increasing their wealth (literally, "objects of enjoyment," *bhogānām*) through virtuous activity of various kinds. He persuades others to think of their eternal happiness after death and admits them to the Order of monks. He wins praise from all, and lives happily, perfectly serene in mind and body. But it is indeed a very difficult task to render service to certain types of individuals. There are people, who have not done anything to accumulate "Roots of Merit" (*kuçala-mūlāni*); others have once lived in great prosperity and affluence, but have fallen on evil days; and then there are the misguided outsiders and heretics. It must be very trying for a *bodhisattva* to do good to such persons, but he does it all the same, and this is his "difficult service" (*duṣkarā artha-caryā*). He also performs a kind of "all-round" service (*sarvato-mukhī*) by conferring the blessing of faith on the unbelievers, and by giving virtue to the wicked, wisdom to the foolish, and a charitable heart to those who are selfish and niggardly. He shows favour and sympathy to those who deserve it, and he punishes and restrains those who deserve to be treated in that manner. He rouses the consciences of those who have fallen into the adverse condition of moral insensibility, and makes them feel noble shame. He preaches the three Ways according to the capacity of the hearers.[593] (*Bo. Bhū.*, fol. 87*b*, 88*a*, 88*b*.)

(*d*) The fourth *vastu* is given as *samān-ārthatā* in Sanskrit and *samānattatā* in Pāli. The form *samārthatā* is also found (*M. S. Al.*, 116.4) There is a great divergence of opinion with regard to the meaning of this word. The following renderings have been suggested :—

Böhtlingk and Roth (s.v. *samānārtha*): "denselben Zweck habend verfolgend."

T. W. Rhys Davids: "Impartiality" ("Dialogues", iii, 145).

T. W. Rhys Davids: "Impartiality to one as to another" ("Dialogues", iii, 184).

S. Lévi: "le sens en commun" (*M. S. Al.*, tr., p. 201).

E. Burnouf: "la qualité d'avoir un bien commun" ("Lotus," pp. 405–6).

S. Yamakami: "Sharing with others" ("Systems", p. 306).

L. de la Vallée Poussin: "Impartialité: son égal intérêt au bien propre et au bien des autres" (Le Muséon, xii, 160).

L de la Vallée Poussin: "Practising ourselves the virtues we recommend to our neighbours" (ERE, ii, 740*a*).

S. Dasgupta: "Sharing the joy and sorrow of others" ("Mysticism", p. 106).

H. Kern: (i) "Pursuit of a common aim" (SBE., vol. xxi, p. 140, note 4). (ii) "Co-operation" ("Manual", p. 67).

J. Alwis: "Regarding all as one's self" (JBTS., 1894, vol. ii, part 2, p. 22).

Pāli Dictionary: "Equanimity, impartiality"... "state of equality, i.e. sensus communis or feeling of common good" (s.v. *samānattatā* and *saṅgaha*).

P. Oltramare: "Ils pratiquent eux-mêmes ce qu'ils conseillent de faire" ("Bouddhique", p. 389).

D. T. Suzuki: "Engaging in the same work" ("Studies", p. 451).

This term has also been explained by some Buddhist writers, and L. de la Vallée Poussin follows the *Bo. Bhū.* in his second rendering, "practising ourselves the virtue we recommend to our neighbours." The *Bo. Bhū.* paraphrases the word thus: "Here the *bodhisattva* himself pursues the same Ideal or Aim and the same Good (Root of Good) as he exhorts others to follow" (*Bo. Bhū.*, fol. 89*a*, line 7, sections 2, 3). In this way, the people believe that he teaches them for their spiritual benefit, as he is consistent in word and deed (*Bo. Bhū.*, fol. 89*b*, line 2, section 2). They cannot reproach him with such words as these: "Thou dost not do well: why dost thou think that others should be exceedingly taught and exhorted by thee? Thou thyself needest admonition and instruction" (fol. 89*b*, 3.3). Thus the *bodhisattva* has the same Ideal or Aim as others have, and he thereby shows his *samān-ārthatā*. The *Bo. Bhū.* is accepted as an authority by L. de la Vallée Poussin, but this interpretation seems to be far-fetched and unconvincing. The author of this treatise lived as late as the fourth century A.D., and he appears to have lost touch with the old tradition.

Another Sanskrit writer explains *samān-ārthatā* in this way: "*Samān-ārthatā*: the pursuit by himself of that (aim) to which he incites others . . . It makes (people) follow. When the others know that the preacher acts as he speaks, they follow the Good (Ideal), for which he has persuaded them to exert themselves" (*M. S. Al.*, p. 116, lines 8, 14, 15). The author of this prose commentary (Vasubandhu) thus seems to offer the same interpretation as the *Bodhisattva-bhūmi*. Both belong to the fourth century.

There was an older tradition with regard to this term, as we learn from the *Mtu.* and the *Saund. Kā.* The *Mtu.* gives the fourth *vastu* as *samāna-sukha-duḥkhatā*, at i, 3, 12 (and not as *samāṇ-ārthatā* at all). Açvaghoṣa speaks of *artha-caryā* and *sāmānyaṃ sukha-duḥkhayoḥ* (*Saund. Ka.*, xi, 17). It is clear that this interpretation is quite different from that of the fourth-century theologians. It harmonises more with the real import of the other three *saṅgraha-vastus*, which refer to personal altruism evinced in the ordinary course of social life. There is a sudden and illogical transition in the plane of thought, if we accept the authority of the *Bodhisattva-bhūmi*. It is preferable to follow the *Mtu.* and translate, "sharing the joys and sorrows of others"; or, "the quality of being the same in one's relation to others in joy and in sorrow."

It may also be suggested that we have here most probably to deal with a wrongly Sanskritised form. The Pāli word is *samānattatā*, which means, "the quality of being of an even mind" (Pāli. Dicy.). Now the correct Sanskrit form would be *samān-ātmatā* (and not *samān-ārthatā*). *Artha* in Sanskrit usually corresponds to *attha* in Pāli (and not to Pāli *atta*). If we adopt this view, the word can be easily explained in the sense suggested by the *Mtu.*: "The quality of having an even mind (in joy and sorrow)"; or, "the quality of having a common mind with others, i.e. sharing their feelings and experiences, and remaining the same in joy and grief." The Tibetan equivalent is *don-ḥthun-pa* (*M. Vy.*, p. 72; J. Rahder, "Glossary," p. 187). S. C. Das gives the form, *don-mthun-pa*, and translates: "*samānārtha*: an assembly having a common interest" (Tib. Dicy., 644). It seems that the Tibetans read *arthatā*, and not *ātmatā*. But their opinion is not decisive.

This virtue may be described as *anuvartaka* (that which follows after, or conforms). A *bodhisattva*, who practises this *vastu*, cultivates faith, virtue, liberality and wisdom, so that his conduct may be in conformity with his precepts (*Bo. Bhū.*, fol. 47*a*).

The object of all the *saṅgraha-vastus* is the conversion of the living beings. The Buddhist authors are unanimous on this point.

"The Equipment of the *saṅgraha-vastus* is for the ripening of the beings" (*Kar. Pu.*, 104.34).

"He matures or ripens the beings" (*Bo. Bhū.*, fol. 32*a*, 3.1).

"One should win (or conquer) the beings by means of the *saṅgrahas*" (*Lka.* 346, verse 656).

"For the proper conversion, training (or discipline) and ripening of the beings" (*Bo. Bhū.*, fol. 47*a*, 4.3).

"The maturing of the beings (is attained) through the *saṅgraha-vastus*" (*Bo. Bhū.*, fol. 90*a*, 1.2).

"The four *saṅgraha-vastus* are a door to the light of the Doctrine, which is for the conversion of the beings. In the case of one who has attained the supreme Wisdom, they are for a thorough and detailed examination of the Doctrine (*Lal. V.*, 35.9).

The four *vastus* are sometimes classified in two groups: material and spiritual (*āmiṣa-saṅgraha*, *dharma-saṅgraha*). *Dāna* is the *vastu* that depends on material objects; while the other three deal with spiritual values (*M. S. Al.*, 116.22).

In the course of development of Buddhist thought, the *saṅgraha-vastus*, like the *brahma-vihāras*, acquired a position of greater importance than was accorded to them in the beginning. The Mahāyāna exhibited a marked tendency to emphasise practical altruism. Thus in the fourth century, the four *vastus* are given the high honour of being mentioned together with *prajñā* (*Bo. Bhū.*, fol. 32*a*, 3.1). According to the *Pr. Pā. Aṣṭa.*, they are included in the six *pāramitās*, which may be regarded as the fundamental factors of a *bodhisattva's* career. They are integral elements in that great virtue, which was subsequently raised to the rank of a *pāramitā*, viz. *upāya-kauçalya*. The author of the *Bo. Bhū.* explicitly declares that the *saṅgraha-vastus* are identical with *upāya* (fol. 46*b*, 5, 2–3). The same writer goes so far so to promise rebirth among the *devas* and even absolute *nirvāṇa* as the reward of the practice of the third *vastu* (*Bo. Bhū.*, 87*b*, 6.3. and 88*a*, 1.1). This is very high praise indeed according to Buddhist ideas. These *saṅgraha-vastus* are spoken of as almost equal in importance to the *pāramitās* in a striking passage of the *Bo. Bhū.*, in which the *pāramitās* are said to be necessary for the personal realisation of the *dharma* of the Buddha, while the *saṅgraha-vastus* are regarded as indispensable for the conversion of others (fol. 90*a*, 1.2).[594] They are also brought into relation with that supreme virtue, *karuṇā*, in which the *bodhisattva* doctrine culminates. We read in the *Jā. Mā.* that "they are really due to the outflow of the *bodhisattva's* compassion" (p. 2., line 1). They are also included in the list of a *bodhisattva's* eighteen *āveṇika-dharmas* (*M. Vy.*, xxix, p. 61). In this way, these altruistic practices are appreciated in an increasing degree, and their final approximation to the *pāramitās* indicates the triumph of the ideal of social service.

According to the scheme of ten *bhūmis*, as outlined in the *Da. Bhū.*, a *bodhisattva* practises *dāna* in the first *bhūmi*, *priya-vāditā* in the second *bhūmi*, *artha-caryā* in the third *bhūmi* and *samān-ārthatā* in the fourth *bhūmi*. Thus these virtues are finally incorporated in the comprehensive synthesis of the Mahāyāna. It is to be understood that a *bodhisattva* acquires them in the first four *bhūmis*, and then continues to cultivate them throughout his many lives, as he devotes himself to preaching and teaching in the *ninth bhūmi*. He has the greatest need of these virtues and practices at that advanced stage of his career.

2. *The Pratisaṃvids.* A *bodhisattva* must acquire the four *pratisaṃvids*. This word has been translated in the following ways :—

Böhtlingk and Roth : " Genaues Verständnis im Einzelnen."

Monier Williams : " An accurate understanding of the particulars of anything " (Skt. Dicy., 621*b*).

T. W. Rhys Davids and W. Stede : Literally, " resolving, continuous breaking up ", i.e. " analysis, analytic insight, discriminating knowledge " . . . " the four branches of logical analysis " (Pāli Dicy., s.v. *paṭisambhidā*).

P. E. Foucaux : (i) " La connaissance distincte " (*Lal V.*, tr., p. 286). (ii) " La science claire et variée " (*Lal. V.*, tr., p. 37.7). (iii) " La connaissance des détails " (*Lal. V.*, tr., p. 246.5).

C. A. F. Rhys Davids : " Analysis " (JRAS., 1906, p. 239).

E. Burnouf : " La connaissance distincte, distributive " (" Lotus ", p. 839).

S. Lévi : " Les Pleins-savoirs-respectifs " (*M. S. Al.*, tr., p. 234).

L. Feer : " La connaissance distincte " (*Ava. Ça.*, tr., p. 425).

F. Max Müller : " Consciousness " (SBE., vol. xlix, *Su. Vy.*, p. 39, line 22).

S. Lefmann : " Das genaue Verständnis " (*Lal. V.*, tr., p. 55).

S. Julien : " Les connaissances " (cited SBE., x, *Dhammapada*, p. 86, note).

M. Walleser : (i) " Die Unterscheidungen " (*Pr. Pā.*, tr., p. 72, line 35). (ii) " Die Erkenntnisse " (ibid., p. 80).

E. J. Thomas : " Analysis " (" Buddha ", p. 275).

P. Oltramare : " Les quatre savoirs parfaits et personnels " (" Bouddhique ", p. 359).

A. B. Keith : " Powers of comprehension and exegesis " (" Philosophy ", p. 131).

T. W. Rhys Davids: "The discriminating knowledge of all the Scriptures" (SBE., xi, p. 111, line 4).

H. Kern: "Special and distinctive gift," "a transcendent faculty" ("Manual", p. 60).

H. C. Warren: "The analytical sciences" ("Buddhism" p. 286).

The Tibetan equivalent, *so-sor-yaṅ-dag-par-rig-pa*, is a very literal rendering (*M. Vy.*, p. 18; *M. S. Al.*, tr., p. 234, note 1). The Tibetan *so-sor* (distinct, separate: Tib. Dicy., Das, 1283*a*) corresponds to Skt. *prati*, *yaṅ-dag-par* to Skt. *sam*, and *rig-pa* to Skt. *vid* (Tib. Dicy., Das, 1177*b*). S. C. Das also gives the form, *so-sor-raṅ-rig-pa*, and translates "accurate understanding" (Tib. Dicy., 1284*a*). J. Rahder mentions another equivalent, *tha dadpa yaṅ dag par çes pa* ("Glossary", p. 119). In this word, Skt. *prati* is rendered by *tha dad pa* (= distinct, separate: Tib. Dicy., Das, 564*b*), and Skt. *vid* by Tib. *çes-pa* (= knowledge, wisdom, science: Tib. Dicy., Das, 1243*a*). It is clear that the Tibetan translators derive the word from Skt. *vid* (to know). S. Lévi thinks that the Chinese equivalent denotes "intelligence sans obstacle" (*M. S. Al.*, tr., p. 234). According to J. Eitel, it means: "unlimited knowledge" (p. 122).

The fourth-century authors of the *M. S. Al.* and the commentary have also exercised their ingenuity in explaining the term. Their fantastic comment may be given in their own words: "When one has reached *samatā* (equality or sameness) in one's own soul, or by oneself, the preaching, that follows for the destruction of all doubts, is designated *pratisaṃvid* . . . By this, the explanation and function of the *pratisaṃvids* are indicated. By super-normal (transcendental) knowledge, one knows the equality or sameness of all things, and subsequently preaches the Scripture and the Doctrine by means of the knowledge acquired afterwards. This is the explanation of *pratisaṃvid*." (*M. S. Al.*, 139.12 ff.) But these obscure words do not throw much light on the real etymology of the word.

It may be argued that *pratisaṃvid* is a wrongly Sanskritised form The Pāli word is *paṭisambhidā*, and the correct Sanskrit equivalent should be *pratisambhid*. The Pāli equivalent is derived from the root *bhid*, and not from the root *vid*. The grammatically incorrect forms *pratisaṃvidāni* and *pratisaṃvidāḥ* are also met with (*Kar. Pu.*, 103.3; *Mtu.*, iii, 167.3). The first prefix is sometimes omitted, and the simpler form *saṃvid* is found at *Pr. Pā. Çata.*, 1471.1. The same word *saṃvid*, with a slightly different connotation, occurs in the *Saund. Kā.* (xi.10–xiii.22). In Kṣemendra's *Avadāna-kalpa-latā*, the poet uses this word *saṃvid* very frequently (i, 823.17; i, 929, 68.1, 913.7; ii, 331.39; ii, 497.42; ii, 281.47, etc.). The forms *pratisaṃvedī*, *pratisaṃvidita* and *pratisaṃvedayati* occur in the *Lal. V.*, the *Mtu.* and the *Divy.* (*Mtu.* iii, 256.5; *Mtu.* i, 228.7; *Divy.*, 567.18; *Lal. V.*, 369.11). But we need not attach any importance to these different forms, as the term *pratisaṃvid* has a peculiar technical sense.

The questions may be asked: "Is the Pāli word *paṭisambhidā* itself a rendering of a Sanskrit term? Have the Pāli writers made a mistake in determining the Pāli equivalent of the original Sanskrit word *pratisaṃvid* (from *vid*)? Is the Sanskrit form earlier than the Pāli?" It is a curious fact that the four *paṭisambhidās* are not mentioned in the *Saṅgīti-suttanta* of the *Dīgha-Nikāya*, which gives a long list of different terms; and the *Saṅgīti-suttanta* must belong to a comparatively late period of early Buddhist history, as it is a kind of systematic catechism. The treatise, *Paṭisambhidā-magga*, which is included in the *Khuddaka-Nikāya*, also cannot be regarded as an early product of Buddhist literature. It may be argued with a certain degree of plausibility that the Buddhists borrowed the Sanskrit term *pratisaṃvid* from some Brahmanic source, and the Pāli writers translated it inaccurately into Pāli. The word *saṃvid* occurs in the *Yoga-sūtras* (*citta-saṃvid*—iii, 34, p. 154), and J. H. Woods translates: "consciousness" (p. 262). It is also found in the *Taittirīya Upaniṣad* (*çriyā deyaṃ hriyā deyaṃ bhiyā deyaṃ saṃvidā deyam.* 1, 11.3, p. 34). *Pratisaṃvid* is mentioned in connection with *vidyā* and *abhijñā* in the *Avadāna-çataka* (i, 96.8). It should also be noted that *pratisaṃvid* is mentioned as a concomitant of the supreme *bodhi* at *Lal. V.*, 343.4.; it suggests the idea of knowledge, and not of analysis. Such texts seem to indicate that the Sanskrit form may be the original one. The term would then connote "knowledge" of some sort (and not "analysis"). It could in that case be translated: "detailed and thorough knowledge." It must also be admitted that this sense seems to suit the context better than "analysis" in many passages, in which the four *pratisaṃvids* are spoken of. They imply thorough knowledge of something for purposes of propaganda.

It should be noted that the prefix *prati* has been interpreted in two ways. Most scholars think that it conveys the notion of detail and distinctness; but P. Oltramare, following Vasubandhu, is of opinion that it connotes personal action, "knowing personally, or by oneself." The former interpretation seems to be more acceptable.[595]

A *bodhisattva* needs the four *pratisaṃvids* for success in his preaching. According to the *M. S. Al.*, they are required in order to remove all the doubts of others (p. 139.16). In the scheme of the ten *bhūmis*, a *bodhisattva* acquires them in the ninth *bhūmi*, when he appears before the world as a preacher. The author of the *Da. Bhū.* distinctly associates the *pratisaṃvids* with a *bodhisattva's* activity as a teacher. He says: "The *bodhisattva*, who is established in this *bhūmi*, which is called *sādhumatī* (Stage of good Thoughts), acts as a preacher of the *dharma* (doctrine, religion), and guards the treasure of the religion of the *Tathāgata*. Having attained the position (or state) of a preacher of the faith, he teaches the Doctrine with practical skill, combined with infinite (or immeasurable) knowledge, and with the speech of a *bodhisattva*, in which the four *pratisaṃvids* have been realised. The four *pratisaṃvids* of a *bodhisattva* constantly and continually abide with him, entire and indivisible." (*Da. Bhū.*, 76, 24 ff.)

The *Karuṇā-puṇḍarīka* also declares that a *bodhisattva's* Equipment of the *pratisaṃvids* (*sambhāraḥ*) serves to destroy the doubts of all creatures (104.28). The *Lal. V.* teaches that the attainment of the *pratisaṃvids* leads to the acquisition of the *dharma-cakṣus* (the "eye" of the Doctrine, *Lal. V.*, 35.16). They also confer a certain power (*bala*) on a *bodhisattva* (*Lal. V.*, 287.10). When he understands all *dharmas* (principles, truths) and can preach them to others, he reaches the final and perfect stage of Knowledge (*Bo. Bhū.*, fol. 100*b*, 2.1). "He has nothing more to learn beyond that. It is the *ne plus ultra* of Knowledge," cries the author of the *Bodhisattva-bhūmi*. The same writer values the *pratisaṃvids* so highly that he regards them as essential elements of *prajñā*, the highest Wisdom. They appertain to that kind of Wisdom, which removes the hostility of other people and induces them to ask a *bodhisattva* for benefits (*Bo. Bhū.*, fol. 85*a*, 4, 3 ff). A *bodhisattva* thus acquires the fivefold practical Wisdom relating to the *skandhas*, the physical elements, the sense-organs and their objects, the formula of Dependent Origination and the relation of specific causation (*Bo. Bhū.*, fol. 100*b*, 1.2–3).

The *Pr. Pā. Çata.* also exalts the *pratisaṃvids* to such a degree that it actually includes them among the permanent attributes of a Buddha, and inserts them right in the middle of the traditional formula of ten *balas*, four *vaiçāradyas* and eighteen *āveṇika-dharmas* (*Pr. Pā. Çata.*, p. 131, line 20). This remarkable innovation shows that the Mahāyānists came to attach great importance to these requisites of successful propaganda.

The four *pratisaṃvids* are given as *dharma-pratisaṃvid*, *artha-*, *nirukti-*, and *pratibhāna-* (*M. Vy.*, xiii, p. 18; *Sam. Rā.*, fol. 98*b*. 5, and fol. 193*b*. 1; *Pr. Pā. Çata.*, 1449; *Dh. S.*, li, p. 11; *Da. Bhū.*, 77.4; *Mtu.*, iii, 321.14, etc.). They are as a rule mentioned in this order, but *artha* is put before *dharma* by the authors of the *Sam. Rā.* and the *Pr. Pā. Çata.*, who follow the Pāli tradition in this respect. The third *pratisaṃvid*, *nirukti*, is omitted at *Bo. Bhū.*, fol. 38*a*, 2.2, though the same treatise discusses all the four at fol. 100*a*. It appears that *dharma* and *artha* existed as a pair of terms before the complete formula was devised, and then *artha* was always placed first. They are often mentioned together (e.g. *artha-vādī dharma-vādī*. *Da. Bhū.*, 24. 19. *Cf. Dhammapada*, 363). *Nirukti* is mentioned without *pratibhāna* at *Su. Vy.*, 59.8; but these two terms were also employed together before they were added on to *dharma* and *artha* as the third and fourth *pratisaṃvids*. Thus only *nirukti* and *pratibhāna* are mentioned in a passage of the *Pr. Pā. Çata.* (1470.20 ff.). We may conclude that the formula consists of two pairs of terms put together.

(*a*) *Dharma-pratisaṃvid*. According to the *M. S. Al.*, this *pratisaṃvid* consists in knowing all the names and mutually convertible terms, which are related to each meaning. The *Bo. Bhū.* offers a very concise and formal definition. It may be rendered as follows:—

" *Dharma-pratisaṃvid* is the reflective, absolute and irrevocable knowledge of all phenomena in all their forms with regard to the extent and manner of their existence." [596] *Dharma* and *artha* are taught by a *bodhisattva*, and these two items are therefore related to each other. A *bodhisattva* knows the essential nature (*sva-lakṣaṇam*) of all things (or phenomena), their body-of-non-existence (i.e. their unreality), their present classification (or division), and their difference. He knows the skill of unmixed classification in the knowledge of the phenomena. He understands that they remain unshaken and unmoved according to one law (or principle). He knows that the various Ways (of the Buddhist faith) meet together in one Way, and he enters into the knowledge of all the spiritual duty and wisdom of a *bodhisattva*. He understands that all the Buddhas are of the same type, and he knows all about them: their speech, their Powers, their Grounds of Self-confidence, their personality, their great compassion, their use of the *pratisaṃvids*, their turning the wheel of the faith (i.e., preaching the doctrine), and their acquisition of Omniscience.[597]

The *Sam. Rā.* appears to connect *dharma-pratisaṃvid* with the knowledge of protective magical formulae, called *dhāraṇīs*; but this is certainly unsound exegesis (*Sam. Rā.*, fol. 106*b*, 6 ff.).

(*b*) *Artha-pratisaṃvid.* This *pratisaṃvid* is defined in the *Bo. Bhū.* as "the reflective, absolute and irrevocable knowledge of all phenomena in all their characteristics (*lakṣaneṣu*) with regard to the extent and manner of their existence."[598] The *M. S. Al.* uses the same word *lakṣaṇa*, and adds, "which name belongs to which meaning."[599] By this *pratisaṃvid*, a *bodhisattva* knows the division (or classification) of all phenomena in the past and the future, and understands their origin and their disappearance (or, their rise and their end). He knows the differences of meaning. He acquires the practical wisdom relating to the elements or substrata of sensory existence, the sense-organs and their objects, the Truths and the formula of Dependent Origination. He knows the distinctive features of the several *yānas*, and also the divisions and distinctions of the scheme of the ten *bhūmis*. He understands the details and characteristics of various times and objects. He knows separately the inclinations, the ruling principles and the resolves of the eighty-four thousand different types of beings, and he understands the word of the Buddha.[600]

It is to be noted that the later Mahāyānist writers transpose the places of *artha* and *dharma* in the formula of the *pratisaṃvids*. Thus the *Sam. Rā.* and the *Pr. Pā. Çata.* follow the Pāli tradition in putting *artha* as the first *pratisaṃvid*; but the *Da. Bhū.*, the *M. Vy.*, the *Dh. S.* and the *M. S. Al.* agree in placing *dharma* first. One can only speculate as to the cause of this alteration. Perhaps the later writers attached more importance to the substance and spirit of the *dharma* than to the letter of the Scriptures. The abstract *dharma* was more and more spiritualised and universalised, while the Scriptures remained concrete and material. We know that Bodhidharma and his school held such views. Thus *dharma* was exalted and *artha* was given the second place.[601]

(*c*) *Nirukti-pratisaṃvid*. The *M. S. Al.* defines this *pratisaṃvid* as the knowledge of the different languages that are spoken in different countries.[602] The *Bo. Bhū.* here does not employ the same term as the *M. S. Al.* (*vākye*), but prefers *nirvacaneṣu*. It explains thus: "*Nirukti-pratisaṃvid* is the reflective, absolute and irrevocable knowledge of all phenomena in all their etymological or linguistic explanations with regard to the extent and manner of their existence." [603] By this *pratisaṃvid*, a *bodhisattva* knows how to preach the pure (unmixed) Doctrine. He teaches the Doctrine without confounding and confusing the past, present and future. He preaches according to the letter, and does not mix up relative truth and the realisation of true knowledge. He speaks with a pleasant voice, which is accessible to the whole world; and he also teaches by writing without uttering a sound. He gives instruction in all the *yānas* without making any distinction among them, and he teaches about the Stages of Perfection, the Way and Concentration. He teaches according to the highest Truth and with proper regard to the divisions. He speaks after the manner of the Buddha's word, and imparts the pure teaching with regard to the duties of all living beings.[604] He also acquires the knowledge of the speech of such non-human beings as *devas*, *nāgas*, *yakṣas*, *gandharvas*, *asuras*, *garuḍas*, *kinnaras* and *mahoragas*.[605]

(*d*) *Pratibhāna-pratisaṃvid*. This word occurs in two forms: *pratibhāna* and *pratibhāṇa*. It is difficult to determine the precise meaning of the word *pratibhāna*. Modern scholars have suggested these renderings:—

S. Lévi: "Présence d'esprit" (*M. S. Al.*, tr., pp. 12 and 234). "Il indique à la fois la rapidité de l'esprit et la facilité."

P. Oltramare: "Intuition" ("Bouddhique", p. 359)

H. Kern: "Readiness in expounding and discussing" ("Manual", p. 60).

S. Julien: "l'Intelligence" (SBE., vol. x, *Dhammapada*, p. 86, note).

L. de la Vallée Poussin: "Clairvoyance" (of Avalokiteçvara). (ERE ii, 259.)

C. Bendall and W. H. D. Rouse: "Word, utterance" (*Çik.* tr., p. 17).

Böhtlingk and Roth: "Einsicht" (Skt. Dicy. Pbg.).

Monier Williams: "Light, splendour, brilliancy; intelligence, understanding, brilliance of conception; confidence, boldness, audacity" (Skt. Diçy., 617*c*).

T. W. Rhys Davids and W. Stede: "Understanding, illumination, intelligence; readiness or confidence of speech; promptitude, wit" (s.v. *paṭibhāna*, Pāli Dicy.).

J. S. Speyer: "Power of expounding" (*Ava. Ça.*, ii, 81, note 1).

E. Burnouf: "Notre mot 'sagesse' serait une meilleure traduction de '*paṭibhāna*' que celui d' 'intelligence'. En résumé, la définition de la quatrième connaissance distincte doit revenir à ceci; la connaissance distincte des trois vérités que sait pénétrer la sagesse" ("Lotus", p. 841).

The Tibetan equivalent is *spobs-pa* (J. Rahder, "Glossary," p. 117; *M. Vy.*, p. 18). It means: "self-reliance and wisdom; courage, self-confidence; fitness, propriety" (Tib. Dicy., Das, 802*b*). As a verb, it signifies "to dare, to venture". The Tibetan word *spobs-pa-can* means "daring, bold" (= Skt. *viçārada*). According to J. Eitel, the Chinese equivalent of Sanskrit *pratibhāna* means "pleasant discourses" (Eitel, 122*b*). The Sanskrit verb *prati-bhā* (Pāli: *paṭibhā*) means: "to appear, to be evident, to come into one's mind, to be clear, to shine." A comparison of several passages of Buddhist Sanskrit literature seems to show that *pratibhāna* refers to courage and boldness in speech rather than to intelligence and understanding (e.g. *Lal. V.*, 35.19; *Mtu.*, i, 119.16; *Da. Bhū.*, 4.2; *Kar. Pu.*, 101.23, 103.18; *Su. Vy.*, 4.4; *Ava. Ça.*, i, 48.10; *Mtu.*, ii, 290.18).

As the third *pratisaṃvid*, *nirukti*, is useful for the purpose of effective preaching, it may be surmised that *pratibhāna* also denotes some quality or advantage relating to speech. If it is interpreted as "intelligence", it seems to be rather out of place as the last *pratisaṃvid*. It is therefore advisable to accept the meaning suggested by the Tibetan equivalent and translate: "courage or boldness in speech, ready address."

According to the *M. S. Al.*, *pratibhāna* denotes readiness of speech with regard to knowledge.[606] The *Bo. Bhū.* defines it as "the reflective, absolute and irrevocable knowledge of the verbal distinctions of all kinds as applied to all phenomena with regard to the extent and manner of their existence".[607] A *bodhisattva* acquires the full knowledge of the attributes of ingenuity by means of this *pratisaṃvid*.[608] In a noteworthy verse, Açvaghoṣa compares Buddha's speech to a cow; the true

Doctrine is her milk, and *pratibhāna* is likened to her horns[609] (*Saund. Kā.*, xviii, 11). Here *pratibhāna* is not spoken of as a *pratisaṃvid*, but its function in propaganda is indicated. Çāntideva mentions four characteristics of *pratibhāna* in a passage, which he quotes from a Mahāyāna *sūtra* (*Çikṣā*, 15.17 ff.). "O Maitreya, *pratibhāna* in this connection is associated with truth, not with falsehood (untruth); it is associated with righteousness, not with unrighteousness; it diminishes (or weakens) sinful desires (or passions), and it does not increase (or intensify) them; it shows the advantages and merits of *nirvāṇa* (Release, Liberation, Freedom), and it does not point out the advantages and merits of *saṃsāra* ('transmigration', 'the succession of births and deaths'; literally, 'faring-on')." The writer here does not refer to *pratibhāna* as a special *pratisaṃvid*, but he describes its general attributes. The *Lal. V.* declares briefly that *pratibhāna* is a door to the light of the Doctrine and serves to please all creatures by means of excellent utterances.[610]

3 *The Dhāraṇīs.* The *Sad. Pu.* declares that a pious preacher is invulnerable. He is immune to danger and disease. Weapons and poison cannot injure him.[611] But such a *bodhisattva* has also special means of protection in the *dhāraṇīs* (protective spells), which he receives from benevolently disposed *devas* and others. The word *mukha* is sometimes added to *dhāraṇī* on the analogy of the term *samādhi-mukha*. The phrase *dhāraṇī-mantra-padāni* (spell-words of *dhāraṇīs*) is also found.[612]

The idea of using strange or meaningless words as charms for protection against disease and danger goes back to very ancient times. L. A. Waddell thinks that they belonged to the pre-Aryan religion of India.[613] The *Atharva-veda* contains short poems, which may be recited as charms; but it also gives spells consisting of unintelligible sounds and syllables, e.g. "*Nidhāyo vā nidhāyo vā oṃ vā oṃ vā oṃ vā. ē ai oṃ svarṇajyotiḥ.*"[614] The *Āṭānāṭiya-suttanta* of the *Dīgha-Nikāya* contains what are called *parittās* (prayers for safety), and a few others are found in the Pāli canon.[615] But the Sanskrit writers attach great importance to mystical charms and spells, which have lost the character of prayers and invocations. The *bodhisattvas* of *Amitābha's* paradise obtain *dhāraṇīs*.[616] *Dhāraṇīs* are even said to confer the *vaiçāradyas* (Grounds of Confidence) on a *bodhisattva*.[617] *Dhāraṇī-pratilabdha* (possessed of *dhāraṇīs*) is a regular epithet of the advanced *bodhisattvas*.[618] They are due to the "Roots of Merit".[619] In the later Mahāyāna, *dhāraṇīs* are mentioned along with such important concepts as *samādhi* and *kṣānti*, and sceptical objectors are severely condemned.[620]

The chief object of the *dhāraṇīs* is said to be the protection of the preachers against all enemies, that may do them harm.[621] They guard and protect a preacher against the non-human beings like the *devas*, *devīs*, *Māras*, *yakṣas*, demons, hobgoblins and ogres of all species.[622] They confer immunity from snake-bite, poison and sickness.[623] They also ward off the attacks of thieves and robbers.[624]

The *dhāraṇīs* are generally uttered and taught by the *devas* and other super-human beings, who promise to protect the preaching *bodhisattvas*. Even benevolent *rākṣasīs* (female demons) volunteer to help the *bodhisattvas* with these spells. But the increasing importance of these formulae is shown by the circumstance that the Buddha himself is said to have uttered two *dhāraṇīs* in the approved style.[625]

The *Bo. Bhū.* divides the *dhāraṇīs* into four classes: the *dhāraṇīs* of *dharma* (the Doctrine), of *artha* (Meaning), of magic spells (*mantra*), and the *dhāraṇī* for the acquisition of *kṣānti* (Forbearance, or, Acquiescence in the Truth: fol. 105*a*, 3). The *Dh. S.* also speaks of four *dhāraṇīs*, two of which are included in the list of the *Bo. Bhū.* (*dharma-dhāraṇī* and *mantra-dhāraṇī*); and the others are *ātma-dhāraṇī* (the *dhāraṇī* for oneself, or for the body) and *grantha-dhāraṇī* (the *dhāraṇī* for the Scriptures or books).[626] The *M. Vy.* mentions twelve *dhāraṇīs*, which are supposed to appertain to a *bodhisattva*.[627] They are named *abhiṣecanī* (consecrating), *jñānavatī* (possessing knowledge), *ananta-varṇā* (of infinite praise), *asaṅga-mukha-praveçā* (entry into the realm of the Unconditioned), etc. etc.

The *dhāraṇīs* generally consist of strings of short meaningless words, which are to be recited in a spirit of solemn piety. The usual forms of the words seem to show that the root-idea is that of invoking some goddess, as most of the words end in the vowel *e*, e.g. *jvale*, *ruhe*, *amale*, *dime*, etc. Faint glimpses of the names of female deities are sometimes to be caught through the thick mists of nonsense. A few words are sometimes intelligible. But the whole formula is usually intended to be mystical and unintelligible. There is plenty of rhyme, too, though not much of reason. The *dhāraṇīs* seem to have gone from bad to worse in course of time. It may not be out of place to close this section with a few specimens of *dhāraṇīs* :—

. . . *tuṭṭe tuṭṭe vuṭṭe vuṭṭe paṭṭe paṭṭe kaṭṭe kaṭṭe amale amale vimale vimale nime nime* . . . *ṭu ṭu ṭu ṭu* . . . *phu phu phu phu svāhā.*

. . . *iti me iti me iti me iti me nime nime nime nime ruhe ruhe ruhe ruhe ruhe stuhe stuhe stuhe stuhe stuhe svāhā.*

. . . *illā cillā cakvo bakvo* . . . *halale halale taṇḍi taṇḍi taḍa taḍa tāḍi tāḍi mala mala sphuta sphuta phutu phutu svāhā.*[628]

VIII, IX, X. The eighth, ninth and tenth *pāramitās* are really superfluous. They are named *praṇidhāna*, *bala*, and *jñāna* respectively. These subjects have been discussed above (*jñāna* being equivalent to *prajñā*).

Chapter VI

THE BHŪMIS

A *bodhisattva's* entire career has been divided into several parts and stages. He rises and advances from one stage to another till he attains Enlightenment. These stages have been called *bhūmis*, and also *vihāras*. The word *bhūmi* means, "earth, place, region; (figuratively), ground, plane, stage, level; state of consciousness" (Pāli Dicy.). In a metaphorical sense, it is employed in a general way to denote "range", "state", "sphere", "station", "condition", "function", etc. We find such phrases as *kāma-bhūmi*, *dānta-bhūmi*, *kumāra-bhūmi*, *nirvāṇa-bhūmi*, *citta-bhūmi*, *kṣānti-bhūmi*, *pṛthag-jana-bhūmi*, *tathatā-bhūmi*, etc. In the *Dhamma-saṅgaṇi*, *bhūmi* is synonymous with *magga* (Way).[1] The *Yoga-sūtras* mention *dṛḍha-bhūmi*, *prānta-bhūmi*, *sārva-bhauma*, etc. (*Yo. Sū.*, 1, 14; ii, 27; ii, 31—pp. 18, 97, 104). *Bhūmi* has thus become a philosophical term, meaning "Stage" (of spiritual progress). Almost all the Buddhist treatises divide a *bodhisattva's* career into *bhūmis*, but the *Bodhisattva-bhūmi* also discusses thirteen *vihāras* (states, stations). The *M. S. Al.* gives a fanciful etymological explanation of *bhūmi*: "*bhūyo bhūyo amitāsu*" ("again and again in the unmeasured stages"); or, "*bhūtānām amitānām*" ("immeasurable number of creatures", to deliver them from fear).[2] Such conceits need not be taken seriously.

There are at least four different schemes of division in the principal Sanskrit treatises. The *Pr. Pā. Çata.*, the *Mahā-vastu* and the *Da. Bhū.* describe ten *bhūmis* in different ways, and the *Bodhisattva-bhūmi* speaks of seven *bhūmis* and thirteen *vihāras*. Candrakīrti's *Madhyamakāvatāra* is not available in Sanskrit and cannot therefore be utilised as one of the sources for this essay.

The idea of establishing "Stages" on the spiritual pilgrim's long journey occurred early to the Buddhist thinkers. The Hīnayānists developed the doctrine of the four Stages, which has already been referred to. Three *vihāras* are also mentioned in the Pāli canon: *dibba-vihāra*, *ariya-vihāra* and *brahma-vihāra* (Divine, Noble and Sublime).[3] The

M. Vy. mentions seven *bhūmis* of the *çrāvakas* (Section 50). The Mahāyānists did not attach much importance to the ten *saṃyojanas* (Fetters) and the four Stages of the Hīnayānists. They tried to devise a scheme of division based chiefly on the *pāramitās*.

The *bhūmis* of the Mahāyāna are now supposed to be ten in number, but it is almost certain that they were only seven in the beginning. The vogue of the *Da. Bhū.* finally fixed the number of the *bhūmis*. But the *Bodhisattva-bhūmi* formally discusses seven *bhūmis* (fol. 136*b*), and the *Laṅkāvatāra-sūtra* speaks of "seven *bhūmis*" without specifying them (p. 28). The *Mahā-vastu* speaks of ten *bhūmis*, but it really describes only seven: it gives no relevant details about the fourth, ninth and tenth. It may therefore be inferred that it recognised only seven *bhūmis* at the outset. Even the *Da. Bhū.* shows clear indications of the original scheme of seven *bhūmis*. A *bodhisattva* is said to practise all the ten *pāramitās* in the seventh *bhūmi*, though only one *pāramitā* is allotted to each Stage. He is also supposed to practise only the seventh *pāramitā* in that *bhūmi*, and this contradiction is left unsolved. There is a great "Prediction" in the eighth *bhūmi*, as if a new epoch commenced at that point, for the *bodhisattva* obtains the first Prediction (*vyākaraṇa*) before starting on his career. It is also stated that a *bodhisattva* can pass away in *nirvāṇa* in the seventh *bhūmi*, if he so desires; but he follows the higher ideal of the Mahāyāna, which is especially realised in the eighth, ninth and tenth *bhūmis*. A *bodhisattva*, who has reached the eighth *bhūmi*, should be honoured like a perfect Buddha! All these details point to an original system of only seven *bhūmis*. This is also the number of the *bhūmis* in the *Yoga-sūtras* (*Yo. Sū.*, ii, 27, p. 97). The probable cause of the change from seven to ten has already been indicated above.

It is a curious circumstance that these different schemes of the *bhūmis* have very little in common with one another. J. Rahder has tried to show that the system of the *Mahā-vastu* is closely related to that of the *Da. Bhū.* He says: "Après avoir mis en lumière l'étroite parenté entre le *Daça-bhumaka* . . . et le *Daça-bhūmika*, qui montre la préparation à la dernière incarnation dans le *Mahā-vastu*, etc."[4] But the only points of contact between the systems of the *Mtu.* and the *Da. Bhū.* are that the sections dealing with the first *bhūmi* mention a few similar virtues, and that one of the *bhūmis* in both schemes is named *durjayā* (*sudurjayā*, in the *Da. Bhū.*). J. Rahder has pointed out that some passages of the *Da. Bhū.* resemble those of the *Mtu.*; but the resemblance is so slight and vague that one cannot speak of "l'étroite parenté". On the contrary, the *Mtu.* has no definite plan, while the *Da. Bhū.* allots a *pāramitā* to each *bhūmi*. The *Mtu.* declares that a *bodhisattva* may fall back into a lower *bhūmi* on account of certain faults, but the *Da. Bhū.* never speaks of the possibility of retrogression and always discusses virtues instead of sins. The *Mtu.* gives certain names to the *bhūmis*, but the *Da. Bhū.* has quite different names (except one). The account in the *Mtu.* is incoherent and confused: the *Da. Bhū.* shows a masterly architectonic faculty. The *Pr. Pā. Çata.* also fails to evolve an intelligible system: it does not even assign any names to the *bhūmis* and mentions the same virtues and sins again and again. The names of the *bhūmis* and the *vihāras* in the *Bo. Bhū.* are also different from those of the *Da. Bhū.*, and there is a fundamental difference between the systems outlined in these two treatises. The author of the *Da. Bhū.* has constructed the framework of his system on the basis of the ten *pāramitās*, but the *Bo. Bhū.* divides a *bodhisattva's* career up to a certain point according to the ancient triple formula of *çīla*, *samādhi* (*citta*) and *prajñā*. The two writers have not the same point of view. It is true that the author of the *Bo. Bhū.* makes an unsuccessful attempt to identify some of his *vihāras* with the *bhūmis* of the *Da. Bhū.* and cites some passages from that treatise. But the principles underlying the two systems remain divergent in all essential respects. It may be inferred that the sections treating of the *bhūmis* in the *Mahā-vastu* and the *Pr. Pā Çata.* represent an early stage in the development of the idea, while the later systems of the *Da. Bhū.* and the *Bo. Bhū.* belong to two different schools or sects. The *Bo. Bhū.* has borrowed several ideas from the *Da. Bhū.* The doctrine of the *bhūmis* was not accepted in the same spirit by all the Mahāyānists. The *M. S. Al.* does not discuss the *bhūmis* in detail, and the *B. C. Ava.* does not mention them at all! The *Çikṣā* speaks incidentally of the first *bhūmi*, but not of the others, though the author lived in the same period as Candrakīrti, who gives an elaborate account of the *bhūmis* in his *Madhyamakāvatāra*. Perhaps the exponents of *çūnyatā* as conditioned Existence attached more importance to the *bhūmis* than the other *Mādhyamikas*, who interpreted it as absolute Non-existence.

It is advisable to discuss the data of each treatise separately and also to accept the *Da. Bhū.* as the standard treatise on the subject. The systems of the other books may be summarised very briefly.

I THE BHŪMIS IN THE MAHĀ-VASTU. (I. 76 ff.)

Kātyāyana, a disciple of Gautama Buddha, explains to Ānanda that each *bhūmi* is " unmeasured ", " infinite " (*aprameyā*), but that there are ten of them.

The first *bhūmi* is called *Durārohā* (Difficult-to-enter). A *bodhisattva* cultivates charity, compassion, indefatigable energy, humility, study of all the branches of Learning (or all the Scriptures), heroism, renunciation of the world, and fortitude. He cannot rise to the second *bhūmi*, if he takes delight in life and its pleasures, or if he is indolent, worldly, timid, weak-willed, and unfriendly to others. He should also cultivate the idea of the impermanence of all things, and refuse to be entangled in worldly affairs. He produces the Thought of Enlightenment in his mind in this *bhūmi* and resolves to attain Enlightenment. Thus he gains much Merit and also accumulates the " Roots of Good or Merit ". He is prepared to suffer in the *avīci* purgatory, if it should be necessary for success in his aim. A wonderful light spreads over the entire universe ; the earth shakes and trembles ; and the *devas* promise protection to such a *bodhisattva*, who is sure not to turn back (*avivartika*). He gives away wealth, limbs, wife and children ; he speaks sweetly to cruel men, who may have threatened to beat, bind or kill him.

In the second *bhūmi* (*Baddhamānā*, " Fastening "), a *bodhisattva* cultivates Aversion to all forms of existence in the three realms (*bhaveṣu arati*). He is full of thoughts of beneficence, love and gentleness. He harbours his great, wonderful and profound purpose with a keen mind. He has uncommon nobility and elevation of spirit. He is noted for his independence and overcomes all obstacles. He is resolute, pure, sincere and steadfast, as his character is such that he is free from sensuous desire and love of pleasure, longs for Enlightenment, and thinks in terms of Infinity. But he cannot rise to the third *bhūmi* and abide in it, if he is avid of gain, honour and fame, or if he is dishonest and cunning. He should also beware of showing disrespect to his teachers and the Triple Jewel, and of using garlands, ornaments and unguents. He should not be satisfied with a little progress, and he should never laud himself or contemn others.

The third *bhūmi* is called *Puṣpa-maṇḍitā* (Adorned-with-flowers). In this *bhūmi*, a *bodhisattva* especially cultivates *tyāga* (charity, liberality). He confers happiness on all creatures without any selfish motive. He also loves Learning so much that he is prepared to make the greatest sacrifices only to hear a single instructive verse or stanza. But he cannot rise to the fourth *bhūmi* and abide in it, if he is addicted to gambling and other similar improper pursuits, or if he is too fond of seclusion and solitude. He should also beware of the habit of obtaining money by political influence, and of complicity in crimes of any kind. He should acquire much knowledge and constantly praise the Buddhas, otherwise he will fall back from the fourth *bhūmi* into the third.

The fourth *bhūmi* is called *Rucirā* (Beautiful, Attractive). In this *bhūmi*, a *bodhisattva* should beware of immoral practices and the exercise of the wonder-working Powers for illegitimate objects. He should be conscientious and develop a sense of noble shame. He should not incite others to wicked deeds. If he does not avoid such faults, he cannot rise to the fifth *bhūmi*.

(Note: The *Mahā-vastu* gives the details about the eighth *bhūmi* in the section on the fourth *bhūmi*! These details will be discussed in connection with the eighth *bhūmi*.)

The fifth *bhūmi* is called *Citta-vistāra* (Expansion of the Heart). A *bodhisattva* now realises that all Existence is consumed with the fire of lust, hatred and delusion, and that it is devoid of protection and happiness. He worships and serves many Buddhas. He cannot rise to the sixth *bhūmi* and abide in it, if he mixes with the followers of other sects, like the *Yogācāras*. He should also not be afraid of ascetic practices, and should constantly cultivate calm and insight.

The sixth *bhūmi* is called *Rūpavatī* ("Beautiful, Lovely"). A *bodhisattva* now feels and knows that this "whirlpool" of the world is very terrible and yields little joy and satisfaction. He cannot rise to the seventh *bhūmi* and abide in it, if he desires to attain the trance of the Cessation-of-perception-and-feeling, or listens complacently to his own praises as a great man and a self-restrained saint.

The seventh *bhūmi* is called *Durjayā* ("Difficult to conquer"). A *bodhisattva* practises self-control in order to do good to many creatures. He especially cultivates compassion, refrains from killing living beings, and also teaches others to observe this precept. He also practises forbearance in all his actions and forgives his enemies. He masters all the arts, sciences, languages and scripts. He learns everything about gold, silver, gems and precious stones, and acquires all knowledge that may be useful to mankind.

The eighth *bhūmi* is called *Janma-nideṣa* (Ascertainment of Birth). A *bodhisattva* is now perfectly pure and may be described as *avaivartaka* (not capable of turning back). He should be honoured in the same way as a Buddha. His chief characteristic is great Love and Compassion. He cannot commit any of the five heinous sins, or do evil of any kind. He does not frustrate the good deeds of others. He follows the ten meritorious Ways of Action. He is gentle and grateful: he does not pluck the leaves of the tree, under which he sits or sleeps. He does not injure others by charms and spells. He is calm and serene: he is not elated in prosperity or dejected in adversity. He cannot be reborn in a state of woe or in a common purgatory.

The ninth and tenth *bhūmis* are named *Yauvarāja* (Installation as Crown-Prince) and *Abhiṣeka* (Coronation) respectively. But no details are given.

It is clear that the account of the *bhūmis* in the *Mahā-vastu* is very confused and incoherent. It is also replete with digressions and repetitions.

II. The Bhūmis in the Pr. Pā Çata. (pp. 1454–73)

This treatise mentions ten *bhūmis*, to which it does not assign any names. In the first *bhūmi*, a *bodhisattva* acquires Merit, cultivates the thought of Omniscience, and thus makes the general "Preparation of Purpose". He maintains the same mental attitude toward all beings by practising the four "infinite" Meditations of friendliness, compassion, sympathetic joy and equanimity. He gives freely in charity, and cherishes and serves his good friends. He studies the Doctrine and adheres to the Mahāyāna. He renounces his home and becomes a monk. He continually thinks of the Buddhas. He preaches the faith to the people, exhorts them to live the higher spiritual life, and instructs them in the different branches of the Scriptures. He is free from pride and arrogance, so that he may never be born in a family of low and humble origin.

He speaks the truth, and his actions are in harmony with his words.

In the second *bhūmi*, a *bodhisattva* purifies his conduct by paying no heed to the doctrines of the Hīnayāna and other systems that are prejudicial to his progress towards Enlightenment. He cultivates the virtues of gratitude, forbearance and harmlessness. He experiences great joy by maturing the living beings in the three Ways and working for their rescue and salvation in a spirit of devotion. He feels such deep compassion for all creatures that he resolves to suffer in the purgatories for their sake. He has faith in his teachers, and reveres and serves them. He devotes himself exclusively and entirely to the practice of the Perfections in order to mature and ripen all beings.

In the third *bhūmi*, a *bodhisattva* acquires a thorough knowledge of the teachings of the Buddhas in all the worlds and universes. He preaches to the people in such an unselfish spirit that he does not even desire Enlightenment as his recompense for the work. He applies and dedicates all his "Roots of Merit" for the purification of the minds of others. He never feels weary or depressed on account of his heavy burden. He feels shame and disgust at the thought of countenancing the tenets of the Hīnayānists.

In the fourth *bhūmi*, he lives in the forest. He has few desires and does not long even for *bodhi*. He is contented, and accepts the profound truths regarding Liberation like a true ascetic. He practises all the modes of Discipline and does not harbour any sensual thoughts. He renounces all things and cultivates the idea of passivity. He sacrifices everything, internal and external, and is indifferent to all objects.

In the fifth *bhūmi*, a *bodhisattva* avoids intercourse with householders and travels from one Buddha-field to another. He does not wish to enjoy the company of the nuns even for a moment. He works for the good of all without distinction. He shuns the society of the Hīnayānists and does not frequent their schools. He does not exalt himself or belittle others. He is never malicious and quarrelsome. He avoids the ten demeritorious Ways of Action, as they cause unhappy rebirths and hinder the attainment of Enlightenment. He eschews pride, arrogance, perverted views, sense-desire, hatred, delusion and doubt.

In the seventh *bhūmi*, a *bodhisattva* abandons the wrong belief in the existence of a permanent substantial *ātman*. He understands that nothing is produced or destroyed, and that nothing is eternal or evanescent. He gets rid of the idea of Cause. He is not attached to *nāma-rūpa* (mind-and-body), to the Aggregates (*skandha*), to all the elements and factors of Existence (*dhātu*), to the Spheres of Sense, and to anything in the triple Universe. He does not indulge in speculation with regard to the Buddha, the Doctrine and the Confraternity. He is not dejected at the thought that all things are empty and conditioned (*çūnya*). He realises the truths of Emptiness, Signlessness and Desirelessness, as he does not entertain the idea of the triple Universe. He fulfils the ten ethical precepts and cultivates compassion and friendliness. He comprehends the equality (sameness) of all things and principles. He destroys all his sins and passions, controls his mind, acquires calm and insight, and obtains " the eye of the Buddha " (perfect Knowledge).

In the eighth *bhūmi*, a *bodhisattva* can read the thoughts of all creatures, acquires the Super-knowledges, sees all the Buddha-fields, serves the Buddhas by serving all beings, and obtains true insight into the nature of the *dharma-kāya* (cosmic spiritual Body). He acquires the sovereignty of the Universe and then renounces it. He knows the higher and lower powers of all, purifies the Buddha-fields, and performs all actions without being attached to anything.

In the ninth *bhūmi*, he attains success in his infinite Resolve and Aspiration. He acquires the two useful powers of *nirukti* (exegesis) and *pratibhāna* (readiness in speech). He understands the speech of the *devas*, *nāgas*, *yakṣas*, *asuras* and other beings. His birth is apparitional, and he is not born through the physical union of a man and a woman. He is always born in a noble family of the warrior-caste or the priestly caste. He belongs to the *gotra* (family) of all the former *bodhisattvas*. He illumines innumerable worlds immediately after his birth and causes them to be shaken in six ways. He renounces his home and becomes a recluse. When he sits under the tree of Enlightenment, the tree appears to be made of gold and precious stones. He attains the Perfection of all the virtues and qualities.

In the tenth *bhūmi*, a *bodhisattva* becomes a Buddha and acquires all the attributes of a perfect Buddha.

It is clear that there is no plan or system in this account of the ten *bhūmis*. Only six *pāramitās* are spoken of, and the same items are mentioned several times.

III. The Bhūmis and Vihāras of the Bodhisattva-bhūmi. (fol. 120*a* ff.)

This important treatise gives a complicated and overlapping system of seven *bhūmis*, which include thirteen *vihāras*. The subject is really discussed in detail in connection with the *vihāras*, to which a long chapter is devoted. But the older scheme of classification in seven *bhūmis* is mentioned in the next chapter, and the relation of the *bhūmis* to the *vihāras* is indicated. The seven *bhūmis* and the thirteen *vihāras* are as follows (*Bo. Bhū.*, 136*b*, 4–7) :—

i. *Gotra-bhūmi*, which is identical with the *gotra-vihāra*.

ii. *Adhimukti-caryā-bhūmi*, which is the same as the *adhimukti-caryā-vihāra*.

iii. *Çuddh-āçaya-bhūmi* (the Stage of Pure Intention or Thought), which is also called the *pramudita-vihāra*.

iv. *Caryā-pratipatti-bhūmi* (the Stage of the practice or performance of the Discipline). This stage is very important, as it includes the following six *vihāras* : *Adhiçīla-vihāra* ; *Adhicitta-vihāra* ; *Adhiprajñā-vihāra* No. 1 ; *Adhiprajñā-vihāra* No. 2 ; *Adhiprajñā-vihāra* No. 3 ; *Sābhoga-nirnimitta-vihāra*.

v. *Niyatā-bhūmi* (the Stage of Certainty and Regulation). This *bhūmi* is identical with the *anābhoga-nirnimitta-vihāra*.

vi. *Niyata-caryā-bhūmi* (the Stage of certain regulated Practice). This *bhūmi* is the same as the *pratisaṃvid-vihāra*.

vii. *Niṣṭhāgamana-bhūmi* (Attainment of the End of Perfection). This *bhūmi* includes two *vihāras* : the *parama-vihāra* and the *tāthāgata-vihāra*.

The subjects *gotra* and *adhimukti* have already been discussed above. The remaining eleven *vihāras* may be described briefly.

(1) *Pramudita-vihāra* (The Station of Joy : *Bo. Bhū.*, fol. 123*a*, 3 ff.).

It is a curious coincidence that the first *bhūmi* in the scheme of the *Da. Bhū.* has the same designation (*pramuditā*). In this Station, a *bodhisattva* is distinguished for purity of thought. He takes the great Vow or Resolve, which is also called the "Thought of Enlightenment". This Resolve is incomparable and inviolable. It aims at saving all beings from pain and raises a *bodhisattva* above the *çrāvakas* and the *pratyeka-buddhas.* It arises in a *bodhisattva's* mind on account of the accumulation of Merit in a previous life and the acquisition of the proper Equipment for Enlightenment. Such a *bodhisattva* may rightly be called " Buddha's son of the breast ". He is full of joy in mind and body, because he is free from anger, malice and excitement, and all fears and dangers have disappeared for him. He understands that there is no permanent Ego and has therefore no notion of Self. He is free from self-love and never thinks of injuring others. He is not proud or covetous. He puts forth great energy, as he is blessed with faith and a pure, unsullied Will. He declares his ten great Aspirations. By virtue of these Aspirations, he subsequently develops many others. He sees many Buddhas, about whom he has read in the Scriptures, or of whom he has thought with faith and devotion. On account of his earnest wish, he is born in the worlds, where a Buddha has made his appearance. He worships and serves those Buddhas and learns the Doctrine from them. He practises virtue and " applies " all his Merit to the attainment of Enlightenment. He " matures " the beings by means of the four *saṅgraha-vastus*, and his " Roots of Merit " are purified. He teaches all creatures in a liberal spirit and withholds nothing from them. He is very strenuous, becomes a homeless monk and acquires many *samādhis* (modes of Concentration). He can see the Buddhas in many Buddha-fields with his supernal organ of sight. He can live for hundreds of *kalpas* (æons) and knows the past and the future. He can create his own phantom-bodies and show them to other *bodhisattvas* who need instruction ; and he can perform many other miracles.

(2) *Adhiçīla-vihāra.* This *vihāra* is said to correspond to the second *bhūmi* of the *Da. Bhū.* A *bodhisattva* purifies his thoughts by serving his teachers and living peacefully and happily with his fellow-*bodhisattvas.* He is master of his mind and conquers all the great and small sins and passions. He does not value the things of the world, thinks of the advantages of Liberation, and continually cultivates the *bodhipakṣya-dharmas.* He is indifferent to worldly gain and honour. He rejects the Hīnayāna and accepts the Mahāyāna. He is virtuous by nature, and does not commit the slightest sin. He follows the ten meritorious Ways of Action, knows the results of good and evil deeds in future rebirths, and exhorts others to the pursuit of righteousness on account of his great compassion for them.

(3) *Adhicitta-vihāra*. This *vihāra* is said to correspond to the third *bhūmi* of the *Da. Bhū*. A *bodhisattva* now knows that his thoughts are permanently pure and cannot be corrupted by attachment to worldly and sinful objects. He cultivates the virtue and wisdom that form the antidote to the *āsravas* (Intoxicants). He cannot be overcome by the hosts of *Māra*. He feels no pain or difficulty in practising severe austerities. He is devoted to the Mahāyāna and takes delight in doing good to all. He realises the dangers and disadvantages of all material things and phenomena, and turns his mind away from them. He longs for the knowledge of the Buddhas, as it would confer wonderful benefits on him. He pities the afflicted creatures and becomes still more strenuous and vigilant. He understands that pure and perfect Knowledge and Wisdom are the only remedies for the evils, from which all living beings suffer. He diligently studies the Scriptures and tries to acquire the *dhyānas*, *samādhis* and *samāpattis* (Attainments). He is ready to sacrifice his wealth, serve his teachers, and endure pain and hardship in order to receive religious instruction, which he values more highly than all the treasures of the entire universe. He is so eager in the pursuit of such knowledge that he would willingly throw himself into the fire in order to learn a single new sentence or maxim relating to the Doctrine and perfect Enlightenment. He is prepared even to suffer in the purgatories, if need be. He acts in accordance with the teaching, and attains the four *dhyānas*, the four non-material *samāpattis*, the four "infinite" Meditations, and the five *abhijñās* (Super-knowledges). He is then reborn at will, wherever he thinks that the interests of the living beings can best be served. He is freed from the bonds of sensuous desire, love of existence, hatred and delusion.

(4) *Adhiprajñā-vihāra* No. 1. This *vihāra* is said to correspond to the fourth *bhūmi* of the *Da. Bhū*. A *bodhisattva* now practises the thirty-seven *bodhipakṣya-dharmas*. He gets rid of the last traces of the wrong belief in the *ātman*. He does all actions that have been praised by the Buddha, and avoids all actions that the Buddha has condemned. He is more compassionate, active, grateful, virtuous, energetic and steadfast than ever before. He is more than a match for all rival teachers belonging to other sects.

(5) *Adhiprajñā-vihāra* No. 2. This *vihāra* is said to correspond to the fifth *bhūmi* of the *Da. Bhū*. A *bodhisattva* makes further progress in knowledge and comprehends the four

Noble Truths in all their aspects. He determines to obtain the full Equipment of Merit and Knowledge in order to liberate all beings. He thinks of nothing else but this duty, and cultivates mindfulness, thoughtfulness, proper deportment and other virtues. He acquires a thorough knowledge of the arts, sciences and technical crafts. He helps the people by bestowing wealth on the poor, healing the sick, and supplying all with appropriate objects of enjoyment. He protects them against such dangerous persons as kings, thieves and robbers. He exhorts them to do what is proper and shun what is improper, to take what is beneficial and reject what is detrimental to them. He teaches them how to live together in love and peace in this life, and attain happiness hereafter.

(6) *Adhiprajñā-vihāra* No. 3. This *vihāra* is said to correspond to the sixth *bhūmi* of the *Da. Bhū.* A *bodhisattva* now comprehends the formula of the *pratītya-samutpāda* and the three "Entrances to Liberation", viz. *çūnyatā*, *ānimitta* and *apraṇihita*. He gets rid of the notions of Doer, Knower, Existence and Non-existence. He realises that the twelve causes of Existence and Pain depend on impure sin and passion (*kleça*). He attains absolute Knowledge and the Perfection of Wisdom, and can therefore perform all ordinary worldly actions without being attached to anything. He cultivates the *kṣānti* that is called *ānulomikī*. He experiences thousands of *samādhis*. He is skilful in the choice of the means for converting and helping others.

(7) *Sābhoga-nirnimitta-vihāra* (The Station of the Unconditioned, accompanied with Mental Effort or Thought).[5] This *vihāra* is supposed to correspond to the seventh *bhūmi* of the *Da. Bhū.* A *bodhisattva* now rises above mere Merit and begins to acquire the Buddha-knowledge in body, speech and mind. He understands the immense scope of Buddhahood and continually tries to be faultless in his deportment, conduct and thoughts. He fulfils the ten *pāramitās* and all the seven Factors of Enlightenment (*bodhy-aṅgāni*). He is completely free from all the sins and passions like sensuous desire, hatred, etc.; or it may be said that he transcends them altogether. He improves and perfects his knowledge of the arts and sciences He is superior to all beings except the Buddhas and the more advanced *bodhisattvas*. He experiences a million *samādhis*. His words, deeds and thoughts are now independent of *nimitta* (cause and motive). He attains the *summum bonum*, but does not disappear in *nirvāṇa*.

(8) *Anābhoga-nirnimitta-vihāra* (The Station of the Unconditioned without Mental Effort or Thought). This *vihāra* is said to correspond to the eighth *bhūmi* of the *Da. Bhū.* In this *vihāra*, a *bodhisattva's* actions are perfectly pure, whereas they were not so in the preceding Stations. He obtains infallible knowledge of the past, present and future. He comprehends that all things are really undefinable and indescribable. There can be no origination and no causation. Thus he acquires the *kṣānti* that is called *anutpattika-dharma-kṣānti.* He is now exhorted by the Buddhas and obtains the ten Powers (*vaçitā*). He can enjoy the *dhyānas* that he wishes to experience. He can get material objects like food and drink merely by thinking of them. All his desires are automatically fulfilled. He can know everything that he wants to know. He is never deprived of communion with the Buddhas.

(9) *Pratisaṃvid-vihāra.* This *vihāra* is said to correspond to the ninth *bhūmi* of the *Da. Bhū.* In this *vihāra*, a *bodhisattva* understands the problem of moral corruption and purification in all its aspects. He becomes a great and successful preacher and teacher. He is protected by the magic spells of the *devas* and acquires the four *pratisaṃvids.*

(10) *Parama-vihāra* (the highest or supreme Station). This *vihāra* is said to correspond to the tenth *bhūmi* of the *Da. Bhū.* A *bodhisattva* now attains the highest *samādhis* and incomparable, innumerable Powers. He destroys the sins and errors of many beings by spiritual instruction. He is like a cloud that sends down rain on the earth ; he lays the dust of passion and promotes the growth of meritorious deeds by his teaching. He is absolutely free from all sins and all hindrances to Knowledge.

(11) *Tāthāgata-vihāra* (the Station of the Buddhas). In this *vihāra*, a *bodhisattva* reaches his goal and acquires Omniscience. He attains final and absolute Enlightenment.

This scheme of thirteen *vihāras* has really very little in common with the ten *bhūmis* of the *Da. Bhū*, though the author of the *Bo. Bhū.* takes great pains to point out that ten of the *vihāras* correspond to the ten *bhūmis* of the *Da. Bhū.* But they do not so correspond. The *Da. Bhū.* allots one *pāramitā* to each *bhūmi* : that is the essential feature of its system. But the author of the *Bo. Bhū.* mentions the word *pāramitā* only twice in the chapter on the *vihāras* (fol. 129*b*, 5.1 and 130*b*, 2.1). He does not attach particular importance to the *dāna-pāramitā* in the *pramudita-vihāra*, which is said to correspond to the first *bhūmi* of the *Da. Bhū.* He omits the Perfection of *kṣānti* altogether. He does not mention the seventh, eighth and ninth *pāramitās* in connection with the *vihāras* that are supposed to correspond to the respective *bhūmis* of the *Da. Bhū.* He goes further and adds the last *vihāra* that does not correspond to any *bhūmi* of the *Da. Bhū.* Here the pretence is dropped. There are other discrepancies too. The *Da. Bhū.* allots one of the *saṅgraha-vastus* to each of the first four *bhūmis*, but the *Bo. Bhū.* puts all of them in the *pramudita-vihāra* (fol. 125*a*, 1.2–3). This system of the *vihāras* is really based on the idea of what is called *nirnimitta-bhāvanā*, and not on the ten *pāramitās*. This is the fundamental difference between the schemes of the *Da. Bhū.* and the *Bo. Bhū.* The *Bo. Bhū.* lays stress on the gradual realisation of the principle of *nirnimitta-bhāvanā* (cultivation of the idea of the Unconditioned, the Uncaused: fol. 121*b*, 5.2 ff.). This *bhāvanā* commences in the *adhimukti-caryā-vihāra* and reaches complete fruition in the last *vihāra*.

In conclusion, the *Bo. Bhū.* declares that all the *vihāras* and *bhūmis* are purified by faith, compassion, friendliness, learning, fortitude, indefatigable zeal and the worship of the Buddhas.

IV. The Bhūmis of the Daça-bhūmika-sūtra

The most systematic treatment of the subject of the *bhūmis* is found in the *Daça-bhūmika-sūtra*. The author takes us through a mighty maze, but it is not without a plan. He manages to place almost all the important concepts and categories of Buddhist philosophy in his scheme of ten *bhūmis*. Thus, for example, he puts the four *saṅgraha-vastus* in the first four *bhūmis*, the four Noble Truths in the fifth *bhūmi*, the formula of Dependent Origination in the sixth *bhūmi*, and so on. But his system exhibits a certain unity of plan on account of the parallelism between the ten *pāramitās* and the ten *bhūmis*. A *bodhisattva* especially cultivates one of the *pāramitās* in each *bhūmi*. Other details are subsidiary. The *Da. Bhū* thus offers a methodical and coherent scheme, which is now accepted as the standard system of division and classification for a *bodhisattva's* career. The *Da. Bhū.* does not speak of the *gotra-bhūmi* and the *adhimukti-caryā-bhūmi*, and differs in this respect from the *Bo. Bhū.* The latter treatise has borrowed from the *Da. Bhū.* the "progressive simile" of gold, which relieves the dreary dullness of the *Da. Bhū.* A *bodhisattva* is compared in each *bhūmi* to gold, which is purified more and more by being heated in the goldsmith's fire till it is at last made into an ornament to be worn on the neck of a powerful monarch.[6] The *bodhisattva's* splendour is likened to the light of the moon and the sun. In each *bhūmi*, a *bodhisattva's* glory and power (*prabhāva*) increase a hundredfold, a thousandfold, a millionfold, and so on. His rebirths exhibit a similar progressive tendency.[7] In the first *bhūmi*, he is as a rule born as the King of India (*Jambudvīpa*, Rose-apple Island). In the second *bhūmi*, he is born as a universal Monarch, ruler of the four *dvīpas* (islands) and owner of the seven "jewels." In the third *bhūmi*, he is born in a heaven as *Indra*, ruler of the thirty-three *devas*. In the fourth *bhūmi*, he is *Suyāma*, King of another class of *devas*. Then he is successively born in the higher heavens as the ruler of the *devas* of the *Tuṣita* heaven, of the *nirmāṇa-rati devas*, and of the *devas* called *paranirmita-vaça-vartins*. Finally, he is born as *Mahābrahmā*, ruler of a thousand worlds and of two thousand worlds, and ends by being born as *Maheçvara* (*Çiva*). This last stage betrays the influence of the *Çaiva* sect, which is also apparent in the list of the heavens in the *M. Vy.* It is also to be noted that a *bodhisattva* is not said to be born in the four non-material heavens (*ārūpya-dhātu*). In fact, the heavens are many, and the *bhūmis* are only ten. So the author of the *Da. Bhū.* mentions only two heavens of the *Brahma-loka*, which, however, belong more to the Pāli than to the Sanskrit tradition (cf. *Majjhima* iii, 101 ff.). He omits the other heavens of the *rūpa-dhātu*, and ends his list with *Maheçvara*, who seems to have ousted *Brahmā* from the highest position.

Such is the general plan of the *Da. Bhū.* A few details about each *bhūmi* may be added.

(1) *First Bhūmi*, called *Pramuditā* (Joyful). The form *muditā* is also found (*Lka.*, p. 375). The *M.S. Al.* explains that the *bhūmi* is so called because a *bodhisattva* feels keen delight (*moda*), when he knows that he will soon attain *bodhi* and promote the good of all beings (p. 181). According to the *Da. Bhū.*, a *bodhisattva* enters this first Stage immediately after the production of the "Thought of Enlightenment". He rejoices exceedingly, as he remembers the teaching of the Buddha and thinks of the discipline of the *bodhisattvas*. He realises that he has

now risen above the life of the foolish common people and is also delivered from the fear of unhappy rebirths. He feels that he is the refuge of all creatures. He is not troubled by the five fears that embitter the lives of other men, viz. the fear of loss of livelihood, of obloquy, of death, of rebirth in a state of woe, and of diffidence in assemblies. He does not think of Self; he does not care for honour; he knows that he will always remain in communion with the Buddhas and the *bodhisattvas* after his death; and he feels that he is superior to others in all assemblies. He is well and firmly established in this *bhūmi* through faith, devotion, aspiration, preparation, mercy, compassion, friendliness, fortitude, conscientiousness, noble shame, gentle forbearance, reverence for Buddha's teaching, and perseverance in accumulating the "Roots of Merit". He cherishes his good friends, takes delight in righteous activity, seeks for learning and knowledge with unabated zeal, ponders well on the Doctrine, and longs for the stage of Enlightenment and the practice of the Perfections. He cultivates honesty, sincerity and truthfulness, and develops the different Factors of Enlightenment. He is firm like a rock in his aspiration for Omniscience. He takes the ten great Vows. He wishes that his Vows may endure and extend as far as the universe and all space and Buddha-knowledge itself. He has deep faith in the Buddhas and all their attributes. He knows that the principles of Buddhahood are profound, absolute, transcendental and ineffable. He sees that the worldly people are the slaves of sins, passions and errors, and therefore endure the pain that is inseparable from life. He pities them and resolves to save and liberate them. He then begins to practise charity and self-sacrifice on an immense scale, as he himself has no desire for anything. He gives away wealth, wife and children, and his own limbs and life. He acquires learning, experience and fortitude. He worships the Buddhas and has the privilege of seeing and serving millions and billions of them. He then "applies" and dedicates all his "Roots of Merit" for Enlightenment. He practises *the Perfection of Giving* (*dāna-pāramitā*) *with zeal* and also cultivates the other Perfections according to his capacity. He pays special attention to the first *saṅgraha-vastu* (Charity). As a skilful caravan-leader obtains full information about the difficulties and perils of the road before starting on a journey, even so a wise *bodhisattva* now learns everything about the discipline and duties of his long career from the Buddha, the *bodhisattvas* and his good friends. He becomes a monk, experiences hundreds of *samādhis*, lives for a hundred aeons, assumes a hundred forms, and performs innumerable miracles.

(2) *Second Bhūmi*, called *Vimalā* (" Pure ", " Free from impurity," " Immaculate "). The *M. S. Al.* explains that this *bhūmi* is so called because a *bodhisattva* is free from the " dirt " of unrighteous conduct and of the Hīnayāna (p. 182). Candrakīrti says : " Possédant les pures qualités de la plénitude de la moralité le *bodhisattva*, même en rêve, abandonne la souillure de l'immoralité " (Le Muséon, 1907, p. 280). According to the *Da. Bhū.*, a *bodhisattva* is now straightforward, tender-hearted, active, self-controlled, calm, beneficent, incorruptible, noble, magnanimous, and free from desire. He is distinguished for such traits of character. He also follows the ten meritorious " Ways of Action ", as *he especially cultivates the çīla-pāramitā in this bhūmi* without neglecting the other *pāramitās*. He knows that the violation of the ten moral Precepts leads to rebirth in the three states of woe and to severe penalties in the case of rebirth as a human being. He exhorts others to observe the ten Precepts, and again resolves to be their friend, guide, protector, teacher and saviour, as they are so deeply enmeshed and engulfed in pain, sorrow, sin and ignorance. He pays special attention to the second *saṅgraha-vastu* (Pleasant Speech) in this *bhūmi*.

(3) *Third Bhūmi*, called *Prabhākarī* (" Light-giving," "Luminous," "Illuminating," "la Terre clarifiante"). W. McGovern translates, "Brightness of Intellect," but the name does not seem to refer to "intellect".[8] The *M. S. Al.* explains that this *bhūmi* is so called, because a *bodhisattva* diffuses the great light of the Doctrine among the living beings (p. 182). But Candrakīrti says : " On nomme cette terre la Lumineuse, parce que, en ce moment, apparaît la lumière du feu, du savoir qui consume entièrement le combustible appelé 'connaissable' " (*Madhyamakāvatāra* : Le Muséon, 1907, p. 294). A *bodhisattva's* thoughts are now pure, constant, unworldly, dispassionate, firm, resolute, ardent, ambitious, noble and magnanimous. He realises that all material compounds are transient, impermanent and momentary. He understands that his body, exposed to grief and pain, is burning with the fire of passion, hatred and error. He therefore cultivates an attitude of still greater aversion and indifference to all things of the world. He longs all the more for Buddha-knowledge, which is incomparable and confers security,

happiness and salvation on all. He again thinks of the misery, sins and folly of the living beings, and again resolves to help, teach and liberate them. He devotes himself night and day to the study of the Scriptures and the teachings of the Buddha in order to gain perfect Knowledge and Wisdom. He practises regular self-examination and meditation. He experiences and acquires the four *dhyānas*, the four non-material *samāpattis*, the four *brahma-vihāras* and the five *abhijñās*. He gets rid of the *āsravas* of sensuous Desire, love of existence, ignorance, and metayphysical speculation. He especially cultivates the Perfection of *kṣānti* (Forbearance and Endurance) in this *bhūmi* without neglecting the others. He pays particular attention to the third *saṅgraha-vastu* (Promoting the good of others).

The section dealing with this *bhūmi* presents a perplexing problem. The *pāramitā* of *kṣānti* is associated with this Stage, but the attributes and qualifications, that are described, belong to *dhyāna* (Musing). It seems probable that the original scheme of division was based on the three *çikṣās* (branches of instruction) of *çīla*, *citta* and *prajñā*. The *Bo. Bhū.* has partially preserved it, though the *Da. Bhū.* ignores it. But this third *bhūmi* appears to deal with *citta* or *samādhi*, and not with *kṣānti*, which is tacked on at the end. The old scheme was recast and expanded in order to secure the symmetrical parallelism of the ten Perfections and the ten Stages.

(4) *Fourth Bhūmi*, called *Arciṣmatī* (Radiant, Effulgent). The *M. S. Al.* explains that this *bhūmi* is so called because the "rays" of the *bodhipakṣya-dharmas* burn up the veil and obstruction of sin and ignorance (p. 182). Candrakīrti says: "Alors, dans le fils du Sugata, par la culture extrême des auxiliares de la parfaite illumination, naît un éclat qui est supérieur au resplendissement de cuivre. . . . Par conséquent, produisant le rayon du feu du savoir parfait, cette terre du *bodhisattva* est appelée *Arciṣmatī*." A *bodhisattva* now gains entrance to the light of the Doctrine by reflecting on the nature of the Worlds of things and living beings, of Space, of Consciousness, of the Truth, of the three realms of sensuous Desire, Form and Formlessness, and of noble and magnanimous Aspiration. He matures and perfects his knowledge by his firm resolution and his faith in the "Triple Jewel". He realises that all things arise and disappear, and that non-production is their nature. He thinks of

Action, Becoming and Birth, of transmigratory existence and Liberation, of the beginning and the end, of non-existence and destruction. He practises the thirty-seven *bodhipakṣya-dharmas*. He gets rid of all wrong ideas based on the belief in a permanent *ātman*. He cultivates and acquires great, inexhaustible, infinite Energy, combined with ardour and zeal for the instruction and development of all beings. He especially cultivates the Perfection of Energy without neglecting the other *pāramitās*. He pays particular attention to the fourth *saṅgraha-vastu* in this *bhūmi* (*samān-ārthatā*).

(5) *Fifth Bhūmi*, called *Sudurjayā* ("Very-difficult-to-conquer," "Dure-à-gagner"). W. McGovern translates, "Difficult to surpass," but this rendering does not convey the right sense of the name.[9] The Stage is not "invincible", as it is interpreted by L. de la Vallée Poussin (ERE. ii, 748). The *M. S. Al.* explains that this *bhūmi* is so called, because a *bodhisattva* performs the difficult feat of maturing others and guarding his own mind (p. 182). But Candrakīrti says: "Le *bodhisattva*, fixé dans la cinquième terre du *bodhisattva*, ne peut être vaincu par les *devaputra Māras*, qui se trouvent dans tous les univers; à plus forte raison par d'autres, serviteurs de *Māra*, etc. C'est pourquoi le nom de cette terre est *Sudurjayā* (*Madhyamakāvatāra:* Le Muséon, 1907, p. 312). A *bodhisattva* regards all the principles of Buddhahood, past, present and future, with pure thought and equanimity. He thinks in the same way of conduct, meditation, doubt, speculation, knowledge of the right Way and the perfection of all beings. He comprehends the four Noble Truths. He also understands other aspects of Truth, e.g. relative Truth, absolute Truth, the Truths of characteristics, of division, of origination, of things and phenomena, of decay, of non-production, of initiation into the knowledge of the Way, and of the appearance of Buddha-knowledge.[10] He thus realises that all things are empty, futile and worthless. He wonders why the foolish worldly people are attached to their perishable bodies and are the slaves of pleasure and pride. He exerts himself all the more for their development and liberation. He acquires the admirable qualities of mindfulness, fortitude, discretion, and skilfulness in the choice of the means for attaining his ends. He practises all the *saṅgraha-vastus* in this *bhūmi*, and especially cultivates the *dhyāna-pāramitā* without neglecting the others. He also acquires a knowledge of the arts and sciences like writing, arithmetic, medicine,

etc. He preaches the Doctrine and obtains the *dhāraṇīs* for his protection.

(6) *Sixth Bhūmi*, called *Abhimukhī* ("Face-to-face," "Turned towards," "Showing the face," "Droit-en-face," "die *Bhūmi* der Klarheit," etc.). The *M. S. Al.* explains that this *bhūmi* is so called because the *bodhisattva*, practising the Perfection of Wisdom, now stands face to face with both *saṃsāra* (transmigratory existence) and *nirvāṇa* (Liberation). But Candrakīrti says: "Parce qu'on y comprend que la nature des choses est semblable à un reflet, parce que les *bodhisattvas* dans la sixième terre s'appuient sur la vérité du chemin, parce qu'elle est tournée vers le principe des parfaits Buddhas, cette terre s'appelle *Abhimukhī*" ("Tournée vers": *Madhyamakāvatāra*, Le Muséon, 1911, p. 272). A *bodhisattva* now understands the ten aspects of the equality and sameness of all things and phenomena. All things and phenomena are signless and have no definite characteristics; they are not produced and not originated; they are unrelated and also uncorrupted since the beginning; they are indescribable; they are neither admitted nor rejected; they are like a dream, an optical illusion, an echo, the disc of the moon seen in the water, an image and a magically created unreal object.[11] They are free from the duality of Existence and Non-existence. When a *bodhisattva* looks upon all things in this way, he acquires the *kṣānti* called *ānulomikī*. He also comprehends the formula of the *pratītya-samutpāda*. He realises that all sins and errors depend on the mind. He understands that all things are empty and characterless. He is absolutely free from Desire. He gets rid of the notions of "I" and "Other", "Doer" and "Knower", "Existence" and "Non-existence." He severs all connection with the "compounded" elements and experiences many *samādhis*, which are related to the principle of Emptiness. His thoughts are now perfectly firm, steady, profound and pure, and he resolutely sets his face towards Buddha-knowledge. He especially cultivates the Perfection of Wisdom (*prajñā*) without neglecting the others.

(7) *Seventh Bhūmi*, called *Dūraṅgamā* ("Far-going," "Far-reaching," "Va-loin," "die *Bhūmi* der weiten Fernsicht," "far-distant Attainment," etc.). The *M. S. Al.* explains that this *bhūmi* is so called because it leads to the end of the only Way, to the consummation of the Discipline (p. 182). A *bodhisattva* now acquires great wisdom in the choice of expedients for

helping others. He understands that all the Buddhas are identical with their spiritual cosmic Body. He participates in the infinite attributes of the Buddhas, and sees their multifarious physical bodies. He discerns the thoughts and feelings of others. He practises all the ten *pāramitās* at each moment. This Stage witnesses the complete fulfilment of the practical aspects of a *bodhisattva's* discipline, and now he begins to attach more importance to its meditative and metaphysical aspects. He has conquered all the passions and sins and is free from them. His thoughts, words and deeds are pure, and he is in possession of all the factors of Enlightenment. He works without effort or ulterior motive. He transcends the lower wisdom of the Hīnayāna. He attains Liberation, but does not realise personal *nirvāṇa*. He enters the great ocean of Buddha-knowledge. He is free from the four *viparyāsas*. *He especially cultivates the pāramitā* " *upāya-kauçalya* " *without neglecting the others.*

(8) *Eighth Bhūmi*, called *Acalā* (" Immovable," " Steadfast "). The *M. S. Al.* explains that this *bhūmi* is so called because a *bodhisattva* cannot be disturbed by the two ideas of Cause and Absence of Cause. A *bodhisattva* now acquires the *kṣānti* called *anutpattika-dharma-kṣānti.* He is not contaminated by any actions. The Buddhas initiate him into infinite Knowledge, otherwise he would enter into *nirvāṇa* instead of persevering in his efforts to gain *bodhi* for the good of all. He understands the process of the evolution and involution of the Universe. He knows the exact number of atoms in the different elements, of which the Universe is composed. He assumes different bodies and shows them to the people as he thinks fit. He acquires the ten *vaçitās* (Powers). This *bhūmi* is so important that it is called the Stage of Perfection, of Birth, of Finality. A *bodhisattva* especially cultivates the Perfection of Aspiration (*praṇidhāna*) without neglecting the others, and he pervades the whole world with the feeling of Friendliness.

(9) *Ninth Bhūmi*, called *Sādhumatī* ("Stage of the good Beings," "Stage of good Thoughts," "de Bon-Esprit," "of Holy Wisdom," " die *bhūmi* des guten Verständnisses," " of the peaceful Mind," etc.). The *M. S. Al.* explains that this *bhūmi* is so called because a *bodhisattva* has good thoughts on account of the *pratisaṃvids* that he acquires. A *bodhisattva* now knows all phenomena and principles truly and certainly, whether they are mundane or supra-mundane, conceivable or inconceivable,

compounded or uncompounded. He knows everything about the minds and hearts of men and about meritorious and demeritorious actions. He becomes a great preacher and acquires the four *pratisaṃvids*. He is protected by the *dhāraṇīs*. He experiences many *samādhis*. *He especially cultivates the Perfection of Strength* (*bala*) without neglecting the others.

(10) *Tenth Bhūmi*, called *Dharma-meghā* ("Cloud of the Doctrine," "Cloud of Virtue," "die *bhūmi* der Gesetz-umwölkung," "Nuage de l'Idéal," etc.). The *M. S. Al.* explains that this *bhūmi* is so called because it is pervaded by the modes of Concentration and magic spells, as space is occupied by clouds (p. 183). *Dharma-meghā* is also the name of a *samādhi* in the *Yoga-sūtras* (*Yo. Sū.*, iv, 29, page 202). A *bodhisattva* now enters on the Stage of *abhiṣeka* (anointing, consecration) and experiences many great *samādhis*. He acquires a glorious body, which is seen in a celestial lotus adorned with jewels. He emits some rays, which destroy the pain and misery of all living beings. He performs many miracles and creates numberless magical bodies of himself. He obtains the ten "Deliverances" of a *bodhisattva*. *He especially cultivates the Perfection of Knowledge* (*jñāna*) without neglecting the others.

An eleventh *bhūmi* is mentioned in the *Lka.* It is called *Tathāgata-bhūmi* (Stage of a Buddha). The *Dh. S.* and the *M. Vy.* give the name *Samanta-prabhā* (universally luminous) to this Stage. The *Dh. S.* also mentions two other *bhūmis*, called *Nirupamā* (unequalled, incomparable) and *Jñānavatī* (possessing knowledge).[12] But these *bhūmis* are not discussed in detail.

CHAPTER VII

THE LAST LIFE AND ENLIGHTENMENT

The life of Gautama Buddha is the basis and starting-point of all the doctrines and theories of Buddhism. The supposed events of his past lives as a *bodhisattva* have been related in the *avadānas* (stories) devoted to that inspiring theme. The doctrine of a *bodhisattva's* career was also promulgated in order to explain and interpret the historic fact of his marvellous virtue and wisdom. In Buddhist philosophy and history, all roads lead to Gautama Buddha. The real and imaginary important incidents of his life have been regarded as the necessary experiences of all advanced *bodhisattvas* in their last lives, during which they attain Enlightenment. All such *bodhisattvas* must be born and must live in the same manner. Gautama Buddha's life is regarded as a concrete instance of the general law relating to a *bodhisattva's* last earthly existence, which he at last reaches after three *asaṅkhyeyas* of aeons.

The biography of Gautama Buddha is inextricably mingled with myth and legend. Exaggerated reverence for the Teacher and lack of scientific education have led to enormous accretions of picturesque mythology, which render it difficult to separate fact from fiction. We shall relate such relevant facts and incidents as have contributed to the development of the general *bodhisattva* doctrine. They are narrated in the *Mahā-vastu*, the *Lal. V.*, the *Buddha-carita* and the *Avadāna-kalpa-latā*. Similar details are given in the *Mtu.* with reference to a Buddha, named Dīpaṅkara (i, 197 ff.). It may not be out of place to indicate the salient features of the legend of Gautama Buddha, which have some bearing on our subject.

(1) The *bodhisattva* descends from a heaven of his own accord and selects his mother. His birth is therefore not due to the law of *karma*.

(2) His reputed father has no connection with his birth. It is a case of "parthenogenesis," and not of "virgin birth", as E. J. Thomas has conclusively proved ("Buddha": pp. 237 ff.).

(3) He is not soiled by impure elements of any kind at his birth, which is also attended with many other marvels.

(4) He is a Superman even in childhood. He is a highly cultured person, excelling in all physical and intellectual accomplishments.

(5) He is free from passion, but he marries in order to conform to the ways of the world and set a good example. His son is born without any sensual indulgence on his part.

(6) He practises severe penance as an ascetic from similar motives

(7) He meets *Māra*, the *deva* of Desire, in a terrific combat, from which he emerges victorious, and then attains Enlightenment.

(8) All through his life, he is helped, served, encouraged and supported by the *devas* of the different heavens, who also rejoice at his success in winning *bodhi*.

The birth of Vipassin and of Gautama Buddha is attended with wonders and miracles even according to the Pāli canon (cf. *Dīgha*, ii, 12 ff. *Mahāpadāna-sutta.—Majjhima*, iii, 118 ff. *Acchariy-abbhuta-dhamma-sutta*). We shall deal with the legend according to the Sanskrit treatises.

I. Birth

The individual, who is known as Gautama Buddha, is said to have taken the vow of becoming a Buddha many æons before his birth as the historic Teacher. There are several versions of the story. He is most frequently said to have been a *brahmin*, Sumedha or Megha, who took the vow in presence of a Buddha, named Dīpaṅkara.[1] But the *Mtu.* also gives his name as Abhiya, a monk; and the Buddha, who predicted his future Enlightenment, was Sarvābhibhū.[2] The same treatise also contains another account, according to which he was a monarch of the four *dvīpas* (islands); and the Buddha, who gave him the *vyākaraṇa*, was Samitāvin.[3] He is also said to have been a *çreṣthin* (chief of a guild), and the Buddha's name was Çākyamuni.[4] According to Kṣemendra, he first conceived the Thought of Enlightenment when he was a king, named Prabhāsa.[5] It is not possible to reconcile these conflicting accounts. It may be inferred that several traditional names were known.

Since that remote period, he was reborn many times as a human being or an animal, till he appeared on earth as Prince Viçvantara. When that prince dies, he is reborn as a *deva* in the

Tuṣita heaven, whence the *bodhisattva* again descends to the earth. He lives there with the *devas*, who are supposed to be his disciples and admirers. It is announced that the time is ripe for the *bodhisattva's* rebirth for the attainment of *bodhi*, as the age of men is about a hundred years and they know what is meant by pain, old age and death. According to Buddhist cosmogony, a Buddha should not be born at the beginning of a great aeon, when men live very long, nor at the end of a world-cycle, when their lives are very short. In both cases, they would be unable to profit by a Buddha's teaching, which deals with pain, old age and death. The *bodhisattva*, having decided to be born, then determines the continent, the country or region, the family and the mother.[6] All the *devas* take part in these deliberations : this is a curious feature of the legend. It is agreed that the *bodhisattva* should be born in India (*Jambu-dvīpa*), in the region of *Madhyadeça* (Middle Country), and in the family of the Çākyas of Kapilavastu. The general law is here stated that a *bodhisattva* is born only in the two higher castes of the *brahmins* or the *kṣatriyas*, according as one or the other of these is predominant. The mention of the *brahmin* caste is due to the influence of Hinduism, as Gautama Buddha was born in a *kṣatriya* family, and he attached no importance to the pretensions of the *brahmins*. The family must also possess social influence and certain moral qualifications. It must have sixty or sixty-four qualities, e.g. knowledge, character, courage, piety, fame, etc. The woman, who is to be the *bodhisattva's* mother, must be endowed with beauty and virtue, and must not have given birth to a child before. She must have thirty-two admirable qualities.[7] Queen Māyā, wife of King Çuddhodana of Kapilavastu, is said to be faultless, tender-hearted, sweet in speech, gentle, good-tempered, modest, conscientious, steadfast, honest, charitable, and free from "the net of women's failings "[8] Here the legend states that Buddha's father was a king ; but he was only a wealthy nobleman, belonging to " an unbroken *kṣatriya* family, rich, of great wealth, of great possessions ", as the earliest Pāli accounts describe him.[9] Royalty was conferred on Buddha's parents in order to heighten the moral effect of his Renunciation. When the initial preparations in the *Tuṣita* heaven are thus completed, the Queen suddenly conceives an aversion to sensual pleasure and asks her husband to be allowed to live quietly in a secluded part of the palace. Celestial nymphs hasten to serve and honour her with music and flowers. She dreams that a white elephant with six tusks has entered her body.[10] On the same night, the *bodhisattva* descends as a white elephant with six tusks and enters her womb on the right side. It was the full-moon night of the month of *Vaiçākha* (April–May). He previously appoints the *bodhisattva* Maitreya as the teacher of the *Tuṣita* heaven. Here a difficult point in the legend must be explained, if it is possible to do so. According to the older account, the Queen only sees the white elephant in a dream; but the *bodhisattva* is also supposed to have assumed the form of a white elephant. The latter idea is rather absurd, as the *bodhisattva* is visible in the mother's womb as a human child and not as a white elephant, as we learn further on. There is a birth-story (*jātaka*) of a six-tusked elephant, but it throws no light on this particular point in the legend (*Jātaka*, v, pp. 36–7). Kṣemendra mentions the dream-elephant, but is silent about the six tusks. He describes *Indra's* elephant, *Airāvata*, as six-tusked. In the *Mtu.*, Yaçoda is also changed into a six-tusked elephant.[11] Elephants with six tusks must be supposed to be very rare (if not altogether non-existent); and the *bodhisattva* may be compared to such an animal, which is a symbol of extreme rarity and excellence. A universal monarch is said to possess a rare elephant. H. Kern thinks that it is a symbol of lightning (SBE, vol. xxi, p. 434, note). But E. Senart identifies it with the clouds, which envelop the sun. He says: "Il est bien évident que cet Éléphant divin' (*āsuro hastin*) a une certaine signification mythologique, et s'il exprime à la fois et resume la force ou la splendeur du *soma*, du soleil et du feu, aucune conception n'en saurait mieux rendre compte que celle du nuage enveloppant le soleil." [12] But the *bodhisattva* is not born covered with the elephant: he is the elephant. E. Senart also refers to a hymn of the *Atharva-veda* (iii, 22; page 43), in which the "splendour of the elephant" is mentioned (*hasti-varcasaṃ prathatām*, etc.). But it is a far cry from the *Atharva-veda* to the *Lal. V.* The "six tusks" are also not accounted for according to E. Senart's hypothesis. E. Windisch has pointed out that the elephant was a symbol of royalty, and he also connects the elephant of this legend with the *Airāvata* of Hindu mythology. He says: "Der Elefant im Traume deutet zunächst auf die Königswürde hin. . . . . In sofern aber der Elefant den *bodhisattva* bedeutet, musste er als der herrlichste, höchste Elefant erscheinen. Als solcher galt den Brahmanen *Indra's* Elefant: nach diesem

Vorbilde, das Vorbild noch übertreffend, wurde der *bodhisattva*-Elefant ausgemalt . . . . . Aber damit ist nicht gesagt dass das eine identisch ist mit dem andern . . . . . In dem Traume der Geburtslegende deutet die Weisse Silberfarbe symbolisch die Reinheit des *bodhisattva* an."[13] A passage in the *Mahābhārata* speaks of a *brahmin*, who falls into a well or pit in a forest and sees an elephant with six mouths (*ṣaḍ-vaktraṃ kṛṣṇa-çabalam . . . . . mahā-gajam.*" *Mahābhārata. Strī-parvan*, xi, 5, 14–15; Bombay Edition, vol v, p. 6). Vidura explains to Dhṛtarāṣṭra that the forest in that parable represents transmigratory existence in the world (*saṃsāra*); the well is the human body; the elephant is the year; and the six faces are the six seasons (xi, 6, 10–11; vol. v, p. 7). It may be inferred that the six-tusked elephant is the sun, whose course in the sky is run during a year with six seasons. The *Mahābhārata* speaks of the elephant as " dark ", and does not speak of tusks. The white colour is regarded as auspicious. The white elephant of the Buddha-legend may have affinities with both *Airāvata* and the solar myth. Angelo de Gubernatis says: " The whole mythical history of the elephant is confined to India. . . . . The elephant generally represents the sun, as it shuts itself up in the cloud or the darkness, or comes out of it, shooting forth rays of light or flashes of lightning."[14] A. B. Keith suggests a different explanation. He says: " The most plausible hypothesis is to refer the dream to the Indian belief that a child before its conception already exists in an intermediate condition, as follows naturally from the doctrine of rebirth, and to find that the six tusks of the elephant arise from a misunderstanding of a phrase denoting 'one who has the six organs of sense under control' ".[15] But this suggestion is more ingenious than convincing.

To proceed with the story. Queen Māyā experiences the serene joy that usually comes of rapt Concentration. On waking, she goes to a grove of *açoka*-trees and sends for the king, who is at first unable to enter the place. The *devas* inform him of what has transpired, and Māyā tells him the dream. The *brahmins*, who are called to interpret the dream, prophesy that a son will be born to the king. He will become a universal monarch or a Buddha. The *bodhisattva* is not contaminated with bile, phlegm, blood or any impure secretions of the malodorous body during the entire pre-natal period. He sits in the womb in the cross-legged posture and is surrounded by a beautiful rectangular canopy, which has four pillars and a seat for the *bodhisattva*.[16]

This jewelled structure (*ratna-vyūha*) is carried off to the heaven of *Brahmā* after the *bodhisattva's* birth. Māyā can see the *bodhisattva* seated in her womb. This curious conceit owes its origin to the idea that the human body is not altogether pure, as it exudes certain foul and filthy fluids. Queen Māyā enjoys excellent health, and her mind is free from all evil dreams, thoughts and inclinations. She can heal the sick and confer happiness on all creatures. The *devas* honour the miniature *bodhisattva* with music and flowers. All these marvels of the pre-natal period are due to the *ṛddhi* (wonder-working Power) of the *bodhisattva* himself.

Queen Māyā bears the *bodhisattva* for ten months. This general law applies to all *bodhisattvas*: their pre-natal period is ten months. When the time comes for her to be delivered, she goes to the Lumbinī grove with her companions. Invisible *devas* follow her. She takes hold of a branch of a *plakṣa-tree* and looks at the sky. The *bodhisattva* is then born from her right side, which remains uninjured, as his body is mind-made.[17] He is serene and self-possessed, and is quite uncontaminated with impure substances of any kind. *Indra* and *Brahmā* take him in their hands and wrap him in fine silk, which is not soiled at all. All these incidents are in conformity with the general law that such a *bodhisattva's* mother is delivered in a standing position, and that his body is perfectly clean and is first taken in the hands of the *devas*, and not of human beings.

Although the *bodhisattva's* body is clean, yet he gets a bath of hot and cold water, which is provided by the *devas*. He then puts his feet on the ground, and a lotus grows out of the earth. A white umbrella is held over him. He stands in the lotus and looks in all directions. Then he takes seven steps in each of the six directions, and utters such exclamations as the following:—

" I am the best and highest being in the whole world. This is my last existence.

" I will put an end to birth, old age, death and pain. I shall destroy *Māra* and his army," etc.[18] At the same time, celestial music, flowers, rain and winds appear to mark the auspicious event of the *bodhisattva's* birth. A great and wonderful light spreads over the entire universe and makes all living beings happy and kind. The blind see, the deaf hear, the wicked love righteous ways, and even the pains of the sufferers in the purgatories are assuaged. But an earthquake is also a necessary incident on such an occasion.[19] A Buddha's life is marked and punctuated with six " earthquakes " : the earth shakes and trembles when he is conceived, when he is born, when he attains Enlightenment, when he begins to preach, when he decides to pass away soon (instead of living for an aeon), and when he dies. Such a *bodhisattva's* mother dies seven days after his birth, because she is so holy that she may not continue to live as an ordinary wife, or because she must be spared the pain of witnessing her son's Renunciation later on.[20] This general law has of course been deduced from the fact of the death of Gautama Buddha's mother. Several other beings, who are subsequently associated with Gautama Buddha's life, are born on the same day, viz. his wife, his charioteer Chandaka, the horse Kaṇṭhaka, and many other princes, servants and horses.

In this account of the birth of the *bodhisattva*, the seven steps and the earthquake seem to have a certain symbolic significance. E. Senart explains even Māyā as a symbolic name, but we need not go so far.[21] He also attaches much importance to the trees in the Lumbinī grove, as he rightly believes that the legend has much in common with the myth of the birth of Apollo at Delos. He says : " Je veux parler de la légende de Delos sur la naissance d'Apollon ; il est aussi impossible d'en nier que d'en expliquer par le hasard l'étonnante conformité avec notre scène, ... une scène toute mythologique, remontant à une époque réculée du developpement légendaire." [22] Apollo also walks about after birth and declares that he must proclaim the will of Zeus ; but it is difficult to conceive how the Greek myth could have become known in India before the Christian era.[23] It does not belong to the mythology of the Aryans before the dispersion of the tribes, and nothing exactly like it is found in the *Vedas*. The idea of being born from the mother's side is referred to in a hymn of the *Ṛgveda* (iv, 18.1, *ayaṃ panthā anuvittaḥ purāṇo*, etc., vol. iii, page 100). It may appear rather strange that an earthquake should mark certain auspicious events. We associate an earthquake with loss of life and property, but it is probable that the Buddhists meant only a slight tremor as a gesture of delight and approval on the part of the *devatā* of the earth. E. Senart and E. Windisch do not offer any suggestion with regard to the earthquake. The earth is regarded as a goddess in the mythology of many races. L. Spence says : " The earth was personalized by early man, who regarded it as the parent of all things dwelling thereon. . . . . Early man seems to have regarded it as his mother. . . . The Earth-Mother, then, would be practically universal. We should expect to find her everywhere, and indeed we do. In the Vedic hymns, the earth is the bride of Dyaus ; in Greece she was known as Gaea . . . In Mexico more than one god was connected with the earth." [24] But earthquakes are seldom mentioned in the myths of the world, and they are usually considered to be calamities due to the action of demons. P. Ehrenreich says : " Erdbeben werden bekanntlich fast überall auf die Bewegungen fabelhafter dämonischer oder tierischer Erdträger zurückgeführt, sei es, dass diese ihren Unwillen äussern oder nur ihre unbequeme Stellung verändern wollen. . . In Afrika gelten auch rein animistische oder manistische Agenzien als Ursache der Erschütterung. Es sind die Seelen mächtiger Häuptlinge, die auch den Charakter von Lokaldämonen annehmen können." [25] But these earthquakes in Buddhist mythology are connected with auspicious events like the conception and birth of a Buddha. It may therefore be permissible to venture on the tentative explanation that has been suggested above. As regards the seven steps, these are certainly of a symbolic character. In a Hindu marriage ceremony, the bride and the bridegroom take seven steps together round the sacred fire.[26] The *Mahā-vastu* offers the prosaic explanation that the *bodhisattva* is tired of sitting in the womb for a long time and therefore walks about. After the seventh step, the *devas* take hold of him.[27] The *Buddha-carita* gives us a better clue, as it compares the *bodhisattva* to the stars of the constellation " Seven *Ṛṣis* ".[28] E. Windisch does not attach much importance to this passage, as he says : " Aus diesem Vergleiche etwa zu schliessen, dass Buddha astraler Natur sei, halte ich für logisch unberechtigt." [29] E. Senart is silent on this point. It may be suggested that the seven steps perhaps correspond to the seven " planets ", which give their names to the days of the week. The *bodhisattva's* movements bear some relation to the solar system as conceived by the ancient world. The number Seven occurs frequently in mythology. A choir of swans flew seven times round Delos after the birth of Apollo. Seven miraculous trees flourished on the Kuen Lün mountains in China.[30]

II. The Superman

As a child, boy and youth, the *bodhisattva* is a prodigy of strength, skill and erudition. The *Lal. V.* also relates that the images of the *devas* fall down before him on the occasion of his visit to the temple.[31] This incident is intended to prove the superiority of the *bodhisattva* to the *devas* and of Buddhism to Hinduism. When the *bodhisattva* is taken to the school, it is found that he knows as many as sixty-four languages and scripts.[32] At a later period, he shows that he is well-versed in all the arts and sciences: archery, swimming, writing, arithmetic, poetry, grammar, painting, drama, music, dancing, history and the technical crafts.[33] The *bodhisattva* is thus represented as a veritable Superman, who possesses the most varied intellectual accomplishments. He has finished the most complete course of liberal education that can be imagined. Aristotle, Plato, Albertus Magnus, Leonardo de Vinci, Mezzofanti, Goethe and other versatile polymaths pale into insignificance in comparison with this *bodhisattva*. The Buddhist writers were indebted to the portraits of the heroes of the *Rāmāyaṇa* and the *Mahābhārata* for this ideal of a perfectly cultured and educated man. The Pāli canon does not speak much of Buddha's knowledge of the arts and sciences. According to the *Lal. V.*, a *bodhisattva* in his last existence is a master of all profane learning. He is also endowed with beauty, strength and physical fitness. His voice is sweet and deep: his body shines like gold, or even more than gold.[34] He is expert in all the sports and exercises of manly youths. He is so strong that he can send a dead elephant flying over the walls of the town by pushing it with his toe.[35] He excels all athletes in running, wrestling, swimming and other sports. He wins a wrestling match against five hundred young men.[36] He surpasses even Arjuna's exploits in archery. His body is not only lovely and powerful, but is also marked by the thirty-two principal signs of the *mahāpuruṣa* (great man) and his eighty secondary or minor characteristics. They are due to his self-control in previous lives (*Sam. Rā.*, fol. 193*a*, 1). The thirty-two principal marks are as follows (according to the *Lal. V.*)[37]:

(1) His head is like a cap in shape (or like a royal turban). E. Burnouf interprets the term *uṣṇīṣa-çīrṣa* as meaning "having a bump on the head"[38] (Pāli: *unhīsa-sīso. sahaj-oṣṇīṣa-mastakaḥ*; *Kṣemendra*, i, 671). E. Senart compares the *uṣṇīṣa* to the *kaparda* of *Çiva* and *Rudra*, and says: "Toutefois, parmi les interprétations auxquelles il donne lieu, l'une fait de *l'uṣṇīṣa* une disposition particulière de la chevelure, ramenée sur le sommet de la tête."

(2) His hair turns towards the right in locks, which are dark-blue like a peacock's tail or mixed collyrium. The *M. Vy.* and *Dh. S.* say nothing about the colour of the hair.

(3) His forehead is even and broad.

(4) Between his eyebrows there is white hair, which has the lustre of snow and silver (*ūrṇā.* Pāli : *uṇṇā*). E. Senart compares the *ūrṇā* to the white hair on the breast of *Viṣṇu* and *Kṛṣṇa*, to the eyebrows of Zeus, the third eye of *Çiva*, etc.[39] But his analogies are generally superficial. It is a curious fact that the *M. Vy.* gives *ūrṇā-keçaḥ* (having woolly hair ?). But Csoma's list has *ūrṇā-koça* ("hair of treasure" on the forehead). This is incorrect, as Tibetan *spu* means "hair" (Tib. Dicy., 798).

(5) His eyelashes are like a cow's (i.e. "completely surrounding the eyes, thick like a black cow's"; or, "bright and soft like a new-born red calf's").

(6) The pupils of his eyes are very dark (*abhinīla*).

(7) He has forty teeth, which are even (or, "of equal size").

(8) There are no gaps or interstices between one tooth and another (*avirala-danta.* Pāli : *avivara*).

(9) He has white teeth (or "very white").

(10) He has an excellent voice (*brahma-svara*).

(11) His sense of taste is very acute and keen (*rasa-rasāgratā*).[40] E. Senart points out that *Agni* in the *Ṛgveda* has many teeth and tongues. E. Burnouf explains : "Il a la supériorité du goût des saveurs" ("Lotus", p. 567).

(12) His tongue is large and slender (*prabhūta-tanu-jihva*).

(13) His jaw is like a lion's. E. Senart refers to the epithet of *Agni* in the *Ṛgveda*.

(14) He has evenly-rounded shoulders. (*Susaṃvṛtta* has also been rendered as "even", "symmetrical," "equally rounded." Pāli : *samavattakkhandho.*) *Skandha* refers to "the exterior of the whole vocal apparatus," and not merely to the trunk or the shoulders. It has also been translated as "bust". E. Foucaux translates : "le bras bien arrondi."

(15) He has seven convex surfaces or prominences. (*sapt-otsada, sapt-occhada*; i.e. the backs of the four limbs, the shoulders and the trunk are well fleshed. Pāli : *sattussado.*) Csoma translates : "Of seven spans in stature" (p. 93).

(16) The space between his shoulders is well filled up (literally, "heaped up"; *cit-āntarāṃsa*).

(17) His skin is fine and of the colour of gold.

(18) When he is standing erect and not bending, his arms reach down to the knees.

(19) The front part of his body is like a lion.

(20) His body has the symmetrical proportions of a banyan-tree (*nyagrodha*). " It was believed that a banyan always measured the same in height and width " (*Dialogues* ii, 15). " The *bodhisattva's* height is equal to his outstretched arms " (E. J. Thomas : " Buddha ", p. 220).

(21) Each hair on his body rises straight upward.

(22) Each hair curls to the right.

(23) His private member is concealed in a sheath.

(24) He has well-rounded thighs.

(25) His legs are like an antelope's.

(26) He has long fingers.

(27) He has long heels.

(28) He has prominent ankles (*utsaṅga-pāda*. Pāli : *ussaṅkha-pādo*). Csoma reads *ucchaṅkha-pāda* and translates : " the joints of the ar'-les do not appear." The Tibetan equivalent is *shabs-kyi loṅ-bu-mi-mṅonpa*, which means, " the ankle-bone of the foot is not conspicuous " (Tib. Dicy. 363, 1224). The Tibetan interpretation is just the opposite of the usual explanation. Other renderings are as follows :—

" His ankles are like rounded shells (*T. W. Rhys Davids* : Dialogues ii, 14 ; iii, 138).

Lord Chalmers : " His ankles are over the exact middle of his tread " (*Majjh.* tr., ii, 72).

E. J. Thomas : " Prominent ankles " (" Buddha ", p. 240).

F. Max Müller : " Having the foot arched " (*Dh. S.*, p. 53).

E. Burnouf : " Il a le cou-de-pied saillant " (" Lotus ", p. 573).

(29) His hands and feet are soft and delicate.

(30) His hands and feet are webbed or netted. (*jāl-āṅguli-hasta-pāda*. Pāli : *jāla-hattha-pādo.*) Other renderings are as follows :—

" Hands and feet like a net " (T. W. Rhys Davids : Dialogues, ii, 14). " Les doigts de ses pieds et de ses mains sont marqués de réseaux " (E. Burnouf, " Lotus," 573–4).

" His fingers and toes spring clean, without webbing between them " (*Majjh.* tr., ii, 72).

" Les doigts de ses pieds et de ses mains sont réunis par une membrane, jusqu'à la première phalange " (P. Foucaux, *Lal. V.*, trsln., p. 96).

"Netted hands and feet" (E. J. Thomas, "Buddha," p. 220).

"His hands have the fingers united by a membrane" (A. B. Keith: "Indian Mythology," p. 195). The Pāli Dicy. explains thus: "having net-like hands and feet, probably with reference to long nails." E. J. Thomas refers to the webbed fingers of some of the Gandhāra statues, and adds: "But this was only a device of the sculptor to give strength to parts likely to be broken, since this feature only occurs when the fingers stand out. Buddhaghoṣa appears to have known this view, as he denies that the fingers were webbed, and says that one with such a defect could not receive ordination. That the network of lines on the hand was originally intended is a sufficient explanation. Buddhaghoṣa's own view is not likely to be the primitive one. He says that the four fingers and five toes were of equal length (as he no doubt saw them on statues), and that when Buddha entwined his fingers, they were like a window with a lattice made by a skilful carpenter" ("Buddha", p. 222). The difficulty seems to be that the Pāli text reads simply *jāla-hattha-pādo* (*Dīgha* ii, 17), but the *M. Vy.* and the *Divy.* give *jāl-āvanaddha-hasta-pādaḥ*. The *Mtu.* has *jāla*, but it does not mention the epithets in their fully developed form, and one manuscript reads *jālī* (*Mtu.*, ii, 30). The *Dh. S.* gives a corrupt reading, which may be understood to stand for *jāl-ābaddh-ānguli-pāṇi-pāda-talatā*. Thus several Sanskrit texts seem to differ from the Pāli in inserting a participle (*avanaddha* or *ābaddha*) after *jāla* and also mentioning the fingers. Perhaps the Pāli and the Sanskrit terms do not mean the same thing. The Sanskritists may have altered the phrase in order to explain the "webbed fingers" of the Gandhāra statues. It is a curious circumstance that Csoma's Tibetan list omits this item altogether. But the Tibetan equivalent is *phyag daṅ shabs dra-bas ḥbrel-ba*, which means "having the hands and feet connected with a web or net". The word *dra-ba* is also employed in a compound, which denotes "web-footed, like a goose or duck"; and the word *ḥbrel-ba* is used in a phrase which means, "her fingers and toes adhered together, like the toes of a goose" (Tib. Dicy., 646, 933).

(31) On the soles of his feet, there are two wheels, white, radiant and luminous, with a thousand spokes, and (complete) with rim and nave (tyre and hub). The *Dh. S.* and *M. Vy.* simply mention that *the hands* and the feet are marked with wheels, and Csoma's Tibetan list agrees with them. The wheel is not described,

as it is in the *Lal. V.* The *Mtu.* omits the wheel altogether (ii, 29).

It has been suggested that the wheel is the symbol of the sun; but it really represents universal sovereignty, as is clearly indicated in the *Mahā-sudassana-sutta* (*Dīgha*, iii, 169 ff.). The word *cakra-vartin* is associated with a "wheel", though *cakra* originally meant "sphere of power" in that word. E. Senart of course discerns a solar attribute in the wheel. He says: "C'est le propre *cakra*, à mille raies, de *Viṣṇu*, un des emblèmes les plus antiques et les plus populaires du soleil ..... Cette roue .... peut même paraître issue d'une conception du soleil considéré directement comme le pied du dieu lumineux ...... Ce pied unique formerait avec la roue unique du char solaire un parallélisme frappant (*Ṛgveda*, i, 164.2)".[41] But the analogy is very defective. The *bodhisattva* bears the figure of the wheel on the soles of both feet, and, according to some accounts, on his hands too. It is not easy to understand why he should bear so many symbols of the sun on his body. A wheel is one of the seven "jewels" of a universal monarch, and a Buddha is also said to "turn the wheel" of the Doctrine. In the sculptures of Bharhut, the wheel represents the preaching of the first sermon by Gautama Buddha.[42] Hence a *bodhisattva*, who is born with this mark, must become either a universal ruler (*cakra-vartin*) or a Buddha (*dharma-cakra-pravartin*). E. J. Thomas has clearly shown the untenability of the solar hypothesis in this case ("Buddha", pp. 219 ff.).

(32) His feet are well-set (well-planted). "The traditional meaning is that the whole under-surface touched the ground at once" (Dialogues, ii, 14).

The eighty secondary marks are similar to these principal characteristics in many respects. They are described in the *Mahā-vastu*, the *Lal. V.*, the *M. Vy.*, and the *Dh. S.*[43]

With regard to the origin of these signs of a *mahāpuruṣa*, it is admitted that the theory of the *mahāpuruṣa* existed before the rise of Buddhism. E. Senart has traced it through the epics and the *Upaniṣads* back to the *Atharva-veda* (x, 2, p. 217), and even to the *Puruṣa-sūkta* of the *Ṛgveda* (x, 90; vol. vi, p. 243). But the theory of the bodily marks of a *mahāpuruṣa* has very little in common with the idea of the primeval mythical *Puruṣa* with a thousand heads, a thousand eyes and a thousand feet. It is more probable that the epithets applied to the heroes of the great epics gave rise to the list of the thirty-two signs. Rāma is described in the

Rāmāyaṇa as *vipul-āṃsa*, *mahā-bāhu*, *mahā-hanu*, *ājānu-bāhu*, *sulalāṭa*, *sama-vibhakt-āṅga*, *pīna-vakṣas*, *viçāl-ākṣa*, etc.[44] The doctrine of the marks is pre-Buddhistic, as the Pāli canon speaks of *brahmins* who profess to interpret them, and it also disapproves of such occupations.[45] Some of the marks indicate the poet's ideal of manly beauty, e.g. white and regular teeth, a broad chest, black hair, dark eyes, rotundity of figure, etc. Others are symbolic: the covered male organ typifies lifelong chastity; the long tongue betokens success as a preacher, or it may be an emblem of the sun's rays. A few marks may be due to some tradition with regard to Gautama Buddha's physiognomy. Some are clearly borrowed from Gandhāra sculpture, which created a figure of Buddha in imitation of the Hellenic statues of Apollo. A. Foucher says: "Aux grands Dieux, aux *bodhisattvas*, au Buddha, ils semblent avoir été d'accord pour réserver le type idéal de Phoebus-Apollon . . . Les Buddha, qui tous ont la tête découverte et la marque de *l'ūrṇā* au front . . . La routine des imitateurs gandhariens vient de créer de toutes pièces la bosse de *l'uṣṇīṣa*, dans l'acception bouddhique et postérieure du mot . . . Une malfaçon de leurs pâles imitateurs fait surgir sur la tête du Maître . . . une protubérance d'un caractère anormal." [46]

The thirty-two marks thus owe their origin to the national æsthetic ideal, spiritual symbolism and Gandhāra art. The eighty minor marks are due chiefly to the fussy fatuity of the Buddhist writers, who could not leave well alone.

III. Marriage, Renunciation and Penance

The *bodhisattva* is thus physically and intellectually a very highly developed man. Even as a boy, he is fond of Meditation and once experiences the first *dhyāna*, as he sits under a tree in rapt Concentration.[47] This incident seems to be an early rehearsal of the final scene under the *bodhi*-tree. His father naturally wishes that the young man should become a powerful monarch, and not a Buddha. He surrounds his son with the greatest comfort and luxury in gorgeous palaces. The *bodhisattva* marries only in order to conform to social custom, as he is free from passion. This general law applies to such a *bodhisattva*. Here the Buddhist writers have made a necessary compromise between fact and theory. They do not go so far as those Jainas, who deny the fact of Mahāvīra's marriage.[48] But they spiritualise the marriage and deduce the general rule for all *bodhisattvas* in their last lives. In the meantime, the *bodhisattva* sees four signs (*nimittāni*) that precede his Renunciation. The *devas* show him an old man, a sick man, a corpse and an ascetic.[49] This incident has been invented as the concrete illustration of a passage in the Pāli canon, in which Buddha declares that he pondered on the realities of old age, sickness and death in the days before the Renunciation.[50] The Buddhas of the universe also exhort and rouse the *bodhisattva* by reminding him of his great Vow and the practice of the Perfections in his past lives.[51] All *bodhisattvas* receive such a *sañcodanā* (instigation, prompting) from these Buddhas before the Renunciation. At last, the *bodhisattva* leaves his home at night and becomes a wandering monk and student. All such *bodhisattvas* take this step. The *devas* help them in their flight by opening the gates, sending the people to sleep, and rendering other services.[52] Gautama Buddha becomes the disciple of two teachers, but this rule does not apply to all *bodhisattvas*, as they are supposed to have mastered all the methods of study and meditation in their previous lives. The next event in the careers of all *bodhisattvas* is the performance of austerities.[53] This rule is derived from the facts of Gautama Buddha's life; but quite new motives for the action are adduced, so that the *bodhisattva* should not be supposed to undergo the penance from lack of wisdom. The *bodhisattva* gives up his austerities, eats proper food, and resolves to seek Enlightenment by Musing and Concentration. He dreams five dreams that seem to augur well for his success. The next day, he goes in the evening to a tree and sits cross-legged under it with the firm determination to win Enlightenment. He is accompanied and praised by many *devas*.[54] All such *bodhisattvas* sit in the same way under a tree on the night of Enlightenment. The seat is called the *bodhi-maṇḍa* (throne of *bodhi*). But the hardest ordeal now remains. The great duel with *Māra* begins at this point. Who and what is this *Māra*, who must be defeated and conquered before *bodhi* can be attained?

IV. Māra and the Bodhisattva

(1) *Māra in the Pāli canon.* The word *Māra* (Pāli: *Māro*) is derived from the root *mṛ* (to die). The *Atharva-veda* mentions a *Māra*, who is associated with *Yama*, Death, and other

evil powers (vi, 93, 1, page 129; *Yamo mṛtyur agha-māro nirṛtho babhruḥ*, etc.). In the post-*Vedic* literature, *Mṛtyu* (Death) is spoken of as *pāpmā* (wicked or evil) in several passages: e.g. *tāny asya garbha' eva santi pāpmā mṛtyur agṛhṇāt*; *sarvāṇi bhūtani pāpmano mṛtyospṛṇavānīti* (*Çatapatha Brāhmaṇa*, viii, 4, 2, pp. 433, 434). As E. Windisch has pointed out, *Pāpman* is also the subject of a hymn in the *Atharva-veda* (vi, 26, page 111; *Ava mā pāpmantsṛja vaçī, etc.*).[55] It may be taken to mean "Misery, Misfortune, Evil". *Māra* is called *Namuci* in Buddhist literature, and *Namuci* is mentioned as an *asura* (demon) in the *Ṛgveda* (x, 131, 4, *yuvaṃ surāmaṃ açvinā namucāv-āsure sacā*). *Māra* has been identified by E. Senart with the ancient symbols of Death, *Yama*, *Mṛtyu*, etc., as the name evidently means "the slayer".[56] H. Kern derives it from *mala* (dirt, impurity) or *marīci* (ray, mirage); but this etymology is merely fantastic.[57] The words, *Māra*, *Namuci* and *pāpman* (Pāli: *pāpimā*) are thus found in pre-Buddhistic literature. In the Pāli canon, *Māra* is also called *kaṇha* (black. *Sutta-nipāta*, 967, page 187), probably because he was in some way associated with the mythology of the aboriginal tribes of India.[58] *Māra* is an important figure in the mythology of the Buddhists. We find the following phrase in many passages of the Pāli canon: "this universe, with the *devas*, *Māra* and *Brahmā*, recluses and *brahmins*."[59] In the *Mahāparinibbāna-sutta*, Buddha tells Ānanda that *Māra* has a regular assembly.[60] In the *Māratajjaniya-sutta* of the *Majjhima-Nikāya*, Mahā-Moggalāna says that he was formerly a *Māra* named *Dūsī*, and committed certain sins in that life (*Majjhima*, i, 333 ff.). In the *Māra-saṃyutta*, *Māra* appears as an elephant and a snake in order to frighten Buddha.[61] He assumes the form of a peasant and disturbs Buddha's preaching.[62] He tries to distract the audience by making a terrific noise. Such half-comic exploits end in his discomfiture, as it appears that he is nonplussed and rendered harmless, if his identity is discovered. *Diṭṭho si* (thou art seen) is the formula that can always be employed against him. He enters Moggallāna's stomach, which feels heavy in consequence; but the saint recognises him.[63] *Māra* also tempts the nuns in the disguise of a man.[64] He goes about as a mist or a cloud of smoke in order to search for the *viññāṇa* of a monk, who has committed suicide.[65] In the *Mahāvagga*, *Māra* appears twice and tries to assert his power over Buddha, who sternly repels and repudiates him.[66] In the *Nidāna-kathā*, he attacks Buddha with nine storms of rain, wind, rocks, weapons, charcoal ashes, sand, mud and darkness; and his elephant is 150 leagues in height.[67]

In all such Pāli texts, *Māra* appears as a living, active and mischievous imp or celestial being. This is his personal aspect: he is a mythological being with a distinct individuality, like *Sakka* and other *devas*. But there is also an impersonal aspect of *Māra*. In many passages, he is regarded merely as the symbol of Evil, Sin, Desire and Temptation. He then belongs more to the realm of Allegory than of Myth. Sensuous pleasure and the sixfold "Sphere of Sense" are said to be his Domain.[68] He cannot obtain entrance (*otāra*), if a monk practises virtue and self-control.[69] *Māra's* three daughters are allegorical, not mythical, creatures: they are named *Taṇhā* (Craving), *Arati* (Aversion) and *Ragā* (*Sutta-nipāta*, verse 835). In the *Padhāna-sutta*, his mythical personality is not prominent: he serves only as a symbol of Temptation.[70] In some passages, phenomenal existence as such is identified with *Māra*, and *Māra* is said to be equivalent to the five *khandhas* and all perishable things and phenomena (*Rādha-saṃyutta*, *Saṃyutta-Nikāya*, iii, 189).[71] In such utterances, the impersonal and allegorical aspect of *Māra* is emphasised, and the personal, mythical aspect seems to be entirely ignored.

(2) In Buddhist Sanskrit literature, *Māra* has also a personal and an impersonal aspect. In his personal aspect, he is the chief of the *devas* who are collectively called "the *mārakāyikas*".[72] There are millions of these *devas*.[73] *Māra* has the old titles: *namuci*, *kṛṣṇa-bandhu*, *pāpīyān*.[74] He is especially the god of Desire and Lust in general; he represents all that is detrimental to progress towards Enlightenment. He is not chiefly or primarily associated with the idea of Death. E. Windisch lays stress on the wrong point, when he says: "Buddha besiegt den Tod, der Tod will sich nicht besiegen lassen; das sind die primären Gedanken, die der Māralegende zu Grunde liegen." [75] But the victory over Death is not emphasised in the same degree as the conquest of *kāma*. *Māra* is first and foremost the god of Lust, Passion, Craving, Desire. One of his daughters is named *Tṛṣṇā*, and he is spoken of as "the Lord of Desire" (*kām-ādhipati*).[76] He is distinctly identified with Cupid (*manmatha*, *kāma-deva*) by Açvaghoṣa and Kṣemendra.[77] He is "the supreme Lord of the eyes of beautiful women."[78] He tempts *Cūḍāmaṇi* and others as the god of Love.[79] Besides *kāma*, *Māra* is most frequently associated with *kleça* (sin,

evil, moral corruption in general).[80] *Kleça* is coupled with *māra-karma* (*Māra's* deeds) in the *Laṅkāvatāra-sūtra* (p. 102.14). He is thus the god of Lust and Sin, but he is not the ruler of the gods of the *kāma-dhātu*, as E. Senart incorrectly assumes ("le chef des dieux de la région des sens).[81] The gods of the *kāma-dhātu* live in six heavens with their separate chiefs. It is indeed a peculiar circumstance that the *devas* of the *Māra* class are not assigned to any heaven in the realm of *kāma*. Their exact position in Buddhist cosmology is not known. In his personal aspect, *Māra* plays many pranks and resorts to various tricks in order to impede every *bodhisattva's* spiritual development. He dissuades a *bodhisattva* from giving alms to the monks or the poor. He even employs the desperate stratagem of creating a phantom *naraka* (purgatory) near the door of the house in order to prevent a charitable householder from going out and helping a monk.[82] He can assume the shape and form of Gautama Buddha and show himself to the monk Upagupta, who is very eager to see Buddha's physical body. Upagupta and he part good friends, and it is even reported that *Māra* is converted and his occupation is thus gone, perhaps for ever.[83] But he can also preach false doctrine and mislead the faithful in this convenient disguise.[84] He sows discord among the *bodhisattvas* and dissuades them from diligence in study.[85] He disturbs the congregations and distracts their attention during a *bodhisattva's* sermons.[86] He appears as a heretical teacher in the great contest of the miracles between Buddha and the other religious preachers.[87] He tries to frighten the *bodhisattvas* by pestering them with fiery meteors (*ulkā-pātān*).[88] He troubles a pious *bodhisattva* by hiding all the water in a certain region.[89] In various ways, he asserts his power and shows that he is alive and at work. But a *bodhisattva* can always defeat him by means of magical spells and circles, and also by the power of Virtue and Wisdom.[90]

The personal aspect of *Māra* is not so important in later Buddhist literature as it is in the *Mahā-vastu* and the *Lal. V.* His interesting and concrete figure is resolved in an increasing degree into the abstract idea of Evil. "*Māra-karma*" does not always denote the actual presence of the *deva Māra* or his myrmidons, just as such English words as "diabolical" and "devilry" are now dissociated from the conception of the Tempter, who talked to Job and Jesus. This impersonal aspect of *Māra* is emphasised by the Buddhist writers, who have devised the formula of the four *Māras*.[91]

In this list, the personal *Māra* is allotted only one place, while the impersonal *Māra* consists of three items. It is clear that the former has receded into the background : he is called *deva-putra-māra*. But the other three *Māras* are identified with the principles of sin, individuality and transiency. They are named *kleça-māra* (Sin, Passion), *skandha-māra* (Aggregates, Components of individual existence) and *mṛtyu-māra* (Death). Here the general term *kleça* has replaced the old narrower word *kāma*. There is a *samādhi*, which can rout these four *Māras*.[92] The *Da. Bhū.* speaks of " the ways of the four *Māras* " (*catur-māra-pathāḥ*).[93] This impersonal triple *Māra* incites a *bodhisattva* to sins and spiritual errors. He is especially noted for fostering Pride in the heart (*māna*, *abhimāna*, *manyanā*), particularly when a *bodhisattva* performs miracles or practises austerities.[94] The *Pr. Pā. Aṣṭa.* earnestly warns a *bodhisattva* against the dangers of Pride in all its forms.[95] The well-known " army of *Māra* " must also be supposed to belong to this impersonal *Māra*, as it only consists of different vices, evils and errors : "lusts, aversion, hunger, thirst, craving, torpor-and-stolidity, fear, doubt, anger, hypocrisy, avarice, love of fame, self-praise, envy and censoriousness." [96] Çāntideva clearly explains the nature of the impersonal *Māra* by enumerating several *māra-karmāṇi*, which are also called " the hooks of *Māra* " (*mār-āṅkuça*). Lack of earnestness and diligence in study ; quarrels and controversies ; anxious thoughts for one's relatives or about the necessaries of life ; discord between teachers and pupils ; indifference to continual spiritual progress among the recluses ; compliance with the advice of bad friends who do not appreciate the ideal of the Mahāyāna, and improper and unsuitable activity : all such things are " the work of *Māra* ".[97] The *Pr. Pā. Aṣṭa.* teaches how this *Māra* can be defeated and frustrated. A *bodhisattva* never abandons the living beings (i.e., continues to serve them) ; he regards all phenomena as empty (*çūnya*) ; his actions are in harmony with his words ; and he is helped and honoured by the Buddhas. These are a *bodhisattva's* four weapons against this *Māra*.[98] *Māra* is also pained and rendered powerless by the practice of self-control and the acceptance of the true faith.[99]

(3) *The Bodhisattva's Last Struggle against Māra.*

In the *bodhisattva's* combat with *Māra*, both the personal and impersonal aspects of *Māra* are emphasised with almost equal force. But the final victory is won over the personal *Māra*, as the mythological element has become more important than the allegory in the *Lal. V.* and the *Mtu.* The *bodhisattva's* last struggle with *Māra* under the tree falls into two parts :—

(i) *Māra's* attempt to persuade the *bodhisattva* to give up the holy life and the pursuit of Enlightenment, and (ii) *Māra's* violent attack on the *bodhisattva* for driving him away from the tree. In the spiritual duel, the impersonal metaphysical *Māra* is predominant. In the real "battle", the personal *Māra* of the myths is the leader of the demon-hordes.

The *Mahā-vastu* suddenly introduces *Māra* without dilating on his motive, but *Māra* explains further on that the *bodhisattva's* success will deprive him of his dominion over the multitude.[100] The *Mtu.* relates several stories to show that the *bodhisattva* had also outwitted and checkmated *Māra* on different occasions in his previous lives. In the *B. Ct.*, *Māra* says that the *bodhisattva* may conquer his realms and make them empty.[101] Kṣemendra also relates that *Māra* comes on his own initiative.[102] But the *Lal. V.* explains that the *bodhisattva* deliberately challenges *Māra* and informs him with regard to the situation, so that he may do his worst and also perhaps learn the true law in the end. His defeat would lead to the submission of all the *devas* of the realm of sensuous Desire and the ultimate conversion of his followers. The *bodhisattva* then emits a ray of light which communicates his message to *Māra*.[103] *Māra* too dreams a dream with thirty-two ominous signs that seem to foretell his doom.[104] *Māra* gets ready to defend his empire. But it must be stated that his house is divided against itself. The *Māra* of the Sanskrit treatises has offspring in both aspects of his dual personality. The impersonal *Māra* has three daughters, who are usually named *Rati* (Lust, Attachment), *Arati* (Aversion, Discontent, Unrest) and *Tṛṣṇā* (Craving).[105] Açvaghoṣa does not follow the Pāli tradition in this respect and gives them other names, viz. *Rati*, *Prīti* (in the sense of Love, Attachment), and *Tṛṣā* (= *Tṛṣṇā*). He also speaks of three sons of *Māra*: *Vibhrama* (Confusion, Error), *Harṣa* (Elation) and *Darpa* (Pride).[106] But the *Lal. V.* creates a numerous family for the personal *Māra*, who is said to have "a thousand sons".[107] Some names are also given, e.g. Sārthavāha, Durmati, Madhuranirghoṣa, Çatabāhu, Subuddhi, Sunetra, Ugratejas, Dīrghabāhu, Bhayaṅkara, etc.[108] It is clear that these names are mythical, and not allegorical. They are modelled on the names of the warriors of the *Rāmāyaṇa* and the *Mahābhārata*. The *Mtu.* simply states that *Māra's* sons Sārthavāha and Janīsuta tried to dissuade him from attacking the *bodhisattva.*[109] But the *Lal. V.* describes a protracted debate between the two parties, into which *Māra's* children are divided on account of differences of opinion with regard to the projected conflict.[110] Some were eager for the fray, while the others counselled prudence and discretion. We seem to hear distant echoes of the scenes in Rāvaṇa's palace in Laṅkā before the struggle with Rāma.[111] It is probable that the *Lal. V.* is indebted to the *Rāmāyaṇa* for this animated discussion.

The account of the *bodhisattva's* last struggle against *Māra* is an amalgam of allegory and myth.

(*a*) *The Allegory*. The struggle between the *bodhisattva* and the impersonal *Māra* is really an allegory, like other similar stories of temptation. The *bodhisattva's* allegorical conflict with this *Māra* begins early in his last existence. When he renounces his home, *Māra* appears and tells him that he should continue to live in the world, as he may obtain the wheel of universal sovereignty after seven days.[112] Later, when the *bodhisattva* practises austerities, *Māra* comes, tries to persuade him to give up his strivings, and says: "Thou art lean, pale and miserable. Death is near thee. Death has a thousand parts of thee: life is only one part. If thou givest alms and sacrificest (to the gods) day and night, thou shalt gain great Merit: what hast thou to do with striving?"[113] The *bodhisattva* repels *Māra* on this occasion. When he sits under the *bodhi*-tree, the last fight begins. The *Mahā-vastu* relates that *Māra* tempts the *bodhisattva* to return to the royal palace and enjoy sensual pleasures, as he is still young and healthy. *Māra* also speaks of the great sacrifices (*mahā-yajñāni*) that should be offered by such a powerful monarch (e.g. *açva-medha*, *puruṣa-medha*, etc.).[114] According to the *Lal. V.*, *Māra* exclaims in an envious mood: "Rise, O Prince, rise. Your Merit is such that you can enjoy sovereignty. But how can you obtain Liberation?"[115] The *bodhisattva* replies that he despises worldly power and grandeur, as he has already sacrificed wealth, limbs and life many times in many existences. The *devatā* of the earth, *Sthāvarā*, rises out of the ground and corroborates the *bodhisattva's* statement.[116] Finally, *Māra* sends his daughters to tempt the *bodhisattva* with their womanly wiles, which are said to be of thirty-two kinds. They engage in a lengthy discussion on the advantages and disadvantages of the *kāmas*, and the *bodhisattva* declares that he is absolutely free from passion and lust.[117] *Māra's* discomfiture is now complete. The *bodhisattva* has withstood the temptations of Sovereignty and Love.

Here the allegory ends, and the myth begins.

(*b*) *The Myth*. *Māra* now attacks the *bodhisattva* with a vast army of hideous and grotesque demons and monsters. It has been suggested that the metaphorical phrase, "*Namuci's* army", which is applied in the *Pādhana-sutta* to several sins and vices, gave rise to the conception of a real fourfold army of warriors. But this is hardly probable. The allegory and the myth are derived from different sources. The allegory is the product of the poetic imagination, like Spenser's Faerie Queene and the *Prabodha-caṇdr-odaya*; but the myth has its roots in the dim and distant past of the race, when the battles between the *devas* and the *asuras*, the Hellenic gods and the Titans, *Indra* and *Vṛtra*, Thor and the Jötunn, were first visualised and described.[118] It is almost impossible to bridge the gulf between the simple allegory and the impressive myth in this case. The few moral faults mentioned in the *Padhāna-sutta* could not have been developed into the terrible horde of ugly, fantastic and repulsive monsters, who are led by *Māra's* general. *Māra* is a king and rides an enormous elephant. The demons and monsters are described in detail in the *Mtu.*, the *Lal. V.*, the *B. Ct.* and the *Avadāna-kalpa-latā*.[119] Some are many-headed, many-armed, many-legged: others have no heads, arms or legs at all. Some vomit serpents; others devour them. Some consume the bones and flesh of men; others belch fire and smoke. The faces and the bodies of some of them are of different colours. Some have faces and ears like those of goats, boars, camels and fishes; the bodies of others resemble those of lions, tigers, monkeys, cats, snakes, tortoises and other beasts. Their bellies are protuberant and speckled. According to Kṣemendra, they number thirty-six *koṭis* (360 millions). These soldiers are armed with arrows, swords, spears, clubs, maces and other deadly weapons. They hurl these at the *bodhisattva* and also throw burning mountains at him. They shout: "Take, capture, bind, smite, tear, hack, slay, destroy this monk Gautama and the tree."[120] But the missiles and the fire are changed into flowers and a halo of light respectively through the power of the *bodhisattva's* Love.[121] The *bodhisattva* has also allies of a sort: the eight *devatās* of the *bodhi*-tree and the *devas* of the Pure

Abode try to discourage and weaken *Māra* by abusing and reviling him and also by predicting his speedy downfall.[122] The *bodhisattva* is not dismayed at all: he is supported by noble pride in his own personality and character (*ārya-māna*). He smiles like a saint and looks round like a lion. Like a lion, too, he coughs and yawns. *Māra* groans and laments in sixteen ways.[123] In the end, *Māra's* army is routed, but the final scene is described in different ways in the principal treatises. According to the *Mahā-vastu*, the *bodhisattva* strokes his head thrice, touches his couch and strikes the earth with his right hand. The earth shakes and gives out a deep and terrible sound; and *Māra's* hosts sink down and disappear. *Māra* writes these words with a reed on the ground: "Gautama will escape from my dominion."[124] This account is purely mythical: the Earth-goddess seems to help the *bodhisattva* in some way. But the *Lal. V.*, which intercalates the moral allegory between two onslaughts by the army, clearly indicates that *Māra* is defeated by the *bodhisattva's* virtue and wisdom. Here the allegory and the myth are strangely intertwined. The army is mythical, but the *bodhisattva's* defensive weapons are unmistakably allegorical. He is full of Love (*maitrī*); he understands by his wisdom that all things, including *Māra's* army, are illusory and non-substantial; and he speaks of the practice of the *pāramitās* in his past lives.[125] He declares that all the Buddhas, *devas* and living beings, and even the *pāramitās*, can bear witness to his fulfilment of a *bodhisattva's* complete discipline. He then touches the earth with his hand: this mythical act is the last incident of the conflict even in the *Lal. V.* *Māra's* army is then dispersed and destroyed. Açvaghoṣa does not mention the act of touching the earth; he puts a long hortatory speech into Gautama's mouth.[126] *Māra* retires, sad and downcast, and his soldiers flee in all directions. In Kṣemendra's account, too, the *bodhisattva* does not touch the earth.[127]

It is clear that both *Māra* and the tree belong to the realm of mythology. They are not mentioned in the earliest Pāli account.[128] According to the Pāli canon, every Buddha has his *bodhi*-tree. *Vipassin's* tree was a *pāṭali*, *Sikhin's* was a *puṇḍarīka*, and so on.[129] E. Senart thinks that the ancient myth about the struggle for ambrosia (*amṛta*) has been converted into history in this Buddhist legend. He says: "Dans le *Mahābhārata*, lors de la lutte que la possession de l'ambroisie soulève entre les Ādityas et les Daityas, ceux-ci sont armés de flêches, de massues, d'armes de tout genre. . . . . . C'est toujours, sous une forme un peu renouvelée, le vieux duel védique ; quelques traits en ont persisté, presque inaltérés jusque dans la légende des Buddhistes . . . . les démons ont les pieds et les mains coupés (*Indra* coupe les mains des *Asuras*) ; chez lui (*Māra*), la synthèse du caractère demoniaque et du caractère divin est justement l'un des traits les plus frappants . . . Le trône de l'arbre de *Bodhi* appartient à *Māra* ; le Buddha prétend l'en dépouiller. . . . . On a plusieurs fois comparé l'histoire de *Çākya* et de *Māra* a cette attaque tentée contre Zarathustra par Aṅro Mainyu . . . . . . La *Chāndogya Upanishad* connait l'*açvattha* qui donne l'ambroisie . . . L'arbre de *Bodhi* est l'arbre céleste . . . . . Toute la scène n'est, en dernière analyse, qu'une version particulière du mythe de la conquête de l'ambroisie . . . . La victoire de *Çākya* est toute solaire. La légende marque le lever du soleil comme l'heure décisive." [130] E. Senart would be more convincing, if he did not attempt to prove too much. H. Kern, who regards the history of Buddha as an allegory of the movements of the sun and other heavenly bodies, identifies *Māra* with the Spirit of Darkness, which is defeated by the Sun. A. B. Keith says: "Amid so much mythology, it seems unfair to reject the obvious conclusion that the tree is no ordinary tree, but the tree of life, and that the conflict with *Māra* represents a nature-myth." [131]

The conflict between Buddha and *Māra* is probably intended to be a replica of the struggle between *Indra* and *Vṛtra*, as it is described in the *Ṛgveda*.[132] The myth is very ancient, as the Zend-Avesta mentions "Verethraghna".[133] The glory of the old god is transferred to Buddha, who supplants him. There are also some echoes of the war between Rāma and Rāvaṇa. The custom of tree-worship has prevailed in many countries. J. G. Frazer says: "In the religious history of the Aryan race in Europe, the worship of trees has played an important part . . . . Tree-worship is well attested for all the great European families of the Aryan stock. Among the Celts, the oak-worship of the Druids is familiar to every one. Sacred groves were common among the ancient Germans . . . . . Proofs of the prevalence of tree-worship in ancient Greece and Italy are abundant. . . . . To the savage, the world in general is animate, and trees are no exception to the rule." [134] Several mysterious trees are also associated with the mythology of different races, e.g. the oak of Dodona, the world-tree of the Chaldaeans, the Yggdrasil of the

Scandinavians, the "Tree of all Seeds" of the Persians, the metal pine of the Japanese, the golden gem-bearing tree of the Egyptians, etc.[135] The *bodhi*-tree must also be added to this group.

V. Enlightenment

When the *bodhisattva* has defeated *Māra's* cohorts, he first experiences the four *dhyānas*. He then acquires the supernal organ of sight in the first watch of the night (*divya-cakṣus*). He thus destroys the Darkness (*tamas*) and produces Light (*ālokam*). In the middle watch of the night, he remembers his past lives and acquires the knowledge that arises from such remembrance (*vidyā*). In the last watch of the night, when dawn is breaking, he acquires and realises the knowledge of the destruction of the *āsravas*. He then reflects on the twelve items of the *pratītya-samutpāda* three times. First, he begins with Old-Age-and-Death, and thinks "What existing, does *jarā-maraṇa* come to be? What is its cause?" He repeats the same question till he comes to *avidyā*. The second time he begins with *avidyā*, and thinks thus: "The *saṃskāras* arise from *avidyā* as cause," and so on, till he reaches the last link of the chain. The third time he starts again with *jarā-maraṇa* and thinks thus: "What not existing, does *jarā-maraṇa* not come to be? What is that, by whose cessation *jarā-maraṇa* ceases?" He proceeds in this way and finishes at *avidyā*. Then he feels that Knowledge, Insight, Wisdom and Light have arisen within him. He knows the fact and the nature of Pain, of the *āsravas*, and of the twelve factors of Dependent Origination; he knows their origin and their cessation, and also the Way that leads to such cessation. Thus he acquires the threefold Knowledge and attains supreme and perfect Enlightenment. He knows, understands, discerns and realises all that is to be known, understood, discerned and realised.

He then rises in the air to the height of seven palm-trees in order to convince the *devas* that he has attained Enlightenment. He utters this verse: "The way is cut off; the dust is laid; the *āsravas* are dried up; they do not flow again. When the Way is cut off, it does not turn. This is called the end of Pain." All Buddhas must show such a sign. The *devas* shower flowers on him in recognition of his Buddhahood. Light and happiness spread in all the worlds, which are shaken in six ways. All the Buddhas praise the new Buddha and present him with jewelled umbrellas, which emit rays of light. All the *bodhisattvas* and *devas* rejoice and praise the Buddha.

This is the account of the events accompanying the Enlightenment as given in the *Lal. V.*[136] In the *B. Ct.*, the *bodhisattva* remembers his previous existences in the first watch of the night and obtains the *divya-cakṣus* in the second. In the *Mahā-vastu*, the events of the night of Enlightenment are briefly described in the same order as in the *Lal. V.*, but the feat of levitation is not mentioned. The first utterance after Enlightenment is also quite different. It runs thus : " The result of Merit is pleasant, and success in one's aims is also realised ; one quickly obtains supreme peace and happiness. The menacing troublesome *devas* of *Māra's* realm, who (stand) in front, cannot hinder him, who has done meritorious deeds." [137] In another passage of the *Mtu.*, the first utterance is given as follows : " Having cut off Craving, I abandon the dirt of passion. The dried-up *āsravas* do not flow. The way, which is cut off, does not turn." These words correspond to the verse in the *Lal. V.*[138]

Our task is done. The *bodhisattva*, who commenced his career with the "Thought of Enlightenment" many æons ago, has now become a perfectly enlightened Buddha. Wherefore we respectfully and regretfully take leave of him.

FINIS.

NOTES AND REFERENCES

(The abbreviations p. and pp. have generally been omitted after the titles of Sanskrit and Pāli works).

CHAPTER I

[1] For the conditions and attributes of *arahatta* in the Pāli canon, cf. *Brahmajāla-sutta* (*Dīgha*, i, 1–46); *Sāmañña-phala-sutta* (*Dīgha*, i, pp. 47–86); *Dīgha*, i, 177 (*Kassapa-sīhanāda-sutta*); *Majjhima*, i, 6–12 (*Sabbāsava-sutta*); *Saṃyutta*, iii, 28, section 13 (*Khandha-saṃyutta*); *Majjhima*, ii, 1–22, (*Mahā-sakuludāyi-sutta*); *Majjhima*, iii, 124–8 (*Bakkula-sutta*); *Sutta-nipāta*, pp. 115–23 (*Vāseṭṭha-sutta*); *Saṃyutta*, iv, 252 (*Jambukhādaka-saṃyutta*); *Saṃyutta*, iv, 151 (*Saḷāyatana-saṃyutta*); *Aṅguttara*, iii, 34 (*Sumana-vagga*); iii, 421, section lxvi (*Devatā-vagga*); *Puggala-paññatti*, 73 (*Nava-puggalā*); *Majjhima*, i, 101 ff. (*Ceto-khila-sutta*); *Dīgha*, iii, 133 (*Pāsādika-sutta*); *Majjhima*, iii, 29 ff. (*Chabbisodhana-sutta*); *Dīgha*, iii, 207 ff. (*Saṅgīti-suttanta*).

[2] *Vinaya*, i, 21: "*Caratha bhikkhave cārikaṃ bahu-jana-hitāya bahu-jana-sukhāya lokānukampāya atthāya hitāya sukhāya deva manussānaṃ.*" *Dhammapada*, 77, 158: "*Ovadeyy' anusāseyya asabbhā ca nivāraye*"; "*attānam eva paṭhamaṃ patirūpe nivesaye, ath' aññam anusāseyya na kilisseyya paṇḍito' ti.*"

[3] Cf. *Dhammapada*, 28: "*Pabbataṭṭho va bhummaṭṭhe dhīro bāle avekkhatī'ti.*"

Sutta-nipata (*Khagga-visāṇa-sutta*), pp. 6–7: "*eko care khagga-visāṇa-kappo.*" "*Mitte suhajje anukampamāno hāpeti atthaṃ paṭibaddha-citto, etaṃ bhayaṃ santhave pekkhamāno eko care,*" etc.

Milinda-pañha, 31: "*Kin-ti mahārāja idaṃ dukkhaṃ nirujjheyya aññañ-ca dukkhaṃ na uppajjeyyāti etadatthā mahārāja amhākaṃ pabbajjā anupādā parinibbānaṃ.*"

Thera-gāthā, No. 245, p. 31: "*Yathā Brahmā tathā eko, yathā devo tathā duve, yathā gāmo tathā tayo, kolāhalaṃ tat' uttarin ti.*"

No. 380, p. 42: "*Yassa c'atthāya pabbajito agārasmā anagāriyam so me attho anuppatto sabba-saṃyojana-kkhayo' ti*" (said by Kassapa).

No. 224: "*tisso vijjā anuppattā kataṃ buddhassa sāsanan ti*" (p. 29), etc.

[4] For the ideal of the *pratyeka-buddha*, cf. *Puggala*, 14, and *Da. Bhū.*, 26, ll. 1–4. The *Puggala-paññatti* describes him thus: "*Idh' ekacco puggalo pubbe ananussutesu dhammesu sāmaṃ saccāni abhisambujjhati na ca tattha sabbaññutaṃ pāpuṇāti na ca phalesu vasībhāvaṃ: ayaṃ vuccati puggalo pacceka-sambuddho.*"

5 *Vinaya*, i, 11, l. 23.

6 Cf. *Dīgha*, i, 46: "*Kāyassa bhedā uddham jīvita-pariyādānā na dakkhinti deva-manussā ti.*"

Sutta-nipāta, No. 235, p. 41: "*Khīṇaṃ purāṇaṃ, navaṃ n'atthi sambhavam,*" etc.

Saṃyutta, iii, 109 ff. (dialogue between Sāriputta and Yamaka). It is denied that Buddha taught annihilation, but it is not affirmed that a monk continues to exist. "*na hi Bhagavā evaṃ vadeyya khināsavo bhikkhu kāyassa bhedā ucchijjati vinassati na hoti param maraṇa*" (p. 110).

Udāna, viii, 3 (p. 80): "*asti bhikkhave ajātaṃ abhūtaṃ akataṃ asaṃkhataṃ.*"

Milinda, 96: "*parinibbuto Bhagavā na ca Bhagavā pūjaṃ sādiyati,*" etc.

7 *Asaṃskṛta-dhātu*. The word *dhātu*, derived from *dhā*, means "a primary element", and also signifies "factor, item, principle"; "natural condition," etc. The Buddhists divide the entire sum of things into seventy-five *dhātus*, of which seventy-two are "compounded, made up" (*saṃskṛta*) and three are "uncompounded" (*asaṃskṛta*). L. de la Vallée Poussin translates *asaṃskṛta* as "inconditionné". The three *dhātus*, which are uncompounded, are: (1) *ākāça* (Space, Ether). (2) *Apratisaṅkhyā-nirodha* (Cessation, which is not due to pre-meditation or deliberate intention) ("suppression non due à la sapience": L. de la Vallée Poussin). (3) *Pratisaṅkhyā-nirodha* (Cessation, which is due to pre-meditation or deliberate intention, i.e. *nirvāṇa*, or the cessation of the production of new thoughts (*Abhidharma-koça*, i, 5, pp. 6 ff.); cf. "Tables of the Elements" in Th. Stcherbatsky's "The Central Conception of Buddhism", p. 106. Th. Stcherbatsky renders *asaṃskṛta* as "immutable", and explains *pratisaṅkhyā-nirodha* thus: "The suppression of the manifestations of an element through the action of understanding (*prajñā*), as, e.g. after having realised that the existence of a personality is an illusion, a kind of eternal blank is substituted for this wrong idea."

8 E. Burnouf, Int., p. 97, l. 10.

9 *Pr. Pā. Çata*, 2, note 2.

10 ERE. ii, 739*a*.

11 *B.C. Ava. Pka.*, 421.

12 P. Oltramare, "Bouddhique," p. 250, note.

13 ERE, ii, 739*a*.

14 RHR., vol. xlii, 1900, p. 360, note.

15 "The *Yoga-darçana*," translated by G. Jha, p. 88 (Bombay, 1907).

16 H. Kern, "Manual," p. 65, note 5; "Histoire," i, 383, note.

17 K. E. Neumann, *Majjh.* tr., vol. i, p. 620, note 5. K. E. Neumann cites other words like *manosatto*, *mānasatto*, *bhavasatto*, etc.

[18] P. Oltramare, "Bouddhique," p. 250.

[19] *Kṣemendra*, i, 3; *M. Vy.*, p. 50; J. Rahder, "Glossary," p. 134.

[20] J. H. Woods, *Yoga*, pp. xvii, xx, 93.

[21] T. W. Rhys Davids, "Buddhist India," pp. 161 ff. (London, 1903); "Dialogues," i, pp. xx, 1.

[22] The word *yāna* is generally translated as "vehicle", also as "boat". *Hīna* is rendered as "lower", "inferior", "lesser", and *Mahā* as "higher", "greater". The Tibetan equivalent is *thegpa,* which means "vehicle" (Tib. Dicy., Das, 585). According to E. J. Eitel, the Chinese also translate *yāna* as "conveyance" (p. 90). But it is doubtful if *yāna* originally meant "vehicle". It denotes "way, path" in the *Vedas* and the *Upaniṣads*, e.g. *Chāndogya Upd.*, v, 3.2 ("*pathor deva-yānasya pitṛ-yānasya ca vyāvartanā*"). In Buddhism, there are more than two *yānas*, and the contrast between *hīna* and *mahā* is not the fundamental point. There is the *yāna* of the *pratyeka-buddhas*, and they surely do not need a "vehicle" for their solitary career. It may be suggested that *yāna* in Buddhism originally denoted "Way, Career", and that the connotation was changed after the publication of the *Sad. Pu.*, with its famous parable of the three *yānas* (chap. iii). That play on words led to the substitution of the idea of "vehicle" for that of "way".

[23] *Saṅkāra-dhāna.* H. Kern translates "heap of dirt". But *dhāna* means "receptacle", not "heap" (from the root *dhā*). *Saṅkāra* is rendered as "Kehricht" by Böhtlingk and Roth.

[24] *Divasa-mudrā.* *Mudrā* means "seal", hence a coin with the superscription on it. Literally, *divasa-mudrā* means "day's coin"

[25] *Tathāgata.* This puzzling word may be construed as *tathā-gata* ("gone thus, in that way"), or *tathā-āgata* ("come thus, in that way"). It has been variously translated as follows: "The Truth-finder" (Chalmers, *Majjh.* tr., i, 46, etc.); "the Accomplished One" (Sīlācāra, *Majjh.* tr., p. 67); "He who has won through to the Truth" (*Dhammasaṅgaṇi* tr., 1099); "The Saint who has attained Truth" (J. E. Carpenter, "Buddhism," p. 259); "Der Vollendete" (H. Oldenberg, "Buddha," p. 145, note; Nyāṇatiloka, *Aṅguttara* tr., vol. v, p. 283). The Jainas employ the term *tattha-gaya* (= *tatra-gata*), which is explained as meaning "he who has attained that world, i.e. emancipation" (SBE., vol. xiii, p. 82). R. O. Franke thinks that *Tathāgata* means "one, who has himself gone on the Way, that he teaches others" ("der so Gegangene," . . . "derjenige, der diesen Weg, den er lehrt, zuerst selbst zurückgelegt hat"; *Dīgha*, p. 287). He also points out that *Tathāgata* simply means "*arhat*, monk, individual" in several passages (*Dīgha*, p. 294). C. A. F. Rhys Davids is of opinion that the word means "thus come", and that Gautama Buddha's disciples gave him that name, because he "was believed to have come as a teacher in an order, according to which others had come" ("Gotama," p. 45.)

H. Beckh explains: "Ein So-gegangener, d.h. einer der den Buddhaweg auch wirklich gegangen ist," "der den gleichen Pfad wie alle Buddhas gewandelt" ("Buddhismus," vol. i, pp. 61, 62). Buddhaghoṣa offers no fewer than eight different explanations, which have been discussed by R. Chalmers in JRAS. 1898, pp. 105 ff.: (*a*) "He who has arrived in such fashion," i.e. who has worked his way upwards to perfection for the world's good in the same fashion as all previous Buddhas. (*b*) "He who walked in such fashion," i.e. (1) he who at birth took the seven steps in the same fashion as all previous Buddhas; or (2) he who in the same way as all previous Buddhas went his way to Buddhahood through the four *Jhānas* and the Paths. (*c*) (*Tatha* and *āgato*), he who by the path of knowledge has come at the real essentials of things. (*d*) (*Tatha* and *āgato*), he who has won Truth. (*e*) He who has discerned Truth. (*f*) (*āgato = āgado*), he who declares Truth. (*g*) (*Gato = pavatto*), he whose words and deeds accord. (*h*) (*Tatha* and *agata*) (*agata = agada*, "medicine, physic"), the great physician, whose physic is all-potent. R. Chalmers derives the word from *tatha* and *āgata* and interprets it as meaning "One who has come at the real truth". Böhtlingk and Roth interpret the word as *tathā-gata* (sich in solcher Lage, in solchem Zustande, befindend; derartig, so beschaffen). *Tathāgata* occurs in several passages of the *Mahābhārata*, e.g. ("*ājagmuḥ sahitās tatra yatra rājā tathāgataḥ*," i, 4879; vol. i, p. 179, Calcutta Edition). It is not probable that the doctrine of a succession of Buddhas would be embodied in a term, which belongs to early Pāli literature. This consideration weakens the argument for the derivation *tathā-āgata*. It seems rather pedantic to discover *tatha* (= Truth) in this word. The simple and natural sense seems to be *tathā-gata*. On the analogy of the Jaina term and the phrases in the *Mahābhārata*, we may explain it as "gone there, i.e. to Liberation, *nirvāṇa*, or whatever the *summun bonum* may be". It would thus mean "The Liberated One", "One who has reached the goal"

[26] *Upadhi* (Pāli: *Upādi*). The word *upadhi* seems to be a wrongly Sanskritized form of Pāli *upādi*, which is derived from the root *dā*. It is closely related to *upādāna*, meaning "fuel", "stuff of life", "substratum of the aggregates." (*khandhas*). *Nirvāṇa* with *upadhi* is attained during life on the extinction of the *āsravas*: *Nirvāṇa* without *upadhi* simply means "the death of such a saint". The Tibetan equivalent is *dṅos* (thing) or *phuṅ-po* (= Skt. *skandha*; Tib. Dicy., Das, 824; *M. S. Al.* tr., p. 27, note 4.) L. de la Vallée Poussin translates "residue" (JRAS. 1906, p. 964). "Daseinsgrundlage" (M. Winternitz in "Lesebuch", p. 279).

[27] *Santāna*. H. Kern translates "intelligence". The word denotes the series of mental states, which constitute the individual.

Kuçala-mūlāni: "roots or bases of goodness or merit" (Pāli Dicy.).

[28] *Divy.*, 50.9; *Lka.*, 65, verse 130; *Ava.-ça.*, i, 65.1; *Pr. Pā. Çata.*, pp. 85, 296; *Kā. Vy.*, 46; *Kṣemendra*, i, 623.50; *Da. Bhū.*, 65.2, etc.

[29] *Auddhatya.* This term occurs in the lists of the *nīvaraṇas* and the *saṃyojanas.* As a *nīvaraṇa*, it is coupled with *kaukṛtya* (Pāli: *uddhacca-kukkuccam*). It has been explained as "recklessness", "pride", "la présomption", "vanity", "excitement". In the *M. S. Al.*, it is mentioned with *laya* (142.9). It seems to denote a mood of exaltation and self-satisfaction as opposed to self-reproach and dejection.

Çīla-vrata-parāmarça (Pāli: *sīlabbata-parāmāsa*). Cf. *Dhamma-saṅgaṇi*, sections 1005, 1174. *Parāmarça*, derived from *mṛç* (with *parā*), means "touching, contact, being under the influence of; contagion". Hence the meaning, "perversion," "infatuation," "inverted judgment."

Sat-kāya-dṛṣṭi (Pāli: *sakkāya-diṭṭhi*). (*Dhammasaṅgaṇi*, section 1003.) This Pāli term is explained in two ways: (1) *sva-kāya-dṛṣṭi*; and (2) *sat-kāya-dṛṣṭi*. The latter Sanskritized form is generally accepted as correct. It has been translated as "Heresy of Individuality", "Delusion of Self", "The Personality View", etc. L. Feer's rendering is perhaps inadmissible: "la persuasion que le corps est une chose bonne" (*Ava.-ça.* tr., p. 14). Literally, *sat-kāya* means "the body in being, the existing body".

[30] *Kleça.* In Buddhist Sanskrit, this term is derived from *kliç* (= "to soil, to stain"). Bad butter is called *sankiliṭṭha* in Pāli (cf. *Dhamma-saṅgaṇi*, section 1229). The word has been rendered as "passion", "sin", "lust", "les corruptions de mal", etc. (Pāli: *kilesa*, *klesa*, *sankilissati*).

[31] *traidhātuka.* L. Feer translates, "sous les trois formes." But the word refers to the three worlds.

[32] *vāsī-candana.* L. Feer translates, "froid comme le sandal"; but perhaps the word *vāsī* corresponds to Pāli *vāsita*, and the idea of "fragrance" seems more appropriate than that of "coldness", or both ideas may be combined; "cold like fragrant sandal-wood". E. Burnouf's interpretation is probably correct: "the sandal-tree and the axe that cuts it down" (*asi*). An *arhat* sees no difference between them. This is a third simile.

[33] *Upendra.* L. Feer translates "Indra, premier et second." But I have followed Monier Williams's Sanskrit Dictionary.

[34] *Sad. Pu.*, 80, ll. 6, 9; 81.1.

[35] *Pr. Pā. Çata.*, 122.10; 130.3 ff.

[36] *anupadhi-çeṣa-nirvāṇa.* See note 26 above (Chap. I).

[37] *M. S. Al.*, 115.7 ff.

[38] *M. S. Al.*, 53.4.

[39] *M. S. Al.*, 53.3.

[40] *B.C. Ava.*, vii, 29; iv, 7; ix, 49; viii, 145. *Bo. Bhū.*,

fol. 9*b*.2 ff. *Pr. Pā. Çata.*, 122, 282, 485. *M. S. Al.*, 40, 98, 168, 171. *Çikṣā*, 61.6, 66.11, 50.13. *Sad. Pu.*, 276.8, 129.9, 47.3, etc.

41 *Lka.*, 66.6.

42 *Su. Vy.*, 15.10 ff.

43 *Pr. Pā. Aṣṭa.*, 375.14 ff.

44 *Çikṣā*, 14.8.

45 *Sad. Pu.*, 116.2, 203.11, 131.12, 378.3. *M. S. Al.*, 6.

46 *B.C. Ava.*, vii, 18.

47 D. T. Suzuki, "Outlines," p. 294. Sīlācāra: *Majjh.* tr., p. 66.

48 *Mtu.*, i, 239.18; *Pr. Pā. Çata.*, 91; *Da. Bhū.*, 25, etc.

49 *Mtu.*, i, 63.2; ii, 394.12.

50 "Outlines," p. 295.

51 *Mtu.*, ii, 341.2, ii, 397.2. *Sam. Rā.*, fol. 1*a*.1. *Lka.*, 299, verse 261, etc.

52 *Pr. Pā. Çata.*, 64, 174, 682. *Divy.*, 143. *Sad. Pu.*, 41.5. *Saund. Kā.*, xvii, 34. *Lka.*, 256. *Pr. Pā. Aṣṭa.*, 397. *Da. Bhū.*, 97, etc.

53 *Pr. Pā. Çata.*, 1326, 1373, 499. *Pr. Pā. Aṣṭa.*, 281.19. *Da. Bhū.*, 95.25. *M. Vy.*, section 1 (p. 2*a*). *Kar. Pu.*, 9.11. *M. S. Al.*, 33.

54 *Divy.*, 127.13; 205.120.

55 *Sad. Pu.*, 308.9.

56 *Bo. Bhū.*, fol. 39*b*.6 (*sarva-tarka-mārga-samatikrāntatvad*).

57 *Bo. Bhū.*, 37*a*.6, and 37*b*.3 (*nirmalam, apratihatam, sarvajñānam, asaṅga-jñānam*). *M. S. Al.*, 33.14.

58 *Bo. Bhū.*, fol. 37*b*. 3.3.

59 *M. S. Al.*, 34.3, 35.14.

60 *M. S. Al.*, 36.19. *Bo. Bhū.*, fol. 39*b*.6 ("*agrā çreṣṭhā varā praṇītā*").

61 *Ava. ça.*, i, 7.5, etc. *Bo. Bhū.*, *fol.* 148*b*.6; 37*b*.5.1. *M. Vy.*, section 11.

These three Fields of Mindfulness are defined as follows: Impartiality or same mental attitude (*sama-cittatā*) towards those who wish to hear or learn, those who do not wish to hear or learn, and those who partake of both characteristics (*çuçrūṣamāṇeṣu-*, etc.). Cf. *Sutta-nipāta*, 383, p. 67. The words may mean "obedient", "disobedient".

62 *Mtu.*, i, 38.14 ff. *Lal. V.*, 5.2, 403.1. *Sad. Pu.*, 81.3.

63 *M. Vy.*, section 7. *Dh. S.*, section 76. *Lal. V.*, 275.10. *Ava.-ça.*, i, 7.5. *M. S. Al.*, 186. Csoma, p. 5. Cf. *Aṅguttara.*, v, 33.7 ff. *Majjhima*, i, 69 ff.

64 *Sthān-āsthāna* (Pāli: *ṭhāṇāṭṭhāṇa*). This term has been interpreted in several ways. Csoma de Körös (p. 5) and Nyāṇatiloka (*Aṅguttara* tr., vol. v, 282) translate: "what is possible or impossible". D. T. Suzuki

renders it as "right and wrong". T. W. Rhys Davids, C. A. F. Rhys Davids and Lord Chalmers are of opinion that it refers to the knowledge of specific causal relations. ("Dialogues," iii, 205; *Dhamma-saṅgaṇi* tr., p. 323; *Majjh.* tr., i, 46.) P. Oltramare translates: "Il sait ce qui est comme étant, ce qui n'est pas comme n'etant pas" ("La Théosophie Bouddhique," p. 241). S. Hardy explains the term as meaning "the wisdom that understands what knowledge is necessary for the right fulfilment of any particular duty, in whatsoever situation" ("Manual," p. 394). F. Max Müller translates: "Knowledge of admissible and inadmissible propositions" (*Dh. S.*, p. 51). Sīlācāra translates: "understands according to truth and fact the true and the false" (*Majjh.* tr., p. 67).

[65] *Adhimukti* (Tibetan: *mos-pa-sna-tsogs*). Csoma de Körös and D. T. Suzuki read *vimukti* ("liberation"). But the Tibetan equivalent shows that this is a wrong reading.

[66] *Dhātu*. See note 7 (Chap. I).

[67] The *M. Vy.* has *indriya-varāvara*. But the *Dh. S.* and the *Pr. Pā. Çata.* read *indriya-parāpara*, which is confirmed by the Pāli text, "*indriya paropariyattam*" (*Aṅguttara*, v, 34). The Tibetan equivalent is *mchog-daṅ-mchog-ma*, but *mchog* corresponds to both Skt. *parama* and *vara* (Tib. Dicy., Das, p. 436). Csoma de Körös translates: "the power of knowing what is and what is not the chief organ." Lord Chalmers renders *indriya* as "hearts".

[68] *Sarvatra-gāminī pratipad*. The Pāli text has *sabbattha-gāminipaṭipadam* (which perhaps points to a possible Sanskrit reading *sarvārtha* instead of *sarvatra*). Csoma de Körös translates: "the power of knowing all the ways of transmigration." F. Max Müller also accepts the alternative reading *sarvārtha* ("leads to all the highest objects"). Nyāṇatiloka translates: "Jedweden Ausgang" (= *sarvatra*). Lord Chalmers thinks that it means "the future to which every course leads" (*Majjh.* tr., i, 47). Sīlācāra renders it as "the way that leads to all states" (*Majjh.* tr., 67). The Tibetan text has *thams-cad-du-ḥgro-ba* (= "going everywhere", Tib. Dicy., Das, p. 300). This shows that *sarv-ārtha-gāminī* was not accepted by the Tibetan translators.

[69] The Pāli text makes it clear that the compound should be divided in this way: *sarva-dhyāna-vimokṣa-samādhi-samāpattīnāṃ saṅkleça-vyavadāna-vyutthāna*. Lord Chalmers translates *vyavādana* as "specific stage" and renders *samāpattīnām* as "achievements of Ecstasy, etc." (*Majjh.* tr., i, 47). But *vyavadāna* (Pāli: *vodāna*) means "purification". Sīlācāra translates *vyutthāna* (Pāli: *vuṭṭhāna*) as "manly endeavour" (without citing any authority), and renders *samāpattīnām* as "those aiming at ecstasy", etc. But *samāpatti* always denotes the four Attainments leading to the formless, non-material worlds (*ārūpya-samāpattayaḥ*). Csoma de Kọrös translates: "Liberation from the

miseries of vice and all sorts of theories" (which is really very wide of the mark).

[70] *Lal. V.*, 344. *Mtu.*, ii, 283.

[71] Cf. *Majjhima*, i, 71. *Aṅguttara*, ii, 9.

[72] Csoma, p. 249. U. Wogihara, *Bo. Bhū.*, p. 42. M. Walleser, *Pr. Pā.* tr., p. 72. S. Lévi, *M. S. Al.*, tr., pp. 13, 303. D. T. Suzuki, "Outlines," p. 327. Nyāṇatiloka, *Aṅguttara* tr., ii, 14. L. Feer, *Ava.-ça.* tr., p. 12, etc. For *viçārada* and *vaiçāradya*, cf. *Sam. Rā.*, fol. 112*a*.6. *Mtu.*, i, 39.13; iii, 386.14. *Lal. V.*, 403.1, 160.14. *Dh. S.*, section 77. *M. Vy.*, section 8. *Kar. Pu.*, 106.12. *Ava.-ça.*, i, 7.5. *Su. Vy.*, 40.1. *Çikṣā*, 351.7. The *Dh. S.* omits the third *vaiçāradya*

[73] *M. Vy.*, p. 10. *M. S. Al.*, tr., p. 27.

[74] *M. S. Al.* tr., p. 27

[75] *dharmāḥ*. Lord Chalmers translates, "mental states" (*Majjh.* tr., i, 48). But this rendering does not suit the context. Sīlācāra translates more correctly, "things" (*Majjh.* tr., p. 68).

[76] Csoma de Körös interprets the third *vaiçāradya* thus: "Boldness to teach or prophesy with certainty the immutability of the immanent virtues" (p. 249). But the Pāli text does not support this rendering.

[77] E. Burnouf, Int., p. 150, note. Nyāṇatiloka says: "Das Wort ist wahrscheinlich auf *ven* (gehen) zurückzuführen" (*Aṅguttara* tr., vol. v, p. 530).

[78] H. Kern, SBE., vol. xxi, p. 31, note. S. Hardy, "Manual," p. 395. Csoma, p. 250. L. Feer, *Ava.-ça.* tr., p. 12. S. Lévi, *M. S. Al.* tr., p. 304. C. F. Koeppen, "Buddha," i, 436. J. Speyer, *Ava.-ça.*, ii, 223.

[79] Pāli Dicy., s.v.

[80] E. Burnouf, Int., p. 150, note.

[81] For the *āveṇika-dharmas*, see *M. Vy.*, section 9. *Divy.*, 148. *M. S. Al.*, 187. *Pr. Pā. Çata.*, 1450. *Lal. V.*, 275.11. *Da. Bhū.*, 13.26; 17.17. *Dh. S.*, section 79. *Mtu.*, i, 160.

[82] *nāsti ravitam*. The *Pr. Pā. Çata.* has the incorrect reading, *caritam*. The Tibetan equivalent is *ca-co-med-pa*, and S. C. Das translates: "free from noise or chatter, without fuss". D. T. Suzuki renders the phrase as "faultless in his speeches" ("Outlines," p. 327); but this is a different idea altogether. H. Jäschke gives the rendering: "not loquacious or talkative" (Tib. Dicy., 138).

[83] D. T. Suzuki translates: "He knows everything, yet he is calmly resigned." The Pāli word *appaṭisaṅkhā* means "want of judgment" (*Dhamma-saṅgaṇi*, section 1346, p. 231, "*idhekacco appaṭisaṅkhā ayoniso āhāraṃ āhāreti*"). (Pāli Dicy., s.v.) Csoma de Körös translates: "no indifference for any undiscussed things." But it is best to follow the Pāli text.

[84] The *M. Vy.* omits *vimukti-jñāna-darçana*, and the *Dh. S.* omits *anāgate 'dhvani* ("knowledge of the future"). The *Pr. Pā. Çata.* includes both these items in its list, and gives nineteen *dharmas* instead of eighteen! D. T. Suzuki arbitrarily omits *samādhi* and includes *vimukti-jñāna-darçana* ("Outlines," p. 327). The *M. Vy.* has *hāniḥ*, but the *Dh. S.*, the *M. S. Al.*, and the *Pr. Pā. Çata.* give the reading *parihāṇiḥ*, which seems to be more correct.

[85] *Asaṅgam apratihataṃ jñāna-darçanam.* P. Oltramare translates: "la connaissance intuitive et sans limitation" ("Bouddhique," p. 241). Csoma de Körös renders the Tibetan text thus: "occupied with the contemplation of the wisdom which has been neither attracted nor hindered by the time that has hitherto elapsed." But this cannot be the correct interpretation according to the Sanskrit text.

[86] *Cāra.* Literally, "motion, walking, doing, behaviour, action, process" (from *car*, *carati*). (Pāli Dicy.)

[87] *M. S. Al.*, 184.3, 187.12. *Pr. Pā. Çata.*, 1472. *Divy.*, 124.11, 126.13. *Lka.*, 12.3. *Kar. Pu.*, 17.2. *Kṣemendra*, i, 907.73; ii, 933.12. *Ava.-ça.*, i, 7.5, etc.

[88] *Sad. Pu.*, 136.4, 108.17, 89.12, 90.2. *M. Vy.*, section 19.

[89] *M. Vy.*, section 10.

[90] *Kathā-vatthu*, xviii, 3, p. 561 (*n'atthi Buddhassa Bhagavato karuṇāti*).

[91] Cf. *Diogenes Laertius*, vol. ii, p. 217, ll. 21 ff. E. Zeller, "Stoics," p. 238, l. 4.

[92] *M. Vy.*, section 12. Cf. *Aṅguttara*, iv, 82 ff. *Dīgha*, iii, 217.

[93] *Sad. Pu.*, 228.4, 229.1, 294.6. *M. Vy.*, section 1. *Divy.*, 391, 126. *Lal. V.*, 131.3. *Mtu.*, i, 200.10. *Kṣemendra*, i, 673.39. *Lal. V.*, 423 ff. *M. S. Al.*, 184 ff.

[94] *Lal. V.*, 5, 260. *M. Vy.*, section 2.

[95] *Lal. V.*, 402.10. *Sad. Pu.*, 385.4. *Su. Pr.*, fol. 14*a*.5. *Su. Vy.*, 10. *M. S. Al.*, 48. *Pr. Pā. Çata.*, 73.17. *Mtu.*, i, 57, etc.

[96] *Kar. Pu.*, 122.10, 119. *Pr. Pā. Çata.*, 111.

[97] *Mtu.*, i, 61.10 ff.

[98] *Lal. V.*, 376.5, 402. *Sad. Pu.*, 238.4. *Lka.*, 234.

[99] *Sad. Pu.*, 144 ff.

[100] *Dīgha*, i, 46.

[101] *Milinda*, 95 ff., "*tisso sampattiyo paṭilabhanti.*"

[102] *Mtu.*, iii, 226.

[103] *Sad. Pu.*, 326.2, 319.1, 323.7.

[104] *Sad. Pu.*, 249.

[105] *Su. Pr.*, fol. 5*a*.1 ff. (*na tu çākya-muner āyuḥ çakyaṃ gaṇayitum*).

[106] *Mtu.*, i, 158.11.

[107] For Buddha's miracles, cf. *Ava.-ça.*, i, 109, 331. *Divy.*, 48 ff., 128, 203, etc.

108 *Mtu.*, i, 167.17 ff. Vasumitra's "Treatise on the Sects," cited by D. T. Suzuki ("Outlines," pp. 249 ff.).

109 L. de la Vallée Poussin (JRAS. 1906, p. 960) has compared the Buddha's bodies to Kṛṣṇa's ordinary and glorified bodies (*Bhagavad-gītā*). But it is not proper to mix up the Buddhist notions of *upāya-kauçalya* and *nirmāṇa* with the entirely different Hindu doctrine of *avatāra* (Incarnation).

110 *Su. Pr.*, fol. 6*a* ff., "*anasthi-rudhira-kāye kuto dhātur bhaviṣyati . . . dharma-kāyā hi sambuddhā dharma-dhātus tathāgataḥ*" (fol. 7*a*.4). *Sam. Rā.*, fol. 95*b*.4, "*na rūpa-kāyatas tathāgataḥ prajñātavyaḥ . . . dharma-kāya-prabhāvitāç ca buddhā bhagavanto,*" etc.

111 *Pr. Pā. Çata*, 1211.4.

112 *Sad. Pu.*, 319.1. *M. S. Al.*, 46.1.

113 *Vajrā.*, 43. *Sad. Pu.*, 143.3. *Da. Bhū.*, 3.27.

114 *Divy.*, 396.28; 158.23. *Çikṣā*, 159.7.

115 *Sam. Rā.*, fol. 95*b*.4.

116 *Pr. Pā. Çata.*, 1470.3, 380.6. *M. S. Al.*, 45.3, 189.1, 36.17.

117 *M. S. Al.*, 77.13 ff.

118 *Çikṣā*, 230. *M. S. Al.*, 40.14.

119 *Pr. Pā. Aṣṭa.*, 512; 307.18.

120 *Pr. Pā. Aṣṭa.*, 307.12.

121 *M. S. Al.*, 48.11, 83.2.

122 *M. S. Al.*, 49.14.

123 *Pr. Pā. Çata.*, 1263.

124 *M. S. Al.*, 83.1.

125 *M. S. Al.*, 45.1, 188.6.

126 *Da. Bhū.*, 83.

127 *Kar. Pu.*, 122. *M. S. Al.*, 189.1.

128 *Saṃyutta*, iii, 120 (*Yo kho Vakkali dhammaṃ passati so maṃ passati*). *Itivuttaka*, p. 91 (*dhammaṃ passanto maṃ passati*).

129 *Vinaya*, i, 14 (*cha loke arahanto honti*).

130 *Majjh.*, i, 482 (*na me te vutta-vādino*, etc.).

131 *Vinaya*, i, 16 (*yathā seṭṭhi . . . yasaṃ kulaputtaṃ na passeyyā*).

132 *Vinaya*, i, 24 ff. (*yena Uruvelā tad avasari*, etc.).

133 *Aṅguttara*, ii, 38–39 (*na kho ahaṃ brāhmaṇa manusso bhavissāmīti; Buddho ti maṃ brāhmaṇa dhārehīti*).

134 *Majjh.*, iii, 15 (*anuppannassa maggassa uppādetā*).

135 *Majjh.*, i, 142, ll. 7–8.

136 *Dīgha*, ii, 133 (*chavi-vaṇṇo pariyodāto*).

137 *Mahāpadāna-sutta* (*Dīgha*, ii, 15). *Majjhima*, ii, 222 ff.

138 *Mahāparinibbāna-sutta* (*Dīgha*, ii, 103) (*kappaṃ vā tiṭṭheyya*, etc.).

139 *Majjh.*, ii, 143 (*Brahmāyu-sutta*, ll. 20–1).

140 *Kathā-vatthu*, xviii, 1–2 (pp. 559, 561); ii, 10 (pp. 221 ff.) (*vohāra-kathā*).

141 J. M. Robertson, "A Short History of Christianity," p. 142 (London, 1913). E. Gibbon, "Decline and Fall of the Roman Empire," vol. iii, 147; iv, 197; v, 36 (ed. J. B. Bury, London, 1896–1900, 7 volumes).

142 *Saṃyutta*, iii, 119 ff. (p. 124).

143 Cf. P. Sabatier, "Life of St. Francis," p. xx (London, 1920).

144 R. H. Thouless, "An Introduction to the Psychology of Religion," pp. 136 ff. (Cambridge, 1923). A. G. Tansley, "The New Psychology," p. 88 (London, 1921). "Extroversion is the thrusting out of the mind on to life, the use of the mind in practical life, the pouring out of the libido on external objects. Introversion, on the other hand, is the turning in of the mind upon itself, involving a withdrawal from the external world and the cultivation of an internal mental life."

CHAPTER II

Notes

[1] S. Kimura, "Study," pp. 59, 60. "Historically, it must be said that Buddha preached his phenomenological doctrines in an exoteric form to the people and his ontological doctrines in the esoteric form were reserved only for advanced or brilliant men."

[2] *Dīgha*, ii, 100.3. *Saṃyutta*, v, 153.18 (*Sati-paṭṭhāna Saṃyutta*, "*na tatth' Ānanda Tathāgatassa dhammesu ācariya-muṭṭhi.*").

[3] M. Winternitz, "Problems," p. 63.

[4] H. Kern, "Manual," p. 122.

[5] E. Senart, "Origines," p. 24.

[6] Ibid., p. 31.

[7] K. J. Saunders, "The Gospel for Asia," p. 59 (London, 1928).

[8] L. de la Vallée Poussin, "Opinions," pp. 21, 22.

[9] *Thera-gāthā* tr., p. xxi. C. A. F. Rhys Davids, "Psalms of the Brethren" (London, 1913).

[10] On *saddhā*, cf. *Majjhima*, i, 142.8. *Dhammapada*, 333, "*sukhā saddhā patiṭṭhitā.*" *Majjhima*, i, 356.2 (*Sekha-sutta*). *Majjhima*, i, 478.29 (*saddhā-vimutta*) (*Kīṭāgiri-sutta*). *Majjhima*, ii, 176.21 (*Caṅkī-sutta*; "*saddhā-bahukārā*"). *Aṅguttara*, iii, 4, ll. 3, 11; iii, 352.20 (*Dhammika-vagga*). *Dīgha*, iii, 239.15; iii, 227.7; iii, 237.5 ff.; iii, 238.2; iii, 113.16 (*Sampasādanīya-suttanta*). *Sutta-nipāta*, 182, 184 (pp. 32, 33), "*Sadd' īdha vittaṃ purisassa seṭṭham*"; "*Saddhāya taratī oghaṃ.*" *Dīgha*, ii, 217.19 (*Jana-vasabha-suttanta*: "*Buddhe avecca-ppasādena samannāgatā*"). *Dhammasaṅgaṇi*, section 12, "*saddhā okappanā abhippasādo.*"

[11] O. C. J. Rosenberg, "Probleme," i, 36. L. de la Vallée Poussin, "Opinions," p. 215.

[12] JRAS. 1906, p. 493.

[13] On the *devas*, cf. *Majjhima*, i ,251 ff. (*Cūḷa-taṇhā-saṅkhaya-sutta*: *Sakka* receives instruction). *Majjhima*, ii, 130.18 (*Kaṇṇakat-thala-sutta*: Some *devas* must be reborn on earth). *Majjhima*, i, 73 (*Mahā-sīha-nāda-sutta*: the *devas* need *nirvāṇa*). *Dīgha*, iii, 218 (*Saṅgīti-suttanta*: The *devas* are not free from sense-desires). *Dīgha*, iii, 28 (*Pāṭika-suttanta*: *Brahmā* is not the creator of the universe). *Dīgha*, ii, 263 ff. (*Sakka-pañha-suttanta*: *Sakka* does homage at Buddha's feet, p. 269; the *devas* desire happiness). *Dīgha*, ii, 208 (*Jana-vasabha-suttanta*: The *devas* honour Buddha). *Aṅguttara*, i, 144 (*Sakka* is subject to death and rebirth, and is not free from desire, hatred and

delusion). *Samyutta*, i, 219 (*Sakka* is not free from anxiety; *Sakka-samyutta*).

14 *Dīgha*, ii, 259 (*Mahāsamaya-sutta*).

15 Cf. K. J. Saunders, "Gospel," p. 171. H. Kern, "Manual," p. 122. H. Raychaudhuri, "Materials," p. 74.

16 *Sad. Pu.*, 89.11, 90.2, 229.11.

17 *Su. Vy.*, 18, 19.

18 The five *ānantaryāṇi* are sins, which are immediately followed by retribution and punishment. These are: (1) parricide, (2) matricide, (3) murder of an *arhat*, (4) causing a schism in the Confraternity, and (5) maliciously wounding a Buddha. (*Dh. S.*, section 13. *M. Vy.*, section 122. *Mtu.*, i, 244. SBE., vol. xlix, pt. ii, p. 197.

19 ERE., xi, 54*b*. P. Dörfler, "Anfänge," pp. 111, 112, "So begegnen uns seit dem 4. Jahrhundert die Formeln," etc.

20 R. A. Nicholson, "Mysticism," pp. 38, 78.

21 ERE. xi, pp. 63, 68.

22 M. Horten, "Islam," vol. i, p. 157.

23 *Dh. S.*, section 12. *M. Vy.*, section 23. *Ava.-ça.*, i, 3.7. *Lal. V.*, 438.6. *Çikṣā*, 297.

24 *Su. Vy.*, 76.8. *Lal. V.*, 366.19. *Mtu.*, ii, 323.14. *Kar. Pu.*, 2.1.

25 *M. Vy.*, section 23. *Sad. Pu.*, 47.2.

26 On the Bhāgavatas and Kṛṣṇa, cf. *Chāndogya Upaniṣad*, iii, 17.6 (p. 185, "*Kṛṣṇāya devakī-putrāya*"). A. Barth, "Religions." p. 166. A. B. Keith in JRAS 1915, pp. 548, 841. H. Raychaudhuri, "Materials," pp. 19 ff. ERE. ii, 540 ff.

27 Between 305 and 297 B.C. ("Camb. Ind.," i, 472).

28 J. W. McCrindle, "India," p. 201, ll. 1–3.

29 Cf. S. Sörensen, "An Index to the Names in the *Mahābhārata*," p. 203 (London, 1904).

30 R. G. Bhandarkar, "Sects.," pp. 116, 117.

31 J. M. McCrindle, "India," p. 200, ll. 5 ff.

32 "Camb. Ind.," i, 225.

33 Ibid., p. 518.

34 Ibid., p. 335. P. V. N. Myers, "General History," p. 61 (Boston, 1919).

35 JRAS. 1915, pp. 63 ff.; 1916, pp. 138 ff.; 1916, pp. 362 ff.

36 V. A. Smith, "Asoka," pp. 140 ff.

37 J. H. Moulton, "Zoroastrianism," pp. 96 ff. A. J. Carnoy, "Iranian Mythology," pp. 260, 261 (Boston, 1917). *Zend-avesta*, SBE., vol. xxiii, pp. 4, 203.

38 R. G. Bhandarkar, "Sects," pp. 153, 157.

39 It has been suggested that this epithet only refers to the descent of the Çākya family from the sun. Even if this were so, it would show that the solar myth had already influenced genealogy. *Māra* is called

Kṛṣṇa-bandhu. So it is probable that *āditya-bandhu* did not refer only to Gautama Buddha's ancestry. (Cf. E. J. Thomas, "Buddha," p. 217.)

[40] R. G. Bhandarkar, "Sects," p. 153.

[41] On Gandhāra art and Buddhism, cf. A. Foucher, "Art," vol. ii, pp. 278–336, 407–21. "Le Gandhāra, sitôt converti, allait rester jusqu'à l'invasion des Musulmans l'une des terres d'élection du Bouddhisme" (p. 411). "La fusion des deux éléments . . . le grec et le bouddhique" (p. 443).

[42] H. G. Rawlinson, "Intercourse," p. 163.

[43] A. J. Edmunds, "Gospels," p. 41.

[44] H. G. Rawlinson, "Intercourse," p. 174. E. W. Hopkins, "India," p. 124.

[45] H. G. Rawlinson, "Intercourse," p. 142. E. J. Thomas, "Buddha," p. 237.

[46] H. G. Rawlinson, "Intercourse," p. 177. A. Lillie, "Buddhism," p. 233.

[47] R. Garbe, "Christentum," pp. 128 ff. E. W. Hopkins, "India," p. 141. A. E. Medlycott, "Thomas," p. 16.

[48] Eusebius, "History," p. 178, ll. 5 ff. ("he advanced even as far as India").

[49] R. Garbe, "Christentum," p. 150. A. J. Edmunds, "Gospels," p. 42.

[50] JRAS. 1911, p. 800.

[51] V. A. Smith, "Asoka," p. 43.

[52] Cf. H. G. Rawlinson, "Intercourse," p. 178. A. J. Edmunds, "Gospels," pp. 53 ff. R. Garbe, "Christentum," pp. 179 ff. E. J. Thomas, "Buddha," pp. 237 ff. R. Seydel, "Legende," pp. 11–15, 22–33. G. A. v.d. Bergh v. Eysinga, "Einflüsse," pp. 21–64: ("Indische Überlieferung höchst wahrscheinlich bereits die altchristliche Evangeliendarstellung beinflusst hat"), p. 102.

[53] ERE. vii, 568*b*. "Barlaam and Ioasaph," p. v.

[54] E. W. Hopkins, "India," pp. 152–62. "The parallels here given are almost too close in thought as in diction to have sprung from two independent sources" (p. 157). "Buddhism borrowed from Hinduism, Hinduism in turn from Buddhism, and both probably from Christianity" (p. 161). F. Lorinser, *Gītā*, pp. 267 ff. "Die Lehren der Bhagavad-gītā . . . mit aus dem Christenthum herübergenommenen Ideen und Sentenzen zum mindesten stark versetzt sind." "Der Verfasser der Bhagavad-gītā auch Einsicht in die Schriften des Neuen Testamentes genommen."

[55] Cf. note No. 52 above.

[56] J. E. Carpenter, "Theism," p. [illegible].

[57] *Majjhima*, i, 17.6; i, 114.24; i, 163.9.

[58] *Kathā-vatthu*, xxiii, 3, p. 623; iv, 7, 8, pp. 283–90.

[59] M. Walleser, *Pr. Pā.* tr., p. 4. W. McGovern, "Outlines," p. 20. K. J. Saunders, "Epochs," p. xiv. *Tāranātha*, p. 58.

[60] *M. Vy.*, sections 26, 28, 29.

[61] *Bo. Bhū.*, fol. 100*b*.2. *Çikṣā*, 7.17. *Da. Bhū.*, 21.15.

[62] *Çikṣā*, 286.

[63] *Çikṣā*, 194 ff. *Sad. Pu.*, 11.13. *Çiṣya-lekha*, 68 ff. *Kar. Pu.*, 104.19.

[64] *Kar. Pu.*, 101 ff. *Kṣemendra*, i, 903.61. *Pr Pā. Çata.*, 1531 ff., 1415 ff.

[65] *Çikṣā*, 14.

[66] *Dh. S.*, section 12.

[67] C. Eliot, "Hinduism and Buddhism," vol. ii, p. 19.

[68] E. W. Hopkins, "Origin and Evolution of Religion," p. 325 (New Haven, 1923).

[69] JRAS. 1927, p. 241.

[70] J. Edkins, "Chinese Buddhism," p. 382 (London, 1880).

[71] E. J. Thomas, JRAS. 1929, p. 359.

[72] K. J. Saunders, "The Gospel for Asia," p. 71 (London, 1928).

[73] M. Winternitz, "Problems," p. 38.

[74] JRAS. 1915, p. 403; 1906, p. 464.

CHAPTER III

Notes

[1] *Da. Bhū.*, 11.
[2] *Bo. Bhū.*, fol. 4*a* ff. *M. S. Al.*, 10 ff.
[3] *Bo. Bhū.*, fol. 120*a* ff.
[4] *M. Vy.*, section 61.
[5] *B.C. Ava.*, Canto ii. *Çikṣā.*, 58, 290.
[6] *Dh. S.*, section 14.
[7] *Aṅguttara*, iv, 373, ll. 7 ff.; v, 23, ll. 7 ff.
[8] *Majjhima*, iii, 256, ll. 7 ff.
[9] *Puggala*, 12, ll. 30 ff.
[10] G. K. Sastri, "A Treatise on Hindu Law," p. 88 (Calcutta, 1927). H. S. Gour, "The Hindu Code," p. 281 (Calcutta, 1923).
[11] *Majjhima*, i, 12 (*dhamma-dāyādā*). *Dīgha*, iii, 84 (*putto oraso mukhato jāto*). *Itivuttaka*, 101 (*puttā orasā mukhato jātā*).
[12] "Le Muséon," 1905, p. 4. P. Oltramare, "Bouddhique," p. 392.
[13] *Da. Bhū.*, 71.19.
[14] The details in this sentence are given on the authority of L. de la Vallée Poussin, "Le Muséon," 1905, p. 4.
[15] *Bo. Bhū.*, fol. 4*a*.1.1. (*dharma-Samādāna-gurukaḥ samparāya-gurukaḥ*).
[16] *Bo. Bhū.*, fol. 4*a*.1.2 (*aṇumātreṣv-avadyeṣu bhaya-darçī*).
[17] *Bo. Bhū.*, fol. 4*a*.2.1 (*kalaha-bhaṇḍana-vigraha-vivādeṣu*).
[18] *Bo. Bhū.*, fol. 4*a*.2.1 (*akṛtyāt*).
[19] *Bo. Bhū.*, fol. 4*a*.3.2 (*ārdra-cittaḥ, bhadratā, satya-gurukaḥ*)
[20] *Bo. Bhū.*, fol. 4*a*.4.1 (*guṇa-priyaḥ*).
[21] *Bo. Bhū.*, fol. 4*a*.5.1.2 (*pareṣām antikād apakāraṃ labdhvā nāghāta-cittatāṃ prāviṣkaroti*).
[22] *Bo. Bhū.*, fol. 4*a*.7.2 (*prakṛtyā utthānavān bhavati . . . abhibhūy-ākartukāmatām ālasyam pratisaṅkhyāya prayujyate*).
[23] *Bo. Bhū.*, fol. 4*a*.8.2–3 (*dṛḍha-niçcayo; bhogānām arjane rakṣaṇe*).
[24] *Bo. Bhū.*, fol. 4*b*.1.2 (*nāpy-ātmānaṃ paribhavati; nātyarthaṃ khedam āpadyate*).
[25] *Bo. Bhū.*, fol. 4*b*.3.2 (*sukhaṃ vata naiṣkramyam; araṇya-vana-prasthānāni*).
[26] *Bo. Bhū.*, fol. 4*b*.4.1 (*prakṛtya manda-kleço manda-nīvaraṇo manda-dauṣṭhulyaḥ*).
[27] *Bo. Bhū.*, fol. 4*b*.4.2 (*pāpakā asad-vitarkāḥ*).

[28] *Bo. Bhū.*, fol. 120*b*.3.1.

[29] *Bo. Bhū.*, fol. 120*b*.4.1.

[30] *M. S. Al.*, 11. 9.

[31] *M. S. Al.*, 11.14.

[32] *Bo. Bhū.*, fol. 5*b*.2 (*kleç-ābhyāsāt tīvra-kleçatā āyatana-kleçatā ca*).

[33] *Bo. Bhū.*, fol. 5*b*.2.1–2 (*mūḍhasy-ākuçalasya pāpa-mitra-aṃçrayaḥ*).

[34] *Bo. Bhū.*, fol. 5*b*.2.2–3 (*rājā-caura-pratyarthik-ādy-abhibhūtasy-āsvātantryam ; citta-vibhramaç ca*).

[35] *Bo. Bhū.*, fol. 5*b*.2.3, 3.1. *M. S. Al.*, 11, 25 (*upakaraṇa-vikalasy-ājīvik-āpekṣā*).

[36] *Bo. Bhū.*, fol. 5*b*.3.3, 4.2, 5.1 (*ādita eva aviparīta-bodhi-mārga-daiçikaṃ mitram ; na çithila-prayogo kusīdo*).

[37] *Bo. Bhū.*, fol. 5*a*.5.2 (*āçu parimucyate*).

[38] *Bo. Bhū.*, fol. 5*a*.5.3 (*na ca tathā tīvrām āpāyikīm duḥkha-vedanāṃ vedayate*).

[39] *Bo. Bhū.*, fol. 5*a*.6.3 (*kāruṇya-cittaṃ pratilabhate*).

[40] *Bo. Bhū.*, fol. 5*a*.2.3, 3.1, 3.2 (*bhadraṃ kalyāṇaṃ çukla-pakṣya- . . . samanvāgatam ; çreṣṭhasy-ācintyasy-ācalasy-ānuttarasya tathāgatasya padasya*).

[41] *M. S. Al.*, 11.19.

[42] *M. S. Al.*, 127.18.

[43] *Bo. Bhū.*, fol. 120*b*.7.2, 6.3.

[44] *Bo. Bhū.*, fol. 121*a*.1.1.

[45] *Bo. Bhū.*, fol. 121*b*.3.3 ; 121*b*.4.1.

[46] *Bo. Bhū.*, fol. 121*b*.6.1. *Çikṣā*, 7.19. *Da. Bhū.*, 11.12.

[47] *Dh. S.*, section 14. *B.C. Ava.*, Canto ii. *Çikṣa*, 161, 169, 313.

[48] *B.C. Ava.*, ii, 24. The word, which is translated as " atom ", is *aṇu*. This is a very small measure of length. A *yojana* is equal to about 7 miles (as much as can be travelled with one yoke of oxen), and it contains 79 × 384000 *aṇus.* (*Lal. V.*, 149 ; W. Kirfel, " Kosmologie," p. 335.)

[49] *B.C. Ava.*, ii, 26, 48, 49. Cf. *Dīgha*, i, 85, l. 13. *Khuddaka-pāṭha*, p. 1. *Aṅguttara*, i, 56, ll. 8–9. *Triratna* may also be rendered as " Triple Jewel ", but the *Dh. S.* speaks of *trīṇi ratnāni*.

[50] *Ava.-ça.*, i, 301.4 ; and passim.

[51] *B.C. Ava.*, ii, 28 ff. *Paçunā*. This reading is supported by the *B.C. Ava. Pka.*, which adds the comment : " *moha-bahulatām ātmano darçayati* " (shows his own excessive folly). (p. 59.)

[52] *B.C. Ava.*, ii, 33 ff.

[53] *Ṛgveda*, vii, 86 (vol. iv, pp. 212 ff.) (*kimāga āsa Varuṇa . . . pra tan me voco* . . . etc.). *Bhagavad-gītā*, xi, 42, 44, 45 (*prasīda deveça jagan-nivāsa*, etc. pp. 166, 167, Anandāçrama Series, 1908).

[54] *Dīgha*, i, 85. Cf. *Saṃyutta*, iv, 317 ff. (*Gāminī-saṃyutta*, section 8). *Majjhima*, i, 440.

[55] *Kṣemendra*, ii, 697.21; i, 1077. *Çikṣā*, 58.15, 290.2, 119.4, 170.20, 156.6, 161 ff. *B.C. Ava. Pka.*, 153, ll. 16 ff.

[56] *B.C. Ava.*, iii, 1–3.

[57] *B.C. Ava.*, iii, 4–5.

[58] *Dh. S.*, section 14.

[59] The two words "pains and sorrows" in the translation stand for only one word in the original, *duḥkha*. *B.C. Ava.*, iii, 6 ff.

[60] L. de la Vallée Poussin translates: "tant qu'il y aura des maladies" (*B.C. Ava.* tr., p. 18). The text is: "*yāvad rog-āpunar-bhavaḥ*" (iii, 7).

[61] L. de la Vallée Poussin renders *vyathā* as "le feu". But it is preferable to translate literally.

[62] *utprāsaka* (iii, 16). A rare word. The *B.C. Ava. Pka.* explains: "*upahāsakā viḍamba-kāriṇo va*" (p. 83, l. 11). Monier Williams translates *utprāsa* as "violent burst of laughter, ridicule" (Dicy. 152*a*). Böhtlingk and Roth cite only one passage from the *Sāhitya-darpaṇa*.

[63] *Saṅkrama*. Böhtlingk and Roth cite several passages from the *Rāmāyaṇa*, in which it means "Brücke, Steg über ein Wasser". The *B.C. Ava. Pka.* gives no explanation.

bhadr-ghaṭa. The *B.C. Ava. Pka.* explains: "*yad yad vastv-abhilaṣitam abhisandhāy-āsmin hastaṃ prakṣipet tat sarvaṃ sampadyate.*" Böhtlingk and Roth give no explanation. L. de la Vallée Poussin translates: "une cruche miraculeuse." But Monier Williams gives the technical sense (also A. A. Macdonnell).

Siddha-vidyā. L. de la Vallée Poussin translates: "une formule souveraine." The *B.C. Ava. Pka.* explains: "*siddha-mantraḥ yad-yat karma tayā kriyate tat sarvaṃ sidhyati.*" Böhtlingk and Roth cite a passage, in which it means "Die Lehre der Glückseligen". L. D. Barnett translates: "a spell of power" *Kāma-dhenu*: "cow of plenty" (L. D. Barnett, "Path," p. 45).

[64] D. T. Suzuki, "Outlines," pp. 311, 303.

[65] M. Anesaki, ERE. v, 450. Cf. L. de la Vallée Poussin's critical remarks in JRAS. 1908, p. 891.

[66] *Lka.*, p. 46, verse 106; p. 158, verse 38.

[67] *Saund. Kā.*, xv, 26; xviii, 27. *Lal. V.*, 412.13. *Çikṣā*, 2.4. *B.C. Ava.*, ix, 163; iv, 15, 16, 20. *Ava.-ça.*, ii, 181.13. *Çiṣya-lekha*, verses 61–3. *Su. Vy.*, 73.9, 75.9.

[68] *M. Vy.*, section 120. *Çiṣya-lekha* adds "*mlecchas*" (verse 62). These are called the eight *akṣaṇas*. Cf. S. Yamakami, "Systems," p. 92.

[69] *Sad. Pu.*, 319.11. *Çikṣā*, 2.5. *Ava.-ça.*, i, 230.5.

[70] *Sad. Pu.*, 463.4. *Saund. Kā.*, xviii, 27. *B.C. Ava.*, iv, 20. The passage translated is taken from the *Majjhima-Nikāya* (iii, 169). Cf. H. De's note in JPTS. 1906–7, p. 174.

71 *Lal. V.*, 173.1 ff.
72 *Jā. Mā.*, 226.23. *Kṣemendra*, i, 615.34.
73 *Jā. Mā.*, 227.1.
74 Ibid., 227.3.
75 Ibid., 227.5.
76 Ibid., 227.8.
77 *Divy.*, 27, 100, 486.
78 *Jā. Mā.*, 228.10.
79 Ibid., 228.14 ff., 231.1.
80 Ibid., 226.17, 226.24, 231.3.
81 *Çikṣā*, 287.14.
82 Ibid., 228.1–5.
83 Ibid., 8.12, 288.6.
84 Ibid., 288.8.
85 *Ibid.*, 288.11, 289.1.
86 *Bo. Bhū.*, 98*b*.1.2.
87 Ibid., 98*b*.2.2, 3.3.
88 Ibid., 7*a*.5.2.
89 Ibid., 7*a*.3.3, 98*b*.3.1.

90 These are the five *kaṣāyas*, which are signs of degeneracy. A Buddha is born to counteract them. Cf. *Kar. Pu.*, 16; *Su. Vy.*, 99; *Sad. Pu.*, 43; *Lal. V.*, 248.13; *Çikṣā.*, 60; *M. Vy.*, section 124; *Dh. S.*, section 91, etc. The Pāli word may literally mean "an astringent decoction of a plant"; it means "astringent" when applied to taste, and "pungent" when applied to smell (*Vinaya*, i, 277, ll. 4–5: "*nipacci kasāva-vaṇṇaṃ kasāva-gandhaṃ kasāva-rasaṃ*"). The old Pāli form is *kasāva* (Pāli Dicy., s.v.). Böhtlingk and Roth cite several passages from *Suçruta*, in which it means "a decoction". But it is difficult to understand the transition from this meaning to the figurative sense, "evils, fundamental faults, calamities". The Tibetan equivalent is *sñigs-ma*, which means "sediment, impurity or defilement in food; impurity" (Tib. Dicy., 501). The Chinese equivalent means "mud" (*M. S. Al.* tr., p. 78). Böhtlingk and Roth also cite several passages, in which *kaṣāya* signifies "sediment, impurity" (e.g. *Chāndogya Upaniṣad*, vii, 26.2, p. 435: "*tasmai mṛdita-kaṣāyāya tamasas paraṃ darçayati bhagavān*"). It is probable that the Buddhist technical term is related to *kaṣāya* in this sense (and not to the meaning "decoction"). It has been rendered as "calamities", "les cinq fanges," "les dégénérescences," "attachments," "depravities," etc. (ERE. i, 189*b*, etc.). The five *kaṣāyas* are enumerated as *āyuḥ-kaṣāya*, *dṛṣṭi-*, *kleça-*, *sattva-*, *kalpa-*. These five show signs of degeneracy. The Jainas employ this term in the sense of "sin", "passion," and reckon four *kaṣāyas*: *krodha* "anger", *māna* "pride", *māyā* "deception or illusion", and *lobha* "avarice": (J. Jaini, "Outlines," p. 94). Cf. *Uttarādhyayana-sūtra*, 31.6 "*vigahā kasāya sannāṇam*" (p. 216).

[91] *Su. Vy.*, 15. *Lal. V.*, 124.22, 181.5. *Jā. Mā.*, 36.19. *Da. Bhū.*, 11.13, etc.

[92] *B.C. Ava.*, iii, 22.23.

[93] *Bo. Bhū.*, fol. 6*a*, 2.2 to 3.1.

[94] *Bo. Bhū.*, fol. 6*a*, 4.1.

[95] *B.C. Ava.*, i, 35.

[96] *Dh. S.*, section 15.

[97] *Çikṣā.*, 356.1. *B.C. Ava.*, i, 19. *Bo. Bhū.*, 9*a*.5.1.

[98] *Pr. Pā. Aṣṭa.*, 437.

[99] *Çikṣā.*, 9.7, 10.5.

[100] *Mtu.*, i, 104, 2.

[101] *Bo. Bhū.*, fol. 6*a*, 5.2.

[102] *Mtu.*, ii, 368.5 ff.

[103] *Mtu.*, i, 40, 97.

[104] *Mtu.*, i, 83.

[105] *Bo. Bhū.*, fol. 90*b*, 2.3, 3.1.

[106] *Da. Bhū.*, 12.1.

[107] *Bo. Bhū.*, fol. 9*b*, 3.1, 4.1, 5.1. *Yakṣa*: "name of certain mythical beings or demi-gods, who are attendants on *Kuvera*, the god of wealth, and employed in the care of his garden and treasures . . . they correspond to the genii or fairies of the fairy-tales . . . Historically, they are remnants of an ancient demonology" (Pāli Dicy.).

[108] *Bo. Bhū.*, fol. 10*a*, 1.2.

[109] *Bo. Bhū.*, fol. 8*a*, 6.2 to 8*b*, 2.3.

[110] *Bo. Bhū.*, fol. 6*a*, 4.2 (*parama-bhadra parama-kalyāṇa*).

[111] *B.C. Ava.*, i, 10; iii, 27 ff. *M. S. Al.*, 16.

[112] *Bo. Bhū.*, fol. 6*b*, 4.2.

[113] *Bo. Bhū.*, fol. 6*b*, 5.1.

[114] *Çikṣā.*, 8.15. *B.C. Ava.*, i, 15.

[115] *Bo. Bhū.*, fol. 6*b*, 6; 7*a*, 2.

[116] *Bo. Bhū.*, fol. 7*a*, 2.1.

[117] *Çikṣā.*, 6, 8.

[118] *M. S. Al.*, 15.2. *Bo. Bhū.*, fol. 7*b*, 2.3. *Ava.-ça.*, i, 211.5. *Pr. Pā. Aṣṭa.*, 396.3.

[119] *Bo. Bhū.*, fol. 7*b*, 4.2, 5.1, 5.3.

[120] *Sam. Rā.*, fol. 112*b*, l. 1.

[121] *Pr. Pā. Çata.*, 937 ff.

[122] *Pr. Pā. Çata.*, 1185 ff. *Bo. Bhū.*, fol. 8*b*, 4.2.

[123] *Da. Bhū.*, 13.21.

[124] *B.C. Ava.*, v, 102 ff.

[125] *Bo. Bhū.*, fol. 8*a*, l. 4, section 3.

[126] Ibid., fol. 8*a*, 5.1.

[127] Ibid., fol. 8*a*, 5.2.

[128] Ibid., fol. 8*a*, 5.3.

[129] *Pr. Pā. Çata.*, 1263.19. *Bo. Bhū.*, fol. 8*b*, 5.3.

130 *Bo. Bhū.*, fol. 8*b*, 6.1.

131 *Bo. Bhū.*, fol. 9*a*, ll. 1, 2, 3.

132 *B.C. Ava.*, iv, 4.

133 *B.C. Ava.*, iii, 25 ff.

134 *B.C. Ava.*, iv, 12.

135 *Pr. Pā. Aṣṭa.*, 328.1, ff.

136 *Çikṣā.*, 67.15.

137 *Pr. Pā. Aṣṭa.*, 435.2.

138 D. T. Suzuki, "Outlines," p. 307.

139 JA. 1881, p. 476, ll. 5–7.

140 *M. S. Al.*, 147.25.

141 *Dh. S.*, section 112.

142 *Pr. Pā. Aṣṭa.*, 435.7 ff.

143 *Ava.-ça.*, i, 4.1; i, 10.1, etc.

144 *Lal. V.*, 161.19, 163.16, 175.13, 361.3 ff., 167.14, 399.17, 414.1.

145 *Su. Vy.*, 11 ff.

146 *Samyaktva* (Pāli : *sammatta*). It is one of the three *rāsis* of Pāii literature. In the Abhidhamma literature, three *rāsis* ("accumulations") are spoken of, viz.: *micchatta-niyato rāsi*, *sammatta-niyato rāsi*, and *aniyato rāsi* ("wrong-doing entailing immutable evil results"; "well-doing entailing immutable good results"; and "everything not so determined"). (Pāli Dicy.) (Cf. *Bo. Bhū.*, 84*b*, 4.)

Kathāvatthu, xxi, 8, p. 611 ("*sabbe kammā niyatā ti*," etc.).

147 *Su. Vy.*, 11.21.

148 *Da. Bhū.*, 14.10 ff. *Çikṣā.*, 291.11 ff. For a literal translation of this long passage, see *Çikṣā.* tr., pp. 265 ff.

149 W. H. D. Rouse translates "place" (*Çikṣā.* tr., p. 266.11), but *bhūmi* in Buddhist Sanskrit means "stage" (of a *bodhisattva's* career).

150 W. H. D. Rouse translates "animal world"; but *sattva* means "living being".

151 *Kṣemendra*, ii, 667.93, 159.26, 107.52, etc.

152 *M. Vy.*, sections 34, 26, 27.

153 *Sad. Pu.*, 65.3, ff.

154 *vidy-ācaraṇa-sampannaḥ*. This phrase may also be translated "endowed with knowledge and good conduct". Lord Chalmers translates rather freely: "walking by knowledge" (*Majjh.* tr., i, 45).

anuttaraḥ. This word should be construed with the following phrase. The *M. Vy.* puts them together (section 1, p. 2*a*). Some scholars take *anuttaraḥ* as a separate epithet.

155 *Ava.-çā.*, i, 7.2 ff.; i, 12.16 ff., etc.

156 *M. S. Al.*, 166.3.

157 *Divy.*, 150.18.

158 *Pr. Pā. Aṣṭa.*, 212.

[159] *Kṣemendra*, ii, 259.32.

[160] *Ava.-ça.*, i, 186; i, 191.11.

[161] *Kṣemendra*, ii, 975, 677, 717.

[162] On the five *gatis*, see *Divy.*, 124.15. *Saund. Kā.*, xi, 62. *Ava.-ça.*, i, 16.12. *Kar. Pu.*, 67.1. *B.C. Ava. Pka.*, 589.15, etc.

Pretas. They are not merely "ghosts of the dead" as A. B. Keith assumes ("Indian Mythology," p. 203. Boston, 1917). They are a special class of beings, born in a state of woe.

[163] On the six *gatis* and the *asuras*, see *Lka.*, 347; *Mtu.*, i, 30; *Çikṣā.*, 253; *Divy.*, 394.10; *Çiṣya-lekhā*, 99; *Kā. Vy.*, 16.3; *Da. Bhū.*, 62.9; *Ava.-ça.*, i, 215.5, etc.

[164] Cf. *Çatapatha-Brāhmaṇa*, ii, 3.3.9 (*iha vai punar-mṛtyuṃ mucyate*, p. 94); x, 1.4.14 (p. 510) "*yajamānaḥ punar-mṛtyum apajayati*" etc. (Vedic Press, Ajmer, *saṃvat* 1959.)

[165] ERE, xii, 434*b*.

[166] *Saṃyutta*, ii, 178 ff. ("*Anamataggāyam bhikkhave saṃsāro*"). Cf. L. de la Vallée Poussin, "Nirvāṇa," pp. 34 ff.; C. A. F. Rhys Davids, "Psychology," pp. 244 ff.

[167] *Skandha* (Pāli: *Khandha*). This word is derived from the root *skand* "to rise", and literally means "shoulder", "upper part of the back"; hence "trunk" of a tree, "bulk or mass in general," "heap," "ingredients or parts," "constituent elements," "sensorial aggregates." It has also been translated as "les épaules", "les appuis", "les troncs", "supports", "Daseinselemente", "les Branches", etc.

[168] *Mtu.*, iii, 335.

[169] L. de la Vallée Poussin, "Opinions," pp. 81, 168. *Le Muséon*, 1905, p. 51. S. Konow, "Lehrbuch," ii, 112. E. Burnouf, "Int.," pp. 423, 449, 573. Nyāṇatiloka, *Aṅguttara* tr., i, 285. SBE., vol. x, pt. i, p. 56, note. Th. Stcherbatsky, "Conception," p. 20. H. Hackmann, "Buddhism," p. 13. F. L. Woodward, "Sayings," p. 29. H. Beckh, "Buddhismus," ii, 81. S. Lévi, *M. S. Al.*, tr. p. 47. E. Senart, RHR. 1900, tome 42, p. 351. C. H. Warren, "Buddhism," p. 116. O. C. J. Rosenberg, "Probleme," ii, 212. K. E. Neumann, *Majjh.* tr., ii, 249. K. J. Saunders, "Epochs," p. 5. H. Oldenberg, "Buddha," p. 274. M. Walleser, *Pr. Pā.* tr., p. 6. T. W. Rhys Davids, "Buddhism," p. 156. Sīlācāra, *Majjh.* tr., p. 126. "Dialogues," ii, 196, ii, 335; iii, 211, 204. J. S. Speyer, *Jā. Mā.* tr., p. 324. E. J. Thomas, "Buddha," p. 89. H. Kern, "Manual," pp. 47, 51. S. Dasgupta, "Yoga," p. 98. R. Franke, *Dīgha*, pp. 307 ff. R. Garbe, *Sāṅkhya*, p. 269. R. Chalmers, *Majjh.* tr., i, 95. M. Winternitz, "Lesebuch," pp. 223, 239, 251. F. Heiler, "Versenkung," p. 11. D. T. Suzuki, "Outlines," p. 150. P. Oltramare, "Bouddhique," p. 161. P. Foucaux, *Lal. V.* tr., p. 349. SBE., vol. xiii, p. 76. Th. Stcherbatsky, "Nirvāna," pp. 184, 197. C. F. Koeppen, "Buddha," i, 603. C. A. F. Rhys Davids, "Psychology," p. 51; "Sakya," p. 378, etc.

170 "Compendium," pp. 94 ff. D. T. Suzuki, "Outlines," p. 151.
171 A. B. Keith, "Philosophy," p. 86.
172 R. O. Franke, *Dīgha*, p. 311.
173 P. Oltramare, "Bouddhique," p. 161, note.
174 *Saṃyutta*, iii, 87, ll. 8 ff. (*khandha-saṃyutta*).
175 *Dīgha*, iii, 217. *Saṃyutta*, ii, 82, ll. 9 ff.
176 *Dhamma-saṅgaṇi*, section 62, p. 18.
177 *Abhidharma-koça*, i, 15*a* (vol. i, p. 28).
178 *M. Vy.*, section 104.
179 *Milinda*, p. 61, l. 20.
180 Th. Stcherbatsky, "Conception," p. 20.
181 C. A. F. Rhys Davids, "Gotama," p. 35. JRAS. 1927, p. 201.
182 *Dhamma-saṅgaṇi*, section 63.
183 *Abhidharma-koça*, i, 16*a* (vol. i, pp. 30–1).
184 *Mdh.*, 366, 341. *Vajra*, 25, 21. *Da. Bhū.*, 55, 49. *M. S. Al.*, 154. *Lka.*, 68. *Pr. Pā. Çata.*, 1509. *Saund. Kā.*, xviii, 15, etc.
185 *Lal. V.*, 419.5 ff. *Mtu.*, iii, 335.12 ff., 338, 447.
186 *M. Vy.*, section 208. *Pr. Pā. Çata.*, 472, 522.
187 *Mdh.* 347.12, 349.9. *Pr. Pā. Çata.*, 582. *Çikṣā*, 242. *B.C. Ava.*, ix, 78.
188 *Lka.*, 253. *Ava.-ça.*, i, 85.10; i, 292.12; ii, 75.11. *Da Bhū.*, 39. *M. S. Al.*, 34. *Mdh.*, 340, 361. *Kar. Pu.*, 1. *Kā. Vy.*, 47. *B.C. Ava.*, ix, 78 ff.
189 *Pr. Pā. Aṣṭa.*, 431.2.
190 *Ava.-ça.*, ii, 75.11, and passim. E. Burnouf, "Int.," p. 235. *M. Vy.*, section 209.
191 *Kṣemendra*, i, 659.53. *Jā. Mā.*, passim.
192 *Da. Bhū.*, 35. *Lal. V.*, 345, etc.
193 *Bṛhadāraṇyaka Upd.*, ii, 5.1. *Kaṭha Upd.*, i, 3.15; i, 2.22. *Muṇḍaka Upd.*, i, 1.6, etc.
194 St. John, iv, 24.
195 *Dīgha*, ii, 63.2 ff.
196 *Saṃyutta* i, 122.10 ff.; iii, 124.9 ff.
197 *M. S. Al.*, 185. *Çikṣā.*, 13. *Mtu.*, ii, 362, 364.
198 *Mtu.*, i, 2; i, 46.
199 *Bo. Bhū.*, fol. 137*b*, 6.2–3. *M. S. Al.*, 183.
200 Cf. *Thera-gāthā*, verse 112, p. 16; verse 115, p. 16; verse 493, p. 51, etc. *Dīgha*, ii, 314–15. *Majjh.*, ii, 103.
201 *Ava.-ça.*, ii, 71.7; ii, 117.9.
202 *Ava.-ça.*, i, 128.6; i, 133.10; i, 162.4.
203 *Da. Bhū.*, 46, 54. *Sad. Pu.*, 207.10, 263.10, 312.1. *Lal. V.*, 124.18, 130.5, 151.20, 271.9, 282.4. *M. S. Al.*, 9.
204 *Mtu.*, i, 55.8; i, 57.5. *Lal. V.*, 215.6. *Sad. Pu.*, 200.12 *M. S. Al.*, 33. *Pr. Pā. Aṣṭa.*, 518.12.
205 *Çikṣā.*, 97.12. *M. Vy.*, section 249.

206 *Mdh.*, 431.5. *M. S. Al.*, 171. *Ava.-ça.*, i, 7. *Bo. Bhū.*, fol. 138*a*, 4.1.

207 W. Kirfel, "Kosmographie," p. 336. S. Hardy, "Manual," p. 6.

208 M. Rémusat, "Mélanges posthumes d'Histoire et de Littérature Orientales," p. 69, l. 8 (Paris, 1843).

209 W. Kirfel, "Kosmographie," p. 336. S. Hardy, "Manual," p. 6.

210 "Buddhist Birth Stories," vol. i, p. 28 (London, 1880).

211 L. de la Vallée Poussin, "Opinions," p. 294; "Morale," p. 224.

212 J. E. Carpenter, "Theism," p. 61.

213 *Lal. V.*, 147. *Abhidharma-koça*, iii, 93*d*–94*a*, pp. 189–90. *M. Vy.*, section 249.

214 *Abhidharma-koça*, iii, 89*d*–93*c*, pp. 181 ff. *Aṅguttara*, ii, 142, section 156.

215 *Mtu.*, i, 77.

CHAPTER IV

Notes

[1] *Nettipakaraṇa*, xxxi. The adjective *bodhipakkhiya* is applied to the five *balas* in *Saṃyutta*, v, 227, and to the seven *bojjhaṅgas* in *Vibhaṅga*, 249.

[2] Ibid., p. 112.

[3] *M. Vy.*, sections 38 ff. *Dh. S.*, section 43. *Da. Bhū.*, 38 ff. *Sam. Rā.*, fol. 193*b*, 3 ff. *Pr. Pā. Çata.*, 1427 ff.

[4] *Divy.*, 207, 208.

[5] SBE. x, pt. i, p. 27.

[6] *Dīgha*, ii, 290. *Majjh.*, i, 55 ff.

[7] "Dialogues," ii, 324.

[8] JPTS. 1915–16, p. 26.

[9] C. A. F. Rhys Davids, "Psychology," p. 91.

[10] *Lal. V.*, 34.15.

[11] *Lal. V.*, 239.2.

[12] *Lal. V.*, 434.16.

[13] *Mtu.*, i, 160.12. *M. Vy.*, section 9.

[14] *Lal. V.*, 273.5.

[15] *Lal. V.*, 8.2.

[16] *Lal. V.*, 373.4.

[17] *Pr. Pā. Aṣṭa.*, 326.7.

[18] *M. S. Al.*, 172.22.

[19] *Jā. Mā.*, 2.24.

[20] *Da. Bhū.*, 8.6; 42.15; 44.18.

[21] *Pr. Pā. Çata.*, 1429.

[22] *Kar. Pu.*, 104.

[23] *Saund. Kā.*, xiv, 1.

[24] Ibid., xiii, 30.

[25] Ibid., xvi, 33.

[26] *Çikṣā.*, 356.9.

[27] *Sam. Rā.*, fol. 85*a*, 3.

[28] *viṣameṣu caran*. E. H. Johnston suggests several explanations: "On uneven ground," and "among the *viṣamas* (*rāga, dveṣa, moha*)". "But *viṣayeṣu* might possibly remain, as the blind man without a guide knocks against things as he walks" (*Saund. Kā.*, p. 157).

[29] *B.C. Ava.*, v, 108. *Ava.-ça.*, i, 244.10. *Sam. Rā.*, fol. 7*b*.4.

30 *Viparyāsa* is translated as "mistakes" by L. de la Vallée Poussin, "Nirvāṇa," p. 152.

31 *Pr. Pā. Çata.*, 1427. *Da. Bhū.*, 38.

32 *Lal. V.*, 33.11.

33 *Lal. V.*, 208; 328.20. *Çikṣā.*, 229, 77, 81. *Pr. Pā. Çata.*, 1430. *Kṣemendra*, ii, 578.

34 *Divy.*, 39.11.

35 *Çikṣā.*, 81.15.

36 *Kṣemendra*, ii, 573.32.

37 *Pr. Pā. Çata.*, 1431. *Çikṣā.*, 228, 209.

38 *Pr. Pā. Çata.*, 1430. *Ava.-ça.*, ii, 191.4. *Saund. Kā.*, ix, 12. Two other elements are sometimes mentioned, viz. *ākāça* (ether, space) and *vijñāna* (mentality).

39 *Çikṣā.*, 210.4 ff. *Pr. Pā.*, *Çata.*, 1430. Cf. *Dīgha*, ii, 293 ff.; *Majjh.*, iii, 90 ff.

40 *Pr. Pā. Çata.*, 1431.2 ff. *Çikṣā.*, 210.

Note.—The word, which is translated as "granaries", is *mṛtotri* in the *Pr. Pā. Çata.*, and *mūṭoḍī* in the *Çikṣā.* In Pāli, it is *mutoḷī* (*Dīgha*, ii, 293). The Tibetan equivalent is *rjaṅma*, which means "store-room" (Tib. Dicy., 463*a*). It has also been translated as "sample-bag", "sack", "bundle", "provision-bag." It has been interpreted as a distortion of Pāli *puṭosā* (see Pāli Dicy., s.v.). But the Tibetan Dicy. gives a better meaning.

41 *Çikṣā.*, 229.

Note.—*Ākāça.* This word is derived from *kāç*, literally "shining forth", "illuminated space". It has also been incorrectly explained as a derivative of *kṛṣ*. It is usually translated as "space" or "ether". But it is better not to translate it.

42 *Çikṣā.*, 229.

43 *Lal. V.*, 328.22. *Saund. Kā.*, ix, 6. *Çikṣā.*, 229, 77.

44 *Saund. Kā.*, ix, 6, 29. *Çikṣā.*, 77.11.

45 *Lal. V.*, 324.7. *Saund. Kā.*, ix, 6.

46 *Kṣemendra*, ii, 211.96.

47 Ibid., i, 959.59.

48 *Saund. Kā.*, ix, 6, 11.

49 *Divy.*, 180.23–4. *Çikṣā.*, 229.12. *Divy.*, 281.30.

50 *Lal. V.*, 208.13. *Çikṣā.*, 228.14.

51 *Saund. Kā.*, ix, 9. *Kṣemendra*, ii, 573.33. *Lal. V.*, 328.22.

52 *Çikṣā.*, 229.11. W. H. D. Rouse translates "despair, thieves", . . . (*Çikṣā.*, tr., p. 217). But the sins and passions are metaphorically spoken of as "thieves": Cf. *B.C. Ava.*, v, 28 (*kleça-taskara-saṅgho 'yam*).

53 *Çikṣā.*, 77.12.

54 *Saund. Kā.*, ix, 12, 13.

[55] *Vipaḍumaka*. Cf. Pāli *puḷuvaka*. The Tibetan equivalent is *rnam-par-ḥbus-gshig-pa*. *Ḥbu* means "worm, insect", and *gshi* seems to mean "residence, abode".
[56] *B. Ct.*, Canto iii. Cf. *Dīgha*, ii, 22.
[57] *Kṣemendra*, i, 689.
[58] *Dīgha*, ii, 295 ff. *Majjh.* iii, 89 ff.
[59] J. Jaini, "Outlines" p. 98.
[60] *Lal. V.*, 32.21.
[61] *Çiṣya-lekha*, verse 88.
[62] *Bo. Bhū.*, fol. 46*a*, 3.2.
[63] *Kṣemendra*, i, 681.77.
[64] *Bo. Bhū.*, fol. 82*a*, 3.1. *Çikṣā.*, p. 209.6.
[65] *Çikṣā.*, 209.12.
[66] *Çikṣā.*, 230.
[67] *Lal. V.*, 263.21.
[68] *Kar. Pu.*, 108.6. *Jā. Mā.*, 158.6. *Kṣemendra*, ii, 51.25.
[69] *Jā. Mā.*, 158.7.
[70] *B.C. Ava.*, v, 70. *Jā. Mā.*, 202.21.
[71] *Jā. Mā.*, 4.6.
[72] *Divy.*, 384.5.
[73] *B.C. Ava.*, v, 66.
[74] *Çikṣā.*, 277.
[75] Ibid., 348–9.
[76] *Kṣemendra*, ii, 939.5.
[77] Ibid., i, 43.89.
[78] Ibid., i, 165.42.
[79] Ibid., i, 29.29; ii, 51.26.
[80] Ibid., ii, 1081.174.
[81] *Sam. Rā.*, fol. 95*a*.5.
[82] *Pr. Pā. Çata.*, 152 ff., 952.
[83] T. W. Rhys Davids, "Dialogues," ii, 128. L. de la Vallée Poussin, "Opinions," p. 81. L. Feer, *Ava.-ça.*, tr., p. 406. P. Oltramare, "Bouddhique," p. 348. P. E. Foucaux ("La perception par les sens"), *Lal. V.*, tr., p. 34.
[84] ERE, v, 455.
[85] *Ava.-ça.*, ii, 192.1 ff.
[86] L. A. Waddell, "Buddhism," p. 116.
[87] R. O. Franke ("Gefühle"), *Dīgha*, p. 187. *Çikṣā.*, tr., p. 218.
[88] *Dhamma-saṅgaṇi*, section 358, p. 73. *Dīgha*, iii, 221, etc.
[89] *Cittaṃ pragṛhṇāti samyak pradadhāti*. Some scholars translate it as one clause, "fixes and controls his mind." But the *Pr. Pā. Çata.* gives two clauses (p. 1436), and there is no strong reason why the second clause should be construed with *citta*.
[90] *Nīvaraṇāni*. The five *nīvaraṇas* are: (1) *Abhidyā* or *Kāmacchanda*: "covetousness, lust." (2) *Vyāpāda*: "malice, ill-will."

(3) *Styāna-middha* (Pāli *thīna-middham*) : " indolence of mind and body ; sloth and torpor ". (4) *Auddhatya-kaukṛtyam* : see note 29, Chap. I. (5) *Vicikitsā* : " doubt." It has also been rendered as " perplexity ", " suspense ", " a wavering mind ", etc. (*Dhamma-saṅgaṇi*, sections 1153 ff.; *M. S. Al.*, 141 ; *Pr. Pā. Aṣṭa.*, 480.6.)

[91] C. A. F. Rhys Davids, " Sakya," p. 236.

[92] *Mtu.*, iii, 321.13. *M. Vy.*, section 16. *Dh. S.*, section 133.

[93] Cf. *Dīgha*, iii, 221. *Majjh.*, i, 103.32 ff. *Aṅguttara*, i, 39.22 ff; ii, 256.25 ff. *Saṃyutta*, v, 254.

[94] *Lal. V.*, 33.17. *M. S. Al.*, 142.15.

Note.—The following adjectival clauses are sometimes added after the description of each *ṛddhipāda* : " based upon detachment (*viveka*), absence of passion (*virāga*), and Cessation, and directed or turned towards renunciation (*vyavasarga-pariṇata*) " ; cf. *Dīgha*, iii, 226.

[95] e.g. five *abhijñās* are mentioned in the following passages: *Jā. Mā.*, 146.4. *Da. Bhū.*, 34 ff. *Ava.-ça.*, i, 210. *Kar. Pu.*, 113.32, 114.28. *Saund. Kā.*, xvi, 1. *Mtu.*, iii, 145.15. *Pr. Pā. Çata.*, 65.9, 97.1. *Divy.*, 152.22. *Kṣemendra*, ii, 21, verse 71, etc.

Six *abhijñās* are mentioned in the following passages : *Sad. Pu.*, 129.10. *M. S. Al.*, 25, 185. *Pr. Pā. Çata.*, 1636. *Kā. Vy.*, 60.5. *B.C. Ava. Pka.*, 428.4. *Divy.*, 44.25, etc.

[96] Cf. *Dīgha*, iii, 281.

[97] Cf. *Dīgha*, i, 84. *Majjh.*, i, 12, etc.

[98] The *Bo. Bhū.* seems to identify the *kleças* with the *āsravas* (fol. 31*a*, 1–3).

[99] *Dhamma-saṅgaṇi*, section 1229.

[100] *Dīgha*, i, 84. *Majjh.*, ii, 39. *Dhamma-saṅgaṇi*, sections 1448, 1096.

[101] The eight " powers " of *Yoga* are as follows :—(1) atomization, (2) levitation, (3) magnification, (4) extension, (5) efficacy, the non-obstruction of desire, (6) mastery, (7) sovereignty, (8) the capacity of determining things according to desire. (J. H. Woods, *Yoga*, p. 278.)

[102] *Pr. Pā. Çata.*, 1453.8. Cf. *Saṃyutta*, ii, 213.33 ff.; *Dīgha*, i, 82 (*Sāmañña-phala-sutta*).

[103] *Pr. Pā. Çata.*, 294. The ten directions are North, South, West, East, North-east, East-south, South-west, West-north, Downward (*nadir*), Upward (zenith).

[104] *Bo. Bhū.*, fol. 29*b*.6.

[105] *Kṣemendra*, ii, 779.22. *Ava.-ça.*, i, 230.13; i, 319.12.

[106] Cf. *Saṃyutta*, ii, 212. *Dīgha*, i, 79.

[107] *Bo. Bhū.*, fol. 29*b*.2.1.

[108] Ibid., fol. 29*b*.4.1–2.

[109] Ibid., fol. 29*b*.5.1.

[110] *Mtu.*, ii, 284.8 ff. *Lal. V.*, 345. *Da. Bhū.*, 35.23 ff.

Lal. V., 375.16. *M. Vy.*, section 15, p. 21. Cf. *Saṃyutta*, ii, 213.16 ff.

[111] *M. S. Al.*, 25.7. *Da. Bhū.*, 70.16.

[112] *Dīgha*, i, 78.1 ff. *Saṃyutta*, ii, 212.19 ff.

[113] *M. Vy.*, section 15. *M. S. Al.*, 26.2. *Da. Bhū.*, 35.

[114] Cf. R. Schmidt, "Fakire und Fakirtum," pp. 42-110 (Berlin, 1908).

[115] *Kāyena vaçe vartayati.* It may also be rendered: "controls the beings as far as."

[116] L. de la Vallée Poussin translates "verts" ("Le Muséon," 1911, p. 156). But the MS. reading is *pīta*, "yellow." Cf. *Mtu.*, iii, 115.18 ff.; iii, 410.5 ff. *Divy.*, 161. *M. Vy.*, section 15. *Da. Bhū.*, 35. The items from (*h*) to (*n*) are given on the authority of L. de la Vallée Poussin's article in "Le Muséon", 1911, p. 157, as the manuscript is illegible.

[117] *Bo. Bhū.*, fol. 34*b*.3.2. *M. S. Al.*, 183.26.

[118] *M. S. Al.*, 20.12.

[119] *Ava.-ça.*, ii, 4.4; i, 3.4.

[120] *Divy.*, 150.5.

[121] *Mtu.*, ii, 315.12.

[122] *Bo. Bhū.*, fol. 6*b*.6.2.

[123] *Lal. V.*, 177.20. *Sad. Pu.*, 380.2.

[124] *Bo. Bhū.*, 35*a*.5.

[125] *Mtu.*, iii, 430.13.

[126] *Sad. Pu.*, 392.9; 17.6, 25.2. *Mtu.*, iii, 116.6.

[127] *Sad. Pu.*, 150.3, 228.5, 313.2. *Divy.*, 150.25.

[128] *Bo. Bhū.*, fol. 62*a*.2.

[129] *Divy.*, pp. 144 ff.

[130] *M. S. Al.*, 25.6.

[131] *Lal. V.*, 407.5, 414.8. *Ava.-ça.*, ii, 117. *Divy.*, 156. *Kar. Pu.*, 115.2. *Lka.*, 4. *Divy.*, 49.

[132] *Mtu.*, i, 71.1.

[133] *Ava.-ça.*, i, 331.12.

[134] *Kar. Pu.*, 5.3. *Ava.-ça.*, ii, 91.3. *Divy.*, 294.

[135] *Ava.-ça.*, i, 190.5

[136] *Pr. Pā. Çata.*, 381.21. *Su. Vy.*, 53.

[137] *Ava.-ça.*, ii, 433; ii, 49.

[138] *Divy.*, 201.10.

[139] *Pr. Pā. Çata.*, 106.22 ff.

[140] SBE., vol. x, pt. i, p. 13.

[141] J. Jaini, "Outlines," p. 93.

[142] J. Jaini, "Outlines," p. 93.

[143] J. Jaini, "Outlines," p. 93.

[144] H. T. Colebrooke, "Essays," vol. i, pp. 447 ff.

[145] *Uttarādhyayana-sūtra*: xviii, 5, p. 137, *jhayai kkhaviyāsave*;

xxxiv, 21, p. 243, *paṃcāsava-ppavatto tīhiṃ agutto*, ; xxviii, 14, p. 194, *puṇṇam pāvāsavā tahā*.

[146] ERE., vii, .7.

[147] A. B. Keith, "Philosophy," p. 128, note 1. L. de la Vallée Poussin, "Théorie des douze Causes," p. 8, note 1 (Gand, 1913).

[148] E. J. Thomas, "Buddha," p. 68, note.

[149] *Bo. Bhū.*, fol. 31*a*.3.1; fol. 31*a*.2.2.

[150] *Bo. Bhū.*, fol. 31*a*, l. 3, section 2.

[151] *Bo. Bhū.*, fol. 31*a*.3.3.

[152] Cf. *Dīgha*, i, 156. *Majjhima*, ii, 39, etc.

[153] *Mtu.*, ii, 406.6. *M. Vy.*, section 225. *Lal. V.*, 206.22 *Pr. Pā. Aṣṭa.*, 488.11. *Mdh.*, 388.15. *Divy.*, 37.20. *Çikṣā*, 281.9, etc.

[154] *Mtu.*, iii, 374.5.

[155] *Dh. S.*, section 24. *Pr. Pā. Çata.*, 671.

[156] *Divy.*, 37.29 ff.

[157] *Karaṅka*. P. E. Foucaux translates "ordure" (*Lal. V.*, tr., 182). But the word means "bone, skull" (Skt. Dicy., M.W.).

[158] *lepena*. P. E. Foucaux translates "piège".

[159] *Çardūla*. I have followed P. E. Foucaux's translation.

[160] *Potaḥ*. P. E. Foucaux translates "matelots"; but the word means "ship".

[161] *āvartyante*. P. E. Foucaux translates, "dompté." But the word means "turn round".

[162] *badhyante*. The translation is conjectural.

[163] *kuçalārtha*. E. B. Cowell translates "the robbers of our happiness and our wealth" (SBE., vol. xlix, p. 112). But it is better to construe thus: "*kuçalam ev-ārthaḥ*."

[164] *Samudra-vastrām*. F. Weller translates from the Tibetan, "die vom Meere umgürtete Erde".

[165] On the *Māndhātṛ* legend, cf. *Divy.*, pp. 213 ff.

[166] On *Nahuṣa*, cf. *Mahābhārata*, v, 527 ff. (Calcutta edition). Also J. Dowson, "Hindu Classical Dictionary," p. 214 (London, 1914). *Mahābhārata, Udyoga-parvan*, ll. 527 ff. (vol. ii, p. 104, Calcutta edition). *Çṛṇu çakra priyaṃ vākyam*, etc.

[167] On *Purūravas*, cf. *Mahābhārata, Ādiparvan*, ll. 3147 ff. (vol. i, p. 113, Calcutta edition). *Tato maharṣibhiḥ kruddhaiḥ*, etc. J. Dowson, "Hindu Classical Dictionary," p. 247.

[168] *Bhāgya-kul-ākula*. F. Weller translates from the Tibetan: "die Sinnesfreuden, die an einer Fülle von Schicksalen voll sind." This seems to suit the context better than E. B. Cowell's translation: "unsettled as to lot or family."

[169] *Anyakāryāḥ*. F. Weller states that the Tibetan text corresponds to *ananya-kāryāḥ*. *Cīra*. E. B. Cowell translates "rags"; but the

sages are often spoken of as clad in the bark of trees, not in rags. F. Weller translates from the Tibetan: "Baumrinde."

[170] *tad-vṛttinām*. The Tibetan reading corresponds to *vratānām*: "they must lead to the violation of vows."

[171] On *Ugrāyudha*, see *Harivaṃça*, chap. xx. *Mahābhārata*, vol. iv, p. 481, ll. 1074 ff. (Calcutta edition). *Ugrāyudhaḥ kasya sutaḥ*, etc.

[172] F. Weller translates thus from the Tibetan: "Wenn man sich (ihnen) vereint, nachdem man der Meinung geworden ist, bei Sinnesgenüssen sei geringer Kummer, (so) ist über die Massen keine Sattigung. Wer (möchte) das Gift zu sich nehmen, das den Namen Sinneslust führt, da die Guten (sie) tadeln und (sie) sicher schlecht ist."

[173] *paripānti* in E. B. Cowell's text. F. Weller translates from the Tibetan: "Kommt zu leid" (= Skt. *pariyānti*). I have adopted the latter reading.

[174] Cf. *Lal. V.*, 325.3.

[175] *Sārameyāḥ*. There is no word in the Tibetan text corresponding to *sārameyāḥ* (F. Weller).

[176] For the idea, cf. *Jā. Mā.*, 122.7.

[177] *āyatana*. The word is derived from the root *yam* (with *ā*), and literally means "stretch, extent, reach", hence "region", "sphere", etc.

[178] F. Weller translates from the Tibetan: "Holzscheit bei der Leichenverbrennung." For such similes, cf. *Mtu.*, i, 73.12; ii, 327.3. *Lal. V.*, 329.8. *Jā. Mā.*, 122.9. *B.C. Ava.*, viii, 84, etc.

[179] F. Weller translates "die Nächtigung". The Tibetan word does not correspond to *çayyā*.

[180] The Tibetan word corresponds to *bhogāḥ* (not *bhogyāḥ*).

[181] *saṃjñā*. E. B. Cowell translates "name". But *saṃjñā* in Buddhist Sanskrit often means "idea, notion.

[182] *Anaikāntikatā*. E. B. Cowell translates: "Since variableness is found in all pleasures." F. Weller translates from the Tibetan: "Weil die Sinneslüste nicht den Charakter des Absoluten haben." A. B. Keith renders the word as "uncertain" ("Philosophy," p. 313).

[183] *agurūṇi*. F. Weller's translation, based on the Tibetan text, is evidently incorrect: "schwere und nicht-schwere Gewänder." The parallelism of the verses is lost, and the words yield no proper sense. *agurūṇi* is intended to correspond to sandal-wood in the next line. E. B. Cowell's rendering is preferable: "aloe-wood".

[184] *anavakṛṣṭa-kāyaḥ*. The Tibetan equivalent is "*bram ze de dag ḥdod pa rnams las lus dben par mi gans* (*Lal. V. Tib.*, p. 215, ll. 13–14). (*dben* = "solitary, lonely, separated", Tib. Dicy., Das, 912).

[185] *Lal. V.*, 323.21.

[186] *Mtu.*, ii, 325.20. *Lal. V.*, 324.4.

[187] *Lal. V.*, 324.14.

188 *Lal. V.*, 325.17.
189 *Lal. V.*, 328.1.
190 *Mtu.*, ii, 324.20.
191 *Mtu.*, ii, 325.15.
192 *Lal. V.*, 416. *Mtu.*, iii, 331.
193 *Divy.*, 37.20 ff.
194 *parikalpa.* The past participle *parikappita* (of Pāli *parikappati*) means " inclined, determined, decided, fixed upon ".
195 *Jā. Mā.*, 114.15. *M. S. Al.*, 167.4. *Mtu.*, iii, 357.13.
196 *Mdh.*, 388.17.
197 *B.C. Ava.*, viii, 40 ff.
198 *B.C. Ava.*, viii, 48, 52, 70.
199 *B.C. Ava.*, viii, 50.
200 *B.C. Ava.*, viii, 53. For *gūtha*, cf. *Mtu.*, ii, 326.3.
201 *B.C. Ava.*, viii, 71 ff.
202 *B.C. Ava.*, viii, 72, 74.
203 *B.C. Ava.*, viii, 76.
204 *B.C. Ava.*, viii, 77.
205 *B.C. Ava.*, viii, 79.
206 *B.C. Ava.*, viii, 80, 81, 83.
207 *Jā. Mā.*, 114.21, 122.7.
208 *Çikṣā.*, 281.14. *Lal. V.*, 326.14. *Kṣemendra*, i, 13.41.
209 *Mtu.*, i, 244.3.
210 *Çikṣā.*, 281.11, 281.16.
211 *Mtu.*, iii, 453.14 ff.
212 Cf. St. Jerome's words : " St. Peter washed off the filth of marriage in the blood of martyrdom " (cited in F. W. Farrar's " Lives of the Fathers ", ii, 329). Pietro Damiani's " Liber Gomorrhianus " (eleventh century A.D.). Also F. W. Farrar, " Lives of the Fathers," vol. ii, p. 400 (Edinburgh, 1889, 2 vols). E. Leigh-Bennett, " Handbook of the early Christian Fathers," pp. 240–1 (London, 1920).
213 *Dh. S.*, sections 127, 128, 129.
214 *Dh. S.*, section 137. *M. Vy.*, section 207. *Mdh.*, 446.10 ff., 586 ff., 536 ff. *Lka.*, 114.
215 Cf. *Dhamma-saṅgaṇi*, sections 1099, 1315–20. *Majjhima*, i, 484. *Dīgha*, i, 13.40.
216 *Jīva* = " vital spirit ", " vital principle " (not " soul ").
217 *Mdh.*, 446, 536.
218 *Lka.*, 114. *Divy.*, 164.
219 L. de la Vallée Poussin, " Opinions," p. 164.
220 *Da. Bhū.*, 64.22. *Pr. Pā. Çata.*, 478. *Divy.*, 124.13. *M. Vy.*, section 109.
221 *Mtu.*, iii, 384.10. *Pr. Pā. Çata.*, 478.
222 *Lka.*, 28. *Kar. Pu.*, 118.17.
223 *Divy.*, 44.24.

[224] *Sad. Pu.*, 135–8 ff.
[225] *Kṣemendra*, ii, 771.71.
[226] *M. S. Al.*, 51.8.
[227] *Pr. Pā. Çata.*, 97.
[228] *Kṣemendra*, ii, 795.91.
[229] *Da. Bhū.*, 34. *Pr. Pā. Çata.*, 1458.
[230] *M.S. Al.*, 183.42.
[231] Cf. *Vinaya*, v, 131.9 ff. *Milinda*, p. 351. *Majjhima*, i, 282; ii, 6.
[232] *M. Vy.*, section 49. *Dh. S.*, section 63. *Pr. Pā. Aṣṭa.*, 387.
[233] *Sam. Rā.*, fol. 121*a*.3 ff.
[234] *Mtu.*, i, 64.15.
[235] *Da. Bhū.*, 98.2. *Çikṣā.*, 191.10.
[236] SBE., vol. xx, p. 90, note 3.
[237] E. Burnouf, "Int.," p. 273.1 ff.
[238] *Dh. S.*, p. 49.
[239] E. Burnouf, "Int.," p. 274.
[240] The Pāli words *ekāsana* and *ekāsanika*, however, often mean "living or sitting alone, one who keeps to himself" (*Mil.*, p. 20). *Ekāsanabhojana* (*Majjh.*, i, 437).
[241] E. Burnouf, "Int.," p. 275.
[242] *Dh. S.*, p. 49.
[243] H. Kern, "Manual," p. 76.
[244] E. Burnouf, "Int.," p. 277.
[245] *Lal. V.*, 354.1, 429.3.
[246] *Lal. V.*, 364.10.
[247] *Lal. V.*, 287.20.
[248] *Mtu.*, 441.1.
[249] *Lal. V.*, 416.20.
[250] *Jā. Mā.*, 60.16.
[251] On Devadatta's proposals, cf. *Vinaya* iii, 171 (*Saṅghādisesa*, x).
[252] *Milinda*, pp. 351–20 ff., 352.2 ff., *aṭṭhārasahi guṇehi samāpetā bhavanti*.
[253] *Kṣemendra*, i, 881.45; ii, 499.48.
[254] *Uttarādhyayana-sūtra*, 29.27, p. 203, *Taveṇam vodānam jaṇayai*. J. Jaini, "Outlines," pp. 100, 131.
[255] *Majjhima*, i, 93; ii, 218.
[256] *Majjh.*, ii, 36.2 (*Cūla-sakuludāyi sutta*).
[257] Diogenes Laertius, vol. ii, pp. 3 ff.
[258] St. Luke, vii, 34. Timothy, ii, iv, 23.
[259] Cf. Montalembert, "Moines," vol. i, pp. 61, 101.
[260] *Mtu.*, ii, 231 ff. *Lal. V.*, 250 ff. Cf. *Majjhima*, i, 77 ff. (*Mahā-sīhanāda-sutta*).
[261] *Da. Bhū.*, 14.21, 86.27. *M. S. Al.*, 50. *Divy.*, 391.
[262] *Lal. V.*, 250.4, 250.21, 256.13, 251.3, 259.1.

263 *Mtu.*, ii, 204.6.

264 *Kṣemendra*, ii, 39.122.

265 *M. S. Al.*, 26.2.

266 *Da. Bhū.*, 70.7 ff. *Dh. S.*, section 74. *M. Vy.*, section 27. *Lka.*, pp. 1, 309, 359.

267 *Dīgha*, iii, 253, 283. *Dhamma-saṅgaṇi*, sections 58, 95. *Aṅguttara*, ii, 141, 142.

268 *Dīgha* ii, 100, 120.

269 *M. Vy.*, section 9. *Mtu.*, i, 160.

270 On five *skandhas*, cf. *M. Vy.*, section 4. *Pr. Pā. Aṣṭa.*, 312.1.

271 *Vibhāṅga*, pp. 122, 124. (*Indriya-vibhaṅgo*).

272 Pāli Dicy., s.v. *indriya*.

273 H. Kern, " Manual," p. 67.

274 *Majjhima*, i, 101.5 ff. (*Ceto-khila-sutta*). *Dīgha*, iii, 237.24 ff.

275 *Vide supra*, note 10, Chap. II.

276 *Lal. V.*, 392.1. *M. Vy.*, section 78.

277 *Ava.-ça.*, i, 205.5.

278 *Lal. V.*, 31.12, 33.17, 33.21.

279 *Da. Bhū.*, 19.21.

280 *Çikṣā.*, 316.

281 *Lal. V.*, 392.17.

282 *Lal. V.*, 400.19.

283 *Divy.*, 35.7. *Kar. Pu.*, 106.22.

284 *Mtu.*, iii, 271.8, 109.25.

285 *Lal. V.*, 31.12.

286 *Lal. V.*, 33.17.

287 *Pr. Pā. Aṣṭa.*, 386.8. *M. S. Al.*, 105.29.

288 *Saund. Kā.*, xviii, 4.

289 *Saund. Kā.*, v, 24. *Kar. Pu.*, 66.

290 *Saund. Kā.*, xii, 37.

291 *Mtu.*, i, 248.4. *Lal. V.*, 412.13.

292 *Mtu.*, iii, 309.9.

293 *Kṣemendra*, i, 1067.20.

294 *Kṣemendra*, ii, 861.1.

295 *Çikṣā.*, 140.10.

296 *Pr. Pā. Aṣṭa.*, 287.1. *Çikṣā.*, 62.8.

297 *Çikṣā.*, 5.10.

298 *Pr. Pā. Aṣṭa.*, 386.8.

299 *Çikṣā.*, 2.14.

300 *Çikṣā.*, 2.18. *Kāṅkṣā.* W. H. D. Rouse translates " desire-expelling ". But *kāṅkṣā* in Buddhist Sanskrit often means " doubt ". Cf. *Mtu.*, i, 85.12 (*Buddhe dharme ca saṅghe ca na kāṅkṣanti kadācana*).

301 *Çikṣā.*, 3.6, 3.13, 4.2, 4.17, 3.10. *M. S. Al.*, 143.19.

302 *Pr. Pā. Çata.*, 1442, 1259.

303 *pratisaṅkhyāna.* The *Dhamma-saṅgaṇi* defines it (section 1353).

304 The wheel was the symbol of universal sovereignty. Hence the idea of establishing the Kingdom of the *dharma*.

305 Cf. *Dīgha*, iii, 106. *Aṅguttara*, iv, 23. *Saṃyutta*, v, 63.

306 *Kar. Pu.*, 104.26.

307 *Mtu.*, ii, 257.16. *Da. Bhū.*, 14.5.

308 L. Poussin, "Morale," p. 154. M. Anesaki, ERE, v, 455.

309 R. Chalmers, *Majjh.*, tr., ii, 7. R. O. Franke, *Dīgha*, p. 184.

310 *Lal. V.*, 34.4.

311 *M. S. Al.*, 144.10.

312 *M. S. Al.*, 106.27.

313 E. R. J. Gooneratne, *Aṅguttara* tr., p. 55. *Aṅguttara-Nikāya*, pts. i–iii, by E. R. J. Gooneratne (Galle, 1913).

314 *Ityukta* in E. Burnouf, "Int.," p. 53, l. 28, and B. Hodgson, "Lit.," p. 15, l. 23. "*Nidāna*" (books on Causation) completes the list.

315 *Dh. S.*, section 26. *Sad. Pu.*, 46.1.

316 *M. S. Al.*, 83.12 ff.

317 *Bo. Bhū.*, fol. 43*b*.5–6.

318 *Pr. Pā. Çata.*, 14.3. *Saund. Kā.*, xiii, 25. *Da. Bhū.*, 12.9.

319 *Sam. Rā.*, fol. 113*b*.5. *Mtu.*, ii, 131.17.

320 *Dhamma-saṅgaṇi*, section 9. Translation, p. 12.

321 *Attha-sālinī*, pp. 115, 116 (section 298, *khuddakā* etc.).

322 *Mtu.*, i, 33.6.

323 *Saund. Kā.*, xiv, 26, 27.

324 *Bo. Bhū.*, 87*b*.6.2.

325 *Divy.*, 48.10. *Ava.-ça.*, i, 32.4.

326 *Da. Bhū.*, 40.19. *Saund. Kā.*, xiii, 24.

327 *Lal.*, V, 34.7.

328 *Saund. Kā.*, xiii, 24.

329 See Chap. V.

330 *Jātaka*, i, 47.

331 *Cariyā-piṭaka*, xv, 4, 11; pp. 102, 103.

332 Section 153; Translation, p. 28.

333 *Jātaka*, i, p. 47, ll. 7 ff.

334 *M. S. Al.*, tr. p. 8, note 8.

335 *Pr. Pā. Çata.*, 58, note 1. *Kṣemendra*, i, 889, verse 43.

336 E. Zeller, "Stoics," pp. 18, 22. Diogenes Laertius, vii, 117; vol. ii, p. 221.

337 *M. S. Al.*, i, 8.14. *Mtu.*, iii, 395.15.

338 *Mtu.*, iii, 422.6. *Kṣemendra*, ii, 897, verse 5; ii, 713, verse 39.

339 *Lal. V.*, 35.9.

340 *M. S. Al.*, 145.1.

341 *Ava.-ça.*, i, 191.4.

342 *Su. Vy.*, 59.3. *Divy.*, 124.17. *Ava.-ça.*, i, 16.13.

343 *Divy.*, 211. *Kā. Vy.*, 17. *Mtu.*, ii, 147.7; ii, 323.22; iii, 112.13. *Lal. V.*, 14. 101.

344 *M. S. Al.*, 144.

345 *Saund. Kā.*, xvii, 58. Cf. *Aṅguttara*, iv, 9 ff.; *Dīgha*, iii, 254.

346 *Lal. V.*, 350.5.

347 *Da. Bhū.*, 42.17.

348 *Sad. Pu.*, 17.13 ff.

349 Cf. *Vinaya*, i, p. 10, ll. 26 ff.

350 *Duḥkha*, "Ill," "Suffering," "Sorrow," etc.

351 *Tṛṣṇā* (Pāli: *taṇhā*), "Thirst," "Desire," "Lust," "Appetite," etc.

352 *M. Vy.*, section 112.

353 *Çikṣā.*, 216.9.

354 *M. Vy.*, section 111. *Mdh.* 475.11. *Da. Bhū.*, 51.6 ff.

355 *Lal. V.*, 417 (cf. *Vinaya*, i, 11). *Pr. Pā. Aṣṭa.*, 426.3. *Divy.*, 205.21, 393.24. *Mtu.*, iii, 241.2.

356 *Anvaya-jñāna*: cf. *Dīgha*, iii, 226; *Saṃyutta*, ii, 58.11 ff.; *Vibhaṅga*, 329.18 ff.

357 *Pr. Pa. Aṣṭa.*, 377.21. *Pr. Pā. Çata.*, 911.1. *Saund. Kā.*, xvi, 14; ix, 39; xv, 44; xvi, 7.

358 H. Kern, "Manual," p. 46; cf. C. A. F. Rhys Davids, "Psychology," pp. 79 ff.

359 *Ava.-ça.*, i, 360.9; ii, 148.9. *Divy.*, 128.22, 129.20.

360 *Çiṣya-lekha*, verse 98.

361 *Kṣemendra*, ii, 669, verse 99.

362 *M. S. Al.*, 126.20.

363 *Çikṣā.*, 281.1. *Pr. Pā. Çata.*, 1264.15.

364 *M. S. Al.*, 110.25.

365 Ibid., 173.3.

366 *Pr. Pā. Çata.*, 194.9 ff., 463.10 ff.

367 *Sū. Pr.*, fol. 13*b*, 1.

368 *Lal. V.*, 416.16 ff. *Mtu.*, iii, 331. Cf. *Vinaya*, i, p. 10, ll. 10 ff.

369 *Ava.-ça.*, i, 232.3 ff. Cf. *Dīgha*, ii, 151.

370 *Ava.-ça.*, i, 16.14.

371 *Kṣemendra*, i, 757, verse 50; i, 249.66. *Lka.*, 204, verse 117.

372 *Lal. V.*, 417. *Mtu.*, iii, 331. *Pr. Pā. Çata.*, 1438. *M. S. Al.*, 145. *M. Vy.*, section 44. *Dh. S.*, section 50.

373 Cf. *Dīgha*, ii, 311. *Majjh.*, iii, 71 ff.; 251 ff. *Dhamma-saṅgaṇi*, sections 297 to 304 (pp. 63–4).

374 Sections 16, 297.

375 *Majjh.*, iii, 22.11 ff.; 71.26 ff.

376 *Pr. Pā. Çata.*, 105.

377 *M. S. Al.*, 145.

378 *Aṅguttara*, ii, 195.27 ff.

379 *Lal. V.*, 34.10.
380 *Dīgha*, iii, 215.7 ff.
381 *Majjh.*, iii, 73, ll. 9 ff.; iii, 251.
382 *M. S. Al.*, 145.
383 *Lal. V.*, 34.11.
384 *Majjh.*, iii, 75, ll. 19 ff.; iii, 251.
385 *Pr. Pā. Aṣṭa.*, 334.3, 427.9.
386 *Dīgha*, 1.8 ff.
387 *Majjh.*, iii, 252. *Dīgha*, ii, 312. *Dhamma-saṅgaṇi*, tr., p. 77.
388 *M. S. Al.*, 145. *Lal. V.*, 34.15.
389 J. Jaini, "Outlines," p. 52.
390 E. Senart, "Origines," p. 20.
391 Aristotle, "Ethics," p. 45, l. 16.

CHAPTER V

Notes

[1] *Sutta-nipāta*, 1018. *mantesu pāramim brūhi* (or *pāramīm*), p. 195. *Jātaka*, i, 45–7 ff.; i, 73. *Nettipakaraṇa*, 87, "*catutthe jhāne pāramitāya.*"

[2] E. Burnouf, "Int.," p. 413. B. Hodgson, "Literature," p. 15, note. M. Vassilief, (German edition), p. 376.

[3] E. Burnouf, "Int.," p. 413.

[4] *Bo. Bhū.*, fol. 138*a*, 4.3 ff.

[5] L. de la Vallée Poussin, "Opinions," p. 311.

[6] Candrakīrti also derives the word from *pāra*. He says in the *Madhyamakāvatāra*: "Dans le mot *pāramitā*, "*pāram*" signifie l'autre bord de l'océan des existences, la qualité de Bouddha qui consiste dans l'abandon complet des obscurcissements de la passion et du connaissable. Le mot *pāramitā*, c'est-a-dire 'Parvenu à l'autre bord' (*pāragata*) est formé par le non-suppression de la désinence casuelle d'après la règle, 'Il n'y a pas élision devant le second terme du composé'; ou bien, appartenant au groupe du type *pṛṣodara*, il présente la fin du second terme (= *pāra-gāmitā*)." (Cf. *Pāṇini*, vi, 3.1, "*alug uttarapade.*" *Pāṇini*, vi, 3.109. "Le Muséon," 1907, pp. 277–8.)

[7] *Lal. V.*, 340.21 ff. *Mtu.*, iii, 226. *Pr. Pā. Aṣṭa.*, 194.15. *Kar. Pu.*, 127.1. *Ava.-ça*, i, 7.4. *M. S. Al.*, 99. *Dh. S.*, section 17. *Sam. Rā.*, fol. 112*a*, 3. *Bo. Bhū.*, fol. 47*a*, 6.

[8] *M. S. Al.*, 181.3. *M. Vy.*, section 34. *Dh. S.*, section 18. *Da. Bhū.*, 57.

[9] *Jātaka*, i, 45–7.

[10] "Ind. Ant.," vol. xvii, 1888, p. 36*b*.

[11] J. G. Bühler, "Indian Paleography," p. 78 (Bombay, 1904).

[12] R. Garbe, *Sāṅkhya*, p. 43.

[13] *Bo. Bhū.*, fol. 40*b*.5.2.

[14] *M. S. Al.*, 180. *M. Vy.*, section 33, etc.

[15] *Dh. S.*, 17. *M. S. Al.*, 99, etc. See note 7 above.

[16] *M. Vy.*, section 34. *M. S. Al.*, 75, 181.

[17] *M. Vy.*, section 4.

[18] *Sam. Rā.*, fol. 133*a*.3. *M. S. Al.*, 54.1. *Mdh.*, 377.13. *M. Vy.*, section 36.

[19] *Dīgha*, i, 110.2; i, 148.7. Cf. *Mtu.*, iii, 357.12; 413.2.

[20] *M. S. Al.*, 100.11 ff., 107.3 ff.

[21] *Bo. Bhū.*, fol. 100*b*.2, 151*b*.5. *M. S. Al.*, 139.18 ff. *Dh. S.*, section 117. *Çikṣā.*, 7.17, 191.4, 287.7. *Lal. V.*, 256.14.

22 *M. S. Al.*, 139–140.
23 *Bo. Bhū.*, fol. 86*a*.1.
24 *Pr. Pā. Aṣṭa.*, 396.15 ff.
25 *Lka.*, 29, verse 62.
26 *M. S. Al.*, 109.16.
27 *M. S. Al.*, 166.18.
28 *M. S. Al.*, 107.9.
29 *M. S. Al.*, 101.12 ff., 115.16 ff.
30 *Lka.*, 237 ff.
31 *M. S. Al.*, 102.3 ff.
32 *Çikṣā.*, 90.
33 *M. Vy.*, sections 93, 80, 51, 78.
34 Cf. *Chāndogya Upd.*, ii, 23.1 (*trayo dharma-skandhā yajño 'dhyayanaṃ dānam iti*, p. 113).
Bṛhadāraṇyaka Upd., vi, 2.16 (*atha ye yajñena dānena tapasā lokāñ jayanti*, p. 816).
35 Cf. *Dīgha*, ii, 354 (*Pāyāsi-sutta*). *Aṅguttara*, vi, 235 (*Dāna-vagga*); i, 91 (*Dāna-vagga*); iii, 32 (*Sumana-vagga*); iv, 60 (*Mahāyañña-vagga*); *Sīhanāda-vagga*, iv, 392. *Itivuttaka*, sections 26, 98, 22 (pp. 19, 98, 16). *Jātaka*, i, 20.45. *Saṃyutta*, v, 351, 392 (*Sotāpatti-saṃyutta*). *Dhammapada*, verses 354, 223. *Sutta-nipāta* (*Māgha-sutta*). *Peta-vatthu*, i, 1 (p. 1); ii, 8.3 (p. 22); ii, 4.9 (p. 17).
36 *Dh. S.*, section 105. *Bo. Bhū.*, fol. 53*b*.2.
37 *Çikṣā.*, 24 ff.
38 *Bo. Bhū.*, fol. 47*b*.2 ff.
39 *Bo. Bhū.*, 47*a*.5.2–3.
40 *M. S. Al.*, 112.14. *Cikṣā.*, 82.15.
41 *Jā. Mā.*, 106.4, 219.10. *Çikṣā.*, 82.15. *Bo. Bhū.*, fol. 54*b*.7.2.
42 *Kṣemendra*, i, 1035.26; ii, 155. *Divy.*, 395. *Kar. Pu.*, 66.2. *Jā. Mā.*, 219.10. *M. S. Al.*, 112.4.
43 *Mtu.*, iii, 405.1. *Jā. Mā.*, 15.4. *Ava-ça.*, i, 248.4; i, 198.11; i, 262.2. *Çikṣā.*, 27.15.
44 *Ava-ça.*, ii, 37.1. *Kṣemendra*, i, 687.94; ii, 263; i, 1121.9. *Divy.*, 295.
45 *Çikṣā.*, 129.1, 127.17.
46 *Ava-ça.*, i, 257; ii, 7.11. *Kā. Vy.*, 28. *Kṣemendra*, i, 1029.3; i, 293.46; ii, 595.3.
47 *Divy.*, 429 ff.
48 *Çikṣā.*, 87.5.
49 *Ava-ça.*, i, 158.10.
50 *Pr. Pā. Aṣṭa.*, 36, 519. *Lal. V.*, 276.15. *Pr. Pā. Çata.*, 73.1; 1354. *Sad. Pu.*, 263.10. *Da. Bhū.*, 18.22. *Mtu.*, iii, 405.1, etc.
51 *Jā. Mā.*, 8. *Bo. Bhū.*, fol. 49*a*.2.3 ff. *Çikṣā.*, 21. *D Bhū.*, 18.

[52] *Ava-ça.*, i, 313 ff.

[53] *Da. Bhū.*, 20.2. *Divy.*, 290.8. *Ava-ça.*, ii, 81.6. *Bo. Bhū.*. fol. 60*b*.3.2. The monk's four requisites (*pariṣkārāḥ*) are given as "*piṇḍapāta-cīvara-çayan-āsana-glāna-pratyaya-bhaiṣajya.*" These are sometimes reckoned as six.

[54] *Bo. Bhū.*, fol. 49*a*.2 (*utpīḍāya, badhāya, bandhanāya*).

[55] *Bo. Bhū.*, fol. 48*b*.4.3.

[56] *Bo. Bhū.*, fol. 48*b*.1.3.and 49*a*.1 (*madya; jāla; yantra*).

[57] *Bo. Bhū.*, 49*a*.1.1.

[58] *Bo. Bhū.*, fol. 49*a*.4.1, 50*a*.7.1, 50*a*.5.2 (*apathyam; yācakānām apratirūpaṃ dānam; prapāta-patanāya; dharmeṇa cāsāhasena*).

[59] *Bo. Bhū.*, fol. 54*b*.5.1 ff. (*parīttam; kṛcchr-ārjitān deya-dharmān*).

[60] *Pr. Pā. Çata.*, 1191.9. *Çikṣā.*, 21, 24.

[61] *Bo. Bhū.*, fol. 47*b*.3.3, 48*a*.4 (*yathā-kāma-karaṇīyaṃ vā paravaçyam para-vidheyam ātmānaṃ pareṣām anuprayacchati*).

[62] *Pr. Pā. Çata.*, 1303. *Da. Bhū.*, 19.1. RPP., 12.14.

[63] *Bo. Bhū.*, 49*a*.6 (*poṣakam; saṃvardhakam*).

[64] *Bo. Bhū.*, fol. 50*a*.1.2. *Jā. Mā.*, 166.15.

[65] *M. S. Al.*, 113.3. *Bo. Bhū.*, fol. 90*b*.2.1, 50*b*.6 (*prasāda-prāmodya-sahagataḥ*). *Jā. Mā.*, 237.5, 52.23, 204.7, etc. *Ava-ça.*, i, 171.9. *Kṣemendra*, ii, 837.27, 127.32, 829.28, etc.

[66] *Bo. Bhū.*, fol. 50*b*.6.3, 31*a*.6 (*avipratisārī*). *Kar. Pu.*, 112.29. *Jā. Mā.*, 222.22.

[67] *Bo. Bhū.*, fol. 50*a*.1.1.

[68] *Bo. Bhū.*, fol. 55*b*.1.2 (*nīca-cittaḥ*).

[69] *Bo. Bhū.*, fol. 56*a*.2.2, 49*b*.5 (*sama-cittaḥ*).

[70] *Bo. Bhū.*, fol. 55*a*.1 ff., 50*a*.2.1 (*uddhatānām asaṃvṛtānām ākroçakānām*, etc.). *M. S. Al.*, 112.5 (*pātra-dānatā apātra-dānatā sarvatra dānatā sarva-kāla-dānatā*).

[71] *Çikṣā.*, 145, 165.

[72] *Jā. Mā.*, 154.5.

[73] *Pr. Pā. Çata.*, 90–1. *Ava-ça.*, i, 317.

[74] *Mtu.*, ii, 79.13, 80.4.

[75] *Bo. Bhū.*, fol. 31*a*.7.1 (*āḍhyo bhavati mahā-bhogo mahā-pakṣo*). *M. S. Al.*, 112.26. *Jā. Mā.*, 14.8. *Divy.*, 388. *Kṣemendra*, i, 123.1, 1055.1; ii, 829.27.

[76] *Bo. Bhū.*, fol. 50*a*.5.1 (*annado balī bhavati vasudo varṇavān bhavati cakṣuṣmān dīpadaḥ*).

[77] *Ava-ça.*, i, 172.8.

[78] *Çikṣā.*, 274.9.

[79] *Mtu.*, ii, 363.12. *Çikṣā.*, 34.5. *Kṣemendra*, i, 877.25, 647.5, 651.19; ii, 81.65, 637.47, 999.4, etc.

[80] *Ava-ça.*, i, 173.6 ff. and passim. *Divy.*, 290.22 ff.

[81] *caraṇa-tala-pratiṣṭhitaḥ.* "The soles of his feet become smooth or well-set." (Cf. the thirty-two *lakṣaṇas* of a *mahāpuruṣa*.)

[82] Cf. *Ava-ça.*, i, 241–88.

[83] *Bo. Bhū.*, fol. 90*b*.1.1, 50*a*.4.1. *M. S. Al.*, 165.3. *Çikṣā.*, 146.10.

[84] *Bo. Bhū.*, fol. 90*b*.1.2. *Jā. Mā.*, 204.3. *Kar. Pu.*, 111.20.

[85] *Bo. Bhū.*, fol. 55*b*.7.2.

[86] *Bo. Bhū.*, fol. 50*b*.2.2.

[87] *Bo. Bhū.*, fol. 54*a*.5.

[88] *Bo. Bhū.*, fol. 50*b*.4.3.

[89] *Lal. V.*, 352.11, 162.6, 180.6. *Mtu.*, i, 78.16; ii, 340.22. *Jā. Mā.*, 41.1, 238.22, 2.18, etc. *Çikṣā.*, 8.2, 232.10, 184.12, etc. *Da. Bhū.*, 11.13, 13.13, 18.17, 19.8, 43.8, 42.12, 46.3, 47.23, 52.10, 52.14, 60.7, 63.24, 70.24, 71.2, 73.16, 78.19, 82.6, 88.12, 90.1, etc. *Pr. Pā. Çata.*, 1455.8, 282.11, 1461.8, etc. *M. S. Al.*, 11.5, 14.3, 31.14, 33.22, 167.42, 84.24, 124.30, 167.39, 172.67, 174.74, etc. *Kṣemendra*, ii, 57.42, 831.6, 909.1, etc.

[90] *Pr. Pā. Çata.*, 1461.8 ff.

[91] *Çikṣā.*, 146.10.

[92] *Jā. Mā.*, 41.1.

[93] *Lal. V.*, 180.18.

[94] *Kṣemendra*, 1.1.

[95] *Lka.*, 244.8. *M. S. Al.*, 123.28. *Ava-ça.*, i, 184.12, i, 209.12. *Sad. Pu.*, 136.4. *Lal. V.*, 280.7. *Çikṣā.*, 287.9. Cf. *Sutta-nipāta*, 149–50 (p. 26): *mātā yathā niyaṃ puttaṃ*, etc.

[96] *M. S. Al.*, 161.6.

[97] *Çikṣā.*, 19.

[98] *M. S. Al.*, 162–4.

[99] *Jā. Mā.*, 155.18.

[100] *Jā. Mā.*, 174.9 ff.

[101] Shakespeare's "Merchant of Venice", Act iv, Scene 1, l. 178.

[102] *Çikṣā.*, 286.8 ff.

[103] *M. S. Al.*, 176.27. *B.C. Ava.*, viii, 90 ff. *Mtu.*, iii, 387.12. *Çikṣā.*, 2.10, 357.16.

[104] *M. S. Al.*, 19.17.

[105] *B.C. Ava.*, viii, 90, 95.

[106] *B.C. Ava.*, viii, 110, 131, 136, 140.

[107] *Bo. Bhū.*, fol. 37*b*.7.2 (*ātma-hitāya para-hitāya*); fol. 151*a*.7.3 (*sva-par-ārthe prayujyate*). *M. S. Al.*, 104.7, 105.21, 108.39, 111.50, etc. *Ava-ça.*, i, 2.4, 23.9, 346.8, etc. *B.C. Ava.*, i, 24. *Kṣemendra*, ii, 667.93, 133.52. *Da. Bhū.*, 20.4. *Lal. V.*, 192.11.

[108] *Bo. Bhū.*, fol. 9*a*, 4.

[109] *Kar. Pu.*, 108.7. *Kṣemendra*, ii, 67.93, 133.52. *Ava-ça.*, ii, 13.5.

[110] *M. S. Al.*, p. 13, verse 12; p. 108, verse 36; p. 111, verse 49. *Çiṣya-lekha*, verses 100 ff. *Pr. Pā. Çata.*, 1462.1. *B.C. Ava.*, v, 84; iii, 17 ff. *Kṣemendra*, ii, 583.72; i, 1133.59; i, 1061.23.

[111] *Jā. Mā.*, 4.24, 11.2, 204.3. *Nāgānanda*, iv, 26 (p. 77).

[112] *Kṣemendra*, ii, 857.59.

[113] *Pr. Pā. Çata.*, 1462.1.

[114] *B.C. Ava.*, viii, 173.

[115] *M. S. Al.*, 19.17 ff., 21.6.

[116] *Kṣemendra*, ii, 955 ff.

[117] Tennyson's "In Memoriam", lv.

[118] *Jā. Mā.*, 169.16.

[119] *Jā. Mā.*, 232.21 ff.

[120] *Jā. Mā.*, 1 ff. *Su. Pr.*, fol. 73*b*, 3 ff. *Kṣemendra*, ii, 53 ff.; ii, 907 ff.

[121] *Ava-ça.*, i, 182 ff. *Jā. Mā.*, 6 ff. *Kṣemendra*, ii, 831 ff. Cf. *Cariyā-piṭaka*, p. 77 (i, 8) *Sivirāja-cariyaṃ*. Pāli *Jātaka*, iv, 401, ll. 10 ff.

[122] *Divy.*, 470 ff. *Kṣemendra*, ii, 53 ff.

[123] *Kṣemendra*, ii, 49 ff.

[124] *Kṣemendra*, ii, 1017 ff. *Kathā-sarit-sāgara*, 84 ff., 441 ff. (Chapters xxii, xc) (*Jimūta-vāhana* is "*jātismara*", "*dāna-vīra*", "*sarvabhūta-hitaḥ*", etc.). *Nāgānanda*, 65 ff.

[125] *Sam. Rā.*, fol. 154*a*.

[126] *Kar. Pu.*, 107 ff. *Kṣemendra*, ii, 154 ff.

[127] *Ava-ça.*, i, 187 ff.

[128] *Kṣemendra*, ii, 119 ff.

[129] *Ava-ça.*, i, 168 ff. *Kṣemendra*, ii, 927 ff.

[130] *Kṣemendra*, i 25.

[131] *Kṣemendra*, i, 61 ff.

[132] *Jā. Mā.*, 41 ff.

[133] *Jā. Mā.*, 33.

[134] *Ava-ça.*, i, 206 ff. *Jā. Mā.*, 27 ff. *Kṣemendra*, ii, 969 ff. Cf. Pāli *Jātaka*, iii, 51, l. 10. *Cariyā-piṭaka*, p. 82 (i, 10).

[135] *Poṣadha.* "Bei den Buddhisten Wiederholung des Gelubdes" (Skt. Dicy. Pbg.). This word corresponds to Pāli *uposatha* (Vedic *upavasatha*, the eve of the Soma sacrifice, day of preparation). It means the day preceding four stages of the moon's waxing and waning, viz.: 1st, 8th, 15th, 23rd nights of the lunar month. On the 15th day of the half-month, the Buddhists held a chapter of the Order. Laymen observed special vows. (Pāli Dicy.)

[136] *Kṣemendra*, ii, 911. *Jā. Mā.*, 200 ff. *Kṣemendra*, ii, 919; ii, 957.

[137] *Jā. Mā.*, 51 ff. *Kṣemendra*, i, 647 ff. Cf. Pāli *Jātaka*, vi. 479 ff. (*Vessantara*). *Cariyā-piṭaka*, p. 78 (i. 9).

[138] *Bo. Bhū.*, fol. 53*a*.5.1 (*aprameya-puṇya-prasotā*). *Lal. V.*, 261.13, *Jā. Mā.*, 237.25. *Vajra*, 24.11. *Çikṣa.*, 275.10. *M. S. Al.*, 139.39.

[139] *Da. Bhū.*, 54.15. *Mtu.*, 86.7. *Vajra*, 21.12, 7.10. *Çikṣā.*, 275.10, 69.16, etc.

140 *Kṣemendra*, i, 1161.87.
141 *Lal. V.*, 312.2, 244.19, 270.16, 352.22.
142 *Mtu.*, i, 30.; ii, 63.16.
143 *Jā. Mā.*, 209.3. *Kṣemendra*, i, 891.14; i, 1111.26; ii, 597.11. *Jā. Mā.*, 226.7.
144 *Ava-ça.*, i, 221. *Kṣemendra*, ii, 645.11, 735.16, 797.97.
145 *Jā. Mā.*, 94, 225.22.
146 *Jā. Mā.*, 28.22.
147 *Çikṣā.*, 31.19. *Kṣemendra*, i, 1089.3.
148 *Jā. Mā.*, 29.1 ff.
149 *Çikṣā.*, 350.5. *Ava-ça.*, i, 313.10. *Kṣemendra*, ii, 899.10.
150 *Bo. Bhū.*, 43*b*.1.1 (*na kṛtānāṃ karmaṇāṃ kalpa-çatair api vipraṇāço bhavati*). *Mdh.*, 390.9.
151 *Ava-ça.*, ii, 85.9, and passim. *Kṣemendra*, ii, 191.56 and passim.
152 *Kṣemendra*, ii, 3 ff.
153 *Kṣemendra*, i, 973.1, 707.169, 969.100; ii, 11.31 ff., 191.46, 505.65, 701.34, 483.103, 43.142, etc.
154 *Kṣemendra*, i, 707.169.
155 *Kṣemendra*, ii, 11.31.
156 Ibid., ii, 11.32.
157 *Saund. Kā.*, xv, 31.
158 Ibid., xv, 40.
159 *Sutta-nipāta*, 166 (p. 128).
160 *Aṅguttara*, i, 287.2.
161 *Dīgha*, i, 55, and passim.
162 *Majjhima*, iii, 203.3.
163 *Milinda.*, 294.17, 295.
164 *Milinda.*, 297.10.
165 JRAS. 1906, pp. 581 ff.; 1907, pp. 665 ff. ERE, xi, 561*b*.
166 Aristotle's "Politics", Book 1, Chap. ii, p. 6. "Nicomachean Ethics," p. 15.
167 *Mtu.*, i, 8.
168 D. T. Suzuki, "Outlines," p. 284. J. E. Carpenter, "Buddhism," p. 272.
169 *Bo. Bhū.*, fol. 50*a*.4.1. *Pr. Pā. Çata.*, 1303.2. *Pr. Pā. Aṣṭa.*, 373.13. *Da. Bhū.*, 20.4. *M. S. Al.*, 112.2. *Çikṣā.*, 170.15.
170 *Pr. Pā. Çata.*, 1303.1. *Çikṣā.*, 29 ff.
171 *Çikṣā.*, 29.
172 *Çikṣā.*, 32.
173 *M. S. Al.*, 181.30. *Çiṣya-lekha*, verse 112. *B.C. Ava.*, pp. 221–5.
174 Cf. H. B. Coxon, "Roman Catholicism" (London, 1911), p. 80. Also J. E. Carpenter, "Buddhism," p. 271 ("The Catholics drew on the treasury of the sufferings and the excellences of the saints").

[175] M. Kale, "Higher Sanskrit Grammar," p. 132 (Bombay, 1918).
[176] *Saund. Kā.*, xiii, 27.
[177] *M. S. Al.*, 101.22.
[178] *M. Vy.*, sections 80, 93, 51, 78.
[179] *Sad. Pu.*, 24.11. *Su. Vy.*, 60.17. *Mtu.*, ii, 357.9.
[180] *Mtu.*, ii, 357.6.
[181] *Saund. Kā.*, xiii, 19 ff.
[182] Ibid.
[183] *Mtu.*, iii, 435.6.
[184] "*Dukūla*," "*çīla-gandha*." *Kṣemendra*, ii, 869.29.
[185] *Da. Bhū.*, 57.4.
[186] *Mdh.*, 143.1. *Lal. V.*, 279.7. *Sad. Pu.*, 681. *Mtu.*, ii, 314.17. *Çiṣya-lekha*, 90. *Ava-ça.*, i, 148. *Pr. Pā. Çata.*, 471. *Da. Bhū.*, 37.
[187] *Dhamma-saṅgaṇi*, sections 1055, 1059. *Dhamma-saṅgaṇi*, tr., pp. 254 ff.
[188] *Divy.*, 154.
[189] *Çikṣā.*, 209. *Pr. Pā. Çata.*, 472.
[190] *Mdh.*, 143.1.
[191] *Dhamma-saṅgaṇi*, section 1060; tr., p. 259.
[192] *Çikṣā.*, 209.
[193] *Dhamma-saṅgaṇi*, section 1061; tr., p. 260.
[194] *Çikṣā.*, 219.
[195] *Lka.*, 90.9.
[196] *Da. Bhū.*, 37.2. *Pr. Pā. Çata.*, 1456. *Saund. Kā.*, xvi, 59 ff.
[197] *Mtu.*, iii, 421.11. *Divy.*, 129.
[198] *Jā. Mā.*, 208.5 ff.
[199] *Su. Vy.*, 58, 61.
[200] *M. S. Al.*, 172 ff.
[201] *Lal. V.*, 223 ff., 180 ff., 274 ff. *M. Vy.*, sections 22, 30.
[202] J. Jaini, "Outlines," pp. 97, 133. In Zoroastrianism, *humata*, *hūkhta*, *huvars'ta* (ERE, vol. v, p. 515*a*). "Good thought, word and deed" (M. L. Buch, "Zoroastrian Ethics," pp. 59, 61, Baroda, 1919).
[203] *Sam. Rā.*, fol. 192*b*.6 ff.
[204] *Bo. Bhū.*, fol. 57*a*.2.1, 58*a*. *M. S. Al.*, 108.
[205] *Bo. Bhū.*, 58*b*.3.1, 58*a*.3.2, 58*a*.2, 58*b*.6.3 ff., 59*a*.1.2, 59*a*.2.
[206] *Sam. Rā.*, fol. 200*a*.2. *Pr. Pā. Çata.*, 110.15, 681.12, 279.16. *Da. Bhū.*, 59.10 ff. In Zoroastrianism, "the virtue most praised is that of purity" (M. L. Buch, op. cit., p. 100). "Evil is always considered as a form of impurity" (ERE, v, 514*a*). "In *Vd.* 19 (20–25), rules are given for the cleansing of Vohumanah" (J. H. Moulton, "Early Zoroastrianism," p. 101).
[207] *M. Vy.*, section 92. *Da. Bhū.*, 23 ff. *Çikṣa.*, 69 ff. *M. S. Al.*, 110. *Pr. Pā. Aṣṭa.*, 324, 427.

[208] *Yo. Sū.*, ii, 30 (p. 102). *Baudhāyana-dharma-sūtra*, ii, 10.18.2 (p. 82, ed. E. Hultzsch, Leipzig, 1922). *Ahiṃsā satyam astainyaṃ maithunasya ca varjanam.*

[209] The Bible, Exodus, chap. xx.

[210] Cf. *Pāsādika-suttanta* (*Dīgha*, iii, 133). *Siṅgālovāda-suttanta* (*Dīgha*, iii, 182, ll. 1–2).

[211] *Dīgha*, 1.3 ff. *Aṅguttara*, ii, 83; i, 273. (*Āpāyika-vagga*).

[212] *Vinaya*, i, 83.

[213] *Ava-ça.*, i, 340.1. *Kṣemendra*, ii, 733.14.

[214] *Pr. Pā. Çata.*, 132. *Ava-çataka*, i, 301.4, 324.10. *Kṣemendra*, i, 859.18.

[215] Cf. *Saṃyutta*, ii, 68. *Aṅguttara*, iii, 203. *Sutta-nipāta*, 394–9 (p. 69). *Aṅguttara*, ii, 66. *Dīgha*, iii, 235.

[216] *Mtu.*, ii, 99.

[217] *Pr. Pā. Aṣṭa.*, 324.

[218] *Jā. Mā.*, 100 ff.

[219] *M. Vy.*, section 267.

[220] *Dh. S.*, section 56. *M. S. Al.*, 110.4. *Da. Bhū.*, 25.17.

[221] *Da. Bhū.*, 23.6. *Pr. Pā. Çata.*, 479.3. *M. Vy.*, section 92.

[222] *Sam. Rā.*, fol. 193*b*.6. *Da. Bhū.*, 23.7.

[223] *Mtu.*, ii, 33.15.

[224] *M. Vy.*, section 92. *Dh. S.*, section 56.

[225] Cf. *Saṃyutta*, iv, 342 ff. *Dīgha*, iii, 74.

[226] *Da. Bhū.*, 23.6.

[227] *Jā. Mā.*, 153.4 ff.

[228] *Bo. Bhū.*, fol. 75*a*.1.1, "*Yathāham-arthī jīvitena na me kaçcij jīvitād vyāparopayet*," etc. *Kṣemendra*, ii, 125.22.

[229] *Kṣemendra*, ii, 841.4.

[230] *Kṣemendra*, i, 85.96; ii, 633.36 ff.; ii, 965.15; ii, 659.

[231] Cf. *Vinaya*, i, 137, "*ekindriyaṃ jivaṃ viheṭhentā bahū*," etc. *Vinaya*, i, 97, ll. 1–3, "*pāṇo jīvitā no voropetabbo.*"

[232] *Kṣemendra*, i, 79.66. *Ava-ça.*, ii, 230.

[233] *Kṣemendra*, i, 807.10; ii, 731.4. *Ava-ça.*, i, 289 ff.; i, 319 ff.

[234] *Çikṣā.*, 159.1.

[235] *Jā. Mā.*, passim.

[236] *Kā. Vy.*, 46.

[237] *B. C. Ava.*, vii, 18. *Çikṣā.*; 284.

[238] *Kṣemendra*, ii, 423.17.

[239] *Divy.*, 382 ff. *Kṣemendra*, ii, 247.166.

[240] *Jā. Mā.*, 217.14. 166.7.

[241] *Çikṣā.*, 144.14, 131.12, 174. *Kṣemendra*, i, 78.

[242] *Lka.*, 244 ff. (245, 246, 248, 257, 259).

[243] *B. C. Ava.*, v, 97. *Çikṣā.*, 134.9.

[244] *Saund. Kā.*, xiv, 1 ff.

245 *Mtu.*, i, 107.14.
246 *Da. Bhū.*, 23.
247 *Pr. Pā. Çata.*, 1258.
248 *Da. Bhū.*, 23. *Kṣemendra*, i, 827.36 ff. *Jā. Mā.*, 85.10.
249 *Da. Bhū.*, 23. *Pr. Pā. Aṣṭa.*, 448.12.
250 *Kṣemendra*, ii, 841.41.
251 *Divy.*, 154. *Ava-ça.*, i, 210.6. *Jā. Mā.*, 96.13. *Kṣemendra*, i, 801; i, 1133; ii, 243; ii, 951.
252 *Da. Bhū.*, 24.
253 *Da. Bhū.*, 24. *Jā. Mā.*, 172.20.
254 *Da. Bhū.*, 24.
255 *Pr. Pā. Aṣṭa.*, 334 ff.
256 *Pr. Pā. Aṣṭa.*, 326.4. *Çikṣā.*, 191.5.
257 *Bo. Bhū.*, fol. 47*a*.2. *M. S. Al.*, 116.
258 *Bo. Bhū.*, fol. 86*a*.2.3. *Pr. Pā. Aṣṭa.*, 323.12, 326.4.
259 *Su. Vy.*, 25.17.
260 *Mtu.*, ii, 64.16.
261 *Bo. Bhū.*, fol. 86*a*.3–4.
262 Ibid., 86*a*.4.3.
263 Ibid., 86*a*.5.2.
264 Ibid., 86*a*.6.3.
265 Ibid., 86*b*.1.
266 Ibid., 86*b*.3.3.
267 Ibid., 87*a*.1.
268 Ibid., 87*a*.2–4.
269 Ibid., 87*a*.4–5.
270 *Da. Bhū.*, 24. *Saund. Kā.*, xiii, 46.
271 *Da. Bhū.*, 25. *Saund. Kā.*, xiii, 47.
272 *Mtu.*, i, 107.15.
273 *Da. Bhū.*, 25.
274 See note 375, Chap. IV.
275 See note 75, Chap. V, above.
276 *Bo. Bhū.*, fol. 75*b*.5.1 (*Mahā-prāmodya-sthitaḥ kālaṃ karoti*).
277 *Dh. S.*, section 122. *Mtu.*, i, 5, 9, 16 ff. *Divy.*, 67. *Ava-ça.*, i, 4.8; 19.4. *Kā. Vy.*, 18, 37, 50. *Mtu.*, i, 373, 384. *Çikṣā.*, 155.14, 156.19, 132.19. W. Kirfel, "Kosmographie," pp. 202 ff.
278 *B. Ct.*, xiv, 11 ff. *Çikṣā.*, 69 ff.
279 *Çikṣā.*, 69 ff. Cf. Dante's Inferno, v, 30 ff.; vi, 10 ff.; vii, 25 ff., etc.
280 *B. Ct.* xiv, 23 ff. *Mtu.*, i, 27 ff.
281 *Ava-ça.*, i, 335.
282 For the *pretas*, cf. *B. Ct.*, xiv, 23 ff.; *Mtu.*, i, 27 ff. For ugliness and misery in life, cf. *Ava-ça.*, ii, 59.2. *Kṣemendra*, i, 877.23. *Da. Bhū.*, 26 ff., etc.
283 *M. S. Al.*, 108.10 ff.

[284] *Bo. Bhū.*, fol. 97*b*.3.3. U. Wogihara, *Bo. Bhū.*, p. 40. *M. Vy.*, section 78.

[285] *Bo. Bhū.*, fol. 97*b*.3 (*avadya-samudācāre ātmana ev-āpratirūpatāṃ viditvā bodhisattvasya lajjā hrīḥ*).

[286] ERE, ii, 750.2.

[287] Liddell and Scott's "Lexicon", p. 34 (8th edition).

[288] *Dhamma-saṅgaṇi*, sections 30, 101.

[289] *M. S. Al.*, 132, 133, 134.

[290] *Lal. V.*, 358.8, 352.10. *Dh. S.*, section 61. *Da. Bhū.*, 13.24. *Mdh.*, 350.15. *Çikṣā.*, 180.

[291] *Jā. Mā.*, 77.1.

[292] Cf. J. Watson, "Selections from Kant," p. 227 (Glasgow, 1919). R. Eucken, "Die Lebensanschauungen der grossen Denker," p. 418 (Leipzig, 1919). "The Thoughts of Marcus Aurelius Antoninus," translated by G. Long, pp. 131, 145 (London, 1913).

[293] *B. C. Ava.*, v, 84.

[294] RPP., 28.

[295] *Çikṣā.*, 167, 168.

[296] *Bo. Bhū.*, fol. 67*b*.3.

[297] Ibid., 67*b*.5.2, 6.2.

[298] Ibid., 67*b*.8.2–3.

[299] Ibid., 68*a*.3, 4, 5.

[300] Ibid., 68*b*, 1, 2, 3.

[301] Ibid., 68*b*.6.

[302] Ibid., 69*a*.1.

[303] *Jā. Mā.*, 73.20 ff.

[304] Ibid., 98.11. *Kṣemendra*, ii, 779.29.

[305] *Kṣemendra*, ii, 695.13.

[306] *Jā. Mā.*, 79.

[307] *Jā. Mā.*, 80.15 ff.

[308] *Kṣemendra*, ii, 565 ff.; ii, 739 ff.

[309] *Divy.*, 407. *Kṣemendra*, ii, 163; i, 827, 819.

[310] *Kṣemendra*, ii, 773 ff.

[311] *Jā. Mā.*, 96.

[312] Ibid., 99.

[313] *Divy.*, 54. *Kṣemendra*, i, 909.79 ff.

[314] *Ava-ça.*, ii, 151; ii, 133 ff.

[315] *Kṣemendra*, ii, 979 ff.

[316] D. T. Suzuki, "Outlines," p. 69. A. B. Keith, "Philosophy," p. 260.

[317] *M. S. Al.*, 101, 166. *Pr. Pā. Çata.*, 95, 276, 1460.

[318] *Pr. Pā. Çata.*, 1410, 1357. *Bo. Bhū.*, fol. 76*a*.4. *M. S. Al.*, 99.

[319] *Bo. Bhū.*, fol. 77*b*.1. *Dh. S.*, section 107. *Divy.*, 39.12. *Da. Bhū.*, 13.19.

[320] *Kṣemendra*, ii, 915.7.

[321] *Kṣānti-sauratya* (Pāli: *soracca*). Not *saurabhya*, as is found at *Mtu.*, ii, 354; *Sad. Pu.*, 234.8, etc. See U. Wogihara, *Bo. Bhū.*, p. 43.

[322] *Bo. Bhū.*, 79*a*.6, "*sarvaṃ cāpakāraṃ kṣamate . . . sarvatra deçe . . . rahasi vā mahājana-samakṣaṃ vā . . . rātrau divā vā*," etc.

[323] *Çikṣā.*, 185. *Mtu.*, i, 85.15.

[324] *Bo. Bhū.*, fol. 77*a*.2, 78*b*.6, 79*a*.1, 79*b*.1, 76*a*.7. *Su. Vy.*, 60.2.

[325] *Bo. Bhū.*, 79*a*.5.

[326] Ibid., 79*a*.4.

[327] Ibid., 76*b*.3.

[328] *Bo. Bhū.*, 76*b*. *Çikṣā.*, 243. *B. C. Ava.*, vi, 27.

[329] *Bo. Bhū.*, 77*a*.3.

[330] *B. C. Ava.*, vi, 22, 25.

[331] *B. C. Ava.*, vi, 42, 46.

[332] *Bo. Bhū.*, 76*a*.7

[333] *B. C. Ava.*, vi, 49, 99, 100.

[334] *Ava-ça.*, i, 180. *Çikṣā.*, 58, 67, 115. *Kṣemendra*, ii, 35.

[335] *B. C. Ava.*, vi, 80, 89, 96.

[336] *Bo. Bhū.*, 79*a*.4.1.

[337] *B. C. Ava.*, vi, 119.

[338] *Bo. Bhū.*, 79*a*.2–3 (*sumanaskaḥ; ānanda-jātaḥ*).

[339] *Sam. Rā.*, fol. 113*a*. *Bo. Bhū.*, fol. 79*a*.4, 80*a*.2.

[340] *Bo. Bhū.*, fol. 77*b*.5.6; 78*a*.1, 2, 3, 6; 78*b*.3; 79*b*.4, 5.

[341] *Bo. Bhū.*, fol. 78*b*.3–5. Cf. *Majjhima*, ii, 175.

[342] *Da. Bhū.*, 60, 64. *M. S. Al.*, 68, 163. *Çikṣā.*, 212. U. Wogihara, *Bo. Bhū.*, p. 20. *Anutpattika-dharma-kṣānti* (*Pr. Pā. Aṣṭa.*, 310.2; *Su. Vy.*, 40.4; *Vajra*, 44.1; *Lka.*, 12.10, 81.3; *Kar. Pu.*, 105.27, etc.). This term has also been rendered as follows:— F. Max Müller: "resignation to things to come" (*Su. Vy.*, tr., 71. SBE., vol. xlix). L. de la Vallée Poussin: "patient contemplation of the absence of birth of things" ("Le Muséon," 1905, p. 52); "Upholding the doctrine of the non-production of things" (ERE, ii, 747*b*).

[343] Cf. *Saṃyutta*, iv, 60. *Majjhima*, iii, 267

[344] *Divy.*, 38 ff. *Kṣemendra*, i, 899 ff.

[345] *Divy.*, 417.22. *Kṣemendra*, ii, 243, verse 160.

[346] *Kṣemendra*, i, 781 ff.; i, 933 ff. *Jā. Mā.*, 181.17 ff. In the *KSS.*, the hermit is wounded by robbers (p. 381).

[347] *Kṣemendra*, ii, 915 ff. *Ava.-ça.*, i, 177.

[348] *Kṣemendra*, ii, 531 ff.

[349] *Kṣemendra*, ii, 945.

[350] *Ava.-ça.*, i, 180.

[351] *M. S. Al.*, 102.1.

[352] *B. C. Ava.*, vii, 2. *Bo. Bhū.*, fol. 80*a*.3.

[353] *Bo. Bhū.*, fol. 80*a*.1.
[354] *B. C. Ava.*, canto iv. *Bo. Bhū.*, fol. 97*b*.5–3.
[355] *Sam. Rā.*, fol. 114*a*.4. *M. S. Al.*, 83. *Bo. Bhū.*, 31*b*.5. *Pr. Pā. Aṣṭa.*, 480.4. *B. C. Ava.*, vii, 2. *Çikṣā.*, 111.
[356] *B. C. Ava.*, vii, 1. *Bo. Bhū.*, 81*a*.1, 82*b*.5. *Pr. Pā. Aṣṭa.*, 186.9. *Çikṣā.*, 275. *Sad. Pu.*, 10.10.
[357] *Bo. Bhū.*, fol. 81*a*.2.
[358] *M. S. Al.*, 114.5. *Kar. Pu.*, 104.10.
[359] *Mtu.*, iii, 436.6.
[360] *Çikṣā.*, 112.8, 357.
[361] *Kṣemendra*, i, 1119.1; ii, 955.1. *Lal. V.*, 373.17, 372.10.
[362] *Lal. V.*, 354.6. *Divy.*, 392. *Ava.-ça.*, i, 22.3.
[363] *M. S. Al.*, 109.1.
[364] *Dh. S.*, section 108.
[365] *B. C. Ava.*, vii, 60, 61, 67. *Bo. Bhū.*, fol. 82*a*.3. *Çikṣā.*, 190.
[366] *Bo. Bhū.*, fol. 81*b*.7 (*skhalitasya ca yathā-dharmaṃ pratikaraṇatāyai*).
[367] *Bo. Bhū.*, 82*a*.5.3.
[368] *Bo. Bhū.*, 82*b*.3.1. *Çikṣā.*, 191.5.
[369] *Bo. Bhū.*, 81*b*.3.3; 82*b*.2. *Da. Bhū.*, 57.6.
[370] *B. C. Ava.*, vii, 18, 25.
[371] *Sad. Pu.*, 218.11.
[372] *Bo. Bhū.*, 98*a*.4. *Çikṣā.*, 190.4.
[373] *Bo. Bhū.*, 40*a*.6, 81*b*.6, 98*a*.3.
[374] *Bo. Bhū.*, 44*a*.5, 116*b*.5.3 (*laukikeṣu sarva-çāstreṣu kauçalam*).
[375] *Bo. Bhū.*, 43*b*.6.2, 44*a*.2.2.
[376] *Bo. Bhū.*, 98*a*.3.3, 6.1. *Da. Bhū.*, 19.22. *Jā. Mā.*, 208.1, 105.15, 88.3, 142.14. *Pr. Pā. Aṣṭa.*, 527.11. *Kṣemendra*, i, 675.51. ii, 323.12.
[377] *Rāmāyaṇa*, p. 1 (edited by T. R. Krishnacarya, Bombay, 1905).
[378] *B. C. Ava.*, v, 47.
[379] *B. C. Ava.*, vii, 16. 28. *Çikṣā.*, 54.2, 20.14, 140.6.
[380] *Bo. Bhū.*, 82*b*.3, 80*b*.5.
[381] Ibid., 82*a*.5.
[382] *Çikṣā.*, 255.
[383] *B. C. Ava.*, vii, 16, 31, 49, 55.
[384] *Çikṣā.*, 278.4.
[385] Ibid., 17.
[386] *Bo. Bhū.*, 80*b*.3.
[387] *B. C. Ava.*, vii, 70, 71, 60.
[388] Aristotle's "Nicomachean Ethics", pp. 18, 23, 25. 29.
[389] *B. C. Ava.*, vii, 62, 63, 65.
[390] *Lal. V.*, 166.11.
[391] *Mtu.*, ii, 90 ff.
[392] *Lal. V.*, 166.20.

393 *Kṣemendra*, ii, 995.
394 *Mtu.*, ii, 94.15 ff.
395 *Kṣemendra*, ii, 319 ff.
396 *Ava.-ça.*, ii, 80.
397 *Ava,-ça.*, ii, 181.
398 Ibid., i, 324.8; i, 344.2.
399 Ibid., i, 336 ff.
400 IHQ., vol. iii, No. 4, p. 691.
401 E. J. Thomas, "Buddha," p. 181, note.
402 "Gotama," p. 78.
403 *Bo. Bhū.*, fol. 82*b*.6.
404 *M. S. Al.*, 102.1.
405 *Pr. Pā. Çata.*, 95. *Jā. Mā.*, 112.3.
406 *Pr. Pā. Çata.*, 276.
407 *Mtu.*, ii, 117.16; ii, 140; iii, 50. *Kar. Pu.*, 111.11.
408 *Pr. Pā. Çata.*, 116, 117. *Pr. Pā. Aṣṭa.*, 333.1 ff.
409 *Da. Bhū.*, 22.13.
410 *Jā. Mā.*, 181.19 ff.
411 Ibid., 231.15 ff.
412 Ibid., 34.3 ff.
413 Ibid., 110.10.
414 Ibid., 107.15, 108.12.
415 *Çikṣā.*, 193.5, 114.3.
416 *Kṣemendra*, ii, 299 ff.; ii, 631.28; ii, 795.84.
417 *Ava.-ça.*, ii, 37; ii, 3; ii, 10; ii, 16, etc.
418 *Kṣemendra*, ii, 690.
419 *Sad. Pu.*, chap. xiii, p. 289. *Çikṣā*, 120.3, 62.12.
420 *Lal. V.*, chap. xii, p. 142.
421 *Sad. Pu.*, chap. xii, pp. 263 ff., 383.1, 378.7.
422 *Ava.-ça.*, ii, 1–51.
423 *Vide supra*, notes 137, 345, Chap. V.
424 *Kṣemendra*, ii, 895.
425 *Sad. Pu.*, 474.1, 263, 264.
426 *Mtu.*, i, 103.10.
427 *B. C. Ava.*, x, 30. *Su. Vy.*, 19. *Lal. V.*, 195.16.
428 *Mtu.*, iii, 387.8. *Saund. Kā.*, canto viii. *B. C. Ava.*, v, 7. *Çiṣya-lekha*, verse 89. *Divy.*, 29.4. *Çikṣā.*, 72. *Kṣemendra*, i, 827.33, 851.46 ff., and *passim*.
429 *Çikṣā.*, 69.7.
430 *Pr. Pā. Çata.*, 1456.
431 *Çikṣā.*, 78.14. *Lal. V.*, 137.
432 *Sad. Pu.*, chap. xiii, p. 279.5, etc.
433 *Çikṣā.*, 11.10, 99.1.
434 *Gautama's Dharma-sūtras* (iii, 2–3), "*Brahma-cārī gṛhastho bhikṣur vaikhānasa iti teṣāṃ gṛhastho yonir aprajananatvād itareṣām*" (p. 22,

Ānandāçrama Series, Poona, 1910). *Manu* (iii, 78), "*tasmāj jyeṣṭhāçramī gṛhī*," etc. (p. 48, ed. J. Jolly, London, 1887).

[435] *Mtu.*, ii, 48 ff.; ii, 67 ff.; ii, 69 ff.; ii, 83 ff.; ii, 89 ff.; ii, 94 ff.

[436] Cf. *Tertullian*: "De Habitu Muliebri"; "You are the devil's gateway," etc., cited in E. M. White's "Woman in World History", p. 307 (London, 1924). *Gregory Nazianzen*: "Fierce is the dragon, cunning the asp; but woman has the malice of both" (ibid., p. 308). *Clement of Alexandria*: "It should bring shame to a woman to reflect of what nature she is," etc. (ibid., p. 308).

[437] *B. C. Ava.*, ix, 164 ff. *Da. Bhū.*, 17.26 ff.

[438] *Sam. Rā.*, fol. 121*a*.5.

[439] *Çikṣā.*, 198. *Ava.-ça.*, i, 207. *Pr. Pā. Aṣṭa.*, 291.11.

[440] *Çiṣya-lekha*, 68. *Sam. Rā.*, fol. 118*b*. *Pr. Pā. Çata.*, 1455. *Sad. Pu.*, 309.10 ff. *Lka.*, 308. Shakespeare, "As You Like It," Act II, Scene i, l. 16.

[441] *Çikṣā.*, 199.10. 200.13 ff.

[442] Ibid., 201.5.

[443] *Majjh.*, ii, 76. *Dīgha*, i, 251. *Aṅguttara*, ii, 129.

[444] *Pr. Pā. Çata.*, 1443, etc. *Jā. Mā.*, 232.4.

[445] *Bo. Bhū.*, fol. 120*a* ff.

[446] C. A. F. Rhys Davids, "Gotama," p. 180. JRAS. 1928, p. 271.

[447] *Mtu.*, iii, 421.

[448] *Pr. Pā. Aṣṭa.*, 426. *Su. Vy.*, 40.3. *Sam. Rā.*, fol. 193*a*.5.

[449] R. Pischel, "Buddha," pp. 72 ff. H. Oldenberg, "Aus dem alten Indien," p. 1. ERE. viii, 159. A. B. Keith, "Philosophy," p. 337*b*. L. de la Vallée Poussin, in "Le Muséon", 1907, p. 226. E. J. Thomas, "Buddha," p. 126.

[450] *Pr. Pā. Çata.*, 1411.1.

[451] *Mettā*: Cf. *Metta-sutta* (*Khuddaka-Pāṭha*, pp. 8–9). *Dhammapada*, 3, 4, 5, 129, 130, 197, 291, 223. *Sutta-nipātā*, 73, 507, 146–51, 967. *Mettā-vagga* (*Aṅguttara*, iv, 150). *Vinaya*, i, 301–2 (Buddha tends a sick monk). *Saṃyutta*, i, 208 (*Yakkha-saṃyutta*). *Tevijja-sutta* (*Dīgha*, i, 250 ff.). *Aṅguttara*, i, 183, and i, 196–7 (Buddha and his disciples practised these meditations). *Aṅguttara*, iii, 196 (advantages of *mettā*). *Jātaka*, i, 47. *Thera-gāthā*, 645–9. *Dhamma-saṅgaṇi*, section 1056, etc.

[452] *Pr. Pā. Çata.*, 1179, 550, etc.

[453] The Sanskrit formula adds more nouns and adjectives to the Pāli text.

[454] *Pr. Pā. Çata.*, 1314, 1444. *M. Vy.*, section 69.

[455] C. A. F. Rhys Davids, "Gotama," p. 181.

[456] *Lal. V.*, 287.9.

[457] *Çikṣā.*, 212.10.

[458] *Ava.-ça.*, i, 291.2; i, 31.15. *Kṣemendra*, i, 1125.25. *Pr. Pā. Çata.*, 256.4.

[459] *Ava.-ça.*, i, 57.10.

[460] *Dh. S.*, section 131. *Çikṣā.*, 212.12 ff.

[461] *Ava.-ça.*, i, 31.9.

[462] *Mtu.*, iii, 523.

[463] *Pr. Pā. Çata.*, 482, 1411. *Çikṣā.*, 183. *M. Vy.*, section 83.

[464] *M. Vy.*, section 72. In connection with these exercises, the regulation of breathing (inhalation and exhalation) is also recommended. This practice is included in the longer list of the *anusmṛtis* (*ānāpān-ānusmṛti*), *Pr. Pā. Çata.*, 1429. Cf. *Majjh.*, iii, ff. 79 (*Ānāpāna-sati-sutta*).

[465] *M. Vy.*, section 68.

[466] *M. Vy.*, section 67. *Pr. Pā. Çata.*, 1443.

[467] *M. Vy.*, section 70. *Dh. S.*, section 59. *Divy.*, 124.18.

[468] *Dīgha*, i, 37 ff.

[469] *Lal. V.*, 244.14.

[470] *Mahā-parinibbāna-sutta* (*Dīgha*, ii, 156).

[471] *Pr. Pā. Çata.*, 1444, and passim.

[472] *Da. Bhū.*, 33 ff. *Pr. Pā. Çata.*, 1443, 1314. *M. Vy.*, sections 67, 68. *Lal. V.*, 343.15 ff.

[473] *niṣprītikam.* This word is not found in the Pāli text.

[474] E. Senart thinks that *pariçuddha* here means " suppressed ", as the commentator Bhoja interprets *pariçuddhi* in *Yo. Sū.*, i, 43, as meaning *pravilaya* (suppression). Thus this fourth *dhyāna* would be equivalent to the ultra-cognitive *samādhi* (*asamprajñāta*). RHR., vol. xlii, 1900, pp. 345–64. But Bhoja lived as late as the eleventh century ! His interpretation of *pariçuddhi* cannot be applied to the old Buddhist texts.

[475] *pratigha* (Resistance, Repulsion). The *Abhidharma-koça* explains thus (chap. i, p. 53) : " On appelle *sapratigha* ce en quoi et à l'égard de quoi la connaissance (*manas*) peut être empêchée de naître par un corps étranger."

[476] C. A. F. Rhys Davids, " Gotama," pp. 25, 139 ff.

[477] *M. Vy.*, section 156. *Pr. Pā. Çata.*, 472, 1534. *Da. Bhū.*, 68. *Kṣemendra*, ii, 601.

[478] *Dīgha*, ii, 57.

[479] This word has been interpreted in different ways. (1) " Who make others' creation serve their own ends " (" Compendium "). (2) " Created by others, but possessed of great power " (Pāli Dicy.). (3) " Having control of Pleasures fashioned by others " (H. C. Warren, " Buddhism," p. 511). The name may mean " who control or exercise power over the creations of the gods immediately below them on the list ".

[480] *Pr. Pā. Çata.*, 292, 1254. *Mtu.*, ii, 314, 348. *Divy*, 68. *Lal. V.*, 149. *Dh. S.*, sections 127, 128, 129. *M. Vy.*, sections 157–163.

[481] On " *avṛhāḥ*, cf. " Compendium ", p. 138.

[482] Cf. *Sāmañña-phala-sutta* (*Dīgha*, i, 70 ff.).
[483] *Sad. Pu.*, 335.8. *Pr. Pā. Aṣṭa.*, 520. *Pr. Pā. Çata.*, 1322.
[484] *Lka.*, 97 ff.
[485] *Sam. Rā.*, fol. 60*b*.3 ff.
[486] *Dh. S.*, sections 161, 136.
[487] *Lka.*, 73.1.
[488] *Pr. Pā. Çata.*, 1531 ff., 1267 ff., 1415 ff.
[489] *Sam. Rā.*, fol. 193*a*.4. *Bo. Bhū.*, fol. 38*a*.4.2. *Pr. Pā. Çata.*, 57.11. *Kā. Vy.*, 86. *M. S. Al.*, 148.77. *Sad. Pu.*, 136.12, etc.
[490] *Çikṣā.*, tr., p. 6.
[491] *M. S. Al.*, 99. *Pr. Pā. Çata.*, 825.
[492] *Divy.*, 42.8. *Kṣemendra*, i, 903.61.
[493] *Kar. Pu.*, 121.19.
[494] *Su. Vy.*, 4. *Lka.*, 73.
[495] *Bo. Bhū.*, 83*b*.6 ("*samyak-sañcodanāya*"; "*bhoga-vihīnānāṃ vineyānām*," etc.).
[496] RHR., vol. xlii, 1900, p. 364.
[497] H. Beckh, "Buddhismus," ii, 11.
[498] R. Garbe, *Sāṅkhya*, p. 39.
[499] *Mtu.*, iii, 384.12. *Aṅguttara*, ii, 10, section 10 (*cattāro yogā*).
[500] *Lka.*, 247, 256.
[501] On the four stages of *Yoga*, see the Commentary on *Yo. Sū.*, iii, 51 (p. 169). (*Abhyāsī*, *Ṛtambhara-prajñaḥ*, etc.)
[502] F. Heiler, "Die buddhistische Versenkung," pp. 51 ff. C. A. F. Rhys Davids, "Psychology," pp. 114 ff.
[503] *Bo. Bhū.*, 32*a*.2.3. *Pr. Pā. Çata.*, 95.
[504] "Histoire," ii, 437.
[505] *Bo. Bhū.*, 84*b*.7. *M. S. Al.*, 82.2. *Dh. S.*, section 110.
[506] *M. Vy.*, sections 41, 42, 78, 80. *Dh. S.*, section 65. Five *cakṣus* are mentioned in Buddhist literature: (1) *Māṃsa-cakṣus* (the physical eye); (2) *Divya-cakṣus* (the supernal organ of sight; this has been described above); (3) *Prajñā-cakṣus* (the eye of Wisdom); (4) *Dharma-cakṣus* (the eye of the Doctrine or Truth); (5) *Buddha-cakṣus* (the eye of the Enlightened One). (*Vajra*, 38; *M. S. Al.* 143; *Pr. Pā. Çata.*, 290, 538; *Mtu.*, i, 158. Cf. E. J. Thomas, "Buddha," p. 213.)
[507] *Bo. Bhū.*, 85*a*.6, 84*b*.7. *Lal. V.*, 179.1, 169.13.
[508] *M. S. Al.*, p. 301, verse 15; p. 109, verse 41.
[509] *Bo. Bhū.*, 84*a*.7.2 (*dharmāṇaṃ pravicayaḥ*). *M. S. Al.*, p. 106, verses 27, 28.
[510] *Bo. Bhū.*, 84*b*.7, 85*a*.3, 85*b*.2.
[511] *M. S. Al.*, 112.
[512] *Pr. Pā. Aṣṭa.*, 1, 2, 405, 529, 396, 525, 344, 431, 282, 311, 398. *Pr. Pā. Çata.*, 1642, 70. *B. C. Ava.*, ix, 1. *Çikṣā.*, 97.
[513] *Sam. Rā.*, fol. 35*a*.3–4. "*astīti nāstīti ubhe 'pi antā.*" etc.

514 *Mdh.*, 135.1.
515 *Lka.*, 54.
516 *Mdh.*, 11.13, 592.7.
517 *Majjhima*, ii, 32 (*Cūḷa-sakuludāyi-sutta*). "*Imasmiṃ sati, idam hoti; imass' uppādā idaṃ upapajjati,*" etc.
518 *Dhamma-saṅgaṇi* section 534. *Majjh.*, iii, 104 ff.
519 E. Burnouf, "Int.," p. 432. *Mdh.*, p. 5.
520 Also *Pr. Pā. Çata.*, 1216 ff. *Çikṣā.*, 219. Cf. *Vinaya*, i, p. 1.
521 *Da. Bhū.*, 48.
522 *Da. Bhū.*, 49.13, 49.19.
523 *Kṣemendra*, ii, 599.
524 It is also represented as a blind camel led by a driver. (L. A. Waddell, "Buddhism," p. 107.)
525 *M. S. Al.*, tr., p. 76. T. W. Rhys Davids, "Buddhism," p. 156.
526 Cf. A. Weber, "History of Philosophy," p. 557 (London, 1919). P. Janet and G. Séailles, "A History of the Problems of Philosophy," vol. ii, p. 337 (London, 1902).
527 *Kṣemendra*, ii, 599.
528 Cf. "The Rubaiyāt," 59, 60.
529 *Da. Bhū.*, 49.20.
530 *Kṣemendra*, ii, 599.
531 *Da. Bhū.*, 49.22.
532 *Mtu.*, iii, 66.
533 *Kar. Pu.*, 66. *Kṣemendra*, i, 299.74.
534 *Pr. Pā. Çata.*, 864.
535 *Lka.*, 323.
536 *Lal. V.*, 378.4.
537 *Da. Bhū.*, 50.7.
538 *Mdh.*, 363.9. *Da. Bhū.*, 50. *Çikṣā.*, 226.
539 *Pr. Pā. Çata.*, 478. Cf. *Dhamma-saṅgaṇi*, section 1213.
540 E. Burnouf, "Int.," p. 434.
541 H. Oldenberg, "Buddha," p. 271.
542 L. A. Waddell, "Buddhism," p. 117.
543 *Da. Bhū.*, 50. *Kṣemendra*, ii, 600.
544 L. A. Waddell, "Buddhism," p. 117.
545 *Pr. Pā. Çata.*, 933. *Lal. V.*, 346.5.
546 *Divy.*, 210.7. *Kā. Vy.*, 21.5. *Pr. Pā. Çata.*, 754.
547 E. J. Thomas, "Buddha," p. 193.
548 *Saṃyutta*, ii, 30.
549 "Compendium," pp. 262 ff.
550 H. Beckh, "Buddhismus," ii, 101.
551 L. de la Vallée Poussin, "Théorie des douze Causes," pp. 2, 3, 39 (Gand, 1913). H. Oldenberg, "Buddha," p. 272.
552 P. Oltramare, "La Formule bouddhique des douze Causes," pp. 31, 48 (Genève, 1909).

553 P. Oltramare, "Bouddhique," p. 194.
554 *Da. Bhū.*, 48.
555 *Lka.*, 1. *M. S. Al.*, 149.2.
556 *Pr. Pā. Çata.*, 842, 1216, 1360, 136, 141, 1197, 1643, 1440.
557 *Vajra*, 21.5, 41.11, 42.8, 43.16, 23.7, 38.9, 37.13.
558 *B. C. Ava.*, ix, 142, 143, 146, 148, 149, 150.
559 *Pr. Pā. Aṣṭa.*, 513. *Mdh.*, 215. *Lka.*, 90. *Sam. Rā.*, fol 202*a*.3. *Pr. Pā. Çata.*, 906. *M. S. Al.*, 62. *Da. Bhū.*, 55, etc.
560 *Pr. Pā. Çata.*, 77, 1417, 886. *Dh. S.*, section 41. *M. Vy.* section 37. Cf. Csoma, p. 12. P. Oltramare translates *anavarāgra* "qui n'a ni cime ni base" ("Bouddhique," p. 225).
561 *Lka.*, 74.5.
562 *Pr. Pā. Aṣṭa.*, 348. *M. S. Al.*, 58.
563 *M. S. Al.*, 60. *Pr. Pā. Çata.*, 93, 187, 335, 765. *Mtu.*, iii, 401.13. *Kṣemendra*, i, 1117.47.
564 Cf. *Taittirīya Upd.*, ii, 9 (p. 96), "*etaṃ ha vāva na tapati kimahaṃ sādhu nākaravam kimahaṃ pāpam akaravam iti.*" *Bṛhadāraṇyaka Upd.*, iv, 3.22, "*atra steno asteno bhavati bhrūṇahā abhrūṇahā . . . tāpaso atāpaso,*" etc. (p. 610).
565 *Mdh.*, 337. *Pr. Pā. Çata.*, 1454.
566 *Lka.*, 131. *Mdh.*, 492. *B. C. Ava.*, ix, 2.
567 *Lka.*, 280, 294.
568 *M. S. Al.*, 54, 59.
569 *B. C. Ava.*, ix, 2.
570 *Pr. Pā. Çata.*, 471. *B. C. Ava.*, ix, 40.
571 *Lal. V.*, 314.16, 263.1.
572 *M. Vy.*, section 34.
573 *Pr. Pā. Çata.*, 1324.
574 *Sad. Pu.*, 12, 14, 19, 380.
575 *Da. Bhū.*, 46.
576 *Pr. Pā. Aṣṭa.*, 325.17.
577 *Kar. Pu.*, 66.1.
578 *Pr. Pā. Aṣṭa.*, 472, 373, 310, 311, 386, 379.
579 *Lka.*, 204.
580 *Bo. Bhū.*, fol. 101*b*.5.
581 Ibid., fol. 102*a*.2.
582 Ibid., fol. 102*a*.2.
583 Cf. F. W. Farrar, "Lives of the Fathers," vol. ii, pp. 625–7 (Edinburgh, 1889).
584 *Sad. Pu.*, 72 ff.
585 *Sad. Pu.*, 101 ff.
586 *Sad. Pu.*, 322. Cf. also *Sad. Pu.*, 187.
587 *Sad. Pu.*, 319.1.
588 *Sad. Pu.*, 273.11. 278.10.
589 *Sad. Pu.*, 279.5, 284.7.

590 *Çikṣā.*, 60.10 ff.

591 *Çikṣā.*, 45.13, 99.8 ff., 101.3, 107.15, 116.4, 158.2, 364.6 ff.

592 *Dīgha*, iii, 152 (section 16). *Aṅguttara*, ii, 32 (section 32).

593 *M. S. Al.*, 116. *Bo. Bhū.*, fol. 87*b* ff.

594 *Bo. Bhū.*, fol. 90*a*.1.2.

595 P. Oltramare, "Bouddhique," 359.

596 *Bo. Bhū.*, fol. 100*a*.5.2.

597 *Da. Bhū.*, 77–8.

598 *Bo. Bhū.*, fol. 100*a*.6.

599 *M. S. Al.*, 139.1.

600 *Da. Bhū.*, 77–8.

601 On *Bodhidharma*, see K. J. Saunders, "Epochs," pp. 134 ff. D. T. Suzuki, "Zen Essays," pp. 163 ff.

602 *M. S. Al.*, 139.

603 *Bo. Bhū.*, fol. 100*a*.6.3.

604 *Da. Bhū.*, 77–8.

605 *Pr. Pā. Çata.*, 1470.

606 *M. S. Al.*, 139.

607 *Bo. Bhū.*, fol. 100*a*.7.2–3.

608 *Pr. Pā. Çata.*, 1470.22.

609 *Saund. Kā.*, xviii, 11.

610 *Lal. V.*, 35.19.

611 *Sad. Pu.*, 293.5.

612 *Pr. Pā. Çata.*, 4.5, 68.3.

613 L. A. Waddell, "Ind. Ant.," 1914, p. 37.

614 A. A. Macdonell, "Lit.," p. 183.

615 *Dīgha*, iii, 195 ff. *Sutta-nipāta* (*Ratana-sutta*), p. 39.

616 *Su. Vy.*, 18.19.

617 *Kar. Pu.*, 8.

618 *Kar. Pu.*, 126.9. *Sad. Pu.*, 2.12.

619 *Su. Vy.*, 26.

620 *Çikṣā.*, 94.11, 96.1.

621 *Sad. Pu.*, 396.3. *Lka.*, 260.4.

622 *Sad. Pu.*, 474. *Lka.*, 260.

623 *Çikṣā.*, 140 ff.

624 Ibid., 142.

625 *Sad. Pu.*, 400. *Lka.*, 260 ff.

626 *Dh. S.*, section 52.

627 *M. Vy.*, section 25.

628 *Svāhā.* This exclamation is borrowed from the ancient Vedic literature. It is associated with prayers and incantations. It means "Heil", "Segen", "Hail", "Blessing", "Amen" (Skt. Dicy. Pbg. and Macdonell). A. A. Macdonell suggests that it is derived from the root *ah*. It is an old indeclinable auspicious word.

CHAPTER VI

Notes

[1] *Dhamma-saṅgaṇi*, section 277 (p. 60). *Saund. Kā.*, xiv, 41. *Pr. Pā. Çata.*, 67. *Lka.*, 10.1, etc.

[2] *M. S. Al.*, 183.

[3] *Dīgha*, iii, 220. Eleven stages of training at *Aṅguttura*, v, 342 ff.

[4] *Da. Bhū.*, vii.

[5] *Ābhoga.* The Pāli word *ābhoga* means "idea", "thought", (probably from the root *bhuj* "to enjoy"). L. de la Vallée Poussin explains *ābhoga* as "acte de se tourner vers", "acte d'attention" (from *bhuj* "to bend"). Cf. *Milinda*, p. 97, l. 10, "*na hi bhante uparatassa vātassa ābhogo vā manasikāro vā.*" Also, *M. S. Al.*, tr., p. 8, note 7. D. T. Suzuki translates *anābhoga* as "effortless, purposeless, not being aware of conscious strivings" ("Studies," p. 378).

[6] *Da. Bhū.*, 20, 30, 37, 41, etc.

[7] *Da. Bhū.*, 21, 30, 37, 41, etc.

[8] W. McGovern, "Introduction," p. 176.

[9] Ibid., p. 176.

[10] Cf. L. de la Vallée Poussin's French translation of these terms in "Le Muséon", 1907, p. 314 (*Madhyamakāvatāra*).

[11] Cf. "Le Muséon," 1911, p. 278 (L. de la Vallée Poussin's French translation).

[12] *Lka.*, 215. *M. Vy.*, section 3. *Dh. S.*, section 65.

CHAPTER VII

Notes

[1] *Mtu.*, i, 239. *Lal. V.*, 393.12, 414.19. *Pr. Pā. Aṣṭa.*, 368.
[2] *Mtu.*, i, 38.
[3] *Mtu.*, i, 49 ff.
[4] *Mtu.*, i, 47.
[5] *Kṣemendra*, ii, 931.
[6] *Lal. V.*, 19.7. *Mtu.*, ii, 1.
[7] *Mtu.*, i, 197. *Lal. V.*, 25.5 ff., 23.10 ff.
[8] *Lal. V.*, 26.15 ff., 28.16.
[9] *Dīgha*, i, 115 ("*samaṇo khalu bho Gotamo ubhato sujāto,*" etc.).
[10] *Lal. V.*, 55.3 ff. *Mtu.*, ii, 8.17.
[11] *Mtu.*, iii, 411.4. *Kṣemendra*, i, 665.7.
[12] E. Senart, "Légende," pp. 254, 255.
[13] W. Windisch "Geburt,", pp. 176, 182.
[14] A. de Gubernatis, "Zoological Mythology," ii, p. 92 (London, 1872).
[15] "Indian Mythology," p. 195 (Boston, 1917). J. S. Speyer has discussed the question in ZDMG. 1903, pp. 305–10. In the sculptures of Bharhut and Bara-buḍur, the elephant has only two tusks. J. S. Speyer is of opinion that the Pāli word *chaddanto* means "Zähmer der Sechs" (*danto* to be derived from "dam"). He rejects the hypothesis that "six" may refer to the six rival teachers, who are mentioned in the Pāli canon. He thinks that the word denotes the six organs of sense, and says: "Wenn von einem Zähmer der Sechs die Rede ist, soll man doch zunächst an die fünf Sinnesorgane und das *manas* denken." The epithet was then applied to the elephant and misunderstood as meaning "six-tusked". But this explanation does not seem to be grammatically sound.
[16] *Mtu.*, i, 213. *Lal. V.*, 60 ff.
[17] *Mtu.*, i, 218.10 ff. *Lal. V.*, 83.10.
[18] *Lal. V.*, 85.1 ff.
[19] *Mtu.*, i, 207. *Divy*, 205. *Lal. V.*, 85.14.
[20] *Lal. V.*, 98.8. *Mtu.*, ii, 3.9.
[21] E. Senart, "Légende," p. 267.
[22] E. Senart, "Legénde," p. 243.
[23] T. Keightley, "The Mythology of Ancient Greece and Italy," p. 102 (London, 1896).
[24] L. Spence, "An Introduction to Mythology," pp. 133–4 (London, 1921).

[25] P. Ehrenreich "Die Allgemeine Mythologie," p. 146 (Leipzig, 1910).

[26] *Āçvalāyana Gṛhya-sūtra*, i, 7.19 ("*ath-ainām . . . sapta-padāny-abhyutkrāmayati*," etc.: p. 33, Bibliotheca Indica Series).

[27] *Mtu.*, ii, 20.18.

[28] *B. Ct.*, i, 33.

[29] E. Windisch, "Geburt," p. 132, note.

[30] T. Keightley, op. cit., p. 103. J. H. Philpott, "The Sacred Tree," p. 118 (London, 1897).

[31] *Lal. V.*, 120.3.

[32] *Lal. V.*, 125.19 ff.

[33] *Lal. V.*, 156.

[34] *Lal. V.*, 122.7.

[35] *Lal. V.*, 145.4 ff.

[36] *Lal. V.*, 153.1 ff.

[37] *Lal. V.*, 105.11 ff. *M. Vy.*, section 17. *Dh. S.*, section 83. *Mtu.*, ii, 29.19 ff. *Kṣemendra*, i, 669.29 ff. (Cf. *Dīgha*, ii, 17; iii, 142.) The items Nos. 21 and 22 may also be interpreted thus: "He has one hair to each pore, and his hair rises straight upward and curls to the right." But the *M. Vy.* says: "Each hair curls to the right and the hairs rise upward." The list in the *M. Vy.* agrees with that given in the *Lal. V.* The *M. Vy.* has only *sama-lalāṭa* (No. 3); the mark No. 7 is divided into two items; the items 5 and 6 are given as one mark; the adjective in No. 9 is *suçukla* (very white); the feet are not described as "even" (*sama*); the wheel is both on the hands and the feet, and it is not described. These are the chief points of difference between the *M. Vy.* and the *Lal. V.* The *Dh. S.* really mentions more than thirty-two signs. The hands are also described as "well-set". Several new items are added: e.g. a "straight body", "a white jaw", "the gait of a swan". The tongue is not described as "slender" (*tanu*); the skin is "white" instead of "fine" (*sūkṣma*); the wheel is on both the hands and the feet. These are the chief points of difference between the *Lal. V.* and the *Dh. S.* The *Mtu.* describes the signs by short adjectives, some of which cannot be clearly understood.

[38] E. Burnouf, "Lotus," p. 553. "Sa tête est couronnée par une protubérance du crâne." E. Senart, "Légende," p. 126.

[39] E. Senart, "Légende," p. 128.

[40] Ibid., p. 134.

[41] Ibid., pp. 139–40.

[42] A. Grünwedel, "Art," p. 67, l. 10.

[43] *Dh. S.*, section 84. *M. Vy.*, section 18. *Mtu.*, ii, 43. *Lal. V.*, 106. The eighty minor marks (*anuvyañjanāni*) are not very important. Some of them may be mentioned here. The nails are of the colour of copper; the fingers are round and beautiful; the gait is like that of a lion, an elephant, a swan and a bull (!); the abdomen is

deep; the lines of the hand are soft, deep, long and straight; the lips are red; the voice is sweet and pleasant; the ears are equal in size; etc. For a complete list in English and French, see *Dh. S.*, pp. 55 ff., and P. Foucaux, *Lal. V.* tr., pp. 96 ff.

44 *Rāmāyaṇa*, p. 1 (i, 1.9–10–11).

45 *Dīgha*, i, 9 (section 21), "*iti evarūpāya tiracchāna-vijjāya paṭivirato Samaṇo Gotamo.*"

46 A. Foucher, "Art," vol. ii, pp. 360, 362, 289, 297. See also the figures of Buddha, vol. ii, pp. 291, 347, 777.

47 *Lal. V.*, 129. *Mtu.*, ii, 45. In the *Lal. V.*, the *bodhisattva* experiences four *dhyānas*.

48 Candra-rāja Bhaṇḍārī, *Bhagavān Mahāvīra*, p. 123 (Bhānpura, 1924).

49 *B. Ct.*, canto iii, pp. 21 ff. *Lal. V.*, 187 ff. *Mtu.*, ii, 150 ff.

50 Cf. *Aṅguttara*, i, 145 (section 38.2).

51 *Lal. V.*, 161 ff.

52 *Lal. V.*, 217 ff.

53 *Lal. V.*, 251 ff. *Mtu.*, ii, 231 ff.

54 *Lal. V.*, 272 ff. *Mtu.*, ii, 264.

55 E. Windisch, "*Māra,*" p. 187.

56 E. Senart, "Légende," p. 180.

57 H. Kern, "Histoire," i, 302.

58 Cf. *Sutta-nipāta*, 355 (p. 62). *Dīgha*, i, 93.10 (*pisāce pi Kaṇhā ti sañjānanti*).

59 *Sutta-nipāta*, p. 15, l. 3. *Majjhima*, iii, 60, l. 29.

60 *Dīgha*, ii, 109 (*aṭṭha kho imā Ānanda parisā*, etc.).

61 *Saṃyutta*, i, 103 ff. (*mahantaṃ hatthirāja-vaṇṇam abhinimminitvā*, etc., p. 104; *mahantaṃ sappa-rāja-vaṇṇam*, p. 106).

62 *Saṃyutta*, i, p. 114 (section 9); p. 112 (section 7).

63 *Majjhima*, i, 332 (*Kin-nu kho me kucchi garugaru*, etc.).

64 *Saṃyutta*, i, 128 ff. (*Bhikkhunī-saṃyutta*).

65 *Saṃyutta*, iii, 124.

66 *Vinaya*, i, pp. 21, 22 (*baddho' si sabba pāsehi*, etc.).

67 *Jātaka*, i, 72–3. N.B.—150 leagues, not 250. (E. J Thomas.)

68 *Saṃyutta*, i, 115 (*tava rūpā tava cakkhu-samphassa*, etc.).

69 *Majjhima*, iii, 94 (*labhati tassa Māro otāraṃ, labhati tassa Māro ārammaṇaṃ*).

70 *Sutta-nipāta*, pp. 74–8 (verses 425 ff.).

71 *Saṃyutta*, iii, 189, "*tvaṃ Rādha rūpam Māro ti passa,*" etc.

72 *Pr. Pā. Çata.*, 71. *Ava.-ça.*, i, 215.7. *Çikṣā*, 244.4.

73 *Lal. V.*, 283.20.

74 *Lal. V.*, 301.3. *Mtu.*, ii, 341.3; ii, 320.5. *Pr. Pā. Çata.*, 112. *Da. Bhū.*, 90. *Lal. V.*, 261.6. 262.20, 263.4.

75 E. Windisch, "*Māra,*" p. 186.

76 *Lal. V.*, 130.8.
77 *Kṣemendra*, ii, 583.61. *B. Ct.*, xiii, 2.
78 *Kṣemendra*, i, 713.1.
79 Ibid., i, 95.136; ii, 323.8.
80 *Da. Bhū.*, 53.18.
81 E. Senart, "Origines," p. 7.
82 *Jā. Mā.*, 19.20 ff.
83 *Divy*, 357, 361, 363.
84 *Pr. Pā. Çata.*, 1186.
85 *Çikṣā*, 49 ff.
86 *Divy*, 357. *Kṣemendra*, ii, 575.42.
87 *Divy*, 145.
88 *Çikṣā*, 38, 40.
89 Ibid., 49.
90 *Çikṣā*, 139.9.
91 *Lal. V.*, 354.11, 224.8. *Da. Bhū.*, 54.17. *Kar. Pu.*, 127.7. *Çikṣā*, 198.10. *Dh. S.*, section 80. *Mtu.*, iii, 281.7. L. de la Vallée Poussin mentions only three *Māras* in his article (ERE. viii, 407*a*), but the Mahāyānists made a fourfold division.
92 *Pr. Pā. Çata.*, 485.
93 *Da. Bhū.*, 62.5.
94 *Pr. Pā. Aṣṭa.*, 385.
95 *Pr. Pā. Aṣṭa.*, chaps. xi and xxiv, pp. 232, 416). *Çikṣā*, 151.
96 *Lal. V.*, 262.14. *Mtu.*, ii, 240.
97 *Çikṣā*, 49 ff.
98 *Pr. Pā. Aṣṭa.*, 448.
99 *Çikṣā*, 42.16.
100 *Mtu.*, ii, 404.20, 408.9, 241.13 ff., 244.5 ff., 246.3 ff., 250.20 ff.
101 *B. Ct.*, xiii, 4–5.
102 *Kṣemendra*, i, 725.44.
103 *Lal. V.*, 300.
104 Ibid., 301.
105 Ibid., 378.4.
106 *B. Ct.*, xiii, 3.
107 *Lal. V.*, 308.15.
108 Ibid., 308 ff.
109 *Mtu.*, ii, 408.10 ff.
110 *Lal. V.*, 308 ff.
111 *Rāmāyaṇa*, *Yuddha-Kāṇḍa*, *sargas* 8, 9, 10, 14, 15, 16 (vol. ii, pp. 113 ff.).
112 *Jātaka*, i, 63 (*mārisa mā nikkhammi*).
113 *Lal. V.*, 261.
114 *Mtu.*, ii, 238.
115 *Lal. V.*, 317.20.

116 *Lal. V.*, 319.3.

117 Ibid., 320 ff.

118 Cf. *Aitareya Brāhmaṇa*, i, 4.6 (p. 98), "*devāsurā vā eṣu lokeṣu samayatanta*," etc. (Ānandāçrama Series, vol. xxxii, pt. i, Poona, 1896). "The Works of Hesiod," translated by J. Banks (London, 1914), p. 33. L. Spence, "Introduction to Mythology," p. 293.

119 *Mtu.*, ii, 410. *Lal. V.*, 305. *B. Ct.*, xiii, 19 ff. *Kṣemendra*, i, 729.

120 *Mtu.*, ii, 282.2. *Lal. V.*, 335.13.

121 *Lal. V.*, 318.11.

122 *Lal. V.*, 333.

123 *Mtu.*, ii, 280.1.

124 *Mtu.*, ii, 283.4.

125 *Lal. V.*, 340.21.

126 *B. Ct.*, xiii, 57 ff.

127 *Kṣemendra*, i, 729 ff.

128 *Majjhima*, i, 247 (*So kho ahaṃ Aggivessana oḷārikaṃ āhāraṃ āhāretva*, etc.).

129 *Dīgha*, ii, 4 (section 8).

130 E. Senart, "Légende," pp. 168, 169, 197, 207. E. Senart summarizes his conclusions thus: "Il (Buddha) est mûr pour sa mission prédestinée: la conquête de l'ambroisie et de la roue, de la pluie et de la lumière fécondes. Il prend possession de l'arbre divin; le démon orageux accourt le lui disputer; . . . la sombre armée de *Māra*, rompue, dechirée, se disperse. Les *Apsaras*, filles du demon, les dernières vapeurs légères qui flottent au ciel, essayent en vain d'enlacer et de retenir le triomphateur. . . . Il paraît dans toutes sa gloire, dans sa splendeur suprême: le dieu a atteint le sommet de sa course" ("La Légende," p. 434).

H. Kern says: "La vérité indeniable de la légende, sauf quelques détails insignifiants, n'est pas celle de l'histoire, mais celle de la mythologie de la nature. . . . Le Buddha est un de ces *avatāras*, celui du dieu solaire. . . . La lutte entre le *bodhisatva* et *Māra*, le répresentant de l'obscurité, appartient, au moins dans ses traits essentiels, aux mythes les plus anciens de notre race. . . . Le Dieu solaire était tantôt loué comme chasseur des ténèbres, comme exterminateur d'êtres méchants, géants et autres monstres, tantôt comme la source abondante de benédictions pour la terre entière, à cause de la lumière bienfaisante dont il illumine la terre et le ciel . . . chez les Indiens, le grand Libérateur du monde est le Dieu solaire. . . ." ("Histoire," i, 50, 239, 241, 243, 245).

131 A. B. Keith, "Mythology," p. 197.

132 *Ṛgveda*, i, 32 (p. 309, vol. i), "*indrasya nu vīryāṇi pravoçam*," etc. Cf. H. D. Griswold, "The Religion of the Ṛgveda" pp. 178–86 (Oxford, 1923). H. Oldenberg, "Die Religion des Veda," pp. 133 ff. (Stuttgart, 1917).

[133] SBE., vol. xxiii, p. 231 (*Bahrām Yaṣt*), "We sacrifice unto Verethraghna," etc.

[134] J. G. Frazer, "The Golden Bough," vol. i, pp. 56, 58 (London, 1894).

[135] J. H. Philpott, "The Sacred Tree," pp. 111, 115, 116 (London, 1897). T. Keightley, op. cit., p. 74.

[136] *Lal. V.*, pp. 343 ff. *B. Ct.*, xiv, 2.

[137] *Mtu.*, ii, 286, 417. Cf. *Lal. V.*, 355.19. *Upasargā devatā.* The Pāli word *upasagga* means "attack, trouble, danger". Cf. *Aṅguttara*, i, 101, "*ye keci upasaggā uppajjanti.*"

[138] *Mtu.*, ii, 416.6.

APPENDIX

Chronological Notes on the Principal Sanskrit Treatises that have been utilised for this Essay (*compiled from various sources*)

(1) *Mahā-vastu* ("The Book of the Great Event or Subject"). In its oldest form, it was probably extant in the early part of the third century B.C. The final redaction probably dates from the sixth or seventh century A.D. (fourth century, according to M. Winternitz and A. B. Keith). Cf. Vassilief, p. 270; ZDMG., vol. lii, 1898, p. 673; *Indologica Pragensia* i, p. 76 (1929); "Journal des Savants," 1899, p. 628; *Tāranātha*, p. 271, l. 1; "Cambridge History of India," vol. i, p. 304; J. N. Farquhar, "Outline," p. 110.

(2) *Lalita-vistara* ("Extended Account of the Sport"). Nos. 159 and 160 in B. Nanjio's catalogue. Translated into Chinese four times: A.D. 221–63, 308, 420–79, and 683. Its oldest parts may be assigned to the third century B.C., and its final redaction to the sixth century A.D. (second century, according to M. Winternitz).

Cf. *Lal. V. Tib.*, vol. ii, p. xvi; *Nettipakaraṇa*, p. xxvii; "Abhandlungen und Vorträge des fünften internationalen Orientalisten-Congresses" (Zweite Hälfte), pp. 107–22 (Berlin, 1882); JRAS. 1856, pp. 242 ff.; JA. 1892, p. 202; A. Foucher, "Art," vol. ii, p. 674; M. Winternitz, "Lit." ii, 200; S. Beal, "Abstract," p. 12; S. Beal, "Catena," p. 13; A. Grünwedel, "Mythologie," p. 4; A. Grünwedel, "Art," p. 85; G. K. Nariman, "Lit." p. 26.

(3) *Sad-dharma-puṇḍarīka* ("The White Lotus of the true Dharma or Faith"). Nos. 134, 136, 138, 139 in B. Nanjio's catalogue. Translated into Chinese in A.D. 255, and later. The earliest part (chaps. i–xx) may belong to the first century B.C., while the supplementary chapters (xxi–xxvi) date from the third century A.D.

(4) *Sukhāvatī-vyūha* ("The Structure or Arrangement of the Region of Bliss"). The word *vyūha* has also been translated as "description". This treatise exists in two recensions, of which the larger was translated into Chinese in A.D. 148–70. Nos. 23 (5), 25, 26, 27 and 863 in B. Nanjio's catalogue. Dates from first century B.C. The smaller treatise may be assigned to the fourth century (Nos. 199, 200 in B. Nanjio's catalogue).

(5) Açvaghoṣa's *Buddha-carita* and *Saundarānanda-Kāvya*. The original *Buddha-carita* is available in Sanskrit only in a truncated form (Cantos i–xiii and 32 verses of Canto xiv). Açvaghoṣa was the preceptor of Kaniṣka, who flourished in the first century A.D.

Cf. Vassilief, p. 77; JA. 1892, p. 203; "I-tsing," p. 481; "Cambridge History of India," vol. i, pp. 582, 583, 703; BEFEO. 1904, p. 56.

(6) *Aṣṭa-sāhasrikā Prajñā-pāramitā* ("The Perfection of Wisdom" in 8,000 "verses"). No. 1 (*e*) in B. Nanjio's catalogue. Translated into Chinese A.D. 179. It may be assigned to the first century B.C.

(7) *Çata-sāhasrikā Prajñā-pāramitā* ("The Perfection of Wisdom" in 100,000 "verses"). No. 1 (*a*) in B. Nanjio's catalogue. Translated into Chinese A.D. 659. Belongs probably to the fifth century A.D. Only chapters i-xii have been utilised.

(8) *Vajra-cchedikā Prajñā-pāramitā* ("The Diamond-Cutter: a Treatise on the Perfection of Wisdom"). Nos. 1 (i), 10, 11, 12, 13, 14 and 15 in B. Nanjio's catalogue. First translated into Chinese about A.D. 400. Dates from the fourth century A.D.

These treatises on *Prajñā-pāramitā* are attributed to Nāgārjuna, who lived in the second century A.D. (according to M. Walleser and S. Beal). But internal evidence proves that they were not written by the same author. We may regard "Nāgārjuna" as a group-name for the pioneers of the Mahāyāna, the most eminent of whom was the philosopher Nāgārjuna.

Cf. *Tāranātha*, pp. 87, 127, 131; Vassilief, p. 213; *Rājataraṅgiṇī*, i, 172–3, p. 8 (ed. M. A. Stein, Bombay, 1892); J. Takakusu in ERE., iv, 838*a*; JRAS. 1905, p. 53; JBTS., vol. v, pt. iv, p. 15; "Lehrbuch," ii, 183; ZII. 1928, p. 224; "Ind. Ant.," xv, 1886, p. 356*b*; "Zeitschrift für Buddhismus," Bd. vi, Heft 2, 1925, p. 242.

(9) *Mūla-madhyamaka-kārikāḥ* ("Verses on the fundamental doctrines of the *Mādhyamika* school"). This treatise is also attributed to Nāgārjuna.

(10) *Dharma-saṅgraha* ("Compendium of the Doctrine"). It is erroneously attributed to Nāgārjuna. It may be assigned to the seventh or eighth century A.D., as it was translated into Chinese in the tenth century. No. 812 in B. Nanjio's catalogue.

(11) *Avadāna-çataka* ("A Century of instructive Stories"). No. 1324 in B. Nanjio's catalogue. First translated into Chinese A.D. 223–53. The word *dīnāra* is mentioned in it. Early second century A.D. The first ten stories are Mahāyānist in spirit; the rest belong to the Hīnayāna.

Cf. "Annales du Musée Guimet," vol. xviii, 1891, pp. ix ff.; T'oung-Pao, 1907, pp. 106, 110; JA. 1879, tome 14, p. 151; JRAS. 1907, pp. 681 ff.; JRAS. 1915, pp. 504 ff.

(12) *Divy-āvadāna* ("The Heavenly Stories"). Nos. 1343, 1344 in B. Nanjio's catalogue. The oldest portions date from the second century B.C.; they were included in the Vinaya of the *Mūla-sarvāstivādin* sect. The final redaction may be assigned to the sixth century A.D. (third century, according to M. Winternitz). Mainly Hīnayāna.

Cf. J. Przyluski, "Asoka," p. 14; A. Gawronski, "Studies," pp. 49, 54; A. B. Keith, "Lit.," p. viii.

(13) *Daça-bhūmika-sūtra* ("The Treatise on the Ten Stages"). Nos. 105 and 110 in B. Nanjio's catalogue. First translated into Chinese in A.D. 265–316. Dates from early third century.

(14) *Mahāyāna-sūtrālaṅkāra* ("The Ornament of the Mahāyāna Texts"), with a prose commentary. The verses are usually attributed to Asaṅga, who lived in the fourth century A.D. But H. Ui has proved that they were written by Maitreyanātha, to whom he assigns the date 270–350. The prose commentary was composed by Vasubandhu, who lived in the first half of the fourth century (according to N. Péri, BEFEO. xi, 1911, p. 384).

Cf. JRAS. 1905, p. 43, ll. 17–19; JA. 1890, tome xvi, p. 553; *M. S. Al.* tr., p. 2; ERE. xiii, 256*a*; U. Wogihara, *Bo. Bhū.*, p. 16; A. Barth in RHR., vol. xxviii (1893), p. 258, note 2; ZII., Bd. 6, Heft 2, 1928, pp. 217, 223, 224.

(15) *Bodhisattva-bhūmi*. This is the only portion of the *Yog-ācārya* (*ācāra*)-*bhūmi-çāstra* that is available in Sanskrit. It has been attributed to Maitreya or Asaṅga (fourth century A.D.). The palm-leaf manuscript dates from the ninth century. Cf. U. Wogihara in ZDMG. 1904, p. 452. In a few passages the MS. reading is corrupt, e.g. fol. 125*a*, l. 4, section 2; fol. 126*b*, 2, 2; fol. 126*b*, 6, 3.

(16) *Laṅk-āvatāra-sūtra* ("The treatise on the Visit to Ceylon"). Nos. 175, 176, 177 in B. Nanjio's catalogue. Translated into Chinese in 443, 513, and 700–4. The versified tenth chapter is not found in the earliest Chinese version. Approximate date: Early fourth century.

Cf. G. Tucci in IHQ., vol. iv, 1928, pp. 546, 551; S. Dasgupta, "History," p. 128, note 1.

(17) *Samādhi-rāja-sūtra* ("Treatise on the King of *Samādhis*, Modes of Concentration"). This treatise is the same as "*Candra-dīpa-samādhi-sūtra*", which is mentioned in B. Nanjio's catalogue (Nos. 191, 192). First translated into Chinese about A.D. 450. Belongs to the fourth century.

(18) *Suvarṇa-prabhāsa* ("The Splendour of Gold"). In its original form, it was translated into Chinese in A.D. 397–439, and again in an expanded version in the seventh century. Nos. 126, 127, 130 in B. Nanjio's catalogue. The earliest recension may be assigned to the fourth century A.D.

(19) *Karuṇā-puṇḍarīka-sūtra* ("The treatise of the White Lotus of Compassion"). No. 142 in B. Nanjio's catalogue. Translated into Chinese in the fifth century. Probable date: Fourth century.

(20) *Jātaka-mālā* ("The Garland of Birth-stories"). It was written by Āryaçura, whom Tāranātha identifies with Açvaghoṣa and Mātṛceta! He may be assigned to the sixth century. An earlier date has been suggested (fourth century) on the ground that one of his treatises

was translated into Chinese in A.D. 434 (Nanjio, No. 1349); but this small pamphlet was almost certainly not written by Āryaçura, especially as the *Jātaka-mālā* was not translated into Chinese. Some verses from this book are quoted in the inscriptions describing the paintings in the Ajanta caves.

Cf. A. O. Ivanovski in RHR., tome 47, 1903, pp. 298 ff.; K. Watanabe in JPTS. 1909, p. 263; *Tāranātha*, pp. 90, 136; JRAS. 1893, p. 306; "I-tsing," pp. 162, 163, 177; RHR., tome 28, 1893, p. 260; Album Kern, pp. 405, 408; J. Burgess, "Report on the Buddhist Cave Temples," 1883, p. 81, l. 16; "Nachrichten von der Königl. Gesellschaft der Wissenschaften zu Göttingen, Phil-Hist. Klasse," 1902, pp. 759, 762; Lady Herringham, "Ajanta," p. 18*a*, l. 45; Vincent A. Smith, "Art," p. 274; *Tāranātha*, p. 5.

(21) *Rāṣṭrapāla-paripṛcchā* ("The Inquiry of Rāṣṭrapāla"). This treatise was translated into Chinese early in the seventh century. No. 23 (18) in B. Nanjio's catalogue. Probable date: Sixth century.

(22) *Nāg-ānanda* ("The Joy of the Nāgas or Serpent-folk"). This play is attributed to King Harṣa (Harṣadeva, Harṣavardhana), who lived in the first half of the seventh century.

(23) *Çikṣā-samuccaya* ("Compendium of Teaching"). The author was Çāntideva, who probably lived in the seventh or eighth century. A Tibetan version of the treatise dates from the early ninth century. Cf. *Tāranātha*, p. 5.

(24) *Bodhi-cary-āvatara* ("The Entrance to the Practice or Career for Enlightenment") This is a poem by Çāntideva. There seems to be no reason to doubt the authenticity of the last canto.

(25) *Çiṣya-lekha* ("Letter to a Disciple"). This short poem is attributed to Candragomin. S. Lévi has shown that this author lived in the seventh century (BEFEO. 1903, p. 38). Cf. *Tāranātha*, p. 151, ll. 14, 15.

(26) *Kāraṇḍa-vyūha* ("Description or Structure of the Basket," of the Virtues and Powers of Avalokiteçvara). No. 782 in B. Nanjio's catalogue. Translated into Chinese in the tenth century. It may be assigned to the eighth or ninth century.

(27) *Mahā-vyutpatti* ("The great Treatise on Etymology"). This compendium of technical terms dates from the ninth century. Cf. L. de la Vallée Poussin, ERE. ii, 257, note.

(28) *Bodhisattv-āvadāna-kalpalatā* ("The wish-fulfilling Creeper of the Stories of the *bodhisattva*"). This treatise contains 108 versified narratives, of which 107 were composed by Kṣemendra and the 108th was added by his son. Kṣemendra lived in the eleventh century. Cf. R. Mitra, "Sanskrit Buddhist Literature of Nepal," p. 57 (Calcutta, 1882).

INDEX

Abhidharma-koça, 71, 72, 78
Abhijñās (Super-knowledges), 1, 106 ff.
Açubha-bhāvanā, 93
Açvaghoṣa, 82, 87, 90, 128, 147
Ahiṃsā, 199
Akuçala-mūlāni (Roots of Evil), three, 194
Altruism and Egoism, 179
Anesaki, M., 58, 97, 222
Ānimitta-samādhi, 234
Anuçayas (evil proclivities), 155
Anutpattika-dharma-kṣānti, 213
Apollo, birth of, 298
Arhat: his attributes, 1–2; distinguished from the *bodhisattva*, 15 ff.
Arians, the, 28
Aristotle, 164, 220, 300
Artha-caryā (altruistic service), 254
Artha-pratisaṃvid, 264
Āryaçūra, 96, 138, 178
Ārya-satyāni (Noble Truths), four, 155 ff.; their twelve *parivartas*, 158
Asaṅkhyeya, 77
Āsravas (*āsavas*: sins and errors), the *arhat* is free from, 3; distinguished from *kleças*, 109; knowledge of their destruction, 116; meaning of the term, 116 ff.
Aṣṭāṅga-mārga (the eightfold Way), 160 ff.
Aṣṭa-sāhasrikā Prajñā-pāramitā, 65, 237, 310
Asuras, 68
Athanasius, 28
Atharva-veda, 267, 295
Ātman, doctrine of, 69, 72, 73
Avadāna-çataka, 15, 65, 183, 186, 190
Avalokiteçvara: meaning of his name, 47; a solar deity, 48; his deeds of mercy, 49 his apotheosis, 46, 49
Āveṇika-dharmas (special attributes), 21 ff.
Avidyā (Ignorance), as an *āsrava*, 133; as a *nidāna*, 239
Avyākṛta-vastūni (unexplained subjects), 133
Āyatanas, 122, 241

Balāni (Powers): a Buddha's ten Powers, 20; five *balas*, 144; a *bodhisattva's* ten *balas*, 148
Beckh, H., 235, 243
Bhakti: its origin in Buddhism, 31; inüuence of Hindu sects, 36; idea of Confession, 56
Bhūmi, meaning of, 270
Bhūmis, seven and ten, 271; in the *Mtu.*, 273; in the *Pr. Pā. Çata*, 275; in the *Bo. Bhū.*, 278; in the *Da.-Bhū.*, 283
Bodhi: meaning of the word, 18; is distinguished from *nirvāṇa*, 11; its characteristics, 19
Bodhi-cary-āvatāra, 57, 88, 192
Bodhi-citta (Thought of Enlightenment), 58, 62
Bodhi-citt-otpāda, 58 ff.; its necessity, 60; its causes and occasions, 62
Bodhi-pakṣyā dharmāḥ, 80 ff.
Bodhisattva: meaning of the word, 4 ff.; is distinct from the

arhats and *pratyeka-buddhas*, 9 ff.; rejects *nirvāṇa*, 14; his Discipline and Career, 75; his great Compassion, 178; his Transfer of Merit, 188; he is not afraid of Pain, 159; is always active, 220; his last existence on earth, 292 ff.; as a Superman, 299 ff.; his thirty-two marks, 300; his struggle with *Māra*, 306 ff.
Bodhisattva-bhūmi, 14, 50, 61, 81, 90, 113, 166, 203, 254
Bodhi-tree, 314
Bodhy-aṅgas (Factors of Enlightenment), seven, 149 ff.; compared to a monarch's *ratnas*, 154
Body, the, its arraignment and appreciation, 92 ff.
Brahma-vihāras (Sublime States), four, 225 ff.
Buddhahood, its theory developed, 24 ff.
Buddhas, the, their attributes: they are innumerable, 24; they are immortal, 25; their *kṣetras*, 25; they are super-human, 26; their *rūpa-kāya* and *dharma-kāya*, 25; their *karuṇā*, 24; miracles at their birth, 297
Burnouf, E., 136, 165, 300

Çaiva sect, 37
Çāntideva, 57, 67, 77, 87, 99
Carpenter, J. E., 43, 192
Caryā, fourfold, 75
Çatapatha-Brāhmaṇa, 68
Çata-sāhasrikā Prajñā-pāramita, 16, 21, 94
Celibacy in Buddhism, 132, 222
Cetaḥ-khilāni (Mental obstructions), five, 144
Cetanā (Will), 71
Christian ascetics, 139
Christianity, influence of, 40 ff.
Çikṣā-padāni (Precepts), five, 198
Çīla (Morality), as a *pāramitā*, 193 ff.; its importance, 194; its basic principles, 195; its relation to *saṃvara* (self-control), 196; the ten Precepts or Ways of Action, 197 ff.; motives for moral conduct, 204; casuistry in Buddhist ethics, 207; stories, 208
Citta (Thought) as a *smṛty-upasthāna*, 98
Çivi, story of, 183
Clement of Alexandria, 41
Comte, Auguste, 244
Confession, 56
Corpse, nine conditions of, 94
Cosmology, Buddhist, 231 ff.; the eighteen heavens, 232; three *dhātus* (spheres), 231
Çraddhā (Faith), importance and advantages of, 145 ff.
Crow, parable of the, 132
Çūnyatā (Emptiness), 237 ff.; as conditioned Existence, 238; as Non-existence, 244; classified, 246; applied to the Perfections, 247
Cynics, the, 139

Daça-bhūmika-sūtra, 66, 228, 283
Dāna (Giving), as a *pāramitā*, 172 ff.; developed by the Mahāyānists, 172; classified, 173; recipients of, 174; methods of, 176; motives of, 177; reward of, 177; stories of, 181 ff.
Dante's Inferno, 205
Death, fear of, 60
Dhanāni (Treasures), seven, 145
Dhāraṇīs (Protective spells), 267 ff.
Dharmākara, his vow, 65
Dharma-kāya (Cosmic Body), 19, 27, 192

Dharma-pratisaṃvid, 263
Dharma-pravicaya, as a *bodhy-aṅga* (Factor of Enlightenment), 150; twelve divisions of Buddhist religious literature, 151
Dharma-smṛty-upasthāna, 99
Dhūta-guṇas (ascetic practices), 134
Dhyāna-pāramitā, 221 ff.
Dhyānas (Processes of Musing), four, 230
Divya-chakṣus (supernal organ of sight), 110
Divya-çrotra (supernal organ of hearing), 111
Divy-āvadāna, 59, 129, 231
Dṛṣṭi (*āsrava*), metaphysical speculation condemned, 133
Duḥkha (Pain), 157; it is universal, 158; its relation to altruism, 159; analysed, 158

Earthquakes, six, 298
Education of a *bodhisattva*, 218
Elephant, six-tusked, 295
Enlightenment, a *bodhisattva's*, 316

Feer, L., 64, 97
Forest-life, love of, 225
Francis, St., 92
Franciscans, the, 29
Franke, R. O., 70, 97

Gandhāra art, 39
Garbe, R., 41, 235
Gatis, five or six, 68
Gautama Buddha, his miracles, 28; as a *bodhisattva*, 43; his prediction about Çāriputra, 67; his second sermon, 72; identified with Viçvantara, 73; his utterance with regard to *kalpas*, 77; his words on *çraddhā*, 146; his first sermon, 157; his *vīrya*, 217; his birth, 297; his Renunciation, 306; his victory over *Māra*, 306 ff.; his Enlightenment, 316
Gnostics, the, 41
Gotra, 51 ff.
Greek Art, 39

Hare, the self-immolating, 186
Hartmann, C. R. E. von, 240
Hīnayāna, its ideal of *arhatship*, 1 ff.; its four Stages, 14; emphasises *maitrī*, 228; its three *vihāras*, 270; avoided by a *bodhisattva*, 276; *bhūmis* of, 271
Hrī (Shame), as an ethical principle, 206

Impurity, meditation on, 93
Indriyas as controlling Principles, five, 141.

Jainas, the, their *açuci-bhāvanā*, 95; their doctrine of *tapas*, 138; their technical term, *āsrava*, 118, 164, 168
Jīmūtavāhana, story of, 184

Kalyāṇa-mitra (a good friend), importance of, 63
Kāmas (pleasures, sense-desire), condemned, 121 ff.
Kāraṇḍa-vyūha, 48
Karma: creates the body, 93; cannot be destroyed, 190; is personal, 191; may be shared, 191
Karuṇā: a Buddha's, 24; produces the Thought of Enlightenment, 61; prompts a *bodhisattva's* self-sacrifice, 178; is the quintessence of religion, 179; its two aspects, 179; its

relation to Egoism and Altruism, 180; is innate in all creatures, 181
Karuṇā-puṇḍarīka, 90, 257
Kaṣāyas, 61
Kathā-vatthu, 24, 43
Kāya-smṛty-upasthāna, 91 ff.
Keith, A. B., 70, 191, 209
Kern, H., 31, 137, 144, 315
Kimura, S., 30
Kleças (sins), 109
Kṛtsnāyatanas, the, 229
Kṣaṇa-sampad, 60
Kṣānti (Forbearance), as a *pāramitā*, 209 ff.; its three aspects, 210; arguments for, 211; stories of, 213 ff.
Kṣāntivādin, story of, 215
Kṣemendra, 66, 96, 223, etc.
Kuçala-karma-pathāḥ, 197 ff.
Kuçala-mūlāni, 61
Kuṇāla, story of, 214

Lalita-vistara, 65, 81, 92, 96, 157, 317, etc.
Laṅkāvatāra-sūtra, 200, 233
Lévi, S., 149, 240

Magi, the, 39, 48
Mahābhārata, the, 296
Mahā-kalpa, 79
Maitrī (Friendliness), as a *brahma-vihāra*, 228
Mañjuçri, 45, 46
Māra, 64, 74; in the Pāli canon, 306; in Sanskrit literature, 308; his conflict with the *bodhisattva*, 310 ff.; his army, 313
Māyā, Queen, 294 ff.
Megasthenes, 37, 38
Milinda-pañha, 72, 81, 138
Muditā (Sympathetic joy), as a *brahma-vihāra*, 228
Mysticism, Christian, 235

Nāgārjuna, 133, 238
Nairātmya doctrine (*phenomenalism*), 72 ff.
Nāma-rūpa, 240
Nidānas (causes), twelve, 1, 239 ff.
Nirukti-pratisaṃvid, 265
Nirvāṇa: an *arhat's* ideal of, 3; a *bodhisattva* rejects, 14; consists in renunciation, 58
Nīvaraṇas (Hindrances), 103, 121

Oghas (floods), four, 134
Oldenberg, H., 242
Oltramare, *P.*, 70, 97, 243

Parable of the Burning House, 249
Parable of the Lost Son, 249
Para-citta-jñāna, 111
Pāramitās (Perfections), meaning of the word, 165; fulfilled by a Buddha, 68; ten *pāramitās* in Pāli, 167; six or ten *pāramitās* in the Mahāyāna, 168; enumerated, 168; their relation to the three *çikṣās*, 169; their general characteristics, 171; detailed discussion of the *pāramitās*, 172 ff.
Pariṇāmanā (Transfer of Merit), 57, 188 ff.
Persian religion, 38
Porphyry, 41
Poussin, L. de la Vallée, 31, 77, 97, 134, 166, 273
Praçrabdhi (tranquillity), 152
Praṇidhāna (Vow), 64 ff.
Pratibhāna-pratisaṃvid, 265
Prātihāryas (miracles), 105
Pratisaṃvids, four, 259 ff.
Pratītya-samutpāda (Formula of Dependent Origination), 239 ff.; its interpretation, 242 ff.
Pratyeka-buddha, 3, 76
Pretas, 68, 89, 206

Prīti (*pīti*), Joy, as a *bodhy-aṅga*, 151
Puggala-paññatti, 3, 51
Punishment for sin, 205
Puṇya (Merit), 44, 148; transfer of, 188; power of, 189; example of *pariṇāmanā*, 192
Purgatories (hells), hot and cold, 205
Pūrṇa, story of, 213
Pūrva-nivās-ānusmṛti-jñāna (knowledge of former lives), 111

Rāmāyaṇa, the, 132, 224, 305, 312
Ṛddhi (wonder-working Power), 112 ff.; two kinds of, 113; its object, 115; how used, 116
Ṛddhi-pādas (Bases of wonder-working Power), 104 ff.
Rebirth, doctrine of, 68 ff.; memory of former existences, 111
Ṛgveda, 18, 298, 315
Rhys Davids, C. A. F., 110, 226, 231, 235
Rhys Davids, T. W., 240, 241, and *passim*
Rukmavatī, story of, 184
Rūpa-kāya (physical body), 27

Saddhā (Faith), 32
Sad-dharma-puṇḍarīka, 12, 14, 81
Saint-worship in Islam and Christianity, 35
Samādhi (mode of Concentration), as a *bodhy-aṅga*, 153
Samādhi-rāja-sūtra, 6, 138, 177, 247
Samān-ārthatā, 255 ff.
Samāpattis (Attainments), 230; lead to the non-material Sphere, 233
Sambhoga-kāya (Body of Bliss), 27
Sampads (Blessings), four, 145
Samprajanya, 88
Saṃskārāḥ, 69 ff., 240
Saṃskṛta-dhātu, 4
Samyak-prahāṇas (Right Efforts), 101 ff.
Saṃyojanāni (Fetters), 1, 15
Saṅgraha-vastūni (Means of Conversion), 251 ff.
Sat-kāya-dṛṣṭi, 73 ff.
Saundarānanda-kāvya (story of Nanda and Sundarī), 129 ff.
Senart, E., 31, 298, 304, 314
Skandhas, 69 ff.
Smṛti (Mindfulness), 85 ff.
Smṛty-upasthānāni, 82 ff.
Soul (= *vijñāna*), 74 ff.
Speech, pleasant, 253
Stoics, the, 154
Sukhāvatī-vyūha, 34, 65
Sutta-nipāta, 190, 307
Suzuki, D. T., 58, 64, 70, 192

Tapas (austerities), 137 ff.; how introduced into Buddhism, 139
Tathāgata, meaning of the word, 12; his existence after death, 133
Tathatā (Reality), 19, 27
Thomas, E. J., 119, 221, 242, 303
Tigress, story of, 181
Time, question of, 76
Tree of *bodhi* (Enlightenment), 314 ff.
Turtle, simile of the, 60

Upāya-kauçalya (Wisdom in choice of means), 248 ff.
Upekṣā (*Upekkhā*), equanimity, 153

Vaçitās (a *bodhisattva's* ten Powers), 140
Vaiçāradyas (Grounds of Self-confidence), 20
Vasubandhu, 42, 71, 90, 98, 155, 169
Vedanā (feeling), 71, 89, 97, 241

Vegetarianism, arguments for, 209
Viçvantara, story of, 187
Vidyā-sthānāni, 218
Vijñāna, 72 ff., 240
Viparyāsas (perversions), antidote to, 90
Vīrya (Energy), as a *bodhy-aṅga*, 151; as a *pāramitā*, 216 ff.; its three aspects, 218; stories of, 220
Vyākaraṇa (Prediction), 67 ff.

Waddell, L. A., 242, 267
Walleser, M., 44
War, condemnation of, 199
Windisch, E., 307
Winternitz, M., 31, 48
Women, their foibles, 224; as *bodhisattvas*, 223

Yānas (Ways), three, 11
Yogācāra School, 45, 237
Yogas (four bonds), 134
Yoga system and *Yoga-sutras*, 9, 45, 159, 164, 235

Zend-avesta, 315
Zoroastrianism, 39, 233

Printed in Great Britain by Stephen Austin & Sons, Ltd., Hertford.